IMAGE PROCESSING AND ANALYSIS

image processing and analysis

variational, PDE, wavelet, and stochastic methods

tony F. chan
university of california, los angeles
los angeles, california

jianhong (jackie) shen
university of minnesota
minneapolis, minnesota

Society for Industrial and Applied Mathematics
Philadelphia

MATLAB® is a trademark of The MathWorks, Inc. and is used with permission. The MathWorks does not warrant the accuracy of the text or exercises in this book. This book's use or discussion of MATLAB® software or related products does not constitute endorsement or sponsorship by The MathWorks of a particular pedagogical approach or particular use of the MATLAB® software. For MATLAB® product information, please contact: The MathWorks, Inc., 3 Apple Hill Drive, Natick, MA 01760-2098 USA, 508-647-7000, Fax: 508-647-7101, info@mathworks.com, www.mathworks.com

Library of Congress Cataloging-in-Publication Data

Chan, Tony F.
    Image processing and analysis : variational, PDE, wavelet, and stochastic methods / Tony F. Chan, Jianhong (Jackie) Shen.
        p. cm.
    Includes bibliographical references and index.
    ISBN 0-89871-589-X (pbk.)
    1. Image processing—Mathematical models. I. Shen, Jianhong, 1971- II. Title.

TA1637.C4775 2005
621.36'7—dc22

2005048960

To Monica, Michelle, Ryan, and Claudia

Contents

6   Image Inpainting   **245**

List of Figures

Preface

No time in human history has ever witnessed such explosive influence and impact of image processing on modern society, sciences, and technologies. From nanotechnologies, astronomy, medicine, vision psychology, remote sensoring, security screening, and the entertainment industry to the digital communication technologies, images have helped mankind to see objects in various environments and scales, to sense and communicate distinct spatial or temporal patterns of the physical world, as well as to make optimal decisions and take right actions. Image processing and understanding are therefore turning into a critical component in contemporary sciences and technologies with many important applications.

As a branch of signal processing, image processing has traditionally been built upon the machinery of Fourier and spectral analysis. In the past few decades, there have emerged numerous novel competing methods and tools for successful image processing. They include, for example, stochastic approaches based upon Gibbs/Markov random fields and Bayesian inference theory, variational methods incorporating various geometric regularities, linear or nonlinear partial differential equations, as well as applied harmonic analysis centered around wavelets.

These diversified approaches are apparently distinct but in fact intrinsically connected. Each method excels from certain interesting angles or levels of approximations but is also inevitably subject to its limitations and applicabilities. On the other hand, at some deeper levels, they share common grounds and roots, from which more efficient *hybrid* tools or methods can be developed. This highlights the necessity of *integrating* this diversity of approaches.

The present book takes a concerted step towards this integration goal by synergistically covering all the aforementioned modern image processing approaches. We strive to reveal the few key common threads connecting all these major methodologies in contemporary image processing and analysis, as well as to highlight some emergent integration efforts that have been proven very successful and enlightening. However, we emphasize that we have made no attempt to be comprehensive in covering each subarea. In addition to the efforts of organizing the vast contemporary literature into a coherent logical structure, the present book also provides some in-depth analysis for those relatively newer areas. Since very few books have attempted this integrative approach, we hope ours will fill a need in the field.

Let u denote an observed image function, and T an image processor, which can be either deterministic or stochastic, as well as linear or nonlinear. Then a typical image processing problem can be expressed by the flow chart

$$(\text{input}) \, u \longrightarrow (\text{processor}) \, T \longrightarrow (\text{output}) \, F = T[u],$$

where F represents important image or visual features of interest. In the present book, we explore all three key aspects of image processing and analysis.

- Modeling: What are the suitable mathematical models for u and T? What are the fundamental principles governing the constructions of such models? What are the key features that have to be properly respected and incorporated?

- Model Analysis: Are the two models for u and T compatible? Is T stable and robust to noises or general perturbations? Does $F = T[u]$ exist, and if so, is it unique? What are the fine properties or structures of the solutions? In many applications, image processors are often formulated as inverse problem solvers, and as a result, issues like stability, existence, and uniqueness become very important.

- Computation and Simulation: How can the models be efficiently computed or simulated? Which numerical regularization techniques should be introduced to ensure stability and convergence? And how should the targeted entities be properly represented?

This view governs the structure and organization of the entire book. The first chapter briefly summarizes the emerging novel field of imaging science, as well as outlines the main tasks and topics of the book. In the next two chapters, we introduce and analyze several universal modern ways for image modeling and representation (for u), which include wavelets, random fields, level sets, etc. Based on this foundation, we then in the subsequent four chapters develop and analyze four specific and significant processing models (for T) including image denoising, image deblurring, inpainting or image interpolation, and image segmentation. Embedded within various image processing models are their computational algorithms, numerical examples, or typical applications.

As the whole spectra of image processing spread so vastly, in this book we can only focus on several most representative problems which emerge frequently from applications. In terms of computer vision and artificial intelligence, these are often loosely categorized as *low-level* vision problems. We do not intend to cover *high-level* vision problems which often involve pattern learning, identification, and representation.

We are enormously grateful to Linda Thiel, Alexa Epstein, Kathleen LeBlanc, Michelle Montgomery, David Riegelhaupt, and Sara Murphy of the SIAM Publisher for their constant encouragement and care throughout the project. It has been such a wonderful experience of planning, communication, and envisaging.

We also owe profound gratitude to the following colleagues whose published works and personal discussions have greatly influenced and shaped the contents and structures of the current book (in alphabetical order): Antonin Chambolle, Ron Coifman, Ingrid Daubechies, Rachid Deriché, Ron DeVore, David Donoho, Stu Geman, Brad Lucier, Jitendra Malik, Yves Meyer, Jean-Michel Morel, David Mumford, Stan Osher, Pietro Perona, Guillermo Sapiro, Jayant Shah, James Sethian, Harry Shum, Steve Smale, Gilbert Strang, Curt Vogel, Yingnian Wu, Alan Yuille, and Song-Chun Zhu, and the list further expands.

The book would be impossible without the generous support and help of many friends: Doug Arnold, Andrea Bertozzi, Carme Calderon, Charles Chui, Babette Dalton, Bjorn

Enquist, Bob Gulliver, Xiaoming Huo, Kate Houser, Yoon-Mo Jung, Dan Kersten, Paul Schrater, Mitch Luskin, Riccardo March, Willard Miller, Peter Olver, Hans Othmer, Fadil Santosa, Zuowei Shen, Chi-Wang Shu, Luminita Vese, Kevin Vixie, Tony Yezzi, Hong-Kai Zhao, and Ding-Xuan Zhou.

Tony Chan would like to personally thank his colleagues for numerous inspirations and interesting discussions: Emmanuel Candes, Raymond Chan, Li-Tien Cheng, Ron Fedkiw, Mark Green, Michael Ng, Stefano Soatto, Xue-Cheng Tai, Richard Tsai, and Wing Wong. Tony Chan is also deeply grateful to the following students and postdoctoral fellows for the privilege of working with them in this new and exciting field: Peter Blomgren, Jamylle Carter, Selim Esedoglu, Sung-Ha Kang, Mark Moelich, Pep Mulet, Fred Park, Berta Sandberg, Jackie Shen, Bing Song, David Strong, Justin Wan, Yalin Wang, Luminita Vese, Chiu-Kwong Wong, Andy Yip, Hao-Min Zhou, and Wei Zhu,

Jackie Shen wishes to personally thank Professors Gilbert Strang, Tony Chan, Stan Osher, David Mumford, and Stu Geman for their profound influence on his scholastic growth in the field, as well as numerous personal friends for warming and shining up each ordinary day during the project: Tianxi Cai, Shanhui Fan, Chuan He, Huiqiang Jiang, Ming Li, Tian-Jun Li, William Li, Chun Liu, Hailiang Liu, Huazhang (Andy) Luo, Conan Leung, Mila Nikolova, Jiaping Wang, Chao Xu, Jianling Yuan, Wen Zhang, and Qiang Zhu.

We are very grateful to Jean-Michel Morel and Kevin Vixie specifically for their insightful and constructive comments on an early version of the manuscript for this book, which have significantly improved the quality.

During this book project, the authors are enormously grateful for the support from the National Science Foundations (NSF-USA), the Office of Naval Research (ONR-USA), as well as the National Institute of Health (NIH-USA). In particular, Tony Chan would like to thank Wen Master (at ONR) for the continuous support to this novel area in applied and computational mathematics.

We also acknowledge the tremendous benefits from the participation of numerous imaging sciences related workshops at the Institute of Pure and Applied Mathematics (IPAM) at UCLA, the Institute of Mathematics and Its Applications (IMA) at the University of Minnesota, the Institute of Mathematical Sciences (IMS) at the National University of Singapore, the Mathematical Sciences Research Institute (MSRI) at Berkeley, as well as the Center of Mathematical Sciences (CMS) at Zhejiang University, China.

Finally, this book project, like all the others in our life, is an intellectual product under numerous constraints, including our busy working schedules and many other scholastic duties. Its contents and structures as presented herein are therefore only optimal subject to such inevitable conditions. All errata and suggestions for improvements will be received gratefully by the authors.

This book is absolutely impossible without the pioneering works of numerous insightful mathematicians and computer scientists and engineers. It would be our great pleasure to see that the book can faithfully reflect many major aspects of contemporary image analysis and processing. But unintentional biases are inevitable due to the limited views and experiences of the authors, and we are happy to hear any criticisms from our dear readers.

Chapter 1

Introduction

The last few decades have witnessed a new era of imaging sciences. From satellite imaging and X-ray imaging to modern computer aided CT, MRI, and PET imaging in medical sciences, mankind's naked vision is no longer restricted by the conventional notions of space, time, scales, and visibility. Consequently, just as Mother Nature has achieved for biological vision, there is tremendous need for developing the virtual *brain structures* for all these imaging areas, i.e., models and algorithms for making these *mechanical* or *artificial* vision systems more efficient, accurate, and stable, as well as artificial intelligence that can successfully process, communicate, and interpret the resultant images. The current book attempts to offer a well-organized view of this rapidly evolving field.

This introductory chapter first gives an overview of this exciting emerging field, and then introduces the scopes and structures of the current book. A detailed guidance on how to efficiently read and use the book is also speculated for different groups of potential readers.

1.1   Dawning of the Era of Imaging Sciences

Imaging sciences consist of three relatively independent components: image acquisition, image processing, and image interpretation. This book mainly focuses on the second subject, though we shall first give a quick overview of all three.

1.1.1   Image Acquisition

Image acquisition (or *formation*) studies the physical mechanisms by which particular types of imaging devices generate image observations, and it also investigates the associated mathematical models and algorithms employed by the computers integrated into such imaging devices.

We now briefly describe several important image acquisition problems.

1

Human Vision

The human vision system is Mother Nature's biological device for carrying out intelligent visual perception. The imaging formation system mainly consists of optical peripherals including the cornea, pupil, iris, and lens, as well as two different types of photoreceptors of the retinas, cones and rods, which are responsible for capturing colors and gray value intensities separately [168, 227]. The left and right retinas make up the frontal end of a complex vision system that transforms light or photons into electrochemical signals and prepares for further image processing and interpretation in the inner visual cortices through optical neuron fibers.

The perceptible light spectra for average naked vision are about between 400 and 700nm (nanometer, or 10^{-9} meter) in terms of wavelengths. On the other hand, human vision achieves astounding sensitivity to a large dynamic range of light intensities due to its delicate adaptive mechanism described by the celebrated Weber's law in vision psychology, psychophysics, and retinal physiology [121, 168, 275, 315].

Night Vision and Thermal Imaging

Wavelengths longer than 700nm belong to the infrared (IR) range. Mother Nature forces human beings to sleep and replenish during the night by making IR light imperceptible to normal naked eyes. However, assisted by proper signal amplification and enhancement devices (e.g., night vision goggles), human beings are capable of perceiving IR images ranging from just above 700nm to a few microns (10^{-6} meter).

Furthermore, the majority of light waves in the IR spectra (ranging from 3 to 30 microns) are not reflected by objects as in the visible spectra but emitted by objects due to their intrinsic thermal and statistical activities at atomic levels. For such weak photons, *thermal imaging devices* can still collect, enhance, and process them, producing the so-called *thermograms* that map the detailed distribution of temperatures of a target scene. Assisted with proper signal processing hardware and software, one can then visualize the otherwise imperceptible images.

Radar Imaging and SAR

Radar is a device that employs RAdio waves to make Detection And Ranging of targets. The signals are in the microwave range between 1cm and 1m wavelengths and polarized. Radar antennas emit these polarized radio wave pulses and receive their echoes reflected from objects. The waiting time between sending and receiving, as well as the strength of the echoes or backscatters, reveal important information such as ranges, local configuration, and material differentiation of the targets.

Applied to imaging, radar becomes a powerful tool for remote sensing. To acquire ground images, a radar device is usually attached to a flight vehicle such as a space shuttle and continuously sends, receives, and processes signalling microwave pulses. The radar image is then constructed along its flight path. The resolution of the acquired image is inversely proportional to the size of the radar; that is, larger antennas result in higher resolution images.

This hardware restriction on image resolution can, however, be effectively loosened using clever models, algorithms, and software that can extract extra spatial information from the correlation among the echoes. This amounts to increasing the *effective* size of the real antenna being employed, and thus the resultant imaging technique is called *synthetic aperture radar* (SAR) imaging. Aperture refers to the opening area of an antenna that collects echoed pulses.

Ultrasound Imaging

Like ultraviolet light, ultrasound refers to acoustic waves whose frequencies are higher than the audible range of normal human ears, i.e., about between 20Hz and 20KHz. Medical ultrasound is often above 1MHz and below 20MHz.

The different responses of the various tissues and structures to ultrasound pulses form the physiological foundation for ultrasound imaging. By measuring the time intervals between emitting and receiving sound pulses, as well as their strengths, the range and local topological information of target physiological entities can be inferred and displayed using computers.

Furthermore, using Doppler shifts, ultrasound imaging can be employed to study organs in real-time motion (e.g., heart valves and blood vessels). Recall that the Doppler shift refers to the phenomenon that the reflected echoes from a moving object have higher or lower frequencies than the incident waves depending on whether the motion is toward or away from the wave source.

Computed (Axial) Tomography (CAT or CT)

Ever since the legendary discovery of X-rays by the German physicist Wilhelm Röntgen in 1895, who was then awarded the first Nobel Prize of physics in 1901, X-rays have become the most useful probing signals in medical imaging and diagnosis. Unlike the visible spectra, IR range for night vision or thermal imaging and the microwaves for radar, X-rays have wavelengths in the nanometer (10^{-9}) or picometer (10^{-12}) scales, which are energetic enough to penetrate most materials including biological tissues. This makes X-rays ideal for noninvasive medical probing and imaging.

Different tissues and organs in the human body absorb X-rays at different rates. Denser structures like the bones absorb more X-rays than softer tissues. Thus conventional X-ray imaging is very similar to ordinary photographing, with a film directly exposed to the penetrated X-rays, and the different intensity patterns on the film differentiate different organs and structures.

Computed (axial) tomography, often referred to as CAT or CT scanning, improves the above conventional X-ray imaging method by more delicate hardware design as well as computer software for reconstructing the final images. CT can be called rotational and localized X-ray imaging technology since it consists of a localized X-ray source and a detector which are put opposite to each other and rotate around the human body's longitudinal central axis. A two-dimensional (2-D) slice image is then synthesized from the collected X-ray signals along all the directions.

Since the mid 1970s, CT scanning has witnessed broad applications in medical imaging and diagnosis, thanks to its fast speed and patient-friendly nature, as well as its unique capability in imaging a wide variety of soft tissues, hard bones, blood vessels, and so on.

Magnetic Resonance Imaging (MRI)

The 2003 Nobel Prize in Physiology or Medicine was awarded to Paul Lauterbur and Peter Mansfield for their contributions on magnetic resonance imaging (MRI). The MRI imaging technology has been built upon the remarkable physical theory of nuclear magnetic resonance (NMR), discovered and developed by two American physicists, Felix Bloch and Edward Purcell, who won the Nobel Prize in 1952.

A nucleon such as a proton or neutron possesses spin, which comes at a multiple of 1/2 with plus or minus differentiation. Paired opposite spins can effectively cancel each other out, leading to no evident observables. In an external magnetic field, unpaired or net spins tend to align with the orientation of the field, and statistical mechanics describes the distribution of two opposite alignments. The two alignments in different energy levels can transit to each other by either absorbing or releasing a photon energy proportional to the external magnetic field. For hydrogen atoms in clinical applications, for example, the frequencies of such photons are in the radio frequency (RF) range, i.e., MHz.

Simply speaking, MRI imaging works as follows. First the atomic spins (e.g., hydrogen nuclei) of the human body are aligned by applying a strong external magnetic field. Then high frequency RF pulses are emitted into a slice plane perpendicular to the external field. By absorbing the photons in the RF waves, the aligned spins can transit from the lower energy alignment to the higher (or excited) one. After the RF waves are turned off, the excited nucleus ensemble starts to gradually resume to its original distribution, a process known as *relaxation*. It is the relaxation time that reveals or differentiates different tissues or body structures. MRI imaging hardware and software measure the distribution of relaxation times and construct the associated spatial images.

MRI technology has many new important developments, including functional MRI (fMRI) for brain mapping [36] and diffusion tensor imaging (DTI) for studying neural fibers [314, 319].

Computer Graphics and Synthesized Images

All the above image acquisition processes concern how to design *hardware* and combine it with powerful *software* to construct targeted images in the *real* three-dimensional (3-D) world.

Computer graphics, on the other hand, is a purely *software*-based image acquisition approach, or rather, an art that creates images of *imaginary* 3-D scenes. As a result, computer graphics has become increasingly important in the movie industry (e.g., popular movies like *Shrek*, *Finding Nemo*, *Titanic*, *The Matrix*, and *The Lord of the Rings*, to name only a few).

Computer graphics can be formulated as follows. With an imaginary scene in mind, a designer first creates the 3-D coordinates G for shapes and geometric information of imaginary objects, as well as their optical properties such as the degree of transparency and surface reflectance R. The designer then designs a light source I for illuminance, which could be a point source or scattered sources such as in a normal daytime environment, and also picks a viewpoint θ of an imaginary observer. The final imaginary image u is then synthesized based on some proper optical relation F:

$$u = F(G, R, I, \theta).$$

If motion is involved, such as in movie production, time t has to be included as well:

$$u(t) = F(G(t), R(t), I(t), \theta(t); t),$$

which then becomes a dynamic process of image sequence generation.

Human dreaming can be considered as Mother Nature's subconscious art of graphics, not by computers but by human visual neurons and cortices.

In addition to all the aforementioned optical, electromagnetic, or nuclear imaging areas, there also exist other imaging techniques such as underwater or geophysical acoustic imaging (see, e.g., Papanicolaou [244]).

1.1.2 Image Processing

Any image processor can be abstractly formulated by an input-output system:

$$u_0 \rightarrow \boxed{T} \rightarrow F = T[u_0].$$

The input u_0 denotes an already acquired image, which could be degraded due to either poor imaging conditions or problems during storage and communication. Mathematically speaking, an image processor T could be any linear or nonlinear operator that operates on the inputs and produces targeted features or patterns F.

The design and development of image processors are often driven by specific applications or tasks. For example, in situations where observed images are degraded, one wishes to restore or enhance them to obtain high-quality images, based upon which other important visual decisions can be made more robustly and safely. Tumor detection from lowly contrasted CT images is such an example, while detecting celestial details such as binary stars from a blurry Hubble telescope image is another one.

The main challenge for designing and computing T is that most image processing problems are ill-posed *inverse problems*. That is, there often exists a *forward* problem that generates an image observation u_0 from the targeted feature variable F if F is known or given. Most image processing problems are, however, to recover or detect F from u_0, and are therefore inverse problems. Ill-posedness often results from the nonuniqueness or instability of direct inversion.

The output $F = T[u_0]$ can be generally any collection of features that are visually meaningful. For example, F could denote the location of corners, the layout of object boundaries, the disjoint regions associated with distinct objects, or the relative order or depth of different objects in a scene. When the input u_0 is a degraded image, the output F could also simply be its enhanced *ideal* version, often denoted by u.

The input u_0 can contain more than one image, such as in surveillance cameras, video or movie processing, and continuous medical monitoring of a single patient. For video or movie processing in particular, the time variable can lead to new features such as velocity distribution (or *optical flows*), dynamic evolution of the shapes and areas of interesting targets (or *target tracking*), and image registration.

This book mainly focuses on image processing, and more specifically, on four classes of processing tasks which frequently arise from numerous applications: denoising, deblurring, inpainting or image interpolation, and segmentation. We shall further elaborate on them in the next major section.

By far it seems that *image processing* can be separated apart from *image acquisition*. This is, however, only partially true and is dependent on the real tasks at hand. A doctor who tries to decipher the image patterns of a patient certainly does not need to know nuclear physics or the physics details of MRI. But knowledge of an image acquisition process can often help develop more powerful image processing models or algorithms. One also must be aware that many image acquisition devices have their built-in image processors in order to construct high-quality images during the image formation stage.

1.1.3 Image Interpretation and Visual Intelligence

The ultimate purpose of imaging sciences is to be able to "see," monitor, and interpret the targeted portion of the world being imaged, whether it is the surface of Mars, the newly discovered tenth planet of the solar system, Sedna, or an MRI image slice of the brain.

Therefore image interpretation is of fundamental importance for imaging sciences and is intrinsically connected to vision-based artificial intelligence.

Classical image processing is often loosely identified with low-level vision, while image interpretation generally belongs to high-level vision. An ideal artificial vision system shall be able to perform all the major functions of the human vision system, including depth perception, motion estimation, and object differentiation and recognition. A combination of image processing and image interpretation is often necessary for these tasks.

Image interpretation is partially the inverse problem of image acquisition. The latter studies how to form 2-D images from 3-D structures and patterns, which are arranged or positioned with relative orders, depths, opaqueness or transparency, etc. Image interpretation, on the other hand, attempts to reconstruct or interpret the 3-D world from 2-D images. For example, a well-trained radiologist can identify some abnormal image patterns in an MRI image with tumor tissues in a real 3-D body.

Mathematically speaking, the foundation of image interpretation is a rapidly growing field called *pattern theory*, which mainly covers pattern modeling and representation, learning theory, and pattern detection and identification. This developing field in mathematics has been pioneered by, for example, S. Geman and D. Geman [130], Grenander [143], Mumford [224], Poggio and Smale [252], and Vapnik [307].

1.2   Image Processing by Examples

This section explains some typical image processing tasks through tangible examples. Some will be explored in later chapters with great details, while others can be found in more classical image processing books [140, 194].

Throughout this section, the working example is the ideal image displayed in Figure 1.1.

1.2.1   Image Contrast Enhancement

Figure 1.2 shows an image with very low contrast, which makes it difficult for human vision to clearly perceive important visual features.

Assume that u is a gray-scale image in the range of 0 (black) and 1 (white). Let M denote the maximum value of u and m the minimum value. Then low contrast often means

Figure 1.1. *An ideal image: noiseless, complete, and in good contrast.*

that M and m are not separated far enough. It may appear that a simple linear transform like

$$u \to v = \frac{u - m}{M - m}$$

can renormalize the range and suffice to enhance the image.

But imagine the following scenario. Let w be a normal image with natural contrast and $w(x) \in [0, 1]$ for any pixel x. Suppose it is distorted by some nonlinear process to a low-contrast image u by

$$u = 0.1 \times (2w - 1)^4 + 0.4. \tag{1.1}$$

Figure 1.2. *A low-contrast version of the ideal image.*

Then for u, $0.4 \leq m \leq M \leq 0.5$, and indeed the contrast is quite low. Furthermore, due to the nonlinearity of the distortion, the simple linear transform $u \to v$ proposed above cannot work faithfully to approximate the original image w.

In real scenarios, there are infinitely many transforms like (1.1) that could lead to low-contrast images. Further complexities may arise when the transforms are pixel dependent. It thus starts to become an interesting and nontrivial problem: without any specific knowledge on low-contrast transforms like (1.1), how could one design a scheme that can *optimally* restore the contrast, and perhaps even more importantly, what are the proper criteria for optimality?

A very important solution to this problem in classical image processing is the *histogram equalization* technique, which can be read in many image processing books (e.g., [140, 194]).

1.2.2 Image Denoising

Figure 1.3 shows a noisy image u_0:

$$u_0(x) = u(x) + n(x), \quad x = (x_1, x_2) \in \Omega,$$

where $n(x)$ denotes additive Gaussian white noise and u the ideal "clean" image. To extract u from its noisy version u_0 is the denoising problem.

The above additive Gaussian white noise model is popular for testing the performance of denoising models and algorithms. Another common noise model is the salt-and-pepper noise, which is nonlinear:

$$u_0(x) = (1 - s(x))u(x) + s(x)c(x),$$

where $u(x) \in [0, 1]$ stands for the ideal clean image, $c(x)$ a random field of independent 0-1 (with probabilities 50%:50%) binary random variables, and $s(x)$ a random field of independent 0-1 binary random variables with $p = \text{Prob}(s(x) = 1)$ fixed for all $x \in \Omega$. c

Figure 1.3. *Degradation by additive Gaussian noise (Chapter 4).*

Figure 1.4. *Salt-and-pepper noise with 10% spatial density (Chapter 4).*

and s are assumed to be independent. A sample of such noises can be simulated as follows. Take any two imaginary coins, one biased for s so that the chance of heads ($s = 1$) is p and the other unbiased for c. At each pixel x, first flip the s-coin. If s is a tail ($s = 0$), leave $u(x)$ as it is and move to an unvisited new pixel. Otherwise (i.e., $s = 1$), further flip the c-coin, and change $u(x)$ to the outcome of c. Repeat this game until each pixel has been visited exactly once. Then the resultant distorted image gives a sample of u_0. Figure 1.4 shows an image degraded by the salt-and-pepper noise with $p = 10\%$.

Chapter 4 will further elaborate on noises and various approaches to suppress them.

1.2.3 Image Deblurring

Figure 1.5 shows a real blurry image out of focus. Blur is a common problem in satellite imaging, remote sensing, and cosmological observations. For instance, before the Hubble telescope was launched into space in 1990, astronomic image observations had always been made by telescopes directly mounted on the surface of the Earth. As a result, images qualities were often inevitably blurred by atmospheric turbulence.

Image blur occurs not only in ground telescope observations but also in other scenarios including fast motion or camera jittering (see Figure 1.6). Chapter 5 further explains in details different types of blurs, and models and algorithms to correct them, which is the problem of image deblurring.

1.2.4 Image Inpainting

Figure 1.7 shows a simulated image with 150 8-by-8 blocks randomly missing. The phenomenon often occurs in image communication where the packets are uncontrollably lost, for example, during wireless transmission. To restore the missing image information is in essence an interpolation problem, and is professionally called the *error concealment* problem by the communication community [166, 266].

Figure 1.5. *Degradation by out-of-focus blur: the digital camera focuses on a fingertip about* 1 *inch away while the target scene is about* 1 *foot away (Chapter 5).*

Figure 1.6. *Degradation by motion blur due to horizontal hand jittering during a single exposure (Chapter 5).*

In Chapter 6, readers see that error concealment is just one particular example of general image interpolation problems, which arise from numerous important applications including restoration of ancient paintings, movie production, image compression and construction, zooming and superresolution, and visual interpolation.

The word "inpainting" is the artistic synonym for image interpolation and has been circulating among museum restoration artists for a long time [112, 312]. It was first introduced into digital image processing in the work of Bertalmio et al. [24] and later further popularized in many other works [23, 67, 61, 116].

Figure 1.7. *150 8-by-8 packets are randomly lost during transmission (Chapter 6). The goal of error concealment (or more generally, inpainting) is to develop models and algorithms that can automatically fill in the blanks* [24, 67, 166].

1.2.5 Image Segmentation

Image segmentation crucially bridges low-level and high-level computer visions. Figure 1.8 shows an ideal image and its visually meaningful partition (or segmentation) of the entire image domain into different regions and boundaries. Almost trivial to human vision, image segmentation still remains one of the most challenging and most studied problems in image processing, image understanding, and artificial intelligence.

A general image segmentation can be formulated as follows. Given on a 2-D domain Ω an image observation u_0, which could be degraded by noise or blur, find a *visually*

Figure 1.8. *Such cartoonish segmentation seems trivial to human vision but still remains the most fundamental and challenging problem in image processing and low-level computer vision (Chapter 7). (The background segment Ω_0 is not shown explicitly here.)*

meaningful partitioning of the image domain,

$$\Omega = \Omega_0 \cup \Omega_1 \cup \cdots \cup \Omega_N,$$

for some image-dependent N, such that each component $\Omega_n (n \geq 1)$ visually corresponds to an "object" (besides the "background" patch Ω_0). Beneath this intuitive description of the segmentation problem lie the unavoidable complications on how to properly characterize the notions of (1) "visually meaningful," (2) image-dependent N, and even (3) "objects." These questions have been partially answered, e.g., in the celebrated works of Geman and Geman [130] and Mumford and Shah [226].

1.3   An Overview of Methodologies in Image Processing

In this section, we give an overview of some major approaches to image processing. It is unfair to say which one is necessarily superior to all the others. The efficiency and advantages of a particular methodology often depend on the concrete tasks at hand, as well as the classes and data structures of the images provided.

1.3.1   Morphological Approach

Since images capture objects, image processing naturally studies operations of objects. 2-D objects can be modelled as sets or domains of the 2-D plane $\mathbb{R}^2$ in a continuum setting or of the 2-D lattice $\mathbb{Z}^2$ in the discrete or digital setting. Equivalently, an object A can be identified with its binary characteristic function:

$$1_A(x) = 1, \quad x \in A; \quad 0, \quad \text{otherwise.}$$

A *morphological* transform T is a map among objects,

$$A \rightarrow B = T(A),$$

which is often *local* in the sense that whether or not a pixel x belongs to B can be completely determined by the local behavior of A in the vicinity of x.

Two most fundamental morphological transforms are the dilation operator D and erosion operator E, both depending on a structure element S, or equivalently, a local neighborhood template. For example in the discrete setting, one could take

$$S = \{(i, j) \in \mathbb{Z}^2 \mid i, j = -1, 0, 1\},$$

which is a 3-by-3 square template. The associated dilation and erosion operators are defined by [140]

$$D_S(A) = \{y \in \mathbb{Z}^2 \mid y + S \cap A \neq \phi\},$$
$$E_S(A) = \{y \in \mathbb{Z}^2 \mid y + S \subseteq A\}.$$

Here ϕ denotes the empty set and $y + S = \{y + s \mid s \in S\}$. It is evident that

$$E_S(A) \subseteq A \subseteq D_S(A),$$

as long as $(0, 0) \in S$, from which come the names "erosion" and "dilation." It is evident that both operators are monotonic:

$$A \subseteq B \quad \Longrightarrow \quad D_S(A) \subseteq D_S(B) \text{ and } E_S(A) \subseteq E_S(B). \tag{1.2}$$

Dilation and erosion provide convenient ways to define the "edge" or boundary of objects. For instance the *dilative* edge of an object can be defined by

$$\partial_S^d A = D_S(A) \setminus A = \{y \notin A \mid y + S \cap A \neq \phi\},$$

while the *erosive* edge can be defined by

$$\partial_S^e A = A \setminus E_S(A) = \{y \in A \mid y + S \cap A^c \neq \phi\}.$$

Edges are very crucial in visual inference and perception [163, 210]. Figures 1.9 and 1.10 show the effect of dilation and erosion on a binary object.

In applications, two other morphological transforms generated from dilation and erosion play even more important roles. The first is the *closing* operator $C_S = E_S \circ D_S$, i.e., with dilation followed by erosion. When applied to shapes, C_S can close small holes or gaps. And the second is the *opening* operator $O_S = D_S \circ E_S$, i.e., with dilation following after erosion. The net effect is that O_S can often erase narrow connectors and open up large holes or caves.

The above binary morphological transforms can be naturally extended to general gray-level images via their level sets. Take the dilation operator D_S for example. Let u be a general gray-level image defined on the lattice $\mathbb{Z}^2$. For each gray-level λ, define the cumulative λ-level set of u by

$$F_\lambda = F_\lambda(u) = \{x \in \mathbb{Z}^2 \mid u(x) \geq \lambda\}.$$

Then one defines another gray-level image $v = D_S(u)$, a dilated version of u, by

$$F_\lambda(v) = F_\lambda(D_S(u)) = D_S(F_\lambda(u)) \quad \forall \lambda. \tag{1.3}$$

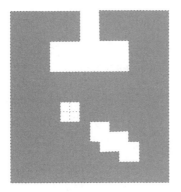

structure element S

a binary image A (or a set)

Figure 1.9. *A binary set A and a structure element S (for dilation and erosion).*

 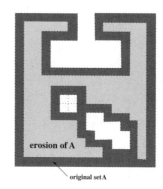

Figure 1.10. *Dilation $D_S(A)$ (left) and erosion $E_S(A)$ (right): dilation closes up small holes or gaps, while erosion opens them up.*

By the monotonicity condition (1.2), $F_\lambda(v)$ defined in this way indeed satisfies the necessary condition for cumulative level sets:

$$\lambda_1 \geq \lambda_2 \quad \Longrightarrow \quad F_{\lambda_1}(v) \subseteq F_{\lambda_2}(v).$$

Therefore v is uniquely determined by the reconstruction formula

$$v(x) = \sup\{\lambda \mid x \in F_\lambda(v)\} \quad \forall\, x \in \mathbb{Z}^2.$$

1.3.2 Fourier and Spectral Analysis

Fourier or spectral analysis has been one of the most powerful and favored tools in classical signal and image processing.

   If an image u is considered as a continuous function on the canonical rectangular domain $\Omega = (0,1)^2$, with periodic extension, the information of u can be completely encoded into its Fourier coefficients:

$$c_n = c_{n_1,n_2} = \langle u(x)\,,\ e^{i2\pi\langle x\,,\,n\rangle}\rangle_{L^2(\Omega)}, \quad n = (n_1, n_2) \in \mathbb{Z}^2 \ \text{and} \ x = (x_1, x_2) \in \Omega.$$

The completeness is in the sense of L^2. Furthermore, in the digital setting when the image domain is actually a finite lattice $\Omega = (0 : N-1) \times (0 : N-1)$ and the image $u = (u_j) = (u_{j_1,j_2})$ with $j = (j_1, j_2) \in \Omega$ a square matrix of data, one resorts to the discrete Fourier transform (DFT):

$$c_n = c_{n_1,n_2} = \sum_{j\in\Omega} u_j e^{i\frac{2\pi}{N}\langle j\,,\,n\rangle}, \quad n \in \Omega. \tag{1.4}$$

DFT is actually an orthonormal transform after a multiplicative scalar renormalization. Furthermore, DFT allows fast implementation known as the *fast Fourier transform* (FFT), which greatly facilitates numerous computational tasks in signal and image processing [237] (see the example in Figure 1.11).

   As in the spectral analysis of linear differential equations, Fourier transforms and their variations (e.g., cosine or sine transforms, and Hilbert transforms [237]) have been

image in the pixel domain

amplitude in the Fourier domain

Figure 1.11. *A digital image and its discrete Fourier transform. The example reveals a couple of salient features of Fourier image analysis:* (1) *most high-amplitude coefficients concentrate on the low-frequency band;* (2) *dominant directional information in the original image is easily recognizable in the Fourier domain; and* (3) *the coefficients, however, decay slowly for Heaviside-type directional edges (i.e., a jump line with distinct constant values along its two shoulders).*

universally applicable in many image processing tasks, including linear filtering and filter design, shift-invariant linear blurs, as well as classical image compression schemes such as the old JPEG protocol.

In image analysis and processing, the Fourier approach has, however, been greatly challenged since the 1980s by another even more powerful tool—wavelet analysis.

1.3.3 Wavelet and Space-Scale Analysis

Fourier transform mixes long-range spatial information, which makes it less ideal for handling localized visual features like edges. One extreme example is Dirac's delta image:

$$u(x) = u(x_1, x_2) = \delta(x_1 - 1/2, x_2 - 1/2), \quad x \in \Omega = (0, 1)^2.$$

Then its Fourier coefficients are

$$c_n = \langle u, \ e^{i2\pi \langle n, \ x \rangle} \rangle = e^{-i\pi(n_1 + n_2)} = \pm 1.$$

That is, all the Fourier coefficients respond indiscriminately despite such a simple image. The harmonics are therefore inefficient in representing and coding localized image information [122].

On the other hand, cognitive and anatomic evidences in vision research have shown that human vision neurons are cleverly organized to be able to resolve localized features more efficiently [122, 152]. Wavelets in a certain sense ideally embody the idea of locality by resorting to localized bases, which are organized according to different scales or resolutions [96, 203]. Simply put, the wavelet representation of a given image u is defined by

$$c_\alpha = \langle u, \ \psi_\alpha \rangle, \quad \alpha \in \Lambda,$$

where ψ_α's are wavelets, with the index set Λ resolving scale-adapted spatial locations.

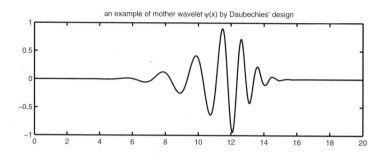

Figure 1.12. *An example of a (mother) wavelet by Daubechies' design* [96]. *Localization and oscillation are characteristic to all wavelets.*

The pioneering works of Nobel laureates Hubel and Wiesel [152] revealed the remarkable physiological fact that the simple and complex cells of human vision system behave like differentiators. Likewise, each wavelet ψ_α possesses the similar differentiation property

$$\langle 1 , \psi_\alpha \rangle = 0 \quad \forall \, \alpha \in \Lambda,$$

implying that it remains dormant to featureless constant images. More generally, wavelets often satisfy the so-called vanishing-moment condition:

$$\langle x_1^{j_1} x_2^{j_2} , \psi_\alpha \rangle = 0 \quad \forall \, j_1 + j_2 \le m$$

for some positive integer m. Coupled with spatial localization (i.e., rapid decay at infinities or being compactly supported [96, 204, 290]), this annihilation property immediately implies that the wavelet coefficients of a generic piecewise smooth image are mostly negligible except for those along important visual cues such as jumps or edges. Thus wavelets are efficient tools for adaptive image representation and data compression. Figure 1.12 displays a typical example of Daubechies' wavelets.

1.3.4   Stochastic Modeling

For images with notable stochastic nature, statistical methods become more suitable than deterministic approaches. There are two different sources leading to the statistical nature of a given image observation u_0.

(a) u_0 is the composition of an ideal (and often deterministic) image u with some random effect X:

$$u_0 = F(u, X),$$

where the function F can be either deterministic or stochastic. For example, $F(u, X) = u + X$, with $X = n$ denoting the Gaussian white noise, represents a noisy image. Or, when X denotes a spatial Poisson process and F is defined by

$$u_0(x) = F(u, X) = \begin{cases} u(x), & X(x) = 0, \\ 0 \text{ or } 1, & X(x) = 1, \end{cases}$$

u_0 becomes a stochastic image with salt-and-pepper noise.

(b) Treat individual images as the typical samples of some random fields, as in Geman and Geman's celebrated work [130] on Gibbs and Markov random fields.

Most *natural* images such as the pictures of trees, cloudy skies, sandy beaches, or other natural landscapes are often more properly handled by the stochastic framework.

For images with statistical nature, stochastic methods are the most ideal and relevant tools for modeling image processing. Especially important are statistical pattern theory [143, 224], learning theory [252], Bayesian inference theory for signal and parameter estimations [176], and stochastic algorithms such as Monte-Carlo simulation, simulated annealing, and the EM algorithm [33]. Combined with filtering techniques, a stochastic approach can become even more powerful in transformed feature spaces than directly in pixel domains.

The Bayesian framework is worth extra highlighting among all stochastic methods due to its fundamental role. Let Q denote some observed data and F some hidden features or patterns embedded within that have generated Q. Bayesian inference of F is to maximize a posteriori probability (MAP):

$$p(F \mid Q) = \frac{p(F)p(Q \mid F)}{p(Q)}.$$

The feature distribution probability $p(F)$ is called the *prior* model since it specifies the a priori bias among the targeted patterns and is independent of data observation. The conditional probability $p(Q \mid F)$ is called the (generative) *data* model since it describes how the observation Q is distributed once F is specified. As far as MAP estimation is concerned, the denominator $p(Q)$ is simply a probability normalization constant and plays no essential role. Without any prior knowledge,

$$\hat{F} = \underset{F}{\operatorname{argmax}} \ p(Q \mid F)$$

alone would also give an optimal feature estimation, and is called the *maximum likelihood* (ML) estimator. In image processing, however, due to the huge degrees of freedom of images as high-dimensional data sets, prior knowledge becomes crucial for effective signal or feature estimation. The Bayesian estimator combines both the prior and data knowledge

$$\hat{F} = \underset{F}{\operatorname{argmax}} \ p(F \mid Q) = \underset{F}{\operatorname{argmax}} \ p(F) \times p(Q \mid F). \tag{1.5}$$

Such a Bayesian principle frequently emerges in numerous image processing models in later chapters.

1.3.5 Variational Methods

Variational approach could be formally considered as the deterministic reflection of the Bayesian framework in the mirror of Gibbs' formula in statistical mechanics [82, 131]:

$$p(F) = \frac{1}{Z} e^{-\beta E[F]},$$

where $\beta = 1/(kT)$ denotes the reciprocal of temperature T multiplied by the Boltzmann constant k, and $Z = Z_\beta$ denotes the partition function for probability normalization. The formula directly expresses the likelihood $p(F)$ of a feature configuration F in terms of its "energy" $E[F]$. Therefore under any given temperature, the Bayesian MAP approach in (1.5) amounts to the minimization of the *posterior* energy:

$$E[F \mid Q] = E[F] + E[Q \mid F],$$

where an additive constant (or ground energy level) independent of F has been dropped. When F and Q belong to certain functional spaces, such as Sobolev or bounded varia-tion (BV) spaces, the minimization of this posterior energy naturally leads to a variational model (see, e.g., the monograph by Aubert and Kornprobst [15]).

We must mention that here F denotes a general feature or pattern variable, which could further contain multiple components, say $F = (F_1, F_2, \ldots, F_N)$. According to the telescoping formula of conditional probabilities, one has

$$p(F) = p(F_1)p(F_2 \mid F_1) \cdots p(F_N \mid F_{N-1}, F_{N-2}, \ldots, F_1).$$

In the important case when the feature components have a natural Markov-chain structure, i.e.,

$$p(F_j \mid F_{j-1}, \ldots, F_1) = p(F_j \mid F_{j-1}), \quad j = 2, 3, \ldots, N,$$

one has

$$p(F) = p(F_1)p(F_2 \mid F_1) \cdots p(F_N \mid F_{N-1}).$$

In terms of energy formulation, it amounts to

$$E[F] = E[F_1] + E[F_2 \mid F_1] + \cdots + E[F_N \mid F_{N-1}]. \tag{1.6}$$

In later chapters, readers will witness this universal structure in several celebrated models including Geman and Geman's mixture image model [130], Mumford and Shah's free boundary segmentation model [226], and Rudin, Osher, and Fatemi's total variation-based image restoration model [258].

As an example, consider the following additive noise model:

$$u_0(x) = u(x) + n(x), \quad x \in \Omega.$$

Assume that

(a) n is a homogeneous field of Gaussian white noise with zero mean; and

(b) ∇u is a homogeneous random field of isotropic Gaussian white vectors with zero means.

By the variational formulation, estimating $F = u$ from $Q = u_0$ can be achieved by

$$\hat{u} = \mathrm{argmin}\, E[u \mid u_0] = \mathrm{argmin}\, \frac{\alpha}{2} \int_\Omega |\nabla u|^2 dx + \frac{\lambda}{2} \int_\Omega (u - u_0)^2 dx, \tag{1.7}$$

where the two weights are inversely proportional to the variances. The preceding stochastic language is a helpful metaphor or rationale for such variational formulations [73, 223, 276]. Figure 1.13 shows an example of applying the above variational model to denoise a smooth signal polluted with noise.

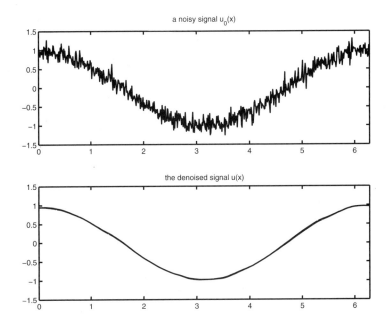

Figure 1.13. *A noisy 1-D signal and its optimal restoration according to* (1.7).

The second theoretical foundation for the variational approach is the Tikhonov regularization technique for solving inverse problems [298]. Many image processing tasks carry the nature of ill-posed inverse problems, and the Tikhonov regularization technique is a powerful tool to make processing tasks well-posed.

In essence, Tikhonov regularization is equivalent to the above Bayesian variational formulation:

$$\min E[F \mid Q] = E[F] + E[Q \mid F],$$

where now the prior model $E[F]$ is understood as the regularization term and the data model $E[Q \mid F]$ as the fitting or fidelity term.

1.3.6 Partial Differential Equations (PDEs)

The successful applications of partial differential equations (PDEs) in image processing can be credited to two main factors. First, many variational problems or their regularized approximations can often be effectively computed from their Euler–Lagrange equations. Second, PDEs as in classical mathematical physics are powerful tools to describe, model, and simulate many dynamic as well as equilibrium phenomena, including diffusion, advection or transport, reaction, and so on [15, 117, 146, 154, 172, 254, 262, 305, 317].

By calculus of variation, for example, the denoising model (1.7) amounts to solving the following elliptic boundary value problem:

$$-\alpha \Delta u + \lambda u = \lambda u_0, \quad x \in \Omega; \quad \partial u / \partial \nu = 0 \text{ along } \partial \Omega, \tag{1.8}$$

or dynamically via gradient descent marching, the diffusion-reaction equation

$$u_t = \alpha \Delta u + \lambda (u_0 - u), \quad x \in \Omega; \quad \partial u / \partial \nu = 0 \text{ along } \partial \Omega \tag{1.9}$$

with some suitable initial condition $u(x, t = 0)$.

On the other hand, PDE modeling in image processing does not have to always follow a variational model. This is well known in physics, with famous examples of Navier–Stokes equations in fluid dynamics, Schrödinger equations in quantum mechanics, and Maxwell equations in electromagnetics.

One most remarkable example of PDEs in image processing is the *mean curvature motion* (MCM) equation [40, 119, 241]

$$\frac{\partial \phi}{\partial t} = |\nabla \phi| \nabla \cdot \left[\frac{\nabla \phi}{|\nabla \phi|} \right], \quad x \in \Omega \subseteq \mathbb{R}^2, \ t > 0, \tag{1.10}$$

under suitable boundary as well as initial conditions.

The MCM equation shares the double features of diffusion and advection. First, note that by naively crossing out the two $|\nabla \phi|$'s, one arrives at the more familiar diffusion equation $\phi_t = \Delta \phi$. On the other hand, define $N = \nabla \phi / |\nabla \phi|$ to be the normal direction of level curves. Then the MCM equation (1.10) can be rewritten as

$$\frac{\partial \phi}{\partial t} + \left(-\nabla \cdot \left[\frac{\nabla \phi}{|\nabla \phi|} \right] N \right) \cdot \nabla \phi = 0,$$

which is in the form of an advection equation with characteristics (i.e., particle motion) given by the curvature motion [117]

$$\frac{dx}{dt} = \kappa N, \quad \kappa = -\nabla \cdot \left[\frac{\nabla \phi}{|\nabla \phi|} \right], \tag{1.11}$$

where at each pixel a, $\kappa(a)$ is precisely the (signed) scalar curvature of the level curve $\{x \mid \phi(x) \equiv \phi(a)\}$.

More interestingly, let s denote the (Euclidean) arc length parameter of a level set and $T = x_s$ its unit tangent vector. Then $\kappa N = T_s = x_{ss}$, and the above particle motion driven by curvature simply becomes

$$x_t = x_{ss}, \quad x = (x_1, x_2) \in \mathbb{R}^2, \tag{1.12}$$

which by itself is a system of two heat equations coupled by the arc length s. Therefore, it is conceivable that under the MCM equation (1.10), all the level curves tend to become more and more regular. As a result, the MCM equation can be employed for tasks such as image denoising. Figure 1.14 displays the evolution of a trefoil shape under the mean curvature motion.

Another important example of PDE processing model is Perona and Malik's anisotropic diffusion for image denoising and enhancement [251, 317]:

$$\frac{\partial u}{\partial t} = \nabla \cdot \left[D(|\nabla u|) \frac{\nabla u}{|\nabla u|} \right],$$

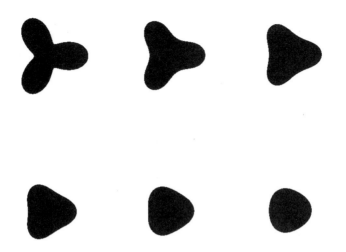

Figure 1.14. *A trefoil evolves under mean-curvature motion* (1.11) *or* (1.12).

where the diffusivity coefficient D depends on the gradient information of u. D often inversely responds to $p = |\nabla u|$, for example, $D(p) = 1/(1 + p^2)$. The Perona–Malik model improves the ordinary constant-coefficient diffusion equation in its adaptivity to edge information: faster diffusion in interior regions where image changes mildly and slower diffusion in the vicinities of object boundaries. Thus the model can maintain sharpness of edges while diminishing the effect of noises, which is desirable for image analysis and processing. Well-posedness of the Perona–Malik model is, however, not so trivial as its intuitive behavior might have suggested (e.g., see the work by Catté et al. [51]).

PDEs involving important geometric features are often called *geometric* PDEs. As one shall see in later chapters, geometric PDEs can usually be constructed by either optimizing some global geometric quantities in the variational setting (e.g., lengths, areas, and total squared curvatures) or by geometric invariance under certain transform groups. High order PDE models also frequently emerge in modern image processing [24, 26, 68, 61, 184, 262].

1.3.7 Different Approaches Are Intrinsically Interconnected

The current book attempts to present most modern image processing approaches and reveal their qualitative or quantitative connections. Some of such efforts have already been made in the literature (see, e.g., [270, 274, 283, 330]).

To illustrate how different approaches are intrinsically connected, Figure 1.15 gives a very specific example on a classical image denoising model, which has just been mentioned in the preceding sections.

In the stochastic setting (*lower left panel* in the figure), the noise model is given by

$$u_0 = u + n, \quad \text{with } n \text{ denoting Gaussian white noise of zero mean.}$$

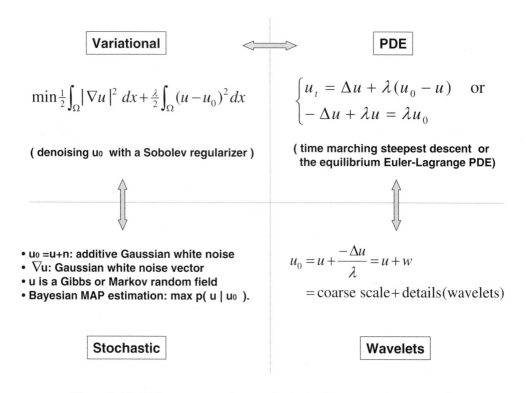

Figure 1.15. *Different approaches are intrinsically connected: an example.*

Given a typical (in the information-theoretic sense [93]) single observation u_0, one attempts to remove noise n and extract the ideal image u. By the Bayesian MAP estimation theory, one attempts to maximize the posterior likelihood

$$\hat{u} = \underset{u}{\mathrm{argmax}}\ p(u \mid u_0) = \mathrm{argmax}\ p(u)p(u_0 \mid u).$$

Since the generative data model is straightforward in the Gaussian white noise case, the performance of such a MAP estimator is therefore mostly determined by the image prior model $p(u)$.

Using Gibbs' ensemble models for images as random fields [130], the prior $p(u)$ is then completely determined by its "energy" $E[u]$. In the case when (i) a standard Cartesian graph (or topological) structure is endowed to the underlying pixel lattice Ω and (ii) the energy $E[u]$ is built upon *dipolar* (or *doubleton cliques*; see Chapter 3) quadratic potentials, the MAP estimator becomes the variational model in the *upper left panel* of Figure 1.15 (after being normalized by some multiplicative constant):

$$\min E[u \mid u_0] = \frac{1}{2} \int_\Omega |\nabla u|^2 dx + \frac{\lambda}{2} \int_\Omega (u - u_0)^2 dx,$$

where the integrals are understood as discrete summations if the pixel domain Ω is a Cartesian lattice. In the continuum limit, it is naturally required that the compatible images u belong to the Sobolev class $H^1(\Omega)$.

Applying the first variation $u \to u + \delta u$ to the energy functional $E[u \mid u_0]$, one then obtains the generalized differential (or Euler–Lagrange equation)

$$\frac{\partial E[u \mid u_0]}{\partial u} = -\Delta u + \lambda(u - u_0) + \frac{\partial u}{\partial n}\bigg|_{\partial\Omega}$$

in the distributional sense. Here the boundary term is understood as an element in the Hilbert space of $L^2(\partial\Omega, \mathcal{H}^1)$, i.e., all boundary functions that are square integrable with respect to the one-dimensional (1-D) Hausdorff measure of $\partial\Omega$. Therefore, by either gradient descent time evolution or directly solving the equilibrium equation, one arrives at the two equations in the *upper right panel* of Figure 1.15. Notice that the boundary term gives rise to the Neumann boundary conditions for both equations.

Finally, from the equilibrium equation

$$-\Delta u + \lambda u = \lambda u_0,$$

one has for the optimally denoised estimator u,

$$u_0 = u + \frac{-\Delta u}{\lambda} = u + w. \tag{1.13}$$

This solution can be understood as a new way to decompose the given image u_0 into two components: u and w. u belongs to the Sobolev space H^1 and is therefore a smooth or regular component. w, on the other hand, is *oscillatory* since it is the distributional Laplacian of u: $w = -\Delta u/\lambda$ and generally belongs only to $L^2(\Omega)$. w is large along edges where u experiences noticeable jumps.

In combination, locality (since differentiation is local), oscillations, and strong responses to edges qualify the w-component as a generalized wavelet projection of u_0 that encodes detailed features. By analogy, the smoother u-component behaves more like a coarse-scale projection in the multiresolution setting of wavelet theory [96, 204, 290]. (The two are, however, not exactly orthogonal.) This brings us to the *lower right panel* of Figure 1.15.

Naive as it may have sounded, this approach indeed led Burt and Adelson [35] to introduce the famous Gauss/Laplace pyramid algorithm for image coding and compression, which has been acknowledged as one of the few earliest wavelets and multiresolution ideas [96, 204, 290]. In Burt and Adelson's pioneering work [35], one should make the following adjustment in (1.13):

$$\lambda = \frac{1}{h} \quad \text{and} \quad u_0 = G_{\sqrt{h}} * u,$$

where $G_\sigma = G_1(x/\sigma)/\sigma^2$ with $G_1(x) = G_1(x_1, x_2)$ denoting the 2-D canonical Gaussian. A similar observation was also made earlier by Gabor in 1960 in the context of image deblurring, as pointed out by Guichard, Moisan, and Morel [146].

In Chapter 3, readers shall also be able to see that for Besov images, there indeed exist precise variational formulations that can lead to Donoho and Johnstone's thresholding-based denoising method in wavelet domains [106, 109]. Such formulations are due to the works of DeVore, Lucier, and their collaborators [55, 101]. Notable efforts have also been made by Steidl et al. [286] to understand the intrinsic connections among wavelets, PDEs, and variational models.

1.4   Organization of the Book

The current book can be divided into three major parts (see Figure 1.16):

(A) Chapter 2: general mathematical, physical, and statistical background for modern image analysis and processing;

(B) Chapter 3: several generic ways to model and represent images; and

(C) Chapters 4, 5, 6, and 7: models and computation of four most common image processing tasks: denoising, deblurring, inpainting or interpolation, and segmentation.

Chapter 2 introduces several general topics significant for modern image analysis and processing, which can be very helpful for understanding the materials of later chapters. It also provides independent reference sources for most contemporary works in the field. These topics are:

(a) differential geometry of curves and surfaces in two and three dimensions;

(b) the space of functions with bounded variations (BV);

(c) elements of statistical mechanics and their implications for image analysis;

(d) an introduction to the general framework of Bayesian estimation theory;

(e) a compact theory of filtering and diffusion; and

(f) elements of wavelet theory.

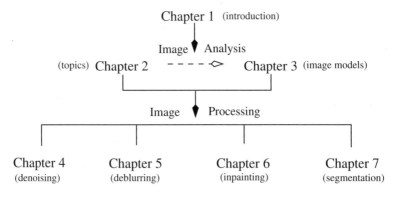

Figure 1.16. *Organization of the book.*

On one hand, these topics reveal the broad scopes of modern image analysis and processing, and on the other, they make the current book more self-contained. Readers can find numerous other monographs for these six individual topics, but few have been exclusively and systematically devoted to image analysis and processing.

Chapter 3 introduces several ways to model and represent images, which in [273] the second author has characterized as the *fundamental problem of image processing*. Proper mathematical models for images are crucial for designing efficient models and algorithms to process them.

Some image models are more general and universal than others. It is, however, often difficult to say which one offers the best model or representation, since optimality is inseparable from the concrete tasks at hand. This is quite similar to the particle-wave duality in quantum mechanics. Particle theory and wave theory are just two different approaches to modeling the same phenomenon of microscopic particles. Particle theory is more convenient in explaining behavior like the mass of photons according to Einstein's equation $E = mc^2$, while wave theory becomes superior in other occasions such as to explain the diffraction phenomenon of electrons through slim slits. To conclude, each model or representation has its own strengths and limitations.

In Chapter 3, we first discuss several deterministic image models in the context of real or functional analysis, including distributions or generalized functions, L^p-functions, Sobolev functions, functions with BV, as well as Besov functions for which the multiscale nature of images can be conveniently revealed using wavelet bases. We then turn to stochastic models of images, as originated from Geman and Geman's celebrated work on Gibbs' image models [130]. It is also discussed how to *learn* image field characteristics by combining filtering techniques with the maximum entropy principle, as first proposed in the remarkable work of Zhu and Mumford [328] and Zhu, Wu, and Mumford [329]. This chapter concludes with two other geometry-based image models: the level-set representation and Mumford and Shah's free boundary image model. These two models play fundamental roles in designing and understanding numerous variational or PDE models in modern image processing.

Based on these preparations, the remaining four chapters study individually four significant image processing tasks and their models: noise and denoising (Chapter 4), blur and deblurring (Chapter 5), inpainting or image interpolation (Chapter 6), and edge extraction and image segmentation (Chapter 7).

All these four tasks are in essence inverse problems. We thus usually start with explaining the corresponding "forward" problems, such as the precise meaning or models of noises, the physical mechanisms leading to various blurs and their mathematical models, as well as how to design generative or synthetic image models leading to multiple segments in general images. We then explore various approaches to their inverse problems, i.e., suppressing embedded noises (denoising), reducing blurry effects (deblurring), completing lost image information (inpainting), and partitioning into different objects (segmentation).

To sum up, the current book has been organized in the logical order of

$$\boxed{\text{image modeling}} \quad \rightarrow \quad \boxed{\text{image processing modeling}},$$

and the central line of philosophy or conclusion is

$$\boxed{\text{good image models lead to good image processors}}.$$

These characteristics well echo the Bayesian inference theory introduced in the preceding section (see (1.5)):

$$\hat{F} = \operatorname{argmax} \, p(F \mid Q) = \operatorname{argmax} \, p(F) \times p(Q \mid F).$$

That is, proper prior knowledge on the target features or patterns F can introduce necessary bias among a large pool of candidates and lead to efficient schemes for estimation and decision making.

1.5   How to Read the Book

A monograph like the present book has multiple purposes:

(a) to demonstrate the intrinsic logical structure behind this nontraditional novel field of image analysis and processing in contemporary applied mathematics;

(b) to offer a well-organized presentation of modern image processing for interested students or scientific researchers in many related disciplines;

(c) to summarize and highlight the most significant contributions by mathematicians during the past few decades, especially for our colleagues in engineering, computer sciences, astronomy, medical imaging and diagnosis, and brain and cognitive sciences;

(d) to explain the vast range of mathematical as well as computational techniques and challenges in contemporary image processing, especially for general applied mathematicians working on computation, modeling, and applied analysis;

(e) to reveal to the mathematicians of other areas many fascinating applications of the knowledge of topology, geometry, real, functional, and harmonic analysis, invariant theory, probability theory, partial differential equations, calculus of variations, and so on, as well as the genuine impact of mathematical power on modern societies and humanity;

(f) to highlight and emphasize the interconnections among different mathematical tools and methodologies in contemporary image processing, with more weight on the variational PDE approach, an area in which the authors have made many contributions; and

(g) as a whole, to serve as an effective communication channel bridging different communities related to image processing, including computer and human vision, computer graphics, signal and data analysis, statistical inference and learning, and numerous aforementioned application fields in medicine, astronomy, and scientific probing and sensoring.

With such a broad range of readers in mind, the authors thus by no means expect a uniformly optimal approach to reading the present book. Each individual reader should come up with his or her own comfortable usage of the book, subject to important factors such as one's background training in imaging sciences or mathematics, one's primary focuses and motivations, as well as potential time pressure, and so on.

Below we try to envision several classes of readers and offer our unnecessarily optimal personal suggestions. These categories are by no means mutually exclusive.

Scientific Workers with Specific Tasks in Image Processing

Some readers are being driven by certain specific image processing tasks at hand. Examples include an astronomy data analyst who is bothered by blurs in telescope images, a medical radiologist who attempts to remove noises in some CT images, or some security developer who engages in designing automatic tracking software for surveillance cameras.

We then recommend such a reader to jump right into the image processing chapters (i.e., Chapters 4 to 7; see Figure 1.16) that are most pertinent to the problem at hand and skip over Chapters 2 and 3 in the beginning. That is, for example, the previously imagined security developer could start directly with Chapter 7 on image segmentation (since segmentation is the most essential ingredient for object tracking).

After getting the general ideas and an integrated picture of those relevant chapters on image processing, the reader can then selectively consult related topics in Chapter 2 and some necessary materials in Chapter 3. Depending on his or her mathematical background, the reader could even consult some external monographs on specific topics there, for example, differential geometry [103], elements of statistical mechanics [82, 131], or partial differential equations [117, 291]. (We have made great efforts in making the current book more self-contained, but real situations often vary among different individuals.) With these investments, the reader can then frequent those image processing chapters that are directly related to the tasks at hand, gain more detailed understanding of the modeling ideas and techniques, and eventually start to develop his or her own novel versions of models or algorithms.

Graduate Student Readers

As far as the current book is concerned, there are mainly two "dual" classes of graduate student readers: (A) one already with some direct experience or knowledge on image processing but less mathematical training and (B) the other with more mathematical training but lacking previous exposure to imaging sciences. For example, an average graduate student in electrical or medical engineering or computer sciences falls into the first category, while a typical mathematics graduate student belongs to the second.

For graduate students of class (A) who are working on some image processing project towards theses, we recommend to first read Chapter 2 on several important mathematical elements or techniques for modern image processing. Afterwards the reader can proceed directly to the image processing chapters (i.e., Chapters 4 to 7) that are intimately connected to his or her current research project. With adequate understanding of the main lines of those chapters, he or she can then further invest time and efforts in Chapter 3 in order to gain more fundamental and systematic understanding of image analysis and modeling, as well as their application in developing good image processing models.

For mathematical graduate students of class (B), we recommend to follow the existent logical structure of the book. The reader can start with Chapter 2 and skip whatever he or she is familiar with and then proceed to Chapter 3 to understand how knowledge in real, functional, harmonic, and stochastic analysis can become very useful in describing various classes of images. Afterwards comes the freedom of order in reading the last four chapters on image processing since Chapters from 4 to 7 are relatively independent. The reader is then suggested to start with whatever topic he or she is more comfortable with. For example, if one is familiar with function interpolation in numerical or approximation theory, the reader can first read Chapter 6 on image inpainting. However, please keep in mind that Chapter 4 on denoising contains many important techniques described earlier and is always a good starting spot if no preference of a specific reading order arises.

General Mathematicians Interested in Image Processing

There are a growing number of mathematicians in pure, applied, or computational mathematics who have no previous direct involvement in image processing research but wish to broaden their own horizon of view by understanding the main ideas of image processing. We then recommend to follow the logical structure of the book (Figure 1.16). They could first *selectively* read topics that are most recognizably connected to their own field of interest, based upon which gradually expand interest into other topics.

A geometer, for example, can first read the geometric topics (Sections 1 and 2) in Chapter 2 and perhaps first skip the details of other sections in order to directly proceed to the similar topics in Chapter 3 with geometric flavors. He or she can then peruse some selected topics in Chapters from 4 to 7 to see how geometric ingredients are built into various image processing models and what the main resultant challenges are in modeling, analysis, and computation.

A computational mathematician, for another instance, may be mainly thirsty for finding challenging models to compute or novel algorithms to analyze. He or she can then quickly go over both Chapters 2 and 3 and focus more on Chapters from 4 to 7 on image processing models and algorithms. To him or her, Chapter 2 or 3 can serve as either intellectual enlightenment on new areas or good reference materials on image processing. There are indeed numerous opportunities in image processing for further computational development.

Other General Scientists Interested in Image Processing

The group could include, for example, psychologists working on human visual perception, computer graphics designers, or scientists who have been mainly working on acoustic signal processing and just recently become curious as to how visual signals (or images) are being processed.

These scientists have already been exposed to signal or image processing concepts previously but never yet had a good chance to adequately acquaint themselves with major image processing ideas and methods. They have no specific image processing tasks at hand and are willing to invest some of their time and efforts because of the kinship between their own fields and image processing.

Some mathematical tools and topics presented in Chapter 2 or 3 may in the beginning sound intimidating, but these readers should always keep in mind that *tools* always follow the footprints of *tasks*. Without good understanding on the real tasks or missions, difficulty could multiply in comprehending the meaning and languages of their tools.

Therefore, such readers can start from Chapters 2 and 3 to get basic tones of the book but should never be discouraged by some of the mathematical details, notations, or formulations that are temporarily beyond their comprehension. They can thus in the beginning spend more time focusing on Chapters 4 to 7 on four very specific but important image processing tasks. The tasks themselves are often relatively much easier to grasp.

When coming to the approaches to carrying out those tasks, the readers then become highly motivated in terms of the main challenges and key ideas. It is from this point on that our readers can start to use Chapters 2 and 3 and gradually understand in depth the real motivations, advantages or disadvantages, and the key ingredients of the mathematical entities. Depending on their mathematical background, these readers are also encouraged to read some external introductory materials on specific mathematical topics in Chapters 2 and 3.

Finally, the authors wish that our readers can genuinely enjoy the numerous unique views and state-of-the-art methods presented in the book. Together we can further advance this exciting novel field which is benefiting profoundly not only contemporary sciences and technologies but also the society, civilization, and the very nature of humanity. *Seeing is not passive watching or reception but active believing, inferencing, and decision making based upon conscious or subconscious computations in the human brain.*

Chapter 2

Some Modern Image Analysis Tools

In this chapter, we help readers review several major tools in modern mathematical image and vision analysis, whose fundamental roles will manifest in later chapters. These topics reveal the geometric, stochastic, real analysis, and harmonic analysis aspects of this emerging field. In addition to providing useful background mathematical knowledge for later chapters, the present chapter can also serve as a valuable reference source for researchers in the field.

2.1 Geometry of Curves and Surfaces

Curves and surfaces are basic geometric elements in image and vision analysis, and computer graphics. For example, they define and reveal the information of an automobile (in automatic traffic control), a star or planet (in astronomic imaging), a human body (in video surveillance), and an internal organ (in medical imaging and 3-D reconstruction). In this section, we review some basic theories on curves and surfaces in two or three dimensions. Readers are also referred to the classical geometry book by do Carmo [103] or some other monographs on geometric image analysis and computation, e.g., Romeny [256] and Kimmel [173].

2.1.1 Geometry of Curves

Local Geometry

A parametric curve is often denoted by $x(t)$, with t varying on an interval and $x = (x_1, x_2)$ or $x = (x_1, x_2, x_3)$ depending on the dimension. Differentiation with respect to t will be denoted by an overhead dot. We shall assume that $x(t)$ is smooth enough, and that the parametrization is *regular*, meaning that $\dot{x}(t)$ is nonzero for all t.

The local infinitesimal displacement is given by $dx = \dot{x}dt$, leading to the Euclidean parameterization $ds = |dx| = |\dot{x}|dt$. Differentiation with respect to the arc length df/ds will be denoted by f' in this section for any function f defined on the curve.

Then $t = t(s) = x'(s)$ is the unit *tangent* vector. In two dimensions, rotation of the tangent by 90 degrees (see Figure 2.1) gives the *normal* vector n. More generally in

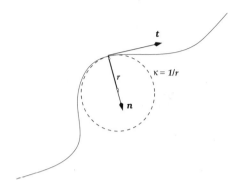

Figure 2.1. *A planar curve: tangent* ***t***, *normal* ***n***, *and curvature* κ.

differential geometry, the normal is a *second* order feature, as manifest in the curvature formula

$$t'(s) = \kappa n, \quad \text{where } \kappa \text{ denotes the curvature.}$$

In three dimensions, the displacement of ***n*** further introduces the third degree of local geometry, i.e., the binormal vector ***b*** and the torsion scalar τ. Concisely, these combine into the well-known frame formula of Frenet [103]:

$$
\begin{aligned}
t' &= & \kappa n, \\
n' &= -\kappa t &+ & \tau b, \\
b' &= & -\tau n.
\end{aligned}
\tag{2.1}
$$

The skew-symmetry of the connection matrix results directly from the orthonormality of the moving frame (t, n, b).

The torsion and binormal often appear in computer graphics and designs, while in 2-D image processing, curvature plays a more explicit role. In vision psychology, it has been observed that human subjects can easily observe and process convex or concave features of shapes and boundaries [163, 170]. That is to say, our biological vision networks are indeed able to evaluate and process the curvature information.

The importance of curvature in image and vision analysis is perhaps rooted in the most fundamental laws of physics. From Newton's law in classical mechanics, Hamiltonian dynamics, and the Second Law in thermodynamics to Schrödinger equations in quantum mechanics, physics seems to be perfectly complete working with up to second order information. Take the Second Law for example; first order derivatives (of free energies) often define some key quantities such as temperature, pressure, and chemical potential, while second order ones well explain their statistical fluctuations and introduce all the rest of the key quantities such as heat capacity and thermal compressibility. Though direct connection has not yet been established, we do believe that curvature-based vision cognition must result from the physics or biophysics of the vision neural networks (see, e.g., the work by Hubel and Wiesel [152]).

Under the arc length parametrization, assuming $\kappa(s) > 0$ and applying the exterior product, we have

$$\kappa(s) = |t \times t'| = |x' \times x''|.$$

Back to the general parametrization $x(t)$, it gives

$$\kappa(t) = \frac{|\dot{x} \times \ddot{x}|}{|\dot{x}|^3}.$$

As an application, consider the graph curve of a function $y = f(x)$ on the x-y plane. Take $t = x$ as the natural parametrization. Then

$$x = (x, y), \quad \dot{x} = (1, \dot{y}), \quad \text{and} \quad \ddot{x} = (0, \ddot{y}).$$

Therefore, the curvature is given by

$$\kappa(x) = \frac{\ddot{y}}{(1 + \dot{y}^2)^{3/2}},$$

with positivity corresponding to convexity.

For some applications in computer graphics or medical imaging (e.g., the action potential and its shock front on a normal heart), one is interested in the behavior of curves on curved 2-D surfaces instead of planes.

One could generally study parametric curves $x(t)$ on a smooth Riemannian manifold M [85, 103]. Then the tangent $\dot{x}$ belongs to the tangent space $T_x M$, which is endowed with some local Riemannian inner product $\langle \cdot , \cdot \rangle$. The arc length parameter is derived from

$$ds = \sqrt{\langle \dot{x} , \dot{x} \rangle} dt = \|\dot{x}\| dt.$$

On a general Riemannaian manifold, high order derivatives are taken based on its Levi–Civita connection D. For a local vector field X defined on a neighborhood of $x \in M$, $D.X$ is a type $(1,1)$ tensor in $T_x M$, meaning that for each $v \in T_x M$, $D_v X \in T_x M$. Thus the Levi–Civita connection generalizes the ordinary (Euclidean) notion of *directional derivative*: $D_v X$ is the rate of change of X along the direction v. In particular, one could define the Levi–Civita derivative $x''_{LC}(s) = D_{x'(s)} x'(s)$. Like straight lines in Euclidean spaces, a curve with $x''_{LC}(s) \equiv 0$ for all s is interpreted as always heading straight forward on M, or simply, a *geodesic*.

In image and vision analysis, most 2-D surfaces are naturally embedded in R^3, and their Levi–Civita connections become more explicit. Let M denote a 2-D surface embedded in R^3, and let $x(t)$ be a parametric curve on M. Then $x(t)$ has a natural representation under the canonical coordinates of R^3: $x = (x, y, z)$. Taking the ordinary first derivative in R^3 gives the tangent $\dot{x}(t) \in T_x M$. Under the arc length parameter s, the second order derivative in R^3: $x''(s) = (x''(s), y''(s), z''(s))$ often "sticks out" from the tangent plane $T_x M$. To obtain the intrinsic or Levi–Civita second order derivative x''_{LC}, one applies an extra step of orthogonal projection:

$$x''_{LC}(s) = x''(s) - \langle x''(s) , N \rangle N,$$

where N is the normal of $T_x M$ in R^3. In particular, a "straight line" with $x''_{LC} \equiv 0$ on M can still bear a hidden degree of bending, namely, along the direction of N. The big circles on a sphere are household examples.

Furthermore, suppose that the surface M is defined as the zero level set of some function ϕ:

$$x \in M \Leftrightarrow \phi(x) = \phi(x, y, z) = 0.$$

Let $x(s)$ be a parametric curve on M with arc length s. Then $\langle x', \nabla\phi \rangle = 0$, where ∇ denotes the gradient. Taking differentiation again leads to

$$\langle x'', \nabla\phi \rangle + D^2\phi(x', x') = 0, \tag{2.2}$$

where D^2 denotes the Hessian operator and the second term for the Hessian bilinear form. Notice that the surface normal is given by $N = \nabla\phi/|\nabla\phi|$. Therefore,

$$
\begin{aligned}
x''_{LC}(s) &= x'' - \left\langle x'', \frac{\nabla\phi}{|\nabla\phi|} \right\rangle \frac{\nabla\phi}{|\nabla\phi|} \\
&= x'' - \langle x'', \nabla\phi \rangle \frac{\nabla\phi}{|\nabla\phi|^2} \\
&= x'' + D^2\phi(x', x') \frac{\nabla\phi}{|\nabla\phi|^2},
\end{aligned}
$$

where the last step follows from (2.2). One clearly sees how the geometry of the surface and that of the curve interact.

Variational Geometry

In many situations, a collection of curves have to be dealt with simultaneously. In image segmentation for example, one attempts to select the "best" candidate among all possible boundary curves [75, 226, 299]; also for image interpolation or disocclusion in computer vision [67, 115, 116, 234], missing or incomplete boundary curves are usually fitted by some optimal candidates.

In such situations, it is more ideal to treat a curve as a "point," out of an ensemble of candidate curves. In order to weigh the quality of each individual curve γ, the first step is to establish some suitable measure $E[\gamma]$.

For curves generated by random walks, E can be specified by probability measures. For Brownian paths for example, the Wiener measure becomes natural and even unique under suitable assumptions. In this section, we shall deal with smooth curves, and regularity functionals are then the ideal candidates for $E[\gamma]$.

Let $x(t)$ be a parametric curve with $t \in [a, b]$. Then the first natural geometric measure is the *length* L:

$$L = \int ds = \int_a^b |\dot{x}| dt.$$

At first sight, it seems necessary that x be C^1, or at least with L^1 integrable $\dot{x}$. But the length L can be interpreted as the *total variation* of $x(t)$, and it therefore suffices that $x(t)$ belongs to the space of *bounded variation* (BV).

Under variational processes, global geometry always points to local geometry. For length, consider a small perturbation of a given curve: $x(t) \to x(t) + \delta x(t)$, $a \le t \le b$. By Taylor expansion, up to the linear order of δx, the change of length δL is given by

$$\delta L = \int_a^b \frac{\dot{x}}{|\dot{x}|} \cdot \dot{\delta x} dt.$$

Integration by parts further leads to

$$\delta L = \int_a^b (-\dot{t}) \cdot \delta x \, dt + t \cdot \delta x \big|_a^b.$$

Thus away from the two ends, the rate of change of the tangent, $-\dot{t}$, characterizes the sensitivity of length growth. Under the arc length parameter s, $-t' = -\kappa n$ exactly defines the curvature information.

A general second order (Euclidean) measure for a smooth curve γ is given by

$$E[\gamma] = \int_\gamma f(\kappa) ds,$$

where $f(\kappa)$ is some suitable function of curvature.

In two dimensions for instance, $f(\kappa) = \kappa$ leads to

$$E_1[\gamma] = \int_0^L \frac{d\theta}{ds} ds = \theta(L) - \theta(0),$$

where θ is the *signed* angle of t with respect to a fixed reference direction (such as the x-axis) and changes continuously. For a closed smooth curve, E_1 has to be an integer multiple of 2π, and is thus called the *total circulation*. In many situations, E_1 is not a good measure since it does not penalize local oscillations as long as they cancel each other.

If $f(\kappa) = |\kappa|$, then the *total absolute curvature*

$$E_2[\gamma] = \int_0^L |\kappa| ds = \int_0^L |\theta'(s)| ds$$

is exactly the *total variation* of the heading direction θ. It is not as *memoryless* as the circulation measure E_1, in that local oscillations do not cancel each other.

The total curvature measure E_2, though capable of memorizing local ripples, still does not effectively discriminate local behavior and global trends. For instance, $E_2[\gamma]$ equals 2π for any simple and closed convex curve γ, including one that contains kinks or corners.

In order to more effectively penalize local singularities, one weighs the arc length element ds by some $w(|\kappa|)$, with w being nonnegative and increasing with respect to $|\kappa|$:

$$E_3[\gamma] = \int_\gamma |\kappa| w(|\kappa|) ds.$$

In the case when $w(|\kappa|) = |\kappa|^{p-1}$ for some $p > 1$, one obtains

$$E_3[\gamma] = \int_\gamma |\kappa|^p ds = \int_\gamma |\theta'(s)|^p ds.$$

A special but very useful case is Euler's elastica measure E_{el}:

$$E_{\text{el}}[\gamma] = \int_\gamma (a + b\kappa^2) ds$$

for some positive constant weights a and b. It first appeared in Euler's work in 1744 on modeling torsion-free elastic rods and has been reintroduced into computer vision by Mumford [222] for measuring the quality of interpolating curves in disocclusion. The ratio a/b indicates the relative importance of the total length versus total squared curvature. Variational calculus leads to the equilibrium equation of the energy E_{el}:

$$2\kappa''(s) + \kappa^3(s) = \frac{a}{b}\kappa(s),$$

which is nonlinear and could be solved explicitly using elliptic functions, as Mumford developed in [222].

2.1.2   Geometry of Surfaces in Three Dimensions

Local Geometry

In abstract differential geometry, surfaces are 2-D Riemannian manifolds on which inner products are defined pointwise and smoothly. Their local differential structures are identical to R^2. Klein bottle is a well-known example which, however, cannot be faithfully visualized in R^3 [103].

In computer graphics and 3-D image reconstructions, surfaces are always naturally embedded in their 3-D environment R^3, which makes their theory and computation relatively simpler.

There are two alternative ways to define a surface embedded in R^3, parametric or implicit. A *parametric* surface is defined as a smooth map $\mathbf{x}(u, v)$ from a parameter domain $\Omega \subseteq \mathbb{R}^2$ to R^3:

$$(u, v) \to \mathbf{x}(u, v) = (x(u, v), y(u, v), z(u, v))$$

with the nondegeneracy condition $\mathbf{x}_u \times \mathbf{x}_v \neq 0$.

As a familiar example in image analysis, a color image could be considered as a parametric surface in the RGB color space, with the two Cartesian coordinates in the image plane as natural parameters.

An *implicit* surface, on the other hand, is defined as a zero level set: $\phi(\mathbf{x}) = 0$ for some suitable function ϕ, often with the nondegeneracy condition $\nabla\phi \neq 0$ on the surface.

By the implicit function theorem, an implicit surface could be locally parameterized. On the other hand, a parametric surface could also be made implicit locally using the distance function. Let $\Sigma \subseteq \mathbb{R}^3$ denote the image of a parametric surface $\mathbf{x}(u, v)$. Define the distance function d_Σ by

$$d_\Sigma(\mathbf{x}) = d(\mathbf{x}, \Sigma) = \min_{y \in \Sigma} |\mathbf{x} - \mathbf{y}|, \qquad \mathbf{x} \in \mathbb{R}^3.$$

Then Σ is exactly the zero level set of d_Σ. The distance function has many applications in image and vision analysis, especially in the level-set method of Osher and Sethian [241].

Consider a parametric surface $\mathbf{x}(u, v) : \Omega \to \mathbb{R}^3$. The tangent plane $T_{\mathbf{x}}$ is spanned by $\mathbf{x}_u$ and $\mathbf{x}_v$. Define

$$E = \langle \mathbf{x}_u , \mathbf{x}_u \rangle, \quad F = \langle \mathbf{x}_u , \mathbf{x}_v \rangle, \quad \text{and} \quad G = \langle \mathbf{x}_v , \mathbf{x}_v \rangle.$$

Then the inner product on $T_{\mathbf{x}}$ is completely determined by the 2-by-2 *structure* matrix $M = (E, F; F, G)$, which contains all the first order information of the surface. A parametric curve on the surface is in the form of $x(u(t), v(t))$. Computing its arc length leads to the so-called *first fundamental form* $I(\cdot, \cdot)$ of the surface:

$$ds^2 = I(dx, dx) = (du, dv)\, M\, (du, dv)^T.$$

Generally, $I(u, v)$ is precisely the inner product for all tangent vectors $u, v \in T_x\Sigma$.

To study the second order geometric information of a surface Σ, one has to understand how to take derivatives for tangent vector fields. In general Riemannian geometry as already mentioned, this is realized by the Levi–Civita connection, or the *covariant* differential operator D. For a given tangent vector field X on Σ and a direction $v \in T_x\Sigma$, $D_v X \in T_x\Sigma$ generalizes the ordinary notion of directional derivative of X along v.

Due to the product rule of the covariant derivative,

$$D_v(fX) = f D_v X + \langle v, \operatorname{grad}(f)\rangle X,$$

and the linearity of D_v on v, it suffices to understand the following four basic actions:

$$D_{x_u} x_u, \quad D_{x_v} x_v, \quad D_{x_u} x_v, \quad \text{and} \quad D_{x_v} x_u.$$

If the surface is flat, these are simply the ordinary second order derivatives x_{uu}, x_{uv}, and x_{vv}.

For a general embedded surface, x_{uu} may stick out from it. But creatures living on the surface cannot sense what is away. Therefore, x_{uu} needs to be projected back onto the surface:

$$D_{x_u} x_u = x_{uu} - \langle x_{uu}, N\rangle N,$$

where N denotes the unit normal in the direction of $x_u \times x_v$. (If the codimension of the embedding is not 1, N has to be replaced by the entire normal space.) This discussion certainly applies to the other three as well.

The quantities $\langle x_{..}, N\rangle$ *completely* measure the deviation of the covariant derivatives from the ordinary ones. Therefore they encode the local information of how far the surface deviates from being a plane, i.e., the bending and curving of the surface. Conventionally, they are denoted by

$$e = \langle x_{uu}, N\rangle, \qquad f = \langle x_{uv}, N\rangle, \qquad \text{and} \quad g = \langle x_{vv}, N\rangle.$$

Since $\langle x_{.}, N\rangle \equiv 0$, one has

$$e = -\langle x_u, N_u\rangle, \qquad f = -\langle x_u, N_v\rangle = -\langle x_v, N_u\rangle, \quad \text{and} \quad g = -\langle x_v, N_v\rangle.$$

In combination, they define the second order geometric information and lead to the second fundamental form II, which is defined as follows.

By abusing the covariant derivative symbol D, for any $v \in T_x\Sigma$, let us denote by $D_v N$ the ordinary directional derivative of N along v in R^3. Since along v (i.e., along a curve segment on Σ which is tangent to v at x), $\langle N, N\rangle \equiv 1$, one must have $\langle D_v N, N\rangle = 0$, implying that $D_v N \in T_x\Sigma$! Thus $D.N$ could be considered as a linear transformation in $T_x\Sigma$. Indeed, $-D.N$ is called the Weingarten linear map [103]. The second fundamental (bilinear) form in $T_x\Sigma$ is then defined as

$$II(u, v) = \langle -D_u N, v\rangle. \tag{2.3}$$

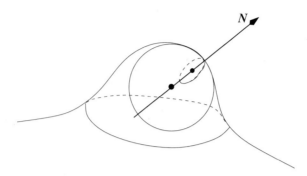

Figure 2.2. *Second order local geometry: surface normal N and two perpendicular principle curvature circles.*

Noticing that $D_{x_u} N = N_u$ and $D_{x_v} N = N_v$, one has

$$e = II(x_u, x_u), \quad f = II(x_u, x_v) = II(x_v, x_u), \quad \text{and} \quad g = II(x_v, x_v).$$

In particular, $dx = x_u du + x_v dv$ and

$$II(dx, dx) = edu^2 + 2fdudv + gdv^2.$$

The second form is thus symmetric as well.

In order to understand how the second fundamental form encodes second order geometric information, consider a *unit* vector $u \in T_x \Sigma$. The two orthonormal vectors u and N span a unique plane though x, which locally intersects Σ along a planar curve γ. Applying Frenet's frame formula (2.1) to γ at x, one has

$$n' = -\kappa t \quad \text{or} \quad \kappa = \langle -n', t \rangle.$$

In the current context, one has

$$N = n, \quad t = u, \quad \text{and} \quad n' = D_u N.$$

Therefore, $II(u, u)$ is exactly the curvature of γ, which is denoted by κ_u and gives the explicit geometric meaning of the second fundamental form.

Furthermore, one can introduce the Rayleigh quotient for the symmetric second form as in linear algebra [138, 289]. For any $u \in T_x \Sigma$ [103], define

$$R(u) = \frac{II(u, u)}{I(u, u)} = \frac{II(u, u)}{|u|^2}.$$

Generically, its maximum κ_1 and minimum κ_2 are called the *principal curvatures* (see Figure 2.2).

Gaussian curvature is defined as $K = \kappa_1 \kappa_2$, while mean curvature $H = (\kappa_1 + \kappa_2)/2$. From the perception point of view, it is unclear to which degree of precision the human vision system can detect these two curvatures. Psychological evidences show that human vision is at least good at detecting the sign of K, which corresponds to the visual differentiability between *ellipticity* (i.e., convexity) and *hyperbolicity* (i.e., saddle structures).

Let M and L denote the two structure matrices of the first and second forms under the natural parametric basis (x_u, x_v):

$$M = \begin{bmatrix} E & F \\ F & G \end{bmatrix} \quad \text{and} \quad L = \begin{bmatrix} e & f \\ f & g \end{bmatrix}.$$

Then from the computational point of view, the two principal curvatures are exactly the two eigenvalues of the generalized eigenvalue problem (L, M): $Lu = \kappa Mu$. Therefore, by linear algebra [139, 289],

$$K = \frac{\det(L)}{\det(M)} \quad \text{and} \quad 2H = \text{trace}(LM^{-1}) = \text{trace}(M^{-1}L),$$

or more explicitly,

$$K = \frac{eg - f^2}{EG - F^2} \quad \text{and} \quad H = \frac{eG - 2fF + gE}{2(EG - F^2)}. \tag{2.4}$$

The ubiquitous denominator $EG - F^2 = \det M$ is the squared area of the parallelogram spanned by x_u and x_v. In particular, if x_u and x_v just happen to be orthonormal at x, then

$$K = eg - f^2 \quad \text{and} \quad H = \frac{e + g}{2}. \tag{2.5}$$

The graph of a gray-scale image $h(u, v) : \Omega \to R$ could be considered as a parametric surface in $(u, v, h) \in R^3$. Then it is easy to establish that

$$K = \frac{h_{uu} h_{vv} - h_{uv}^2}{(1 + h_u^2 + h_v^2)^2}, \tag{2.6}$$

which is the determinant of the Hessian of h, normalized by the graph area element $\sqrt{1 + h_u^2 + h_v^2}$. Similarly for the mean curvature,

$$H = \frac{h_{uu}(1 + h_v^2) - 2h_{uv}h_u h_v + h_{vv}(1 + h_u^2)}{2(1 + h_u^2 + h_v^2)^{3/2}}. \tag{2.7}$$

Figure 2.3 shows a surface patch and its associated Gauss and mean curvatures.

Now consider an implicit surface Σ defined by a potential function ϕ:

$$x = (x, y, z) \in \Sigma \Leftrightarrow \phi(x) = 0.$$

Working near a fixed target point x, one may take any parametrization $x(u, v)$ locally near x on Σ. In addition, assume that at this target point (only!), (x_u, x_v) is an orthonormal system of $T_x\Sigma$. Differentiating $\phi(x(u, v)) = 0$ gives the first order information:

$$\langle \nabla\phi, x_u \rangle = 0 \quad \text{and} \quad \langle \nabla\phi, x_v \rangle = 0.$$

Taking differentiation again to the first equation with respect to u gives

$$\langle \nabla\phi, x_{uu} \rangle + D^2\phi(x_u, x_u) = 0,$$

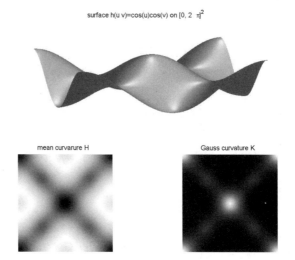

Figure 2.3. *A surface patch $z = h(u, v) = \cos(u)\cos(v)$ (top), its mean curvature field H (lower left), and Gauss curvature field K (lower right).*

where $D^2\phi$ denotes the Hessian matrix in R^3 and its associated bilinear form. Noticing that the surface normal $N = \nabla\phi/|\nabla\phi|$, we obtain the formula for e in the second form:

$$e = \langle x_{uu} , N \rangle = |\nabla\phi|^{-1}\langle x_{uu} , \nabla\phi \rangle = -|\nabla\phi|^{-1}D^2\phi(x_u, x_u).$$

Similarly, one has

$$g = -|\nabla\phi|^{-1}D^2\phi(x_v, x_v) \quad \text{and} \quad f = -|\nabla\phi|^{-1}D^2\phi(x_u, x_v).$$

Since (x_u, x_v) is an orthonormal frame at the target point x, (2.5) leads to

$$K = |\nabla\phi|^{-2} \det \left(D^2\phi\big|_{\phi=0} \right) \quad \text{and} \quad -2H = |\nabla\phi|^{-1}\text{trace} \left(D^2\phi\big|_{\phi=0} \right). \tag{2.8}$$

These two beautiful formulae are independent of the parametrization and completely self-contained.

The mean curvature H has been frequently studied in dynamical processing of shapes and surfaces, mainly due to its variational meaning (see the coming subsection). In the literature, another more explicit formula for H is also commonly used based on the trace formula

$$\text{trace} \left(D^2\phi\big|_{\phi=0} \right) = \text{trace}(D^2\phi) - D^2\phi(N, N).$$

The first term is exactly the 3-D Laplacian

$$\nabla^2\phi = \nabla \cdot \nabla\phi = \phi_{xx} + \phi_{yy} + \phi_{zz}.$$

Therefore, $-2H$ equals

$$\frac{\nabla^2\phi}{|\nabla\phi|} - \frac{1}{|\nabla\phi|^3}D^2\phi(\nabla\phi, \nabla\phi) = \frac{1}{|\nabla\phi|} \nabla \cdot \nabla\phi + \nabla\phi \cdot \nabla\left[\frac{1}{|\nabla\phi|}\right] = \nabla \cdot \left[\frac{\nabla\phi}{|\nabla\phi|}\right], \tag{2.9}$$

and the mean curvature is thus the divergence of the normal field N (up to a constant)!

Variational Geometry

One common global feature of a given surface Σ is its area A. Under the parametric form $\boldsymbol{x}(u, v) : \Omega \to \Sigma$, the area element is given by $da = |\boldsymbol{x}_u \times \boldsymbol{x}_v| dudv$. Thus

$$A = A(\Sigma) = \int_\Sigma da = \int_\Omega |\boldsymbol{x}_u \times \boldsymbol{x}_v| dudv.$$

As for curve length, under a small perturbation,

$$\boldsymbol{x}(u, v) \to \boldsymbol{x}(u, v) + \delta\boldsymbol{x}(u, v),$$

the first order variation of A must be in the form of

$$\delta A = \int_\Sigma \langle \boldsymbol{H} , \delta\boldsymbol{x} \rangle da = \int_\Omega \langle \boldsymbol{H} , \delta\boldsymbol{x} \rangle |\boldsymbol{x}_u \times \boldsymbol{x}_v| dudv, \qquad (2.10)$$

where $\boldsymbol{H}$ is a vector field on Σ that takes values in R^3. Its exact form can be worked out as follows.

Let $X = \boldsymbol{x}_u \times \boldsymbol{x}_v$. Then the normal is $N = X/|X|$. Notice that $\delta|X| = \langle N , \delta X \rangle$ and

$$\delta A = \int_\Omega \delta|X| dudv = \int_\Omega \langle N , \delta X \rangle dudv.$$

From the vector calculus of inner and exterior products, one has

$$\langle N , \delta(\boldsymbol{x}_u \times \boldsymbol{x}_v) \rangle = \langle N , \delta\boldsymbol{x}_u \times \boldsymbol{x}_v \rangle + \langle N , \boldsymbol{x}_u \times \delta\boldsymbol{x}_v \rangle$$
$$= \langle -N \times \boldsymbol{x}_v , \delta\boldsymbol{x}_u \rangle + \langle N \times \boldsymbol{x}_u , \delta\boldsymbol{x}_v \rangle.$$

Applying integration by parts and noticing that $\delta\boldsymbol{x}(u, v)$ has been assumed compactly supported, one has

$$\delta A = \int_\Omega \langle (N \times \boldsymbol{x}_v)_u - (N \times \boldsymbol{x}_u)_v , \delta\boldsymbol{x} \rangle dudv$$
$$= \int_\Omega \langle N_u \times \boldsymbol{x}_v - N_v \times \boldsymbol{x}_u , \delta\boldsymbol{x} \rangle dudv.$$

Compared with (2.10), it gives

$$\boldsymbol{H} |\boldsymbol{x}_u \times \boldsymbol{x}_v| = N_u \times \boldsymbol{x}_v - N_v \times \boldsymbol{x}_u. \qquad (2.11)$$

Notice that all the four vectors on the right are in the tangent plane $T_x \Sigma$. Therefore the two exterior products are both in the normal direction N. Assume

$$\boldsymbol{H} = \tilde{H} N$$

for some scalar $\tilde{H}$. Then by (2.11),

$$\tilde{H} = \langle \boldsymbol{H} , N \rangle = \frac{1}{|\boldsymbol{x}_u \times \boldsymbol{x}_v|^2} \langle N_u \times \boldsymbol{x}_v - N_v \times \boldsymbol{x}_u , \boldsymbol{x}_u \times \boldsymbol{x}_v \rangle.$$

Notice that the denominator is exactly $EG - F^2$ from the first fundamental form. Applying the two rules in vector calculus

$$(A \times B) \cdot C = A \cdot B \times C \quad \text{and} \quad A \times (B \times C) = B(A \cdot C) - C(A \cdot B),$$

one establishes that

$$\langle N_u \times \boldsymbol{x}_v - N_v \times \boldsymbol{x}_u , \ \boldsymbol{x}_u \times \boldsymbol{x}_v \rangle = -(eG + gE - 2fF), \qquad (2.12)$$

where e, f, and g are the coefficients of the second form. Referring to the mean curvature formula (2.4), we end up with

$$\tilde{H} = -2H.$$

Therefore, we have shown that

$$\delta A(\Sigma) = -2 \int_{\Sigma} \langle H \, N , \ \delta \boldsymbol{x} \rangle da, \qquad (2.13)$$

which is the global (or variational) meaning for the local mean curvature H. It also indicates that the most area-efficient displacements are along the normals, which well coincides with the daily life intuition. Consider, for example, the (top) surface area of a glass of still water. Smooth and slow rotation (i.e., $\delta \boldsymbol{x}$'s are on the tangent planes) brings no noticeable change of surface area, but any wave ripples in the vertical direction do.

A surface with mean curvature $H \equiv 0$ is called a minimal surface, which has been a fascinating subject in geometry, geometric measure theory, and nonlinear PDEs ever since J. L. Lagrange [233]. Minimal surfaces are also very useful in computer graphics and geometric designs [92].

In image analysis, one often considers the graph surface Σ_h of a given gray-scale image $h(u, v)$ on an image domain Ω. Then the area is given by

$$A(h) = A(\Sigma_h) = \int_{\Omega} |\nabla h|_1 du dv,$$

where the convenient notation $|X|_a$ denotes $\sqrt{a^2 + |X|^2}$ for any vector X. In this situation, we are interested in the sensitivity of $A(h)$ with respect to small changes of h: $h \to h + \delta h$. Noticing that $\delta |X|_1 = \langle X/|X|_1 , \ \delta X \rangle$, we have for the first order variation of $A(h)$

$$\delta A = \int_{\Omega} \left\langle \frac{\nabla h}{|\nabla h|_1} , \ \delta \nabla h \right\rangle du dv = - \int_{\Omega} \nabla \cdot \left[\frac{\nabla h}{|\nabla h|_1} \right] \delta h \, du dv, \qquad (2.14)$$

where the perturbation δh has been assumed to be compactly supported. It was first derived by Lagrange in 1762 (see more detailed discussion in [233] for example).

Notice that for image graphs, $\boldsymbol{x} = (u, v, h(u, v))$, $\delta \boldsymbol{x} = (0, 0, \delta h)$, and $\langle N , \ \delta \boldsymbol{x} \rangle = \delta h/|\nabla h|_1$. Comparing (2.14) with the most general form (2.13), one concludes that the surface mean curvature is given by

$$H = \frac{1}{2} \nabla \cdot \left[\frac{\nabla h}{|\nabla h|_1} \right]. \qquad (2.15)$$

For smooth surfaces, we could consider high order global features as well. For example, the total curvature

$$E_1[\Sigma] = \int_\Sigma K \, da,$$

the total absolute curvature

$$E_2[\Sigma] = \int_\Sigma |K| \, da,$$

and the total squared curvature

$$E_3[\Sigma] = \int_\Sigma K^2 \, da.$$

More generally, let $f(K, H) = g(\kappa_1, \kappa_2)$ be a proper function of the two principal curvatures. Then one could attempt to minimize the cost function

$$E_4[\Sigma] = \int_\Sigma f(K, H) \, da.$$

Many interesting results exist regarding these energies. For example, suppose the Gaussian curvature K does not change signs. Then from the Gauss map theorem [103]

$$N_u \times N_v = K \, \boldsymbol{x}_u \times \boldsymbol{x}_v, \tag{2.16}$$

one has

$$\pm E_1 = E_2 = \int_\Omega |N_u \times N_v| \, du \, dv,$$

which is exactly the total parametric area of the normal map $N : \Omega \to S^2$. Suppose N is injective. Then this latter area could never be bigger than 4π, the total area of S^2, which implies that $E_2 \leq 4\pi$ in this situation.

Sometimes one may also become interested in energies that are not intrinsically geometric, meaning that they do depend upon specific representations. For example, for a graph surface representation $\boldsymbol{x}(u, v) = (u, v, h(u, v))$, one could attempt to minimize

$$E = \int_\Omega \det{}^2(D^2 h) \, du \, dv = \int_\Omega [h_{uu} h_{vv} - h_{uv}^2]^2 \, du \, dv.$$

By the total curvature formula (2.6),

$$E = \int_\Sigma K^2 |\nabla h|_1^7 \, da,$$

which is not intrinsic due to the h-factor but is indeed a close approximation to the total squared curvature E_3 when ∇h is small.

Finally, we would like to mention that besides curves and surfaces, high-dimensional differential or Riemannian geometry could also be very useful in image processing (see, e.g., [174]).

2.1.3 Hausdorff Measures and Dimensions

In image and vision analysis, one has to deal with curves and surfaces that are less regular, for example, fractal landscapes. Then differential geometry often demands too much, while the notions of Hausdorff measures and dimensions can become more powerful.

Let E be a given set in R^2 or R^3, or more generally any subset in a metric space with distance function. Suppose it is known a priori that E is a d-dimensional object, with $d = 1.618$ say. Then a natural question is how to measure its d-dimensional "volume." Hausdorff measure $\mathcal{H}^d$ provides one good answer.

A covering $\mathcal{A}$ of E is a (countable) collection of subsets A's whose union includes E as a subset. The scale $\|\mathcal{A}\|$ of $\mathcal{A}$ is defined as

$$\|\mathcal{A}\| = \sup_{A \in \mathcal{A}} \operatorname{diam}(A),$$

where $\operatorname{diam}(A)$ stands for the diameter of A. Furthermore, one defines

$$m_d(\mathcal{A}) = \sum_{A \in \mathcal{A}} \operatorname{diam}(A)^d.$$

Then the d-dimensional Hausdorff measure $\mathcal{H}^d(E)$ is defined as

$$\mathcal{H}^d(E) = \lim_{\epsilon \to 0} \inf_{\|\mathcal{A}\| < \epsilon} m_d(\mathcal{A}), \tag{2.17}$$

where $\mathcal{A}$'s must be coverings of E. Notice that the ϵ limit is well defined since the infimum as a function of ϵ is nonincreasing. That is to say, the ϵ limit process is in fact a supremum one. Thus the definition is a minimax statement.

It is easy to see that all the ingredients in the definition are natural.

(a) When d is an integer and A is an ordinary d-dimensional cube or ball, $\operatorname{diam}(A)^d$ correctly measures the volume up to a multiplicative constant.

(b) Taking infimum is to diminish the effect caused by inefficient overcovering or repetition.

(c) Finally, by demanding ϵ to vanish, a Hausdorff measure can potentially resolve details at all scales (see Figure 2.4).

From the measure-theoretic point of view, $\mathcal{H}^d$ defined above is only an "outer" measure. Any outer measure, once restricted on the class of measurable sets, becomes a true measure.

It is easy to see that for any $d, t > 0$,

$$m_{d+t}(\mathcal{A}) \le \|\mathcal{A}\|^t m_d(\mathcal{A}),$$

from which one has, for any $\epsilon > 0$,

$$\mathcal{H}^{d+t}(E) \le \epsilon^t \mathcal{H}^d(E).$$

Therefore, as long as $\mathcal{H}^d(E)$ is finite for some d, $\mathcal{H}^s(E) = 0$ for all $s > d$. Therefore, there exists *at most* one d, so that $\mathcal{H}^d(E)$ is nonzero and finite, which leads to the notion of *Hausdorff dimension* $\dim_H$:

$$\dim_H(E) = \inf\{d \mid \mathcal{H}^d(E) = 0\}.$$

If $\dim_H(E) > 0$, then for any $t \in [0, \dim_H(E))$, $\mathcal{H}^t(E) = +\infty$ (see Figure 2.5).

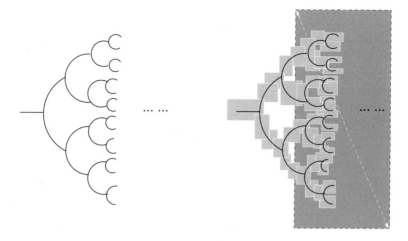

Figure 2.4. *A set E (left) and a covering A (right). Covering elements like the huge box with dashed borders (right) fail to faithfully capture small-scale details. The definition of Hausdorff measures forces covering scales to tend to zero.*

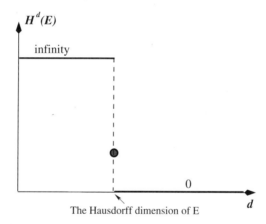

Figure 2.5. *The Hausdorff dimension $\dim_H(E)$ of a set E is the critical d, above which E appears too "thin," while below it appears too "fat."*

2.2   Functions with Bounded Variations

Functions with bounded variations (BVs) are ideal deterministic image models which allow the existence of jumps or edges, and are, however, still mathematically tractable. Theory of BV functions and its extensions [7, 9, 118, 195, 137] provide the necessary mathematical foundations for celebrated image processing models such as Rudin, Osher, and Fatemi's total variation denoising scheme [257, 258] and Mumford and Shah's segmentation model [226].

2.2.1 Total Variation as a Radon Measure

Let $\Omega \subseteq \mathbb{R}^2$ denote a bounded open domain and $u = u(x, y)$ belong to $L^1(\Omega)$. Motivated by both analysis and image processing, Ω is often assumed to be a Lipschitz domain. If u is smooth, then its *total variation* (TV) TV$[u]$ is defined as

$$\text{TV}[u] = \int_\Omega |\nabla u| dx dy, \quad \nabla u = (u_x, u_y). \tag{2.18}$$

A function (or an image) u with TV$[u] < \infty$ is said to have BV. The notation BV(Ω) denotes all functions in $L^1(\Omega)$ with BV.

How smooth should a function be for the definition (2.18) to make sense? At first sight, it appears that at least u should belong to the Sobolev space $W^{1,1}(\Omega)$, i.e., functions with integrable first order partial derivatives. But the power of TV and BV in image analysis exactly arises from the relaxation of such constraints. That is, the space BV(Ω) is in fact much larger than $W^{1,1}(\Omega)$ to include many interesting image functions.

To get acquainted with such relaxation, let us first look at a related but simpler example. For any function $f(x, y) \in L^1(\Omega)$, we could define the total integral I by

$$I[f] = \int_\Omega f dx dy.$$

The condition L^1 seems natural but not exclusively necessary for $I[f]$ to be well defined. For example, assume that $(0, 0) \in \Omega$, and denote by $\delta(x, y)$ the Dirac delta function. Then one can still define

$$I[\delta] = \int_\Omega \delta(x, y) dx dy = 1.$$

More generally, let μ be a nonnegative measure on all Borel sets of Ω with $\mu(K) < \infty$ for all compact subsets $K \subseteq \Omega$. Such measures are examples of Radon measure [126, 118]. Then one could still define, as for Dirac's delta,

$$I[\mu] = \int_\Omega 1 d\mu = \mu(\Omega),$$

where μ could be generally a signed Radon measure. Signed Radon measures generalize the space of $L^1_{\text{loc}}(\Omega)$. Furthermore, in a certain proper sense (i.e., linear functionals) [126], it could be shown that signed Radon measures are indeed the most general class of mathematical entities for $I[\cdot]$ to be well defined.

The same story applies to the TV functional. In some sense, TV$[u]$ is the integrated version of $I[f]$ by taking $f = \nabla u$. Consider the case in R^1 when $f(x) = \delta(x)$. Then $u' = \delta$ would imply that $u = H(x)$—the Heaviside 0-1 function, provided that $u(-\infty) = 0$. Since $H(x)$ contains a jump at the origin, it stays outside the locally Sobolev class $W^{1,1}_{\text{loc}}$. Inspired by the discussion on I, one could, however, still define

$$\text{TV}[H] = \int_{R^1} |H'(x)| dx = \int_{R^1} \delta(x) dx = I[\delta] = 1.$$

Generally, let $\mu(x)$ be any finite and signed Radon measure in R^1, and let $u = u(x)$ denote its cumulative distribution function (c.d.f. in probability theory). One could then define

$$\text{TV}[u] = \int_{R^1} d|\mu| = |\mu|(R^1).$$

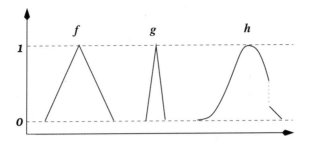

Figure 2.6. *Three 1-D images with* $\mathrm{TV}[f] = \mathrm{TV}[g] = \mathrm{TV}[h] = 2$.

Here $|\mu|$ denotes the TV measure of μ. That is, if $\mu = \mu^+ - \mu^-$ denotes the Jordan decomposition into two mutually singular and nonnegative Radon measures [126], then $|\mu| = \mu^+ + \mu^-$. Figure 2.6 shows the TVs of three 1-D signals.

With these insights in mind, we now formalize the definitions of $\mathrm{TV}[u]$ and $\mathrm{BV}(\Omega)$. Let $U \subseteq \Omega \subseteq \mathbb{R}^2$ denote any open set of Ω. For any $u \in L^1(\Omega)$, define

$$\int_U |D^*u| = \sup_{g \in C_c^1(U,B^2)} \int_U u \, \nabla \cdot g \, dxdy, \qquad (2.19)$$

where B^2 denotes the open unit disk in R^2, and the admissible class $C_c^1(U, B^2)$ denotes

$$\left\{ g = (g_1, g_2) \mid g \text{ is } C^1 \text{ and compactly supported in } U, \text{ and } |g| = \sqrt{g_1^2 + g_2^2} < 1 \right\}. \qquad (2.20)$$

If $\int |D^*u| < \infty$ for any open subset U with *compact* closure contained within Ω, we say that *locally* u has BV and denote by $\mathrm{BV}_{\mathrm{loc}}(\Omega)$ the collection of all such functions in $L^1(\Omega)$.

For any $u \in \mathrm{BV}_{\mathrm{loc}}(\Omega)$, by the standard practice in measure theory, one could construct an *outer* measure by defining, for any subset $E \subseteq \Omega$,

$$\int_E |D^*u| = \inf_{U:E \subseteq U} \int_U |D^*u|,$$

where U are open subsets. Restricted on measurable sets, it becomes a Radon measure on Ω, which shall be denoted by $\int |Du|$, and defines the TV of u (on Ω) by

$$\mathrm{TV}[u] = |Du|(\Omega) = \int_\Omega |Du|.$$

The notation $\mathrm{BV}(\Omega)$ denotes the collections of all functions with finite TVs in $L^1(\Omega)$.

Assume that $u \in W^{1,1}(\Omega)$. Then for any $g \in C_c^1(\Omega, B^2)$,

$$\int_\Omega u \, \nabla \cdot g \, dxdy = -\int_\Omega g \cdot \nabla u \, dxdy$$

by the Gauss–Green divergence theorem (or integration by parts). Since B^2 is closed under radial reflection $g \to -g$, one has

$$\int_\Omega |Du| = \sup_{g \in C_c^1(\Omega, B^2)} \int_\Omega g \cdot \nabla u \, dxdy \le \int_\Omega |\nabla u| \, dxdy.$$

On the other hand, by Lusin's continuity characterization, Uryson's extension lemma, and the mollification technique [126], for any specified precision ϵ and δ, we could always take some $g \in C_c^1(\Omega, B^2)$, so that

$$m\left((x, y) : \ |\nabla u(x, y)| \ne 0 \text{ and } \left| g - \frac{\nabla u}{|\nabla u|} \right| \ge \epsilon \right) < \delta,$$

where m denotes the Lebesgue measure. Therefore, in fact, one must have

$$\int_\Omega |Du| = \int_\Omega |\nabla u| \, dxdy,$$

which implies that TV generalizes the Sobolev norm and $W^{1,1}(\Omega) \subseteq \mathrm{BV}(\Omega)$.

In exactly the same fashion, Du can be defined as a (vector-valued) Radon measure for any $u \in \mathrm{BV}_{\mathrm{loc}}(\Omega)$, and it could be shown that $|Du|$ is exactly the TV of Du in the context of measure theory [118, 126]. In R^2, Du naturally contains two signed Radon measures (u_x, u_y).

Example. Let $\Omega = (0, 1) \times (c, d)$ denote an open box in R^2, and define $u(x, y) = AH(x - 1/2)$, a product of an amplitude constant $A > 0$ and the shifted Heaviside function. It represents a binary black-white image of two adjacent vertical bands. Then

$$\int_\Omega |Du| = (d - c)A \int_{(0,1)} |D^1 H(x - 1/2)| = (d - c)A \int_{(0,1)} \delta(x - 1/2) dx = A(d - c),$$

where D^1 means 1-D TV. It is not a coincidence in this case that the TV measure is the product of the size $d - c$ and strength A of the target *edge*.

Example. Let $\Omega = R^2$, and let aB^2 denote the disk centered at the origin with radius $a > 0$. Let $\chi_{aB^2} = \chi_{aB^2}(x, y)$ be its indicator function. Then by definition,

$$\int_{R^2} |D\chi_{aB^2}| = \sup_{g \in C_c^1(R^2, B^2)} \int_{aB^2} \nabla \cdot g \, dxdy$$

$$= \sup_{g \in C_c^1(R^2, B^2)} \int_{\partial(aB^2)} g \cdot n d\mathcal{H}^1$$

$$\le \int_{\partial(aB^2)} d\mathcal{H}^1 = 2\pi a,$$

where $\partial(A)$ stands for the (topological) boundary of a set A, $\mathcal{H}^1$ the 1-D Hausdorff measure, and n the outer normal. On the other hand, it is easy to construct a $g \in C_c^1(R^2, B^2)$, so that $g|_{\partial(aB^2)} \equiv n$. Therefore,

$$\int_{R^2} |D\chi_{aB^2}| = 2\pi a, \quad \text{the perimeter of } aB^2.$$

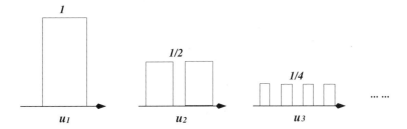

Figure 2.7. *An example of L^1-lower semicontinuity. The sequence (u_n) of 1-D images on $[0, 1]$ converges to $u = 0$ in L^1 since $\|u_{n+1} - u\|_{L^1} \leq 2^{-n}$. Notice that $\mathrm{TV}(u) = 0$ while $\mathrm{TV}(u_n) \equiv 2$, which is consistent with the property of lower semicontinuity: $\mathrm{TV}(u) \leq \liminf_n \mathrm{TV}(u_n)$. In particular, strict inequality is indeed realizable.*

This result holds for any smooth domain E; namely, the TV of its indicator function χ_E is exactly its perimeter. In fact, this approach leads to a more general definition of perimeters for nonsmooth domains [137, 195].

2.2.2 Basic Properties of BV Functions

In this section, we discuss several major properties of BV functions that are important in image analysis. They are L^1-lower semicontinuity, completeness (i.e., Banach), trace and divergence theorem, smoothness and regularity, and relative compactness in L^1.

Theorem 2.1 (L^1-Lower Semicontinuity). *Suppose $u_n(x, y) \to u(x, y)$ in $L^1(\Omega)$. Then*

$$\int_\Omega |Du| \leq \liminf_n \int_\Omega |Du_n|.$$

In particular, if $(u_n)_n$ is a bounded sequence in $\mathrm{BV}(\Omega)$, then u belongs to $\mathrm{BV}(\Omega)$ as well.

The proof almost immediately follows from the definition of TV. For any $g \in C_c^1(\Omega, B^2)$,

$$\int_\Omega u \, \nabla \cdot g \, dxdy = \lim_n \int_\Omega u_n \, \nabla \cdot g \, dxdy \leq \liminf_n \int_\Omega |Du_n|.$$

Taking supremum confirms Theorem 2.1 (see Figure 2.7).

Among the many interesting results that Theorem 2.1 makes contribution to, perhaps the most fundamental one is that $\mathrm{BV}(\Omega)$ is a Banach space. First, it is easy to see that $\mathrm{BV}(\Omega)$ is a normed linear space under the BV norm:

$$\|u\|_{\mathrm{BV}} = \int_\Omega |u(x, y)| \, dxdy + \int_\Omega |Du|,$$

which is stronger than the L^1 norm. To establish the completeness, let $(u_n)_n$ be a Cauchy sequence under $\|\cdot\|_{\mathrm{BV}}$. Then $(u_n)_n$ is also Cauchy in L^1, and let $u \in L^1$ be its limit. By semicontinuity, $u \in \mathrm{BV}(\Omega)$. Furthermore, applying semicontinuity again to $(u_m - u_n)_n$ with m fixed, we have

$$\int_{\Omega} |Du_m - Du| \leq \liminf_{n} \int_{\Omega} |Du_m - Du_n|,$$

which converges to 0 as $m \to \infty$ since $(u_n)_n$ is a Cauchy sequence. Thus $u_n \to u$ in $\mathrm{BV}(\Omega)$ under $\| \cdot \|_{\mathrm{BV}}$.

The behavior of a BV function $u \in \mathrm{BV}(\Omega)$ near the boundary $\partial\Omega$ is reflected in the notion of *trace* $f_u = T(u) \in L^1(\partial\Omega, \mathcal{H}^1)$. In what follows, we shall assume that Ω is a Lipschitz domain.

Roughly speaking, the definability of $f_u = T(u)$ indicates that a BV function u cannot oscillate too much near the boundary $\partial\Omega$. Instead, it converges to some function (in a certain suitable sense) f along $\partial\Omega$. To see clearly why this is the case, let $K_1 \subseteq K_2 \subseteq \cdots$ be a sequence of compact sets so that $\Omega = \bigcup_{n}^{\infty} K_n$. Then by the basic continuity property of a finite measure,

$$\int_{\Omega \setminus K_n} |Du| \to 0, \quad n \to \infty.$$

Therefore, roughness indeed gradually fades away on the "narrow rings" $\Omega \setminus K_n$, and the function tends to converge. More explicitly, as far as a local segment of rectifiable boundary is concerned, one could "zoom in" and simply assume that $\Omega = R \times (0, \infty)$. Take $K_\epsilon = R \times (\varepsilon, \infty)$, $\varepsilon > 0$, and define $f^\varepsilon(x) = u(x, \varepsilon)$ in the L^1 sense (by Fubini's theorem). For any $\delta < \varepsilon$,

$$|f^\varepsilon(x) - f^\delta(x)| \leq \int_{\delta}^{\varepsilon} |D_y u(x, y)|,$$

$$\int_R |f^\varepsilon(x) - f^\delta(x)| dx \leq \int_{R \times (\delta, \varepsilon)} |D_y u(x, y)| dx \leq \int_{R \times (\delta, \varepsilon)} |Du| \to 0 \quad \text{as } \varepsilon \to 0.$$

Therefore $(f^\varepsilon)_\varepsilon$ is a Cauchy sequence in $L^1(R)$, and the trace $f_u = T(u)$ along the boundary is defined as its L^1 limit.

The concept of trace leads to the Gauss–Green divergence theorem for BV images. Suppose that $u \in \mathrm{BV}(\Omega)$, $U \Subset \Omega$ (i.e., $\bar{U}$ is compact in Ω) and is Lipschitz, and $\boldsymbol{g} \in C_0^1(\Omega, \mathbb{R}^2)$. Then

$$\int_U \boldsymbol{g} \cdot Du = -\int_U u \nabla \cdot \boldsymbol{g} \, dx dy + \int_{\partial U} f_u \boldsymbol{g} \cdot \boldsymbol{n} d\mathcal{H}^1,$$

where $\boldsymbol{n}$ denotes the outer normal of ∂U.

As a Radon measure, for any compact set $K \subseteq \Omega$,

$$\int_{\Omega} |Du| = \int_{\Omega \setminus K} |Du| + \int_K |Du|.$$

In image analysis and processing, of particular interest is the case when K is a compact piece of Lipschitz curve γ. γ is said to be *singular* for a given image u if

$$|Du|(\gamma) = \int_{\gamma} |Du| > 0.$$

Notice that under the 2-D Lebesgue measure, γ is always only a null set.

Let f^+ and f^- denote the corresponding traces of u along the two sides of γ. Then one can show that

$$\int_\gamma |Du| = \int_\gamma |f^+ - f^-| d\mathcal{H}^1, \qquad (2.21)$$

the integration under the Hausdorff measure of the jumps along the curve! In image and vision analysis, intensity "jumps," usually referred to as "edges," have been considered as crucial visual cues. Equation (2.21) therefore partially explains why the TV measure and the BV space could have become so convenient and powerful in image analysis and processing.

Another key question is how close $W^{1,1}(\Omega)$ is to $BV(\Omega)$. By adaptive mollification based on the partition of unity [126], one could establish the following result.

Theorem 2.2 (Mollification of BV). *For any $u \in BV(\Omega)$, one can find a sequence of approximations $(u_n)_n$ such that*

1. *$u_n \in C^\infty(\Omega)$ for $n = 1, 2, \ldots$;*
2. *$u_n \to u$ in $L^1(\Omega)$ as $n \to \infty$;*
3. *$\int_\Omega |Du_n| \to \int_\Omega |Du|$, and their traces $g_n \equiv g$ for $n = 1, 2, \ldots$.*

Theorem 2.2 is the best that one could wish for, since for a general BV image u it is infeasible to ask for a sequence of smooth functions $(u_n)_n$ so that

$$\int_\Omega |Du_n - Du| \to 0, \quad n \to \infty.$$

This could be easily explained by (2.21). Suppose $u \in BV(\Omega)$ and that a compact regular curve $\gamma \subseteq \Omega$ is singular, i.e., $\int_\gamma |Du| = a > 0$. Then for any smooth function u_n,

$$\int_\gamma |D(u_n - u)| = \int_\gamma |(f_n^+ - f^+) - (f_n^- - f^-)| d\mathcal{H}^1$$

$$= \int_\gamma |f^+ - f^-| d\mathcal{H}^1 = \int_\gamma |Du| = a.$$

That is, convergence under the TV seminorm is impossible for such an image.

However, mollification provided by Theorem 2.2 has already been quite powerful. It allows one to conveniently transplant many results from the classical Sobolev space $W^{1,1}(\Omega)$.

Let $u \in BV(\Omega)$ and $f = T(u)$ be its trace. A functional $L[u, f]$ on $BV(\Omega)$ is said to be L^1-lower semicontinuous if, for any sequence $(u_n)_n \in BV(\Omega)$ with $u_n \to u$ in $L^1(\Omega)$ and $f_n \equiv f$ as $n \to \infty$, one has

$$L[u, f] \le \liminf_n L[u_n, f].$$

Corollary 2.3 (Sobolev-BV Transition). *Suppose $L[u, f]$ is an L^1-lower semicontinuous functional in $BV(\Omega)$ and that $E = E(t)$ is a continuous function of $t \in [0, \infty)$. If*

$$L[u, f] \le E(|Du|(\Omega)) \qquad \text{for any } u \in W^{1,1}(\Omega),$$

then the same inequality must hold for all $u \in BV(\Omega)$.

The proof follows readily from the semicontinuity property and Theorem 2.2 on mollification approximation.

As an application, define in R^n (with $n > 1$) $p = \frac{n}{n-1}$, and

$$L[u, f] = \left(\int_\Omega |u|^p dx \right)^{1/p} \quad \text{and} \quad E = |Du|(\Omega) = c \int_\Omega |Du|.$$

Then the celebrated Sobolev inequality in $W^{1,1}(R^n)$ states that $L \leq E$ for all compactly supported $u \in W^{1,1}(R^n)$ for some suitable constant c which depends only on n. By the preceding corollary, the same inequality must hold for any compactly supported $u \in \mathrm{BV}(\Omega)$ as well.

The second most important application of the mollification theorem (Theorem 2.2) is the *weak compactness* property, which has become a fundamental tool for establishing the existence of solutions to various BV-based image processing models.

Theorem 2.4 (Weak Compactness of BV). *Let $(u_n)_n$ be a bounded sequence in $\mathrm{BV}(\Omega)$ where Ω is a Lipschitz domain. There must exist a subsequence which converges in $L^1(\Omega)$.*

The proof is again immediate from the mollification theorem (Theorem 2.2) and the weak compactness of $W^{1,1}(\Omega)$ in $L^1(\Omega)$. By Theorem 2.2, we could approximate u_n by $w_n \in W^{1,1}(\Omega)$ such that

$$\int_\Omega |u_n - w_n| \, dx dy \leq 1/n \quad \text{and} \quad \int_\Omega |\nabla w_n| \, dx dy \leq \int_\Omega |Du_n| + 1$$

for each n. Thus $(w_n)_n$ must be bounded in $W^{1,1}(\Omega)$. By the weak compactness property of $W^{1,1}(\Omega)$ (or the Rellich theorem [3, 137, 193]), $(w_n)_n$ contains a subsequence indexed by $n(k)$, $k = 1, 2, \ldots$, which converges in $L^1(\Omega)$. Then the subsequence of $(u_n)_n$ with the same indices $n(k)$ must also converge in $L^1(\Omega)$.

2.2.3 The Co-Area Formula

This beautiful formula was initially due to Fleming and Rishel [125], and De Giorgi gave the complete proof [134, 137]. It reveals the geometric essence of the TV measure, which has been fundamental for numerous applications in image analysis and processing.

For smooth functions, it essentially results from a special change of variables, at least locally. Let $u(x, y)$ denote a smooth image on a domain Ω. Assume that $\nabla u(x_0, y_0) \neq 0$. Say $u_y(x_0, y_0) \neq 0$, without loss of generality. Then by the implicit function theorem, locally near (x_0, y_0), we could explicitly solve y:

$$u(x, y) = \lambda \Leftrightarrow y = y(x, \lambda).$$

For each given λ, one could reparameterize the λ-level curve $(x, y(x, \lambda))$ using arc length s, so that

$$x = x(s) \quad \text{and} \quad y = y(x(s), \lambda).$$

Since the reference points with $s = 0$ may also depend on λ, one has

$$x = x(s, \lambda) \quad \text{and} \quad y = y(s, \lambda),$$

which is well defined at least locally. In summary, this change of variables is governed by

$$\lambda = u(x(s, \lambda), y(s, \lambda)) \text{ and } x_s^2 + y_s^2 = 1. \tag{2.22}$$

In the (s, λ) system, taking partial derivatives with respect to s and λ in the first equation gives

$$0 = (x_s, y_s) \cdot \nabla u \text{ and } 1 = (x_\lambda, y_\lambda) \cdot \nabla u.$$

The first identity, combined with the second one in (2.22), gives $\nabla u = \pm |\nabla u|(-y_s, x_s)$. Therefore, the second identity becomes

$$1 = \pm |\nabla u|(x_s y_\lambda - y_s x_\lambda) = \pm |\nabla u| \frac{\partial(x, y)}{\partial(s, \lambda)},$$

and with the Jacobian, we are able to conclude that

$$|\nabla u| \, dx dy = ds d\lambda.$$

Assuming that this change of variables is global on Ω, one has

$$\int_\Omega |\nabla u| \, dx dy = \int ds d\lambda,$$

where the second integral is over an appropriate domain in the (s, λ) plane. Let γ_λ denote the λ-level curve. Then

$$\int_\Omega |\nabla u| \, dx dy = \int_{-\infty}^{\infty} \text{length}(\gamma_\lambda) d\lambda,$$

which is the celebrated co-area formula for regular functions. More generally, for any function $\phi = \phi(u)$, we have

$$\int_\Omega \phi(u)|\nabla u| \, dx dy = \int_{-\infty}^{\infty} \text{length}(\gamma_\lambda)\phi(\lambda) d\lambda. \tag{2.23}$$

For general BV functions, the above ideal argument has to be polished. One has to first answer the following two natural questions:

1. What do we mean by a level curve $\gamma_\lambda : u \equiv \lambda$? A BV function could be discontinuous, and its range may contain many gaps. Moreover, as an L^1 function, it is only defined in the sense of Lebesgue, and its values along any given curve could be freely alternated.

2. The regularity of γ_λ is not guaranteed. How do we properly define its "length"?

It turns out that the two are intrinsically connected. Instead of the level curve $\gamma_\lambda : u \equiv \lambda$, one defines a *level domain* (or cumulative level set)

$$E_\lambda = \{(x, y) \in \Omega | \ u < \lambda\}.$$

Notice that when the image u is smooth, $\gamma_\lambda = \partial E_\lambda$. For each level domain, one defines its perimeter by

$$\text{Per}(E_\lambda) = \int_\Omega |D\chi_{E_\lambda}|,$$

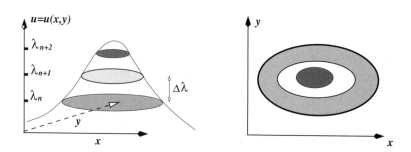

Figure 2.8. *Geometric meaning of TV: the co-area formula. For smooth images,* TV[u] *is to sum up the lengths of all the level curves, weighted by the Lebesgue element* $d\lambda$. *Plotted here is a discrete approximation:* TV[u] $\simeq \sum_n$ length$(u \equiv \lambda_n)\Delta\lambda$.

i.e., the TV of the indicator function. For smooth images, it coincides with the 1-D Hausdorff measure $\mathcal{H}^1(\gamma_\lambda)$.

Theorem 2.5 (Co-Area Formula). *Suppose* $u \in \mathrm{BV}(\Omega)$. *Then*

$$\int_\Omega |Du| = \int_{-\infty}^\infty \mathrm{Per}(E_\lambda)\, d\lambda.$$

The rigorous proof could be found in [137], for example. Figure 2.8 helps visualize the co-area formula.

Intuitively speaking, the co-area formula shows that the TV measure is a natural way for summing up the lengths of *all* level curves simultaneously. Furthermore, one of the most crucial visual cues, edges, could be treated as a "condensed" collection of level curves, rising from the bottom value λ_0 to its top value λ_1. Edges are thus automatically taken care of by the TV measure since the co-area formula shows that the λ-integration is over the entire edge "wall."

Numerous applications of the TV measure and the space of BV functions will be frequently witnessed throughout the book.

2.3   Elements of Thermodynamics and Statistical Mechanics

From Shannon's information and communication theory [272, 93] to the pioneering works of Geman and Geman [130], Zhu and Mumford [328], and Zhu, Wu, and Mumford [329] on Gibbs's random fields in image modeling, it is unsurprising to see the growing importance of ideas and techniques from thermodynamics and statistical mechanics [33, 82]. In this section, we attempt to give a brief introduction to the relevant physics, often blended with some modern views of image and pattern analysis [143].

2.3.1 Essentials of Thermodynamics

The fundamental principle of classical thermodynamics is that a system of many microscopic particles in equilibrium could be well described by only a few key macroscopic quantities, such as the total energy E, temperature T, pressure p, volume V, entropy S, etc. (The usage of these standard symbols therefore will be kept consistently throughout this section.)

To the community of image and pattern analysis, the astounding similarity in terms of missions and goals can be instantly felt: we are also trying to compress the information of complex visual patterns and distributions down to a few visually crucial features. The technical resonance between the two fields has thus been profoundly driven by the characteristics they happen to share.

More generally, in terms of data compression and dimensionality reduction, thermodynamics offers the underlying quasi-physics rationale. Consider a box of dilute ideal gas with one mole of molecules, i.e., 6.022×10^{23} molecules, the Avogadro number. Then the classical microscopic phase space has the astronomical dimension of $6 \times 6.022 \times 10^{23}$: even ignoring the exact atomic configuration of each molecule, one still has 3 for the position of each molecule and 3 for the velocity or momentum. Thus in the language of data compression, equilibrium thermodynamics achieves a stunning compression rate (or *dimensionality reduction*)! It is certainly a very lossy description but sufficient in most macroscopic applications when the specific behavior of individual molecules is of no specific interest.

With this basic link in mind, we now explore the essential ingredients of thermodynamics that are most pertinent to the goals of the current book.

Equilibrium thermodynamics applies to quasi-static or *reversible* processes, which are controllable in terms of the few macroscopic key quantities mentioned in the beginning. Processes such as explosion or a sudden release of a concentrated mass of particles are therefore excluded.

The First Law balances the energy budget:

$$dE = \bar{d}Q + \boldsymbol{F} \cdot d\boldsymbol{X}, \tag{2.24}$$

where $\bar{d}Q$ denotes the "heat" energy absorbed during the infinitesimal process, and $dW = \boldsymbol{F} \cdot d\boldsymbol{X} = f_1 dX_1 + \cdots + f_k dX_k$ specifies the work done to the system by all the relevant generalized pressures f_i's and generalized volumes X_i's. The overhead bar indicates that the heat Q itself is not a well-definable physical quantity, rather, only associated with the particular process at hand. For the work, one could take, for example, in most applications $X_1 = V$ to be the volume, $X_2 = n$ the mole number of particles, $f_1 = -p$ with p the pressure, and $f_2 = \mu$ the chemical potential. The negative sign for pressure results from the negative work done to the system when volume expands.

Acknowledged by the First Law, the true meaning of the absorbed "heat" only comes clear in the Second Law after the historical discovery of the quantity S called *entropy*:

$$\bar{d}Q = T dS \quad \text{and} \quad dE = T dS + \boldsymbol{F} \cdot d\boldsymbol{X}. \tag{2.25}$$

Since generally the temperature $T = T(S, \boldsymbol{X}) \neq T(S)$, $\bar{d}Q$ is therefore not a total differential.

The Second Law further states that

1. entropy $S = S(E, \boldsymbol{X})$ is nondecreasing with respect to the energy E; and
2. if an equilibrium state II is *adiabatically* accessible from state I, then $S_{\mathrm{II}} \geq S_{\mathrm{I}}$.

The first one implies that the temperature $T = [\partial E / \partial S]_X$ cannot be negative. The second statement characterizes the "direction" of thermodynamic processes.

In combination, the two laws spell out a complete set of macroscopic variables for equilibrium systems:

$$S, \ X_1, \ X_2, \ \ldots, X_k.$$

For systems such as dilute gases, these are typically given by

$$S \text{(entropy)}, \quad V \text{(volume)}, \quad \text{and} \quad n \text{(mole number)},$$

and therefore

$$dE = TdS - pdV + \mu dn, \tag{2.26}$$

or, equivalently,

$$T = \left(\frac{\partial E}{\partial S} \right)_{V,n}, \quad -p = \left(\frac{\partial E}{\partial V} \right)_{S,n}, \quad \text{and} \quad \mu = \left(\frac{\partial E}{\partial n} \right)_{S,V}.$$

(T, p, μ) are said to be *conjugate* to (S, V, n). In what follows, we shall focus on (2.26) only.

For image and pattern analysis, these thermodynamic variables teach good lessons. Variables such as E, S, V, and n are said to be *extensive* and the conjugates T, p, and μ *intensive*. A thermal variable X is extensive if it is additive:

$$X_{I \oplus II} = X_I + X_{II},$$

where $I \oplus II$ denotes the direct noninteractive union of two separate systems I and II. It is apparent that energy, volume, and mole number are additive. The additivity of entropy has even more profound meaning in probability and information theory [93]. On the other hand, a thermal variable f is said to be intensive if it does not depend on the system sizes:

$$f_{I \oplus II} = f_I = f_{II}$$

for any two systems in equilibrium. Suppose that X and Y are both extensive; then

$$f = \left(\frac{\partial X}{\partial Y} \right)_Z, \quad \text{with respect to other appropriate variables } Z,$$

must be intensive. Therefore, temperature T, pressure p, and chemical potential μ are all intensive variables. Being intensive is crucial for measurement. Because of the independence of system sizes, thermometers and barometers could be made conveniently small.

In image and visual pattern analysis, one central task is also to successfully identify the few intrinsic features independent of image sizes, which carry crucial visual information and are often sufficient for efficient reconstruction.

2.3.2   Entropy and Potentials

Among all the thermal variables, the one drawing much attention is entropy S. By the Second Law, entropy makes thermodynamics *variational*. Since the variational principle has become very effective in image and vision analysis, let us proceed with more detailed discussion on the variational meaning of entropy.

Since the temperature $T = \partial E / \partial S$ is positive, by the implicit function theorem, one could use (E, V, n) as the complete set of macroscopic variables for equilibrium systems, in place of the original one (S, V, n) as in (2.26). Then $S = S(E, V, n)$.

Imagine that an equilibrium system described by (E, V, n) is to be perturbed internally (by controlled regrouping or repartitioning). Assume that the internal perturbation has been created in such a way that the net work done to the system is all thermally leaked, i.e., $\bar{d}Q + dW = 0$. Therefore, by the First Law, the perturbed system shares the same set of extensive quantities (E, V, n). However, one has to introduce other collection of new variables Y to describe the perturbed system:

$$(E, V, n; \ Y) \quad \text{or} \quad (E, V, n; \ \text{internal controls}).$$

After removing all the internal controls, the system will eventually relax to the original equilibrium state (adiabatically). Then by the Second Law,

$$S(E, V, n) \geq S(E, V, n; Y). \tag{2.27}$$

This is the variational statement of equilibrium—a natural equilibrium state without any internal controls must boost the entropy to its maximum.

One of the most significant consequences of this variational formulation is the necessary set of conditions for two contacting systems to be in equilibrium. It reveals the "forces" associated with all the intensive variables. That is to say, the gradient of an intensive variable could cause macroscopic fluxes between the two contacting systems. As in classical mechanics, therefore, all the intensive variables are potentials. Pressure p is a familiar one, whose gradient even drives the well-known Navier–Stokes flows in fluid dynamics [2].

As an example, let us apply the variational principle (2.27) to derive the condition of thermal equilibrium between two systems contacting along a (heat) conducting interface, which is, however, mechanically fixed and chemically unpenetrable. Suppose the two systems are described by (E_i, V_i, n_i), $i = 1, 2$, separately. Then the V's and n's are all frozen, and only energy can exchange via pure heat flows through the interface. Therefore, $dE_1 + dE_2 = 0$, or equivalently, the combined total energy is fixed. We now show that if the combined system is in thermal equilibrium, then $T_1 = T_2$. Assume otherwise $T_1 > T_2$. One could create some internal perturbation of energies so that $dE_2 = -dE_1 > 0$ (by some external heat bath, say). On the other hand, by the First Law,

$$dS_1 = \frac{1}{T_1} dE_1 \quad \text{and} \quad dS_2 = \frac{1}{T_2} dE_2,$$

since both V's and n's are frozen. Let $S = S_1 + S_2$ denote the total entropy of the combined system. Then

$$dS = dS_1 + dS_2 = \left(\frac{1}{T_2} - \frac{1}{T_1} \right) dE_2 > 0. \tag{2.28}$$

It violates the Second Law since the perturbed system has *increased* the entropy of the original combined system in equilibrium, contrasting to (2.27).

Similarly, for mechanical equilibrium (with a mobile interface which is adiabatic and impenetrable), one must have the pressure identity $p_1 = p_2$.

The above argument also shows the natural dynamical direction for two contacting systems settling down to a new equilibrium state. According to (2.28), heat must flow from the higher temperature system to the lower one to meet the Second Law requirement. Thus it is the gradient or differentiation of temperatures that drives the heat flow. The three intensive variables, temperature, pressure, and chemical potential, are thus all potentials whose gradients are some kind of forces driving dynamics.

In terms of visual patterns, we speculate that this line of analysis could inspire ideal definitions of "visual potentials." Visual potentials should be a set of key intrinsic (or intensive) features, so that when two image patterns with identical potentials are placed adjacent to each other, *visual equilibrium* can be reached in the human visual system, and a normal observer will find it very difficult to differentiate the two.

2.3.3   Statistical Mechanics of Ensembles

Thermodynamics and statistical mechanics are both about stochastic fluctuations of many-body systems. A system in thermodynamic equilibrium still undergoes constant microscopic evolution and reconfiguration. Therefore, a macroscopic state actually corresponds to a collection of microscopic configurations, which is called the associated ensemble. Statistical mechanics reveals the statistical structures and properties of these ensembles and interprets all the macroscopic measurements and observations.

A *microcanonical* ensemble (MCE) refers to the collection of all possible microscopic configurations of a completely isolated equilibrium macroscopic system. Complete isolation means that there are no thermal, mechanical, or chemical exchanges with the environment. Thus all the macroscopic features such as E, V, and n are fixed. The fundamental postulation of statistical mechanics is that

"All microscopic states in a canonical ensemble are equally possible."

Imagine that each state is represented by a dot in the classical phase space (with astronomical dimensions). Then the postulation could be visually interpreted as that all dots in the MCE are uniformly distributed along a band (defined by the macroscopic constraints).

A *canonical* ensemble (CE) refers to all possible microscopic states of an equilibrium system in a heat bath, which is, however, both mechanically and chemically isolated. That is to say, the system has fixed volume V, mole number n, and temperature T. But the energy E could fluctuate due to spontaneous heat exchanges with the ambient heat bath, and is thus a random variable. By quantum mechanics, E is quantized to some discrete levels: $E_0, E_1, \ldots$, with each E_ν corresponding to an MCE. However, the sizes of all these "bands" (which are by themselves MCEs) in the classical phase space are different, equivalently saying their probabilities

$$p_\nu = \text{Prob}(E = E_\nu), \quad \nu = 0, 1, 2, \ldots$$

are not uniform. To discover the exact distribution of $(p_\nu)_\nu$ is therefore the most fundamental task of CEs.

This task has witnessed a beautiful solution by Gibbs. The celebrated Gibbs' distribution law, obtained by perturbing the MCE consisting of both the target system and its

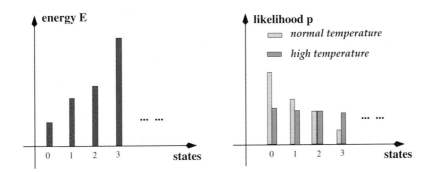

Figure 2.9. *Gibbs' CE: higher temperature T corresponds to smaller β and more uniform distribution; on the other hand, when T ≃ 0, the system exclusively remains at the ground state (leading to superfluids or superconductance in physics).*

ambient heat bath, states that (see Figure 2.9)

$$p_\nu \propto e^{-\beta E_\nu} \quad \text{and} \quad p_\nu = \frac{1}{Z} e^{-\beta E_\nu}, \tag{2.29}$$

where $\beta = 1/\kappa T$ is the reciprocal of temperature T normalized by the Boltzmann constant κ, and Z is the partition function for probability normalization:

$$Z = Z_\beta = \sum_\nu e^{-\beta E_\nu}.$$

It is also convenient to define $A = -(1/\beta) \ln Z$ or $Z = e^{-\beta A}$. By dimensionality analysis, A plays the role of energy, and indeed physically it is Helmholtz's free energy.

Let $\langle X \rangle$ denote the mean value of a random variable X. Then by Gibbs' law (2.29), the average energy is

$$\langle E \rangle = \sum_\nu p_\nu E_\nu = \frac{1}{Z} \sum_\nu e^{-\beta E_\nu} E_\nu$$

$$= \frac{1}{Z} \frac{dZ}{d(-\beta)} = \frac{d(-\ln Z)}{d\beta} = \frac{d(\beta A)}{d\beta}.$$

Strictly speaking, all the differentials are partial with respect to V and n, which are of course frozen in canonical ensembles. It could be further worked out that $A = \langle E \rangle - TS$, the Legendre transform of the mean energy $\langle E \rangle = \langle E \rangle (S, V, n)$ with respect to entropy S.

In the same fashion, the mean squared fluctuation of energy for Gibbs' distributions can be worked out to be

$$\langle \delta E^2 \rangle = \langle E^2 \rangle - \langle E \rangle^2 = \frac{d^2(-\beta A)}{d\beta^2} = -\frac{d\langle E \rangle}{d\beta}. \tag{2.30}$$

Physically, this is exactly the heat capacity C_V of the material up to a temperature-related multiplier. Thus the formula beautifully connects microscopic fluctuations to macroscopic

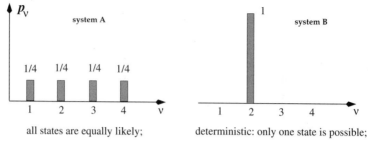

all states are equally likely;   deterministic: only one state is possible;

very chaotic; entropy is maximum S=ln 4   no uncertainty; entropy is minimum: S=0

Figure 2.10. *Gibbs' entropies for two imaginary 4-state systems (with κ set to 1). Entropy generally measures the degrees of freedom of a system. A lower entropy therefore means that the target system is more restrained. (This observation led Shannon [272] to define negative entropies as information metrics, since less randomness implies more information.)*

material properties. Though we will not go further deeper into the underlying physics, it does imply that high order statistics could be very meaningful for image and pattern analysis.

Physically, Gibbs' distribution law comes from the first order perturbation of MCEs and their uniformity postulation discussed above. It could also be derived from the variational statement of the Second Law in the preceding section, namely, the law of maximum entropy. This approach is more general and therefore even applicable to image and pattern analysis.

The starting point is Gibbs' celebrated entropy formula,

$$S = -\kappa \sum_{\nu} p_\nu \ln p_\nu, \qquad (2.31)$$

where κ is again the Boltzmann constant, and ν runs through all possible MCEs corresponding to different energy levels E_ν (or both energy levels E_ν and mole numbers n_ν for *grand* canonical ensembles). Figure 2.10 compares the entropies of two imaginary 4-state systems.

In what follows, we shall work with the grand canonical ensemble (GCE) to illustrate the generality of this variational approach. By the Second Law of macroscopic thermodynamics, the distribution $(p_\nu)_\nu$ should maximize the entropy S when all the other equilibrium variables are prescribed:

$$\bar{E} = \langle E \rangle, \quad \bar{n} = \langle n \rangle, \quad \text{and} \quad V \text{ fixed}$$

in the case of GCE. This leads to the beautiful mathematical abstraction of statistical mechanics—variational optimization with constraints. Thus, for example, the distribution $(p_\nu)_\nu$ of a GCE could be obtained by solving

$$\max_{(p_\nu)} -\sum_{\nu} p_\nu \ln p_\nu \quad \text{subject to} \quad \sum_{\nu} p_\nu E_\nu = \bar{E} \quad \text{and} \quad \sum_{\nu} p_\nu n_\nu = \bar{n}. \qquad (2.32)$$

Of course $(p_\nu)_\nu$ as a probability distribution must also satisfy the natural conditions of nonnegativity and unity. By introducing Lagrange multipliers β for E, μ for n, and δ for unity normalization, we are led to the unconstrained optimization problem

$$\max_{(p_\nu)} \left(-\sum_\nu p_\nu \ln p_\nu + \beta \sum_\nu E_\nu p_\nu + \mu \sum_\nu n_\nu p_\nu + \delta \sum_\nu p_\nu \right).$$

Taking derivatives along each p_ν gives

$$-\ln p_\nu - 1 + \beta E_\nu + \mu n_\nu + \delta = 0, \quad \nu = 0, 1, \ldots,$$

which implies that

$$p_\nu = \frac{1}{Z_{\beta,\mu}} e^{-\beta E_\nu - \mu n_\nu}, \quad \nu = 0, 1, \ldots,$$

where the partition function Z (initially contributed from δ) has been connected to β and μ for probability normalization:

$$Z_{\beta,\mu} = \sum_\nu e^{-\beta E_\nu - \mu n_\nu}.$$

This is Gibbs' distribution law for GCEs. Without particle exchanges, it reproduces Gibbs' law (2.29) for CEs.

This elegant approach to statistical mechanics has very much inspired the general framework of image pattern analysis developed by Geman and Geman, Mumford, and Zhu, et al. The new and challenging ingredient for image analysis is again to properly define visually meaningful features, ones that are parallel to both extensive and intensive variables in thermodynamics and statistical mechanics.

2.4 Bayesian Statistical Inference

This section briefly explains the fundamental role of Bayesian inference theory in image and vision analysis.

2.4.1 Image Processing or Visual Perception as Inference

Image processing or visual perception can be abstractly formulated as an inference problem: given observed image data Q, determine the key patterns or features F embedded within. If the image data Q are considered, at least conceptually, as the samples of stochastic distributions that are either parameterized by or generated from the feature variable F, such decision making naturally falls into the realm of *statistical inference*. Here both Q and F can contain multiple components; e.g., Q denotes a sequence of images in a video segment or from the continuous CT scanning of a patient.

First, suppose F is an on-or-off binary feature, i.e., representing a certain feature being present or absent. Let $F = 0$ and 1 denote the feature being on and off separately. Then the inference on the values of F given Q can be achieved by *significance test*.

A significance test leads to a choice between the so-called *null hypothesis* (i.e., $F = 0$), assuming the target feature is present, and the *alternative* one(s) (i.e., $F = 1$), based upon some criterion statistics $T = T(Q \mid F = 0)$ and its associated threshold t_c. Given a particular sample $Q = q$ of image data, the decision rule of a significance test could be

$$T(q \mid F = 0) < t_c \Rightarrow \text{accept } F = 0; \quad \text{otherwise,} \quad \Rightarrow \text{accept } F = 1.$$

t_c is therefore often called the decision boundary.

For example, suppose that Q denotes the light intensity at some fixed pixel, and $F = 0$ corresponds to the hypothesis that Q is generated from a Gaussian $N(\mu = 90, \sigma^2 = 100)$, while $F = 1$ otherwise. Then the pair $(\mu = 90, \sigma = 10)$ is the target pattern in the current scenario. Define the criterion statistics to be

$$T_0 = \frac{Q - \mu}{\sigma} = \frac{Q - 90}{10} \quad \text{and} \quad T = |T_0|.$$

The critical decision boundary t_c could be, for example, the 95th symmetric percentile, i.e., the unique value t_c so that

$$\text{Prob}(|T_0| \geq t_c) = 5\% = 0.05, \quad \text{if indeed } T_0 \sim N(0, 1).$$

By this criterion, the chance of *miss* (i.e., failure to detect the target pattern while it is actually present) is controlled under 5 percent.

For a more general competition among multiple exclusive hypotheses,

$$F = f_1, f_2, \ldots, \text{or } f_N,$$

another popular inference method is the *maximum likelihood* (ML) criterion. Under the ML principle, given any observed image data $Q = q$, the hidden feature is estimated by

$$\hat{F} = \underset{f_i \in f_{1:N}}{\text{argmax}} \; p(Q = q \mid F = f_i);$$

i.e., the embedded feature is identified with the one leading to the ML of the observed image data.

For instance, suppose that a low-quality image $Q = u_0$ under a night vision goggle captures a walking man F with a baseball hat and that this man is known to be one of the twins named f_1 =Mike and f_2 =Jack. Mike and Jack share almost the same physical appearance, as well as clothes, except that Mike is fond of baseball hats while Jack only occasionally wears one. As a model, for example, assume that

$$p(u_0 \mid F = f_1) = p(\text{wearing a hat} \mid \text{Mike}) = 50\%,$$
$$p(u_0 \mid F = f_2) = p(\text{wearing a hat} \mid \text{Jack}) = 10\%,$$

meaning in the sense of a frequentist that Mike wears a baseball hat every other day while Jack wears one for only three days per month. Thus according to the ML criterion, the person (or pattern) in the image is $\hat{F} = f_1$ =Mike.

2.4.2 Bayesian Inference: Bias Due to Prior Knowledge

Such decision making can become more involved if other information is available about the unknown target patterns.

Following the preceding example, suppose in addition that the twins are residing in their hometown of Boston and that

(a) the particular image $Q = u_0$ was taken at Paris, France; and

(b) Mike as a school teacher travels only occasionally, while Jack as a salesman in a renowned international company travels much more frequently.

To make things easier, assume that the twins travel only between Boston and Paris and that

$$p(F = f_1 \mid \text{in Paris}) = p(F = \text{Mike} \mid \text{one of the twins in Paris}) = 10\%, \quad \text{and}$$
$$p(F = f_2 \mid \text{in Paris}) = p(F = \text{Jack} \mid \text{one of the twins in Paris}) = 90\%.$$

Since the picture $Q = u_0$ is known to be taken in Paris, one could simply drop the conditional symbol and write

$$p(F = f_1) = 10\% \quad \text{and} \quad p(F = f_2) = 90\%.$$

With this new piece of information, the ML method introduced in the preceding section apparently becomes insufficient. Consider the imaginary extreme case when

$$p(F = f_1) = 0 \quad \text{and} \quad p(F = f_2) = 100\%,$$

meaning that Mike never leaves Boston. Then it becomes irrational to identify the guy in image u_0 as Mike, as just inferred previously by the ML principle. A more reasonable inference strategy has to profit from the new a priori information $p(F = f)$.

The distribution $p(F = f)$ is said to be the *prior* information since it is available *prior to* the acquisition of data Q—the image u_0 taken in Paris in our case. That is, the prior probabilities of Mike and Jack in Paris are not affected by whether or not a photo is taken in Paris. (The *conditional* or *posterior* probabilities are, however, indeed influenced.)

Consequently, in terms of stochastic modeling, the distribution $p(F = f)$ of the target pattern or feature F is called the *prior model*, while the likelihood distribution $p(Q = u_0 \mid F = f)$ central to the ML inference procedure is called the *data model*, or *data generative model* to emphasize that F generates Q: $F \to Q$.

With prior knowledge available, a reasonable inference scheme should rely on both the prior model and data model. The central issue is how to properly combine the two, and one convenient answer would be simply to weigh their product:

$$g(F = f \mid Q = q) = \text{prior model} \times \text{data model} = p(F = f) \times p(Q = q \mid F = f). \tag{2.33}$$

One then identifies the target pattern as the one that maximizes this product:

$$\hat{F} = \underset{f \in f_{1:N}}{\operatorname{argmax}} \ g(F = f \mid Q = q).$$

Compared with the preceding section, this new inference strategy can be called the *biased* ML method and in fact is precisely the celebrated Bayesian inference approach. Continuing on the above thought-experiment on Mike and Jack, Bayesian inference compares the magnitude of

$$g(F = f_1 \mid Q = u_0) = 50\% \times 10\% = 5\% \quad \text{and} \quad g(F = f_2 \mid Q = u_0) = 10\% \times 90\% = 9\%$$

and draws the conclusion that the guy with a baseball hat in image u_0 is (more likely) Jack, which is completely opposite to the earlier ML estimator.

The legitimacy of the product form $g(F = f \mid Q = q)$ in (2.33) as a proper way to combine both the prior and data models is justified by the Bayesian formula for conditional probabilities:

$$p(F = f \mid Q = q) = \frac{p(F = f)p(Q = q \mid F = f)}{p(Q = q)},$$

or even more generally, for any two random events A and B,

$$p(A \mid B) = \frac{p(A)p(B \mid A)}{p(B)}.$$

Therefore, the product form g is precisely the *posterior* probability $p(F = f \mid Q = q)$ up to the denominator factor $p(Q = q)$, which is, however, a constant once a specific observation q is acquired. Indeed the denominator is merely a probability normalization constant:

$$p(Q = q) = \sum_{f \in f_{1:N}} p(F = f)p(Q = q \mid F = f).$$

Compared with the ML method in the preceding section, the Bayesian approach therefore maximizes the *posterior* likelihood, or equivalently, detects the most likely target pattern $F = f$ based (or conditioned) on the acquired image data $Q = q$.

The information-theoretic foundation [93] for the Bayesian approach can be understood as follows. The observed data Q is believed to contain some information about the target F, and therefore F should be readable or detectable from Q in some optimal way. In the case when Q contains no information about F, the data becomes useless, and Bayesian inference on F degenerates to a sheer maximization of the prior distribution $p(F = f)$. The above intuitive concepts of "information" or "mutual information" can be well quantified by information theory [93]. For example, the mutual information $I(F, Q)$ of F and Q is defined as

$$I(F, Q) = H(F) - H(F \mid Q) = H(Q) - H(Q \mid F) = H(F) + H(Q) - H(F, Q),$$

where $H(F)$, $H(Q)$, and $H(F, Q)$ are individual or joint entropies defined as in the preceding section on thermodynamics and statistical mechanics, while $H(F \mid Q)$ and $H(Q \mid F)$ are conditional entropies. We refer the reader to [93] for further details on these concepts.

2.4.3 Bayesian Method in Image Processing

Bayesian method has played a central role across the entire spectra of image processing and visual perception. See, for example, the monograph *Perception as Bayesian Inference* edited by Knill and Richards [176].

Regarding the two building blocks of a generic Bayesian inference model, the prior model $p(F = f)$ and the data model $p(Q = q \mid F = f)$, the former usually imposes major challenges and hence stays at the heart of many modeling tasks in image and vision analysis.

In terms of image processing, constructing sound image prior models in essence amounts to properly defining the very meaning of "images," which in [273] the second author identifies as the *fundamental problem* of image processing. Most image estimation tasks are usually ill-posed, and it is often the prior knowledge on images that introduces necessary bias, as well as significantly reduces the size of the ensemble of image candidates.

There are generally two ways of constructing image prior models: by learning or by direct modeling.

With large image data banks readily available in this information era, it is possible to learn the common features embedded in generic images based on statistical learning. For example, Zhu and Mumford [328], and Zhu, Wu, and Mumford [329] combined the maximum entropy principle with proper local visual filters to learn the dominant statistics of natural images. Learning theory, despite its long recognized central role in a number of disciplines, still remains a young field and needs much more attention and efforts from contemporary scientists. We refer the reader to the recent survey article by Poggio and Smale [252] as well as the classic monograph by Vapnik [307] for a good overview on the learning theory.

A less computationally expensive approach to image prior models is by direct construction, which is typically based on either some common visual experiences or some related physics principles for image formation.

For instance, for an ensemble of images randomly generated by some 2-phase crystal display devices, Ising's lattice model in statistical mechanics offers a natural image prior model [82]. More general image prior models can be similarly constructed using, for example, Gibbs' ensembles and Markov random fields, as studied in the celebrated work of Geman and Geman [130]. On the other hand, inspired by some common experiences in image perception, including translation invariance and scale invariance, Mumford and Gidas proposed image prior models based on a few fundamental axioms [225].

Computationally less demanding compared with the learning approach, the image prior models from such direct construction clearly lack data adaptivity and most often can only be employed as lower order approximations.

The next chapter shall reveal more details on both approaches to the construction of image prior models. The remaining chapters then further demonstrate the significant roles of such image prior information in many areas of image processing.

2.5 Linear and Nonlinear Filtering and Diffusion

In this section, we explore the main ideas underlying one of the most powerful tools in image and vision analysis—filtering. Mathematically, filtering is closely connected to the mollification operator in real analysis and the diffusion phenomenon in the PDE theory. Stochastically, filtering can be realized by random walks of microscopic particles.

2.5.1 Point Spreading and Markov Transition

For simplicity, first assume the ideal image domain is R^2 so that no unnecessary boundary technicality shall arise.

A 2-D *point spreading function* (PSF) $K(x, y)$ is a smooth function satisfying

(a) $\int_{R^2} K(x, y) = 1$, or equivalently, $\hat{K}(0, 0) = 1$;

(b) $\hat{K}(\omega_1, \omega_2)$ decays sufficiently fast as $|\omega| = \sqrt{\omega_1^2 + \omega_2^2} \to \infty$.

Here $\hat{K}$ stands for the 2-D Fourier transform

$$\hat{K}(\omega) = \hat{K}(\omega_1, \omega_2) = \int_{R^2} K(x, y)e^{-i(\omega_1 x + \omega_2 y)} \, dxdy.$$

In signal processing, they are called the *lowpass* conditions, since in combination when applied to images, such PSFs almost preserve low frequency components (condition (a)) while suppressing high frequency ones (condition (b)).

A *radially* symmetric PSF K is said to be *isotropic*. That is, there exists a single variable function $k(r^2)$ so that $K(x, y) = k(x^2 + y^2)$. More generally, K is said to be orientation selective or polarized, if

$$K(x, y) = k((x, y)A(x, y)^T) = k(ax^2 + 2bxy + cy^2),$$

for some positive definite matrix $A = [a, b; b, c]$.

A *nonnegative* PSF $K(x, y) \geq 0$ for $(x, y) \in \mathbb{R}^2$ could be naturally treated as a probability density function due to condition (a), which is also equivalent to the Markov condition for Markov transitions, as to be made clear below.

Given a PSF $K(x, y)$, the associated spreading or blurring transform for images is given by the convolution

$$v(x, y) = K * u(x, y) = \int_{R^2} K(x - p, y - q)u(p, q) \, dpdq. \qquad (2.34)$$

In the Fourier domain, it is simply $\hat{v} = \hat{K} \cdot \hat{u}$. In particular, $\hat{v}(0, 0) = \hat{u}(0, 0)$, which is exactly the conservation law if $u(x, y)$ is understood as a photon density function for optical signals:

$$\int_{R^2} v(x, y) \, dxdy = \int_{R^2} u(x, y) \, dxdy.$$

The spreading behavior could be easily visualized in the ideal case when $u = 1_R(x, y)$ and $K = 1_r(x, y)/(\pi r^2)$, the indicator functions of disks B_R and B_r centered at $(0, 0)$ with radii R and r. Then it can be easily shown that $v = K * u$ is supported over B_{R+r} and vanishes outside. That is, the original image information on B_R spreads out to an expanded region B_{R+r}.

When K is nonnegative, point spreading carries the beautiful stochastic interpretation by Markov transitions or random walks. Assume that $u(x, y)$ denotes the spatial density of photons. Imagine (which may not be physically plausible!) that each photon is moving randomly in the (x, y)-visual field and is subject to the one-step transition law

$$P(x, y|p, q)dxdy = K(x - p, y - q)dxdy, \qquad (2.35)$$

which describes the percentage of photons in the infinitesimal box $(p, p+dp) \times (q, q+dq)$ to be observed within $(x, x + dx) \times (y, y + dy)$ after one step. The Markov condition for random walks is then automatically satisfied:

$$\int_{R^2} P(x, y|p, q) \, dxdy = 1 \qquad \text{for any } (p, q),$$

which simply says that no photons are created or annihilated, and each photon either stays at the original place or transits to a new location after one step. Suppose the initial photon distribution is given by $u(x, y)$, and denote the new distribution after one step by $v(x, y)$. By the transition law, out of $u(p, q)dpdq$ photons, $P(x, y|p, q)dxdy$ percentage would be transferred to $(x, x + dx) \times (y, y + dy)$. Therefore,

$$v(x, y) \, dxdy = dxdy \int_{R^2} P(x, y|p, q)u(p, q) \, dpdq, \qquad (2.36)$$

which is exactly the spreading transform of u when P is given by (2.35).

Notice that so far the actual time lapse δt of the single transition step has been ignored. In the continuous and evolutionary setting, the transition should be time dependent:

$$P = P_t(x, y|p, q), \quad t \geq 0.$$

For Brownian motion [164, 228] for example, one has $P_{t+s} = P_t \circ P_s$, when P_t is understood as density transform operators as in (2.36). Furthermore, the dynamic transition law for Brownian motion is well known to be

$$P_t(x, y|p, q) = \frac{1}{2\pi t} e^{-\frac{(x-p)^2 + (y-q)^2}{2t}},$$

the 2-D isotropic Gaussian with variance $2t$ (one t from each dimension).

More generally in image and vision analysis, point spreading via random walks could be realized by the associated infinitesimal generators of parabolic PDEs, which we will now discuss.

2.5.2 Linear Filtering and Diffusion

Let us start with the digital setting of which (u_{ij}) is a given digital image defined on the canonical Cartesian lattice $(i, j) \in Z^2$. In the linear filtering theory, one has

$$\tilde{u}_{ij} = u_{ij} + \varepsilon \sum_{(k,l) \sim (i,j)} h_{ij,kl} \, u_{kl},$$

where $\varepsilon > 0$ is a constant weight, and h's are filter coefficients. The notation $(k, l) \sim (i, j)$ refers to all pixels (k, l) that are "connected" to (i, j). Connectivity is usually established by specifying neighboring windows, or edges in graph theory [87]. To respect the conservation law, the filter h must be *highpass* in the sense of

$$\sum_{(k,l) \sim (i,j)} h_{ij,kl} = 0 \qquad \text{at each } (i, j).$$

Consider, for example, the 5-pixel stencil

$$(k, l) \sim (i, j) \quad \text{if and only if} \quad |k - i| + |l - j| \leq 1 \qquad (2.37)$$

and the associated Laplacian filter

$$h_{ij,kl} = 1 \text{ if } |k - i| + |l - j| = 1; \quad \text{and} \quad h_{ij,ij} = -4.$$

original image

anisotropic diffusion: **vertical:horizontal=10:1**

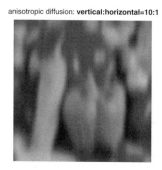

Figure 2.11. *An example of linear anisotropic diffusion by (2.38) with diagonal diffusivity matrix $D = \mathrm{diag}(D_x, D_y)$ and $D_y : D_x = 10 : 1$. The image thus diffuses much faster along the vertical y-direction.*

Then one has

$$\tilde{u}_{ij} - u_{ij} = \varepsilon\big[(u_{i+1,j} + u_{i-1,j} - 2u_{ij}) + (u_{i,j+1} + u_{i,j-1} - 2u_{ij})\big].$$

Introducing spatial step $\Delta x = \Delta y$ and time step Δt, we choose $\varepsilon = D\Delta t/(\Delta x)^2$ in such a way that D is a fixed constant of order 1. Then

$$\frac{\tilde{u}_{ij} - u_{ij}}{\Delta t} = D\left(\frac{u_{i+1,j} + u_{i-1,j} - 2u_{ij}}{(\Delta x)^2} + \frac{u_{i,j+1} + u_{i,j-1} - 2u_{ij}}{(\Delta y)^2}\right).$$

Letting Δt and $\Delta x = \Delta y$ pass towards 0, one ends up with the standard heat equation

$$\frac{\partial u}{\partial t} = D\left(\frac{\partial^2 u}{\partial x^2} + \frac{\partial^2 u}{\partial y^2}\right) = D\nabla^2 u,$$

provided that $u_{ij} = u(i\Delta x, j\Delta y, t)$ and $\tilde{u}_{ij} = u(i\Delta x, j\Delta y, t + \Delta t)$. Thus the iteration of this classical linear filter is tantamount to the diffusion process. More generally, by allowing $D = D(x, y)$ to vary spatially, or even to be a 2-by-2 positive definite matrix $D = [a(x, y), b(x, y); b(x, y), c(x, y)]$, one obtains the PDE version of spatially varying linear stationary filters:

$$u_t = \nabla \cdot [D\nabla u] = (au_x)_x + (bu_y)_x + (bu_x)_y + (cu_y)_y. \tag{2.38}$$

These equations are accompanied by suitable boundary conditions as well as the initial condition $u(x, y, 0) = u_0(x, y)$—the given image. Figure 2.11 shows an example.

Physically, diffusion is a typical self-driven evolutionary process, and the driving "force" is spatial inhomogeneity. It is also manifest in the flux formula

$$\mathbf{j} = -D\,\nabla u = -D(u_x, u_y)^T.$$

As long as $D = D(x, y) = [a, b; b, d]$ is positive definite, such flux must be gradient descent, since

$$\frac{\partial u}{\partial \mathbf{j}} = \mathbf{j} \cdot \nabla u = -(\nabla u)^T D(\nabla u) < 0.$$

Therefore, diffusion discourages the development of large gradients and diminishes fast local oscillations caused by random noise.

Furthermore, during a linear diffusion process, oscillations with different spatial wave numbers decay in different rates. For simplicity, first consider the case when $\Omega = \mathbb{R}^2$ and $D = [a, b; b, c]$ is a positive definite constant matrix. Denote by L the spatial linear operator $\nabla \cdot D \nabla$. A monochromatic oscillation in the direction of θ with spatial frequency k is given by $\phi(x) = e^{i\langle k, x\rangle}$, with $k = (k\cos\theta, k\sin\theta)$ and $x = (x, y)$. Then

$$L\phi = -kDk^T e^{i\langle k, x\rangle} = -\lambda\phi, \tag{2.39}$$

with $\lambda = kDk^T > 0$. Thus ϕ is L-invariant since $L\phi$ is still in the "direction" of ϕ, or loosely speaking, ϕ is the eigenvector of L associated with the eigenvalue λ. Invariance allows one to restrict the diffusion process $u_t = Lu$ within the ϕ-space and to try a solution in the form of $u(x, t) = g(t)\phi(x)$. Then

$$g'(t) = -\lambda g(t) \quad \text{and} \quad g(t) = g(0)e^{-\lambda t}, \tag{2.40}$$

which shows that the decaying rate for $\phi = e^{i\langle k, x\rangle}$ is $\lambda = kDk^T$. Since D is a fixed positive definite matrix, one has $\lambda = O(k^2)$, confirming the earlier assertion that faster oscillations die out faster during the diffusion process.

The above analysis beautifully carries on to linear diffusion processes on general *bounded* image domains with proper boundary conditions. The starting point is to first solve the invariant equations (2.39): $L\phi = \lambda\phi$ for suitable λ's to characterize different oscillatory modes on the domain. It is an eigenvalue problem since L, together with boundary conditions, behaves very much like a nonnegative matrix. The squared frequencies are generally quantized to

$$0 \le \lambda_1 \le \lambda_2 \le \cdots,$$

and their associated eigenfunctions depict the associated spatial patterns. Then the decay law (2.40) still holds.

Following this line, one observes the striking feature of diffusion: as $t \to \infty$, all oscillatory components with nonzero λ's must vanish. Under the Neumann adiabatic boundary condition for instance, only the direct-current component $\phi_1 \equiv 1$ associated with $\lambda_1 = 0$ remains in the end. Furthermore, by the conservation law (guaranteed by the adiabatic condition), one must have

$$u(x, t) \to c_1\phi_1 = \frac{1}{\text{area}(\Omega)} \int_\Omega u_0(x)dx \qquad \text{as } t \to \infty.$$

It is of course unwanted in image processing since all image features are wiped out.

Therefore in both practice and theory, it is a crucial problem to decide when to turn off the diffusion process before all major image features and visual patterns are gone. This time T_s is called the *optimal stopping time*. The answer clearly depends on the task at hand. For the removal of white noise with variance σ^2 for example, it could be shown that $T_s = O(\sigma^2)$. For spatially inhomogeneous noises, one could imagine that a uniform stopping time T_s cannot be sufficient to fully characterize the spatial inhomogeneity, unless the diffusivity coefficient D has already been adapted to the noise.

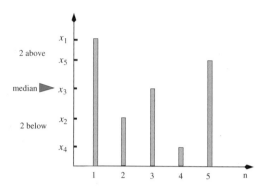

Figure 2.12. *The median of a 5-component segment from an imaginary 1-D signal* (x_n).

2.5.3   Nonlinear Filtering and Diffusion

Compared with most acoustic or sound signals, images differ in that they are discontinuous functions. The discontinuities in 2-D images are commonly associated with the boundaries of objects in the 3-D world, and therefore intrinsic and visually important. Effective filtering and diffusion processes must be able to distinguish such singularities from noisy oscillations. Linear diffusions fail on this aspect due to the lack of adaptivity to given images. Thus nonlinearity is naturally demanded in image analysis and processing.

The most well known and simplest nonlinear filter is perhaps the *median filter*:

$$\tilde{u}_{ij} = \text{median}\{u_{kl} : (k, l) \sim (i, j)\}. \tag{2.41}$$

Here as in the preceding subsections, interpixel connectivity $\sim$ is often specified by a local window, for example, the 5-by-5 Cartesian neighborhood. Figure 2.12 shows a 1-D example with a window of size 5.

Median filtering is a special example of the more general class of *order-statistics* filtering. Recall that for $2n + 1$ observations $(x_{-n}, \ldots, x_0, \ldots, x_n)$ (a window at index 0), the order statistics $x_{(-n)} \leq x_{(-n+1)} \leq \cdots \leq x_{(n)}$ are established by sorting the data in increasing order. Then a general lowpass order statistic filter H is specified by

$$\tilde{x}_0 = H(x_{-n}, \ldots, x_n) = h_{-n}x_{(-n)} + \cdots + h_n x_{(n)} \tag{2.42}$$

for some suitable set of filter coefficients h's. Notice that nonlinearity is caused by the association of the fixed filter coefficients with the order statistics, instead of with the original raw data. (The choice of $\tilde{x}_0$ is purely for the sake of illustration, and in principle one could use the same expression to update the value at any fixed index m between $-n$ and n.) For median filtering, $h_k = \delta_k$, the discrete Dirac delta sequence.

Due to its statistical nature (i.e., inside a window with enough data samples), median filter easily applies to noise removal. But why is it capable of preserving edges? As an example consider a simple 1-D "cliff" or Heaviside-type signal:

$$x = (\ldots, 1.4, \; 1.3, \; 1.2, \; 1.1, \; 1, \; 0, \; 0.1, \; 0.2, \; 0.3, \; 0.4, \ldots).$$

Assume that $x_0 = 1$, where the cliff is located. Applying the median filter with a symmetric window of length 5 (i.e., $n = 2$), one obtains the output sequence near the cliff,

$$\tilde{x}_{-2} = 1.2, \; \tilde{x}_{-1} = 1.1, \; \tilde{x}_0 = 1, \; \tilde{x}_1 = 0.2, \; \tilde{x}_2 = 0.2.$$

salt & pepper noise with 40% spatial density   a single pass of median filtering with a 7x7 window

Figure 2.13. *An example of using the median filter (with 7×7 centered square window) to denoise an image with severe salt-and-pepper noise. Notice the outstanding feature of median filtering: the edges in the restored image are not blurry.*

Although the values at $m = 1$ and 2 seem to be updated unwisely for such a piecewise smooth signal, the steep cliff at $m = 0$ is indeed well preserved. Figure 2.13 shows an example of image denoising via median filtering.

Now consider a general ideal 2-D Heaviside cliff defined by

$$u(x, y) = H(ax + by + c), \qquad (x, y) \in \mathbb{R}^2,$$

where a, b, c are constants and $H = H(s)$ is the Heaviside function: $H(s) = 1, s \geq 0$, and $H(s) = 0$ otherwise. The cliff spreads out along the straight line $ax + by + c = 0$. For any pixel (x_+, y_+) so that $ax_+ + by_+ + c > 0$, any median filter with a radially symmetric window (i.e., a disk) would lead to

$$\tilde{u}(x_+, y_+) = 1 = u(x_+, y_+),$$

simply because more pixels inside the disk window carry the value 1 than 0. Similarly, for any pixel (x_-, y_-) with $ax_- + by_- + c < 0$,

$$\tilde{u}(x_-, y_-) = 0 = u(x_-, y_-).$$

Therefore, the output from median filtering preserves the cliff in this highly idealized case.

Nonlinear filtering has become a very important research topic in digital signal and image processing [63]. We now turn to the class of nonlinear digital filters which are associated with nonlinear diffusions.

In order to macroscopically preserve edges, the randomly walking particles must not go across edge "cliffs." Thus in the density transition formula

$$\tilde{u}_{ij} = \sum_{(k,l) \sim (i,j)} P^\varepsilon_{ij,kl} u_{kl},$$

the transition probabilities $P^\varepsilon_{ij,kl}$'s have to be adaptive. For example, considering u as an energy function, as motivated by Gibbs' distribution law in the preceding section, one may define

$$P^\varepsilon_{ij,kl} = P^\varepsilon_{ij,kl}(u) = \frac{1}{Z^\varepsilon} e^{-\frac{|u_{ij} - u_{kl}|^\alpha}{\varepsilon}}, \qquad (k, l) \sim (i, j). \tag{2.43}$$

Here the controlling parameter ε plays the role of temperature, and the partition function Z^ε normalizes the total outgoing transition probability to 1:

$$\sum_{(i,j)\sim(k,l)} P^\varepsilon_{ij,kl} = 1 \qquad \text{for any } (k,l). \tag{2.44}$$

The power parameter α is also tunable. By this law, transitions between two neighboring pixels with huge difference in u are highly unlikely.

To derive the macroscopic diffusion PDEs, assume that $u_{ij} = u(ih, jh)$ with $\Delta x = \Delta y = h$ and that the lowpass condition holds:

$$\sum_{(k,l)\sim(i,j)} P^\varepsilon_{ij,kl} = 1 \qquad \text{at any } (i, j). \tag{2.45}$$

(P satisfying both (2.44) and (2.45) is said to be doubly stochastic.) Then the above density transition formula becomes

$$\tilde{u}_{ij} - u_{ij} = \sum_{(k,l)\sim(i,j)} P^\varepsilon_{ij,kl}(u_{kl} - u_{ij}).$$

Suppose the neighboring connectivity is specified by 5-pixel stencils as in the linear case before, and the transition probabilities bear the nonlinear form of

$$P^\varepsilon_{ij,kl} = P^\varepsilon\left(u_{\frac{i+k}{2},\frac{j+l}{2}},\ \nabla u_{\frac{i+k}{2},\frac{j+l}{2}}\right) \tag{2.46}$$

for some suitable continuous function $P^\varepsilon(u, \nabla u)$. To be precise, we now adopt the notation of $P^\varepsilon_{\frac{i+k}{2},\frac{j+l}{2}}$ for such $P^\varepsilon_{ij,kl}$. Then

$$\tilde{u}_{ij} - u_{ij} = P^\varepsilon_{i+\frac{1}{2},j}\,(u_{i+1,j} - u_{ij}) - P^\varepsilon_{i-\frac{1}{2},j}\,(u_{ij} - u_{i-1,j}) + \cdots$$

$$\simeq h\left[(P^\varepsilon \partial_x u)_{i+\frac{1}{2},j} - (P^\varepsilon \partial_x u)_{i-\frac{1}{2},j}\right] + \cdots$$

$$\simeq h^2 \partial_x(P^\varepsilon \partial_x u) + h^2 \partial_y(P^\varepsilon \partial_y u).$$

Here the two difference-differential approximations are both accurate to the leading orders on h. We now choose P^ε so that

$$P^\varepsilon = P^\varepsilon(u, \nabla u) = \frac{\varepsilon}{h^2} D(u, \nabla u) \qquad \text{for some fixed positive function } D.$$

By identifying $u_{ij} = u(ih, jh, t)$ and $\tilde{u}_{ij} = u(ih, jh, t + \varepsilon)$, we therefore obtain the nonlinear diffusion equation in the limit $\varepsilon, h \to 0$:

$$u_t = \nabla \cdot D(u, \nabla u)\,\nabla u.$$

Notice that to make the lowpass condition (2.45) valid, it suffices to require $P^\varepsilon \leq 1/4$, or $\varepsilon \|D\|_\infty / h^2 \leq 1/4$. In computational PDEs, this is well known to be the CFL condition named after Courant, Friedrichs, and Lewy [287]. In [251], Perona and Malik first proposed to properly choose the dependence of D on ∇u in order to preserve edges in images.

Similarly in the preceding example (2.43) inspired by Gibbs' distribution law, take $\varepsilon = h^\alpha / \beta$ for some fixed parameter β of order 1. Then to the leading order of h as $h \to 0$,

$$P^\varepsilon_{ij,(i\pm 1,j)} = \frac{1}{Z^\varepsilon} e^{-\beta |u_x|^\alpha_{i\pm\frac{1}{2},j}}, \qquad P^\varepsilon_{ij,(i,j\pm 1)} = \frac{1}{Z^\varepsilon} e^{-\beta |u_y|^\alpha_{i,j\pm\frac{1}{2}}}.$$

Define

$$D_1(\nabla u) = \frac{h^2}{\Delta t\, Z^\varepsilon} e^{-\beta |u_x|^\alpha}, \qquad D_2(\nabla u) = \frac{h^2}{\Delta t\, Z^\varepsilon} e^{-\beta |u_y|^\alpha},$$

with Δt denoting the time lapse to be associated with a single-step transition of the process. Let $\Delta t, h \to 0$ in such a way so that D_1 and D_2 both converge. Then we obtain the nonlinear anisotropic diffusion

$$u_t = \nabla \cdot D \nabla u = (D_1(\nabla u)u_x)_x + (D_2(\nabla u)u_y)_y,$$

with $D = \mathrm{diag}(D_1, D_2)$ being a diagonal matrix. Furthermore, as $h \to 0$, the partition function Z^ε converges to

$$Z = 1 + 2\left(e^{-\beta |u_x|^\alpha} + e^{-\beta |u_y|^\alpha}\right).$$

Thus if we let $h, \Delta t \to 0$ so that $h^2/\Delta t \to 3$, then

$$D_1 = \frac{3e^{-\beta |u_x|^\alpha}}{1 + 2\left(e^{-\beta |u_x|^\alpha} + e^{-\beta |u_y|^\alpha}\right)}, \qquad D_2 = \frac{3e^{-\beta |u_y|^\alpha}}{1 + 2\left(e^{-\beta |u_x|^\alpha} + e^{-\beta |u_y|^\alpha}\right)}. \tag{2.47}$$

The artificial choice of 3 leads to the simple yet tight estimation: $D_1 < 1$ and $D_2 < 1$.

2.6 Wavelets and Multiresolution Analysis

In this section, we intend to give a concise introduction to the *classical* wavelet theory [96, 204, 215, 290]. The most recent developments on geometric and nonlinear wavelets can be read in, e.g., [41, 107, 108, 155, 248].

2.6.1 Quest for New Image Analysis Tools

Unlike many other signals, images result from the random positioning of individual objects in the 3-D world. The most striking features of these objects are manifest in the large dynamic range of spatial scales and their easily recognizable (to human vision) differences in terms of surface geometry, reflectance, and various patterns of surface textures.

Being able to easily decorrelate and identify individual image objects and their patterns is thus demanded by image and vision analysis. Wavelets and their associated techniques have so far met such requirements most satisfactorily.

An individual wavelet, literally speaking, is a localized small wave. It acts as a virtual neuron that fires strongly whenever localized visual features are presented to it. Due to localization, it can respond strongly only when its window captures the target feature within.

Wavelet analysis studies how to design, organize, and analyze such wavelets and achieve efficient computational schemes. A significant portion of its mission is to scientifically model human and machine vision and to effectively perform various image processing tasks.

To better understand and appreciate the characteristics and advantages of wavelets, let us first briefly return to the analysis of conventional signals that are generated by typical physical systems. Near their equilibrium states, such systems could usually be well approximated by linear systems. An input f and output u are then connected by a linear system $\mathcal{A}$:

$$u = \mathcal{A}f \qquad \text{in the absence of noise.}$$

For any system such as a string of a guitar, the vocal channel of a human being, or the surface of a drum, the spatial part of $\mathcal{A}$ could often be well modelled by a second order elliptic operator

$$L = -\nabla \cdot D(x, t) \nabla + b(x, t),$$

where x and t denote the spatial and temporal variables, and D and b specify the physical nature of the target system. In practice, suitable boundary conditions have to be specified as well.

If the nature of the system is independent of time t: $D = D(x)$ and $b = b(x)$, its intrinsic states or eigenmodes are L-invariant and specified by the eigenvalue problem

$$L\phi_\lambda = \lambda\phi_\lambda \qquad \text{with suitable boundary conditions,}$$

where the eigenvalue λ reflects the energy level of the associated state. Generically, the system possesses a collection of eigenmodes,

$$(\phi_n, \lambda_n), \quad \text{ordered by } \lambda_0 \leq \lambda_1 \leq \cdots.$$

The general theory of second order linear elliptic operators [117, 132] claims that $\lambda_n \to \infty$ as $n \to \infty$, and $(\phi_n)_n$ provides a natural linear basis for studying signal generation and evolution under the linear system $\mathcal{A}$, which is typically connected to $\partial_t - L$ if $\mathcal{A}$ is purely *diffusive* or $\partial_{tt} - L$ if $\mathcal{A}$ is purely *convective*.

For instance, consider the small-amplitude vibration of a string with length a and two ends fastened. Its eigenmodes are given by

$$-u_{xx} = \lambda u, \qquad u(0) = u(a) = 0.$$

Then it is well known that

$$\lambda_n = \left(\frac{\pi}{a}\right)^2 n^2, \quad n = 1, 2, \ldots \text{ and } \phi_n = \sqrt{\frac{2}{a}} \sin\left(\frac{n\pi}{a}x\right), \tag{2.48}$$

so that $(\phi_n)_n$ is an orthonormal basis of harmonic waves for $L^2(0, a)$. As is clear from the expressions, these harmonic modes neatly combine both the motion law (of strings) and the global geometry (i.e., size a), and therefore cannot be local.

The nonlocality can be further made explicit by considering the signal diffusion problem

$$u_t = u_{xx}, \ 0 < x < a, \qquad u(0) = u(a) = 0,$$

with the initial shape given by Dirac's delta $u(x, 0) = f = \delta(x - a/2)$, an idealized local impulse at the middle point. The signal diffusion can be expressed by $u(x, t) = \sum_{n=1}^{\infty} a_n(t)\phi_n(x)$. Notice that the initial impulse equally contaminates *all* the odd eigenmodes since

$$a_{2n+1}(0) = \langle \phi_{2n+1} , \delta(x - a/2) \rangle = \pm \sqrt{\frac{2}{a}}.$$

Spatial localization is therefore not intrinsic for such systems. One has to turn to wavelets for localized signal analysis or processing.

2.6.2 Early Edge Theory and Marr's Wavelets

Edge is the most common and significant visual feature in images, which defines and differentiates objects and leaves crucial cues for 3-D spatial orders [234]. Consequently, it is one of the most fundamental problems in image and vision analysis to properly define and extract edges from 2-D images, as initiated by Marr [210], and Marr and Hildreth [211] and further advanced by many others [44, 130, 165, 226].

Marr defined edges of an image u to be the locations where $\Delta u_\sigma = 0$, the zero-crossings of the Laplacian of the image u mollified to the scale of σ. More specifically, let $x = (x_1, x_2)$ and $r = |x|$, and let

$$G(x) = \frac{1}{2\pi} e^{-\frac{x^2}{2}} \quad \text{and} \quad G_\sigma(x) = \frac{1}{\sigma^2} G\left(\frac{x}{\sigma}\right) = \frac{1}{2\pi\sigma^2} e^{-\frac{x^2}{2\sigma^2}}, \qquad (2.49)$$

so that G_σ is a radially symmetric probability density with variance $2\sigma^2$. Then $u_\sigma = u * G_\sigma$, and

$$\Delta u_\sigma = u * \Delta G_\sigma = u * \psi_\sigma,$$

where $\psi_\sigma = \Delta G_\sigma$ is now often called Marr's wavelet:

$$\psi_\sigma = \frac{1}{\pi\sigma^4} \left(\frac{x^2}{2\sigma^2} - 1\right) e^{-\frac{x^2}{2\sigma^2}} = \frac{1}{\sigma^4} \psi_1\left(\frac{x}{\sigma}\right). \qquad (2.50)$$

Notice that ψ_σ satisfies the *highpass* condition $\int_{R^2} \psi_\sigma = 0$. Plotted in Figure 2.14 are two examples of Marr's wavelets with different σ's.

The intuition behind Marr's zero-crossing edge theory is as follows. Suppose u has an ideal step edge along a straight line segment l. Let t denote the unit tangent

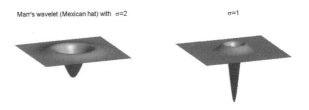

Figure 2.14. *Two examples of Marr's wavelets ("Mexican hats") as in (2.50).*

direction of l and n its unit normal. Then (t, n) provides a local Cartesian coordinates and

$$\Delta = \frac{\partial^2}{\partial t^2} + \frac{\partial^2}{\partial n^2},$$

due to the rotational invariance of the Laplacian. Suppose $\sigma \ll \text{length}(l)$. Then u_σ is still translation-invariant along the t-direction (up to an exponentially small deviation). Therefore, we have

$$\frac{\partial u}{\partial t} \simeq 0, \quad \frac{\partial^2 u}{\partial t^2} \simeq 0, \quad \text{and} \quad \Delta u_\sigma \simeq \frac{\partial^2 u_\sigma}{\partial n^2}.$$

Thus the zero-crossings of Δu_σ are the inflection points in the n-direction where $|\nabla u_\sigma| = |\partial u_\sigma / \partial n|$ reaches the maxima. For general images, to distinguish nontrivial inflection edge points from trivial ones in slowly varying regions, it seems necessary to keep track of the gradient information ∇u_σ as well [44].

In this well-known example, Marr's wavelets ψ_σ's are merely used as local detection tools. The term "wavelet" is used here in the broadest sense of Kronland-Martinet, Morlet, and Grossmann [185], namely, any function $\psi(x)$ that decays sufficiently fast at ∞, and satisfies the highpass condition $\int_{R^2} \psi = 0$.

2.6.3 Windowed Frequency Analysis and Gabor Wavelets

Compared with the conventional (Fourier) frequency analysis, windowed frequency analysis promotes locality by applying Fourier transform to the windowed image signal $w(x-a)u(x)$, where $w(x) = w(x_1, x_2)$ stands for a local window and $a = (a_1, a_2)$ its moving center. A window $w(x)$ is often a rapidly decaying real function with $\int_{R^2} w^2 = 1$. The windowed Fourier transform (wFT) of a given image $u(x) = u(x_1, x_2)$ is defined to be

$$U(a, k) = \int_{R^2} u(x)w(x - a)e^{-i\langle k, x\rangle} \, dx, \qquad (2.51)$$

which is a four-dimensional (4-D) function of location $a = (a_1, a_2)$ and spatial frequency $k = (k_1, k_2)$. It could be approximately understood as the strength of spatial frequency k locally at $x = a$.

The wFT (2.51) is also the projection of the image u onto a collection of localized waves

$$\psi_{a,k}(x) = w(x - a)e^{i\langle k, x\rangle}, \qquad a, k \in \mathbb{R}^2, \qquad (2.52)$$

with moving center a and local frequency k. Therefore, $\psi_{a,k}$'s are naturally called wavelets. When w is a scaled Gaussian, they are popularly known as the Gabor wavelets.

The reconstruction procedure is carried out as if $(\psi_{a,k})_{a,k}$ were an orthonormal basis:

$$u(x) = \int_{R^2} \int_{R^2} U(a, k)\psi_{a,k}(x) \, \frac{dk \, da}{(2\pi)^2}, \qquad (2.53)$$

mainly thanks to the facts that by (2.51) the inverse Fourier transform on x alone can recover $w(x - a)u(x)$ and that

$$\int_{R^2} w^2(x - a)da = \int_{R^2} w^2 = 1.$$

As for Marr's wavelets, one could also introduce multiple scales into wFT by rescaling the given window. Define

$$w_\sigma(x_1, x_2) = \frac{1}{\sigma} w\left(\frac{x}{\sigma}\right)$$

and $\psi_{a,k,\sigma}(x) = w_\sigma(x - a)e^{i\langle k, x\rangle}$, which lead to the most general Gabor wavelets. Then multiscale wFT is defined as

$$U_\sigma(a, k) = \langle u(x), \psi_{a,k,\sigma}(x)\rangle.$$

As before, $u(x)$ could be perfectly reconstructed from U_σ at any single scale.

The most serious drawback of such Gabor wavelets is that the scale σ and the spatial frequency k are combined in a rather crude manner (i.e., via uncorrelated tensor product). In practice, they should be coupled: high frequencies are more necessary for resolving small-scale features, while low frequencies alone usually suffice for large-scale ones.

Another issue concerns the redundancy in the analysis step (2.51) and the stability in the synthesis step (2.53). The 4-D space-frequency parameter space $(a, k) \in \mathbb{R}^2 \times \mathbb{R}^2$ apparently looks redundant for encoding 2-D images. Moreover, lack of orthogonality (or near orthogonality) could potentially cause serious stability problems due to image noises or approximation errors.

These considerations have inspired further advancement in wavelet theory.

2.6.4 Frequency-Window Coupling: Malvar–Wilson Wavelets

For simplicity, we shall only work with 1-D signals on the entire real axis $\mathbb{R}$. Suppose we have a collection of windows

$$w_n(x), \quad n = 0, \pm 1, \pm 2, \ldots$$

covering the whole space so that supp $w_n = [a_n, b_n]$ are finite intervals with *variable* lengths $l_n = b_n - a_n$.

Then each windowed image $u_n(x) = w_n(x)u(x)$ is chopped onto $[a_n, b_n]$. By l_n-periodic extension, $u_n(x) \to \hat{u}_n(x)$, $\hat{u}_n$ could be perfectly recovered (in $L^2(a_n, b_n)$) by the Fourier coefficients:

$$U(n, k) = \langle \hat{u}_n(x), e^{i\frac{2\pi}{l_n}kx}\rangle = \langle u(x), \psi_{n,k}(x)\rangle, \tag{2.54}$$

where the first inner product is in $L^2(a_n, b_n)$, and $\psi_{n,k}(x) = w_n(x)e^{i\frac{2\pi}{l_n}kx}$ are new wavelets. Notice the coupling between window sizes l_n and the frequency components.

Assume as before that $\sum_n w_n^2(x) = 1$ for all $x \in \mathbb{R}$. Then

$$\sum_{n\in Z}\sum_{k\in Z} \frac{1}{l_n} U(n, k)\psi_{n,k}(x) = \sum_{n\in Z} w_n(x) \sum_{k\in Z} \frac{1}{l_n}\langle \hat{u}_n(y), e^{i\frac{2\pi}{l_n}ky}\rangle e^{i\frac{2\pi}{l_n}kx}$$

$$= \sum_{n\in Z} w_n(x)\hat{u}_n(x) = \sum_{n\in Z} u_n(x)w_n(x)$$

$$= u(x) \sum_{n\in Z} w_n^2(x) = u(x).$$

That is, perfect reconstruction is again achieved from the wavelet coefficients $U(n, k)$, $n, k \in Z$. Compared with the continuous wFT $U(a, k)$, $a, k \in \mathbb{R}$ discussed in the previous section, redundancy has been substantially reduced though not completely removed. More importantly, in the new set of wavelets $\psi_{n,k}(x)$, spatial resolution has been made more efficient after the incorporation of the window sizes l_n into the harmonics.

How could redundancy still remain in this improved version of discretized wFT? It is rooted in the inevitable overlapping of the windows as demanded by the normalization condition

$$\sum_{n \in Z} w_n^2(x) = 1, \qquad x \in \mathbb{R},$$

and the necessary regularity conditions imposed on the windows for a number of analytical as well as computational reasons.

In the case when the windows $(w_n)_n$ are "hard cutters,"

$$w_n(x) = 1_{[a_n, a_{n+1})}(x), \qquad \cdots < a_n < a_{n+1} < \cdots , \tag{2.55}$$

i.e., nonsmooth indicator functions associated with a partition of the whole space, one could easily show that indeed redundancy is completely gotten rid of since $(\psi_{n,k}/\sqrt{l_n})_{n,k}$ is an orthonormal basis of $L^2(R)$. But such cheap orthonormality comes at the heavy cost of approximation precision: for a generic smooth image $u(x)$, a simple nonconstant linear function for example, the approximation error decays at a sluggish rate of $O(|k|^{-1})$. Therefore, much "softer" or smoother windows are preferred for securing high order accuracy in image analysis and synthesis.

The key questions are, Using smooth windows, can one indeed design an orthonormal basis that is very similar to $(\psi_{n,k})_{n,k}$? and In which aspects can $\psi_{n,k}$'s be further polished? The answer to the feasibility part is affirmative. Among many of the existing designs, we now give a brief introduction to the remarkable approach of Malvar [205] and Wilson [321], which leads to what are called Malvar–Wilson wavelets and their variants [91, 215].

First, choose a smooth window template $w(x)$ which satisfies (see Figure 2.15):

1. w is supported on $[-\pi, 3\pi]$ and symmetric around $x = \pi$: $w(2\pi - x) = w(x)$;
2. restricted on $[-\pi, \pi]$, $w(x)$ satisfies the nonaliasing condition $w^2(x) + w^2(-x) = 1$.

Generate a sequence of windows by 2π-translations: $w_n(x) = w(x - 2n\pi)$, $n = 0, \pm 1, \pm 2,$ .... Then the symmetry and nonaliasing condition lead to

$$\sum_n w_n^2(x) = 1, \qquad x \in \mathbb{R}.$$

Notice that the infinite sum consists only of at most two terms since supp w_n and supp w_m never overlap for $|n - m| > 1$.

If the old construction (2.54) were to be followed, one would have to utilize $e^{i\frac{k}{2}x}$, $k \in Z$, to be associated with each window $w_n(x)$ since $l_n \equiv l_0 = 4\pi$, or equivalently,

$$\left\{ \cos \frac{k}{2}x : k = 0, 1, \ldots \right\} \quad \text{and} \quad \left\{ \sin \frac{k}{2}x : k = 1, 2, \ldots \right\}. \tag{2.56}$$

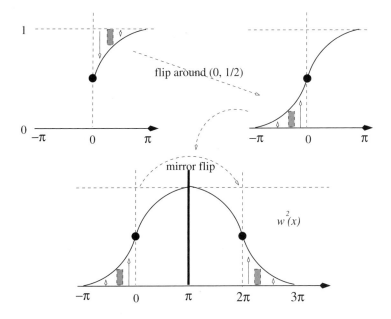

Figure 2.15. *A generic approach to designing the window template $w(x)$ via symmetrically constructing the profile of its square $w^2(x)$.*

But two adjacent windows w_n and w_{n+1} do clearly overlap and inevitably introduce redundancy, which can, however, be cleverly removed by an *alternated* "downsampling" of factor 2. That is, associated with any even window $w_{2n}(x)$, one applies only half from (2.56),

$$\left\{ \cos \frac{k}{2}x : k = 0, 1, \ldots \right\},$$

while for any odd window w_{2n+1}, one applies the other half,

$$\left\{ \sin \frac{k}{2}x : k = 1, 2, \ldots \right\}.$$

Therefore, we have derived the set of so-called Malvar–Wilson wavelets:

$$\psi_{2n,k} = c_k w_{2n}(x) \cos \frac{k}{2}x, \quad k \geq 0, \quad \text{and} \quad \psi_{2n+1,k} = c_k w_{2n+1}(x) \sin \frac{k}{2}x, \tag{2.57}$$

where $c_0 = 1$ and $c_k = \sqrt{2}, k \geq 1$ for L^2 normalization.

The beautiful fact is that the Malvar–Wilson wavelets $(\psi_{n,k})_{n,k}$ consist into an orthonormal basis in $L^2(R)$! The interorthogonality between two adjacent wavelets

$$\langle \psi_{n,k}(x), \psi_{n+1,l}(x) \rangle = 0$$

results from the symmetry (or evenness) of the template $w(x)$ and the oddness of the product of a cosine with a sine, while the intraorthogonality between two wavelets within a common window

$$\langle \psi_{n,k}(x) , \ \psi_{n,l}(x) \rangle = 0$$

is guaranteed by the nonaliasing condition of the template as well as the fact that both

$$\left\{ c_k \cos \frac{k}{2}x : \ k = 0, 1, \ldots \right\} \quad \text{and} \quad \left\{ c_k \sin \frac{k}{2}x : \ k = 1, 2, \ldots \right\}$$

are orthonormal bases for $L^2[0, 2\pi]$. The very last statement follows from the fact that these cosines are exactly the eigenmodes of the Sturm–Liouville system

$$-u_{xx} = \lambda u, \ \ 0 \leq x \leq 2\pi, \ \ u'(0) = u'(2\pi) = 0,$$

while the sines are the eigenmodes of

$$-u_{xx} = \lambda u, \ \ 0 \leq x \leq 2\pi, \ \ u(0) = u(2\pi) = 0.$$

This alternated cosine-sine association was first suggested by Nobel laureate Kenneth Wilson in the study of renormalization group theory [321], was later systematically developed in the remarkable paper by Daubechies, Jaffard, and Journé [97], and was also independently rediscovered in digital signal processing by Malvar [205].

The Malvar–Wilson wavelets could be extended into a broad class of orthonormal space-frequency wavelets, as done by Coifman and Meyer [91]. For example, one could replace the translation invariance of the windows

$$w_n(x) = w(x - na) \quad \text{for some suitable } a$$

by dilation invariance

$$w_n(x) = w(\lambda^n x) \quad \text{for some } \lambda > 0, \ \ \lambda = 2 \text{ for example.}$$

Such windows have variable window lengths, and accordingly the associated cosine and sine waves should be scaled proportionally. Much more generally, one could completely abandon a single-window template and the translation- or scaling-invariant property and individually design each window w_n. As long as one

1. maintains the nonaliasing condition for intraorthogonality and
2. well coordinates the symmetry behavior of any pair of adjacent windows and their associated harmonic waves in the overlapping region for interorthogonality,

an orthonormal basis of space-frequency wavelets is still easily achievable by this design.

2.6.5 The Framework of Multiresolution Analysis (MRA)

From the designs of Gabor to Malvar–Wilson, wavelets still live in the mighty shadow of Fourier frequency analysis. Historically, the situation did not make an energetic turn until Meyer and Mallat introduced the independent and general framework of multiresolution analysis (MRA). Though mainly originated from methodologies in signal and image processing, MRA does not look completely strange to scientists working on multiscale phenomena such as multiscale turbulence flows and multigrid methods.

The contributions of the MRA framework to the development of wavelets have been extraordinary for a number of crucial reasons. First, woven into the core principles of MRA are a few ingenious novel ideas in modern signal and image processing. Second, MRA provides a systematic approach for wavelet construction and analysis. More remarkably, it allows fast and efficient digital implementations for image analysis and synthesis by wavelets. Finally and above all, it lifts wavelet theory out of the shadow of Fourier frequency analysis and puts it on the solid and self-contained foundation of multiscale analysis.

MRA is an elegant mathematical framework for representing and analyzing images and general signals in multiple scales. An orthonormal MRA of $L^2(R)$ is an ordered chain of closed subpspaces:

$$\cdots \subseteq V_{-1} \subseteq V_0 \subseteq V_1 \subseteq \cdots, \tag{2.58}$$

which satisfies the following three conditions:

1. [Completeness] $\overline{\lim_{j \to \infty} V_j} = L^2(R)$, and $\lim_{j \to -\infty} V_j = \{0\}$.
2. [Dyadic Similarity] $u(x) \in V_j \Leftrightarrow u(2x) \in V_{j+1}$.
3. [Translation Seed]   There exists a function $\phi \in V_0$, so that $(\phi(x - k))_k$ is an orthonormal basis of V_0.

Thus if such an MRA indeed exists, the entire $L^2(R)$ world can be coded by a single "seed" function ϕ. In fact, define

$$\phi_{j,k} = 2^{j/2}\phi(2^j x - k), \qquad j, k \in Z.$$

By dyadic similarity, $(\phi_{j,k})_k$ is also an orthonormal basis of V_j. By the completeness postulation, any image $u(x) \in L^2(R)$ can be well approximated to any desired precision by its projection $u_j = P_j u$ onto V_j:

$$u_j = P_j u = \sum_k \langle u, \phi_{j,k} \rangle \phi_{j,k}.$$

In this sense, in the early days of wavelet theory, ϕ was often called the "father" wavelet. It is now usually called the *scaling function*, or the *shape function* by some computational scientists.

As a necessary condition, the scaling function must satisfy the two-scale similarity condition

$$\phi(x) = 2 \sum_k h_k \phi(2x - k) = \sum_k (\sqrt{2}h_k)\phi_{1,k} \tag{2.59}$$

with the coefficients $(h_k)_k$ given by

$$h_k = \frac{1}{\sqrt{2}} \langle \phi, \phi_{1,k} \rangle, \qquad k \in Z.$$

In practice, (2.59) provides the equation for designing the scaling function $\phi(x)$ from appropriate coefficients $(h_k)_k$ and is often called the *two-scale relation*, the *refinement equation*, or the *dilation equation*.

Another characteristic condition on the scaling function is that $\int_R \phi \neq 0$, assuming that $\phi \in L^2(R) \bigcap L^1(R)$. To avoid unnecessary technicality, assume for simplicity that ϕ is compactly supported. (Generally, a moderate decay rate such as $\phi = O(|x|^{-1-\epsilon})$ at $x = \pm\infty$, combined with tools such as the Lebesgue dominated convergence theorem, will still be able to accomplish the following proof.) Suppose otherwise $\int_R \phi = 0$. Then

$$\int_R \phi_{j,k} = 0, \qquad j, k \in Z.$$

Take any image $u \in L^2$ that is compactly supported and $\int_R u = 1$. Then at any given scale level j with $u_j = P_j u$,

$$\int_R u_j = \sum_k \langle u , \phi_{j,k} \rangle \int_R \phi_{j,k} = 0, \tag{2.60}$$

since the infinite sum is actually finite. On the other hand, by the completeness postulation of MRA, $u_j \to u$ in L^2 as $j \to +\infty$. Since all $(u_j)_{j \geq 0}$ can be easily shown to be uniformly compactly supported, one must have, as $j \to \infty$,

$$u_j \to u \text{ in } L^1 \text{ and } \int_R u_j \to \int_R u = 1,$$

which contradicts (2.60).

This seemingly trivial condition has profound influences. First, it allows one to normalize the scaling function by $\int_R \phi = 1$. Then the dilation equation (2.59) implies that

$$1 = \sum_k h_k,$$

which is called the *lowpass* condition in digital signal processing when $h = (h_k)_k$ is considered as a digital filter. Second, applying Fourier transform to the dilation equation (2.59) leads to

$$\hat{\phi}(\omega) = H\left(\frac{\omega}{2}\right) \hat{\phi}\left(\frac{\omega}{2}\right), \tag{2.61}$$

where $H(\omega) = \sum_k h_k e^{-ik\omega}$ is the impulse response of the filter h. In combination with $\hat{\phi}(0) = 1$, iteration of (2.61) gives the explicit expression of the scaling function in the frequency domain:

$$\hat{\phi}(\omega) = H\left(\frac{\omega}{2}\right) H\left(\frac{\omega}{4}\right) \cdots = \prod_{j=1}^{\infty} H\left(\frac{\omega}{2^j}\right). \tag{2.62}$$

Thus the scaling function is completely determined by the lowpass filter h.

Consequently, it can be expected that the orthonormality condition on $(\phi(x - k))_k$ should be reflected by the filter $h = (h_k)_k$ as well. To validate this expectation, first define a 2π-periodic function

$$A(\omega) = \sum_n |\hat{\phi}|^2 (\omega + 2n\pi). \tag{2.63}$$

By the two-scale relation in the frequency domain (2.61), we have

$$A(2\omega) = \sum_n |\hat{\phi}|^2(2\omega + 2n\pi)$$

$$= \sum_{n=2m} |H|^2(\omega)|\hat{\phi}|^2(\omega + 2m\pi) + \sum_{n=2m+1} |H|^2(\omega + \pi)|\hat{\phi}|^2(\omega + \pi + 2m\pi).$$

Therefore, we obtain one of the most important equations in MRA:

$$A(2\omega) = |H|^2(\omega)A(\omega) + |H|^2(\omega + \pi)A(\omega + \pi). \tag{2.64}$$

On the other hand, since $(\phi(x - k)_k)$ are orthonormal, one has

$$\langle \phi(x) , \phi(x - k) \rangle = \delta_k, \qquad \text{or equivalently,} \quad \frac{1}{2\pi}\langle \hat{\phi} , e^{-ik\omega}\hat{\phi} \rangle = \delta_k.$$

Still denote the inner product in $L^2(0, 2\pi)$ by $\langle \cdot , \cdot \rangle$. The last identity is then equivalent to

$$\frac{1}{2\pi}\langle A(\omega) , e^{-ik\omega} \rangle = \delta_k,$$

which immediately implies that

$$A(\omega) \equiv 1 \quad \text{in } L^2(0, 2\pi).$$

By the general identity (2.64), we have thus derived a necessary condition on the lowpass filter $h = (h_k)_k$ in an orthonormal MRA:

$$1 = |H|^2(\omega) + |H|^2(\omega + \pi), \qquad \omega \in (0, \pi). \tag{2.65}$$

The lowpass condition $H(0) = 1$ then immediately implies that $H(\pi) = 0$, and the digital filter indeed suppresses high frequencies. In practice, identity (2.65) provides a good starting point of designing orthonormal MRA [96].

Thus far we have only discussed the scaling function ϕ and its associated lowpass filter $h = (h_k)_k$. The real beauty of MRA of course cannot terminate here since wavelets have not yet emerged from the analysis.

In MRA, wavelets correspond to the details that are lost during the transfers from fine scales to coarser ones. Due to the dyadic scale similarity in MRA, it is sufficient to focus on a representative pair of adjacent scales: $V_0 \subseteq V_1$. V_1 has finer details, and the orthogonal projection of an image $u_1 \in V_1$ onto $u_0 \in V_0$: $u_0 = P_0 u_1$ is to wipe out some details of u_1 that are impossible to detect in V_0. Let W_0 denote the range of $(I - P_0)|_{V_1}$, or equivalently, the space of "details." Then

$$V_1 = V_0 \oplus W_0, \qquad P_0 W_0 = \{0\}. \tag{2.66}$$

Generally, let W_j denote the space of details at scale $\lambda = 2^{-j}$, i.e., $V_{j+1} = V_j \oplus W_j$. Then it is easy to see that the dyadic scale similarity of MRA is faithfully inherited:

$$\eta(x) \in W_j \Leftrightarrow \eta(2x) \in W_{j+1}, \quad j \in Z.$$

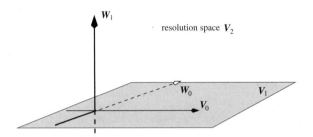

Figure 2.16. *MRA as (Hilbert) space decompositions: the finer resolution space V_2 is decomposed to the detail (or wavelet) space W_1 and coarser resolution space V_1. The same process applies to V_1 and all other V_j's* [290].

The completeness of MRA is now read as

$$L^2(R) = V_J \oplus \sum_{j \geq J} W_j = \sum_{j=-\infty}^{\infty} W_j, \qquad (2.67)$$

where J is any arbitrary reference scale level, and the two infinite sums always denote the smallest closed subspaces of $L^2(R)$ that contain all the relevant wavelet spaces. The formula shows that a general image $u(x) \in L^2(R)$ is the accumulated effect of its details at all scales. Figure 2.16 gives a low-dimensional visualization to the relations among different subspaces.

Introduce the dilation notation for a given subspace $U \subseteq L^2(R)$,

$$U(2x) = \{f(2x)| f \in U\}.$$

Then (2.67) could also be written as

$$L^2(R) = \sum_{j=-\infty}^{\infty} W_0(2^j x),$$

which clearly shows that W_0 completely determines the representation and analysis of images in $L^2(R)$.

To further reveal the structure of W_0, consider a general element $\eta(x) \in W_0$. By (2.66), one must have

$$\eta(x) = 2 \sum_k g_k \phi(2x - k) = \sum_k (\sqrt{2} g_k) \phi_{1,k}, \qquad g_k = \frac{1}{\sqrt{2}} \langle \eta, \phi_{1,k} \rangle, \qquad (2.68)$$

or, in the frequency domain,

$$\hat{\eta}(\omega) = G\left(\frac{\omega}{2}\right) \hat{\phi}\left(\frac{\omega}{2}\right). \qquad (2.69)$$

The set of coefficients $g = (g_k)_k$ have to reflect the nature of "details," i.e., $W_0 \perp V_0$, which amounts to $\langle \eta, \phi(x + k) \rangle = 0, k \in Z$, or in the frequency domain,

$$\left\langle (\hat{\eta}\overline{\hat{\phi}})(\omega), e^{ik\omega} \right\rangle = 0, \quad k \in Z.$$

After 2π-periodization, it leads to

$$\sum_n \left(\hat{\eta}\overline{\hat{\phi}}\right)(\omega + 2n\pi) = 0 \quad \text{in } L^2(0, 2\pi).$$

Having ω replaced by 2ω, and applying the two-scale relations (2.61) and (2.69), we obtain

$$G(\omega)\bar{H}(\omega)A(\omega) + G(\omega + \pi)\bar{H}(\omega + \pi)A(\omega + \pi) = 0,$$

where A is as given in (2.63). Since $A(\omega) \equiv 1$ due to the orthonormality of $(\phi(x - k))_k$, we have

$$G(\omega)\bar{H}(\omega) + G(\omega + \pi)\bar{H}(\omega + \pi) = 0. \tag{2.70}$$

Define $\lambda(\omega) = G(\omega)e^{iL\omega}/\bar{H}(\omega + \pi)$ for a fixed *odd* integer L. Then the last equation becomes

$$\lambda(\omega) = \lambda(\omega + \pi),$$

implying that $\lambda(\omega)$ must be a π-periodic function, or $C(\omega) = \lambda(\omega/2)$ 2π-periodic. Define a template

$$G_0(\omega) = e^{-i\omega L}\bar{H}(\omega + \pi).$$

Then $G(\omega) = G_0(\omega)C(2\omega)$, and

$$\hat{\eta}(\omega) = C(\omega)G_0\left(\frac{\omega}{2}\right)\hat{\phi}\left(\frac{\omega}{2}\right) = C(\omega)\hat{\psi}(\omega),$$

where $\psi = (G_0(\frac{\omega}{2})\hat{\phi}(\frac{\omega}{2}))^\vee$, defined by the template G_0, is called the *mother wavelet*. Assume the Fourier coefficients of $C(\omega)$ are $(c_k)_k$. Then it has been established that a general detail element $\eta \in W_0$ must be in the form of

$$\eta(x) = \sum_k c_k \psi(x - k).$$

Therefore, the detail space W_0 is spanned by all the integer translates of the mother wavelet $\psi(x)$.

We further show that $(\psi(x - k))_k$ is in fact an orthonormal basis of W_0. As for the scaling function, define

$$B(\omega) = \sum_n |\hat{\psi}|^2(\omega + 2n\pi).$$

Then it is adequate to show that $B(\omega) = 1$. Similar to the scaling function, the two-scale relation (2.69) easily leads to

$$\begin{aligned}
B(2\omega) &= |G_0|^2(\omega)A(\omega) + |G_0|^2(\omega + \pi)A(\omega + \pi) \\
&= |H|^2(\omega + \pi)A(\omega) + |H|^2(\omega)A(\omega + \pi) \\
&= |H|^2(\omega + \pi) + |H|^2(\omega) = 1.
\end{aligned}$$

Here we have applied $A(\omega) \equiv 1$ and (2.65).

By scale similarity,

$$\{\psi_{j,k} = 2^{j/2}\psi(2^j - k) \mid j, k \in Z\}$$

is an orthonormal basis for $L^2(R)$, in which sense that ψ has been fondly called the mother wavelet. It satisfies the so-called *wavelet equation*

$$\psi(x) = 2 \sum_k g_k \phi(2x - k) \qquad (2.71)$$

for a set of suitable coefficients $g = (g_k)$ as discussed above. Let $G(\omega)$ denote the Fourier transform of g. Then the necessary condition (2.70), combined with $H(0) = 1$ and $H(\pi) = 0$, leads to

$$G(0) = 0 \quad \text{and} \quad \hat{\psi}(0) = G(0)\hat{\phi}(0) = 0,$$

implying that $\int_R \psi = 0$. These conditions on G and ψ are called the *highpass* conditions of wavelets, since they both filter out low frequency components near $\omega \approx 0$.

In summary, an orthonormal MRA carries four pieces of crucial data: the scaling function ϕ and its lowpass filter h connected by the dilation equation

$$\phi(x) = 2 \sum_k h_k \phi(2x - k) \qquad (2.72)$$

and the mother wavelet ψ and its highpass filter g connected to the scaling function by the wavelet equation

$$\psi(x) = 2 \sum_k g_k \phi(2x - k). \qquad (2.73)$$

For orthonormality, the two filters must satisfy

$$1 = |H|^2(\omega) + |H|^2(\omega + \pi), \qquad (2.74)$$
$$0 = (G\bar{H})(\omega) + (G\bar{H})(\omega + \pi). \qquad (2.75)$$

The actual design of orthonormal MRA starts from these last two equations on the lowpass filter h and highpass filter g. In most applications in signal and image processing both h and g contain only a finite number of nonzero coefficients; then it essentially becomes a polynomial (or Laurent polynomial) design problem [95, 96, 290]. Such filters are said to have finite impulse responses (FIR) in digital signal processing [237]. Figure 2.17 shows a pair of scaling function and mother wavelet.

2.6.6 Fast Image Analysis and Synthesis via Filter Banks

We now further explain how the MRA framework leads to efficient computational algorithms for multiscale image analysis and synthesis.

By the completeness postulation, any image $u(x) \in L^2(R)$ could be approximated to any precision by its projections $u_j = P_j u$ onto increased resolutions V_j:

$$u_j = \sum_k c_k^j \phi_{j,k}, \qquad c_k^j = \langle u, \phi_{j,k} \rangle. \qquad (2.76)$$

The efficiency of MRA very much results from the intrinsic connections of such expansions at different scales, as nourished by the dyadic similarity postulation in the design of MRA. Thus in situations where multiple users are interested in different tasks and scales, there is a universal data storage and retrieval structure which could efficiently meet most of the

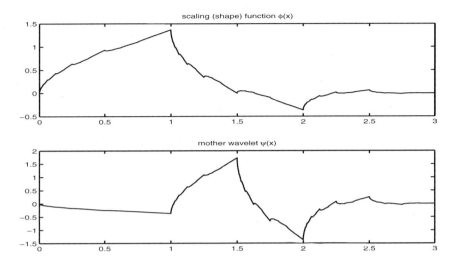

Figure 2.17. *A pair of compactly supported scaling function $\phi(x)$ and mother wavelet $\psi(x)$ by Daubechies' design* [96].

demands. In particular, it becomes unnecessary to work out the expensive integrals for *all* j and k in (2.76).

Such efficiency results from the two fundamental equations (2.72) and (2.73). By the dyadic similarity postulation, one has

$$\phi_{j,k} = \sum_l h_l\, \phi_{j+1,2k+l} \ \text{ and } \ \psi_{j,k} = \sum_l g_l\, \phi_{j+1,2k+l}.$$

Suppose that $u_{j+1} = u_j + w_j \in V_j \oplus W_j$. Then

$$c_k^j = \langle u\,,\ \phi_{j,k}\rangle = \left\langle u\,,\ \sum_l h_l \phi_{j+1,2k+l}\right\rangle = \sum_l h_l\, c_{2k+l}^{j+1}.$$

Similarly for the wavelet coefficients,

$$d_k^j = \langle u\,,\ \psi_{j,k}\rangle = \sum_l g_l\, c_{2k+l}^{j+1}.$$

Define the *transposes* of the two (real-valued) filters by spatial reversal:

$$\tilde{g}_l = g_{-l} \ \text{ and } \ \tilde{h}_l = h_{-l},$$

and as in digital signal processing also define the *downsampling* operator in l^2:

$$(\downarrow 2)c = (\downarrow 2)(\ldots, c_{-2}, c_{-1}, c_0, c_1, c_2, \ldots) = (\ldots, c_{-2}, c_0, c_2, \ldots) \tag{2.77}$$

by dumping all the odd components. Then the above results can be concisely expressed by

$$c^j = (\downarrow 2)(\tilde{h} * c^{j+1}) \ \text{ and } \ d^j = (\downarrow 2)(\tilde{g} * c^{j+1}), \tag{2.78}$$

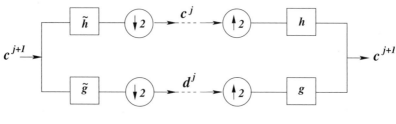

Analysis Bank   Synthesis Bank

Figure 2.18. *Fast wavelet transform via filter banks: the two-channel analysis (or decomposition) and synthesis (or reconstruction) banks.*

where the asterisk symbols denote discrete convolutions of sequences. It is exactly here that the mathematical framework of MRA neatly meets modern digital signal processing (DSP). In DSP, these two identities lead to a two-channel *analysis* filter bank $(\tilde{h}, \tilde{g})$, which takes c^{j+1} as the input and (c^j, d^j) as the output.

The iteration of this simple DSP unit leads to fast wavelet decomposition: starting from any fine scale $\lambda = 2^{-J}$,

$$c^J \to (d^{J-1}, c^{J-1}) \to \cdots \to (d^{J-1}, d^{J-2}, \ldots, d^0, c^0). \tag{2.79}$$

Therefore, once the representation at a fine scale is available, all the coarser-scale decompositions can be obtained by simply cascading the two-channel analysis bank, which spares the costly computation of all the inner product integrals.

The analysis bank (in Figure 2.18) is accompanied by its companion synthesis or reconstruction bank. In the orthonormal MRA framework, the synthesis bank is the "transpose" of the analysis bank, very much like the well-known linear algebra fact that inverting an orthogonal matrix amounts to transposing it. The transpose of the analysis filter pair $(\tilde{h}, \tilde{g})$ is simply (h, g), the original filter pair in the dilation and wavelet equations. The transpose of the downsampling operator $(\downarrow 2)$, as also well known in multigrid methods [34], is the upsampling operator $(\uparrow 2)$:

$$(\uparrow 2)\, c = (\uparrow 2)\, (\ldots, c_{-1}, c_0, c_1, \ldots) = (\ldots, c_{-1}, 0, c_0, 0, c_1, 0, \ldots).$$

Then the synthesis formula is given by (see Figure 2.18)

$$c^{j+1} = h * (\uparrow 2)(c^j) + g * (\uparrow 2)(d^j).$$

In combination, MRA goes completely digital, and in between the analysis bank and the synthesis bank in Figure 2.18, i.e., on the wavelet domain, lies the vast freedom for image coding, transmission, processing, or analysis.

The filter bank structure also immediately suggests the way for designing the so-called biorthogonal MRA in which $(\psi_{j,k})_{j,k}$ is only a Riesz basis for $L^2(R)$ and $(\phi_{j,k})_k$ for V_j. Digitally, it means that the synthesis filter pair (h_s, g_s) is no longer required to be the transpose of the analysis pair (h_a, g_a). Instead, a biorthogonal MRA imposes only the condition of *perfect* or *lossless* reconstruction:

$$(h_s*)(\uparrow 2)\,(\downarrow 2)(h_a*) + (g_s*)(\uparrow 2)\,(\downarrow 2)(g_a*) = \text{Id}, \quad \text{the identity operator.}$$

Of course, like computing the inverse of a general affine matrix A in linear algebra, one has to make sure that filter banks are well conditioned, so that both the analysis and synthesis steps are stable. The notion of biorthogonality greatly expands the family of MRA-based wavelets. And even more remarkably, it allows the scaling functions, wavelets, and their filters to be symmetric or to have even phases [290], a crucial technical virtue in signal and especially image processing.

Chapter 3

Image Modeling and Representation

The goal of image modeling or representation is to find proper ways to mathematically describe and analyze images. It is therefore the most fundamental step in image processing. One, however, must realize that there is no absolutely *the* best representation, since optimality inevitably depends upon specific processing tasks, as in the case of different representations of natural numbers: the decimal system is more convenient than the dyadic one in daily life, but the latter is more natural for digital or quantum computers. The current chapter introduces five general and useful approaches to image representation, based upon which many successful image processors are to be developed in later chapters.

3.1   Modeling and Representation: What, Why, and How

Digital images are most commonly presented as a matrix of scalars for gray-scale images or vectors for color images, since they are often captured by charge coupled device (CCD) arrays (as in digital cameras) or displayed by liquid crystal arrays (as for laptop or pocket computers). Pixel-matrix representation is, however, by no means the most efficient from the information-theoretic point of view. In what follows, we shall call such direct matrix representation $u = (u_{i,j})$ or its analog idealization $u = u(x, y)$ with $(x, y) \in \Omega = (a, b) \times (c, d)$, the *physical* image.

A *representation* of a given class U of physical images refers to a *transform* $\mathcal{T}$ under which any image u from the class is transformed to a new data type or structure $w = \mathcal{T}u$. Let W denote the range space of $\mathcal{T}$, which is also called the *transform space*. Then we have, for short,

$$\mathcal{T} : U \to W, \quad u \to w = \mathcal{T}u.$$

A *representation* is said to be *linear* if

1. both the image class U and its transform space W are *linear* spaces, or convex cones of linear spaces, so that for example, $au_1 + bu_2$ belongs to U as long as u_1 and u_2 do and $a, b \in \mathbb{R}$ or R^+; and

2. the transform is *linear*:

$$\mathcal{T}[au_1 + bu_2] = a\mathcal{T}u_1 + b\mathcal{T}u_2.$$

For instance, consider the class of all two-pixel images: $U = \{u = (s, t) : s, t \in \mathbb{R}^+\}$, which is a convex cone in R^2 (i.e., the first quadrant). Let the transform space be $w = (a, d) \in W = R^2$, and let $\mathcal{T}$ be the average-difference transform of Haar [96, 290]:

$$w = \mathcal{T}u : a = \frac{s + t}{2} \quad \text{and} \quad d = \frac{s - t}{2}. \tag{3.1}$$

It is the key linear transform for the construction of Haar's wavelets [96, 290].

Mathematically, even the human vision system could be considered as a (biological) representation operator $\mathcal{T}_h$. The photoreceptors (i.e., cones and rods) of the two retinas are indeed laid out very much in a 2-D manner. Let U denote the class of images $u = (u_l, u_r)$ projected onto the retinas of both left and right eyes. Let W denote the class of electrochemical signals encoded by all the major visual cortices (e.g., V1 and MT [227, 168]). Then the human vision system (from the photoreceptors, ganglion cells, and lateral geniculate nucleus (LGN) to the primary visual cortex V1 and so on) is a biological transform $\mathcal{T}_h$ realized by this complex neural and cellular network. Numerous evidences show that it is nonlinear [150, 152].

How does one judge whether a particular type of image representation is good for image and vision analysis? Images as a special class of signals carry rich material, geometric, and positional information about the 3-D world. A good representation should be able to highlight such information and efficiently catch the associated key visual features. This is the most general guideline for efficient image modeling or representation.

A representation $\mathcal{T}$ is said to be *lossless* if any u can be perfectly reconstructed from its representation $w = \mathcal{T}u$. That is, there exists another (reconstruction) transform $\mathcal{R}$ from W to U so that

$$u = \mathcal{R}[\mathcal{T}[u]] \qquad \text{for any} \quad u \in U.$$

A necessary condition for a representation $\mathcal{T}$ being lossless is being injective; namely, two distinct images u and v should be transformed into different $\mathcal{T}u$ and $\mathcal{T}v$, since $\mathcal{T}u = \mathcal{T}v$ would immediately imply

$$u = \mathcal{R}[\mathcal{T}[u]] = \mathcal{R}[\mathcal{T}[v]] = v.$$

Haar's representation in (3.1) is apparently lossless since the reconstruction $\mathcal{R}$ is easily realized by

$$s = a + d \quad \text{and} \quad t = a - d.$$

More generally in terms of linear algebra, the lossless nature of Haar's representation is guaranteed by the invertibility of the associated matrices.

In signal and image analysis, the two transforms $\mathcal{T}$ and $\mathcal{R}$ are usually called the *analysis* and *synthesis* transforms separately. Analysis is to analyze a given image signal and extract its key features and information, while synthesis is the effort of reconstructing the original signal from the output of the analysis step.

If one has a complete code book or dictionary at hand, being injective is already sufficient to be lossless. For instance, if 10 complicated images have been a priori stored and labelled by $u_1, u_2, \ldots, u_{10}$, the simple injective representation

$$\mathcal{T} : u_k \to k$$

is already sufficient to reconstruct the images as long as the code book is available. Imagining that the number $k = 3$ is received, one can then simply turn to the code book to retrieve the image u_3.

Unlike any national language whose vocabulary is relatively stable and finite, it is practically impossible to create a dictionary which contains *all* the images of the world. As a result, the preceding dictionary-based representation idea can never work effectively in the real world.

Instead, most good representations focus on catching the *intrinsic* visual features of images. By ignoring visually unimportant image information, a good representation is inevitably lossy instead of being lossless. However, the associated reconstruction processes often lead to reasonably good synthesis since no significant visual information has been ignored. This is indeed the case in the wavelet-based JPEG2000.

3.2 Deterministic Image Models

We first discuss several deterministic image models that prevail in the literature. They are all mathematical models that approximate real images to certain levels of faithfulness.

3.2.1 Images as Distributions (Generalized Functions)

Treating images as distributions or generalized functions is the broadest approach for deterministic modeling [225] and has profound merits in image understanding as explained below.

As before, let Ω denote an open and bounded 2-D Lipschitz image domain. The set of test functions are defined as

$$D(\Omega) = \{\phi \in C^\infty(\Omega) | \text{supp}\phi \subseteq \Omega\}.$$

Each test function $\phi \in D(\Omega)$ could be considered as a linear *sensor* for capturing image signals.

An image u on Ω, being treated as a distribution, is a linear functional on $D(\Omega)$:

$$u : \phi \to \langle u , \phi \rangle,$$

where the inner product symbol has been used formally, as is customary in distributional theory [3, 193]. Thus the image space is the distribution space $D'(\Omega)$.

Though such an image u may not look like any familiar function at all, it definitely outputs a single response $\langle u , \phi \rangle$ for any sensor $\phi \in D(\Omega)$, which attempts to sense the existence and features of the image u. Furthermore, the sensing is linear:

$$\langle u , a\phi + b\psi \rangle = a\langle u , \phi \rangle + b\langle u , \psi \rangle \quad \forall \phi, \psi \in D(\Omega), \quad a, b \in \mathbb{R}.$$

The notion of distribution is so flexible that one can take derivatives to any order. In the 2-D case for example, let α_1 and α_2 be two nonnegative integers. Then for any distribution $u \in D'(\Omega)$, its derivative $v = \partial_1^{\alpha_1} \partial_2^{\alpha_2} u$ is defined as a new distribution (or linear functional) so that for any test sensor $\phi \in D(\Omega)$,

$$\langle v , \phi \rangle = (-1)^{\alpha_1 + \alpha_2} \langle u , \partial_1^{\alpha_1} \partial_2^{\alpha_2} \phi \rangle.$$

Since the test space $D(\Omega)$ is closed under differentiation, the new distribution is well defined.

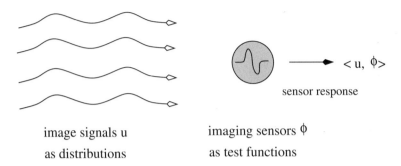

Figure 3.1. *Images as distributions or generalized functions. Test functions then model various biological or digital sensors, such as retinal photoreceptors of human vision or coupled charge devices in CCD cameras.*

The very positive news about the notion of distributional images is as follows (see Figure 3.1).

1. Generalized functions seem to meet the expectation of highly *diversified* images in many disciplines. Notice that historically the notion of generalized functions also arose from the insufficiency of ordinary functions in mathematical analysis.

2. The definition of a distribution seems to resonate well with the physical interpretation of an image. That is, an image u does not exist by itself in the world; rather, it is only observed or acquired through its responses to sensors (e.g., CCD cameras or the human vision system).

Interesting examples of distributional images include

1. a bright spot ideally concentrated at the origin (assuming $(0, 0) \in \Omega$):

$$u(x) = u(x_1, x_2) = \delta(x),$$

where δ stands for Dirac's delta function or point sampler, so that

$$\langle u, \phi \rangle = \phi(0, 0) \qquad \text{for any sensor} \quad \phi \in D(\Omega);$$

2. an ideal uniform step edge: $u(x_1, x_2) = H(x_1)$, where $H(t)$ is the Heaviside 0-1 step function;

3. a uniform bright line (or a beam [107]): $u(x_1, x_2) = \delta(x_1)$, so that for any sensor $\phi \in D(\Omega)$,

$$\langle u, \phi \rangle = \int_R \phi(0, x_2) dx_2.$$

A nonuniform bright line could be modelled as $u(x_1, x_2) = \delta(x_1)v(x_2)$, where $v(x_2)$ stands for a 1-D distribution, so that

$$\langle u, \phi \rangle = \langle v(x_2), \phi(0, x_2) \rangle.$$

Notice that the images in examples 1 and 3 cannot be described by classical functions.

The disadvantage is that distributional images are so broad that one could hardly derive any exciting image features from them. Thus further regularity conditions must be properly incorporated to model practical images.

One interesting condition noteworthy for image analysis is *positivity*.

Definition 3.1 (Positive Distribution). *A distributional image u is said to be positive if for any sensor $\phi \in D(\Omega)$ with $\phi(x) \geq 0$, one has $\langle u , \phi \rangle \geq 0$.*

The remarkable effect of being positive is the continuity property.

Theorem 3.2. *Suppose u is a positive distributional image on Ω. Then for any compact set $K \subseteq \Omega$, there exists a constant $C = C_K(u) > 0$, so that for any sensor $\phi \in D(\Omega)$ with $\operatorname{supp}\phi \subseteq K$,*

$$\langle u , \phi \rangle \leq C \|\phi\|_\infty.$$

The proof is trivial, as one could always construct a nonnegative sensor $\psi \in D(\Omega)$ which equals 1 on K. As a result, $\|\phi\|_\infty \psi - \phi$ is also a nonnegative sensor for any ϕ supported on K.

Positivity necessarily means that the distribution must not involve any derivatives of a sensor, because the norm $\|\phi\|_\infty$ has no control over its derivatives. As a result, for example, $v(x_1) = \delta'(x_1)$ cannot be a positive 1-D distribution.

A very intriguing result out of positivity is the celebrated *Riesz representation theorem* (see, e.g., [118, 126]).

Theorem 3.3 (Riesz Representation Theorem on Radon Measures). *u is a positive distributional image if and only if there exists a (unique) Radon measure μ on Ω, such that for any sensor $\phi \in D(\Omega)$,*

$$\langle u , \phi \rangle = \int_\Omega \phi(x) \, d\mu.$$

Since Ω is a subset of R^2, a Radon measure on Ω is simply a Borel measure that is finite on any compact subset [118, 126]. Therefore, an ideal bright spot and a uniform beam in the preceding examples are both positive distributional images.

Physically, if one treats the pointwise values of an image as the *numbers* of photons projected onto the pixels, the positivity condition then becomes very natural.

We now discuss how to properly quantify the information content of a distributional image. Let U denote any open subset of Ω. Define the *total mass* of u on U by

$$\|u\|_U = \sup\{\langle u , \phi \rangle \ : \ \phi \in D(\Omega); \ \operatorname{supp}\phi \subseteq U; \ \|\phi\|_\infty \leq 1\}.$$

Generally, this could be ∞. It must be finite when U is precompact (i.e., its relative closure in Ω is compact) and u is positive.

Notice that the total mass measure does not carry the *differential* nature. Namely, a constant image such as $u \equiv 1$ on Ω has a nonzero information content: $\|u\|_\Omega = |\Omega|$. This is inappropriate from the vision point of view because many visual neurons in the primary cortex are known to only respond to spatial changes and features (see, e.g., the work of Nobel laureates Huble and Wiesel [152]). To improve, we could define the following information measure instead, by restricting the sensors to those that are differentiating:

$$\|u\|_U^* = \sup\{\langle u \, , \, \phi \rangle \, : \, \phi \in D(\Omega); \ \mathrm{supp}\phi \subseteq U; \ \|\phi\|_\infty \le 1; \ \langle 1 \, , \, \phi \rangle = 0\}.$$

Zero total integral over Ω necessarily means that ϕ must be oscillatory. Thus in some sense these are wavelet sensors.

It is then clear that for any featureless constant image u, the information content $\|u\|_U^* = 0$. On the other hand, there is still a degree of freedom left even in the new definition, namely, the choice of the class of differential sensors. If it is substituted by the class

$$\{\phi \in D(\Omega) \, : \, \phi = \nabla \cdot \boldsymbol{g}, \boldsymbol{g} = (g_1, g_2) \in D(\Omega) \times D(\Omega), \|\boldsymbol{g}\|_\infty \le 1\},$$

then we end up with a new norm $\| \nabla u \|_U^*$ (the gradient operator is in the distributional sense), which is precisely the TV measure $|Du|(U)$ if u is in $L_{\mathrm{loc}}^1(\Omega)$ (see Section 2.2).

3.2.2 L^p Images

L^p images carry more structures than distributional or Radon-measure images. Recall that for any $p \in [0, \infty]$, the Lebesgue L^p function space is defined as

$$L^p(\Omega) = \left\{u \, : \, \int_\Omega |u(x)|^p dx < \infty\right\}.$$

When $p = \infty$, an L^∞ image is understood as an *essentially* bounded function. These are all Banach spaces under the norms

$$\|u\|_p = \left[\int_\Omega |u|^p dx\right]^{1/p}.$$

The remarkable property of L^p images is again expressed by the Riesz representation theorem. Recall that p and p^* are said to be conjugate if

$$\frac{1}{p} + \frac{1}{p^*} = 1.$$

Theorem 3.4 (Riesz Representation Theorem on L^p Images). *Assume $1 \le p < \infty$. Then the dual of $L^p(\Omega)$ is $L^{p^*}(\Omega)$. That is, any continuous linear functional L on $L^p(\Omega)$ must be given by the integration form*

$$L(u) = \int_\Omega v_L(x)u(x)dx$$

for some unique $v_L \in L^{p^*}(\Omega)$. Furthermore, the operational norm of L and the L^{p^*} norm of the representative v_L are identical: $\|L\| = \|v_L\|_{p^*}$.

For $p = \infty$, although L^1 is isometrically embedded into the dual space $(L^\infty)^*$, $(L^\infty)^*$ is, however, much bigger [126, 193].

By applying Hölder's inequality,

$$\left| \int_\Omega f(x)g(x)dx \right| \leq \|f\|_q \|g\|_{q^*}, \tag{3.2}$$

to $f = |u|^p$, $g = 1$, and $q = p_+/p$, one concludes that for any $p_+ \geq p \geq 1$,

$$L^{p_+}(\Omega) \subseteq L^p(\Omega),$$

since the image domain Ω has been assumed bounded. In this sense L^1 images are the most general class among all L^p's.

L^p images are naturally distributional images. Since $D(\Omega)$ is dense in L^{p^*} for $1 \leq p^* < \infty$, any L^p image $(1 < p < \infty)$ must be completely determined by its distributional behavior in $D'(\Omega)$. But L^p images carry more structures than general distributional images.

One particularly interesting structure of L^p images is their blowup behavior. By applying Fubini's theorem to $g(t, x) = pt^{p-1}1_{|u(x)|>t}$ with the product measure $dx \times dt$ on $\Omega \times (0, \infty)$, one could directly obtain the following remarkable identity:

$$\int_\Omega |u(x)|^p dx = p \int_0^\infty t^{p-1} |\{x : |u(x)| > t\}| dt, \tag{3.3}$$

where the notation $|A|$ on the right denotes the Lebesgue measure of a set A. This is often cheerfully called the "layer-cake representation" (see, e.g., Lieb and Loss [193]).

Since Ω is bounded, $w(t) = |\{x : |u(x)| > t\}|$ is bounded as well. Thus the convergence on the right side of the layer-cake representation (3.3) is determined by the decay rate of $w(t)$ as $t \to \infty$.

1. As a by-product, we again obtain $L^{p_+}(\Omega) \subseteq L^p(\Omega)$ for any $p_+ \geq p \geq 1$.

2. Suppose that a particular L^p image u has a power law decay $w(t) = |\{x : |u(x)| > t\}| = O(t^{-\alpha})$. Then we must have $\alpha > p$.

We now discuss how to properly measure the information content of a general L^p image. Given any measurable subset $U \subseteq \Omega$ with positive Lebesgue measure $|U|$, define the mean $\langle u \rangle_U$ of u on U by

$$\langle u \rangle_U = \frac{1}{|U|} \int_U u(x)dx.$$

The (average) information content of u on U is then defined by the p-mean oscillation $\sigma_p(u|U)$:

$$\sigma_p(u|U) = \left(\frac{1}{|U|} \int_U |u - \langle u \rangle_U|^p dx \right)^{1/p}. \tag{3.4}$$

When $p = 2$, this is the canonical definition for empirical standard deviation in statistics. Furthermore by applying Hölder's inequality (3.2), one could easily show that

$$\sigma_p(u|U) \leq \sigma_q(u|U) \quad \text{for } 1 \leq p \leq q.$$

As an interesting note in real analysis, any image u with

$$\sup_{\text{any cube } U \subseteq \Omega} \sigma_p(u|U) < \infty$$

is said to have *bounded p-mean oscillations*, and all such images are denoted by BMO(Ω). It turns out that the space of BMO is independent of $p \geq 1$ [216, 324].

3.2.3 Sobolev Images $H^n(\Omega)$

An L^2 image u on Ω is naturally a distribution when the Hilbert inner product is applied to u and the test sensors in $D(\Omega)$. Thus its distributional derivatives $\partial_1^{\alpha_1} \partial_2^{\alpha_2} u$ are well defined.

Such an image u is said to be Sobolev H^1 if its first order derivatives (as distributions) belong to $L^2(\Omega)$ as well, or equivalently in combination, its gradient ∇u belongs to $L^2 \times L^2$. That is to say, there exist two L^2 functions u_1 and u_2, so that for any test sensor vector $\boldsymbol{\phi} = (\phi_1, \phi_2) \in D(\Omega) \times D(\Omega)$,

$$\langle \nabla u , \boldsymbol{\phi} \rangle = \langle \partial_1 u , \phi_1 \rangle + \langle \partial_2 u , \phi_2 \rangle \equiv - \int_\Omega (u_1 \partial_1 \phi_1 + u_2 \partial_2 \phi_2) dx. \qquad (3.5)$$

$H^1(\Omega)$ is a Hilbert space under the inner product,

$$\langle u , v \rangle_{H^1} = \langle u , v \rangle_{L^2} + \langle \nabla u , \nabla v \rangle_{L^2 \times L^2},$$

which induces the linear norm

$$\|u\|_{H^1} = \sqrt{\|u\|_{L^2}^2 + \|\nabla u\|_{L^2 \times L^2}^2}.$$

For H^1 images, it seems natural to measure image information by

$$\|\nabla u\|_{L^2 \times L^2} = \left(\int_\Omega ((\partial_1 u)^2 + (\partial_2 u)^2) dx \right)^{1/2}.$$

Higher order Sobolev image spaces $H^n(\Omega)$ ($n = 2, 3, \ldots$) are defined in a similar fashion and carry the natural Hilbert space structures as in (3.5). On the other hand, if the L^2 norm used to constrain the derivatives is replaced by some L^p ($p \geq 1$) norm, the resultant Sobolev image spaces are often denoted by $W^{n,p}(\Omega)$ [3, 126, 193].

3.2.4 BV Images

From general distributions to L^p images, and further to Sobolev images, each time when more regularities are added, the spaces become more specific and better manageable. However, there is a tradeoff between the regularity of image spaces and the fidelity of image modeling. An optimal solution is to find the balance, namely, to construct an image space that is both mathematically tractable and practically faithful in representing the key features of general images. This is the space of BV images, as already introduced in the preceding chapter, whose role in image analysis and processing has been fundamental and influential ever since the well-known work of Rudin and Osher [257], and Rudin, Osher, and Fatemi [258].

From the distributional point of view, an L^1 image u belongs to BV(Ω) if and only if its distributional gradient ∇u satisfies

$$\sup_{\boldsymbol{\phi} \in D(\Omega) \times D(\Omega); \|\boldsymbol{\phi}\|_\infty \leq 1} \langle \nabla u , \boldsymbol{\phi} \rangle < \infty,$$

where $\|\boldsymbol{\phi}\|_\infty = \sup_{x \in \Omega} (\phi_1^2(x) + \phi_2^2(x))^{1/2}$. If so, this supremum is called the TV of u and denoted by TV$[u]$ or $|Du|(\Omega)$. BV(Ω) is a Banach space under the natural norm

$$\|u\|_{\text{BV}} = \|u\|_{L^1} + \text{TV}[u].$$

The remarkable features of BV images are characterized as follows.

1. All $W^{1,1}$ images (including H^1 as a subspace since Ω is bounded) are BV images, but the former do not allow edges (i.e., intensity jumps along curves). From the very beginning of artificial intelligence research, edges have been recognized as crucial visual cues in perception and image understanding [44, 183, 210, 226].

2. While L^p images also permit edges, they keep no specific track of local oscillatory irregularities. But BV images do.

Thus the notion of BV images indeed achieves a reasonably good balance between penalizing irregularities (often due to noise) and respecting intrinsic image features such as edges.

The concept of BV images is also compatible to the occlusion-generative imaging process of Lee, Mumford, and Huang [191]. Most objects in the 3-D world are not transparent, causing the generic phenomenon of occlusion. On a 2-D image domain Ω, occlusion is modelled as follows. Suppose there are N Lipschitz subdomains of Ω, ordered from foreground to background:

$$Q_1, \ Q_2, \ \ldots, \ Q_N,$$

whose boundaries all have finite 1-D Hausdorff measures. Assume that each Q_n has a constant gray level of u_n, $n = 1 : N$. Then the synthetic image u generated from such a scene is

$$u(x) = u_1 1_{Q_1}(x) + u_2 1_{Q_2 \setminus Q_1}(x) + u_3 1_{Q_3 \setminus Q_2 \cup Q_1}(x) + \cdots,$$

provided that the background intensity is 0. Then the TV is

$$|Du|(\Omega) \leq \left(\max_{0 \leq i < j \leq N} |u_i - u_j| \right) \sum_{n=1}^{N} \mathcal{H}^1(\partial Q_n) < \infty, \tag{3.6}$$

implying that such a synthetic image must belong to $BV(\Omega)$. If the u_n's are allowed to be smooth functions instead of constants, the resultant image u is piecewise smooth and still belongs to $BV(\Omega)$.

3.3 Wavelets and Multiscale Representation

In this section, following the basic knowledge prepared in the preceding chapter [86, 96, 290], we further explore the role of wavelets as efficient tools for multiscale image modeling and representation.

3.3.1 Construction of 2-D Wavelets

We first introduce two different approaches for constructing 2-D wavelets from 1-D ones.

Approach I: Three Mother Wavelets at Equal Scales

As in the preceding chapter, let $\psi(t)$ and $\phi(t)$ denote the mother wavelet and scaling function for an orthonormal multiresolution analysis in $\mathbb{R}^1$:

$$\cdots \subseteq V_{-1} \subseteq V_0 \subseteq V_1 \subseteq \cdots$$

so that $(\phi(t-k) \mid k \in \mathbb{Z})$ is an orthonormal basis for V_0, and $(\psi(t-k) \mid k \in \mathbb{Z})$ for the wavelet space W_0, which orthogonally complements V_0 in the more "detailed" space V_1. Then

$$\{\psi_{j,k} = 2^{j/2}\psi(2^j t - k) \mid j, k \in \mathbb{Z}\}$$

is an orthonormal wavelet basis for $L^2(R)$.

To avoid complication, it shall be assumed in this section that the image domain $\Omega = \mathbb{R}^2$. In practice, many ways exist for extending image data on a bounded square domain to $\mathbb{R}^2$, such as zero-padding, symmetric reflection, periodic extension, extrapolation, etc (see, e.g., Strang and Nguyen [290]). There also exist rigorous ways of constructing wavelets on bounded domains (see, e.g., the celebrated work of Cohen et al. [89]).

Recall that the tensor product of two linear spaces X and Y is defined by

$$X \otimes Y = \mathrm{span}\{x \otimes y : x \in X \text{ and } y \in Y\}.$$

If both X and Y are Banach spaces of infinite dimensions, the above definition should be followed by a further completion process so that $X \otimes Y$ is Banach as well.

If X and Y are both Hilbert spaces, and $(x_n \mid n \in \mathbb{Z})$ and $(y_m \mid m \in \mathbb{Z})$ are their orthonormal bases separately, then under the natural tensor-product extension of inner products,

$$\langle x \otimes y \,,\, u \otimes v \rangle := \langle x \,,\, u \rangle \times \langle y \,,\, v \rangle,$$

the tensor products of the bases vectors

$$z_{n,m} = x_n \otimes y_m, \quad n, m \in \mathbb{Z}, \tag{3.7}$$

become an orthonormal basis for $X \otimes Y$.

The construction of 2-D MRA starts from the following relation.

Theorem 3.5 (Separability). *Treating $\mathbb{R}^2 = \mathbb{R} \oplus \mathbb{R}$ (direct sum of vector spaces), one has, under Lebesgue measures,*

$$L^2(\mathbb{R} \oplus \mathbb{R}) = L^2(\mathbb{R}) \otimes L^2(\mathbb{R}). \tag{3.8}$$

It claims that for any $f(x) = f(x_1, x_2) \in L^2(\mathbb{R}^2)$, and $\varepsilon > 0$, there exists a function $f_\varepsilon(x)$ in the form of

$$f_\varepsilon(x) = \sum_{k=1}^{K} c_k g_k(x_1) e_k(x_2), \quad g_k, e_k \in L^2(\mathbb{R}), \text{ and } c_k \in \mathbb{R},$$

so that $\|f - f_\varepsilon\|_{L^2(\mathbb{R}^2)} < \varepsilon$. There are many different approaches leading to this fact, and perhaps none could be more convenient than the Fourier transform.

Proof. Notice that the test functions $D(\mathbb{R}^2)$ (i.e., smooth functions with compact supports) are dense in $L^2(\mathbb{R}^2)$. For any test function $\phi(x_1, x_2)$, assumed to be supported on the canonical open square $Q = (-\pi, \pi)^2$ without loss of generality, we form its Q-periodic extension $\Phi(x)$ so that $\Phi(x)|_Q = \phi(x)$. Notice that $\Phi(x)$ equals zero on a neighborhood of Q's boundary. Then $\Phi(x)$ can be approximated to any precision (in L^2 or uniformly) by a finite truncation of its Fourier series

$$\sum_{(n,m)\in\Lambda} c_{n,m} e^{inx_1} e^{imx_2},$$

where $\Lambda \subseteq \mathbb{Z}^2$ denotes some suitable finite subset. Define

$$g_n(x_1) = e^{inx_1} 1_{(-\pi,\pi)}(x_1) \in L^2(\mathbb{R}) \quad \text{and} \quad e_m(x_2) = e^{imx_2} 1_{(-\pi,\pi)}(x_2) \in L^2(\mathbb{R}).$$

Then it easily follows that $\phi(x_1, x_2)$ can be approximated to any precision in $L^2(\mathbb{R})$ by the span of $g_n \otimes e_m$'s. $\square$

For each (logarithmic) scale $j \in \mathbb{Z}$, define a closed subspace of $L^2(\mathbb{R}^2)$ by

$$V_{(j)} = V_j \otimes V_j = \text{closure}\big(\text{span}\{f_1(x_1)f_2(x_2) \mid f_1, f_2 \in V_j\}\big).$$

Since $V_{j-1} \subseteq V_j$, one must have as well

$$V_{(j-1)} \subseteq V_{(j)}. \tag{3.9}$$

The dilation similarity in 1-D MRA also holds in two dimensions:

$$f(x) \in V_{(j-1)} \Leftrightarrow f(2x) = f(2x_1, 2x_2) \in V_{(j)}. \tag{3.10}$$

Notice that the dilation factors (i.e., 2's) are the same for both x_1 and x_2, which is said to be isotropic. Finally, by Theorem 3.5 and the completeness of 1-D MRA,

$$\text{closure}\left(\lim_{j\to\infty} V_{(j)}\right) = L^2(\mathbb{R}^2). \tag{3.11}$$

To further study the representation of these multiresolution spaces, define

$$\psi^{(0,0)}(x) = \phi(x_1) \otimes \phi(x_2), \quad \psi^{(0,1)}(x) = \phi(x_1) \otimes \psi(x_2), \tag{3.12}$$

$$\psi^{(1,0)}(x) = \psi(x_1) \otimes \phi(x_2), \quad \psi^{(1,1)}(x) = \psi(x_1) \otimes \psi(x_2). \tag{3.13}$$

Then $\psi^{(0,0)}$ is lowpass (i.e., with total integral equal to 1) and is the 2-D scaling function, and the other three are all highpass (i.e., with zero total integrals) and are the 2-D mother wavelets.

For any scale level $j \in \mathbb{Z}$, and location $\boldsymbol{k} = (k_1, k_2) \in \mathbb{Z}^2$, define

$$\psi^\alpha_{j,\boldsymbol{k}}(x) = 2^j \psi^\alpha(2^j x - \boldsymbol{k}), \tag{3.14}$$

where $\alpha = (a, b)$ denotes the four types. Then the following theorem is straightforward.

Theorem 3.6 (2-D Wavelet Decomposition).

1. *At any scale j, $(\psi_{j,k}^{(0,0)} \mid k \in \mathbb{Z}^2)$ is an orthonormal basis for $V_{(j)}$.*
2. *Let $W_{(j)}$ denote the orthogonal complement of $V_{(j)}$ in $V_{(j+1)}$. Then*

$$\{\psi_{j,k}^{\alpha} \ : \ k \in \mathbb{Z}^2, |\alpha| = a + b > 0\}$$

   is an orthonormal basis for $W_{(j)}$.
3. *Thus $V_{(1)} = V_{(0)} \oplus W_{(0)}$ has two sets of orthonormal bases: $(\psi_{1,k}^{(0,0)} \mid k \in \mathbb{Z}^2)$ and the combination of othornormal bases from $V_{(0)}$ and $W_{(0)}$ just established above. They are connected by the two-scale relations*

$$\psi^{\alpha} = \sum_{k \in \mathbb{Z}^2} h_k^{\alpha} \psi_{1,k}^{(0,0)}, \tag{3.15}$$

   where h^{α}'s are four digital filters, lowpass for $\alpha = (0, 0)$ and highpass for the other three.

Computationally, the four 2-D digital filters h^{α}'s are also the tensor products of the two 1-D digital filters defining the scaling function and wavelet in 1-D MRA. Therefore, the filter bank realizing the above change of bases is the tensor product as well. More precisely, suppose $u \in V_{(j+1)}$ has the representation

$$u(x_1, x_2) = \sum_k c_{j+1,k}^{(0,0)} \psi_{j+1,k}^{(0,0)}(x_1, x_2).$$

After passing through the 1-D *analysis* filter bank (i.e., lowpass and highpass channels with downsampling; see Section 2.6) along the k_1-direction for any fixed k_2, $(c_{j+1,k}^{(0,0)} \mid k \in \mathbb{Z}^2)$ splits into two intermediate fields of coefficients:

$$c_{(j,j+1),k}^{(0,0)} \quad \text{and} \quad c_{(j,j+1),k}^{(1,0)},$$

where the uniform scale index splits into $(j, j + 1)$ since the k_2-direction is still in the scale level of $j + 1$. Next, after passing through the same 1-D filter bank along the k_2-direction for each fixed k_1, the two intermediate fields further split into the desired four fields of coefficients of u in the bases $\{\psi_{j,k}^{\alpha} \mid k \in \mathbb{Z}^2, \alpha = (0|1, \ 0|1)\}$:

$$\{c_{j,k}^{\alpha} \mid k \in \mathbb{Z}^2\}, \quad \alpha = (0|1, 0|1).$$

Example. As an example, consider the 2-D Haar wavelets:

$$\begin{aligned}
\psi^{(0,0)}(x) &= 1_{[0,1)^2}(x_1, x_2), \\
\psi^{(0,1)}(x) &= 1_{[0,1)}(x_1) \otimes \left(1_{[0,1/2)}(x_2) - 1_{[1/2,1)}(x_2)\right), \\
\psi^{(1,0)}(x) &= \psi^{(0,1)}(x_2, x_1), \\
\psi^{(1,1)}(x) &= \left(1_{[0,1/2)}(x_1) - 1_{[1/2,1)}(x_1)\right) \otimes \left(1_{[0,1/2)}(x_2) - 1_{[1/2,1)}(x_2)\right).
\end{aligned} \tag{3.16}$$

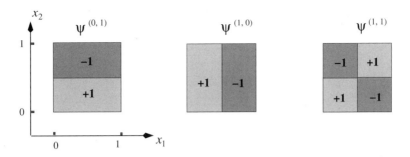

Figure 3.2. *Three Haar mother wavelets in two dimensions via tensor products.*

Figure 3.2 helps visualize these mother wavelets. What looks very appealing is that the three wavelets imitate the three differential operators (under the finite difference scheme)

$$\partial_y, \quad \partial_x, \quad \partial_y \partial_x,$$

up to some multiplicative constants.

Finally, let us go to the spatial frequency domain to understand the very nature of such 2-D MRA.

Either in the case of Shannon wavelets [96, 204, 216] or in terms of the asymptotic behavior of Daubechies's family of wavelets [280, 281], MRA clearly parallels Littlewood and Paley's theory on dyadic partitioning of the Fourier domain [127].

Thus in the 1-D case, each resolution space V_j can be approximately thought of representing all signals bandlimited to $|\omega| \leq 2^j \pi$ and its orthogonal complement W_j in V_{j+1} all signals bandlimited to the high frequency band $|\omega| \in \pi(2^j, 2^{j+1}]$. In fact, it is the primary change of notion in wavelet theory to think of these bands as scale resolutions instead of individual frequencies [96, 204, 215].

This view naturally extends to the 2-D MRA just constructed above. The mechanism of tensor product implies that each resolution $V_{(j)}$ *approximately* represents all 2-D images bandlimited to the dyadic cube

$$Q_j = [-2^j \pi, \ 2^j \pi] \times [-2^j \pi, \ 2^j \pi],$$

and its wavelet complement $W_{(j)}$ denotes the high frequency Cartesian ring inside Q_{j+1} but outside Q_j.

Each wavelet space $W_{(j)}$ further orthogonally splits into three subspaces represented by the three mother wavelets

$$W_{(j)} = W_{(j)}^{(0,1)} \oplus W_{(j)}^{(1,0)} \oplus W_{(j)}^{(1,1)},$$

corresponding to the further partitioning of the Cartesian ring into three bands:

$$R_j^{(0,1)} = \{(\omega_1, \omega_2) : |\omega_1| \leq \pi 2^j, \ \pi 2^j < |\omega_2| \leq \pi 2^{j+1}\},$$
$$R_j^{(1,0)} = \{(\omega_1, \omega_2) : |\omega_2| \leq \pi 2^j, \ \pi 2^j < |\omega_1| \leq \pi 2^{j+1}\}, \qquad (3.17)$$
$$R_j^{(1,1)} = \{(\omega_1, \omega_2) : \pi 2^j < |\omega_1| \text{ and } |\omega_2| \leq \pi 2^{j+1}\}.$$

Approach II: Single Mother Wavelet and Anisotropic Scale Mixing

One characteristic feature of the above construction is that each space $V_{(j)}$ exactly corresponds to a single resolution level j in both directions of x_1 and x_2. There exists, however, another way of tensor-product-based construction that allows anisotropic scale mixing.

In addition to the translation vector $\boldsymbol{k} = (k_1, k_2)$, define $\boldsymbol{j} = (j_1, j_2) \in \mathbb{Z}^2$ to be the anisotropic resolution vector. According to the general construction formula (3.7), the tensor products

$$\psi_{\boldsymbol{j},\boldsymbol{k}}(x) = \psi_{j_1,k_1}(x_1) \otimes \psi_{j_2,k_2}(x_2), \quad \boldsymbol{j}, \boldsymbol{k} \in \mathbb{Z}^2,$$

consist into an orthonormal basis for $L^2(\mathbb{R}^2)$. To further investigate the intrinsic structures of this family of 2-D wavelets, for each anisotropic resolution vector $\boldsymbol{j} = (j_1, j_2)$, define the diagonal matrix

$$J = \begin{pmatrix} j_1 & 0 \\ 0 & j_2 \end{pmatrix}.$$

Then from linear algebra,

$$2^J = e^{J \ln 2} = \begin{pmatrix} e^{j_1 \ln 2} & 0 \\ 0 & e^{j_2 \ln 2} \end{pmatrix} = \begin{pmatrix} 2^{j_1} & 0 \\ 0 & 2^{j_2} \end{pmatrix}.$$

Treating the continuous pixel variable $x \in \mathbb{R}^2$ as a column vector $(x_1, x_2)^T$ and $\boldsymbol{k} = (k_1, k_2)^T$ as well, we then have for each $\boldsymbol{j} \in \mathbb{Z}^2$,

$$\psi_{\boldsymbol{j},\boldsymbol{k}}(x) = \sqrt{\det 2^J}\, \psi_{\boldsymbol{0},\boldsymbol{0}}(2^J x - \boldsymbol{k}),$$

which looks more like the 1-D formula.

For each anisotropic resolution vector $\boldsymbol{j} = (j_1, j_2)$, define its associated wavelet subspace

$$W_{\boldsymbol{j}} = \mathrm{closure}\big(\mathrm{span}\{\psi_{\boldsymbol{j},\boldsymbol{k}} \mid \boldsymbol{k} \in \mathbb{Z}^2\}\big).$$

Following the discussion in the preceding subsection, in the Fourier domain, $W_{\boldsymbol{j}}$ corresponds to the four rectangles of high frequencies:

$$Q_{\boldsymbol{j}} = \{(\omega_1, \omega_2) \,:\, 2^{j_1}\pi < |\omega_1| \le 2^{j_1+1}\pi \ \text{ and } \ 2^{j_2}\pi < |\omega_2| \le 2^{j_2+1}\pi\}.$$

If $|j_1 - j_2| \gg 1$, $Q_{\boldsymbol{j}}$ represents a rectangle with large aspect ratio, resolving image features that are relatively highly oscillatory in one direction while smoother in the other. Thus, one could imagine that this second construction is particularly efficient in representing images structures such as thin silky cloud, hair or fur, tall grass, or straws. In the physical domain, such structures must also bear large aspect ratios according to Heisenberg's uncertainty principle [288].

3.3.2　Wavelet Responses to Typical Image Features

In this section, we discuss wavelet responses to typical image features: smoothness and edges. To illustrate the main ideas, we shall restrict the analysis only to the 1-D case.

Response to Smooth Images

A mother wavelet $\psi(x) \in L^2(\mathbb{R})$ is said to be r-regular if it belongs to $C^r(\mathbb{R})$. For orthonormal MRA, there is a beautiful theorem connecting the smoothness of the mother wavelet to the number of its vanishing moments, belonging to Meyer [216], Battle [18], and Daubechies [96]. An improvement on Daubechies' result was also made by Cai and Shen [38].

Theorem 3.7 (Vanishing Moments [96, 38]). *Suppose the mother wavelet $\psi(x)$ is r-regular. In addition,* (i) *ψ has up to rth order moments, and* (ii) *$|\psi(x)| \le C(1 + |x|)^r$, $x \in \mathbb{R}$, for some fixed constant C. Then all the moments vanish up to the rth order:*

$$\int_{\mathbb{R}} x^k \psi(x) dx = 0, \quad k = 0 : r. \tag{3.18}$$

See Daubechies [96] and Cai and Shen [38] for a proof. Notice that conditions (i) and (ii) are trivially satisfied for compactly supported wavelets, which are the most common in applications [95]. In particular, we have the following results.

Theorem 3.8 (Decaying Rate and Smoothness of Wavelets).

(1) *A compactly supported mother wavelet ψ cannot be C^∞.*

(2) *More generally, a mother wavelet ψ that decays at certain exponential rate (i.e., $O(e^{-a|x|})$ for some $a > 0$ at $x = \infty$) cannot be C^∞.*

(1) results from (2), while the proof of (2) is straightforward from the preceding theorem; otherwise, all moments of ψ would vanish, or equivalently, all the Taylor coefficients of $\hat{\psi}$ (Fourier transform) vanish at the origin, which is impossible as $\hat{\psi}$ is a nonzero function and analytic on a horizontal stripe containing the real axis (due to the exponential decay).

In what follows, we shall assume that the mother wavelet ψ is r-regular and compactly supported on some finite interval $[a, b]$. As for Daubechies' wavelets [96, 95], r could be any desired integer order.

Suppose $u(x)$ is any given C^m 1-D image with $0 \le m \le r+1$. We expect the wavelet coefficients to be small in small scales (i.e., large j) when the signal behaves smoothly relative to the tiny wavelets.

By definition, the wavelet coefficient $c_{j,k}$ is

$$c_{j,k} = \int_{\mathbb{R}} u(x)\psi_{j,k}(x)dx = 2^{-j/2} \int_a^b \psi(y)u(x_0 + 2^{-j}y)dy, \tag{3.19}$$

where $x_0 = x_{j,k}$ denotes $2^{-j}k$. By Taylor's expansion at x_0,

$$u(x_0 + t) = \sum_{n=0}^{m-1} \frac{u^{(n)}(x_0)}{n!} t^n + \int_0^t \frac{(t-s)^{m-1}}{(m-1)!} u^{(m)}(x_0 + s)ds = P_{m-1}(t) + R_{m-1}(t).$$

For convenience assume that $C_m = C_m(u) = \|u^{(m)}\|_\infty < \infty$. Then the residual R_m can be easily bounded:

$$|R_{m-1}(t)| \le \frac{C_m}{m!} |t|^m.$$

On the other hand, since $r \geq m - 1$, the inner product of $\psi(y)$ and $P_{m-1}(2^{-j}y)$ must vanish. Therefore,

$$c_{j,k} = 2^{-j/2} \int_a^b \psi(y) R_{m-1}(2^{-j}y) dy.$$

Define the mth order absolute moment M_m of ψ by

$$M_m = M_m(\psi) = \int_a^b |\psi(y)| \, |y|^m dy.$$

Then we have established the estimation for the wavelet coefficients

$$|c_{j,k}| \leq 2^{-j(m+1/2)} \frac{C_m(u)}{m!} M_m(\psi) \text{ or } c_{jk} = O(h_j^{m+1/2}), \tag{3.20}$$

where as in computational PDEs, h_j denotes the scale 2^{-j} at level j.

Let D_j denote the orthogonal projection from L^2 to the wavelet space W_j, and $w_j(x) = D_j u(x)$. Due to the limited overlapping among $\psi_{j,k}$'s at each fixed resolution j, the estimation in (3.20) immediately implies that

$$\|w_j\|_\infty = O(h_j^m). \tag{3.21}$$

Notice that the extra factor $h_j^{1/2}$ bounding $c_{j,k}$'s in (3.20) has been cancelled out by the normalization factor $h_j^{-1/2}$ in $\psi_{j,k}(x) = h_j^{-1/2} \psi\left(h_j^{-1}(x - x_{j,k})\right)$.

In both formulae (3.20) and (3.21), $O(\cdot)$ can be improved to $o(\cdot)$ after some small modification of the argument [38].

Besides this classical or pointwise approach, estimations such as (3.21) can be established for Sobolev images in even more convenient ways, which we now explain.

In terms of its Fourier transform $\hat{u}(\omega)$ [193], the condition $u \in H^m(\mathbb{R})$ is equivalent to

$$\int_{\mathbb{R}} |\hat{u}|^2 (1 + 4\pi^2 \omega^2)^m d\omega < \infty. \tag{3.22}$$

Assume that $\hat{u}$ has a power law decay

$$\hat{u}(\omega) = O(|\omega|^{-\alpha})$$

for some optimal α. Then (3.22) implies that (in one dimension)

$$\alpha - m > 1/2 \text{ or } \alpha > m + 1/2.$$

Suppose the regularity r of the mother wavelet ψ is much larger than m. Then in the Fourier domain, the jth level wavelet component w_j of u is approximately equivalent to (with $\alpha - m - 1/2$ denoted by $\varepsilon > 0$)

$$\hat{w}_j(\omega) \simeq \hat{u}(\omega) \cdot 1_{[2^j \pi, 2^{j+1} \pi]}(|\omega|) = O(|\omega|^{-(m+1/2+\varepsilon)}) \cdot 1_{[2^j \pi, 2^{j+1} \pi]}(|\omega|),$$

where in reality the indicator function should be replaced by a smooth function (depending on the construction of the associated MRA [96, 216]). Therefore, for some constant C,

$$\|w_j\|_\infty \leq C \|\hat{w}_j\|_{L^1} = O(h_j^{m-1/2+\varepsilon}). \tag{3.23}$$

Thus from the approximation theory point of view, for smooth images, high resolution wavelet coefficients and components can all be set to 0.

Response to Image Edges

Consider a normalized ideal edge of a 1-D Heaviside image

$$u(x) = H(x) = 1_{[x_e,\infty)}(x),$$

where x_e is the edge or jump pixel. As in the preceding section, write $x_{j,k} = 2^{-j}k$ and $h_j = 2^{-j}$, and assume that supp$\psi = [a, b]$. Then the wavelet coefficient is

$$c_{j,k} = \langle u , \psi_{j,k} \rangle = h_j^{1/2} \int_a^b \psi(y) u(x_{j,k} + h_j y) dy. \tag{3.24}$$

If the edge pixel $x_e \notin x_{j,k} + h_j[a, b]$, one has $c_{j,k} = 0$ due to the constancy of the Heaviside image away from its edge. Otherwise, defining $y_{j,k} = (x_e - x_{j,k})/h_j$, one has

$$c_{j,k} = h_j^{1/2} \int_{y_{j,k}}^b \psi(y) dy \leq h_j^{1/2} \|\psi\|_{L^1}.$$

Since $y_{j,k} - y_{j,k+1} = 1$, there are at most $N = \lfloor b - a \rfloor + 1$ number of nonzero wavelet coefficients at each resolution level j. Notice that N is independent of j. Thus on the space-scale plane (i.e., x versus $-\log_2 h$ plane with $x = 2^{-j}k$ and $h = 2^{-j}$), the influence domain of such an ideal edge bears a parasol shape [96, 290].

More generally, if the 1-D image signal u is piecewise smooth and has many edge points, then each edge point carries its own parasol influence domain, and they overlap at coarse resolutions. Within each parasol, the wavelet coefficients are bounded by

$$|c_{j,k}| \leq h_j^{1/2} \|u\|_\infty \|\psi\|_1, \tag{3.25}$$

while all the rest are still subject to the estimation developed in the preceding section.

3.3.3   Besov Images and Sparse Wavelet Representation

As a multiscale tool, wavelets are particularly powerful for studying a class of images known as Besov images, whose multiscale nature is intrinsic from their definitions.

A Besov class on $\mathbb{R}$ is often denoted by $B_q^\alpha(L^p)$, with three indices α, p, and q:

1. α is called the *regularity* index (or power), measuring the degree of smoothness.
2. $L^p = L^p(\mathbb{R})$ denotes the *intrascale* metric controlling the finite differences at each scale. We shall call p the *intrascale* index.
3. q or $L^q(dh/h, \mathbb{R}^+)$ denotes the *interscale* metric (on the scale space $h \in \mathbb{R}^+$ with the logarithmic measure dh/h) that controls the overall regularity *across* all scales. We thus call q the *interscale* index.

In what follows, we shall start out with the classical definition of Besov spaces and then state the equivalent one under wavelet representations. For simplicity, we focus on the 1-D case when the image domain $\Omega = \mathbb{R}$.

Besov Images and Multiscale Characterization

It shall be assumed throughout this section that the regularity index $\alpha \in [0, 1)$ and $u(x) \in L^p(\mathbb{R})$. For any scale $h > 0$, define the p-modulus of continuity of u to be

$$\omega_p(u, h) = \sup_{|a| \le h} \|u(x + a) - u(x)\|_{L^p(\mathbb{R})}. \tag{3.26}$$

It is uniformly bounded by $2\|u\|_{L^p}$ due to the triangular formula of L^p norms. An image u is said to belong to the Besov class $B_q^\alpha(L^p)$ if

$$\left[\int_0^\infty \frac{\omega_p(u, h)^q}{h^{\alpha q}} \frac{dh}{h} \right]^{\frac{1}{q}} < \infty.$$

If so, the *homogeneous* Besov (semi-)norm of $B_q^\alpha(L^p)$ is defined to be

$$\|\|u\|\| = \left[\int_0^\infty \frac{\omega_p(u, h)^q}{h^{\alpha q}} \frac{dh}{h} \right]^{\frac{1}{q}} = \|\omega_p(u, h)h^{-\alpha}\|_{L^q(dh/h)}, \tag{3.27}$$

and the true norm of $B_q^\alpha(L^p)$ is defined by

$$\|u\|_{B_q^\alpha(L^p)} = \|u\|_p + \|\|u\|\|. \tag{3.28}$$

As in the classical L^p theory, if either p or q is ∞, the corresponding norm is understood in the sense of essential supremum [126, 193]. Figure 3.3 helps visualize the meaning of the three parameters α, p, and q in the definition of Besov norms.

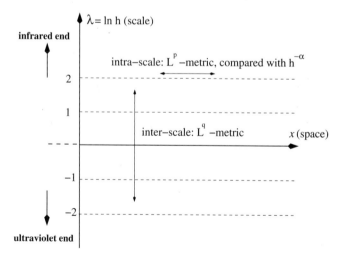

Figure 3.3. *Besov norms in $B_q^\alpha(L^p)$'s measure the strength of signals in the space-scale plane: L^p for intrascale variations, L^q for inter- or cross-scale variations (in terms of $d\lambda = dh/h$), while $h^{-\alpha}$ for comparison with Hölder continuity.*

In the definition, $h = \infty$ causes no problem in the integral of (3.27) as long as α and q are both positive. The sensitive end is the *ultraviolet* limit (borrowing Mumford and Gidas's insightful terminology [225]) as the "wavelength" $h \to 0$. Suppose for a given image $u \in B_q^\alpha(L^p)$, its p-modulus of continuity has a strict power law decay at the ultraviolet end:

$$\omega_p(u, h) = O(h^\beta).$$

Then the decay has to be faster than α: $\beta > \alpha$; otherwise, the ultraviolet end will cause blowup in the integral (3.27). It is out of this consideration that α is called the regularity index.

It is easy to see that $B_\infty^\alpha(L^\infty)$ is precisely the Hölder space H^α, which is usually defined by the single formula

$$\sup_{x,y \in \mathbb{R}} \frac{|u(x) - u(y)|}{|x - y|^\alpha} < \infty.$$

Thus Besov spaces naturally generalize Hölder spaces.

If the scale space $h \in \mathbb{R}^+$ is endowed with the measure $d\mu_{\alpha,q}(h) = h^{-1-\alpha q}dh$, then the Besov condition simply becomes $\omega_p(u, \cdot) \in L^q(\mathbb{R}^+, d\mu_{\alpha,q})$. Or, if one introduces the logarithmic scale level $\lambda = -\ln h \in \mathbb{R}$ and writes $\omega_p(u, \lambda) = \omega_p(u, h)$, then the Besov condition becomes

$$\int_{\mathbb{R}} \omega_p(u, \lambda)^q \, e^{\lambda \alpha q} d\lambda < \infty,$$

from which the ultraviolet sensitivity as $\lambda \to +\infty$ also becomes evident. Furthermore, parallel to MRA, the natural logarithm can be replaced by the binary one, and the Besov condition is equivalent to

$$\int_{\mathbb{R}} \omega_p(u, \lambda)^q \, 2^{\lambda \alpha q} \, d\lambda < \infty. \tag{3.29}$$

If one formally discretizes the integral with $d\lambda = 1$ on the integer grid $\mathbb{Z}$, the Besov condition simply becomes

$$\sum_{j \in \mathbb{Z}} \omega_p(u, j)^q \, 2^{j\alpha q} < \infty. \tag{3.30}$$

As a matter of fact, a rigorous proof of the equivalence is straightforward simply by noticing that $\omega_p(u, h) = \omega_p(u, \lambda)$ is monotonically increasing with respect to scale h, or equivalently, decreasing with respect to λ. Therefore, on each interval $\lambda \in [j, j+1)$,

$$\omega_p(u, j+1)^q \, 2^{j\alpha q} \le \omega_p(u, \lambda)^q \, 2^{\lambda \alpha q} \le \omega_p(u, j)^q \, 2^{(j+1)\alpha q},$$

and a summation leads to $2^{-\alpha q} I_d \le I \le 2^{\alpha q} I_d$, if I and I_d denote the integral and discrete sum separately in formulae (3.29) and (3.30).

Furthermore, since $\omega_p(u, j) \le 2\|u\|_p$, and $\alpha, q > 0$,

$$\sum_{j<0} \omega_p(u, j)^q 2^{j\alpha q} \le \frac{2^q}{2^{\alpha q} - 1} \|u\|_p^q.$$

This establishes the following theorem.

Theorem 3.9. *The Besov norm* (3.28) *is equivalent to*

$$\|u\|_p + \left(\sum_{j \geq 0} 2^{j\alpha q} \omega_p(u, j)^q \right)^{1/q}.$$

In the above it has been assumed that the regularity index $\alpha \in [0, 1)$. If $\alpha \in [n-1, n)$ for some positive integer n, the definition of Besov space $B_q^\alpha(L^p)$ continues to hold as long as the the first order finite difference operator $\Delta_a u = u(x + a) - u(x) = (T_a - I)u$, where T_a denotes the backward translation operator and I the identity, is replaced by the nth order finite difference operator

$$\Delta_a^n = (T_a - I)^n = \sum_{m=0}^{n} (-1)^{n-m} \binom{n}{m} T_{ma},$$

and the p-modulus of continuity $\omega_p(u, h)$ in (3.26) is updated to

$$\omega_{p,n}(u, h) = \sup_{|a| \leq h} \|\Delta_a^n u\|_p. \tag{3.31}$$

For more details on Besov spaces, we refer the reader to Meyer [216] and Wojtaszczyk [324]. For example, one could even allow α to be negative by duality, and on the other hand, as long as $\alpha < n$, the definition of $B_q^\alpha(L^p)$ is independent of n.

Wavelet Characterization of Besov Images

Given an orthogonal MRA chain

$$\cdots \subseteq V_{-1} \subseteq V_0 \subseteq V_1 \subseteq \cdots,$$

let E_j and D_j denote the orthogonal projections from $L^2(\mathbb{R})$ to V_j and the wavelet spaces W_j separately. As before, it shall be assumed that the mother wavelet ψ is r-regular, and r can be any desired order.

For any given image u, let u_j denote the wavelet component $D_j u$ for any $j \in \mathbb{Z}$:

$$u_j(x) = \sum_k d_{j,k} \psi_{j,k}(x).$$

Due to the condition of vanishing moments in (3.18), the mother wavelet ψ looks like the differential operator d^{r+1}/dx^{r+1}. Furthermore, the projection D_j looks like the finite difference operator at scale $h_j = 2^{-j}$: $\Delta_{h_j}^{r+1}$, which implies that the p-modulus of continuity in (3.31), $\omega_{p,r}(u, j)$, is approximately equivalent to $\|u_j\|_p$. Following Theorem 3.9, this convenient (but heuristic) argument leads to a new characterization of Besov images in terms of their wavelet components:

$$\|E_0 u\|_p + \left(\sum_{j \geq 0} 2^{j\alpha q} \|u_j\|_p^q \right)^{1/q} < \infty. \tag{3.32}$$

Notice that $\|u\|_p$ in Theorem 3.9 has been replaced by the p-norm of its lowpass projection $E_0 u$, which seems weaker but in fact equivalent. This is because $\|u_j\|_p = \|D_j u\|_p \leq C2^{-j\alpha}$, where C denotes the entire second term in (3.32), and the convergence of

$$u = E_0 u + D_0 u + D_1 u + \cdots$$

in L^p is therefore geometric and strong, implying that $u \in L^p$ and its norm $\|u\|_p$ is indeed controlled by the left-hand side in (3.32). A detailed rigorous proof for the claims in this paragraph can be found in the nice book [324].

We are in a good position to introduce the main result of this section, which has also been a renowned result in wavelet theory [215]. That is, the p-norms of the wavelet components $\|u_j\|_p$ can be directly characterized by their wavelet coefficients $(d_{j,k} \mid k \in \mathbb{Z})$.

Theorem 3.10 (Norm Equivalence Between L^p and l^p). *There exist two constants C_1 and C_2, both dependent only on the mother wavelet ψ, such that for each resolution j,*

$$C_1 \|u_j\|_p \leq 2^{j(1/2-1/p)} \|(d_{j,k} \mid k \in \mathbb{Z})\|_{l^p} \leq C_2 \|u_j\|_p. \tag{3.33}$$

First, we claim that if the equivalence holds for the reference scale $j = 0$, it must hold automatically for all j's. For any j,

$$u_j(x) = \sum_{k \in \mathbb{Z}} d_{j,k} 2^{j/2} \psi(2^j x - k).$$

Therefore, $v(x) = 2^{-j/2} u_j(2^{-j}x) \in W_0$ with wavelet coefficients $(d_{j,k} \mid k \in \mathbb{Z})$. Applying the equivalence to $v(x)$ for $j = 0$, we have

$$C_1 \|2^{-j/2} u_j(2^{-j}x)\|_p \leq \|(d_{j,k} \mid k \in \mathbb{Z})\|_{l^p} \leq C_2 \|2^{-j/2} u_j(2^{-j}x)\|_p.$$

The claim is thus validated since $\|f(2^{-j}x)\|_p = 2^{j/p}\|f(x)\|_p$. (In addition, this argument shows that if the image domain $\Omega = \mathbb{R}^n$, then the weighting factor $2^{j(1/2-1/p)}$ should be replaced by $2^{jn(1/2-1/p)}$.)

Consequently, in order to establish Theorem 3.10, it suffices only to prove the following general result.

Theorem 3.11. *Suppose $w(x)$ is a continuous function such that*

1. *as $x \to \infty$, $w(x) = O(|x|^{-\beta})$ for some $\beta > 1$, and*
2. *$(w(x - k) \mid k \in \mathbb{Z})$ are orthonormal.*

Then there exist two constants C_1 and C_2, depending only on $w(x)$ and $p \geq 1$, such that for any function $f(x) = \sum_{k \in \mathbb{Z}} c(k) w(x - k)$,

$$C_1 \|f\|_{L^p} \leq \|(c(k) \mid k \in \mathbb{Z})\|_{l^p} \leq C_2 \|f\|_{L^p}.$$

To start, we first prove a general lemma.

Lemma 3.12. *Let $d\mu_x$ and $d\mu_y$ be two measures supported on $x \in \mathbb{R}$ and $y \in \mathbb{R}$. Suppose $K(x, y)$ is a measurable function on the product measure space $(\mathbb{R}^2, d\mu_x \times d\mu_y)$,*

$g(x) \in L^q(d\mu_x)$, *and* $c(y) \in L^p(d\mu_y)$ *with* $p, q \geq 1$ *that are conjugate to each other:* $p^{-1} + q^{-1} = 1$. *Then*

$$\left| \int_{\mathbb{R}^2} K(x, y)c(y)g(x)d\mu_x d\mu_y \right| \leq \|L(x)\|_\infty^{1/q} \|R(y)\|_\infty^{1/p} \|g\|_q \|c\|_p, \qquad (3.34)$$

where

$$L(x) = \int_{\mathbb{R}} |K(x, y)| d\mu_y \quad and \quad R(y) = \int_{\mathbb{R}} |K(x, y)| d\mu_x, \qquad (3.35)$$

both assumed to be finite.

In fact, the inequality (3.34) results directly from Hölder's inequality,

$$\int_{\Omega} |F \cdot G| d\nu \leq \|F\|_{L^p(d\nu)} \|G\|_{L^q(d\nu)},$$

as applied to $\Omega = \mathbb{R} \times \mathbb{R}$, $F(x, y) = c(y)$, $G(x, y) = g(x)$, and the $|K|$-weighted product measure $d\nu = |K| d\mu_x d\mu_y$.

To prove Theorem 3.11 from the lemma, first notice that

$$c(k) = \int_{\mathbb{R}} w(x - k)f(x)dx, \quad k \in \mathbb{Z}.$$

On the other hand, by introducing the δ-train measure

$$d\mu_y = \sum_{k \in \mathbb{Z}} \delta(y - k) \quad \text{with Dirac's } \delta,$$

one has

$$f(x) = \int_{\mathbb{R}} w(x - y)c(y)d\mu_y,$$

where $c(y)$ can be any extension of $c(k)$ from $\mathbb{Z}$ to $\mathbb{R}$ as $\mathbb{R}\backslash\mathbb{Z}$ is a null set of $d\mu_y$. Furthermore, almost surely according to $d\mu_y$, the $f \to c$ equation can be rewritten as

$$c(y) = \int_{\mathbb{R}} w(x - y)f(x)dx.$$

Thus by applying the lemma to $K(x, y) = w(x - y)$, $c(y) \in L^p(d\mu_y)$, and any arbitrary $g(x) \in L^q(d\mu_x = dx)$, one obtains

$$\left| \int_{\mathbb{R}} f(x)g(x)dx \right| \leq \|L\|_\infty^{1/q} \|R\|_\infty^{1/p} \|c\|_{l^p} \|g\|_q,$$

which immediately implies that $\|f\|_p \leq \|L\|_\infty^{1/q} \|R\|_\infty^{1/p} \|c\|_{l^p}$. Since the roles of f and c are perfectly symmetric in the above argument, the other direction must hold as well. Finally, both $\|L\|_\infty$ and $\|R\|_\infty$ are indeed finite since

$$L(x) = \int_{\mathbb{R}} |K(x, y)| d\mu_y = \sum_k |w(x - k)| \quad \text{is continuous and periodic with period 1},$$

$$R(y) = \int_{\mathbb{R}} |K(x, y)| d\mu_x = \int_{\mathbb{R}} |w(x - y)| dx \equiv \|w\|_1.$$

To conclude, following (3.32), we have been able to establish the equivalent characterization of a Besov image $u \in B_q^\alpha(L^p)$ in terms of its wavelet coefficients $d_{j,k}$'s and lowpass coefficients $c_{0,k}$'s at the reference scale $j = 0$:

$$\|c_{0,\cdot}\|_{l^p} + \left(\sum_{j \geq 0} 2^{jq(\alpha+1/2-1/p)} \|d_{j,\cdot}\|_{l^p}^q \right)^{1/q} < \infty. \tag{3.36}$$

Sparsity of Wavelet Representation and Image Compression

Besov images allow convenient analysis of wavelet representation and approximation. We refer the reader to, e.g., the remarkable papers [55, 101, 102] for more details.

One particularly interesting class of Besov images is $B_p^\alpha(L^p)$, of which the intrascale index p equals the interscale index q, and the Besov norm can be defined as

$$\|u\|_{B_p^\alpha(L^p)} = \left(\sum_{k \in \mathbb{Z}} |c_{0,k}|^p \right)^{1/p} + \left(\sum_{j \geq 0, k \in \mathbb{Z}} 2^{jp(\alpha+1/2-1/p)} |d_{j,k}|^p \right)^{1/p}. \tag{3.37}$$

In particular, when $p = q$ and $\alpha + 1/2 = 1/p$ (in one dimension), the weighted sum on wavelet coefficients becomes completely decoupled across all the scales:

$$\|u\|_{B_p^\alpha(L^p)} = \left(\sum_{k \in \mathbb{Z}} |c_{0,k}|^p \right)^{1/p} + \left(\sum_{j \geq 0, k \in \mathbb{Z}} |d_{j,k}|^p \right)^{1/p}. \tag{3.38}$$

These are the image models frequently studied in the literature of image compression and wavelet approximation (see, e.g., [55, 101, 102]).

As an example, first consider the efficiency of *linear* wavelet compression. A classical linear compression scheme is to choose a target resolution level J, such that all wavelet components finer than J are dumped. That is, the compressed image u_J for a given image u is defined as

$$u_J = E_0 u + \sum_{0 \leq j \leq J} D_j u.$$

The compression error, measured in the L^2 metric, is given by

$$\|u - u_J\|_2^2 = \sum_{j > J} \|D_j u\|_2^2 = \sum_{j > J, k \in \mathbb{Z}} |d_{j,k}|^2.$$

Following [55], suppose u is a Besov image $B_2^\alpha(L^2)$ for some $\alpha > 0$, which according to (3.37) implies

$$\sum_{j \geq 0, k \in \mathbb{Z}} 2^{2j\alpha} |d_{j,k}|^2 \leq \|u\|_{B_2^\alpha(L^2)}^2.$$

Therefore, the L^2 error for such a linear compression scheme is controlled by

$$\|u - u_J\|_2^2 = \sum_{j>J, k \in \mathbb{Z}} |d_{j,k}|^2$$

$$\leq 2^{-2J\alpha} \sum_{j>J, k \in \mathbb{Z}} 2^{2j\alpha} |d_{j,k}|^2$$

$$\leq 2^{-2J\alpha} \|u\|_{B_2^\alpha(L^2)}^2,$$

or simply,

$$\|u - u_J\|_2 \leq 2^{-J\alpha} \|u\|_{B_2^\alpha(L^2)} = h_J^\alpha \|u\|_{B_2^\alpha(L^2)},$$

where $h_J = 2^{-J}$ is the spatial resolution finer than which all wavelet coefficients are set to 0. It is clear from this example that the efficiency of the linear compression scheme is proportional to the regularity (i.e., α) of the given image.

Following [55, 101], let us now consider a popular *nonlinear* compression scheme realized by only retaining the N largest wavelet coefficients.

Assume u is a Besov image belonging to $B_p^\alpha(L^p)$ with $\alpha + 1/2 = 1/p$ (in one dimension; or $\alpha/2 + 1/2 = 1/p$ in two dimensions; either case implies $p < 2$). Then by (3.38),

$$\sum_{k \in \mathbb{Z}} |c_{0,k}|^p + \sum_{j \geq 0, k \in \mathbb{Z}} |d_{j,k}|^p \leq \|u\|_{B_p^\alpha(L^p)}^p.$$

The nonlinear compression scheme starts with the reordering of all the coefficients $(c_{0,k} \mid k \in \mathbb{Z})$ and $(d_{j,k} \mid j \geq 0, k \in \mathbb{Z})$ by the descending order of their absolute values:

$$a_1, a_2, \ldots, a_{N-1}, a_N, a_{N+1}, \ldots \quad \text{with} \quad |a_1| \geq |a_2| \geq |a_3| \geq \cdots.$$

The compressed image is defined to be

$$u_N(x) = \sum_{n=1}^{N} a_n g_n(x),$$

where g_n denotes either $\phi_{0,k}$ or $\psi_{j,k}$ if $a_n = c_{0,k}$ or $d_{j,k}$.

To estimate the approximation error of such a nonlinear compression scheme, first write $\lambda_N = |a_N|$, and notice

$$N\lambda_N^p \leq \sum_{n=1}^{\infty} |a_n|^p = \sum_{k \in \mathbb{Z}} |c_{0,k}|^p + \sum_{j \geq 0, k \in \mathbb{Z}} |d_{j,k}|^p \leq \|u\|_{B_p^\alpha(L^p)}^p,$$

which implies that

$$\lambda_N^p \leq N^{-1} \|u\|_{B_p^\alpha(L^p)}^p.$$

Therefore, by noticing that $\alpha = 2/p - 1$, we have

$$\|u - u_N\|_2^2 \leq \sum_{n > N} |a_n|^2 \leq \lambda_N^{2-p} \sum_{n > N} |a_n|^p$$

$$\leq \lambda_N^{2-p} \sum_{n=1:\infty} |a_n|^p$$

$$\leq (\lambda_N^p)^{(2/p-1)} \|u\|_{B_p^\alpha(L^p)}^p$$

$$\leq N^{-\alpha} \|u\|_{B_p^\alpha(L^p)}^2,$$

or simply,

$$\|u - u_N\|_2 \leq N^{-\alpha/2} \|u\|_{B_p^\alpha(L^p)} = O(N^{-\alpha/2}). \tag{3.39}$$

As in the case of linear compression, the approximation error is directly controlled by the smoothness index α.

Moreover, as shown by DeVore, Jawerth, and Popov [102], the last error control formula is invertible. Roughly speaking, it means that if for a given image u, there exists a constant $C > 0$ and $\alpha > 0$, such that the above nonlinear compression scheme yields

$$\|u - u_N\|_2 \leq C N^{-\alpha/2},$$

then $u \in B_p^\alpha(L^p)$ for p with $1/p = \alpha + 1/2$ (in one dimension; or $1/p = \alpha/2 + 1/2$ in two dimensions).

In the next chapter, we shall explain the role of Besov images in image denoising.

3.4   Lattice and Random Field Representation

Away from all the previous more deterministic approaches to image modeling, in this section we discuss stochastic methods based on Gibbs or Markov random fields [130, 328, 329].

3.4.1   Natural Images of Mother Nature

Looking at a typical picture taken during a beach vacation trip, we are often able to immediately identify the ocean, blue sky, sand beach, palm trees, and so on. No sand beaches are identical in two different cities, due to the variation in sand size, color, grain type, and purity. Nevertheless, a normal human vision system never finds it too challenging to identify them.

Apparently, the vision system has to be able to calculate and analyze certain statistically invariant properties in order to maintain such robustness, which points to the significance of properly modeling the stochastic characteristics of natural images.

The word "natural" has been widely used in image and vision analysis [122, 123, 142, 225]. Though lacking a uniform definition, it intuitively refers to images that randomly capture scenes in the nature, such as sandy beaches mentioned above or green lawns. Natural images are also often called "textures." Unlike "artificial" images mostly capturing man-made smooth scenes, textures are often rough and fluctuating as far as the image functions are concerned.

The roughness and fluctuation in natural images result directly from those in Mother Nature. These features are usually not directly *painted* on 2-D regular surfaces by Mother

Nature; rather, they are *carved* into the 3-D world by numerous random physical forces such as tides rolling, rain washing, wind motion, and weather regulated biological growth. The resulting 3-D roughness and fluctuation in surface geometry are then captured by 2-D images and become 2-D textures. Sand beaches, trees, grasslands, and hilly scenes are all such examples.

There do exist some exceptions to roughness- (or surface geometry-) based textures. Those are in some sense truly painted by Mother Nature on relatively smoother surfaces. Familiar examples include the wooden texture on a smoothly cut section of a trunk and numerous animal skin patterns (e.g., zebras, leopards, snakes) generated by biochemical mechanisms (e.g., Turing's reaction-diffusion models [304]).

In conclusion, 2-D textures are truly the mirror images of Mother Nature, with faithful reflection of Her randomness and fluctuations. Consequently, stochastic tools are intrinsically necessary for the proper representation and analysis of natural images.

3.4.2   Images as Ensembles and Distributions

Unlike the deterministic view by which each image is an image on its own right, the statistical view treats each image as a sample from the ensemble it belongs to.

Therefore, for example, although a lawn picture taken in Paris may look in every detail quite different from the one taken in the New York City, they are still easily recognizable as grass images, or two different samples from the ensemble of images commonly named by the word "grass."

On the other hand, human vision is also advanced enough to easily tell apart a typical sand beach image from a typical grass image. That is, it has the remarkable capability of classifying different image ensembles.

Even at the ensemble level, unlike the deterministic view, different ensembles of images unnecessarily have to carry clear cut decision boundaries. There do exist certain image samples that may look like both grass images and sand beach images. For instance, typically near an unpaved and undeveloped natural beach area, as one walks away from the coast line into land, the pure sand beach may gradually carry more soil and allow the growth of more grass. As a result, in terms of their images, the sandy features may slowly fade away while those of the grass grow stronger. At a certain point, even to human vision a binary decision of sand or grass becomes very difficult.

Thus, if $\mathcal{I} = \mathcal{I}(\Omega)$ denotes *all* possible images on a 2-D domain Ω, the stochastic view does not intend to partition $\mathcal{I}$ into *disjoint* distinct subsets such as

$$\mathcal{I} = \mathcal{I}_{\text{grass}} \bigcup \mathcal{I}_{\text{tree}} \bigcup \mathcal{I}_{\text{sand beach}} \bigcup \cdots$$

with each collection exclusively representing a specific category.

Instead, any image in $\mathcal{I}$ is believed to have certain likelihood of being labelled as a grass image, even it may look "entirely" tree-like to human vision, and vice versa. Mathematically, this implies that each ensemble is really a probability distribution μ on $\mathcal{I}$, and different categories correspond to different distributions. For example, we may have μ_{grass}, μ_{tree}, and $\mu_{\text{sandbeach}}$ for the ensembles of grass, tree, and sand beach.

Therefore, the mission of stochastic representation and analysis of natural images is to properly develop and model these ensemble distributions μ's. It has broad applications in contemporary sciences and technologies, for example, ground reading for auto piloting, target detection and recognition in military, and automatic detection of abnormal tissues in medical imaging, just to name a few.

What are called in daily life image "features" or "patterns" correspond to the characteristics of such ensemble distributions μ's.

This stochastic view has been in fact very fundamental in the classical signal detection theory in sensory psychology and psychophysics, not merely for visual signal analysis. Below we discuss a simple example.

Consider the signal detection of two spots: one brighter and the other dimmer. In real experiments, they may be generated by controlling the light emission of a light source in a dark room. Due to electric or environmental fluctuations, the light intensities of the two spots fluctuate as well and are typically modeled by Gaussian distributions, for example,

$$p^b(i) = \frac{1}{\sqrt{2\pi\sigma_b^2}}\ e^{-\frac{(i-4)^2}{2\sigma_b^2}} \quad \text{and} \quad p^d(i) = \frac{1}{\sqrt{2\pi\sigma_b^2}}\ e^{-\frac{(i-2)^2}{2\sigma_d^2}}. \qquad (3.40)$$

The bright spot has mean intensity $m_b = 4$ and spreading rate (or fuzziness) σ_b, while the dimmer one has mean intensity $m_d = 2$ and spreading rate σ_d. This is the stochastic view of two seemingly deterministic spots. When $\sigma_b = \sigma_d = 0$, these are two ideal deterministic spots.

Assume now that $\sigma_b = \sigma_d = 1$, and one particular measurement gives $i_0 = 3$. Then, without bias from any other factors, an experimenter will have difficulty in determining which spot has been present. This is the fuzziness in detecting signal patterns, precisely analogous to pattern recognition: the supports of the two probability distributions can overlap.

In this example, the signal patterns "bright" and "dim" are really characterized by the feature pair (mean, variance) $= (m, \sigma)$ in the Gaussian model (3.40). As a result, a complete and efficient representation of a spot is not to record all the individual samples i's, rather, to only store the two key feature numbers: the mean and variance. This is again analogous to what needs to be done for stochastic image representation and analysis: to extract the least amount of key statistical information so that the target image ensembles can be efficiently characterized.

Below we introduce the remarkable works of Geman and Geman [130], Zhu and Mumford [328], and Zhu, Wu, and Mumford [329] on the stochastic modeling of image patterns.

3.4.3 Images as Gibbs' Ensembles

In most digital applications, the imaging or display devices often consist of 2-D arrays of pixels, most of which are Cartesian. After pixel rescaling, let the integer lattice

$$\mathbb{Z}^2 = \{(n, m) : n, m = 0, \pm1, \pm2, \ldots\}$$

denote the canonical image array. Then a finite domain Ω is a subset of $\mathbb{Z}^2$, and typically a square in most digital applications:

$$\Omega = \{(i, j) : 0 \le i \le I - 1 \text{ and } 0 \le j \le J - 1\},$$

which shall be assumed below unless otherwise stated.

As before, let $\mathcal{I}(\Omega)$ denote all digital images on Ω:

$$\mathcal{I}(\Omega) = \{u = (u_{ij}) : \Omega \to \mathbb{R} \mid u_{ij} \in \mathbb{R}\}.$$

Formally, these are simply all the I-by-J matrices with real entries, and therefore $\mathcal{I} = \mathbb{R}^{I \times J}$. One, however, must realize that the formal matrix structure of a digital image is rarely employed in the sense of linear algebra.

The mission of stochastic modeling of an image class is to model the underlying probability distribution p on $\mathcal{I}(\Omega)$. Obviously, p_{grass} should be reasonably different from $p_{\text{sand beach}}$.

One familiar distribution on $\mathcal{I}(\Omega)$ is the homogeneous Gaussian

$$p(u) = \frac{1}{(2\pi\sigma^2)^{IJ/2}} \ \exp\left(-\frac{1}{2\sigma^2}\sum_{ij \in \Omega} u_{ij}^2\right) = \frac{1}{(2\pi\sigma^2)^{IJ/2}} \exp\left(-\frac{\|u\|^2}{2\sigma^2}\right), \qquad (3.41)$$

where $\|\cdot\|$ stands for the Euclidean norm in $\mathcal{I}$ as the Euclidean space $R^{I \times J}$. Unfortunately, a typical sample from this distribution usually looks noisy and uninteresting.

However, there are some features of the Gaussian expression that are in fact shared by many other more useful image distributions. Define

$$E[u] = \frac{\|u\|^2}{2}, \quad \beta = \frac{1}{\sigma^2}, \ \text{ and } \ Z = (2\pi\sigma^2)^{\frac{IJ}{2}}.$$

Then the Gaussian distribution (3.41) could be written as

$$p(u) = p_\beta(u) = \frac{1}{Z} \exp(-\beta E[u]). \qquad (3.42)$$

Formally calling $E[u]$ the "energy" of u, we have obtained the Gibbs CE in statistical mechanics (see the preceding chapter).

In statistical mechanics, u denotes a microscopic state of a target ensemble of particles and $E[u]$ the energy level of that particular state. If a 2-D lattice of particles all freely move in one fixed direction, and u_{ij} is associated with the velocity of the particle labelled by (ij), then the Gaussian distribution (3.41) becomes the celebrated Maxwell–Boltzmann distribution law assuming that the mass of each particle is one unit [82, 131].

On the other hand, in statistical mechanics, the parameter β is called the "inverse" temperature as it is explicitly given by $\beta = 1/(kT)$, with k denoting the Boltzmann constant and T the absolute temperature.

Finally, the constant Z is called the *partition function* and is uniquely determined by β for probability normalization

$$Z = Z(\beta) = \sum_{u \in \mathcal{I}} \exp(-\beta E[u]) \ \text{ or } \ \int_{u \in I} \exp(-\beta E[u])du,$$

once the energy is specified. Here the summation applies when u is quantized to finite gray-scale levels and $\mathcal{I}$ is a finite set, while the integration when u's are continuous and $\mathcal{I}$ is an open subset in $\mathbb{R}^{I \times J}$. Physically, the partition function generally contains important information of free energies and fluctuations [82, 131].

For image modeling, it is often not enough merely working with a single energy.

Definition 3.13 (Gibbs' Image Models (Geman and Geman [130])). *A Gibbs' field or ensemble model of an image class refers to any probability distribution $p(u)$ on the image space $\mathcal{I}$ given by the following form:*

$$p(u) = p_{\boldsymbol{\beta}}(u) = \frac{1}{Z} \exp(-\boldsymbol{\beta} \cdot \boldsymbol{E}[u]), \qquad (3.43)$$

where for some finite m,

$$\boldsymbol{\beta} = (\beta_1, \beta_2, \dots, \beta_m) \quad and \quad \boldsymbol{E}[u] = (E_1[u], E_2[u], \dots, E_m[u]) \qquad (3.44)$$

are some proper parameter vector and "energy" function vector separately, and the partition function is given by

$$Z = Z(\boldsymbol{\beta}) = \sum_{u \in \mathcal{I}} \exp(-\boldsymbol{\beta} \cdot \boldsymbol{E}[u]).$$

As in statistical mechanics and the preceding chapter, we shall call each $E_k[u]$ a generalized energy and its dual parameter β_k a generalized potential. In thermodynamics for example, one can have

$$\boldsymbol{E} = (E, V, n),$$

with the internal energy E, the volume V, and the mole number n of particles, and

$$\boldsymbol{\beta} = (\beta, \ p, \ \mu)$$

corresponding to the inverse temperature β, the pressure p, and the chemical potential μ.

The primary challenge for Gibbs' image modeling is to properly design these generalized energy functions and their dual potentials.

3.4.4 Images as Markov Random Fields

There is a special class of energies whose associated Gibbs' ensembles are Markov random fields. The converse is also true, which is a remarkable result in stochastic modeling and analysis due to Hammersley and Clifford (see, e.g., [33]).

As before, let Ω denote a discrete set of pixels, upon which an intensity image $u : \Omega \to \mathbb{R}$ is defined. Suppose that associated with each pixel $\alpha \in \Omega$, there is a unique *neighborhood* $N_\alpha \subseteq \Omega \setminus \{\alpha\}$. For instance, for the canonical Cartesian grid $\Omega = \mathbb{Z}^2$, a familiar choice is to define for each pixel $\alpha = (i, j)$,

$$N_\alpha = \{\beta = (k, l) \in \Omega \ : \ |k - i| + |l - j| = 1\} = \{(i, j \pm 1), (i \pm 1, j)\}. \qquad (3.45)$$

Notice that α is excluded from its neighborhood. Then the collection of all neighborhoods

$$\mathcal{N} = \{N_\alpha \mid \alpha \in \Omega\}$$

is called a *neighborhood system*, which will always be assumed *symmetric* in the sense of

$$\beta \in N_\alpha \quad \text{if and only if} \quad \alpha \in N_\beta, \quad \alpha, \beta \in \Omega.$$

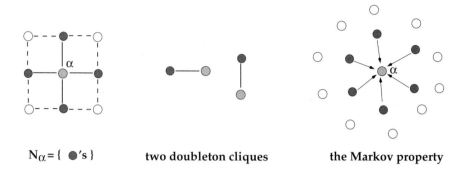

$N_\alpha = \{\, \bullet\text{'s} \,\}$ **two doubleton cliques**   **the Markov property**

Figure 3.4. *Ingredients of Markov random fields by examples: a neighborhood N_α (left), two doubleton cliques $C \in \mathcal{C}$ (middle), and locality of conditional inference $p(u_\alpha \mid u_{\Omega \setminus \alpha}) = p(u_\alpha \mid u_{N_\alpha})$ (right).*

Then the couple $(\Omega, \mathcal{N})$ is said to be a *graph* or *topological* pixel domain. We shall also denote $\beta \in N_\alpha$ by $\beta \sim \alpha$ or $\beta \sim_{\mathcal{N}} \alpha$. In graph theory, the neighborhood system $\mathcal{N}$ is also equivalent to the edge system $E_\Omega \subseteq \Omega \times \Omega$ with

$$E_\Omega = \{(\alpha, \beta) \in \Omega \times \Omega \mid \beta \sim \alpha\}.$$

For simplicity in notation, the same symbol u shall denote both a random image field and any of its particular samples.

Definition 3.14 (Markov Property). *A random field u on a pixel domain Ω is said to be Markovian with respect to a neighborhood system $\mathcal{N}$ if it is local, i.e., in terms of conditional probabilities, for any pixel $\alpha \in \Omega$,*

$$p(u_\alpha \mid u_{\Omega \setminus \{\alpha\}}) = p(u_\alpha \mid u_{N_\alpha}).$$

That is, the image information at any given pixel α, given the rest of the image, actually depends only on its neighborhood N_α (see Figure 3.4).

Locality is desirable for both theoretical analysis and efficient computation (such as parallelization), and Markov random fields have thus played significant roles in studying spatial patterns across a number of disciplines.

To state the Gibbs–Markov equivalence theorem mentioned in the beginning, it is necessary to introduce the notion of *cliques* (see Figure 3.4).

Definition 3.15 (Cliques). *A clique C of a graph $(\Omega, \mathcal{N})$ is a set of pixels such that for any two distinct pixels $\alpha, \beta \in C$,*

$$\alpha \in N_\beta \quad (\text{and as a result of symmetry, } \beta \in N_\alpha).$$

Let $\mathcal{C} = \mathcal{C}(\Omega, \mathcal{N})$ denote the collection of all cliques. Then $\mathcal{C}$ is naturally *stratified* according to the sizes of cliques:

$$\mathcal{C} = \mathcal{C}_0 \cup \mathcal{C}_1 \cup \mathcal{C}_2 \cup \cdots,$$

where for $k = 0, 1, \ldots,$

$$\mathcal{C}_k = \{C \in \mathcal{C} \mid \#C = k\}, \quad \text{the collection of all } k\text{-cliques.}$$

Notice that $\mathcal{C}_0$ contains only the empty clique, and $\mathcal{C}_1$ consists of all singleton cliques, and both are therefore trivial and independent of the neighborhood system $\mathcal{N}$. The first nontrivial stratum $\mathcal{C}_2$ is the collection of all doubleton cliques. For instance, for the canonical Cartesian domain $\mathbb{Z}^2$ with the cross neighborhood system defined as in (3.45),

$$\mathcal{C}_2 = \{\{(i, j), (i + 1, j)\} \mid (i, j) \in \mathbb{Z}^2\} \cup \{\{(i, j), (i, j + 1)\} \mid (i, j) \in \mathbb{Z}^2\}.$$

Notice that any clique C must be covered by N_α for any $\alpha \in C$, and thus has to be local.

Definition 3.16 (Cliquish Potentials). *A spatial statistics (or real functional) $V_C[u]$, which assigns a real value $V_C[u]$ to any sample image u, is said to be a cliquish potential mounted on a clique C if for any two image samples u and w,*

$$V_C[u] = V_C[w], \quad \text{whenever } u\big|_C = w\big|_C.$$

That is, in essence $V_C[u]$ is only a function of $u\big|_C$.

The remarkable theorem of Hammersley and Clifford on Gibbs–Markov equivalence is stated as follows.

Theorem 3.17 (Gibbs–Markov Equivalence). *Let u denote a Gibbs' ensemble on Ω:*

$$p(u) = \frac{1}{Z} \exp(-\beta E[u]),$$

as in (3.42), and $\mathcal{N}$ a given neighborhood system on Ω. Suppose that the energy $E[u]$ is a superposition of cliquish potentials:

$$E[u] = \sum_{C \in \mathcal{C}} V_C[u].$$

Then u is a Markov random field on $(\Omega, \mathcal{N})$. Conversely, under a mild positivity condition [144], any Markov random field can be designed in this manner, with a unique set of cliquish potentials under some suitable normalization procedure.

The proof for the first half is relatively straightforward based on the definitions, while the second part often relies on the Möbius formula for (combinatorial) lattice inversion. We refer the reader to Brémaud [33] and Grimmett [144] for more details on the proof.

To conclude, local cliquish potentials and Gibbs' ensembles consist into a convenient machinery for designing Markov random images. We shall return to this topic in the segmentation chapter when the celebrated work of Geman and Geman [130] is further explained.

3.4.5 Visual Filters and Filter Banks

The preceding sections have made the exciting connections between stochastic image modeling and Gibbs' ensembles. The main challenge now is how to design properly the generalized energies and their associated potentials.

What seems natural and necessary is that these energies and potentials must be related to the key ingredients of human visual perception, including, for example, scale, orientation, and frequency. Therefore, we shall call them *visual* energies and *visual* potentials.

From Marr's edge theory to modern wavelet analysis, one outstanding attribute of visual perception seems to be the *differentiation* capability. That is, a constant image $u \equiv c$ usually looks uninteresting and has zero energy. Thus it is reasonable to expect that for any visual energy E,

$$E[c] = 0 \text{ for } c \in \mathbb{R} \text{ as a constant image.}$$

This also suggests that it may be wiser to build visual energies directly in feature spaces. Let F be a feature extraction operator which extracts a feature vector or function Fu for any given image u, and it is highpass in the sense that Fc is a zero feature vector or function for any constant image c. Then it is desirable to have an energy in the form of

$$E[u] = V[Fu]$$

for some suitable function (when Fu is a vector) or functional (when Fu is a function) $V[\cdot]$ in the feature space with $V[0] = 0$.

Example. Suppose (Ω, E_Ω) is the pixel graph carrying all the targeted images. Take edge differencing as the feature extraction operator, i.e., $w = Fu$ is the vector indexed by all the edges and defined by, for any graph edge $e : x \sim y$,

$$w_e = |u(x) - u(y)|.$$

Take V in the form of

$$V[w] = V_q[w] = \sum_{e \in E_\Omega} w_e^q.$$

When $q = 2$ this energy leads to two important quantities of the graph: the incidence matrix and the graph Laplacian [87]. For $q = 1$, the energy is the *separable* TV energy of u.

More generally, as motivated by vision analysis, one could have many feature extraction operators $(F^\alpha : \alpha \in \mathcal{A})$, where $\mathcal{A}$ is a finite labelling alphabet and typically in the order of tens [328, 329]. Let u^α denote the feature output $F^\alpha u$ for each $\alpha \in \mathcal{A}$ and image u.

In image and vision analysis, feature extraction is usually assisted by highpass filters.

Definition 3.18 (Linear Highpass Filter). *A feature extraction operator F from the image space $\mathcal{I} = \mathcal{I}(\Omega)$ to some linear feature space V is said to be linear and highpass if*

$$F(au + bv) = aFu + bFv$$

for any two constants a and b and images u and v, and

$$Fc \equiv 0$$

for any constant image c.

Example. As before, suppose (Ω, E_Ω) is the carrying graph of images. For each pixel $x \in \Omega$, define its degree by

$$d(x) = \#\{y \in \Omega \setminus \{x\} : y \sim x\} = \#N_x,$$

i.e., the number of nearby pixels with direct edge access to x. Define the Laplacian operator or filter $w = Fu$ by

$$w(x) = -d(x)u(x) + \sum_{y \in N_x} u(y). \tag{3.46}$$

Then it is easy to verify that the Laplacian filter is indeed linear and highpass. It plays a central role in the graph spectral theory [87]. An energy built upon the Laplacian filter can be given by

$$E[u] = \sum_\Omega |w(x)|^q$$

for some fixed power $q \geq 1$.

In signal and image analysis, a *filter bank* refers to a collection of filters, often designed to achieve a common goal.

Suppose $(F^\alpha : \alpha \in \mathcal{A})$ is a bank of linear highpass filters capable of extracting all major visual features that a normal human vision system cares about. That means, it should be able to resolve key features such as local spatial frequencies, orientations, etc. Then it would be reasonable to assume that a faithful stochastic model should depend *only* on the filter responses of such a filter bank. But the question is how to characterize such dependence.

One approach, whose genesis and rigorous derivation will be given in the next subsection, formally assumes that all the filter outputs $(u^\alpha : \alpha \in \mathcal{A})$ are somewhat *independent*, and therefore their individual energies $E_\alpha[u^\alpha]$ behave like the independent extensive variables E (internal energy), V (volume), and n (mole numbers) in a typical GCE in statistical mechanics (see Section 2.3). That is to say, the Gibbs image model takes the following form:

$$p(u) = \frac{1}{Z} \exp\left(-\sum_{\alpha \in \mathcal{A}} \beta_\alpha E_\alpha[u^\alpha]\right), \tag{3.47}$$

where β_a's are the associated potentials. In fact, even more generally, for each feature class $\alpha \in \mathcal{A}$, one could allow both E_α and β_a to be vectors:

$$E_\alpha = [E_\alpha^1, E_\alpha^2, \ldots, E_\alpha^{m_\alpha}] \quad \text{and} \quad \boldsymbol{\beta}_\alpha = [\beta_\alpha^1, \beta_\alpha^2, \ldots, \beta_\alpha^{m_\alpha}].$$

Then the Gibbs image model is given by

$$p(u) = \frac{1}{Z} \exp\left(-\sum_{\alpha \in \mathcal{A}} \boldsymbol{\beta}_\alpha \cdot \boldsymbol{E}_\alpha[u^\alpha]\right). \tag{3.48}$$

This is the most general form of Gibbs' image models in the literature.

3.4.6   Entropy-Based Learning of Image Patterns

In this section, we give a brief introduction to Zhu, Mumford, and Wu's approach to learning Gibbs' image models based upon the *maximum entropy principle* [328, 329].

Following the general Gibbs model (3.48) in the preceding subsection, we are led to the following three questions:

1. What is a good filter bank $(F^\alpha : \alpha \in \mathcal{A})$ that captures visual features sufficiently well?

2. What are the visual energies (extensive variables) E_α for each channel of feature extraction $u^\alpha = \mathcal{F}^\alpha u$?

3. What are appropriate visual potentials (or dual intensive variables) β_α associated with the energies?

Recall as in Section 2.3 that a quantity $X = X[u|\Omega]$ is said to be *extensive* if for any two *disjoint* image domains Ω_1 and Ω_2, and an image u in "equilibrium,"

$$X\left[u|\Omega_1 \bigcup \Omega_2\right] = X[u|\Omega_1] + X[u|\Omega_2].$$

Similarly, X is called an *intensive* variable if instead,

$$X\left[u|\Omega_1 \bigcup \Omega_2\right] = X[u|\Omega_1] = X[u|\Omega_2].$$

Following statistical mechanics, they should both be understood in the asymptotic sense when the sizes of the domains are sufficiently large.

On the other hand, unlike statistical mechanics where equilibria (e.g., thermal, mechanical, or chemical) are naturally defined through physical contact (e.g., via thermal contact, a mechanical piston, or a permeable membrane), the definition of the equilibrium of two portions of an image or two separate images is much less obvious. What seems natural for image and vision analysis is that the notion of equilibrium must be in the sense of visual discrimination. Intuitively speaking, two images are said to be in (visual) equilibrium if one cannot distinguish one from the other when having them placed next to each other.

In the most ideal scenario, a class of natural images are best characterized by a learning process that could learn all the three elements of Gibbs modeling: the visual filters $(F^\alpha : \alpha \in \mathcal{A})$, the extensive "energy" variables $(E_\alpha : \alpha \in \mathcal{A})$, and the intensive visual potentials $(\beta_\alpha : \alpha \in \mathcal{A})$. Such a learning process is, however, conceivably expensive.

In the work of Zhu and Mumford [328], and Zhu, Wu, and Mumford [329], a learning model is proposed for the visual potentials, provided that two dictionaries are given or chosen a priori for the visual filters and extensive energy variables. It is beautifully rooted in Gibbs' variational formulation of statistical mechanics—the principle of *maximum entropy*, as introduced in Section 2.3.

The filter bank used consists of multiscale Gabor linear filters. Thus for example, a feature index α is associated with a triple of scale $\sigma > 0$, orientation $\theta \in (-\pi, \pi]$, and spatial frequency $k > 0$:

$$\alpha = (\sigma, \ \theta, \ k) \in \mathbb{R}^3,$$

and $\mathcal{A}$ is a quantized finite subset in $\mathbb{R}^3$. Then for each $\alpha \in \mathcal{A}$, $u^\alpha = F^\alpha u$ is a feature distribution on the scaled domain $\Omega_\alpha = \Omega_\sigma$, which is given by, for example,

$$\Omega_2 = \{(2i, 2j) \in \mathbb{Z}^2 : 0 \le i \le (I - 1)/2 \text{ and } 0 \le j \le (J - 1)/2\},$$
$$\Omega_4 = \{(4i, 4j) \in \mathbb{Z}^2 : 0 \le i \le (I - 1)/4 \text{ and } 0 \le j \le (J - 1)/4\}, \quad \cdots$$

assuming that the original image domain is $\Omega = (0 : I - 1) \times (0 : J - 1)$. Notice that here the scale indices 2 and 4 are the zoom-out scales. In practice, often several scale levels are sufficient for general image analysis. For the moment, we will ignore boundary effects by using reflective or periodic extensions. In addition, we shall call Ω_α the *carrier* of feature type α.

The extensive energy variables in Zhu, Mumford, and Wu's Gibbs' image modeling are the histograms of the feature distributions.

First, the range of each feature distribution u^α is equally quantized to certain finite levels (denoted by the partition symbol π):

$$\pi : \cdots < b < a < c < \cdots,$$

where the quantization step or bin size $h = a - b = c - a = \cdots$ may depend on the feature type α. For each bin index a, define the *level band* Ω_α^a by

$$\Omega_\alpha^a = \{x \in \Omega_\alpha : a - h/2 \le u^\alpha(x) < a + h/2\}.$$

Then the (unnormalized) histogram vector $\boldsymbol{H}_\alpha$ for feature type α under the quantization scheme π is defined as

$$\boldsymbol{H}_\alpha = (\ldots, H_\alpha^b, H_\alpha^a, H_\alpha^c, \ldots), \quad \text{with } H_\alpha^a = \#\Omega_\alpha^a.$$

Notice that for each feature type α, $\boldsymbol{H}_\alpha = \boldsymbol{H}_\alpha[u]$ is indeed a (nonlinear) vector function of the original image u. In Zhu, Mumford, and Wu's model [328, 329], these are taken to be the energies $\boldsymbol{E}_\alpha$'s for the general Gibbs ensemble model (3.48). It is trivial to verify that each $\boldsymbol{H}_\alpha$ is extensive, once the filter type α and its quantization scheme are given.

Finally, we are led to the proper determination of the associated potentials. For the reason that will immediately come clear afterwards, these potentials will be denoted by $\lambda_\alpha(a)$ instead of the general notation β_α^a in the preceding subsection and are learned by Gibbs' formulation of maximum entropy.

First, notice that the histograms $\boldsymbol{H}_\alpha$'s are random vectors since the images are assumed to be random fields. Suppose we have a sufficiently large bank $\mathcal{C}$ of a target class of natural images. Then the statistics of the histograms can be obtained by empirical ensemble averaging, for example, the means

$$\langle \boldsymbol{H}_\alpha \rangle_{(\mathcal{I}, p)} \simeq \langle \boldsymbol{H}_a[u] \rangle_{u \in \mathcal{C}} = \boldsymbol{h}_\alpha, \quad \alpha \in \mathcal{A}. \tag{3.49}$$

If instead, these are imposed as exact constraints on the random field distribution $p(u)$ to be modelled, as analogous to the GCE formulation (2.32) in statistical mechanics, then Gibbs' maximum entropy principle naturally leads to the Gibbs field model

$$p(u) = p_\Lambda(u) = \frac{1}{Z} \exp\left(-\sum_{\alpha \in \mathcal{A}} \lambda_\alpha \cdot \boldsymbol{H}_\alpha[u]\right),$$

where $\Lambda = (\lambda_\alpha : \alpha \in \mathcal{A})$ collects all the Lagrange multipliers for the constrained maximization of Gibbs' entropy (2.31), which are called visual potentials.

To determine or learn these visual potentials, one notices that the partition function depends on the visual potentials

$$Z = Z_\Lambda = \sum_{u \in \mathcal{I}} \exp\left(-\sum_{\alpha \in \mathcal{A}} \lambda_\alpha \cdot H_\alpha[u]\right),$$

where it has been assumed that the image gray scales are quantized as well (e.g., 8 or 16 bits quantization), and consequently $\mathcal{I} = \mathcal{I}(\Omega)$ consists of finitely many images. Furthermore, we have as in statistical mechanics (Section 1.3.3)

$$\frac{-\partial \ln Z_\Lambda}{\partial \lambda_\alpha} = \langle H_\alpha \rangle_{(\mathcal{I}, p_\Lambda)} = h_\alpha, \quad \alpha \in \mathcal{A}. \tag{3.50}$$

These are the equations for the unknown visual potentials $\Lambda = (\lambda_\alpha : \alpha \in \mathcal{A})$ and can be statistically solved using Gibbs' samplers [33].

Write $\lambda_\alpha(a) = \lambda_\alpha^a$ for any quantization level a of feature class α, and extend it to a piecewise constant function $\lambda_\alpha(y)$ consistent with the quantization scheme $\pi : \cdots < b < a < c < \cdots : \lambda_\alpha(y) = \lambda_\alpha^a$ for any $y \in [(b+a)/2, (a+c)/2)$. Then

$$\lambda_\alpha \cdot H_\alpha = \sum_{\cdots < b < a < c < \cdots} \lambda_\alpha(a) \times \#\Omega_\alpha^a = \sum_{y \in \Omega_\alpha} \lambda_\alpha(u^\alpha(y)).$$

Thus for continuous domains, with a possible constant multiplier, it becomes

$$\lambda_\alpha \cdot H_\alpha \to \int_{\Omega_\alpha} \lambda_\alpha(u^\alpha(y)) dy,$$

which leads to the familiar form of "free energies" used by the community of variational/PDE image processing:

$$\sum_{\alpha \in \mathcal{A}} \lambda_\alpha \cdot H_\alpha \to \sum_{\alpha \in \mathcal{A}} \int_{\Omega_\alpha} \lambda_\alpha(u^\alpha(y)) dy.$$

For example, choosing a priori the gradient highpass filter

$$u^\alpha(y) = |\nabla u(y)|, \quad y \in \Omega = \Omega_\alpha,$$

and the visual potential $\lambda_\alpha(a) \equiv a$ formally leads to the BV image model of Rudin, Osher, and Fatemi [258], and Rudin and Osher [257] introduced in the preceding chapter.

3.5 Level-Set Representation

An image as a function can be understood as a collection of isophotes, or equivalently, level sets. This view leads to the *level-set representation* of images and is closely connected to the celebrated level-set *computational* technology of Osher and Sethian [241], Osher and Fedkiw [243], Osher and Paragios [239], and Sethian [269]. We must emphasize that the level-set representation can also be considered as the continuum limit of the morphological approach in classical discrete image processing, as briefly introduced in Chapter 1 (also see, e.g., [48, 147, 267]).

3.5.1 Classical Level Sets

Consider a gray-scale image $u = u(x)$ as a function on a 2-D bounded open domain $x \in \Omega$, which is typically a square domain in most digital applications.

For each real value λ, define the λ-level set of u to be

$$\gamma_\lambda = \{x \in \Omega : u(x) = \lambda\}. \tag{3.51}$$

Then the classical level-set representation of u is the one-parameter family of all the level sets

$$\Gamma_u = \{\gamma_\lambda : \lambda \in \mathbb{R}\}. \tag{3.52}$$

Notice that Γ_u is a partitioning of the image domain, meaning that

$$\Omega = \cup_{\lambda \in \mathbb{R}} \gamma_\lambda, \quad \gamma_\lambda \cap \gamma_\mu = \phi, \quad \lambda \neq \mu.$$

Assume first that u is smooth enough (after an infinitesimal heat diffusion, say). Then differential topology is helpful in understanding the general behavior of the level-set representation [218].

A value λ is said to be *regular* if the gradient of u never vanishes anywhere along γ_λ. If so, the level set γ_λ must be a 1-D submanifold of Ω, meaning that locally it looks like (after some differential deformation) the interval $(-1, 1) \times \{0\}$ embedded in the square $Q = (-1, 1) \times (-1, 1)$, no branching or termination. For convenience, such a 1-D submanifold is often simply called a *regular* curve, though it may consist of many connected components.

Otherwise, a value λ is said to be *singular*. Any pixel $x_0 \in \gamma_\lambda$ with $\nabla u(x_0) = \mathbf{0}$ is consequently said to be *critical*. A critical point is where a local minimum or maximum (valley or peak) resides. It could also be a saddle point where along one direction the image gets darker while along its perpendicular direction it gets brighter. These are the only three generic situations in two dimensions. Moreover, a generic critical point is always isolated.

By differential topology [218], the set of regular values of a smooth image u is *open* and *dense* in $\mathbb{R}$. It implies that for any value λ one randomly chooses, it is almost certain (in the Lebesgue sense) that the associated level set γ_λ is a regular curve.

3.5.2 Cumulative Level Sets

In reality, images are rarely smooth functions. Instead, they are assumed to be in certain functional spaces such as $L^1(\Omega)$ or $L^2(\Omega)$, etc. Then the pointwise values are not that crucial since they are always modifiable over a set of zero (Lebesgue) measure. Thus the individual level sets may make less sense.

The classical pointwise level sets can be modified to the *cumulative level sets* F_λ defined by

$$F_\lambda = F_\lambda(u) = \{x \in \Omega : u(x) \leq \lambda\}. \tag{3.53}$$

Each cumulative level set is well defined in the measure-theoretic sense since if $u(x) = v(x)$, almost surely $x \in \Omega$, the symmetric difference

$$F_\lambda(u) \ominus F_\lambda(v) = (F_\lambda(u) - F_\lambda(v)) \cup (F_\lambda(v) - F_\lambda(u))$$

has zero measure as well. The *cumulative* level-set representation of a given image u is the one-parameter family

$$\mathcal{F}_u = \{F_\lambda : \lambda \in \mathbb{R}\}.$$

Notice that the two notions of level sets are related by

$$F_\lambda = \cup_{\mu \leq \lambda} \gamma_\lambda.$$

If the image u is a continuous function on Ω, each F_λ is a (relatively) closed set and its topological boundary $\partial F_\lambda = \gamma_\lambda$. For a general Lebesgue measurable image, each of its level sets must be measurable as well.

The regularity of a level set γ_λ or F_λ can be measured in various ways. The lowest order is the *length* measurement length(γ_λ), which is well defined if γ_λ is smooth or Lipschitz. More generally, the concept of length is extended to the *perimeter* via cumulative level sets

$$\text{Per}(F_\lambda|\Omega) = \int_\Omega |D\chi_{F_\lambda}|, \tag{3.54}$$

i.e., the TV of the indictor function. By the co-area formula in Section 2.2, one has

$$\int_\Omega |Du| = \int_{-\infty}^\infty \text{Per}(F_\lambda|\Omega)d\lambda. \tag{3.55}$$

When u is smooth, this simply becomes

$$\int_\Omega |\nabla u|dx = \int_{-\infty}^\infty \text{length}(\gamma_\lambda)d\lambda.$$

For the level-set representation, the beautiful identity (3.55) due to De Giorgi [134] and Fleming and Rishel [125] is analogous to the famous Parseval identity in Fourier analysis [193],

$$\int_{R^2} |u(x)|^2 dx = \int_{R^2} |\hat{u}(\omega)|^2 d\omega,$$

where the 2-D Fourier transform is defined as

$$\hat{u}(\omega) = \int_{R^2} u(x)e^{-i2\pi\omega \cdot x}dx, \quad \omega \cdot x = \omega_1 x_1 + \omega_2 x_2.$$

The analogy is made more explicit by the correspondence,

$$\lambda \longleftrightarrow \omega,$$
$$F_\lambda \text{ or } \gamma_\lambda \longleftrightarrow \hat{u}(\omega),$$
$$\text{Per}(\cdot) \text{ or } \text{length}(\cdot) \longleftrightarrow |\cdot|^2.$$

Thus the level-set representation preserves the TV "energy," just as the Fourier representation does to the L^2 energy. But unlike the Fourier transform, the level-set representation is nonlinear.

3.5.3 Level-Set Synthesis

Under the level-set representation, any given image u is transformed to a one-parameter family of (cumulative) level sets $\mathcal{F}_u = \{F_\lambda(u) : \lambda \in \mathbb{R}\}$. This is the *analysis* step. We now discuss the *synthesis* step, i.e., how to synthesize an image from the information of its level sets.

Conversely, given any such one-parameter family of Lebesgue measurable sets $\mathcal{F} = \{F_\lambda : \lambda \in \mathbb{R}\}$, as long as it satisfies the following two compatibility conditions:

1. for any $\lambda \le \mu$, $F_\lambda \subseteq F_\mu$ (monotonicity) and (right continuity)

$$F_\lambda = \cap_{\mu > \lambda} F_\mu = \lim_{\mu \to \lambda^+} F_\mu,$$

2. $F_{-\infty} := \lim_{\lambda \to -\infty} F_\lambda$ is an empty set and $F_\infty := \lim_{\lambda \to \infty} F_\lambda = \Omega$,

there must exist a unique Lebesgue measurable image u on Ω such that $\mathcal{F}_u = \mathcal{F}$. Uniqueness is of course in the measure-theoretic sense. Let us discuss this theorem in more details.

The synthesis of u can be realized by, for any given pixel $x \in \Omega$,

$$u(x) = \inf\{\mu : x \in F_\mu\}. \tag{3.56}$$

The second compatibility condition guarantees that $u(x)$ is well defined everywhere on Ω and always finite.

We now show that for the image u synthesized by (3.56),

$$F_\lambda(u) = F_\lambda \quad \text{for any } \lambda \in \mathbb{R}.$$

First, $x \in F_\lambda(u)$ implies that $u(x) \le \lambda$. By definition (3.56), $x \in F_\mu$ for any $\mu > \lambda$. Then by the first compatibility condition, $x \in F_\lambda$, implying that $F_\lambda(u) \subseteq F_\lambda$. Conversely, if $x \in F_\lambda$, by definition, $u(x) \le \lambda$. As a result $x \in F_\lambda(u)$, and $F_\lambda \subseteq F_\lambda(u)$. This proves that $F_\lambda(u) \equiv F_\lambda$ for any $\lambda \in \mathbb{R}$. In particular, the synthesized image is indeed Lebesgue measurable.

To show the uniqueness, suppose two images u and v both satisfy

$$F_\lambda(u) \equiv F_\lambda \equiv F_\lambda(v) \quad \text{for any } \lambda \in \mathbb{R}.$$

Then for any pixel $x \in \Omega$, $u(x) \le \lambda$ if and only if $v(x) \le \lambda$. Thus if there exists some pixel $x \in \Omega$ such that $u(x) < v(x)$, taking $\lambda = (u(x) + v(x))/2$ would lead to immediate contradiction.

Thus the level-set representation is lossless and the reconstruction by (3.56) is exact.

3.5.4 An Example: Level Sets of Piecewise Constant Images

As an example, consider a piecewise constant image u given by

$$u(x) = \sum_{n-1}^{N} c_n \chi_{\Omega_n}(x), \quad \text{with } c_1 \le c_2 \le \cdots \le c_N,$$

where $\Omega = \cup_{n=1}^{N} \Omega_n$ is a partition. For such a class of images, the cumulative level-set representation is explicitly given by

$$F_\lambda = \cup_{m \leq n} \Omega_m \ \text{ for } \ c_n \leq \lambda < c_{n+1},$$

with the assumption that $c_0 = -\infty$ and $c_{N+1} = +\infty$.
    Define

$$s(\lambda) = \mathrm{Per}(F_\lambda | \Omega)$$

to be the perimeter of each level set of u. Let

$$s_n = \mathrm{Per}(\cup_{m \leq n} \Omega_m | \Omega) \ \text{ for } \ 1 \leq n \leq N.$$

Notice that $s_N = \mathrm{Per}(\Omega | \Omega) = 0$. Then $s(\lambda)$ as a piecewise constant function is given by

$$s(\lambda) = \sum_{n=1}^{N} s_n \chi_{[c_n, c_{n+1})}(\lambda).$$

Thus, by the co-area formula (3.55) (and $s_N = 0$),

$$\int_\Omega |Du| = \int_{-\infty}^{\infty} s(\lambda) d\lambda = \sum_{n=1}^{N-1} s_n (c_{n+1} - c_n).$$

One could easily show that the last expression is equivalent to weighting the length of each jump segment by its jump magnitude in the original image u.

    From the realistic coding point of view, for such piecewise constant images, it is redundant trying to code all the level sets F_λ since most of them are identical. If the TV norm is accepted as a faithful visual measurement, the last identity suggests to only encode the addresses of all the jump segments (assuming that each Ω_n is Lipschitz) and their associated signed jumps. It could then be shown that up to a uniform gray-scale shift, the original piecewise constant image u can be perfectly decoded or synthesized.

3.5.5 High Order Regularity of Level Sets

In some applications such as disocclusion [234] and image inpainting [61, 116], the length or perimeter energy for level sets is insufficient for visually faithful outputs. Then, as in the classical interpolation theory, one has to take into account higher order geometric regularities.

    In this subsection u will be assumed smooth (at least C^2, say). Let λ be a *regular* value and γ_λ the associated level set, which is a smooth regular curve in Ω. The naturally signed curvature of γ_λ at any of its pixel x is given by

$$\kappa = \kappa(x | \gamma_\lambda) = \nabla \cdot \left[\frac{\nabla u}{|\nabla u|} \right].$$

One could easily verify that κ is negative near a peak (or local maximum) while positive near a valley, since the normalized gradient field $\nabla u / |\nabla u|$ is contractive and expansive, respectively.

In studying the geometric shape of a torsion-free thin elastic rod, Euler in 1744 [196] first introduced the elastica energy for a 2-D curve γ:

$$e[\gamma] = \int_\gamma (\alpha + \beta\kappa^2)ds, \qquad (3.57)$$

where α and β are proper weight constants and ds the arc length element. In terms of image and vision analysis, the two mechanical weights α and β could be considered as the visual balance between being straight and curvy. Under proper boundary conditions, Birkhoff and De Boor called the equilibrium curves of $e[\gamma]$ *nonlinear splines* in approximation theory [27]. Euler's elastica energy was first introduced into computer vision by Mumford [222] as a good candidate for visual interpolant and has been recently applied to image processing tasks by Masnou and Morel [214], Chan, Kang, and Shen [61], Esedoglu and Shen [116], and Shah [271].

By imposing Euler's elastica energy on each individual level curve γ_λ and weighing them uniformly, one obtains a regularity measure in the level-set space:

$$E[\Gamma_u] = \int_{-\infty}^{\infty} e[\gamma_\lambda]d\lambda.$$

For a smooth image u, by applying the same technique as for the derivation of the co-area formula, one realizes that the regularity measure could be directly expressed by the image itself:

$$E[\Gamma_u] = E[u] = \int_\Omega \left(\alpha + \beta\left(\nabla\cdot\left[\frac{\nabla u}{|\nabla u|}\right]\right)^2\right)|\nabla u|\,dx.$$

For general images, however, theoretical study of this nonquadratic high order geometric energy is more challenging than TV.

3.5.6 Statistics of Level Sets of Natural Images

We now briefly present the remarkable work of Gousseau and Morel [142] on the statistics of cumulative level sets of *natural* images and their important implications in image modeling. We shall slightly alter their presentation (e.g., notions and notations) to fit the flow of the current book.

For each intensity level λ and a positive jump $\Delta\lambda = h \ll 1$, define

$$L_{\lambda,h}(u) = F_{\lambda+h}(u) \setminus F_\lambda(u) = \{x \in \Omega \mid u(x) \in (\lambda, \lambda+h]\}.$$

$L_{\lambda,h}$ shall be called an h-branch of u. Then for any h, the image domain Ω can be partitioned into nonoverlapping h-branches for any given image u:

$$\Omega = \bigcup_{n\in\mathbb{Z}} L_{nh,h}(u).$$

Any *connected* component of an h-branch $L_{nh,h}(u)$ shall be called an h-leaflet of u (see Figure 3.5).

Let a denote the nonnegative real variable for the area of a general leaflet. Define

$$\rho(a \mid h)da = \mathrm{E}_u\left[\frac{\#\text{ of }h\text{-leaflets whose areas are between }(a, a+da)}{\text{total }\#\text{ of }h\text{-leaflets}}\right].$$

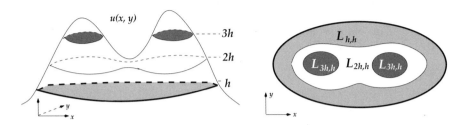

Figure 3.5. *An example of branches* $L_{\lambda, \Delta\lambda}$*'s with* $\Delta\lambda = h$ *and* $\lambda = nh$. *The branch* $L_{3h,h}$ *contains two leaflets.*

Here u is treated as a random field (and often assumed to be invariant under gray-level shift: $u \to u + \lambda$), and E_u denotes the corresponding ensemble average. For real natural images, E_u is often approximated by an empirical mean as in [142] under the ergodicity assumption.

Statistical study on natural image banks by Gousseau and Morel reveals the following scaling law near the ultraviolet limit (i.e., $a \to 0^+$):

$$\rho(a \mid h) = \frac{C(h)}{a^\alpha} \qquad \text{with the exponent } \alpha \text{ close to 2.}$$

Here $C(h)$ denotes a positive constant depending only on h. It is this important statistical scaling law that has enabled Gousseau and Morel to conclude that natural images do not precisely have BVs. We refer the reader to [142] for further details.

3.6 The Mumford–Shah Free Boundary Image Model

Images are the 2-D optical projections of the 3-D world, which is full of individual objects. Under a common light source, the image (or reflected light intensity) of each object is completely characterized by its surface material (i.e., reflectance) as well as topographic properties (i.e., shape geometry). Since most often each 3-D object has approximately uniform surface properties (such as the hands of a person or an orange), its image is accordingly uniform and distinct from the images of other objects.

Consequently, with surface texture details of each individual object neglected or blurred, such images can be well approximated by piecewise constant or smooth functions, with each piece corresponding to the image of an individual 3-D object. This is the qualitative description of the Mumford–Shah image model.

3.6.1 Piecewise Constant 1-D Images: Analysis and Synthesis

We begin the discussion with this simplest but intriguing case. Consider a 1-D image $u(x)$ defined on the entire real axis $x \in \Omega = R^1$, with $\lim_{x \to \pm\infty} u(x) = 0$.

Definition 3.19 (Piecewise Constant Image). *A 1-D image* $u(x)$ *is said to be piecewise constant if for any pixel* x_0, *there is a neighborhood* $|x - x_0| < \varepsilon$ *on which*

$$u(x) = a + b \, H(x - x_0)$$

for two scalars a and b (x_0 dependent). Here $H(s)$ stands for the Heaviside 0-1 canonical template:

$$H(s) = \begin{cases} 0, & s < 0, \\ 1, & s \geq 0. \end{cases}$$

Notice that technically it has been implicitly assumed that the image u is right continuous, which is not crucial in the Lebesgue sense.

If $b = [u]_{x_0} = u(x_0^+) - u(x_0^-)$ is *nonzero*, it shall be called the *jump* at x_0, and x_0 a jump or edge pixel. Let J denote the jump set

$$J = J_u = \{x : [u]_x \neq 0\}.$$

Theorem 3.20. *The jump set J_u of any piecewise constant image u is closed and isolated.*

In particular, $J \cap [A, B]$ is a finite set for any bounded interval $[A, B] \subseteq \mathbb{R}^1$, and J can be enumerated by

$$\cdots < x_n < x_{n+1} < \cdots$$

with $\lim_{n \to \pm\infty} x_n = \pm\infty$ if the sequence is infinite in either direction.

With the jump set enumerated as above, the image u could be uniquely written as

$$u(x) = \sum_n c_n \chi_{[x_n, x_{n+1})}(x), \tag{3.58}$$

where the summation in either direction could be finite or infinite according to J_u.

Taking the generalized or distributional derivative on (3.58), one obtains

$$Du = \sum_n b_n \delta(x - x_n), \tag{3.59}$$

where $b_n = c_n - c_{n-1} = [u]_{x_n} \neq 0$ are the jumps, and δ is Dirac's point measure.

The very last equation gives an efficient way to represent a 1-D piecewise constant (and right continuous) image. That is, it suffices to only encode the addresses and values of all the jumps:

$$\{(x_n, b_n) : n\} = \{(z, [u]_z) : z \in J_u\},$$

instead of the entire 1-D function.

This representation is indeed *lossless* as it allows a perfect reconstruction scheme:

$$\tilde{u}(x) := \tilde{u}(0) + \int_{(0,x]} Du = \tilde{u}(0) + \sum_{x_n \in (0,x]} b_n.$$

Since it has been assumed that $u(\pm\infty) = 0$, the unknown constant $\tilde{u}(0)$ is explicitly given by

$$\tilde{u}(0) = -\lim_{K \to +\infty} \sum_{x_n \in (0,K]} b_n.$$

Then the synthesis must be exact: $\tilde{u} = u$.

3.6.2 Piecewise Smooth 1-D Images: First Order Representation

For technical simplicity, all images in this subsection are assumed to be *compactly supported*.

Definition 3.21 (Piecewise Smooth Images). *A right continuous image $u(x)$ on R^1 is said to be piecewise smooth if at each pixel x_0, there is a neighborhood $|x - x_0| < \varepsilon$ on which*

$$u(x) = a(x) + b(x)H(x - x_0),$$

where $a(x)$ and $b(x)$ are C^1 functions on the neighborhood.

Unlike the piecewise constant case, generally $a(x)$ and $b(x)$ are not unique. However, $b(x_0)$ and $b'(x_0)$ are indeed unique since they can be completely characterized in terms of the image itself:

$$b(x_0) = [u]_{x_0} = u(x_0^+) - u(x_0^-),$$
$$b'(x_0) = [u']_{x_0} = u'(x_0^+) - u'(x_0^-).$$

Define the jump set J_u to be

$$J_u = \{z \in \mathbb{R} : [u]_z \neq 0\}.$$

As in the piecewise constant case, J_u is closed and isolated and can be finitely enumerated as (due to the assumption of compact support)

$$x_1 < x_2 < \cdots < x_N.$$

Define $u_n^\pm = u(x_n^\pm)$ and $b_n = [u]_n = u_n^+ - u_n^-$ for all $1 \leq n \leq N$. Furthermore, define $x_0 = -\infty$ and $x_{N+1} = +\infty$. Then on each interval (x_n, x_{n+1}) with $0 \leq n \leq N$, $g_n(x) = u'(x)$ belongs to $L^2(x_n, x_{n+1}) \cap L^1(x_n, x_{n+1})$.

A good representation of such an image is given by the following set of data:

$$g_0(x) \quad \text{and} \quad (x_n, b_n, g_n(x)) \quad \text{with } 1 \leq n \leq N. \tag{3.60}$$

Notice that both g_0 and g_N are compactly supported. This representation could lead to efficient coding schemes when the associated image u is almost piecewise constant, that is, when

$$\max_{0 \leq n \leq N} \int_{(x_n, x_{n+1})} |g_n(x)| dx \ll 1.$$

In this case, the g_n's could be coded using very low bit rates. In the extreme scenario when no bits are allocated at all to the g_n's, it is equivalent to approximating the original image u by a piecewise constant image. Generally the g_n's can be well approximated by lower order polynomials or splines. Figure 3.6 shows a typical example to highlight the underlying ideas.

The representation (3.60) is lossless as it permits a perfect reconstruction scheme given by

$$\tilde{u}(x) = \sum_{x_n \in (-\infty, x]} b_n + \int_{-\infty}^{x} \sum_{0}^{N} g_n(y) \chi_{(x_n, x_{n+1})}(y) dy.$$

Since both $\tilde{u}$ and u are zeros near $-\infty$ and right continuous with identical distributional derivatives $D\tilde{u} = Du$, indeed the perfect synthesis must hold: $\tilde{u}(x) \equiv u(x)$.

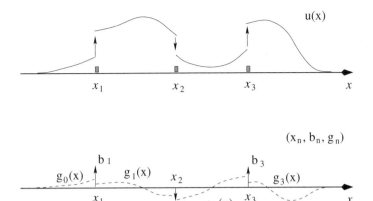

Figure 3.6. *The (x_n, b_n, g_n)-representation of a (compactly supported) piecewise smooth signal u. On smooth regions where the signal u varies slowly, g_n is often small and only a few bits suffice to code them.*

3.6.3   Piecewise Smooth 1-D Images: Poisson Representation

Another perhaps more interesting representation resulting from the preceding section is the *Poisson representation*, as motivated by the theory of linear elliptic PDEs.

Assume that u is Sobolev H^2 on each interval (x_n, x_{n+1}) between two adjacent jump points. That is, $f_n(x) = u''(x) \in L^2(x_n, x_{n+1})$. Then the Poisson representation of u refers to the following set of data:

$$f_0(x) \quad \text{and} \quad (x_n, u_n^+, u_n^-, f_n(x)) \quad \text{with} \ \ 1 \le n \le N. \tag{3.61}$$

As in the preceding section, notice that both f_0 and f_N are compactly supported.

This representation could be very efficient when the target image u is almost linear on each interval (x_n, x_{n+1}), in which case one has

$$\max_{0 \le n \le N} \int_{(x_n, x_{n+1})} |f_n(x)|^2 dx \ll 1.$$

Therefore, all the f_n's can be encoded using very low bits. When f_n's are all wiped out to zeros, it is tantamount to approximating the original image u by a piecewise linear function.

The Poisson representation (3.61) is lossless as well since perfect reconstruction can be achieved by solving the Poisson equations with Dirichlet boundary data: on each interval $x \in (x_n, x_{n+1})$,

$$\tilde{u}''(x) = f_n(x) \quad \text{with} \ \ \tilde{u}(x_n^+) = u_n^+ \ \ \text{and} \ \ \tilde{u}(x_{n+1}^-) = u_{n+1}^-. \tag{3.62}$$

All the necessary data for setting up these equations are available from the Poisson representation (3.61). By the theory of linear elliptic equations, the weak H^1 solutions exist and are unique for each system. Thus after gluing all the $\tilde{u}$ pieces according to the right continuous assumption, one must have the perfect reconstruction: $\tilde{u}(x) \equiv u(x)$ (see Figure 3.7).

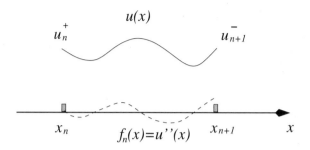

Figure 3.7. *Poisson representation of a piecewise smooth signal u. Shown here is only a single representative interval. The signal u is represented by the two boundary values u_n^+ and u_{n+1}^- and its second order derivative $f = u''$ (corresponding to the source distribution in electromagnetism). Reconstructing u on the interval then amounts to solving the Poisson equation* (3.62). *The advantage of such representation is that f is often small (just like wavelet coefficients) for smooth signals and demands fewer bits compared with u.*

3.6.4   Piecewise Smooth 2-D Images

In two dimensions, the main challenge arises from the geometric complexity of the jump set J_u. Following the initial discussion of the current section, the jump set of the image should approximately capture the projected boundaries of 3-D objects. Due to opaqueness and occlusion, the collective behavior of the jump set could be very involved. Corners, T-junctions, incomplete edges, and oscillatory boundaries are just some typical examples.

   Tremendous challenges still exist to date in terms of both theoretical analysis and computational approaches, which one could get a glimpse of from both the following subsection and the last chapter. In what follows, some necessary simplification has been made to facilitate the discussion.

Definition 3.22 (Lipschitz Partition of a Domain). *Let $\Omega \subseteq \mathbb{R}^2$ be the target image domain which is bounded, open, and Lipschitz (often a square). A Lipschitz partition of Ω refers to a finite set partition*

$$\Omega = \bigcup_{n=1}^{N} \Omega_n \bigcup \Gamma \tag{3.63}$$

which satisfies the following:

1. *Each Ω_n is a* connected *open Lipschitz domain.*
2. *Γ is relatively closed in Ω and has a finite 1-D Hausdorff measure $\mathcal{H}^1(\Gamma) < \infty$.*

Theorem 3.23. *Suppose a Lipschitz partition of Ω is given by* (3.63). *For any subset X of Ω, let $\partial_\Omega X$ denote its relative topological boundary in Ω. Then*

(1) *$\partial_\Omega \Gamma = \Gamma$;*
(2) *$\partial_\Omega \Omega_n \subseteq \Gamma$ for $n = 1 : N$.*
(3) *$\Gamma = \bigcup_{n=1}^{N} \partial_\Omega \Omega_n$.*

Proof. (1) is true since the interior of Γ must be empty; otherwise its 1-D Hausdorff measure would be infinite. (2) must hold since $\partial_\Omega \Omega_n \cap \Omega_m$ must be empty for each pair of (n, m). (2) implies that

$$\bigcup_{n=1}^{N} \partial_\Omega \Omega_n \subseteq \Gamma.$$

On the other hand, for any pixel $z \in \Gamma = \partial_\Omega \Gamma$, there exist at least one sequence of pixels $(x_k)_{k=1}^{\infty} \subseteq \Omega \setminus \Gamma$, so that $x_k \to z$ as $k \to \infty$. Since N is finite, there must exist certain m, so that the sequence visits Ω_m infinitely often. This implies $z \in \partial_\Omega \Omega_m$ and consequently,

$$\Gamma \subseteq \bigcup_{n=1}^{N} \partial_\Omega \Omega_n.$$

Thus (3) must be true as well. $\square$

This theorem confirms that for a Lipschitz partition, the set Γ indeed models the boundaries of different "objects."

Definition 3.24. *An image u on Ω is said to be piecewise smooth if there exist a Lipschitz partition of Ω as given in (3.63) and N smooth functions on Ω: $U_1(x), U_2(x), \ldots, U_N(x)$, such that*

$$u(x) = \sum_{n=1}^{N} U_n(x)\chi_n(x), \quad x \in \Omega \setminus \Gamma,$$

where $\chi_n(x) = \chi_{\Omega_n}(x)$ are the indicators.

Notice that the definition does not specify the image values along the boundary set Γ. This works fine in the measure-theoretic sense since Γ is a 2-D Lebesgue null set.

As in the 1-D case, here the term "smooth" could refer to at least the classical C^1 regularity, or more generally the Sobolev H^1 regularity. Each $u_n(x) = U_n(x)\chi_n(x)$ models the relatively homogeneous interior of a single "object."

Similar to the 1-D case, a *Poisson representation* or coder could be built up as follows. Assume that each "object" u_n belongs to $H^2(\Omega_n)$. Then the Laplacian $f_n(x) = \Delta u_n$ belongs to $L^2(\Omega_n)$. In the situation when each u_n is almost harmonic on Ω_n, one has

$$\sum_{n=1}^{N} \int_{\Omega_n} |f_n(x)|^2 dx \ll 1,$$

and consequently, only low bit rates are needed for encoding the f_n's.

On the other hand, according to the theory of Sobolev spaces, since each Ω_n is assumed to be a Lipschitz domain, the trace of $u_n(x)$ against $\gamma_n = \partial \Omega_n$ is well defined. Let it be denoted by $\phi_n(x)$, defined along γ_n. Notice that in R^2,

$$\bigcup_{n=1}^{N} \gamma_n = \partial \Omega \bigcup \Gamma.$$

Then a Poisson representation for such a piecewise smooth image u consists of the following set of data:

$$\{(\gamma_n, \phi_n(x), f_n(x)) : \quad 1 \le n \le N\}. \tag{3.64}$$

Notice that $\phi_n(x)$'s are in essence 1-D functions (defined along γ_n's). Compared with the direct coding of u_n's, f_n's are often small and require only low bit rate coding for almost harmonic objects.

The Poisson representation (3.64) is lossless as it permits a perfect reconstruction scheme in the measure-theoretic sense. That is, on $\Omega \setminus \Gamma$, the original image u could be perfectly reconstructed. This is realized by the Poisson solver on each Lipschitz component Ω_n:

$$\Delta \tilde{u}(x) = f_n(x) \quad \text{for} \quad x \in \Omega_n \quad \text{and} \quad \tilde{u}(y) = \phi_n(y) \quad \text{for} \quad y \in \gamma_n.$$

According to the existence and uniqueness theorem for linear elliptic equations with Dirichlet data on Lipschitz domains, the perfect reconstruction is indeed true: $\tilde{u}(x) \equiv u(x)$ for any $x \in \Omega \setminus \Gamma$.

A *harmonic* representation would consist only of the following 1-D data:

$$\{(\gamma_n, \phi_n(x)) : \quad 1 \le n \le N\} \tag{3.65}$$

with f_n's all set to zero. Harmonic representation is therefore lossy and approximate, the necessary price to pay for becoming highly data compressive.

3.6.5 The Mumford–Shah Model

A critical issue still remains for real applications and computation: given a piecewise smooth image u, how could one actually extract its associated object-boundary decomposition?

As previously stated, images are the optical projections of 3-D scenes full of individual objects. Thus the extraction process is an *inverse* problem that aims at recovering objects from images, or more properly, 2-D occupation regions of individual objects from images. Such a process is therefore often called the *segmentation* problem.

As an inverse problem, segmentation is invariably achieved by two essentially equivalent methods: statistical estimation via *maximum likelihood* (ML) or *maximum a posteriori probabilities* (MAPs), and deterministic estimation via energy-based variational optimization. The celebrated Mumford–Shah segmentation model [226] belongs to the latter category and is closely inspired by and connected to earlier statistical models, for example, by Geman and Geman [130] and Blake and Zisserman [29].

In what follows, we give a brief introduction to the Mumford–Shah image model, and more details related to its applications and computation will appear in the last chapter.

Let u_0 denote an acquired image on a Lipschitz domain Ω. In most applications, it is improper to directly assume that u_0 is piecewise smooth, even if the 3-D scene from which u_0 has been acquired indeed consists of individual objects with smoothly varying surfaces and reflectance properties. First, during the imaging process, *noise* is often inevitable as caused by various random factors, such as moving human bodies or organs (like the heart) in medical imaging, inhomogeneity of spatial media like water for underwater imaging, and natural biochemical fluctuations in the cellular neural networks of the human vision system. Second, as in astronomical imaging or sports photographs, blurring effect caused by local media interference or motion correlation is also frequently present.

Such complexity of real environments has inspired many successful models. One of the most popular approaches is to separate an imaging process into different layers, for example,

$$\boxed{\text{3-D scene}} \rightarrow \boxed{\text{ideal image } u} \rightarrow \boxed{\text{blur } K} \rightarrow \boxed{\text{noise } n} \rightarrow \boxed{\text{observed image } u_0} \; .$$

Thus for instance, assuming the noise is additive, one has

$$u_0 = n + K[u], \tag{3.66}$$

where the blur operator could be either linear or nonlinear.

It is the image u that can be assumed piecewise smooth, at least as a good approximation when the 3-D scene consists mainly of objects without much texture. The mission of image segmentation is to extract or estimate the object-boundary information from a single degraded observation u_0.

We now explain the key ingredients of the objective function $E[u, \Gamma | u_0]$ in the Mumford–Shah segmentation decision.

Suppose the ideal image u is built upon the Lipschitz partition

$$\Omega = \bigcup_{m=1}^{M} \Omega_m \bigcup \Gamma,$$

as defined in the previous section, with the smooth components

$$u_m = u|_{\Omega_m} \in H^1(\Omega_m), \quad m = 1 : M.$$

In an additive fashion (which is well justified from the probability point of view), the regularity energy of u is specified as

$$E[u, \Gamma] = E[\Gamma] + E[u|\Gamma].$$

The edge set Γ can be naturally evaluated by length, or more generally, the 1-D Hausdorff measure $E[\Gamma] = \mathcal{H}^1(\Gamma)$. On the other hand, all the patches $(u_m)_{m=1}^{M}$ can be evaluated by their Sobolev norms:

$$E[u|\Gamma] \propto \sum_{m=1}^{M} E[u_m|\Omega_m] = \sum_{m=1}^{M} \int_{\Omega_m} |\nabla u_m|^2 dx = \int_{\Omega \backslash \Gamma} |\nabla u|^2 dx.$$

In combination, the regularity energy of an ideal piecewise image u with an edge set Γ is given by

$$E[u, \Gamma] = \alpha \mathcal{H}^1(\Gamma) + \beta \int_{\Omega \backslash \Gamma} |\nabla u|^2 dx, \tag{3.67}$$

with proper constant weights α and β to model the corresponding visual sensitivities.

Finally, assume that the additive noise n in the imaging model (3.66) is homogeneous Gaussian white noise with variance σ^2. Then the variance could be well approximated by its empirical estimator

$$\sigma^2 \simeq \frac{1}{|\Omega|} \int_{\Omega} (u_0 - K[u])^2 dx, \tag{3.68}$$

where $|\Omega|$ denotes the Lebesgue area, provided that u is known.

Then the Mumford–Shah segmentation estimator is to

$$\text{minimize} \quad E[u, \Gamma] \quad \text{subject to the noise constraint (3.68).}$$

By introducing a Lagrange multiplier λ for the constraint, the Mumford–Shah model is to minimize the single objective functional given an observation u_0:

$$E[u, \Gamma | u_0] = \alpha \mathcal{H}^1(\Gamma) + \beta \int_{\Omega \setminus \Gamma} |\nabla u|^2 dx + +\lambda \int_{\Omega} (u_0 - K[u])^2 dx. \tag{3.69}$$

With the last third term symbolized by $E[u_0 | u, \Gamma]$, it simply becomes

$$E[u, \Gamma | u_0] = E[u, \Gamma] + E[u_0 | u, \Gamma],$$

which clearly indicates the Bayesian rationale of the Mumford–Shah model—the piecewise smooth image prior model $E[u, \Gamma]$ and the image acquisition model $E[u_0 | u, \Gamma]$ are formally combined.

3.6.6   The Role of Special BV Images

The challenge for the piecewise smooth representation and the Mumford–Shah segmentation model is the edge set Γ, or the geometric ingredient of the model.

Consider the collection of *all* such edge sets. No natural linear structure seems obvious to make it a Banach or Hilbert space, causing the difficulty in identifying a convenient admissible space for the Mumford–Shah objective functional. As a result, most tools for conventional optimization cannot be directly applied.

There is, however, one linear function space that is intrinsically pertinent to the Mumford–Shah model. It is a subspace of BV(Ω) consisting of the so-called *special* BV (SBV) functions, and it is denoted by SBV(Ω) [7].

Let u be a Mumford–Shah admissible image with, for simplicity, a piecewise C^1 edge set Γ. Let $\mathcal{H}^1$ denote the 1-D Hausdorff measure along Γ. Then, $\mathcal{H}^1$ almost surely, one could define a piecewise continuous unit normal vector field ν along Γ. For each edge pixel x in a C^1 component of Γ, as in the 1-D case, define the jump $[u]_x$ to be

$$[u]_x = \lim_{\varepsilon \to 0^+} u(x + \varepsilon \nu_x) - u(x - \varepsilon \nu_x).$$

Here the limits are understood in the trace sense since each $u_m = u|_{\Omega_m}$ is assumed in $H^1(\Omega_m)$. Then restricted upon the edge set Γ only,

$$J_u = [u] \, \nu \, d\mathcal{H}^1$$

defines a vectorial measure by, for any Borel subset $\gamma \subseteq \Gamma$,

$$J_u(\gamma) := \int_{\gamma} [u]_x \nu_x d\mathcal{H}^1_x.$$

It could be easily shown under the C^1-regularity assumption that the vectorial Radon measure Du when restricted upon the closed edge set Γ is precisely J_u. On the other hand, on each open component Ω_m, by the admissibility condition of the Mumford–Shah model, $u_m \in H^1(\Omega_m)$, one has $Du = \nabla u \in L^2(\Omega_m)$. In combination, we have

$$Du = \nabla u|_{\Omega \setminus \Gamma} + J_u|_{\Gamma}. \tag{3.70}$$

This argument is almost nonheuristic, as long as the C^1 condition is relaxed to the more general condition of finite $\mathcal{H}^1$ measure as in the Mumford–Shah model and that both $[u]$ and ν are properly defined.

We now ask how general the structure of the two-component decomposition (3.70) is in $\mathrm{BV}(\Omega)$. In the blessed case when any BV function allowed such representation, the space $\mathrm{BV}(\Omega)$ would become perfect for studying the Mumford–Shah model. But this is not the real case.

Let $u \in \mathrm{BV}(\Omega)$ be a general image with BV. According to the Radon–Nikodym–Lebesgue decomposition, one could write

$$Du = \nabla u + D_s u,$$

where $\nabla u = Du/dx$ is the Radon–Nikodym derivative and encodes image information that can be captured by the Lebesgue measure $dx = dx_1 dx_2$, while $D_s u$ is *singular* to the Lebesgue measure and only supported on a Lebesgue null set. Roughly speaking, the Hausdorff dimension of this null set must be less than 2 for planar images. It is this singular component that complicates a general BV image.

This Lebesgue singular part could be further decomposed into

$$D_s u = D_1 u + D_c u, \tag{3.71}$$

where, heuristically speaking, $D_1 u$ encodes 1-D information that can be captured by scattered 1-D Hausdorff measures $\mathcal{H}^1$ on the image domain, while $D_c u$ stores information that is supported on a set whose Hausdorff dimension is strictly in between 1 and 2. The subscript "c" stands for "Cantor" since the Cantor function [126] $f(x)$ is historically the most well known example in one dimension that is almost (in the one dimension Lebesgue sense) always flat on $[0, 1]$ but magically increases in a continuous fashion from $f(0) = 0$ to $f(1) = 1$. The increment is achieved on the Cantor set which has a fractal dimension. Thus $D_c u$ is often called the *Cantor singular component* for a general BV image u.

Without any explicit specification of the edge set Γ as in the Mumford–Shah model, how could the 1-D feature $D_1 u$ be properly detected or defined for a general BV image u? This is beautifully done through the notion of the jump set S_u and its properties.

Given a gray-scale level λ, a pixel $z \in \Omega$, and a small radius $\rho > 0$, define a subset of the disk $B_{z,\rho} = \{x : |x - z| < \rho\}$ by

$$\{u > \lambda\}_{z,\rho} = \{x \in \Omega \cap B_{z,\rho} : u(x) > \lambda\}.$$

The same definition extends to the $<$ sign as well.

Definition 3.25 (Essentially No Greater Than or No Less Than). *u is said to be (Lebesgue)* essentially *no greater than* λ *at* x *if*

$$\lim_{\rho \to 0^+} \frac{|\{u > \lambda\}_{x,\rho}|}{|B_{x,\rho}|} = 0,$$

where $| \cdot |$ *stands for the 2-D Lebesgue measure on* Ω. *If so, we write* $u \preceq_x \lambda$. *The same definition and notation naturally extend to "being essentially no greater than."*

The intuition is crystal clear: if u is essentially no greater than λ at x, as one zooms into the neighborhood, the opposite event $u > \lambda$ should become rarer and rarer, until in the end it is completely extinguished in the measure-theoretic sense.

Definition 3.26 (Upper and Lower Functions). *Given a measurable function u on Ω, we define its* upper *function by*

$$u_+(x) = \inf\{\lambda \in \mathbb{R} : u \preceq_x \lambda\},$$

the lower bound of all values that are essentially no less than u at x, and similarly its lower *function by*

$$u_-(x) = \sup\{\lambda \in \mathbb{R} : u(x) \succeq_x \lambda\},$$

the upper bound of all values essentially no greater than u at x.

It is easy to show that if $u \preceq_x \lambda$ and $u \succeq_x \mu$, then $\mu \leq \lambda$. Therefore, we must have $u_-(x) \leq u_+(x)$ at any pixel x. In a natural sense, we could think that u is *essentially* bounded between $u_-(x)$ and $u_+(x)$ at x. On the other hand, both $u_+(x)$ and $u_-(x)$ are achievable in the following sense. For any $\lambda < u_+(x)$, there exists a sequence $\rho_k \to 0$ ($k \to \infty$), and some constant $r > 0$, so that

$$\lim_{k \to \infty} \frac{|\{u > \lambda\}_{x, \rho_k}|}{|B_{x, \rho_k}|} = r > 0.$$

The same can be said about $u_-(x)$.

The jump set S_u of a BV image $u \in BV(\Omega)$ is then defined as

$$S_u = \{x \in \Omega : u_+(x) > u_-(x)\}. \tag{3.72}$$

Driving this definition is the plain intuition that a jump point is a pixel where there occurs an *essential* jump. S_u is thus introduced as a candidate for the edge set Γ in the Mumford–Shah model. Notice, however, that the definition of S_u is completely intrinsic, independent of any a priori knowledge of a 1-D Hausdorff measurable edge set. Meanwhile, (3.72) could also be considered as the algorithm for extracting the support of the singular measure $D_1 u$.

The remarkable fact about BV images is that the jump set S_u indeed carries nice regularity property. In fact, modulo an $\mathcal{H}^1$ null set, S_u is a countable union of rectifiable curves [137]:

$$S_u \setminus (\text{an } \mathcal{H}^1 \text{ null set}) = \bigcup_{k=1}^{\infty} \gamma_k,$$

where each γ_k is a compact subset of some C^1 curve. As a result, one could define the jump $[u] = u_+ - u_-$ and a proper normal vector field ν along S_u modulo an $\mathcal{H}^1$ null set. Then it could be shown that

$$D_1 u = [u] \, \nu \, d\mathcal{H}^1 = J_u,$$

supported on S_u.

In summary, we have shown that the vector Radon measure Du of a general BV image u can be written as

$$Du = \nabla u + J_u + D_c u.$$

Compared with the decomposition formula (3.70) for an ideal Mumford–Shah image, except for the delicate difference between the closed 1-D Hausdorff edge set Γ and the jump set S_u, a BV image u seems to be an ideal candidate for the Mumford–Shah model as long as its Cantor component $D_c u$ vanishes. This is the key observation leading to many theoretical results about the Mumford–Shah segmentation model.

Definition 3.27 (Special BV Images). *A BV image u on Ω is said to be special if its Cantor component vanishes everywhere. The subspace of all such special BV images is denoted by* SBV(Ω).

Relaxing the compact $\mathcal{H}^1$-summable edge set Γ to the jump set S_u, one obtains the *weak* Mumford–Shah energy on SBV(Ω):

$$E[u \mid u \in \text{SBV}, u_0 \text{ given}] = \alpha \mathcal{H}^1(S_u) + \beta \int_\Omega |\nabla u|^2 dx + \gamma \int_\Omega (u_0 - K[u])^2 dx. \quad (3.73)$$

The existence of this weak Mumford–Shah segmentation is confirmed in the work of Ambrosio [7]. With further characterization of the fine properties of the jump set S_u of the weak solution, De Giorgi, Carriero, and Leaci [136], Dal Maso, Morel, and Solimini [94], and Morel and Solimini [221] proved that $(u, \Gamma = \overline{S_u})$ is in fact a minimizer for the original strong formulation. Chapter 7 further explores the celebrated Mumford–Shah segmentation model.

Chapter 4

Image Denoising

Image processors could be categorized into different levels by the human vision standard. Lower-level ones are to clean and enhance observations, interpolate missing image data, or identify regions occupied by objects without telling what they are. For example, counting the number of cells in a blood-sample image falls into this category. Higher-level processors are to recognize object features and identify the associated hidden real-world contexts, such as face recognition for video surveillance and terrain reading for automatic piloting.

In this sense, the human vision system, involving both optical and neuronal activities, is a highly advanced and complex system of image processors. The present book focuses only on lower-level vision activities and their associated image processors such as denoising, deblurring, inpainting and interpolation, and segmentation. Not only do they frequently emerge in a variety of scientific or industrial applications, but also there have been accumulated numerous significant contributions by applied mathematicians and imaging scientists.

In this chapter, we illustrate how to develop efficient image *denoising* schemes based upon appropriate image models or representations discussed in the previous chapters.

4.1 Noise: Origins, Physics, and Models

4.1.1 Origins and Physics of Noise

Noise is ubiquitous and noisy but not always annoying.

From the standpoint of statistical mechanics, noise is intrinsic to any multibody system. For image and vision analysis, such a system can be an electric current of many electrons flowing through a resistor or a circuit (in electrical imaging devices), a beam of photons striking the layers of the two retinas, and the resultant electrochemical currents of various ions (e.g., Na^+, K^+, Ca^{2+}) propagating over the neuronal membranes in the visual pathways. In particular, the universal presence of noise implies that the human vision system must biologically employ certain denoising schemes.

Noises or fluctuations are often not as bad as their names might suggest. In equilibrium thermodynamics as well as statistical mechanics, noise is the key ingredient underlying the

Second Law (i.e., *law of maximum entropy*) and is crucial for maintaining the stability of target systems.

Consider for instance a box of gas molecules with *fixed* volume V, mole numbers N, and temperature T (or equivalently, the inverse temperature $\beta = 1/(kT)$ with Boltzmann constant k). The constancy of temperature is maintained by requiring the rigid and impermeable walls to be heat conductive and the box bathed in a huge ambient heat reservoir. Such a system belongs to Gibbs and Boltzmann's CEs [82, 131], as explained in the previous chapters.

Let E_ν denote the quantal energy of the system in a quantum state ν. Then in thermal equilibrium, E. is a random variable, and Gibbs' distribution formula specifies its probability distribution:

$$p_\nu = \frac{1}{Z} \exp(-\beta E_\nu) \qquad \text{for all (microscopic) quantum states } \nu\text{'s.}$$

Macroscopically one observes the average energy

$$\langle E. \rangle = \sum_\nu E_\nu p_\nu.$$

It is well known in statistical mechanics that the microscopic noise level (i.e., the variance $\langle \delta E^2 \rangle$) is connected to macroscopic thermal quantities by (see (2.30))

$$\left(\frac{\partial \langle E. \rangle}{\partial \beta} \right)_{V,N \text{ fixed}} = -\langle \delta E^2 \rangle.$$

In particular, the thermodynamic derivative on the left always remains nonpositive, which bears the profound implication that the system is thermodynamically stable since $\langle E. \rangle$ and β are dual variables for entropy S and $\partial \beta / \partial \langle E. \rangle = \partial^2 S / \partial \langle E. \rangle^2$. Furthermore, it allows one to define a very useful positive thermodynamic quantity called *heat capacity*, which echoes the Second Law by saying that you always need *input* heat to increase the temperature of such a system, not otherwise (which leads to catastrophic blowups) [82, 131].

From the signal analysis point of view, a particular observation E_ν consists of two components:

$$E_\nu = \langle E. \rangle + \delta E_\nu,$$

where the mean energy could be considered as *the signal* and the thermal fluctuation as *the noise*. It can be easily derived that for an N-body system, the signal-to-noise ratio (SNR) is in the order of $O(\sqrt{N})$:

$$\frac{\langle E. \rangle}{\langle \delta E^2 \rangle^{1/2}} = O(\sqrt{N}).$$

Simply put, this is because that both $\langle E. \rangle$ and $\partial \langle E. \rangle / \partial \beta$ are *extensive* (see Section 2.3), and are therefore proportional to the system size:

$$\langle E. \rangle, \quad \frac{\partial \langle E. \rangle}{\partial \beta} \propto N.$$

Thus thermal noises are often relatively low, and macroscopic states in thermal equilibrium usually appear invariant.

Noises also have broad applications in electrical and optical system engineering. For instance, for electric circuits, using noisy inputs of voltages or currents, one can deduce many system properties from the measurement of the corresponding outputs [238].

In image and vision analysis, noises in images are caused by many sources. For example,

1. in astronomical imaging: atmospheric inhomogeneity in terms of density, temperature, index of refraction, and so on;

2. in medical imaging: spontaneous motion and material inhomogeneity of tissues or organs;

3. in night vision: fluctuation in heat, temperature, and infrared radiation;

4. in general image acquisition: inherent thermal noises in electrooptical imaging devices, physical or chemical noises of the target systems to be imaged, and the inhomogeneity of intermediate media.

If the noise is *additive*, a generic expression or model for such processes is

$$u_0 = u + n,$$

where u denotes the imaginary ideal image, n noise, and u_0 the real observation. In some situations, SNR = $\langle u \rangle / \langle n^2 \rangle^{1/2}$ could be very low (assuming $\langle n \rangle = 0$). Watching such an image u_0, even human vision can have difficulty in spotting important features or patterns, despite its unmatched superiority and efficiency. Such failures could be either clinically fatal (as in tumor detecting) or scientifically costly.

Therefore, the task of denoising has become an important subject ever since the beginning of signal and image processing.

4.1.2 A Brief Overview of 1-D Stochastic Signals

Noises are necessarily stochastic or random, but random observations do not have to be noises. In fact, in the stochastic framework, all signals or images, whether looking more randomized or deterministic, are treated as random processes or fields. In this section, we give a brief overview of the theory of 1-D stochastic signals.

A (real) stochastic signal $s(t)$ with $t \in \mathbb{R}$ is a random process, or a collection of real random variables parameterized by the "time" parameter t. Interesting stochastic signals are not those obtained by merely stacking up a collection of random variables without temporal correlations. For example, for a canonical Brownian motion $W(t)$ starting from $W(0) \equiv 0$ [164], one has the important correlation formula

$$E[W(t_1)W(t_2)] = t_1 \wedge t_2 = \min(t_1, t_2). \tag{4.1}$$

Moreover, a stochastic signal could be treated as a random vector which is infinitely long, and a complete description thus has to depend on the joint probability distributions. For any finite set of sampling times

$$t_1 < t_2 < \cdots < t_N,$$

let $P_{t_1,\ldots,t_N}(s_1, \ldots, s_N)$ denote the joint distribution function (either density function or cumulative function) of the random vector $(s(t_1), \ldots, s(t_N))$. Then all such functions lead to a complete description of the target stochastic signal.

A stochastic signal $s(t)$ is said to be *stationary* if its statistical properties bear no temporal memory. Equivalently speaking, one cannot try such a signal as a clock by only measuring its statistics. For a stationary signal, any finite joint distribution function is time-delay invariant:

$$P_{t_1,\ldots,t_N}(s_1,\ldots,s_N) = P_{t_1+\tau,\ldots,t_N+\tau}(s_1,\ldots,s_N) \tag{4.2}$$

for any delay $\tau \geq 0$ and any time marks $t_1, \ldots, t_N$. In particular, for a stationary signal, the probability distribution of any singleton $s(t)$ is fixed.

The mean m and variance σ^2 of a stochastic signal s are two deterministic functions of time:

$$m(t) = \mathrm{E}[s(t)], \qquad \sigma^2(t) = \mathrm{E}[(s(t) - m(t))^2].$$

Both are constant for a stationary signal.

More generally, for a real stochastic signal $s(t)$, one could define its autocorrelation function by

$$R_{ss}(t_1, t_2) = \mathrm{E}[s(t_1)s(t_2)], \quad t_1, t_2 \in \mathbb{R}, \tag{4.3}$$

which is a second order statistics.

In classical signal analysis, there is a weaker but more popular notion of being stationary, which is called "wide sense stationary (WSS)" [237, 306]. A stochastic signal s is said to be WSS if its mean remains constant while its autocorrelation function is also memoryless:

$$R_{ss}(t_1, t_2) = R_{ss}(t_1 + \tau, t_2 + \tau), \quad \text{or equivalently,} \quad R_{ss}(t_1, t_2) = R_{ss}(0, t_2 - t_1).$$

Thus for a WSS signal, the autocorrelation simplifies to a single-variable function $R_{ss}(\tau)$ with $\tau = t_2 - t_1 \in \mathbb{R}$.

If the signal is temporally discrete, $s_n, n = 0, 1, \ldots$, all the preceding notions for continuous signals naturally hold. For example, for a WSS discrete signal, the autocorrelation matrix $R_{ss}(n, m)$ (instead of a bivariate function) reduces to a sequence $R_{ss}(k = m - n)$.

Notice that for real WSS signals, both $R_{ss}(\tau)$ and $R_{ss}(k)$ are even. All the above notions also naturally extend to 2-D signals or images.

Example. Let A be a Gaussian random variable of type $N(0, 1)$, and let θ be uniformly distributed over $(0, 2\pi)$ and independent of A. Define a stochastic sinusoidal signal by

$$s(t) = A \sin(t + \theta), \quad t \in \mathbb{R}.$$

Any fixed delay τ can be absorbed into θ since

$$(t + \tau) + \theta = t + (\tau + \theta).$$

Since the sine is 2π-periodic and the uniform distribution is translation-invariant modulo 2π, we conclude that the signal is temporally memoryless, or (strongly) stationary.

For a WSS signal $s(t)$, let $R(t)$ denote its autocorrelation function $R_{ss}(t)$. Then its power spectral density is defined to be the Fourier transform of $R(t)$:

$$S(\omega) = \int_{\mathbb{R}} R(t) \exp(-i\omega t)dt. \tag{4.4}$$

Assuming that the long-range correlation gets very weak so that $R(t)$ decays fast enough, the Fourier transform is well defined in L^2 or other proper senses.

By Fourier inversion, one has in particular,

$$\mathrm{E}[s(t)^2] \equiv R(0) = \frac{1}{2\pi} \int_{\mathbb{R}} S(\omega)d\omega. \tag{4.5}$$

Since the leftmost term is the mean power of the target signal, and $S \geq 0$, the last formula can be interpreted as follows: the mean power is distributed over the entire spectra with density function $S(\omega)$. This has naturally given $S(\omega)$ the name "power spectral density."

Finally, for two stochastic signals $s_a(t)$ and $s_b(t)$, one can define their *cross-correlation* function by

$$R_{ab}(t_a, t_b) = \mathrm{E}[s_a(t_a)s_b(t_b)] \tag{4.6}$$

for any $t_a, t_b \in \mathbb{R}$. Suppose R_{ab} is delay-invariant; then it is a single-variable function of $\tau = t_a - t_b$, and its Fourier transform is denoted by $S_{ab}(\omega)$. Two stationary signals with delay invariant cross-correlation are said to be *cross-stationary*.

We now briefly comment on the behavior of stochastic signals processed by linear systems. Let $h(t)$ denote a real linear system and $H(\omega)$ its impulse response. Let $x(t)$ denote an input stochastic signal to the system, so that the output $y(t)$ is a new stochastic signal given by

$$y(t) = \int_{\mathbb{R}} h(u)x(t-u)du = h * x(t), \quad t \in \mathbb{R}. \tag{4.7}$$

By definition it is easy to verify the following results [237, 306].

1. If the input signal $x(t)$ is WSS, so is the output $y(t)$, and the cross-correlation function R_{yx} is delay-invariant as well.

2. The power spectral densities are connected by

$$S_{yy}(\omega) = |H(\omega)|^2 S_{xx}(\omega) \quad \text{and} \quad S_{yx}(\omega) = H(\omega)S_{xx}(\omega) = S_{xy}(-\omega). \tag{4.8}$$

The same discussion applies to discrete-time linear systems. As an application, suppose the input signal x is a white noise so that $S_{xx}(\omega) \equiv 1$. Then the first identity in (4.8) provides a way for identifying the linear system if it is unknown a priori. That is, the system can be partially identified from the power spectral density $S_{yy}(\omega)$ of the output and completely identified if the system is further known to be symmetric so that the frequency response $H(\omega)$ is a generic real smooth function.

To conclude this section, we briefly comment on the ensemble nature of statistical signals.

The basic assumption of all the above definitions and computation is that there indeed exists a consistent way to specify the stochastic distribution of the infinitely long random "vector" $s(t)$ indexed by t. Theoretically this does not seem so obvious because there are also infinitely many finite marginal distributions,

$$P_{t_1,\dots,t_N}(s_1, \dots, s_N),$$

which have to satisfy consistency constraints such as, (a) if $A \subseteq B$, then P_A is P_B's marginal, and (b) if $C \subseteq A \cap B$, then P_A and P_B should reproduce identical marginal distributions on C, etc. This is the problem of the *existence* of a specific stochastic signal and is highly nontrivial as in the case of Brownian motions [164, 228].

To be more specific, consider a stochastic signal $s(t)$ with a finite duration $t \in [0, \infty)$. Suppose, for any arbitrary experiment labelled by α, the observed sample signal $s(t; \alpha)$ is invariably continuous (or almost surely with respect to some measure/probability). Let $\mathcal{A}$ denote the collection of all such experiments, or more generally and yet perhaps in a more straightforward manner, all the continuous functions on $[0, \infty)$. That is, $\mathcal{A} = C[0, \infty)$. Then, to characterize or define a random signal $s(t)$ is tantamount to specifying a probability measure μ on $\mathcal{A}$, or an *ensemble* supported on $\mathcal{A}$, which of course is highly nontrivial since $\mathcal{A}$ is not a conventional space like $\mathbb{R}^n$.

Physically, such ensembles may be naturally generated by a multibody system as in thermodynamics and statistical mechanics. On the other hand, from the modeling and computation point of view, one usually tends to prefer simple generative rules, which are often local and self-replicative, leading to the global ensemble μ. The connection between Gibbs' ensembles and their Markovian properties in image modeling and processing is such a remarkable example [130, 328].

4.1.3   Stochastic Models of Noises

As often done in the literature [237], we shall use the same symbol $s(t)$ to denote both a stochastic signal and any one of its empirical samples.

In applications, noises are often modelled as WSS stochastic signals with mean zero. Additional structures are often imposed in terms of the behavior of their power spectral densities.

The first popular noise model is called *white noise*, as inspired by the notion of *white color*. A shade of white color results from approximately equal mixture of different visible color spectra ranging from 400nm to 700nm.

Definition 4.1 (White Noise). *A WSS stochastic signal $n(t)$ with mean zero is called a white noise if its power spectral density $S_{nn}(\omega)$ is a constant σ^2 over all the spectra: $\omega \in \mathbb{R}$. More generally, such a signal is said to be a* bandlimited *white noise if $S_{nn}(\omega)$ is constant over certain spectral bands, and zero outside.*

It is easier to first understand discrete-time white noises. Suppose $n(k), k \in \mathbb{Z}$, is a white noise, whose autocorrelation sequence is defined by

$$R(m) = R_{nn}(m) = \mathrm{E}[n(k)n(k + m)], \quad m \in \mathbb{Z}.$$

Then demanding its power spectral density function $S_{nn}(\omega) \equiv \sigma^2$ is equivalent to asking for

$$R(m) = \sigma^2 \delta_m \quad \text{with Dirac's delta sequence } \delta_m. \tag{4.9}$$

That is, for any nonzero delay m, $n(k)$ and $n(k + m)$ as two random variables are always uncorrelated, which is automatic if the two are independent (since the means are assumed to be zero).

A white noise $n(k)$ is said to be Gaussian if all the finite marginal distributions are Gaussian. As is well known in probability theory, for two Gaussian random variables of mean zero, being uncorrelated is equivalent to independency. Gaussian white noise is perhaps the most popular noise model in many areas of image processing, partially due to the celebrated *central limit theorem* in probability theory.

All the above definitions and comments on white noises naturally extend to two dimensions for image analysis and processing. From the application point of view, whether for 1-D or 2-D signals, one central issue is how to test the hypothesis that a given stochastic signal is indeed white noise. In order to answer the question, the very first step is to be able to *actually* compute the correlation function or sequence. The difficulty lies in the scarcity of signal samples, either due to the high cost of measurement or the one-time nature of physical occurrences (such as seismic signals).

That is where the assumption of ergodicity plays a key role. If the noise $n(k)$ is assumed to be ergodic, then any ensemble statistics can be estimated from any of its empirical samples (almost surely). That is, for any statistics $F = F(n)$,

$$E[F(n)] = \lim_{N \to \infty} \frac{1}{N} \sum_{k=0}^{N-1} F(n(k)).$$

In particular, the autocorrelation sequence can be estimated by

$$R(m) = \lim_{N \to \infty} \frac{1}{N} \sum_{k=0}^{N-1} n(k)n(k+m).$$

In applications, it is of course only approximate since any digital signal has finite length, and one has to employ properly truncation windows.

4.1.4 Analog White Noises as Random Generalized Functions

Compared with discrete-time ones, analog white noises attract deeper theoretical attention from the modeling point of view.

By definition, if $n(t)$ is a white noise, its power spectral density $S_{nn}(\omega) \equiv \sigma^2$. As a result, the autocorrelation function $R_{nn}(t)$ must be $\sigma^2 \delta(t)$, Dirac's delta function, which is a generalized function or distribution (see Section 3.2.1). The same holds for 2-D white noises. Naturally one asks if it is possible to directly characterize white noises via the notion of generalized functions, and the answer turns out to be confirmative.

Recall as in Section 3.2.1 that an ordinary 2-D function $f(x)$ can be extended to a generalized function F in the distribution theory, so that for each sensor $\phi \in D(\mathbb{R}^2)$,

$$F(\phi) = \langle f, \phi \rangle.$$

The notion of white noise can also be generalized in the same fashion. A white noise $N(\phi)$ in the distributional sense is a random linear functional on the sensors $\phi \in D(\mathbb{R}^2)$, so that (a) for each sensor ϕ,

$$N(\phi) = \langle n, \phi \rangle$$

is a random variable with zero mean and variance $\sigma^2 \|\phi\|^2$; (b) more generally, for any two different sensors ϕ and $\psi \in D(\mathbb{R}^2)$, the two random variables are subject to

$$E[N(\phi)N(\psi)] = \sigma^2 \langle \phi, \psi \rangle, \tag{4.10}$$

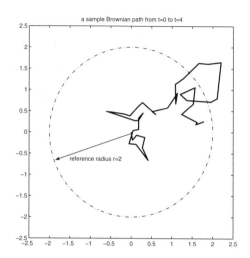

Figure 4.1. *A sample 2-D Brownian path $W(t)$ with $0 < t < 4$, and the reference circle with radius $2 = \sqrt{4}$, the standard deviation of $W(4)$.*

where the latter inner product is not symbolic but actually in $L^2(\mathbb{R}^2)$. Thus if ϕ and ψ are orthogonal, $N(\phi)$ and $N(\psi)$ must be uncorrelated. In particular, the last condition generalizes

$$\mathrm{E}[n(t)n(t + \tau)] \equiv 0 \quad \text{for any } \tau \neq 0,$$

since ϕ and ψ can be local sampling sensors near t and $t + \tau$ with nonoverlapping supports.

On the other hand, Gaussian white noise allows even more explicit expression under the notion of generalized functions. It can be treated as the generalized or distributional derivative of the canonical Brownian motion or Wiener process (see Figure 4.1).

It is well known that almost surely (over all sample paths), $W(t)$ is nowhere differentiable. However, since $W(t)$ is a continuous and therefore locally L^1, its distributional derivative $W'(t)$ is well defined and is subject to

$$\langle W' , \phi \rangle = -\langle W , \phi' \rangle = - \int_0^\infty W(t)\phi'(t)dt \qquad (4.11)$$

for any test sensor $\phi \in D(0, \infty)$. Then W' is identified with the analog Gaussian white noise $n_g(t)$ on $(0, \infty)$.

The following lines validate the relation (4.10) for n_g:

$$E[\langle n_g, \phi \rangle \langle n_g, \psi \rangle] = E[\langle W, \phi' \rangle \langle W, \psi' \rangle] = E \int_{\mathbb{R}^+ \times \mathbb{R}^+} W(t) W(s) \phi'(t) \psi'(s) \, dt ds$$

$$= \int_{\mathbb{R}^+ \times \mathbb{R}^+} t \wedge s \, \phi'(t) \psi'(s) \, dt ds$$

$$= \int_{t \leq s} t \phi'(t) \psi'(s) \, dt ds + \int_{s \leq t} s \phi'(t) \psi'(s) \, dt ds$$

$$= \int_{t \leq s} [t \phi'(t) \psi'(s) + t \psi'(t) \phi'(s)] \, dt ds$$

$$= - \int_{\mathbb{R}^+} [t \phi'(t) \psi(t) + t \phi(t) \psi'(t)] \, dt$$

$$= - \int_{\mathbb{R}^+} [(t \phi(t) \psi(t))' - \phi(t) \psi(t)] \, dt = \langle \phi, \psi \rangle.$$

Notice that for the canonical Brownian motion, $\sigma^2 = 1$. The above lines essentially show that, in the distributional sense,

$$\frac{\partial^2 (t \wedge s)}{\partial t \partial s} = \delta(t - s).$$

4.1.5   Random Signals from Stochastic Differential Equations

One important class of generative models for random signals are stochastic differential equations (SDEs) [186, 235]. Many random physical signals can be simulated using SDEs.

A general first order SDE for a sequential random signal $X(t)$ is in the form of

$$dX = b(X, t)dt + \sigma(X, t)dW, \quad X(0) = X_0, \tag{4.12}$$

where $W = W(t)$ denotes the canonical Wiener process or Brownian motion. The coefficient $b = b(X, t)$ reveals the general motion or advection trend, while $\sigma = \sigma(X, t)$ signifies the strength of random fluctuations.

At each time t,

$$dX(t) = X(t + dt) - X(t) \quad \text{and} \quad dW(t) = W(t + dt) - W(t).$$

By the definition of canonical Brownian motion, $E(dW) = 0$ and $E(dW)^2 = dt$. Assume that the initial value X_0, which by itself could be a random variable, is independent of $W(t)$. Then at each t, $dW(t)$ is independent of $X(t)$, and as a result,

$$dE(X) = E(dX) = dt E(b(X, t)).$$

In particular, suppose $b(x, t) = X\phi(t)$ is linear and separable; then the mean curve $x(t) = E(X(t))$ solves the following ordinary differential equation (ODE):

$$\frac{dx}{dt} = x\phi(t), \quad x(0) = x_0 = E(X_0). \tag{4.13}$$

We now discuss two familiar examples of SDEs. The first one is called the *Ornstein–Uhlenbeck process* and is given by

$$dX = -\alpha X dt + \sigma dW, \quad X_0 \equiv x_0, \quad (4.14)$$

where α and σ are fixed positive constants. Similar to the solution techniques for ODEs, the factor $e^{\alpha t}$ simplifies the equation to

$$d(e^{\alpha t} X) = \sigma e^{\alpha t} dW,$$

a direction integration of which leads to the solution

$$X = X(t) = e^{-\alpha t} x_0 + \sigma \int_0^t e^{-\alpha(t-\tau)} dW(\tau).$$

The second example will highlight the difference between ordinary ODE calculus and SDE calculus:

$$dX = bX dt + \sigma X dW, \quad X_0 \equiv x_0, \quad (4.15)$$

where b and σ are two constants. Separation of variables leads to

$$\frac{dX}{X} = b dt + \sigma dW. \quad (4.16)$$

However, for SDEs and stochastic analysis, the following well-known identity in classical calculus and ODE theories no longer holds:

$$\frac{dx}{x} = d \ln x.$$

Instead, if $X = X(t)$ is a general solution to the SDE (4.12) and $f(x)$ a smooth deterministic function, Itô's formula says

$$df(X) = f'(X)dX + \frac{1}{2}\sigma^2(X, t) f''(X)dt$$

$$= (b(X, t)f'(X) + \frac{1}{2}\sigma^2(X, t)f''(X))dt + \sigma(X, t)f'(X)dW.$$

The formula results directly from the classical Taylor expansion after noticing that $(dX)^2$, or equivalently $\sigma^2(X, t)(dW)^2$, is of order dt. With Itô's formula, (4.16) becomes

$$d \ln X - \frac{1}{2}\sigma^2 X^2(-X^{-2})dt = b dt + \sigma dW,$$

which leads to the explicit solution

$$X = X(t) = x_0 e^{(b - \frac{\sigma^2}{2})t + \sigma W(t)}.$$

Figure 4.2 shows a sample signal $X(t)$ for such a generating system with $x_0 = 1, b = 2$, and $\sigma - 1$.

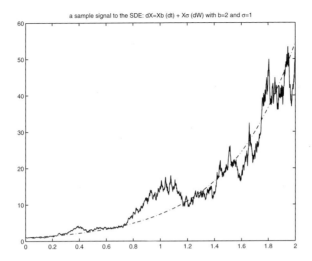

Figure 4.2. *A sample random signal generated by the SDE $dX = 2X dt + X dW$ with $X(0) = 1$. The smooth dashed curve denotes the mean curve $x(t) = \mathrm{E}X(t) = e^{2t}$. The random signal is clearly not stationary since both the means and variances of $X(t)$ evolve.*

4.1.6 2-D Stochastic Spatial Signals: Random Fields

The theory on 1-D temporal stochastic signals naturally extends to 2-D spatial signals such as images. In this section, we quickly collect all the facts on 2-D stochastic images that are parallel to the above discussion on 1-D signals. For convenience, it shall be assumed that the carrying domain is either $\mathbb{R}^2$ for analog images or $\mathbb{Z}^2$ for digital ones. General pixels in $\mathbb{R}^2$ or $\mathbb{Z}^2$ will be denoted by $x = (x_1, x_2)$, y, or z.

Analogous to the notion of "stationary," a stochastic image $u(x)$ is said to be (spatially) *homogeneous* if any of its finite marginal distributions carries no spatial memory, or equivalently, is translation-invariant:

$$P_{x+z,\ldots,y+z}(u, \ldots, v) \equiv P_{x,\ldots,y}(u, \ldots, v).$$

Gibbs' random fields with translation-invariant potentials, or equivalently, Markov random fields with translation invariant graph structures and local conditionals are familiar sources for homogeneous images [33, 130]. Homogeneity is an appropriate concept for modeling certain ideal single-species textures such as sandy beaches or grasslands.

As for 1-D (real) signals, u is said to be wide sense homogeneous (WSH) if its two-point autocorrelation function

$$R_{uu}(x, y) = \mathrm{E}[u(x)u(y)]$$

is translation-invariant: for any relocation z,

$$R_{uu}(x + z, y + z) = R_{uu}(x, y).$$

Thus if u is WSH, its autocorrelation function is essentially a single-pixel function: $R_{uu}(x - y) = R_{uu}(x, y)$. Let $\omega = (\omega_1, \omega_2)$ denote the harmonic frequency. Then the power spectral density $S_{uu}(\omega)$ is the Fourier transform of the autocorrelation function.

A WSH image $n(x)$ is said to be *white noise* if $S_{nn}(\omega) \equiv \sigma^2$, or equivalently its autocorrelation function $R_{nn}(z)$ is a multiple of Dirac's delta function $\sigma^2 \delta(x)$.

Two WSH images u and v are said to be *cross*-WSH if their cross-correlation function is translation-invariant as well:

$$R_{uv}(x, y) = \mathrm{E}[u(x)v(y)] = R_{uv}(x - y). \tag{4.17}$$

Define the cross-WSH set of a given WSH image u to be

$$\Lambda_u = \{v \mid v \text{ is cross-WSH to } u \}. \tag{4.18}$$

Then $u \in \Lambda_u$. The following list of properties are straightforward but useful.

Theorem 4.2. *Suppose u is a WSH stochastic image and Λ_u its cross-WSH set. Then*

1. *Λ_u is a linear space, i.e., closed under additions and multiplications;*
2. *Λ_u is closed under spatial relocation:*

$$v(\cdot) \in \Lambda_u \Rightarrow v(\cdot + z) \in \Lambda_u$$

   for any relocation z;
3. *Λ_u is closed under linear filtering:*

$$v \in \Lambda_u \Rightarrow h * v \in \Lambda_u$$

   for any filter $h = h(x)$. Let $H(\omega)$ denote the impulse response of h. Then

$$R_{h*v,u}(x) = h * R_{vu}(x) \quad and \quad S_{h*v,u}(\omega) = H(\omega)S_{vu}(\omega).$$

4.2   Linear Denoising: Lowpass Filtering

4.2.1   Signal vs. Noise

Consider for convenience 1-D temporal signals. Let $s(t) : t \in \mathbb{R}$ denote a "clean" signal and $n(t)$ an additive white noise. Then the noisy signal

$$s_0(t) = s(t) + n(t), \quad t \in \mathbb{R},$$

strictly speaking, is a random process no matter whether $s(t)$ is a single deterministic signal or by itself a stochastic signal. In what follows, we shall assume that $s(t)$ is a single deterministic signal.

The goal of denoising is to reconstruct the original signal $s(t)$ from the noisy one $s_0(t)$. From the statistical point of view, such reconstruction is necessarily an estimation problem since generally the original signal $s(t)$ is either unknown or impossible to acquire, though some partial information is often available. The same could be said about the noise.

Practically, a denoising task often has to be carried out based only on a single observation of $s_0(t)$. Insufficiency of data and correlation sources further worsens the ill-posedness of the denoising process as an inverse problem. The key to successful denoising therefore lies in the so-called *prior* information about the signal $s(t)$ and the noising mechanism and properties (i.e., the generative data model in the Bayesian framework).

Ideally, one would go for a simple linear denoising operator, say A, operating on all signals, so that

$$A\,s = s, \ \mathrm{E}[A\,n] = 0 \ \text{and} \ \mathrm{E}(An)^2 = o(\mathrm{E}[n^2]),$$

where the little o symbol means that the ratio of the two involved is practically small (e.g., 5 percent, say). Then $\tilde{s} = As_0$ becomes an unbiased estimator for the signal s.

To have the signal as a *strict* fixed point, the design of A has to depend on the *full* knowledge of the signal itself, which is impossible for most applications. *Partial* information on the signal necessarily brings in uncertainties, and as a result $As = s$ could only be expected to hold approximately. Together with the stochastic nature of the noise, this introduces a tradeoff between the fidelity of the recovered signal and the reduction of the noise.

We shall call such a tradeoff *the entanglement between signals and noises*, which is reflected by the brilliant maxim circulated among signal processing experts,

> *"What to one is a noise is often a signal to another."*

4.2.2 Denoising via Linear Filters and Diffusion

Assume that a target 1-D image signal $u(t)$ is smooth, or in the ideal case, bandlimited and therefore analytical. Let a be the upper bound which is known a priori so that the Fourier transform of $u(t)$ is supported on $(-a, a)$. Then one could simply design the denoising linear operator A based on the spectral truncation operator, so that the Fourier transform of Au is $1_{(-a,a)}(\omega) \cdot \hat{u}(\omega)$. That is, A is the convolution operator with the kernel function

$$k_a(x) = \frac{a}{\pi} \mathrm{sinc}\left(\frac{a}{\pi} x\right),$$

with sinc denoting Shannon's interpolating function $\sin(\pi x)/(\pi x)$ [272]. In signal processing, a linear convolution kernel is usually called a *filter*, and a digitized sequence as a discrete convolution kernel is called a *digital* filter.

If, instead of the hard truncation operator, one employs a softer or smoother window, often in the class of Schwartz functions [126, 193], then the kernel function $k(x)$ also decays fast, and in fact still belongs to the Schwartz class.

Among all linear filters, Gaussian filter perhaps plays the most important role in both theory and applications. In two dimensions, a Gaussian filter is given by

$$G_\sigma(x) = G_\sigma(x_1, x_2) = \frac{1}{2\pi\sigma^2} \exp\left(-\frac{x^2}{2\sigma^2}\right) = \frac{1}{\sigma^2} G_1\left(\frac{x}{\sigma}\right).$$

Notice that $G_\sigma(x)$ is precisely the probability density function of a 2-D Gaussian random variable with variance $2\sigma^2$.

The scaling parameter σ bears insightful interpretation. In terms of local averaging, σ indicates the *scale* level at which averaging is being carried out. Therefore, if

$$u_\sigma(x) = G_\sigma * u_0(x) \tag{4.19}$$

denotes the filtering output at the scale σ, it is intuitively conceivable that only those features that are larger than $O(\sigma)$ are still readable in $u_\sigma(x)$. Features of size smaller than $O(\sigma)$ have been treated as noise or distorted significantly.

Gaussian filtering (4.19) is remarkably associated with the linear heat diffusion process:

$$u_t(x, t) = \frac{1}{2}\Delta u(x, t) = \frac{1}{2}(u_{x_1 x_1} + u_{x_2 x_2}), \quad u(x, 0) = u_0(x),$$

for which the Gaussian kernel $G_{\sqrt{t}}(x)$ is the Green's function, and the diffusion process is precisely the linear filtering:

$$u(x, t) = G_{\sqrt{t}} * u_0(x) = \frac{1}{2\pi t}\int_{\mathbb{R}^2} u_0(y)\ \exp\left(-\frac{(x - y)^2}{2t}\right) dy.$$

The Laplacian infinitesimal generator for Gaussian filtering also suggests a convenient digital implementation for digital images. Let $u_{ij}^n = u(ih, jh, n\tau)$ denote the digital sample of a continuous image sequence $u(x_1, x_2, t)$ on a Cartesian grid of resolution h and with temporal sampling rate τ. Under the central-difference scheme, the Laplacian is digitized to

$$(u_{i+1,j}^n + u_{i-1,j}^n + u_{i,j+1}^n + u_{i,j-1}^n - 4u_{ij}^n)/h^2.$$

Then the forward Euler scheme in the temporal direction leads to the digital Gaussian filtering formula

$$u_{ij}^{n+1} = \lambda(u_{i+1,j}^n + u_{i-1,j}^n + u_{i,j+1}^n + u_{i,j-1}^n) + (1 - 4\lambda)u_{ij}^n, \tag{4.20}$$

where $\lambda = \tau/2h^2$. For stability reason (i.e., the CFL condition), it is required that $\lambda \le 1/4$, under which (4.20) is simply an iterated process of moving average.

The key issue arising from diffusion-based denoising schemes is the problem of *optimal stopping time*, that is, to decide when to stop the process to achieve a well-balanced performance of suppressing the noise while retaining the fidelity of the target signal. Without termination at certain finite time T, by the conservation law of adiabatic diffusion, as $t \to \infty$, $u(x, t)$ will only be able to tell a single scalar feature of the target signal—the mean $\langle u \rangle$ over the image domain Ω, as discussed in Section 2.5.

From the preceding discussion, it seems natural that the optimal stopping time T should be roughly in the order of $O(\sigma^2)$, provided that one does know that most interesting features of the target image are no less than the scale order $O(\sigma)$.

But such a connection is nothing more than a relay of problems, instead of a genuine offer of true solutions, because the identification of σ is no cheaper at all than the optimal stopping time T. In fact, the two are in some sense identical.

Therefore, in either case one ends up with the problem of parameter estimation. As commonly practiced in statistical inference, a general way must rely on a cost or risk function $R(T)$ (or $R(\sigma)$), properly defined to faithfully reflect human or machine visual perception. For instance, convenient but not unique, the following is a good candidate:

$$R_\alpha(t) = \alpha \int_\Omega |\nabla u(x, t)|^2 dx + \int_\Omega (u(x, t) - u_0(x))^2 dx, \tag{4.21}$$

and the optimal stopping time is defined to be $T = T_\alpha = \operatorname{argmin} R_\alpha(t)$. Here the weight α models visual sensitivity to local ripples in images.

4.3   Data-Driven Optimal Filtering: Wiener Filters

The above linear filtering and diffusion have been built upon preselected filters. Ideally, the filter should instead be learned from or driven by the given image data, which leads to another historically important class of filters proposed by Wiener [320].

Assume that a clean image $u(x)$, $x \in \mathbb{R}^2$, is polluted by an independent and additive white noise $n(x)$ with mean zero and variance σ^2:

$$u_0(x) = u(x) + n(x), \quad x \in \mathbb{R}^2.$$

Independence implies that $\mathrm{E}[u(x)n(y)] = \mathrm{E}[u(x)]\mathrm{E}[n(y)] \equiv 0$ or that the cross-correlation $R_{un} \equiv 0$. In addition, the approach of Wiener filtering requires that the image signal u is WSH (see previous sections).

Wiener's approach assumes that the denoising estimator $\hat{u}$ is a filtered version of the observation u_0, using some optimal filter $w(x)$:

$$\hat{u}_w = w * u_0.$$

The optimality of w is in the sense of minimizing the mean squared estimation error $e_w(x) = \hat{u}_w(x) - u(x)$:

$$w = \operatorname*{argmin}_h \mathrm{E}[e_h^2] = \operatorname*{argmin}_h \mathrm{E}(h * u_0(x) - u(x))^2. \tag{4.22}$$

Notice that the Wiener filter is independent of the particular pixel x used in the above definition since e_h is easily seen to be WSH for any fixed real filter $h = h(x)$.

The optimal design (4.22) is in essence variational as $\mathrm{E}[e_h^2]$ is a functional of h. Variation on the optimal Wiener filter $h = w$: $w \to w + \delta h$ gives the "equilibrium" equation

$$\mathrm{E}[(w * u_0(x) - u(x)) \cdot (\delta h) * u_0(x)] = 0.$$

Taking localized small variation $\delta h(x) = \varepsilon \delta(x - a)$ for some $\varepsilon \ll 1$ and localization a, we can rewrite the equation to

$$\mathrm{E}[(w * u_0(x) - u(x))u_0(x - a)] = 0.$$

Since a is arbitrary, it is equivalent to saying that for any two pixels x and y,

$$\mathrm{E}[(w * u_0(x) - u(x))u_0(y)] = 0. \tag{4.23}$$

This is known as the *orthogonal condition* for the Wiener filter.

By Theorem 4.2 in the preceding section, in terms of the correlations functions, the equation becomes

$$w * R_{u_0 u_0}(z) = R_{u u_0}(z), \quad z = x - y \in \mathbb{R}^2.$$

According to the power spectral densities and the impulse response $W(\omega)$ of w, one has

$$W(\omega) S_{u_0 u_0}(\omega) = S_{u u_0}(\omega).$$

Since the noise is independent of the signal,

$$R_{u u_0}(z) = R_{uu}(z) \text{ and } S_{u u_0}(\omega) = S_{uu}(\omega).$$

Similarly, $S_{u_0 u_0}(\omega) = S_{uu}(\omega) + S_{nn}(\omega)$. Therefore we have obtained the explicit formula for the Wiener filter.

Theorem 4.3 (Wiener Filter for Denoising). *The optimal Wiener filter w that minimizes the mean squared denoising error is unique, and its frequency response $W(\omega)$ is given by*

$$W(\omega) = \frac{S_{uu}(\omega)}{S_{u_0 u_0}(\omega)} = \frac{S_{uu}(\omega)}{S_{uu}(\omega) + S_{nn}(\omega)} = \frac{S_{u_0 u_0}(\omega) - S_{nn}(\omega)}{S_{u_0 u_0}(\omega)},$$

where for white noise, $S_{nn} \equiv \sigma^2$ and $S_{u_0 u_0} \geq \sigma^2 > 0$.

As implied from the formulation, Wiener filtering is not only applicable to denoising but also general image restoration problems such as deblurring, which shall be studied in the next chapter.

Compared with linear filtering with prefixed filters, Wiener filtering is data-driven and thus more adaptive. On the other hand, the above computation crucially relies on the stationary (in one dimension) or homogeneous (for two dimensions) assumption on the target signal. For nonstationary signals with dynamic evolution, Wiener filters can be generalized to Kalman filters [162], another remarkable class of filters that have proven to be extremely powerful in many fields, including object tracking in battle fields and weather forecasting.

We now discuss important nonlinear mechanisms for image denoising.

4.4   Wavelet Shrinkage Denoising

The intuition behind wavelet–shrinkage-based signal and image denoising is as follows. Under Besov norms (Section 3.3.3), the magnitudes of wavelet coefficients are directly proportional to the irregularity of a given image. When noises are involved, such irregularity grows in the wavelet coefficients. Thus by properly suppressing such irregular growth due to noises from the wavelet coefficients, the goal of denoising can be naturally achieved.

The central issues are, (1) What are the theoretical foundations for noise-signal separation in wavelet domains? and (2) How should such separation be actually implemented?

The theoretical foundations consist of both Donoho and Johnstone's statistical estimation theory [106, 109] and the variational optimization theory in Besov spaces due to Chambolle et al. [55] and DeVore, Jawerth, and Lucier [101]. Both are implemented by the wavelet shrinkage or truncation mechanisms.

The following presentation tightly follows the aforementioned works, except for some slight modifications to smoothen the flow of the current book.

4.4.1   Shrinkage: Quasi-statistical Estimation of Singletons

Eventually the shrinkage operator is applied to *all* the wavelet coefficients of a given signal or image. In these coming two subsections, we first study the behavior of the shrinkage operator when applied to singletons, i.e., signals with only one component.

Shrinkage $S_\lambda(t)$ is a nonlinear operator defined for any scalar $t \in \mathbb{R}$ with λ as the threshold. It resets any t to zero if $|t|$ is below the threshold, while to $t - \text{sign}(t)\lambda$ otherwise. Or as in [106, 109] and the spline theory, define $t_+ = t H(t)$ with the Heaviside function

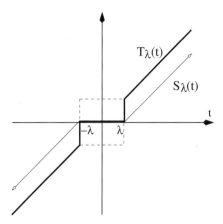

Figure 4.3. *Hard thresholding $T_\lambda(t)$ and soft shrinkage $S_\lambda(t)$.*

$H(t)$. Then the shrinkage operator is simply

$$\hat{t}_* = S_\lambda(t) = \text{sign}(t)(|t| - \lambda)_+. \tag{4.24}$$

Notice that unlike the hard thresholding operator

$$T_\lambda(t) = t \cdot H(|t| - \lambda),$$

the shrinkage operator is continuous, and thus often referred to as the *soft* thresholding operator in the literature (see Figure 4.3).

There are two ways to connect shrinkage to wavelet-based signal and image denoising: statistical and variational.

First, following Donoho and Johnstone [109], consider the following model problem of statistical estimation:

$$a_0 = a + \sigma w,$$

where a is the target signal (a single number in this case) to be estimated, w an additive nuisance (or noise) only known to be between -1 and 1, and σ a known nuisance level.

The signal is bounded by the observation by

$$a_0 - \sigma \leq a \leq a_0 + \sigma.$$

Suppose the SNR is large: $|a|/\sigma \gg 1$. Then $a_0 - \sigma$ and $a_0 + \sigma$ are of the same sign, and we define the estimator $\hat{a}$ to be the one with smaller magnitude. If the assumption of large SNR is invalid, the two bounds can then have opposite signs. Whenever this happens, we define the estimator $\hat{a}_* = 0$. It is then trivial to see that such an estimator is precisely the shrinkage operator $\hat{a}_* = S_\sigma(a_0)$, and the estimator satisfies the *uniform shrinkage condition*

$$|\hat{a}_*| = |S_\sigma(a_0)| \leq |a| \quad \forall a \in \mathbb{R},\ w \in [-1, 1]. \tag{4.25}$$

Since the magnitude of wavelet coefficients measures the irregularity of the target signal, the uniform shrinkage condition guarantees that the estimator is no rougher than the signal itself.

Among all the estimators satisfying the uniform shrinkage condition, the shrinkage estimator is optimal.

Theorem 4.4 (Donoho [106]). *Among all estimators $\hat{a}$ satisfying the uniform shrinkage condition, the shrinkage estimator $\hat{a}_*$ achieves the* minimum shrinkage performance *(i.e., with the largest magnitude),*

$$|\hat{a}(a_0)| \leq |\hat{a}_*(a_0)| \qquad \forall\, a_0,$$

and the minimum worst estimation error,

$$\max_{w \in [-1,1]} |\hat{a} - a| \geq \max_{w \in [-1,1]} |\hat{a}_* - a|,$$

for any signal $a \in \mathbb{R}$.

Proof. Here we give a construction-based proof. Consider only $a \geq 0$ due to the sign symmetry. First, notice

$$a_0 = \hat{a}_* + (a_0 - \hat{a}_*) = \hat{a}_* + \sigma w.$$

One must have $w \in [-1, 1]$ since

$$|\hat{a}_*(a_0) - a_0| = |a_0| \wedge \sigma \leq \sigma.$$

Therefore, for any estimator $\hat{a}$ satisfying the uniform shrinkage condition,

$$|\hat{a}| = |\hat{a}(a_0)| = |\hat{a}(\hat{a}_* + \sigma w)| \leq |\hat{a}_*|,$$

which is the statement of minimum shrinkage.

For the shrinkage estimator $\hat{a}_*$, it is easy to see that the worst estimation error for $a \geq 0$ occurs when the observation happens to be

$$a_0^w = a - a \wedge \sigma = (a - \sigma)_+, \quad a \geq 0,$$

in which case the shrinkage estimation

$$\hat{a}_*(a_0^w) = (a_0^w - \sigma)_+ = (a - 2\sigma)_+,$$

and the associated error realizes the worst scenario:

$$\max_{w \in [-1,1]} |\hat{a}_* - a| = |\hat{a}_*(a_0^w) - a| = a \wedge 2\sigma.$$

Finally, combined with the minimum shrinkage property just established, the worst observation a_0^w for $\hat{a}_*$ also bounds the performance of any arbitrary estimator $\hat{a}$:

$$\max_{w \in [-1,1]} |\hat{a} - a| \geq |\hat{a}(a_0^w) - a| \geq a - |\hat{a}(a_0^w)| \geq a - |\hat{a}_*(a_0^w)| = |a - \hat{a}_*(a_0^w)| = \max_{w \in [-1,1]} |\hat{a}_* - a|.$$

This completes the proof. Figure 4.4 can be helpful to visualize the proof. $\square$

This theorem paves the way for noise reduction based on statistical wavelet shrinkage, as well as points to the fact that wavelet shrinkage naturally achieves optimality in a certain minimax sense [106, 109].

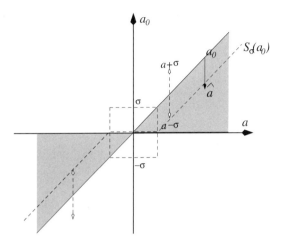

Figure 4.4. *The shrinkage operator* $\hat{a}_* = S_\sigma(a_0)$ *achieves minimum shrinkage (Theorem 4.4) among all the estimators $\hat{a}$ that satisfy the* uniform shrinkage condition (4.25).

4.4.2 Shrinkage: Variational Estimation of Singletons

The variational approach was first developed by Chambolle et al. [55] and DeVore, Jawerth, and Lucier [101]. It reveals the role of the shrinkage operator for denoising with a more deterministic flavor. Again this section reveals the theory from the singleton point of view.

As in the preceding statistical theory, we consider the singleton noise model

$$a_0 = a + z,$$

where a is the target singleton signal and z is Gaussian noise. In terms of wavelet decomposition, a represents an individual wavelet coefficient and z the noise of that component.

In the variational formulation, the optimal estimator $\hat{a}$ from the observation a_0 is the minimizer of the following error function:

$$e_p(t|a_0) = \frac{\lambda}{2}(a_0 - t)^2 + \mu|t|^p. \tag{4.26}$$

The parameter $\lambda > 0$ serves the role of a Lagrange multiplier for a constrained optimization formulation, while $\mu > 0$ controls the decay rate of wavelet coefficients, or equivalently, Besov regularity. In practice μ could depend on the scales, regularity, and the power $p \geq 1$.

Theorem 4.5. *The optimal estimator*

$$\hat{a} = \hat{a}(a_0) = \underset{t}{\mathrm{argmin}}\ e_p(t|a_0)$$

exists and is unique. Moreover, $a_0 \cdot \hat{a} \geq 0$.

Proof. For any t with $a_0 t < 0$, it is easy to see that

$$e_p(-t|a_0) < e_p(t|a_0).$$

Thus the minimizer $\hat{a}$ must satisfy the same-sign condition as claimed,

Furthermore, this allows us to consider only the case when $a_0 > 0$ (noticing that $a_0 = 0$ is trivial) and $t \geq 0$. As a result,

$$e_p(t|a_0) = \frac{\lambda}{2}(t - a_0)^2 + \mu t^p,$$

$$e'_p(t|a_0) = \lambda(t - a_0) + \mu p t^{p-1},$$

$$e''_p(t|a_0) = \lambda + \mu p(p - 1)t^{p-2} > 0.$$

The strict convexity ensures the uniqueness of the optimal estimation $\hat{a}$, while existence is trivial as the error function is continuous and blows up at $t = +\infty$.   □

We now show that the *exact* solution $\hat{a}$ for $p = 1$ is precisely realized by a suitably defined shrinkage operator $S_\sigma(a_0)$, and for a general $p \geq 1$, a hard truncation operator $T_\sigma(a_0)$ yields good approximation to the exact estimator.

In the case of $p = 1$, the optimal estimator must satisfy $e'_1(\hat{a}|a_0) = 0$:

$$\lambda(\hat{a} - a_0) + \mu = 0, \qquad\qquad (4.27)$$

or otherwise $\hat{a} = 0$. Define $\sigma = \mu/\lambda$ to be the *modulated noise level*. We say so because if σ_z^2 denotes the variance of noise z, then in the Bayesian framework [63, 71, 67], λ is in the order of $O(\sigma_z^{-2})$. On the other hand, for (2-D) Besov images $B_1^\alpha(L^1)$, at any working scale $h_j = 2^{-j}$, μ is in the order of $O(h_j^{-(\alpha-1)})$ (see Section 3.3.3) and $s = \mu^{-1}$ could be considered as the typical signal strength (at scale j in the wavelet domain). In combination one has

$$\sigma = \frac{\mu}{\lambda} \propto \frac{\sigma_z^2}{s} = \frac{\sigma_z}{s} \cdot \sigma_z.$$

Therefore, σ is indeed the noise level modulated by the SNR s/σ_z.

If $a_0 > \sigma$, the optimal estimator $\hat{a} = a_0 - \sigma > 0$. Otherwise, $e'(t|a_0) > 0$ for all $t > 0$, and the minimum is reached at the "boundary" $t = \hat{a} = 0$ (see Figure 4.5).

Therefore, combined with $a_0 \leq 0$, for $p = 1$, the optimal estimator is precisely the shrinkage operator:

$$\hat{a} = \hat{a}(a_0) = S_\sigma(a_0) = \text{sign}(a_0)(|a_0| - \sigma)_+. \qquad\qquad (4.28)$$

In the case of $p = 2$, if one defines $\gamma = \lambda/(\lambda + 2\mu) < 1$, the optimal estimator also has a simple and explicit form:

$$\hat{a} = \hat{a}(a_0) = \gamma a_0,$$

which is a uniform multiplicative shrinkage.

Finally, for general $p \in (1, 2)$, we define a hard truncation estimator $\hat{a}$ which is almost optimal [55]. Define the truncation threshold

$$\sigma = \left(\frac{2\mu}{\lambda}\right)^{\frac{1}{2-p}},$$

and

$$\hat{a}(a_0) = T_\sigma(a_0) = a_0 H(|a_0| - \sigma).$$

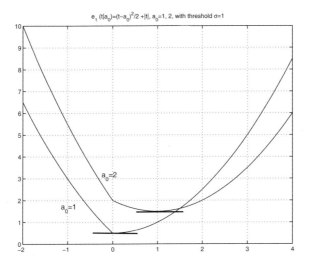

Figure 4.5. *Two singleton error functions $e_1(t|a_0)$ with $\lambda = \mu = 1$ and $a_0 = 1, 2$. Notice that the optimal estimators (i.e., the valleys) $\hat{a} = 0, 1$ are precisely the shrinkages $S_\sigma(a_0)$ with $\sigma = \mu/\lambda = 1$.*

This estimator goes for 0 if $|a_0| \leq \sigma$, or equivalently, $a_0^2 \lambda/2 \leq \mu|a_0|^p$, and for a_0 otherwise. To see the near optimality, consider only $a_0 \geq 0$ again. For all $t \leq a_0/2$,

$$e_p(t|a_0) \geq \frac{\lambda}{2}(a_0 - a_0/2)^2 = \frac{\lambda a_0^2}{8} = \frac{1}{4}e_p(0|a_0);$$

and for any $t \geq a_0/2$,

$$e_p(t|a_0) \geq \mu\left(\frac{a_0}{2}\right)^p = \frac{1}{2^p}e_p(a_0|a_0).$$

Therefore,

$$(4 \vee 2^p)\min_t e_p(t|a_0) \geq e_p(0|a_0) \wedge e_p(a_0|a_0). \tag{4.29}$$

By design of the hard threshold σ, the right-hand side is precisely the error $e(\hat{a}|a_0)$ associated with the estimator. This shows that $\hat{a}$ is indeed almost optimal up to a constant factor.

4.4.3   Denoising via Shrinking Noisy Wavelet Components

Donoho and Johnstone's wavelet–shrinkage-based denoising scheme takes the following form:

$$\hat{u}^* = W^{-1}S_\lambda W(u_0),$$

where $W(u_0)$ is the wavelet transform which represents a noisy image

$$u_0(x) = u(x) + n(x)$$

by its wavelet coefficients and W^{-1} the inverse wavelet transform that resumes to the pixel space. As in the preceding sections, S_λ denotes the singleton shrinkage operator, componentwise applied to all the wavelet coefficients. That is, S_λ is "diagonal" in the wavelet domain. For L^2 images and orthonormal wavelet transforms, the denoising operator K_λ is thus orthogonally similar to the shrinkage operator. Finally, $\hat{u}_*(u_0) = K_\lambda u_0$ is nonlinear since S_λ is.

The shrinkage theory naturally focuses on two key issues: (a) how to properly choose the threshold λ for a given noisy image and (b) how to justify such approach, or equivalently, how to show that such an estimator $\hat{u}_*(u_0)$ is nearly optimal in a certain (statistical) sense. We refer the reader to the papers by Dohono and Johnstone for all the details [106, 109]. Presented below is a slightly different approach from that in [106, 109]. The two main characteristics of our approach are the following:

1. The nature of analog white noises is respected, and as a result, their projections on the multiresolution spaces are *not* assumed to be scale dependent as in [106, 109].

2. To avoid the technicality in [106, 109] associated with a finite domain and discrete samples (also see [55, 89]), our approach has been consistently kept analog.

We shall illustrate the idea of wavelet shrinkage via 1-D images. Assume the noise model is given by

$$u_0(x) = u(x) + n(x), \quad x \in \mathbb{R},$$

where $n(x)$ is an analog white noise with variance σ^2, and the target signal $u(x)$ is assumed to belong to the class

$$\tilde{\mathcal{F}}(A, B) = \{u \in L^2(\mathbb{R}) \mid u \text{ is compactly supported on } [A, B]\}$$

for some fixed $A < B$. Unlike [106, 109], we do not restrict wavelet decomposition in $L^2(A, B)$, but treat $\tilde{\mathcal{F}}(A, B) = L^2(A, B)$ as a subspace of $L^2(\mathbb{R})$, and apply the multiresolution of the latter.

For the multiresolution analysis, assume that both the scaling function $\phi(x)$ and mother wavelet $\psi(x)$ are r-regular for some $r \geq 1$ and both compactly supported on some finite interval $[a, b]$.

For each resolution level $j \geq 0$, define the influence domain I_j of the interval (A, B) associated with the wavelets by

$$I_j = \left\{ (j, k) \mid k \in \mathbb{Z}, \int_{(A,B)} |\psi_{j,k}(x)| dx > 0 \right\}, \quad j = 0, 1, \dots. \tag{4.30}$$

In addition, for notational convenience, define, for the scaling function ϕ,

$$I_{-1} = \left\{ (-1, k) \mid k \in \mathbb{Z}, \int_{(A,B)} |\phi(x - k)| dx > 0 \right\}. \tag{4.31}$$

Notice that each $I_j : j \geq -1$ is a finite set due to the compactness assumption on both ϕ and ψ.

For each $u \in L^2(\mathbb{R})$, denote its wavelet decomposition by

$$u = \sum_{j \geq -1, k \in \mathbb{Z}} d_{j,k}(u) \psi_{j,k},$$

where as in (4.31), the index -1 is actually for the scaling function ϕ; that is, $\psi_{-1,k}$ denote $\phi(x - k)$, and $d_{-1,k}$'s are in fact the lowpass coefficients $\langle u, \phi(x - k) \rangle$. This novel way of indexing may be different from the conventional ones but is convenient as one does not need to spell out each time the ϕ components separately.

For each scale level $J \geq 0$, define a subspace of $L^2(\mathbb{R})$ by

$$\mathcal{F}_J(A, B) = \{u \in L^2(\mathbb{R}) \mid d_{j,k}(u) \neq 0 \text{ at most for } (j, k) \in I_j, J > j \geq -1\}. \quad (4.32)$$

It is easy to see that each $\mathcal{F}_J$ is a closed subspace in $L^2(\mathbb{R})$. Moreover, as $J \to \infty$, $\mathcal{F}_J$'s monotonically converge to

$$\tilde{\mathcal{F}}(A, B) = \{u \in L^2(\mathbb{R}) \mid d_{j,k}(u) \neq 0 \text{ at most for } (j, k) \in I_j, j \geq -1\}. \quad (4.33)$$

By the definition of I_j's, it is then clear that

$$\tilde{\mathcal{F}}(A, B) \subseteq \mathcal{F}(A, B).$$

Notice that $\mathcal{F}(A, B)$ is a closed subspace as well. The reason we introduce $\mathcal{F}(A, B)$ and will work with it instead of $\tilde{\mathcal{F}}(A, B)$ can be traced to Donoho's solid and orthosymmetric condition [106, 109] so that minimax type of estimation results can be developed later.

Theorem 4.6 (Donoho's Solid and Orthosymmetric Condition). *Both the subspaces $\mathcal{F}_J(A, B)$ and $\mathcal{F}(A, B)$ satisfy Donoho's solid and orthosymmetric condition in the wavelet domain. That is, if $(d_{j,k})_{j \geq -1, k \in \mathbb{Z}}$ are the wavelet coefficients of some image in $\mathcal{F}_J$ or $\mathcal{F}$, so are $(s_{j,k}d_{j,k})_{j \geq -1, k \in \mathbb{Z}}$ for any sequence $(s_{j,k})$ with $|s_{j,k}| \leq 1$ for all $j \geq -1, k \in \mathbb{Z}$.*

The verification is straightforward. From now on, we shall focus on the denoising problem for images from the $\mathcal{F}_J(A, B)$'s and $\mathcal{F}(A, B)$.

The noise model $u_0(x) = u(x) + n(x)$ is now transformed into

$$d^0_{j,k} = d_{j,k} + z_{j,k}, \quad j \geq -1, k \in \mathbb{Z}, \quad (4.34)$$

in terms of the wavelet coefficients. Special attention should be paid to the noisy components $z_{j,k}$. Recall that the Gaussian white noise $n(x)$, assumed to have variance σ^2, as a random generalized function satisfies (see Section 4.1.4)

$$\mathrm{E}[z_{j,k}z_{j',k'}] = \mathrm{E}[\langle n, \psi_{j,k}\rangle \langle n, \psi_{j',k'}\rangle] = \sigma^2 \langle \psi_{j,k}, \psi_{j',k'}\rangle = \sigma^2 \delta_{jk,j'k'}. \quad (4.35)$$

That is, the projections $(z_{j,k})$ constitute into a discrete Gaussian white noise of variance σ^2. This is the major difference of our approach from Donoho and Johnstone's, of which the projections are assumed to have scale-dependent variances (i.e., $2^{-J}\sigma^2 = \sigma^2/N$ instead of σ^2) [106, 109].

Fix a fine-scale level $J \gg 1$ (e.g., $J = 8, 10$ for most digital images of moderate sizes), and assume that the target image $u \in \mathcal{F}_J(A, B)$. Define the influence index set associated with the fine scale J to be

$$I_{(J)} = I_{J-1} \cup I_{J-2} \cup \cdots \cup I_0 \cup I_{-1}. \quad (4.36)$$

It is a priori known that $d_{j,k} \equiv 0$ for all $(j, k) \notin I_{(J)}$. This prior knowledge allows us to focus only on those wavelet coefficients whose indices belong to $I_{(J)}$.

Theorem 4.7 (Size of $I_{(J)}$). *Suppose* $\text{supp}\,\psi = \text{supp}\,\phi = [a, b]$ *(identical supports simplify the statement of the theorem, but are not essential) and* $l = b - a$. *Also define* $L = B - A$, $M = \#I_{(J)}$, *and* $N = 2^J$. *Then*

$$NL + (l - 1)(\ln N + 1) \leq M < NL + (l + 1)(\ln N + 1). \tag{4.37}$$

Proof. By the definition of I_j's in (4.30) and (4.31), and $f_{j,k} = 2^{j/2} f(2^j x - k)$, we conclude that for any $j \geq 0$, $(j, k) \in I_j$ if and only if the two intervals $2^j(A, B) - k$ and (a, b) have nonempty intersection. This is equivalent to

$$a < 2^j B - k < 2^j A - k < b \quad \text{or} \quad 2^j A - b < k < 2^j B - a.$$

Therefore, $\#I_j$ satisfies

$$2^j L + l - 1 \leq \#I_j < 2^j L + l + 1, \quad j \geq 0.$$

Notice that I_{-1} satisfies the same estimation as I_0. Hence,

$$L + l - 1 + \sum_{j=0}^{J-1}(2^j L + l - 1) \leq M < L + l - 1 + \sum_{j=0}^{J-1}(2^j L + l + 1),$$

or equivalently,

$$2^J L + (l - 1)(J + 1) \leq M < 2^J L + (l + 1)(J + 1),$$

which is precisely the inequality (4.37).   □

To apply the singleton shrinkage results developed in the preceding sections, one employs the following key fact about a finite set of Gaussian i.i.d.'s (see, e.g., Donoho [106] and Leadbetter, Lindgren, and Rootzen [190]).

Theorem 4.8. *Let* $(z_k)_{k=1}^{\infty}$ *be a sequence of Gaussian i.i.d.'s of mean zero and variance* σ^2. *Then*

$$\pi_M = \Pr\left(\max_{1 \leq k \leq M} |z_k| \leq \sigma\sqrt{2\ln M}\right) \to 1, \quad M \to \infty. \tag{4.38}$$

It is worth mentioning that the cutoff $\lambda = \sigma\sqrt{2\ln M}$ is optimal in the sense that for any $\gamma < 1$, $\gamma\sigma\sqrt{2\ln M}$ will cause $\lim_{M \to \infty} \pi_M = 0$. On the other hand, $\gamma > 1$ causes no problem in terms of the theorem itself but may lead to oversmoothing in the forthcoming shrinkage-based denoising.

We now define the *supervised* shrinkage operator $\tilde{S}_\lambda$ in the wavelet domain for noisy images generated from $\mathcal{F}_J(A, B)$. Inspired by the preceding theorem, one sets the threshold $\lambda = \sigma\sqrt{2\ln M}$ (further improvement later in [106]). First, for any noised wavelet coefficient $d_{j,k}^0$ with index $(j, k) \notin I_{(J)}$, set

$$\hat{d}_{j,k}^* = \tilde{S}_\lambda(d_{j,k}^0) = 0,$$

which is the supervised truncation since the target image $u \in \mathcal{F}_J(A, B)$. For noised wavelet coefficients supported on $I_{(J)}$, one applies the ordinary singleton shrinkage operator

$$\hat{d}_{j,k}^* = \dot{S}_\lambda(d_{j,k}^0) = S_\lambda(d_{j,k}^0) = \text{sign}(d_{j,k}^0)(d_{j,k}^0 - \lambda)_+.$$

Thus in combination, the denoised image estimation $\hat{u}$ is

$$\hat{u}^* = W^{-1}\tilde{S}_\lambda W(u_0) = W^{-1}(\hat{d}^*_{j,k} \mid j \geq -1, k \in \mathbb{Z}). \tag{4.39}$$

Here W and W^{-1} denote the forward and inverse wavelet transforms.

Notice that asymptotically as J or $M \to \infty$, Theorem 4.7 shows that

$$\ln M = \ln N + \ln L + O\left(\frac{\ln N}{N}\right).$$

Recall that $L = B - A$ is the continuum pixel length of the target class of 1-D images. The examples in [106, 55] are both about the unit interval (or the unit square in two dimensions) for which $L = 1$ and $\ln L = 0$. Then $\ln M = \ln N(1 + O(N^{-1})) \approx \ln N$, and the threshold takes the familiar form $\lambda = \sigma\sqrt{2\ln N}$. For instance, for $J = 8$ (very typical in real applications), $\lambda \approx 3.33\sigma$. But when the target image signals are supported on a relatively longer interval (e.g., $(A, B) = (-25, 25)$ with $L = B - A = 50$), and the working finest scale level J is still like 8, then for real applications or implementations one has to consider the effect of $\ln L$ and take $\ln M = \ln N + \ln L$ as a good approximation. (For $L = 50$ and $J = 8$ for example, $\lambda \approx 4.35\sigma$.) Also interestingly notice from the above formula that $\ln M$ does not sensitively depend upon the support length l of the mother wavelet or scaling function.

Following the properties on the singleton shrinkage operator, it is then easy to investigate the behavior of the supervised wavelet-shrinkage estimation $\hat{u}$ in (4.39).

Theorem 4.9. *For any target image $u \in \mathcal{F}_J(A, B)$, with probability at least no less than π_M (as defined in (4.38)), the supervised shrinkage estimator $\hat{u} = W^{-1}\tilde{S}_\lambda W(u_0)$ is smoother than u in terms of any applicable Besov norm $B^\alpha_q(L^p(\mathbb{R}))$ expressed in terms of wavelet coefficients as in (3.37). That is,*

$$\text{Prob}\left(\|\hat{u}^*\|_{B^\alpha_q(L^p)} \leq \|u\|_{B^\alpha_q(L^p)}\right) \geq \pi_M \to 1, \quad M \to \infty.$$

Proof. Both the theorem and its proof are essentially adapted from [106].

Suppose $u \in B^\alpha_q(L^p(\mathbb{R})) \cap \mathcal{F}_J(A, B)$. The supervision of shrinkage gives $\hat{d}^*_{j,k} = d_{j,k} \equiv 0$ for any index $(j, k) \notin I_{(J)}$. This is always true independent of noise due to supervision (i.e., the knowledge on J).

For any index (j, k) belonging to the influence set $I_{(J)}$, $\hat{S}_\lambda$ is the singleton shrinkage operator S_λ on $d^0_{j,k} = d_{j,k} + z_{j,k}$. Therefore, by the uniform shrinkage condition of S_λ expressed in (4.25), as long as $|z_{j,k}| \leq \lambda$,

$$|\hat{d}^*_{j,k}| = |\tilde{S}_\lambda(d^0_{j,k})| = |S_\lambda(d^0_{j,k})| \leq |d_{j,k}|, \quad (j, k) \in I_{(J)}.$$

Now according to Theorem 4.8, with confidence π_M ($M = \#I_{(J)}$), all the pure noisy components $z_{j,k}$ are indeed bounded in $[-\lambda, \lambda]$. Therefore, with at least confidence π_M,

$$|\hat{d}^*_{j,k}| \leq |d_{j,k}| \quad \forall j \geq -1, \ k \in \mathbb{Z}.$$

Then the theorem follows since in the wavelet domain Besov norms are increasing functions of the magnitude of any wavelet coefficient (see (3.37)). $\square$

Finally, following [106], we investigate the near optimality of the above wavelet–shrinkage-based denoising estimator $\hat{u}^*$.

Definition 4.10 (Componentwise Wavelet-Based Denoiser (CWBD)). *A general denoising estimator $u_0 \to \hat{u} = \hat{u}(u_0)$ is called a* componentwise wavelet-based denoiser *(CWBD) if*

$$d_{j,k}(\hat{u}) = \hat{d}_{j,k}(d_{j,k}^0) \quad \forall j \geq -1, \; k \in \mathbb{Z}.$$

That is, each wavelet coefficient of the denoised estimator depends only on the corresponding wavelet coefficient of the noisy image. (Thus such estimators do not take into account the correlations among wavelet coefficients.)

For the image space $\mathcal{F}_J(A, B)$, a CWBD $\hat{u}$ is said to be *supervised* if

$$\hat{d}_{j,k} \equiv 0 \quad \forall (j, k) \notin I_{(J)}.$$

In particular, $\hat{u}(u_0) \in L^2(\mathbb{R})$ for any noisy image $u_0 = u + n$ because only a finite number of wavelet coefficients are nonzero.

Suppose $\hat{u}$ is a supervised CWBD (or S-CWBD) for $\mathcal{F}_J(A, B)$. Define its mean squared estimation error for a given image $u \in \mathcal{F}_J(A, B)$ by

$$e_J(u|\hat{u}) = \mathrm{E}\|\hat{u} - u\|_{L^2}^2$$

and its worst estimation error by

$$e_J(\hat{u}) = \sup_{u \in \mathcal{F}_J(A,B)} e_J(u|\hat{u}).$$

Notice that the shrinkage estimator $\hat{u}^*$ defined previously is a S-CWBD. Finally, among all S-CWBDs of $\mathcal{F}_J(A, B)$, define the best performance error by

$$e_J^* = \inf_{\hat{u} \in \mathrm{S-CWBD}} e_J(\hat{u}).$$

Theorem 4.11 (Uniform Near-Optimality). *The shrinkage estimator $\hat{u}^*$ in (4.39) is near-optimal:*

$$e_J(u|\hat{u}^*) \leq (2\log M + 1)(\sigma^2 + 2.22 e_J^*) \quad \forall u \in \mathcal{F}_J(A, B),$$

where as before $M = \#I_{(J)}$, and σ^2 denotes the noise level.

Proof. From Theorem 4.6, the target image space $\mathcal{F}_J(A, B)$ is solid and orthosymmetric [106]. In combination with the definition of S-CWBD, it allows one to go to the wavelet domain and employ Theorem 4.2 in [106]. Notice that the notion of supervision essentially reduces the whole continuous setting (i.e., in L^2) to the finite index set $I_{(J)}$. □

More discussion on the near-optimality of $\hat{u}^*$ can be developed following the pioneering works in [106, 109], where more information on choosing an optimal threshold λ can also be found. Figures 4.6 and 4.7 show two examples of shrinkage-based image denoising.

4.4.4 Variational Denoising of Noisy Besov Images

The variational approach to wavelet shrinkage denoising has been studied, for example, in [55, 101, 199]. It brings the wavelet shrinkage technique closer to the variational, functional, and PDE methodologies in image processing (e.g., [73]).

To some degree, the variational approach is simpler than the preceding statistical estimation theory. The hidden cost is that the target image signals have to be a priori assumed in certain Besov spaces, and Besov regularity serves as the prior model in the variational Bayesian formulation. The preceding statistical estimation theory and near-optimal type of assertions can be, however, applied to more general image classes. When applied to a real given image, such generality sometimes causes the oversmoothing effect (see, for example, the discussion in [55]).

Again assume the noise model (for 1-D images)

$$u_0(x) = u(x) + n(x), \quad x \in \mathbb{R},$$

ideal image between 0 and 1

Gaussian noise with σ=0.1

4–level uniform shrinkage: λ=0.25

over–shrinkage: λ_o=0.49

under–shrinkage: λ_u=0.089

Figure 4.6. *An example of shrinkage-based image denoising, with Gaussian white noise level σ = 0.1, and four levels of wavelet decompositions based on one of Daubechies' orthonormal wavelets [96]. The three bottom panels demonstrate the effect of the threshold parameter λ on the shrinkage operator S_λ: a too large λ causes overshrinkage and oversmoothing, while a too small one leads to the opposite.*

ideal image between 0 and 1

Gaussian noise with σ=0.2

4–level uniform shrinkage: λ=0.44

over–shrinkage: λ_o=0.88

under–shrinkage: λ_u=0.16

Figure 4.7. *Same example as in Figure* 4.6 *with increased Gaussian noise level* $\sigma = 0.2$.

with the target image $u \in B_q^\alpha(L^p)$. To illustrate the connection to the preceding statistical estimation theory of Donoho and Johnstone, we assume $p = q \geq 1$ following [55].

Unlike the statistical theory of white noise, in the variational approach, the noisy component $n(x)$ is treated as a highly oscillatory function in $L^2(\mathbb{R})$. Being square integrable necessarily implies that n decays with some moderate rate at $x = \pm\infty$, which means it cannot be stationary in the statistical sense.

Given a single observation u_0, the cost function of a variational estimation scheme takes the form of

$$E[u \mid u_0] = E[u] + E[u_0 \mid u] + const.$$

The particular prior model $u \in B_p^\alpha(L^p)$ is specified by the Besov norm (see (3.36) and (3.37) in the preceding chapter):

$$E[u] = \sum_{j \geq -1} 2^{jp(\alpha+1/2-1/p)} |d_{j,k}|^p, \qquad (4.40)$$

where as in the preceding section, $d_{-1,k}$'s conveniently denote the lowpass coefficients which are more commonly denoted by $c_{0,k} = \langle u \, , \, \phi_{0,k} \rangle$ in the literature. (Also for two dimensions, $1/2 - 1/p$ should be doubled.) Following the Gaussian noise model, the data generative model $E[u_0 \mid u]$ is specified by

$$E[u_0 \mid u] = \frac{\lambda}{2} \int_{\mathbb{R}} (u_0(x) - u(x))^2 dx = \frac{\lambda}{2} \sum_{j \geq -1, k \in \mathbb{Z}} (d^0_{j,k} - d_{j,k})^2.$$

The weight constant λ, as evident from Gaussian distributions, is inversely proportional to the variance of the noise. Then in the variational formulation, the denoiser $\hat{u}$ is obtained by

$$\hat{u} = \text{argmin } E[u|u_0] = \text{argmin } \sum_{j \geq -1, k} 2^{jp(\alpha+1/2-1/p)} |d_{j,k}|^p + \frac{\lambda}{2} \sum_{j \geq -1, k} (d^0_{j,k} - d_{j,k})^2.$$

(4.41)

The cost function is completely decoupled in the wavelet domain. That is, (4.41) is equivalent to componentwise minimizing each univariate cost function:

$$\hat{d}_{j,k} = \text{argmin } e_{j,k}(d_{j,k}|d^0_{j,k}) = \text{argmin } \frac{\lambda}{2}(d^0_{j,k} - d_{j,k})^2 + \mu_j |d_{j,k}|^p \quad \forall j, k. \quad (4.42)$$

Here $\mu_j = 2^{jp(\alpha+1/2-1/p)}$ is independent of the location index k.

The last formula is precisely in the singleton form (4.26), and all the discussion in Section 4.4.2 thus smoothly applies. In particular, we have the following result.

Theorem 4.12. *In one dimension with $p = q = 1$ and $\mu_j = 2^{j(\alpha-1/2)}$, define the modulated noise level $\sigma_j = \mu_j/\lambda$ as in (4.27). Then the optimal denoiser $\hat{u}$ for the cost function $E[u|u_0]$ in (4.41) is explicitly given by the shrinkage operator*

$$\hat{d}_{j,k} = d_{j,k}(\hat{u}) = S_{\sigma_j}(d^0_{j,k}) = \text{sign}(d^0_{j,k})(d^0_{j,k} - \sigma_j)_+ \quad \forall j \geq -1, k \in \mathbb{Z}.$$

Notice that when $\alpha = 1/2$, the thresholds $\sigma_j \equiv 1/\lambda$ become independent of the resolution levels, which leads to *uniform* or *global* shrinkage (see Figures 4.6 and 4.7).

Similarly as in Section 4.4.2, for all $p \in [1, 2)$, define

$$\sigma_j = \left(\frac{2\mu_j}{\lambda}\right)^{\frac{1}{2-p}},$$

and the hard truncation estimator

$$\hat{d}_{j,k} = T_{\sigma_j}(d^0_{j,k}) = d^0_{j,k} H(|d^0_{j,k}| - \sigma_j) \quad \forall j \geq -1, k \in \mathbb{Z},$$

where $H = H(t)$ denotes the Heaviside 0-1 function. Then

$$\hat{u} = W^{-1}(\hat{d}_{j,k} \mid j \geq -1, k \in \mathbb{Z}), \quad \text{the inverse wavelet transform},$$

is near-optimal for the cost function $E[u|u_0]$ in (4.41). That is,

$$E[\hat{u}|u_0] \leq (4 \vee 2^p) \, \text{min } E[u|u_0].$$

The proof is straightforward according to (4.29).

Thus the variational estimation theory for Besov images with Gaussian noises provides the most ideal environment for understanding wavelet denoising schemes based on the (soft) shrinkage and (hard) truncation mechanisms. We refer the reader to [55, 101] for further details.

4.5 Variational Denoising Based on BV Image Model

4.5.1 TV, Robust Statistics, and Median

TV is a powerful notion in robust statistics and robust signal estimation [153, 177]. Consider a set of independent observations $\{x_1, x_2, \ldots, x_N\}$ generated from a hidden but fixed scalar x (due to noise or random perturbations). If one considers the mean squared estimation error function

$$e_2(x) = \frac{1}{N} \sum_{k=1}^{N} (x - x_k)^2,$$

the best estimator $\hat{x}^{(2)} = \operatorname{argmin} e_2(x)$ is precisely the mean of the samples

$$\hat{x}^{(2)} = \langle x. \rangle = \frac{1}{N} \sum_{k=1}^{N} x_k.$$

If the hidden noise process is Gaussian, the mean squared error is then appropriate and the mean is precisely the ML estimator.

But if the probability distribution of perturbations does not penalize large deviations as harshly as the Gaussian, then any spontaneous large deviation can destroy the robustness of the mean estimator. For instance, suppose for a set of 10 observations, the mean estimator is $\langle x. \rangle = 10$. Now suppose another experimenter obtains a very similar set of 10 observations: all data are identical except for the last datum x_{10} which is increased by 100 (say, due to some unexpected erratic behavior of the measurement instrument at that particular moment). Then the least square estimator undergoes a substantial change from 10 to 20. In this sense, the mean is not a robust estimator—any erratic change of a small fraction of the data set can cause a major change in the estimator, and thus ruin the values of the majority.

A slight modification of the estimation error $e_2(x)$ can substantially improve robustness. Define the TV error to be

$$e_1(x) = \sum_{k=1}^{N} |x - x_k|.$$

Then the associated optimal estimator is precisely the median of the samples:

$$\hat{x}^{(1)} = \operatorname{median}\{x.\} = x_{(N/2)}.$$

Recall that the order statistics are the monotonically sorted data:

$$x_{(1)} \le x_{(2)} \le \cdots \le x_{(N)}.$$

(If N is odd, $N/2$ is understood as the nearest integer(s).) Figure 4.8 shows the difference between the median and mean processors.

For the scenario just discussed above, the change in the optimal estimator is bounded by the mutual spacing of the majority, and is thus insensitive to any single trouble maker.

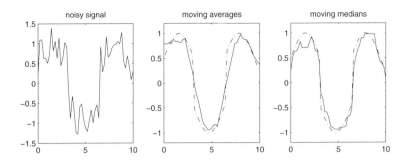

Figure 4.8. *Denoising effects of moving means vs. moving medians. Both employ the same symmetric (moving) window of four neighbors on either side. As expected, the median filter preserves sharp edges better than the mean filter. (The dashed curve denotes the ideal clean signal.)*

4.5.2 The Role of TV and BV Image Model

The TV denoising model was first introduced by Rudin and Osher [257] and Rudin, Osher, and Fatemi [258] in 1992. Ever since, there have been numerous works and extensions based upon the TV denoising and restoration model [1, 16, 56, 60, 62, 66, 71, 67, 104, 276, 275, 198, 302, 301, 308, 309]. The BV image model and the associated TV Radon measure can conveniently handle the most fundamental class of visual features in 2-D images—edges.

Already highlighted several times, edges are respected in many well-known works on image analysis and processing. In Geman and Geman's Gibbs fields-based Bayesian image restoration, images are modelled as the mixture of both intensity and edge distributions. In Mumford and Shah's deterministic segmentation model [226], edges are again singled out explicitly and impose the most challenging role in terms of both theory and computation.

The convenience of the BV image model manifests in that it admits edges without having them explicitly singled out. The BV image model in some sense is the ideal deterministic crystallization of Geman and Geman's mixture prior model and is also a weaker form for Mumford and Shah's free boundary image prior. In fact, for the latter case, the viewpoint of weaker formulation turns out to be essential in many works on the existence theory of Mumford–Shah segmentation (e.g., [5, 7, 11, 12, 94, 136]; also see Chapter 7). Thus the BV image model is especially useful in applications where edges are to be respected but not explicitly sought for as an output, e.g., denoising, deblurring, and inpainting.

4.5.3 Biased Iterated Median Filtering

To motivate Rudin, Osher, and Fatemi's TV denoising model [258], we first introduce the biased iterated median filtering procedure, whose convergent solutions naturally connect to the TV denoising model.

Consider a 1-D discretized image signal on [0, 1]:

$$x[k]: \quad k = 0, 1, \ldots, N,$$

assumed to be the pointwise samples of a continuous signal $x(t)$: $x[k] = x(k/N)$. Suppose the signal has been polluted by white noise $n[k]$ with variance σ^2:

$$x_0[k] = x[k] + n[k].$$

Starting with an initial guess $x^{(0)}$, we perform an iterated estimation process based on localized and biased (by the given observation x_0) median filtering. At any pixel k, define the localized and biased TV estimation error to be as follows: for $k = 1 : N - 1$,

$$e_\lambda(z \mid x^{(n)}[k-1], x^{(n)}[k+1]; x_0[k]) = |z - x^{(n)}[k-1]| + |z - x^{(n)}[k+1]| + \lambda|z - x_0[k]|,$$

where λ is the bias toward the observed noisy signal. For the two boundary nodes $k = 0$ and N, the same definition holds by dropping off nonexisting terms (i.e., $x^{(n)}[-1]$ and $x^{(n)}[N + 1]$).

We then define the updated estimator to be

$$x^{(n+1)}[k] = \operatorname*{argmin}_z\ e_\lambda(z \mid x^{(n)}[k-1], x^{(n)}[k+1]; x_0[k]) \quad \text{for } k = 0 : N. \qquad (4.43)$$

Notice that when $\lambda = 1$,

$$x^{(n+1)}[k] = \operatorname{median}(x^{(n)}[k-1], x^{(n)}[k+1], x_0[k]),$$

as discussed in the first subsection. The iteration from $x^{(n)}$ to $x^{(n+1)}$ is therefore called the biased median filtering.

For $z = z[k]$, $k = 0 : N$, define the overall cost function to be

$$\tilde{E}_\lambda[z \mid x^{(n)}; x_0] = \sum_{k=0}^{N} e_\lambda(z[k] \mid x^{(n)}[k-1], x^{(n)}[k+1]; x_0[k]), \qquad (4.44)$$

which is decoupled in terms of the components of z. Therefore,

$$x^{(n+1)} = \operatorname{argmin}\ \tilde{E}_\lambda[z \mid x^{(n)}; x_0] \quad \forall n = 0, 1, \ldots. \qquad (4.45)$$

Theorem 4.13. *If the above iterated filtering process converges, say,*

$$\lim_{n \to \infty} x^{(n)}[k] = \hat{x}[k], \quad k = 0 : N,$$

the limit $\hat{x}$ must be the critical point of the cost function

$$E_\lambda[z|x_0] = \sum_{k=0}^{N-1} |z[k+1] - z[k]| + \lambda \sum_{k=0}^{N} |z[k] - x_0[k]|. \qquad (4.46)$$

We must point out that as $n \to \infty$, $\tilde{E}_\lambda[z|x^{(n)}; x_0]$ converges to $\tilde{E}_\lambda[z|z; x_0]$, which is, however, not $E_\lambda[z|x_0]$ in the theorem since

$$\tilde{E}_\lambda[z|z; x_0] = \sum_{k=0}^{N} e_\lambda(z[k] \mid z[k-1], z[k+1]; x_0[k])$$

$$= 2 \sum_{k=0}^{N-1} |z[k+1] - z[k]| + \lambda \sum_{k=0}^{N} |z[k] - x_0[k]|.$$

Notice that the factor 2 comes from the double counting of $|z[k+1] - z[k]|$ at both k and $k+1$.

Proof. From the definition of the filtering process (4.43), the limit estimation $\hat{x}$ satisfies

$$\hat{x}[k] = \underset{t}{\text{argmin}} \ e_\lambda(t \mid \hat{x}[k+1], \hat{x}[k-1]; x_0[k]) \quad \forall k,$$

which shares the same equation of critical point x_c as E_λ (for the corresponding component). That is, for any k,

$$0 = \frac{de_\lambda}{dt}(t = x_c[k] \mid x_c[k+1], x_c[k-1]; x_0[k]) = \frac{\partial E_\lambda}{\partial z[k]}(z = x_c \mid x_0). \quad \square$$

Notice the flavor of Gibbs/Markov random fields in the above presentation [130], if the cost functions are interpreted as the energy functions in Gibbs' distributions.

4.5.4 Rudin, Osher, and Fatemi's TV Denoising Model

Properly scaling the bias parameter λ according to the discretization space $h = 1/N$, and passing N to ∞, the error function $E_\lambda[z \mid x_0]$ in (4.46) converges to

$$E_\lambda[z(t) \mid x_0(t)] = \int_0^1 |z'(t)| dt + \lambda \int_0^1 |z(t) - x_0(t)| dt.$$

Or more generally,

$$E_{\lambda, p}[z \mid x_0] = \int_0^1 |z'(t)| dt + \lambda \int_0^1 |z(t) - x_0(t)|^p dt,$$

for some $p \geq 1$. On the other hand, if the noise $n(t)$ is known to be additive and Gaussian with variance σ^2, then both the maximum likelihood (ML) and the maximum a posteriori probability (MAP) estimation suggest to take $p = 2$ and take λ to be inversely proportional to the variance. The associated denoising estimator is taken to be the minimizer:

$$\hat{x}_{\lambda, p} = \underset{z}{\text{argmin}} \ E_{\lambda, p}[z \mid x_0].$$

The important feature about the last model is that the discrete median filtering mechanism has been implicitly built in because of the TV seminorm:

$$\text{TV}[z] = \int_0^1 |z'(t)| dt.$$

For 2-D noisy images $u_0(x)$ on a square domain $x = (x_1, x_2) \in \Omega$ with additive Gaussian white noise, the last model is precisely Rudin, Osher, and Fatemi's TV denoising model:

$$E_{\text{tv}}[u \mid u_0] = \int_\Omega |\nabla u| dx + \frac{\lambda}{2} \int_\Omega (u_0(x) - u(x))^2 dx, \quad (4.47)$$

where the factor 2 has been incorporated for computational convenience. The minimizer of E_{tv} may not be attainable if u is restricted in the Sobolev space $W^{1,1}(\Omega)$. The existence theory goes smoothly, however, if one extends the admissible space to a larger and more convenient one, the space of functions with BV, and rigorously writes the energy in terms of the TV Radon measure (see Section 2.2):

$$E_{tv}[u \mid u_0] = \int_\Omega |Du| + \frac{\lambda}{2} \int_\Omega (u_0(x) - u(x))^2 dx. \tag{4.48}$$

Theorem 4.14 (Existence and Uniqueness of TV Denoising). *Assume that the noisy image sample $u_0 \in L^2(\Omega)$. Then the minimizer $\hat{u}$ of E_{tv} in $BV(\Omega)$ exists and is unique.*

Proof. Uniqueness follows directly from the strict convexity of E_{tv}. (Notice that the TV measure is not strictly convex but the squared fitting error is.) Existence easily comes from the following three facts: (a) E_{tv} is finite for at least one BV image u, e.g., $u(x) \equiv \langle u_0 \rangle$; (b) a sequence of images in $BV(\Omega)$ with bounded E_{tv} values must be bounded as well in $BV(\Omega)$ (i.e., in terms of the BV norm); (c) $BV(\Omega)$ is compactly embedded in $L^1(\Omega)$, and both the L^2 norm and the TV Radon measure are lower semicontinuous with respect to the $L^1(\Omega)$ topology. We refer the reader to, e.g., [1, 16, 56, 137], or Chapter 2, for more details. $\square$

The parameter λ balances the TV regularization term and the fitting term. By the Gaussian rationale, it is clear that λ should be inversely proportional to the variance of the noise. Ideally, its optimal value should be estimated as well, as done in [167] for example. In most practical applications, it often serves as a tunable parameter to balance the fidelity of the restored image features and the suppression of oscillatory image noises. We refer the reader to Vogel's book for more discussion on this issue [310].

4.5.5   Computational Approaches to TV Denoising

In this section, we discuss various computational aspects of Rudin, Osher, and Fatemi's TV denoising model [1, 16, 56, 62, 63, 105, 258]: its formal Euler–Lagrange equations, numerical regularization and conditioning techniques, the lagged diffusivity fixed-point algorithm, and its simple digital implementation on Cartesian grids. In the next section, we shall also discuss the dual method for TV denoising. Interested readers are also referred to the recent excellent monograph by Vogel [310] on TV related computation.

The Euler–Lagrange Equations

Computationally the TV denoising model (4.48) is usually solved via its formal Euler–Lagrange equations. Assume that u belongs to the more regular Sobolev space $W^{1,1}(\Omega)$. Then the first variation, $E_{tv} \rightarrow E_{tv} + \delta E_{tv}$, under $u \rightarrow u + \delta u$ is given by (see (2.14))

$$\delta E_{tv} = -\int_\Omega \nabla \cdot \left[\frac{\nabla u}{|\nabla u|} \right] \delta u dx + \lambda \int_\Omega (u - u_0) \delta u dx + \int_{\partial\Omega} \frac{1}{|\nabla u|} \frac{\partial u}{\partial \boldsymbol{n}} \delta u \, d\mathcal{H}^1, \tag{4.49}$$

where $\boldsymbol{n}$ denotes the outer normal along the boundary $\partial\Omega$, and $d\mathcal{H}^1$ is the 1-D Hausdorff measure supported on $\partial\Omega$. In addition, the divergence in the first term is understood in the

original image

noisy image u$_0$

TV denoising u

residual image v=u$_0$−u

Figure 4.9. *An example of Rudin, Osher, and Fatemi's TV denoising.*

distributional sense. Therefore, if the unique minimizer is C^1 or $W^{1,1}$, it must satisfy the Euler–Lagrange equation

$$0 = -\nabla \cdot \left[\frac{\nabla u}{|\nabla u|}\right] + \lambda(u - u_0) \quad \text{with} \quad \left.\frac{\partial u}{\partial \boldsymbol{n}}\right|_{\partial\Omega} = 0 \qquad (4.50)$$

in the distributional sense.

Alternatively as in Rudin, Osher, and Fatemi [258], one could also adopt the steepest descent marching with artificial time t:

$$u_t(x, t) = -\frac{\partial E_{\text{tv}}}{\partial u} = \nabla \cdot \left[\frac{\nabla u}{|\nabla u|}\right] - \lambda(u(x, t) - u_0(x)), \qquad (4.51)$$

with the same Neumann boundary condition along $\partial\Omega$, and some suitable initial guess $u(x, 0)$ (e.g., $u(x, 0) = u_0(x)$). Figure 4.9 shows the performance of TV denoising on a test image.

The nonlinear Euler–Lagrange equations (4.50) and (4.51) are both of elliptic type but degenerate due to the gradient term in the denominators. Consider the gradient descent marching equation for example, where the diffusivity coefficient D is given by $D = |\nabla u|^{-1}$.

1. In homogeneous regions where $u \simeq 0$, D is unbounded from above and the diffusion could go infinitely strong.

2. Near edges where ∇u behaves like a Dirac beam distribution (e.g., canonical Dirac beam along the x_2-direction: $g(x_2)\delta(x_1)$ for some function g), the diffusivity coefficient vanishes and diffusion activity dies out.

For image processing, these slow and fast diffusion mechanisms are necessary and advantageous for edge adaptive smoothing techniques.

Computational Regularization Techniques

There are many ways to overcome such degeneracy (e.g., [1, 56, 129, 209]). From the computational point of view, Marquina and Osher [209] proposed to tame the direct steepest descent marching (4.51) by the factor $|\nabla u|$, leading to the new nonlinear evolutionary equation

$$u_t = |\nabla u|\, \nabla \cdot \left[\frac{\nabla u}{|\nabla u|}\right] - \lambda |\nabla u|(u - u_0), \tag{4.52}$$

still with the Neumann boundary condition. It is easy to see that smooth and homogeneous regions now cause no problem at all due to the cancellation of the gradients. This simple conditioning technique works surprisingly well computationally [209].

The second common conditioning technique connects TV denoising to the minimum surface problem. Instead of $D = |\nabla u|^{-1}$ being the diffusivity coefficient, one now replaces it by

$$D_* = |\nabla u|_a^{-1}, \quad \text{with} \quad |x|_a := \sqrt{x^2 + a^2}, \tag{4.53}$$

for some small conditioning parameter $a > 0$. Thus the equilibrium equation (4.50) is now conditioned to

$$0 = -\nabla \cdot \left[\frac{\nabla u}{|\nabla u|_a}\right] + \lambda(u - u_0), \quad \text{with} \quad \frac{\partial u}{\partial \boldsymbol{n}}\Big|_{\partial\Omega} = 0, \tag{4.54}$$

which is precisely the equilibrium Euler–Lagrange equation to the modified cost function

$$E_*[u \mid u_0] = \int_\Omega |\nabla u|_a dx + \frac{\lambda}{2}\int_\Omega (u_0(x) - u(x))^2 dx. \tag{4.55}$$

Notice that if one goes to one extra dimension higher,

$$x = (x_1, x_2) \to \tilde{x} = (x, z) = (x_1, x_2, z), \quad z \in (0, 1),$$

and defines $\tilde{\Omega} = \Omega \times (0, 1)$, and

$$\tilde{u}(\tilde{x}) = az - u(x) \quad \text{and} \quad \tilde{u}_0(\tilde{x}) = az - u_0(x),$$

then the conditioned energy E_* is precisely

$$\tilde{E}[\tilde{u} \mid \tilde{u}_0] = \int_{\tilde{\Omega}} |\nabla \tilde{u}| d\tilde{x} + \frac{\lambda}{2}\int_{\tilde{\Omega}} (\tilde{u}_0 - \tilde{u})^2 d\tilde{x},$$

which is a 3-D version of E_{tv}! If $\tilde{u}$ is understood as a configuration variable (e.g., orientation in liquid crystals [114]) and $a \ll 1$, then the new energy $\tilde{E}$ resembles a *thin-film* model (on the thin film $\Omega \times (0, a)$), and $\tilde{u}_0$ is a layered external potential [19].

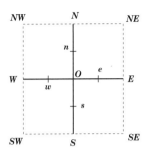

Figure 4.10. *A target pixel O and its neighbors.*

On the other hand, if one considers the parametric surface on Ω defined by

$$0 = az - u(x) \ \text{ or } \ z = \frac{1}{a}u(x_1, x_2),$$

the conditioned energy E_*, (4.55), then becomes a *biased* (by the fitting term involving u_0) *minimum surface model* with λ also properly scaled by a [137, 233].

Digital Implementation via Lagged Diffusivity Fixed-Point Iteration

We now detail explicitly the numerical scheme for implementing the TV denoising model on Cartesian grids, which is based on simple finite difference schemes and the lagged diffusivity fixed-point iteration [1, 56] for the Euler–Lagrange equation (4.50):

$$0 = -\nabla \cdot \left[\frac{\nabla u}{|\nabla u|}\right] + \lambda(u - u_0) \ \text{ with } \ \left.\frac{\partial u}{\partial \boldsymbol{n}}\right|_{\partial\Omega} = 0.$$

The lagged (diffusivity) fixed-point iteration method [1, 56, 62] linearizes the above nonlinear equation at each iteration $u^{(n)} \to v = u^{(n+1)}$:

$$0 = -\nabla \cdot \left(D^{(n)} \nabla v\right) + \lambda(v - u_0) \ \text{ with } \ \left.\frac{\partial v}{\partial \boldsymbol{n}}\right|_{\partial\Omega} = 0,$$

where the diffusivity coefficient $D^{(n)} = 1/|\nabla u^{(n)}|$ is frozen or lagged for the current step. It amounts to the optimization of the following quadratic energy:

$$E[v \mid u^{(n)}, u_0] = \frac{1}{2}\int_\Omega D^{(n)}|\nabla v|^2 dx + \frac{\lambda}{2}\int_\Omega (v - u_0)^2 dx.$$

The convergence analysis of the algorithm can be found in, e.g., [1, 56, 62]. Below we further detail its pixelwise implementation.

As in Figure 4.10, at a given target pixel O, let E, N, W, S denote its four adjacent pixels and e, n, w, s the corresponding four midway points (not directly available from the digital image). Write the neighborhood

$$\Lambda_O = \{E, N, W, S\}.$$

Let $\boldsymbol{v} = (v^1, v^2) = \nabla u / |\nabla u|$. Then the divergence is first discretized by central differencing:

$$\nabla \cdot \boldsymbol{v} = \frac{\partial v^1}{\partial x} + \frac{\partial v^2}{\partial y} \tag{4.56}$$

$$\simeq \frac{v_e^1 - v_w^1}{h} + \frac{v_n^2 - v_s^2}{h}, \tag{4.57}$$

where h denotes the grid size, which is always taken to be 1 in image processing. Next, we generate further approximations at the midway points, where image information is not directly available. Take the midpoint e for example,

$$v_e^1 = \frac{1}{|\nabla u_e|} \left[\frac{\partial u}{\partial x} \right]_e \simeq \frac{1}{|\nabla u_e|} \frac{u_E - u_O}{h}, \tag{4.58}$$

$$|\nabla u_e| \simeq \frac{1}{h} \sqrt{(u_E - u_O)^2 + [(u_{NE} + u_N - u_S - u_{SE})/4]^2}. \tag{4.59}$$

Namely, we approximate $[\partial u / \partial x]_e$ by the central difference scheme and $[\partial u / \partial y]_e$ by the average of $(u_{NE} - u_{SE})/2h$ and $(u_N - u_S)/2h$. Similar discussion applies to the other three directions N, W, and S.

Therefore, at a pixel O the Euler–Lagrange equation (4.50) is discretized to

$$0 = \sum_{P \in \Lambda_O} \frac{1}{|\nabla u_p|} (u_O - u_P) + \lambda \left(u_O - u_O^0 \right), \tag{4.60}$$

where, for example, if $P = E$, then p denotes e. Define

$$w_P = \frac{1}{|\nabla u_p|}, \qquad P \in \Lambda_O, \tag{4.61}$$

$$h_{OP} = \frac{w_P}{\sum_{Q \in \Lambda_O} w_Q + \lambda}, \tag{4.62}$$

$$h_{OO} = \frac{\lambda}{\sum_{Q \in \Lambda_O} w_Q + \lambda}. \tag{4.63}$$

Then (4.60) becomes

$$u_O = \sum_{P \in \Lambda_O} h_{OP} u_P + h_{OO} u_O^0, \tag{4.64}$$

with

$$\sum_{P \in \Lambda_O} h_{OP} + h_{OO} = 1.$$

Equation (4.64) is in the form of a *lowpass* filter, which is of course in reality a system of nonlinear equations since the filter coefficients all depend on u.

Inspired by the lagged diffusivity fixed-point iteration algorithm stated in the beginning, in combination with the Gauss–Jacobi iteration scheme for linear systems [138, 289], one can iteratively update $u^{(n)}$ to $u^{(n+1)}$ by

$$u_O^{(n+1)} = \sum_{P \in \Lambda_O} h_{OP}^{(n)} u_P^{(n)} + h_{OO}^{(n)} u_O^{(n)}, \tag{4.65}$$

where $h^{(n)} = h(u^{(n)})$. Since h is a lowpass filter, the iterative algorithm is stable and satisfies the *maximum principle* [63, 117]. In particular, the gray value range [0, 1] is always preserved during the iterating process. Moreover, due to the locality nature of (4.65), the scheme can be easily implemented in parallel computers. A more self-contained digital version of the scheme can be found in the works of Chan, Osher, and Shen [63] and Osher and Shen [242], where even more general graph domains other than Cartesian grids are also allowed.

Useful variations of the scheme can be obtained by altering the definition w_P or $|\nabla u_p|$ in (4.61). For instance, instead of (4.59), one could also try

$$|\nabla u_e| \simeq \frac{1}{h}\sqrt{(u_E - u_O)^2 + [(u_{NE} - u_{SE})/2]^2}.$$

Moreover, as discussed in the preceding subsection, the weights w_P's are also "lifted" to

$$w_P = \frac{1}{|\nabla u_p|_a} = \frac{1}{\sqrt{a^2 + |\nabla u_p|^2}} \tag{4.66}$$

for some small scalar $a > 0$ to regularize the denominators in smooth regions.

More computational techniques for nonlinear diffusion equations in image processing can be found in, e.g., [317, 318].

4.5.6 Duality for the TV Denoising Model

The discussions so far, based on the minimization of E_{tv} in (4.48), can be viewed as the *primal* approach to solving the TV denoising problem. In this approach, the independent variable u in (4.48) is the *primal* variable of both the optimization problem and the associated Euler–Lagrange equation. In this section, we shall discuss briefly the *dual* formulation of the optimization problem. While the dual formulation is not as well developed as the primal one, it does have some inherent advantages and has been receiving increasing interest recently. It offers an alternative formulation which can lead to effective computational algorithms, in addition to those discussed in the preceding section.

Following [45], we now derive the dual formulation of the primal problem

$$\min_u \int_\Omega |Du| + \frac{\lambda}{2} \int_\Omega (u_0 - u)^2 dx.$$

Writing the TV term using the definition in (2.19), we have

$$\min_u \left(\sup_{g \in C_c^1(\Omega, B^2)} \int_\Omega u \nabla \cdot g\, dx \right) + \frac{\lambda}{2} \int_\Omega (u_0 - u)^2 dx,$$

where B^2 denotes the unit disk in $\mathbb{R}^2$. Since the second term does not involve g, it can be regrouped as

$$\min_u \sup_{g \in C_c^1(\Omega, B^2)} \left(\int_\Omega u \nabla \cdot g\, dx + \frac{\lambda}{2} \int_\Omega (u_0 - u)^2 dx \right).$$

Formally exchanging the min and the sup (see the general theory on convex optimization, e.g., [32]), we have

$$\sup_{g \in C_c^1(\Omega, B^2)} \min_u \left(\int_\Omega u \, \nabla \cdot g \, dx + \frac{\lambda}{2} \int_\Omega (u_0 - u)^2 dx \right). \tag{4.67}$$

Now the "min" problem in u is quadratic and can be easily solved by setting the gradient of the "min" objective function to zero, yielding

$$u = u_0 - \lambda^{-1} \nabla \cdot g. \tag{4.68}$$

Substituting this back into (4.67), we get the dual formulation

$$\sup_{g \in C_c^1(\Omega, B^2)} \int_\Omega u_0 \, \nabla \cdot g \, dx - (2\lambda)^{-1} \int_\Omega (\nabla \cdot g)^2 dx. \tag{4.69}$$

In principle, once g is known, (4.68) gives the solution for the primal variable u.

Note that the objective function in (4.69) is smooth and differentiable in g, unlike for the primal formulation, where the objective function is not differentiable when $\nabla u = 0$. This is one of the main advantages of the dual formulation over the primal. On the other hand, the dual formulation is a constrained optimization problem, and the constraints require special attention to deal with in a solution procedure. Thus, one can view the tradeoff between the primal and dual formulations as exchanging an unconstrained nondifferentiable optimization problem for a constrained quadratic one.

The derivation of the dual problem can be generalized to cases where the fidelity term is not just the least squares error but a general function of u:

$$\min_u \int_\Omega |Du| + \lambda \int_\Omega F(u) dx.$$

Such situations arise when one uses a different norm (e.g., L^1) or when one models textures using the Meyer decomposition [216, 309]. In this general setting, one can use the techniques of subgradients and convex conjugates to derive the dual formulation (see [54]).

The dual formulation can be used to derive efficient computational algorithms for the TV denoising problem. Following Chambolle [54], we can take the Lagrangian $L[g, \mu]$ of the dual problem (4.69) with the Lagrange multiplier (function) $\mu = \mu(x)$:

$$L[g, \mu] = \int_\Omega \left(u_0 \nabla \cdot g - (2\lambda)^{-1}(\nabla \cdot g)^2 + \frac{\mu}{2}(1 - g^2) \right) dx.$$

Setting the gradient of L with respect to g to zero, we get the necessary condition for optimality:

$$-\nabla \left(u_0 - \lambda^{-1} \nabla \cdot g \right) - \mu g = 0. \tag{4.70}$$

The complementary condition of the Lagrange multiplier implies that if $|g| = 1$ at the optimum, then $\mu > 0$, whereas if $|g| < 1$, then $\mu = 0$. Now the key observation is that, in any case, we have

$$\mu = |H(g)|,$$

where $H(g) = -\nabla(u_0 - \lambda^{-1}\nabla \cdot g)$. Thus (4.70) can be written as

$$H(g) - |H(g)|g = 0.$$

This is a nonlinear equation in g which can be solved in many ways. Chambolle [54] used the following implicit artificial time marching scheme (i.e., steepest ascent for $L[g, \mu]$):

$$g^{(n+1)} = g^{(n)} + dt\left(H(g^{(n)}) - |H(g^{(n)})|g^{(n+1)}\right),$$

which leads to the updating scheme:

$$g^{(n+1)} = \frac{g^{(n)} + dt\,H(g^{(n)})}{1 + dt\,|H(g^{(n)})|}.$$

Another approach to exploit the dual variable g in deriving efficient computational algorithm is to use both u and g simultaneously (the primal-dual method). We shall describe the approach used in [58]. This approach starts directly from the Euler–Lagrange equation (4.50) and uses a regularization of the $|\nabla u|$ term in the denominator (as in the preceding section):

$$-\nabla\left[\frac{\nabla u}{|\nabla u|_a}\right] + \lambda(u - u_0) = 0. \tag{4.71}$$

Now define a new variable:

$$w = \frac{\nabla u}{|\nabla u|_a}. \tag{4.72}$$

Note that if $\nabla u \neq 0$ at the optimum, then $|w| \to 1$ as $a \to 0$, and hence w can be viewed as a regularized version of the dual variable g. Now we rewrite (4.71) and (4.72) as a system of nonlinear equations in (u, w):

$$-\nabla \cdot w + \lambda(u - u_0) = 0 \quad \text{and} \quad w|\nabla u|_a - \nabla u = 0, \tag{4.73}$$

for which we can proceed by applying Newton's method to derive an iterative method. A further simplification can be obtained by eliminating the updates for w in the iteration in the resulting linear Newton's equation, resulting in the need for solving only a linear equation for the update of u in each Newton iteration, at a cost approximately equal to each step of the fixed-point method discussed in the preceding section. Empirically, this primal-dual method is much more robust than applying Newton's method directly to the primal problem in u only. In practice, the convergence behavior is very robust and quadratic convergence is almost always achieved, requiring only a few iterations for reasonable tolerances. For further details, we refer the reader to [58].

4.5.7   Solution Structures of the TV Denoising Model

In this section, we briefly discuss some interesting analytical results regarding the solution structures of the TV denoising model of Rudin, Osher, and Fatemi [258],

$$\hat{u} = \underset{u}{\arg\min} \int_\Omega |Du| + \lambda \int_\Omega (u - f)^2 dx, \tag{4.74}$$

given an image f. More details can be read in Strong and Chan [293], Bellettini, Caselles, and Novaga [20], and Meyer [216]. In particular, the development below very much follows Meyer's remarkable lecture notes [216], with some slight modification to fit the flow of the present book.

In [216], Meyer models the image observation f as an element in the space of

$$G = \mathrm{div}(L^\infty(\Omega, \mathbb{R}^2)); \tag{4.75}$$

i.e., there exists some $\boldsymbol{g}(x) = (g_1(x), g_2(x))$ such that in the distributional sense,

$$f = \nabla \cdot \boldsymbol{g} = \partial_1 g_1 + \partial_2 g_2 \ \text{ and } \ \|\boldsymbol{g}\|_\infty = \sup_{x \in \Omega} \sqrt{g_1^2 + g_2^2} < \infty.$$

By distributional sense, we mean that for any smooth test function ϕ that is compactly supported in Ω,

$$\langle f , \phi \rangle = -\langle \boldsymbol{g} , \nabla\phi \rangle = -\int_\Omega \boldsymbol{g} \cdot \nabla\phi dx.$$

Following Meyer's notation, such an image f shall be conveniently called a G-image later. For each G-image f, define all its *generative* flows by

$$G_f = \{\boldsymbol{g} \in L^\infty(\Omega, \mathbb{R}^2) \mid \nabla \cdot \boldsymbol{g} = f\}. \tag{4.76}$$

Theorem 4.15. *Let f be a G-image. Then G_f is an infinite-dimensional affine space.*

Proof. Suppose $f = \nabla \cdot \boldsymbol{g}_0$. Then $G_f = \boldsymbol{g}_0 + G_0$ with

$$G_0 = \{\boldsymbol{g} \in L^\infty(\Omega, \mathbb{R}^2) \mid \nabla \cdot \boldsymbol{g} = 0\},$$

i.e., all divergence-free (in the distributional sense) bounded vector fields. It is evident that G_0 is a linear space, and thus G_f is affine. In two dimensions,

$$G_0 \supseteq \left(\mathrm{grad}(W^{1,\infty}(\Omega))\right)^\perp = \{(\nabla\psi)^\perp \mid \psi \in W^{1,\infty}(\Omega)\},$$

where $\perp$ denotes the counterclockwise 90-degree planar rotation and $W^{1,\infty}$ the Sobolev space of all Lebesgue measurable functions with bounded first order distributional derivatives. Thus G_0 and G_f must be infinite-dimensional.   □

Definition 4.16 (Meyer's G-Norm $\|\cdot\|_*$). *Let f be a given G-image. Define the G-norm $\|f\|_*$ by*

$$\|f\|_* = \inf_{\boldsymbol{g} \in G_f} \|\boldsymbol{g}\|_\infty. \tag{4.77}$$

Theorem 4.17 (Realizability of the G-Norm). *If f is a G-image, there exists some $\boldsymbol{g} \in G_f$ such that*

$$\|f\|_* = \|\boldsymbol{g}\|_\infty.$$

Proof. Suppose $g_n \in G_f$, such that

$$\|g_n\|_\infty \to \|f\|_*, \quad n \to \infty.$$

Then (g_n) is a bounded sequence in $L^\infty(\Omega, \mathbb{R}^2)$, which is the dual space of the separable Banach space $L^1(\Omega, \mathbb{R}^2)$. Thus there exists a subsequence, for convenience still denoted by (g_n), such that

$$g_n \xrightarrow{w^*} g \in L^\infty(\Omega, \mathbb{R}^2).$$

Here the weak-star topology w^* refers to the following: for any $h \in L^1(\Omega, \mathbb{R}^2)$, $\langle g_n , h \rangle \to \langle g , h \rangle$ when $n \to \infty$. Lower semicontinuity of a dual norm under weak-star convergence implies

$$\|g\|_\infty \leq \liminf_{n \to \infty} \|g_n\|_\infty = \|f\|_*,$$

and continuity of distributional derivatives under weak-star convergence implies

$$f \equiv \nabla \cdot g_n \to \nabla \cdot g \quad \text{in the distributional sense.}$$

In combination, $g \in G_f$ and $\|g\|_\infty = \|f\|_*$. $\square$

Theorem 4.18 (Completeness of $(G, \| \cdot \|_*)$). *The collection of all G-images is a Banach space under the G-norm $\| \cdot \|_*$.*

Proof. First, it is easy to verify that the G-norm is indeed a norm since

$$G_{\lambda f} = \lambda G_f \quad \text{and} \quad G_{f_1 + f_2} \supseteq G_{f_1} + G_{f_2},$$

as well as that $\|f\|_* = 0$ implies $\|g\|_\infty = 0$ from the preceding theorem.

Let (f_n) be any given Cauchy sequence in $(G, \| \cdot \|_*)$. To prove the Banach property, it suffices to show that there exist some $f \in G$ and a subsequence (f_{n_k}), such that f_{n_k} converges to f in the G-norm. Suppose $g_n \in G_{f_n}$ such that $\|g_n\|_\infty = \|f_n\|_*$ for each n. Then (g_n) is bounded in $L^\infty(\Omega, \mathbb{R}^2)$. By the weak-star compactness of a bounded sequence in a dual space, there exist a subsequence (g_{n_k}) and some $g \in L^\infty(\Omega, \mathbb{R}^2)$, such that

$$g_{n_k} \xrightarrow{w^*} g \quad \text{as } k \to \infty.$$

Let $f = \nabla \cdot g$. Then $f_{n_k} \to f$ as $k \to \infty$ in the distributional sense. It now remains to show that $\|f_{n_k} - f\|_* \to 0$ as $k \to \infty$.

Fixing k, for each $l \geq k$ let $g_{l,k}$ denote the element such that

$$\nabla \cdot g_{l,k} = f_{n_l} - f_{n_k} \quad \text{and} \quad \|g_{l,k}\|_\infty = \|f_{n_l} - f_{n_k}\|_* = \varepsilon_{l,k}.$$

Notice that $\varepsilon_{l,k} \to 0$ as $l \geq k \to \infty$ since (f_n) is a Cauchy sequence. Define $g_{l|k} = g_{n_k} + g_{l,k}$. Then

$$\nabla \cdot g_{l|k} = f_{n_k} + (f_{n_l} - f_{n_k}) = f_{n_l}, \quad l \geq k.$$

For any given k, since $(g_{l|k})_{l \geq k}$ is a bounded sequence in $L^\infty(\Omega, \mathbb{R}^2)$, it has a subsequence, still denoted by $(g_{l|k})_{l \geq k}$ to avoid messy notation, and some $g_{|k}$ such that

$$g_{l|k} \xrightarrow{w^*} g_{|k}, \quad l \to \infty.$$

Then $f_{n_l} \to \nabla \cdot g_{|k}$ in the distributional sense as $l \to \infty$. By the uniqueness of distributional limit, $f = \nabla \cdot g_{|k}$. Therefore,

$$\|f_{n_k} - f\|_* \le \|g_{n_k} - g_{|k}\|_\infty$$

$$\le \liminf_{l \to \infty} \|g_{n_k} - g_{l|k}\|_\infty$$

$$= \liminf_{l \to \infty} \|g_{l,k}\|_\infty$$

$$= \liminf_{l \to \infty} \varepsilon_{l,k},$$

which goes to zero as $k \to \infty$, and the proof is complete. $\square$

Notice that the above proof is purely functional and generally applies to any space G in the form of $G = T(B^*)$, where B is an arbitrary separable Banach space, B^* its dual space, and T a linear operator that is continuous with respect to weak-star convergence in B^*. In our example, T is the divergence operator and $B = L^1(\Omega, \mathbb{R}^2)$.

Theorem 4.19 (Duality Inequality). *Suppose $v \in G \cap L^2(\Omega)$ and $u \in \mathrm{BV}(\Omega)$ with zero trace along $\partial \Omega$. Then*

$$\langle u, v \rangle = \int_\Omega uv dx \le \|v\|_* |Du|(\Omega). \tag{4.78}$$

Proof. The inequality holds by mere definition when $u = \phi$ is a test function. It thus must hold for all Sobolev functions $u \in W_0^{1,1}(\Omega)$ with zero traces since both sides (of the inequality) are continuous functionals in $W_0^{1,1}$ and test functions are dense. The extension to a general BV image u with zero trace is then achieved by standard mollification procedures (see, e.g., Theorem 2.2 or Giusti [137]). $\square$

Note that when $\Omega = \mathbb{R}^2$, the zero-trace condition in the theorem can be dropped since $\mathrm{BV}(\mathbb{R}^2)$ automatically requires u to (weakly) vanish at infinity, which, as far as the mollification process is concerned, serves the same purpose as the zero-trace condition on bounded regular domains. We now discuss the case when $\Omega = \mathbb{R}^2$. The following two remarkable characterization theorems belong to Meyer [216].

Theorem 4.20 (Underfitting (Meyer [216])). *For the Rudin–Osher–Fatemi model*

$$(\hat{u}, \hat{v}) = \operatorname*{argmin}_{u \in \mathrm{BV}, u+v=f} E[u, v \mid f] = |Du|(\mathbb{R}^2) + \lambda \|v\|_2^2, \tag{4.79}$$

if the fitting parameter λ is too small (i.e., underfitting) so that

$$\lambda \|f\|_* \le \frac{1}{2},$$

the optimal decomposition is then given by $(\hat{u}, \hat{v}) = (0, f)$.

Proof. The key tool is the duality inequality. One has, for any admissible decomposition (u, v) with $f = u + v$,

$$
\begin{aligned}
E[u, v \mid f] &= |Du|(\mathbb{R}^2) + \lambda \|v\|_2^2 \\
&= |Du|(\mathbb{R}^2) + \lambda \|f - u\|_2^2 \\
&= |Du|(\mathbb{R}^2) - 2\lambda \langle f, u \rangle + \lambda \|u\|_2^2 + \lambda \|f\|_2^2 \\
&\geq |Du|(\mathbb{R}^2) - 2\lambda \|f\|_* |Du|(\mathbb{R}^2) + \lambda \|u\|_2^2 + \lambda \|f\|_2^2 \\
&\geq \lambda \|f\|_2^2 = E[0, f \mid f],
\end{aligned}
$$

and the equality holds $E[u, v \mid f] = E[0, f \mid f]$ if and only if $u = 0$. This completes the proof. $\square$

This quantitative result well echoes the qualitative behavior of the model. When the fitting weight λ is too small, it is less expensive to introduce more v-component (traditionally identified as noise) than the smooth u-component (often identified as the feature).

What will happen when the given image observation f gets much rougher, or more specifically, $\|f\|_*$ grows beyond $1/(2\lambda)$? An intuitive answer seems to be that $\|v\|_*$ should grow proportionally since rougher f implies more noise. It is, however, not the case according to Meyer's next remarkable theorem, which in spirit reveals the extraordinary connection to Donoho and Johnstone's thresholding technique introduced in earlier sections.

Theorem 4.21 (Thresholding for Overfitting (Meyer [216])). *Following the preceding theorem, suppose the fitting parameter λ is too large (i.e., overfitting) for a given image observation f so that*

$$
\lambda \|f\|_* \geq \frac{1}{2}.
$$

Then the optimal decomposition pair $(u, v) = (\hat{u}, \hat{v})$ is completely *characterized by the following three properties: $f = u + v$,*

$$
\|v\|_* = \frac{1}{2\lambda}, \quad and \quad \langle u, v \rangle = \|v\|_* |Du|(\mathbb{R}^2). \tag{4.80}
$$

That is, any pair satisfying these three conditions must be the (unique) optimal pair, and vice versa.

Notice that for a given λ, $\|\hat{v}\|_*$ is fixed and does not depend proportionally on $\|f\|_*$, as the intuition would suggest earlier. Thus $1/(2\lambda)$ puts a ceiling on the traditional "noise" component $\hat{v}$, which is the remarkable thresholding phenomenon. We refer the reader to Meyer [216] for the proof and more interesting discussion.

In combination of the preceding two theorems, we thus conclude that for the optimal decomposition pair $(\hat{u}, \hat{v})$,

$$
\|\hat{v}\|_* = \frac{1}{2\lambda} \wedge \|f\|_* = \min\left(\frac{1}{2\lambda}, \|f\|_*\right). \tag{4.81}
$$

The second characterization theorem gives a simple solution to a canonical test problem which has been studied by Strong and Chan [293], Meyer [216], and Bellettini, Caselles, and Novaga [20]. We statc it as a theorem following Meyer.

Theorem 4.22. *Let $r > 0$ be a fixed positive radius and $B_r = B_r(0)$ the open disk centered at the origin with radius r. Let $f = 1_{B_r}(x)$, the indicator function of B_r, be the test image for the Rudin–Osher–Fatemi model. Then the optimal decomposition is given by*

$$\hat{u} = (1 - (\lambda r)^{-1}) 1_{B_r}(x) \quad \text{and} \quad \hat{v} = (\lambda r)^{-1} 1_{B_r}(x) \tag{4.82}$$

if $\lambda r \geq 1$; otherwise, if $\lambda r < 1$,

$$\hat{u} = 0 \quad \text{and} \quad \hat{v} = \hat{f} = 1_{B_r}(x). \tag{4.83}$$

It is remarkable in the first case that despite the offsets in intensity values, the edge location is perfectly preserved, which is crucial in image and vision analysis.

Proof. To prove these two results based on Meyer's two theorems, one needs only the following numerical identity (see Meyer [216]):

$$\|1_{B_r}(x)\|_* = \frac{r}{2}. \tag{4.84}$$

This can be established as follows. First,

$$\text{Area}(B_r) = \int 1_{B_r} dx = \langle 1_{B_r}, 1_{B_r} \rangle \leq \|1_{B_r}\|_* |D 1_{B_r}|(\mathbb{R}^2) = \|1_{B_r}\|_* \text{Per}(B_r),$$

which implies that

$$\|1_{B_r}\|_* \geq \frac{\text{Area}(B_r)}{\text{Per}(B_r)} = \frac{r}{2}. \tag{4.85}$$

For the other direction, construct the continuous vector field

$$\boldsymbol{g} = \frac{x}{2} \left(1_{B_r}(x) - \frac{r^2}{|x|^2} 1_{\mathbb{R}^2 \setminus B_r}(x) \right), \quad x = (x_1, x_2).$$

Then $\nabla \cdot \boldsymbol{g} = 1_{B_r}(x)$, since $\ln|x|$ is harmonic on $\mathbb{R}^2 \setminus \{0\}$ and $\nabla \ln|x| = x/|x|^2$. Therefore,

$$\|1_{B_r}\|_* \leq \|\boldsymbol{g}\|_\infty = \frac{r}{2},$$

which establishes the identity (4.84).

We are now ready to prove (4.82) and (4.83). When $\lambda r < 1$, one has

$$\|f\|_* = \|1_{B_r}\|_* = \frac{r}{2} < \frac{1}{2\lambda}.$$

Thus by Meyer's first theorem, $\hat{u} = 0$ and $\hat{v} = f = 1_{B_r}$, which is (4.83). Similarly, the condition $\lambda r \geq 1$ is equivalent to $\|f\|_* \geq 1/(2\lambda)$, and it then suffices to verify that the pair in (4.82) does satisfy the characterization in Meyer's second theorem. The computation is straightforward and left to the readers. $\square$

When the image domain is finite, $\Omega = B_R = B_R(0)$ for some $R > r$, Strong and Chan established the following theorem.

Theorem 4.23 (Strong and Chan [293]). *If the image domain $\Omega = B_R$ and the test image $f(x) = 1_{B_r}(x)$, with $r < R$, then there exists some λ_*, such that for any fitting parameter $\lambda > \lambda_*$, the optimal pair is given by*

$$\hat{u} = (1 - \delta_1)1_{B_r}(x) + \delta_2 1_{B_R \backslash B_r}(x), \quad \hat{v} = \delta_1 1_{B_r}(x) - \delta_2 1_{B_R \backslash B_r}(x),$$

with $\delta_1 = 1/(\lambda r)$ and $\delta_2 = r/(\lambda(R^2 - r^2))$.

Thus as $R \to \infty$, Strong and Chan's result is consistent with what has just been established for $\Omega = \mathbb{R}^2$. Furthermore, this "noiseless" theorem even holds when limited noises are present [293].

This remarkable property of edge preservation is further generalized by Bellettini, Caselles, and Novaga [20].

Theorem 4.24 (Bellettini, Caselles, and Novaga [20]). *Suppose the image domain $\Omega = \mathbb{R}^2$ is the entire plane, and the test image $f(x) = 1_B(x)$, where B is a convex domain with $C^{1,1}$ boundary. In addition, suppose the boundary curvature satisfies*

$$\text{ess-}\sup_{x \in \partial B} \kappa(x) \leq \frac{\text{Per}(B)}{2\text{Area}(B)}.$$

Then there exists some λ_* such that for all $\lambda > \lambda_*$, the optimal pair is given by

$$\hat{u} = \left(1 - \frac{\text{Per}(B)}{2\lambda \text{Area}(B)}\right) 1_B(x), \quad \hat{v} = f - \hat{u}.$$

As a result, the edge preservation property becomes unguaranteed if the target edge contains *corners* where the curvatures κ's blow up. A well-known example is a square domain for which the TV model unavoidably "chops" off the corners [216].

Rudin, Osher, and Fatemi's TV denoising model has been energy based and variational. Next we discuss another extraordinary denoising machinery which is purely based on PDEs.

4.6 Denoising via Nonlinear Diffusion and Scale-Space Theory

4.6.1 Perona and Malik's Nonlinear Diffusion Model

Linear diffusions or linear scale spaces (see Witkin [322]) in the form of

$$u_t = \nabla \cdot D(x) \nabla u, \quad x \in \Omega, u(x, 0) = \text{noisy image } u_0(x),$$

unavoidably smear sharp edges embedded in u_0 while filtering out noises. To remedy this shortcoming, Perona and Malik in their seminal paper [251] allowed the diffusivity coefficient D to be adapted to the image itself, instead of being prefixed:

$$D = D(x, u, \nabla u).$$

More specifically, a desirable diffusivity coefficient D must qualitatively attain edge selectivity:

$$D = \begin{cases} \text{large,} & \text{when } |\nabla u| \text{ is small on intraregions;} \\ \text{small,} & \text{when } |\nabla u| \text{ is large on interregions or near edges.} \end{cases}$$

That is, qualitatively D must be inversely proportional to $p = |\nabla u|$. As a result, Perona and Malik made the choice of

$$D = g(p^2) = g(|\nabla u|^2), \quad \text{with } g(0^+) = a > 0, \quad g(+\infty) = 0, \quad \text{and } g'(s) \leq 0, \ s > 0, \tag{4.86}$$

where $g = g(s)$ is a smooth function for $s \geq 0$. With a proper scaling of diffusion time t, one could for simplicity assume that $a = 1$.

For instance, Perona and Malik experimented with the Gaussian law

$$D = g(p^2) = e^{-\frac{p^2}{2\sigma^2}}, \tag{4.87}$$

as well as the Cauchy law

$$D = g(p^2) = \frac{1}{1 + bp^2}, \quad b > 0. \tag{4.88}$$

Noticing that $p^2 = |\nabla u|^2 = (\nabla u)^2$, the divergence form of the Perona and Malik model can be expanded as

$$\nabla \cdot (g(p^2)\nabla u) = g(p^2)\Delta u + 2g'(p^2)D^2u(\nabla u, \nabla u). \tag{4.89}$$

Let $\boldsymbol{n}(x) = \nabla u/|\nabla u|$ denote the unit normal to the level set of u passing through x, and $T = T(x)$ is the tangent space of the level set at x. Define the tangential Laplacian $\Delta^T u$ by

$$\Delta^T u = \text{trace}(D^2u\big|_T).$$

Then $\Delta u = \Delta^T u + D^2u(\boldsymbol{n}, \boldsymbol{n})$, and

$$\nabla \cdot (g(p^2)\nabla u) = g(p^2)\Delta^T u + (g(p^2) + 2p^2g'(p^2))D^2u(\boldsymbol{n}, \boldsymbol{n}). \tag{4.90}$$

Let η denote the signed arc length parameter along the normal line passing through x. Then one could easily show that

$$u_{\eta\eta} = D^2u(\boldsymbol{n}, \boldsymbol{n}), \quad \text{when } u \text{ is restricted along the normal and treated as a function of } \eta.$$

Then formula (4.90) clearly explains the adaptive feature of the Perona–Malik diffusion. On intraregions where $p \ll 1$, the diffusion is the ordinary isotropic Laplacian Δu, provided that $a = g(0^+) = 1$. The situation changes near edges with $p \gg 1$, where the two directions start to compete: the diffusion along the tangent space T via $u_t = g(p^2)\Delta^T u$ and that along the normal direction $\boldsymbol{n}$ via the second term in (4.90).

The fine competition between the two is controlled by the ratio of the two weights in (4.90):

$$r = \frac{g(p^2) + 2p^2g'(p^2)}{g(p^2)} = 1 + 2s\frac{d \ln g}{ds}, \quad s = p^2. \tag{4.91}$$

As a result, to discourage the relative diffusion across edges or along their normal directions, one could further require

$$r = r(s) \to 0, \quad s \to \infty.$$

Notice that $r \leq 1$ since $g' \leq 0$ due to the monotonicity assumption. On the other hand, to prevent instability along the normal direction arising from potential backward diffusion, one must also assume

$$g(p^2) + 2p^2 g'(p^2) \geq 0, \quad \text{or equivalently,} \quad r \geq 0.$$

For any continuous function $r(s)$ on $s \in [1, \infty)$ satisfying $r(s) \in [0, 1]$ and $r(s \to +\infty) = 0$, define

$$g(s) = g(1) \exp\left(-\int_1^s \frac{1 - r(t)}{2t} \, dt\right), \quad s \geq 1, \tag{4.92}$$

which is the solution to the ODE (4.91) on $s \geq 1$. Since $r(s) \to 0$, the asymptotic behavior of $g(s) = g(p^2)$ is therefore given by

$$g(s) \propto \frac{1}{\sqrt{s}}, \quad \text{or equivalently,} \quad D = g(p^2) \propto \frac{1}{p} = \frac{1}{|\nabla u|}.$$

Thus asymptotically it has to be the diffusivity coefficient induced by the TV energy discussed in the preceding section. In fact, when $r(s) \equiv 0$ for all $s > 0$, one precisely attains the gradient descent diffusion equation of the TV energy:

$$u_t = g(p^2)\Delta^T u = \frac{1}{|\nabla u|} D^2 u(T, T) = \nabla \cdot \left[\frac{1}{|\nabla u|} \nabla u\right],$$

where for 2-D image domains, T denotes the tangent of level sets.

For a general nonzero r, one has, with $s = p^2 = |\nabla u|^2$,

$$D = g(s) = g(1) \frac{1}{\sqrt{s}} \exp\int_1^s \frac{r(t)}{2t} dt \tag{4.93}$$

with the TV diffusivity coefficient weighted by an extra factor. For instance, if taking

$$r(s) = \frac{2\sqrt{s}}{1 + s} = \frac{2p}{1 + p^2} \in [0, 1], \quad s = p^2 \geq 0,$$

one has

$$\exp\int_1^s \frac{r(t)}{2t} dt = const. \, e^{2\tan^{-1}\sqrt{s}} = const. \, e^{2\tan^{-1} p}. \tag{4.94}$$

To our best knowledge, this form has never appeared previously in the literature (see Figure 4.11).

Theoretically, the original Perona–Malik model

$$u_t = \nabla \cdot (g(|\nabla u|^2) \nabla u), \quad u(x, 0) = u_0(x),$$

encounters the following challenge: how to robustly compute the diffusivity coefficient $D = g(|\nabla u|^2)$ in the very beginning of the initial value problem if u_0 is highly oscillatory

Figure 4.11. *An example of applying Perona and Malik's anisotropic diffusion to a noisy image. The nonlinear diffusivity coefficient $D(|\nabla u|)$ for this example is the one in (4.93) and (4.94). Notice the remarkable feature of edge preservation, as contrast to linear heat diffusions that invariably blur sharp edges while removing noises.*

due to noise. This issue was investigated in the work by Catté et al. [51], in which the original Perona–Malik model is replaced by its progressively mollified version:

$$u_t = \nabla \cdot (g(|\nabla G_\sigma * u|^2)\,\nabla u), \quad u(x,0) = u_0(x),$$

where G_σ denotes the canonical Gaussian kernel with zero mean and variance σ^2. The well-posedness of this regularized Perona–Malik model is established in [51] in terms of existence and uniqueness. More extensive discussion on the behavior of the Perona–Malik model can be found in [171, 317].

4.6.2   Axiomatic Scale-Space Theory

The contributions of the scale-space theory to image analysis and processing have been monumental (see, e.g., the contemporary series [175, 230]). The *axiomatic* scale-space theory of Alvarez et al. [6] significantly generalizes Witkin's classical linear theory [322] (based on the linear heat equation), as well as Perona and Malik's nonlinear diffusion model [251] just introduced above. The mathematical beauty of the approach lies in its rigorous derivation based on a few core principles or axioms, as started by Euclid in geometry.

A slightly simplified version of the theory starts from the general form

$$u_t = F(D^2u, \nabla u, u, x, t) = F(H, \boldsymbol{p}, \lambda, x, t), \quad x = (x_1, x_2), \quad (4.95)$$

where H, $\boldsymbol{p}$, and λ denote the Hessian matrix (or operator), gradient, and intensity value, respectively. Witkin's linear scale-space theory and Perona and Malik's nonlinear diffusion model (see (4.89)) are special cases corresponding to

$$F(H, \boldsymbol{p}, \lambda, x, t) = F(H) = \text{trace}(H),$$

$$F(H, \boldsymbol{p}, \lambda, x, t) = F(H, \boldsymbol{p}) = g(p^2)\,\text{trace}(H) + 2g'(p^2)H(\boldsymbol{p}, \boldsymbol{p}).$$

F shall be called the *infinitesimal generator* of the scale space to be developed and is always assumed to be *continuous* with respect to its arguments.

We now introduce the axioms one by one that will put more constraints on the infinitesimal generator F and thus make it more specific.

Translation Invariance

Translation invariance (in the pixel space) requires

$$F(H, \boldsymbol{p}, \lambda, x + z, t) = F(H, \boldsymbol{p}, \lambda, x, t) \quad \forall\, z \in \mathbb{R}^2.$$

Therefore, one must have $F = F(H, \boldsymbol{p}, \lambda, t)$. Translation invariance makes a general image processor irrelevant to the origin one chooses, which should be the case since different users may work with different origins.

Gray-Level Shift Invariance

This axiom further requires

$$F(H, \boldsymbol{p}, \lambda + \mu, t) = F(H, \boldsymbol{p}, \lambda, t) \quad \forall\, \mu \in \mathbb{R}.$$

Then one must have $F = F(H, \boldsymbol{p}, t)$. Gray-level shift invariance implies that the processor depends only on the relative variance of an image (via its differentials) but not on its absolute gray values. This axiom is therefore well supported by the crucial physiological discovery of the vision system: vision neurons are mostly differentiative and only fire strongly along edges and jumps (see, e.g., the work of Nobel laureates Hubel and Wiesel [152]).

Rotation Invariance

Rotation invariance further requires, for any rotation $Q \in O(2)$,

$$F(Q^T H Q, Q^T \boldsymbol{p}, t) = F(H, \boldsymbol{p}, t),$$

where $\boldsymbol{p} = \nabla u = (\partial_{x_1}u, \partial_{x_2}u)^T$ is treated as a column vector. Define the *geometric* Hessian matrix

$$G = (\boldsymbol{p}, \boldsymbol{p}^\perp)^T H (\boldsymbol{p}, \boldsymbol{p}^\perp) \quad \text{with } \boldsymbol{p}^\perp = (-p_2, p_1)^T, \quad \boldsymbol{p} = (p_1, p_2)^T.$$

Then it is evident that $(H, \boldsymbol{p}) \longleftrightarrow (G, \boldsymbol{p})$ is a one-to-one change of coordinates whenever $\boldsymbol{p} \neq \boldsymbol{0}$. Thus one must have $F = F(G, \boldsymbol{p}, t)$.

More importantly, it is easy to verify that G is invariant under rotation. Thus rotation invariance demands

$$F(G, Q^T \boldsymbol{p}, t) = F(G, \boldsymbol{p}, t) \qquad \forall \ Q \in O(2),$$

implying that $F = F(G, p, t)$ with $p = |\nabla \boldsymbol{p}|$.

For $p \neq 0$, further renormalize the three elements of the geometric Hessian $G = (G_{ij})$ by

$$\sigma = p^{-3} G_{11} = \frac{1}{p} H(\boldsymbol{n}, \boldsymbol{n}), \quad \boldsymbol{n} = \frac{\boldsymbol{p}}{p},$$

$$\kappa = p^{-3} G_{22} = \frac{1}{p} H(\boldsymbol{t}, \boldsymbol{t}), \quad \boldsymbol{t} = \boldsymbol{n}^{\perp} = \frac{\boldsymbol{p}^{\perp}}{p}, \tag{4.96}$$

$$\tau = p^{-3} G_{12} = \frac{1}{p} H(\boldsymbol{n}, \boldsymbol{t}).$$

As well known in image analysis (e.g., Chapter 2), κ is the (signed) curvature of the level sets of a given image u when $H = D^2 u$ and $\boldsymbol{p} = \nabla u$, and τ is the curvature of the gradient lines. Since $\Delta u = \text{trace}(D^2 u)$, one has

$$p(\sigma + \kappa) = H(\boldsymbol{n}, \boldsymbol{n}) + H(\boldsymbol{t}, \boldsymbol{t}) = \text{trace}(H) = \Delta u.$$

In combination, under the previous three axioms, one must have

$$F = F(\sigma, \kappa, \tau, p, t).$$

Morphological Invariance

This axiom is also often nicknamed "flashing invariance." It requires the invariance under a general morphological transform or monotone flashing: $u \to v = \phi(u)$ for any monotonically increasing smooth function ϕ:

$$u_t = F(\text{given } u) \to v_t = F(\text{given } v), \tag{4.97}$$

or equivalently, $F(\text{given } v) = \phi'(u) F(\text{given } u)$ since $v_t = \phi'(u) u_t$.

Define $\mu = \phi' > 0$ and $\eta = \phi''$. Using subscripts to indicate association with u or v, one has

$$\boldsymbol{p}_v = \nabla v = \mu \nabla u = \mu \boldsymbol{p}_u,$$
$$H_v = D^2 v = \mu D^2 u + \eta \nabla u \otimes \nabla u = \mu H_u + \eta \boldsymbol{p}_u \otimes \boldsymbol{p}_u.$$

Consequently, $p_v = \mu p_u$, $\boldsymbol{n}_v = \boldsymbol{n}_u$, and $\boldsymbol{t}_v = \boldsymbol{t}_u$. By the definitions of σ, κ, and τ in (4.96), one has

$$\sigma_v = \sigma_u + \frac{\eta}{\mu} p_u,$$

$$\kappa_v = \kappa_u + \frac{\eta}{\mu p_u} \boldsymbol{p}_u \otimes \boldsymbol{p}_u(\boldsymbol{t}, \boldsymbol{t}) = \kappa_u,$$

$$\tau_v = \tau_v + \frac{\eta}{\mu p_u} \boldsymbol{p}_u \otimes \boldsymbol{p}_u(\boldsymbol{n}, \boldsymbol{t}) = \tau_u,$$

since $\boldsymbol{p} \cdot \boldsymbol{t} = p \, \boldsymbol{n} \cdot \boldsymbol{t} = 0$.

In combination, morphological invariance (4.97) further requires

$$F(\sigma + \zeta p, \kappa, \tau, \mu p, t) = \mu F(\sigma, \kappa, \tau, p, t)$$

for any $\mu > 0$ and $\zeta \in \mathbb{R}$. Since the right-hand side is independent of ζ, F therefore cannot depend upon σ, and

$$F(\kappa, \tau, \mu p, t) = \mu F(\kappa, \tau, p, t).$$

Taking $p = 1$, one ends up with

$$F(\kappa, \tau, \mu, t) = \mu F(\kappa, \tau, 1, t) = \mu f(\kappa, \tau, t),$$

or simply, $F = p f(\kappa, \tau, t)$, for some continuous function f.

Stability or Ellipticity

By far, the previous axioms have led to

$$F = F(H, \boldsymbol{p}, t) = p f(\kappa, \tau, t).$$

The stability or ellipticity axiom requires F to be monotone with respect to H:

$$F(H, \boldsymbol{p}, t) \geq F(L, \boldsymbol{p}, t) \quad \forall \ H \geq L, \tag{4.98}$$

where $H \geq L$ means that the difference matrix $H - L$ is semipositive definite. We now prove that this ellipticity axiom further implies

$$f = f(\kappa, t), \quad \text{independent of } \tau! \tag{4.99}$$

Due to rotational invariance, assume $p = 1$, $\boldsymbol{n} = \boldsymbol{p}/p = (1, 0)^T$, and $\boldsymbol{t} = (0, 1)^T$. Then

$$H = \begin{bmatrix} \sigma & \tau \\ \tau & \kappa \end{bmatrix}.$$

Define

$$H_\varepsilon^+ = \begin{bmatrix} \sigma_\varepsilon^+ & 0 \\ 0 & \kappa + \varepsilon \end{bmatrix} \quad \text{and} \quad H_\varepsilon^- = \begin{bmatrix} \sigma_\varepsilon^- & 0 \\ 0 & \kappa - \varepsilon \end{bmatrix}$$

with $0 < \varepsilon \ll 1$ and $\sigma_\varepsilon^\pm$ to be chosen momentarily. Then

$$H_\varepsilon^+ - H = \begin{bmatrix} \sigma_\varepsilon^+ - \sigma & -\tau \\ -\tau & \varepsilon \end{bmatrix} \quad \text{and} \quad H - H_\varepsilon^- = \begin{bmatrix} \sigma - \sigma_\varepsilon^- & \tau \\ \tau & \varepsilon \end{bmatrix}.$$

Therefore, as long as $\sigma_\varepsilon^\pm$ are chosen in such a way that

$$(\sigma_\varepsilon^+ - \sigma)\varepsilon \quad \text{and} \quad (\sigma - \sigma_\varepsilon^-)\varepsilon \geq \tau^2,$$

one has $H_\varepsilon^+ \geq H \geq H_\varepsilon^-$. As a result, the ellipticity axiom implies

$$f(\kappa - \varepsilon, 0, t) \leq f(\kappa, \tau, t) \leq f(\kappa + \varepsilon, 0, t)$$

for any $\varepsilon > 0$. Passing $\varepsilon \to 0$, and noticing that f is continuous, one must have

$$f(\kappa, \tau, t) = f(\kappa, 0, t),$$

which is precisely the claim (4.99) that f is independent of τ.

In combination, we have established the most general form of the scale-space theory.

Theorem 4.25 (Scale-Space Equation).   *Under the preceding five axioms, a generic scale-space equation must satisfy $F = pf(\kappa, t)$, or equivalently,*

$$u_t = |\nabla u| f(\kappa, t),$$

where the curvature scalar

$$\kappa = \frac{1}{p} H(t, t) = \frac{1}{|\nabla u|} D^2 u(t, t) = \nabla \cdot \left[\frac{\nabla u}{|\nabla u|}\right].$$

Furthermore, since the first identity clearly shows that κ is a nondecreasing function of $H = D^2 u$, the stability condition requires $f(\kappa, t)$ to be a nondecreasing function of κ.

As an example, taking $f(\kappa, t) = \kappa$, one obtains the celebrated mean curvature motion equation [39, 40, 84, 119]:

$$u_t = |\nabla u| \nabla \cdot \left[\frac{\nabla u}{|\nabla u|}\right].$$

Scaling Invariance

Scaling invariance requires that for any scaling $h > 0$, $v(x, t) = u(hx, ht)$ is still a scale-space solution, provided that u is. Define $\tau = ht$. Then scaling invariance implies

$$v_t = hu_\tau(hx, \tau) = hp_u(hx, \tau) f(\kappa_u(hx, \tau), \tau)$$

$$= p_v f(h^{-1} \kappa_v, ht), \text{ which must equal } p_v f(\kappa_v, t).$$

As a result, by taking $h = t^{-1}$, one must have

$$f(\kappa, t) = f(t\kappa, 1).$$

Thus combined with Theorem 4.25, a scaling-invariant scale space on $\mathbb{R}^2$ is given by

$$u_t = |\nabla u| f(t\kappa) \quad \text{for some continuous and nondecreasing function } f.$$

For other additional axioms such as affine invariance, we refer the reader to, e.g., Faugeras and Keriven [120], Calabi, Olver, and Tannenbaum [40], and Sapiro and Tannenbaum [264].

4.7   Denoising Salt-and-Pepper Noise

Most of the previous denoising models apply only to additive or multiplicative noises. In the last section of the current chapter, we discuss another popular class of noises—the salt-and-pepper noises and their denoising schemes. For the related subjects on impulsive noises and more details on modeling and computation, we refer the reader to, e.g., Nikolova [231, 232] and Chan, Ho, and Nikolova [57].

Salt-and-pepper noise is the mostly studied type of *nonlinear* noise. By *linear* noise, we mean a noise generation mechanism M in the form of

$$u^0 = M(u, n) = A(u) + B(u)n,$$

where $A(u)$ and $B(u)$ are suitable transforms of an input ideal image u. For example,

(a) additive noise: $A(u) = u$ and $B(u) = 1$, often with $\mathrm{E}(n) = 0$; and

(b) multiplicative (or speckle) noise: $A(u) = 0$ and $B(u) = u$, often with $\mathrm{E}(n) = 1$.

For salt-and-pepper noise, it is usually assumed that the gray levels of the ideal image u vary between a and b with $a < b$ and both are reachable. In the 8-bit digital setting, for example, $a = 0$ and $b = 2^8 - 1 = 255$. For convenience we shall work with the analog range when $a = 0$ and $b = 1$, and u could take any value in between. Then 0 corresponds to dark color or "black pepper," while 1 corresponds to bright color or "salt."

In addition to the image field u and noise field n, the generation of a salt-and-pepper type of noise also depends on a switch random field ω which is binary: at each pixel x, $\omega(x) = 0$ or 1. More specifically,

$$u^0(x) = M(u, n, \omega)(x) = \begin{cases} u(x), & \omega(x) = 0, \\ n(x), & \omega(x) = 1. \end{cases} \qquad (4.100)$$

In addition, the noise field n is also binary, corresponding to "salt" when $n = 1$ and "black pepper" when $n = 0$.

Suppose that u, n, and ω are independent random fields and that n and ω both consist of i.i.d.'s across the entire pixel domain. Then the noise generation mechanism is completely characterized by two probabilities:

$$p = \mathrm{Prob}(\omega(x) = 1) = \mathrm{E}\omega(x) \ \text{ and } \ \alpha = \mathrm{Prob}(n(x) = 1) = \mathrm{E}n(x),$$

which are independent of x. p is often called the *spatial density* of the salt-and-pepper noise, while physically α reveals the percentage of "salt" in a salt-pepper mixture.

Below we consider two approaches to suppressing salt-and-pepper noises, corresponding separately to low spatial density (i.e., p is closer to 0) and high spatial density (i.e., p is closer to 1).

Median Filtering for Low Spatial Density Noises

Median filtering is a convenient and cheap approach for removing low spatial density salt-and-pepper noises.

Take the ideal Cartesian digital domain $\Omega = \mathbb{Z}^2$ for example. Fixing the two size parameters n and m, one defines a moving window at any pixel (i, j) by

$$U_{i,j} = \{u^0_{i-k,j-l} \mid -n \leq k \leq n, \; -m \leq l \leq m\}.$$

Then there are $N = (2n+1)(2m+1)$ samples within each window. The median filter is to estimate the ideal image $u_{i,j}$ by the median:

$$\hat{u}_{i,j} = \text{median}(U_{i,j}), \quad (i, j) \in \Omega.$$

To understand the effectiveness of median filtering, consider qualitatively the following mean-field analysis. Suppose $N \gg 1$ in the statistical sense. Then within each window $U_{i,j}$, *on average* there are

$$\#Np(1-\alpha) \; \text{0's}, \quad \#N(1-p) \; u\text{'s}, \quad \text{and} \quad \#Np\alpha \; \text{1's}.$$

Suppose that

$$\max(Np(1-\alpha), Np\alpha) < N/2, \quad \text{or equivalently}, \quad \max(p(1-\alpha), p\alpha) < 1/2. \quad (4.101)$$

Then on average, the median estimator $\hat{u}_{i,j}$ should always be one of the $u_{k,l}$'s inside the window. It stays very close to the ideal value $u_{i,j}$ by Taylor expansion when the target image u is smooth. Notice that the condition (4.101) holds for any α when $p < 1/2$, i.e., when the spatial density is low.

More quantitatively, we have the following characterization theorem, which has not appeared before in the literature to our best knowledge.

Theorem 4.26. *Assume for convenience that the salt density $\alpha = 1/2$ and that generically $0 < u_{i,j} < 1$ at any pixel (i, j). Then for large window size N,*

$$\text{Prob}(\hat{u}_{i,j} \neq some \; u_{k,l} \; in \; U_{i,j}) \leq C_N \, (4q(1-q))^{N/2}\sqrt{2N/\pi}, \quad C_N \to 1, \quad (4.102)$$

where $q = p\alpha = p/2 \leq 1/2$.

The proof can be established based on Stirling's celebrated asymptotic formula,

$$N! = N^N e^{-N} \sqrt{2\pi N} \, (1 + O(N^{-1})),$$

as well as the fact that

$$\begin{aligned}
&\text{Prob}(\hat{u}_{i,j} \neq \text{some } u_{k,l} \text{ in } U_{i,j}) \\
&= \text{Prob}(\hat{u}_{i,j} = 0 \; \text{or} \; 1) \\
&= \text{Prob}(\#0\text{'s} \geq N/2 \; \text{or} \; \#1\text{'s} \geq N/2) \\
&\leq \text{Prob}(\#0\text{'s} \geq N/2) + \text{Prob}(\#1\text{'s} \geq N/2) \\
&= 2\,\text{Prob}(\#1\text{'s} \geq N/2).
\end{aligned}$$

Then the estimation essentially becomes a binomial problem.

Notice that the exponential factor in the theorem dominates since

$$4q(1-q) = \left(2\sqrt{q}\sqrt{1-q}\right)^2 \le (q + (1-q))^2 = 1.$$

For equally mixed (i.e., $\alpha = 1/2$) salt-and-pepper noises, $p \in (0, 1)$ and $q < 1/2 < 1 - q$. As a result, one must have the strict inequality $4q(1-q) < 1$. Also pay attention that the assumption $\alpha = 1/2$ is not essential and the same analysis goes through as long as $q = p/2$ is replaced by $q = p \max(\alpha, 1 - \alpha)$.

Although the Stirling formula is an asymptotic one, it works remarkably well even for relatively small numbers, which implies that the constant C_N in the upper-bound formula (4.102) can be virtually set to 1.

To appreciate the theorem, let us consider a specific low-density example when $p = 20\%$ and $\alpha = 1/2$. Then $q = p\alpha = 0.1$. Suppose a moving window of size 7-by-7 is employed. Then $N = 49$, and

$$\text{right-hand side of formula (4.102)} \simeq (0.36)^{24.5}\sqrt{31.19} = 7.52 \times 10^{-11}.$$

The probability is indeed negligibly thin! For a 5-by-5 window, one has $N = 25$, and

$$\text{right-hand side of formula (4.102)} \simeq (0.36)^{12.5}\sqrt{15.92} = 1.13 \times 10^{-5},$$

which is still very small for an ordinary image of size 256-by-256 since

$$256 \times 256 \times 1.13 \times 10^{-5} = 0.74.$$

It implies, in a frequentist's view, that *on average* there can exist at most *one* pixel (i, j) (over the entire pixel domain) where the median estimator $\hat{u}_{i,j}$ is not some $u_{k,l}$ within its window $U_{i,j}$.

The theorem also points out the potential problem with median filtering when the spatial density p is large, in which case $p \simeq 1$, $q = p/2 \simeq 1/2$, and the exponential factor no longer dominates since

$$4q(1-q) \simeq 4 \times 1/2 \times 1/2 = 1.$$

Thus high-density salt-and-pepper noises call for new approaches other than median filtering. Figure 4.12 shows the performance of median filtering for removing low- and high-density salt-and-pepper noises.

Inpainting Approach for High Spatial Density Noises

When the density is high, say $p = 80\%$, one approach is to apply the inpainting or interpolation approach, which will be more extensively discussed in Chapter 6.

Assume that the underlying ideal image u is generic so that the two boundary level sets

$$\{x \in \Omega \mid u(x) = 0\} \quad \text{and} \quad \{x \in \Omega \mid u(x) = 1\}$$

both are null sets in terms of the 2-D Lebesgue measure. In the digital setting, from the implementation point of view, one could simply assume that their joint percentage is significantly below $1 - p$.

salt & pepper noise with 20% spatial density   median filtering with a 5x5 window

with 60% spatial density   median filtering with a 5x5 window

Figure 4.12. *Two examples of salt-and-pepper noises and the denoising performance of median filtering. As consistent with theoretical analysis, median filtering works very efficiently for low spatial densities but poorly for high ones.*

Assume that $u^0 = M(u, n, \omega)$ is an observed image sample with salt-and-pepper noise as generated in (4.100). Define the inpainting region

$$K = \{x \in \Omega \mid u^0(x) = 0 \ \text{ or } \ 1\}.$$

Since the image has been assumed to be *generic*, K almost surely (in the Lebesgue sense) captures all the pixels where the original image information has been replaced by salt-and-pepper powder.

Thus almost surely,

$$u\big|_{\Omega \backslash K} = u^0\big|_{\Omega \backslash K},$$

and it suffices only to recover the image information on the region K. This reduces the denoising problem to an image interpolation, or *inpainting* problem, which can be solved for example, using Chan and Shen's TV inpainting model:

$$\hat{u} = \min_u \int_\Omega |Du| + \frac{\lambda}{2} \int_{\Omega \backslash K} (u - u^0)^2 dx \qquad (4.103)$$

with $\lambda \gg 1$. Since in the noise generation model (4.100), the information on $\Omega \setminus K$ has not been distorted at all, one could ideally request $\lambda = \infty$ for perfect fitting. However, as in the *minimal surface theory*, allowing large but finite λ makes the interpolation model (4.103) better posed in terms of existence and solutions. Figure 4.13 shows the performance of the model when the density is as high as $p = 80\%$.

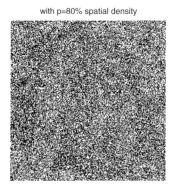
with p=80% spatial density

denoised image via TV inpainting

Figure 4.13. *An example of applying the TV inpainting technique* (4.103) *(also see Chan and Shen [67] or Chapter 6) to the denoising of high-density salt-and-pepper noises.*

4.8 Multichannel TV Denoising

In this section, we briefly discuss extensions of the TV denoising model to multichannel images. More details can be read in the related works, e.g., of Blomgren and Chan [30], Chan, Kang, and Shen [60], Chan and Shen [66], and Sapiro and Ringach [263].

Below we explore only the *linear* multichannel case when the range space is linear, affine, or convex. For the nonlinear or nonflat applications when the multiple channels are confined on general Riemannian manifolds, we refer the reader to, e.g., [66, 60, 250, 297, 301, 302].

4.8.1 Variational TV Denoising of Multichannel Images

Color images or hyperspectral satellite images are typical examples of multichannel images. Generally, a multichannel image u is defined on a 2-D domain Ω and takes vectorial values. That is,

$$u : \Omega \to \mathbb{R}^p, \quad x = (x_1, x_2) \to u(x) = (u_1(x), \dots, u_p(x)) \in \mathbb{R}^p,$$

where each scalar component u_i is called a channel and p the total number of channels.

Since matrix-vector notations will emerge later, we shall always assume in this section that u denotes a *row* vector.

For multichannel images, an additive Gaussian noise model is given by

$$u_0(x) = u(x) + n(x), \quad x \in \Omega,$$

where at each pixel x, $n(x)$ is a Gaussian vector in $\mathbb{R}^p$. Assume that the lower order statistics of the noise are known or modelled a priori to be

$$En(x) = \mathbf{0} \quad \text{and} \quad En^T(x)n(x) = M, \tag{4.104}$$

where M is the p-by-p covariance matrix, and assumed to be spatially invariant for convenience.

Following Section 4.5, a general TV-based denoising model can be naturally specified by

$$\min E[\boldsymbol{u} \mid \boldsymbol{u}_0, M] = \text{TV}[\boldsymbol{u}] + \frac{\lambda}{2} \int_\Omega (\boldsymbol{u} - \boldsymbol{u}_0)^T M^{-1} (\boldsymbol{u} - \boldsymbol{u}_0) dx, \tag{4.105}$$

where the Lagrange multiplier (or fitting weight) λ is independent of the noise. In most applications [30, 66], the Gaussian noise is assumed to be isotropic. Then $M = \sigma^2 I_{p \times p}$ is a diagonal matrix, and the second fitting term leads to the canonical least square penalty.

Thus the key issue is how to properly define the total variation $\text{TV}[\boldsymbol{u}]$ for a general multichannel image $\boldsymbol{u}$.

4.8.2   Three Versions of TV[u]

In this subsection, we discuss three natural versions of $\text{TV}[\boldsymbol{u}]$, labelled separately by $\text{TV}_1[\boldsymbol{u}]$, $\text{TV}_2[\boldsymbol{u}]$, and $\text{TV}_3[\boldsymbol{u}]$. As before, for each channel, $\text{TV}[u_i]$ denotes the ordinary scalar TV on Ω.

The first version is *decoupled* and defined by

$$\text{TV}_1[\boldsymbol{u}] = \sum_{i=1}^p \text{TV}[u_i] = \sum_{i=1}^p \int_\Omega |\nabla u_i| dx = \int_\Omega \left(\sum_{i=1}^p |\nabla u_i| \right) dx. \tag{4.106}$$

Following the general formulation in (4.105), let E_1 denote the energy E when the TV regularity is specified by TV_1. Then it is easy to obtain the system of Euler–Lagrange equations:

$$-\nabla \cdot \left[\frac{\nabla u_i}{|\nabla u_i|} \right] + \lambda (\boldsymbol{u} - \boldsymbol{u}_0) M^{-1} \boldsymbol{e}_i^T = 0, \quad i = 1 : p. \tag{4.107}$$

Here $\boldsymbol{e}_i = (0, \ldots, 0, 1, 0, \ldots, 0)$ denotes the ith canonical Cartesian basis vector.

Notice that the first (geometric) term is completely decoupled among the channels, while statistical coupling is still present in the second (fitting) term when the covariance matrix M is nondiagonal. Thus TV_1 is not very attractive for real applications since there exists no geometric communication among different channels.

The second version, first proposed by Blomgren and Chan in [30], is defined by

$$\text{TV}_2[\boldsymbol{u}] = \left[\sum_{i=1}^p \text{TV}[u_i]^2 \right]^{1/2} = \left[\sum_{i=1}^p \left(\int_\Omega |Du_i| \right)^2 \right]^{1/2}. \tag{4.108}$$

Let E_2 denote the energy E in (4.105) when the TV is specified by TV_2. For a given $\boldsymbol{u}$ and each channel i, define a *global* constant

$$\alpha_i = \alpha_i[\boldsymbol{u}] = \frac{\text{TV}[u_i]}{\text{TV}_2[\boldsymbol{u}]} \geq 0, \quad i = 1 : p.$$

Then $\alpha_1^2 + \cdots + \alpha_p^2 = 1$. The Euler–Lagrange equilibrium system associated with E_2 can be worked out to be

$$-\alpha_i[\boldsymbol{u}] \nabla \cdot \left[\frac{\nabla u_i}{|\nabla u_i|} \right] + \lambda (\boldsymbol{u} - \boldsymbol{u}_0) M^{-1} \boldsymbol{e}_i^T = 0, \quad i = 1 : p. \tag{4.109}$$

Unlike the previous version, now the constants α_i's introduce coupling among different channels.

Since each $\alpha_i[\boldsymbol{u}]$ depends on the *global* behavior of $\boldsymbol{u}$ on the entire image domain Ω, the system (4.109) is difficult for direct parallel implementation. However, following Section 4.5.5, parallel implementation becomes possible when the following lagged diffusivity fixed-point iteration scheme is adopted:

$$-\alpha_i[\boldsymbol{u}^{(n)}] \nabla \cdot \left[\frac{\nabla u_i^{(n+1)}}{|\nabla u_i^{(n)}|} \right] + \lambda(\boldsymbol{u}^{(n+1)} - \boldsymbol{u}_0) M^{-1} \boldsymbol{e}_i^T = 0, \quad i = 1 : p.$$

This special lag helps *localize* the linearized system.

The third version $\mathrm{TV}_3[\boldsymbol{u}]$, studied by Sapiro and Ringach [263], is defined by

$$\mathrm{TV}_3[\boldsymbol{u}] = \int_\Omega \left(\sum_{i=1}^p |\nabla u_i|^2 \right)^{1/2} dx = \int_\Omega \left(\sum_{i,j} u_{i,j}^2 \right)^{1/2} dx, \qquad (4.110)$$

where $u_{i,j}$ denotes $\partial u_i/\partial x_j$. It is the most natural extension of the scalar TV since it also results from the *dual* definition of the TV measure [118, 137], as explained below.

Let $\boldsymbol{g} = (\boldsymbol{g}_1, \ldots, \boldsymbol{g}_p) \in (\mathbb{R}^2)^p = \mathbb{R}^{2 \times p}$ denote a general $2 \times p$ matrix, or equivalently, p number of 2-D (column) vectors. Then

$$\nabla \boldsymbol{u} = (\nabla u_1, \ldots, \nabla u_p) \in \mathbb{R}^{2 \times p} \quad \text{as well,}$$

as long as the scalar gradients are understood as column vectors. The linear space $\mathbb{R}^{2 \times p}$ carries the natural Euclidean structure via

$$\langle \boldsymbol{g}, \boldsymbol{h} \rangle = \sum_{i=1}^p \langle \boldsymbol{g}_i, \boldsymbol{h}_i \rangle = \sum_{i,j} g_{ij} h_{ij}, \qquad (4.111)$$

assuming that $\boldsymbol{g}_i = (g_{i1}, g_{i2})^T$. The induced norm is given by

$$\|\boldsymbol{g}\| = \sqrt{\langle \boldsymbol{g}, \boldsymbol{g} \rangle}. \qquad (4.112)$$

Then

$$\langle \nabla \boldsymbol{u}, \boldsymbol{g} \rangle = \sum_{i=1}^p \langle \nabla u_i, \boldsymbol{g}_i \rangle.$$

When $\boldsymbol{g}$ is compactly supported and C^1: $\boldsymbol{g} \in C_c^1(\Omega, \mathbb{R}^{2 \times p})$, integration by parts gives

$$\int_\Omega \langle \nabla \boldsymbol{u}, \boldsymbol{g} \rangle dx = \sum_{i=1}^p \int_\Omega \langle \nabla u_i, \boldsymbol{g}_i \rangle dx = -\int_\Omega \sum_{i=1}^p \langle u_i, \nabla \cdot \boldsymbol{g}_i \rangle dx = -\int_\Omega \langle \boldsymbol{u}, \nabla \cdot \boldsymbol{g} \rangle dx.$$

Here the divergence operator $\nabla \cdot$ in the last expression is understood as

$$\nabla \cdot \boldsymbol{g} = (\nabla \cdot \boldsymbol{g}_1, \ldots, \nabla \cdot \boldsymbol{g}_p): \quad C_c^1(\Omega, \mathbb{R}^{2 \times p}) \to C_c^1(\Omega, \mathbb{R}^p).$$

Therefore, the third version of TV allows the dual formulation

$$\mathrm{TV}_3[\boldsymbol{u}] = \sup_{\boldsymbol{g} \in C_c^1(\Omega, B^{2 \times p})} \int_\Omega \langle \boldsymbol{u}, \; \nabla \cdot \boldsymbol{g} \rangle dx,$$

where $B^{2 \times p}$ denotes the unit ball in $\mathbb{R}^{2 \times p}$ under the norm (4.112).

Let $E_3[\boldsymbol{u} \mid \boldsymbol{u}_0, M]$ denote the energy in the general formulation (4.105) when the TV is given by TV_3. Then the Euler–Lagrange equation is given by

$$-\nabla \cdot \left[\frac{\nabla u_i}{\| \nabla \boldsymbol{u} \|} \right] + \lambda(\boldsymbol{u} - \boldsymbol{u}_0) M^{-1} \boldsymbol{e}_i^T = 0, \quad i = 1 : p.$$

Or collecting these p equations as a row vector, one has simply

$$-\nabla \cdot \left[\frac{\nabla \boldsymbol{u}}{\| \nabla \boldsymbol{u} \|} \right] + \lambda(\boldsymbol{u} - \boldsymbol{u}_0) M^{-1} = 0.$$

Formerly it looks exactly the same as the scalar TV case.

For TV_3 as proposed in [263], one can say more based on linear algebra [138, 289]. Treating $\boldsymbol{g} \in \mathbb{R}^{2 \times p}$ as a matrix, one realizes that the Euclidean norm (4.112) is precisely the Frobenius norm defined by

$$\|\boldsymbol{g}\|_F = \sqrt{\mathrm{trace}(\boldsymbol{g}\boldsymbol{g}^T)} = \sqrt{\sum_{i,j} g_{ij}^2}.$$

Let $\sigma_+ \geq \sigma_-$ denote the two singular values of $\boldsymbol{g}$ (noticing that all the other singular values must vanish since the rank is no bigger than 2). Then one has

$$\|\boldsymbol{g}\|_F = \sqrt{\sigma_+^2 + \sigma_-^2} := \phi(\sigma_+, \sigma_-).$$

Applying any general nonnegative function $\phi(\sigma_+, \sigma_-)$ can therefore potentially lead to new alternatives for the TV measure, as suggested in [263]. However, the seminorm properties (especially, the triangle inequality) may fail to hold.

Chapter 5

Image Deblurring

To recover a sharp image from its blurry observation is the problem known as *image deblurring*. Like denoising, it frequently arises in imaging sciences and technologies, including optical, medical, and astronomical applications, and is often a crucial step towards successful detection of important patterns such as abnormal tissues or the surface details of some distant planets.

Mathematically, image deblurring is intimately connected to backward diffusion processes (e.g., inverting the heat equation), which are notoriously unstable. As inverse problem solvers, deblurring models therefore crucially depend upon proper regularizers or conditioners that help secure stability, often at the necessary cost of losing certain high frequency details of the ideal images. Such regularization techniques can result in the existence or uniqueness of deblurred images.

In this chapter, we present the physics foundations of some common types of blurs, classify deblurring problems, and develop both mathematical analysis on several deblurring models and their associated computational methods.

5.1 Blur: Physical Origins and Mathematical Models

5.1.1 Physical Origins

There are three major categories of blurs according to their physical background: *optical, mechanical,* and *medium-induced.*

Optical blur is also often called *out-of-focus* blur and is due to the deviation of an imaging plane from the focus of an optical lens. For instance, for a nearsighted eye, the retina falls slightly behind the focus of the pupil lens. On the other hand, when capturing an outdoor scene with many objects in notably different ranges, the lens of a digital camera can only focus on a single target or a group of interest while leaving the rest out of focus.

Mechanical blur arises from the rapid mechanical motions of either target objects or imaging devices during image acquisition processes. Both types of motions could lead to the *motion blur* as often called in the literature. When the relative motion between an imaging device and its targeted objects is intense enough, the image of an object point could travel many pixels wide on the imaging plane during a single exposure. Such spreading and mixture of spatial information are the roots to mechanical or motion blurs.

Medium-induced blur is due to the scattering or optical turbulence of photonic media through which light rays travel. The influence of the atmosphere on satellite imaging is a well-studied example and is often called *atmospheric blur*.

Spatiotemporal variations of physical properties such as the temperature and density of the atmosphere could result in randomly fluctuating distributions of the *index of refraction*, the phenomenon known as *optical turbulence*.

Meanwhile, chemical substances of different sizes can also introduce various types of scattering to light waves with different wavelengths. In atmospheric sciences, the phenomenon is often called *aerosol scattering*, i.e., scattering due to various chemical species floating in the air. Familiar examples include the salt just above sea level in marine atmosphere, soil-based dusts in continental atmosphere, and various chemicals from vegetation. In the sunlight, for example, clouds and fogs often appear white since they mainly contain particles of large sizes and most visible light waves are equally scattered.

Both optical turbulence and aerosol scattering could lead to the mixture of spatial information, or blur. Atmospheric blur has been a significant topic in atmospheric sciences, satellite imaging, and remote sensing.

5.1.2   Mathematical Models of Blurs

We now develop the mathematical models for the aforementioned common blurs.

Modeling Motion Blur

Within a very short period of exposure time, most motions can be well approximated by constant velocities, as justified by Taylor expansion. One still has to distinguish two different types of constant motions—those of objects in 3-D scenes and those of imaging devices (e.g., digital cameras and camcorders).

The latter type is often caused by mechanical vibrations or sudden hand jittering during an imaging process and results in uniform blurring on the entire image. *Spatial uniformity* is characteristic for this type of motion blur (see Figure 5.1).

Under the first type of motion, on the other hand, when imaging devices are kept static, the induced motion blurs are typically nonuniform since different objects can move in distinct speeds. For instance, distant far backgrounds are often approximately static with respect to a digital camera, while running automobiles or jumping basketball players within closer distance move noticeably fast. As a result, such motion blurs are typically *localized* to the vicinities of individual objects.

While the two types of motions lead to different global blurry patterns, the underlying local blurring mechanisms are, however, essentially the same. By ignoring the physical complexity of imaging lenses, as well as the motion components that are perpendicular to imaging planes (related to out-of-focus blurs), such local blurs could be modelled as follows.

Suppose against a dark background, a single bright spot (the image of a physical point) moves from its initial point O to an endpoint A during a single exposure in some uniform velocity. Let $[O, A]$ denote the straight line segment and $L = |A - O|$ the travel distance

Figure 5.1. *An example of motion blur (due to camera jittering).*

on the imaging plane (see Figure 5.2). In addition, denote by T the time lapse of a single exposure and by I the illuminance of the bright physical point.

Assume that each imaging sensor is linear and accumulative, so that without motion the image response at O after a single exposure would be proportional to both I and T:

$$u(O) = \mu \times I \times T = \mu \int_0^T I dt,$$

where μ is a response constant determined by the imaging device. The assumption of being accumulative is often a valid approximation under most normal signalling or illuminance conditions. For instance, before a firing, the soma of a neuron is often modelled as accumulative in mathematical biology and neural networks [168], i.e., adding up all the responses received from its dendrites.

Now consider some fixed motion with speed $v = L/T$. Label all the imaging sensors by $1, \ldots, N$ along $[O, A]$. Assume that each sensor spans an effective physical distance ε on the imaging plane and $L = N \times \varepsilon$ (Figure 5.2). Then the image response k_n for the nth sensor would be

$$k_n = \mu \times I \times \frac{\varepsilon}{v} = \mu I T \times \frac{\varepsilon}{L} = u(O) \times \frac{\varepsilon}{L}, \quad n = 1 : N.$$

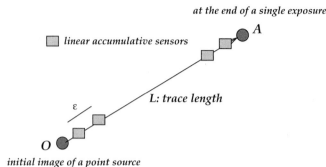

Figure 5.2. *Motion blur of the image of a point source.*

In particular,

$$u(O) = \sum_{n=1}^{N} k_n, \qquad (5.1)$$

which is the blurring model for a single spot—an otherwise static point source is now spread out along its trace.

In the continuum limit, the above spot model implies that a unit spot at the origin O, as modelled by Dirac's delta measure, $\delta(\boldsymbol{x}) = \delta(x, y)$, is spread out to the uniform measure $k(\boldsymbol{x})$ along the interval $[O, A]$. Notice that if $[O, A]$ is rotated to the standard horizontal interval $[0, L] \times \{0\}$ along the x-axis, the uniform measure can be expressed by

$$k(\boldsymbol{x}) = \frac{1}{L} 1_{[0,L]}(x) \times \delta(y).$$

Generally, let $\boldsymbol{t}$ denote the unit vector of motion velocity and $\boldsymbol{n}$ the unit normal perpendicular to $\boldsymbol{t}$. Then the unit amount of information at O, i.e., $\delta(\boldsymbol{x} - O)$, is spread out to the line measure

$$k_{O,t}(\boldsymbol{x}) = \frac{1}{L} 1_{[0,L]}((\boldsymbol{x} - O) \cdot \boldsymbol{t}) \times \delta((\boldsymbol{x} - O) \cdot \boldsymbol{n}) = k_t(\boldsymbol{x} - O), \qquad (5.2)$$

where $k_t(\boldsymbol{x})$ corresponds to the spreading of $O = (0, 0)$.

To extend such a single-spot blur model to the entire imaging plane, we first assume that during a single exposure the entire image scene moves at a common constant speed in direction $\boldsymbol{t}$ and with a distance d. Assume the ideal static image is $u(\boldsymbol{y})$, defined on the entire imaging plane of $\mathbb{R}^2$. Consider any target image pixel $\boldsymbol{x}$ with an imaging sensor. The linear assumption on the sensors implies that the contribution of a *source* pixel $\boldsymbol{y}$ to the field pixel $\boldsymbol{x}$ is the amount of

$$u(\boldsymbol{y}) \times k_{y,t}(\boldsymbol{x}) = u(\boldsymbol{y}) \times k_t(\boldsymbol{x} - \boldsymbol{y}),$$

according to (5.2). Let $u_0(\boldsymbol{x})$ denote the blurred image at a field point $\boldsymbol{x}$. Then

$$u_0(\boldsymbol{x}) = \int_{\mathbb{R}^2} k_t(\boldsymbol{x} - \boldsymbol{y}) u(\boldsymbol{y}) d\boldsymbol{y} = k_t * u(\boldsymbol{x}), \qquad (5.3)$$

which is precisely the convolution of the ideal static image u with the PSF (point spreading function) kernel

$$k_t(x) = \frac{1}{L} 1_{[0,L]}(x \cdot t) \times \delta(x \cdot n).$$

It then becomes manifest that (5.3) amounts to the line integral

$$u_0(x) = \frac{1}{L} \int_0^L u(x - st)ds = \int_{\mathbb{R}^2} u(y)d\mu_{x,t}(y), \tag{5.4}$$

where $d\mu_{x,t}$ denotes the uniform line measure on the interval $[x - Lt, x]$.

We make two further remarks before concluding the discussion on modeling motion blurs.

(1) Suppose the imaging sensors are linear, but the motion during a single exposure is not uniform across the entire imaging plane. Then the direction t and the total travel distance d could depend on individual pixels, and consequently the uniform line measures $d\mu_{x,t}$ in the blur model (5.4) are no longer shift-invariant. This is the case when the motion blur is mainly caused by individual objects in fast motions.

(2) In reality, imaging sensors can often be nonlinear. For example, the photoreceptors of human retinas are well known to be logarithmic due to Weber's law [121, 275, 279, 315]. Moreover, many digital or biological imaging sensors are often saturated at certain thresholding levels [168, 279], leading to another type of nonlinear complexity. For instance, suppose the illuminance I of a single bright spot is so strong that $\varepsilon/L \times I$ already exceeds the saturation level. Then the spreading formula (5.1) is revised to

$$u(O) = k_1 = \cdots = k_N \equiv \text{the saturated response of the sensors,}$$

which is not averaging or lowpass, and consequently cannot be expressed by convolution. In this situation, the target bright spot is simply copied over along its path.

Modeling Out-of-Focus Blur

Consider aperture imaging through an aberration-free and convex thin lens. Let d denote the distance from an object point to the lens plane, f the focal length of the lens, and e the distance from the image point to the lens plane (see Figure 5.4). Then the ideal *lens law* says (e.g., [83])

$$\frac{1}{d} + \frac{1}{e} = \frac{1}{f}. \tag{5.5}$$

Let h denote the distance between the lens plane and the imaging plane. If $h = e$, the image of the object point is sharply focused on the imaging plane. Otherwise, a single physical point at distance d could be blurred to a fat spot on the imaging plane (Figure 5.4).

By similarity of triangles, it is easy to show in Figure 5.4 that this blurred spot is a disk area as long as the rim of the lens is circular. Let r and a denote the radii of the blurred spot and the lens separately. Then one could expect that among the parameters some relation holds such as

$$r = r(a, f, d, h).$$

Figure 5.3. *An example of out-of-focus blur.*

In fact, by the similarity of the two triangles OAD and BCD in Figure 5.4,

$$\frac{r}{a} = \frac{h-e}{e} = h\left(\frac{1}{e} - \frac{1}{h}\right).$$

According to the lens law (5.5), one obtains an explicit formula

$$r = ah\left(\frac{1}{f} - \frac{1}{d} - \frac{1}{h}\right). \tag{5.6}$$

Thus sharp vision occurs with no blur, $r = 0$, if and only if the lens law holds. For most imaging devices, the lens constants a and f are fixed. Then the degree of blur is a function of d and h only.

To summarize, for a fixed out-of-focus imaging plane and any object in a fixed range plane, the associated PSF is the indicator function of a disk with radius r:

$$k(\boldsymbol{x}) = k_r(\boldsymbol{x}) = \frac{1}{\pi r^2} 1_{B_r}(\boldsymbol{x}), \quad B_r = \{\boldsymbol{x} \in \mathbb{R}^2 \ : \ \|\boldsymbol{x}\| < r\}.$$

In reality the above analysis based on both geometric optics and the ideal lens assumption is only approximative due to the diffraction phenomenon and optic aberration. Different wavelengths are diffracted at different rates and can cancel out or strengthen each other, so that the net out-of-focus effect is a smoothly decaying circular blob on the imaging plane instead of a clear cut disk area obtained above via geometric optics. As well studied

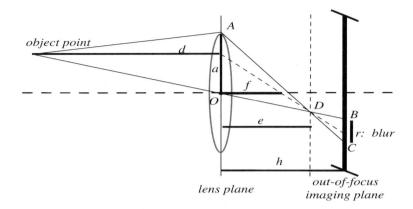

Figure 5.4. *Geometric optics of out-of-focus imaging.*

in many works [83, 141, 249, 265], the blurred blob could be approximated by the Gaussian PSF:

$$k_\sigma(\boldsymbol{x}) = k_\sigma(x, y) = \frac{1}{2\pi\sigma^2} \exp\left(-\frac{x^2 + y^2}{2\sigma^2}\right).$$

The statistical radius σ is proportional to the geometric radius r in (5.6) by [83]: $\sigma = \rho r$, with the constant ρ determined by the imaging device. Thus

$$\sigma = \rho a h \left(\frac{1}{f} - \frac{1}{d} - \frac{1}{h}\right),$$

and any otherwise clearly focused image $u(\boldsymbol{x})$ is blurred to

$$u_0(\boldsymbol{x}) = k_\sigma * u(\boldsymbol{x}) = \int_{\mathbb{R}^2} u(\boldsymbol{y}) k_\sigma(\boldsymbol{x} - \boldsymbol{y}) d\boldsymbol{y} \qquad (5.7)$$

in the ideal setting when the imaging plane is $\mathbb{R}^2$. This is the most commonly used blur model in image processing. Figure 5.3 shows a real example of out-of-focus blur.

Modeling Atmospheric Blur

Due to the complexity of atmospheric turbulence and aerosol scattering, mathematical modeling of atmospheric blur is much more involved than the previous two cases, and it has been studied carefully in many important areas including adaptive optics, satellite imaging, and remote sensing (e.g., [149, 255, 310]).

In most models, the atmosphere is approximated by a linear system, and atmospheric blur is modelled to be shift-invariant with a *point spread function* (PSF) $k(\boldsymbol{x})$, so that an observed blurred image $u_0(\boldsymbol{x})$ is related to the ideal sharp image $u(\boldsymbol{x})$ by

$$u_0(\boldsymbol{x}) = k(\boldsymbol{x}) * u(\boldsymbol{x}).$$

In optics, the Fourier transform $K(\boldsymbol{\omega}) = K(\omega_1, \omega_2)$ of the PSF $k(\boldsymbol{x})$ is often called the *optical transfer function* (OTF), and most atmospheric blur models are defined in terms of their OTFs.

For instance, as profited from Kolmogrov's turbulence theory, the OTF could be modelled by [140, 149]

$$K(\boldsymbol{\omega}) = \exp\left(-\beta\|\boldsymbol{\omega}\|^{\frac{5}{3}}\right). \tag{5.8}$$

Recall that the Fourier transform is defined by

$$K(\boldsymbol{\omega}) = \int_{\mathbb{R}^2} k(\boldsymbol{x})e^{-i\boldsymbol{\omega}\cdot\boldsymbol{x}}d\boldsymbol{x}.$$

In a more specific setting of telescope imaging through a thin boundary layer of atmosphere [255, 310], the PSF has also been modelled by

$$k(\boldsymbol{x}) = |(Ae^{i\phi})^\vee|^2, \quad \cdot^\vee \text{ denoting the inverse Fourier transform.} \tag{5.9}$$

Here A is the aperture function of the telescope and ϕ the phase factor. The phase distribution ϕ encodes the net optical effect of a thin layer of turbulent atmosphere and can be obtained by measuring the phase distortion of a planar wavefront from a distant star or a guided laser beam. The associated OTF is often bandlimited since the aperture function is compactly supported in the Fourier domain (e.g., Vogel [310]).

5.1.3   Linear vs. Nonlinear Blurs

All the above three models are linear. A general linear blur is in the form of $u_0 = K[u]$, with K standing for the linear blur operator. In most applications noise is inevitable, and a real observation is thus often given by

$$u_0 = K[u] + n,$$

provided that the noise n is additive.

A linear operator K is said to be *shift-invariant* if for any $\boldsymbol{a} \in \mathbb{R}^2$,

$$u_0(\boldsymbol{x}) = K[u(\boldsymbol{x})] \quad \text{implies that} \quad u_0(\boldsymbol{x} - \boldsymbol{a}) = K[u(\boldsymbol{x} - \boldsymbol{a})].$$

It is well known in signal processing as well as system theory [237, 238] that a shift-invariant linear operator must be in the form of convolution:

$$K[u] = k * u(\boldsymbol{x}) = \int_{\mathbb{R}^2} k(\boldsymbol{x} - \boldsymbol{y})u(\boldsymbol{y})d\boldsymbol{y} \tag{5.10}$$

for some suitable kernel function $k(\boldsymbol{x})$, which is called the *PSF* in the context of atmospheric imaging. (Without extra information on regularity, a shift-invariant linear operator could be differential operators, or in the Fourier domain, polynomial multipliers.)

More generally, if K is linear, then at any fixed pixel $\boldsymbol{x}$ in the pixel domain Ω,

$$L_{\boldsymbol{x}} : u \to K[u](\boldsymbol{x})$$

must be a linear functional on u, or a generalized function. Denote it symbolically by $k(\boldsymbol{x}, \cdot)$ so that as in distribution theory [292], one has

$$L_{\boldsymbol{x}}[u] = \langle k(\boldsymbol{x}, \cdot) , \ u(\cdot) \rangle.$$

Suppose that the distribution $k(x, \cdot)$ is actually representable by an ordinary measurable function in $L^1(\Omega)$. Then the linear blur becomes a location-dependent ordinary integral:

$$u_0(x) = \int_\Omega k(x, y)u(y)dy.$$

For analysis purposes, u can be assumed belonging to $L^p(\Omega)$ with $p \in [1, +\infty]$, and K is a (bounded) linear operator from $L^p(\Omega)$ to $L^q(\Omega)$ with some $q \in [1, +\infty]$. As a result, the adjoint K^* is defined from $(L^q)^*$ to $(L^p)^*$, the dual spaces. (One must be aware, however, that $(L^\infty)^* \neq L^1$ [193].) In what follows, the values of p and q shall be adjusted as necessary.

Not any linear operator could be called a blur, however, whether it is shift-invariant or not. The *least* requirement for being a blur operator is the DC-condition:

$$K[1] = 1, \qquad \text{treating} \quad 1 \in L^\infty(\Omega). \tag{5.11}$$

As in electrical engineering [237, 238], DC stands for *direct current* since the Fourier transform of a constant contains no nonzero frequencies. By the dual formula for the adjoint

$$\langle K[u], v \rangle = \langle u, K^*[v] \rangle,$$

the DC-condition on K amounts to the *mean-preservation condition* on K^*:

$$\langle K^*[v] \rangle = \langle v \rangle, \quad \text{by setting } u = 1; \quad \text{or} \quad \int_\Omega K^*[v](x)dx = \int_\Omega v(x)dx, \tag{5.12}$$

if both v and $K^*[v]$ belong to $L^1(\Omega)$.

By the DC-condition, ordinary differentiation operators in particular cannot be treated as blurs, which include the gradient ∇, divergence $\nabla\cdot$, and Laplacian Δ.

For a shift-invariant linear blur with kernel k, the DC-condition requires

$$\int_{\mathbb{R}^2} k(x)dx = 1, \quad \text{or in terms of its Fourier transform,} \quad K(0) = 1.$$

In addition, a more genuine blur operator has to be *lowpass* [237, 290], meaning in the shift-invariant case that $K(\omega)$ decays rapidly for large frequencies.

Finally, blurs do not have to be linear, though linear models have been pervasive in the literature. Consider, for example, the minimum surface diffusion model:

$$v_t = \nabla \cdot \left[\frac{1}{\sqrt{1 + |\nabla v|^2}} \nabla v \right], \qquad v\big|_{t=0} = u(x). \tag{5.13}$$

Let the solution be denoted by $v(x, t)$. For any fixed finite time $T > 0$, define a nonlinear operator K by

$$u_0 = K[u] = v(x, T).$$

Nonlinearity is evident since, for example, $K[\lambda u] \neq \lambda K[u]$ for general u and $\lambda \neq 0$. But the operator K apparently satisfies the DC-condition. Furthermore, (5.13) is the gradient descent equation of the minimum surface energy

$$E[v] = \int_{\mathbb{R}^2} \sqrt{1 + |\nabla v|^2}dx.$$

Thus it is evident that small-scale features and oscillations of u are wiped out in $u_0 = K[u]$, making u_0 a visually blurred and mollified version of the original ideal image u. This data-dependent nonlinear blur model is, however, shift-invariant.

5.2   Ill-posedness and Regularization

The ill-posedness of the deblurring problem can be well understood from four distinct but closely correlated angles.

Deblurring Is to Invert Lowpass Filtering

From the classical signal processing point of view, in the Fourier spectral domain, a blur operator is often a lowpass filter that diminishes high frequency details via vanishing multipliers. As a result, to deblur a blurry image, one has to in certain degree multiply the reciprocals of the vanishing multipliers, which becomes understandably unstable to noises or other high frequency small perturbations in the image data.

Deblurring Is a Backward Diffusion Process

By the canonical theory of linear parabolic PDEs, to blur an image with a Gaussian kernel amounts to running the heat diffusion equation for some time with a given image as the initial data. Therefore, to deblur is naturally equivalent to inverting the diffusion process, which is well known to be unstable.

Deblurring Is to Decrease Entropy

The goal of deblurring is to reconstruct the detailed image features from a mollified blurry image. Thus from the statistical mechanics point of view, deblurring is a process to increase (Shannon) information, or equivalently, to decrease entropy, which according to the Second Law of statistical mechanics [82, 131] can never occur *naturally*. That is, extra work has to be done to the system, mechanically speaking.

Deblurring Is to Invert Compact Operators

In terms of abstract functional analysis, a blurring process is often a *compact* operator. A compact operator is one that maps any bounded set (according to the associated Hilbert or Banach norms of the target image spaces) to a much better behaved set which is precompact. To achieve this goal, intuitively speaking, a compact operator has to mix spatial information or introduce many coherent structures, which is often realized by *essential* dimensionality reduction based on vanishing eigenvalues or singular values. Therefore, to invert a compact operator is again equivalent to decorrelating spatial coherence or reconstructing formerly suppressed dimensions (during the blurring process) of features and information, which is unstable.

Regularization Is Crucial for Deblurring

To conclude, proper regularization techniques have to be introduced to better condition the deblurring process.

Two universal regularization approaches, which are essentially mutual mirror images in the two dual worlds of deterministic and stochastic methodologies, are Tikhonov regularization [298] and Bayesian theory of decision making or inference [176]. Their intimate connection is explained in, for example, Mumford [223] and Chan, Shen, and Vese [73].

In essence, both approaches introduce some a priori knowledge about the target images u to be reconstructed. In the Bayesian framework, it is to introduce some proper probability distribution over all possible image candidates, and therefore necessary bias (i.e., regularization) is encouraged to favor more likely ones. In the Tikhonov setting, the prior knowledge is often reflected through some properly designed "energy" formulations, e.g., a quadratic energy term like $a\|u\|^2$ under certain suitable norm.

The following sections will give more detailed account on how regularization can actually be carried out in the variational (or deterministic) setting. To be complete, we shall start with the most popular deblurring approach—Wiener filtering in the stochastic setting, which in essence is variational as well.

5.3 Deblurring with Wiener Filters

In this section, we explore deblurring models based on Wiener's filters.

Consider a linear shift-invariant blur model with additive noise

$$u_0 = k * u + n,$$

where the PSF $k(x)$ is assumed to be known with Fourier transform (or OTF) $K(\omega)$.

From now on, instead of the black-faced symbols x and ω, a general pixel will be denoted by $x = (x_1, x_2)$ and its frequency dual by $\omega = (\omega_1, \omega_2)$.

5.3.1 Intuition on Filter-Based Deblurring

Deblurring via filtering is to estimate the ideal clear image u from its blurry observation u_0 by some filtering estimator

$$\hat{u} = \hat{u}_w = w * u_0 \quad \text{with a suitable filter } w.$$

For pure denoising without blur, linear filtering seems a natural tool for suppressing noise via moving average (i.e., convolution). For deblurring, however, it appears a little risky trying to *remove* a convolution (i.e., $k*$) by another convolution (i.e., $w*$). For instance in the noise-free case, the ideal solution would be, as conveniently expressed in the Fourier domain,

$$W(\omega) = \frac{1}{K(\omega)}, \tag{5.14}$$

so that $\hat{u} = w * u_0 \equiv u$ for any clear image u, and *perfect reconstruction* seems to be cheaply established. However, (5.14) is a rather unnerving formula since a typical blur k is often a *lowpass* filter and $K(\omega)$ decays rapidly at high frequencies, leading to unstable blowups in the deblurring filter $W(\omega)$. Such a deblurring filter therefore can exaggeratedly amplify any tiny error in high frequencies.

To overcome this potential risk of unstable restoration, in the noise-free case one rewrites (5.14) as

$$W(\omega) = \frac{K^*(\omega)}{K(\omega)K^*(\omega)} = \frac{K^*}{|K|^2}, \quad \text{where * denotes complex conjugacy.}$$

Then one may try to regularize the potentially vanishing denominator at high frequencies by adding some positive factor $r = r(\omega)$:

$$W \rightarrow W_r = \frac{K^*}{|K|^2 + r}.$$

Let $\hat{u}_r$ denote the resulted estimator. Then (in the noise-free setting)

$$\hat{u}_r = w_r * k * u,$$

or in the Fourier domain, the net reconstruction operator becomes the multiplier

$$W_r(\omega)K(\omega) = \frac{|K(\omega)|^2}{|K(\omega)|^2 + r(\omega)}. \tag{5.15}$$

By this formula, the restoration indeed well approximates the identity operator on low frequencies where $r \ll |K|^2$. High frequencies are, however, distorted by suppression since K almost vanishes and $|K|^2 \ll r$. Thus the regularizer r plays a role of cutoff or threshold. Equation (5.15) is a typical example for *regularized inverse filtering*.

Now the question is how to choose wisely an optimal regularizer r. It turns out that for this purpose noise can make significant contribution instead of being annoying. This is accomplished by Wiener's principle of least mean squared error.

5.3.2 Wiener Filtering

As for denoising in Section 4.3, Wiener filtering assumes that the deblurred estimator $\hat{u}$ is a filtered version of the observation u_0, using some optimal filter $w(x)$:

$$\hat{u}_w = w * u_0.$$

Wiener's filter w is to minimize the mean squared estimation error $e_w(x) = \hat{u}_w(x) - u(x)$:

$$w = \operatorname*{argmin}_h \mathrm{E}[e_h^2] = \operatorname*{argmin}_h \mathrm{E}(h * u_0(x) - u(x))^2. \tag{5.16}$$

As derived previously for denoising in Section 4.3, (5.16) leads to the orthogonal condition

$$\mathrm{E}[(w * u_0(x) - u(x))u_0(y)] = 0 \quad \forall x, y \in \Omega, \tag{5.17}$$

which in terms of the correlation functions becomes

$$w * R_{u_0 u_0}(z) = R_{u u_0}(z), \qquad z \in \mathbb{R}^2.$$

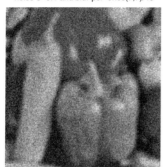
noise σ=0.1 and blur psf=ones(7,7)/49

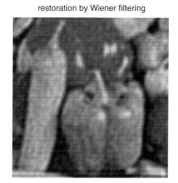
restoration by Wiener filtering

Figure 5.5. *An example of Wiener filtering for both denoising and deblurring.*

Consequently the explicit formula for the optimal Wiener filter is

$$W(\omega) = \frac{S_{uu_0}(\omega)}{S_{u_0u_0}(\omega)},$$ (5.18)

expressed in terms of the cross- and autopower spectral densities. For the blur model,

$$u_0 = k * u + n,$$

one has, according to Theorem 4.2,

$$S_{uu_0} = K^*(\omega)S_{uu}(\omega) \quad \text{and} \quad S_{u_0u_0} = |K(\omega)|^2 S_{uu}(\omega) + S_{nn}(\omega).$$

Therefore, we have established the following theorem.

Theorem 5.1 (Wiener Filter for Deblurring). *The optimal Wiener filter is given by, in the Fourier domain,*

$$W(\omega) = \frac{K^* S_{uu}}{|K|^2 S_{uu} + S_{nn}} = \frac{K^*}{|K|^2 + r_w},$$ (5.19)

where the regularizer $r_w = S_{nn}/S_{uu}$ is the squared noise-to-signal ratio.

In particular for a Gaussian white noise with variance σ^2, one has $S_{nn}(\omega) \equiv \sigma^2$. Since S_{uu} is often bounded, the Wiener regularizer r_w is therefore well bounded above zero. Figure 5.5 shows the performance of Wiener filtering for a blurry and noisy test image.

We conclude this section by two comments on the main features as well as limits of Wiener deblurring.

(a) The blur has to be shift-invariant (or spatially homogeneous) and the PSF explicitly known.

(b) Both the noise and ideal image have to be wide sense homogeneous (WSH), and their statistical properties (i.e., S_{nn} and S_{uu}) have been estimated in advance.

These issues have partially been addressed by some polished versions of Wiener filters which are local or adaptive (see, e.g., [151, 192]).

5.4   Deblurring of BV Images with Known PSF

In this section, we discuss how to enhance and restore blurry images with BVs when the blur is linear and shift-invariant, and the PSF is known. Shift-invariance reduces such blurring processes to convolution operators, and deblurring is therefore also called deconvolution in this context [77, 104].

5.4.1   The Variational Model

Consider the blur model with shift-invariant blur and additive white noise:

$$u_0(x) = k * u(x) + n(x), \quad x = (x_1, x_2) \in \mathbb{R}^2.$$

Assume that the PSF k is either known explicitly, estimated in advance, or modelled properly as done in the beginning of the current chapter. Moreover, in this section it is assumed that the ideal image u has bounded TV, or equivalently, belongs to the space $\mathrm{BV}(\mathbb{R}^2)$ (see, e.g., [118, 137]).

As an estimation problem, deblurring could be carried out in the light of Bayesian principle or MAP:

$$\hat{u} = \max \mathrm{Prob}(u \mid u_0, k),$$

or equivalently, in terms of the logarithmic energy $E = -\log p$,

$$\hat{u} = \min E[u \mid u_0, k].$$

The Bayesian formula with known PSF $k(x)$ is expressed by

$$\mathrm{Prob}(u \mid u_0, k) = \mathrm{Prob}(u \mid k)\mathrm{Prob}(u_0 \mid u, k)/\mathrm{Prob}(u_0 \mid k).$$

Given an image observation u_0, the denominator is simply a fixed probability normalization constant. Thus effectively one seeks an estimator $\hat{u}$ to minimize the product of the *prior* model $\mathrm{Prob}(u \mid k)$ and the data (or fidelity) model $\mathrm{Prob}(u_0 \mid u, k)$. Since images and blurs are often independent, one has $\mathrm{Prob}(u \mid k) = \mathrm{Prob}(u)$. Therefore in terms of the energy formulation, one attempts to minimize the posterior energy

$$E[u \mid u_0, k] = E[u] + E[u_0 \mid u, k].$$

Under the assumptions of independent white noise and the BV prior, the posterior energy is in the form of

$$\begin{aligned} E[u \mid u_0, k] &= E[u] + E[u_0 \mid u, k] \\ &= \alpha \int_\Omega |Du| + \frac{\lambda}{2} \int_\Omega (k * u - u_0)^2 dx \end{aligned} \tag{5.20}$$

with $x = (x_1, x_2) \in \Omega = \mathbb{R}^2$ and two suitable positive weights α and λ. This was the restoration model originally proposed and computed by Rudin, Osher, and Fatemi [257, 258], and later theoretically studied by Chambolle and Lions [56].

We will study its existence and uniqueness in the upcoming section. In what follows, two important issues are first addressed—one on the choice of weighting parameters and the other on the finiteness of domains in most practical applications.

First, as far as energy minimization is concerned, only the ratio $r = \alpha/\lambda$ contributes to the solution process. (But just as in projective geometry, placing α and λ side by side is convenient and flexible in applications.) As for parametric estimation in statistics, one could treat r as an unknown as well and expand the energy to $E[u, r \mid u_0, k]$ by absorbing some prior knowledge $E[r]$ on r.

On the other hand, from the visual perception point of view, there may exist no single optimal parameter r at all, since different observers can have distinct visual sensitivities and subsequently weight differently on the prior and the other fidelity term. It therefore does no harm to leave *tunable* the two weights or their relative ratio r, and let users experiment with their own choices. (For instance, the weights could be quite different in the following two scenarios: (1) harsh legal or financial penalty if missing any detailed features (as for tumor detection in medical decision) and (2) harsh penalty on unpleasant noisy fluctuations (as for commercial pictures or videos that advertise some skin-lotion product).)

As inspired by Wiener's filter (5.19) in the preceding section, however, it seems natural to assume that the ratio $r = \alpha/\lambda$ is in the same order of the squared noise-to-signal ratio r_w. In particular, r should be proportional to the variance σ^2 of the noise, which is natural since by the Bayesian rationale for least square fidelities, one has $\lambda = O(1/\sigma^2)$ as in Gaussian distributions.

The second issue concerns the finiteness of image domains in most practical applications. In model (5.20), it has been conveniently assumed that the image domain Ω is the entire plane $\mathbb{R}^2$ to facilitate the notion of shift-invariance. In real applications, however, Ω is often finite such as a disk or a square, in which case the blur

$$K[u] = k * u(x) = \int_{\mathbb{R}^2} k(x - y)u(y)dy, \qquad x \in \Omega,$$

has to be properly defined since u is only available on Ω.

There are two common ways to overcome this obstacle. First, one may modify the assumption of shift invariance by allowing shift variance on Ω. Then the blur operator $K[u]$ remains linear but can have a shift-variant PSF such as

$$k(x, y) = \frac{k(x - y)}{\int_{\Omega} k(x - z)dz} \qquad \forall x, y \in \Omega, \tag{5.21}$$

for which the linear blur is updated to

$$K[u] = \int_{\Omega} k(x, y)u(y)dy.$$

It has been assumed here that the original PSF $k(x)$ is nonnegative, and $x = (0, 0)$ belongs to the support of the measure $d\mu(x) = k(x)dx$. That is, the integral of $k(x)$ on any neighborhood of $(0, 0)$ is positive. Even the motion blur model in (5.4), for example, satisfies this condition, of which k is a generalized function involving Dirac's delta. Then the denominator in the definition (5.21) always stays nonzero.

It is trivial to see that the modified blur model K or $k(x, y)$ as in (5.21) indeed satisfies the DC-condition (5.11), $K[1] = 1$.

The second approach to handle a finite domain Ω is to extrapolate u beyond Ω, instead of modifying the shift-invariant kernel within Ω as just done above. Let

$$Q : u|_{\Omega} \to \tilde{u} = Q[u]|_{\mathbb{R}^2}$$

be a suitable linear extrapolation operator which extends u on Ω onto the entire plane. (Functionally, Q could be some linear operator from, e.g., $W^{1,\infty}(\Omega)$ to $W^{1,\infty}(\mathbb{R}^2)$.) Then one modifies the blur to

$$K[u](x) = k * \tilde{u}(x) = k * Q[u](x) \quad \forall x \in \Omega, \tag{5.22}$$

or equivalently, $K = 1_\Omega \cdot (k * Q)$, where $1_\Omega(x)$ is treated as a multiplier.

The DC-condition is satisfied if and only if $k * Q[1] \equiv 1$ when restricted in Ω. In particular, the natural condition $Q[1] \equiv 1$ would suffice since k satisfies the DC-condition on $\mathbb{R}^2$.

More generally, suppose Q is represented by some kernel $g(x, y)$ with $y \in \Omega$ and $x \in \mathbb{R}^2$. Then the modified K is represented by

$$k(x, y) = \int_{\mathbb{R}^2} k(x - z)g(z, y)dz, \quad x, y \in \Omega.$$

Therefore the DC-condition is satisfied when g and k meet the compatibility condition

$$\int_\Omega \int_{\mathbb{R}^2} k(x - z)g(z, y)dzdy \equiv 1 \quad \forall x \in \Omega. \tag{5.23}$$

Another less traditional approach to handle a finite domain is based on the inpainting technique [23, 24, 67, 68, 70, 69, 71, 61, 116]. Let us briefly explain the idea here. Suppose $k(x)$ is compactly supported on a disk $B_\rho(0) = \{x \in \mathbb{R}^2 \mid |x| < \rho\}$ for some positive radius ρ. Define the ρ-neighborhood of Ω by

$$\Omega_\rho = \{x \in \mathbb{R}^2 \mid \text{dist}(x, \Omega) < \rho\}.$$

Suppose that the ideal image $u \in \text{BV}(\Omega)$ and, instead of the original model (5.20), one attempts to minimize

$$E[u \mid u_0, k] = \alpha \int_{\Omega_\rho} |Du| + \frac{\lambda}{2} \int_\Omega (k * u - u_0)^2 dx. \tag{5.24}$$

Now the convolution inside the fidelity term does not stir up any problem. We could call this approach the *boundary-layer approach* since a layer of thickness ρ is glued to the boundary of Ω.

To conclude, both the restricted-kernel method (5.21) and the image-extrapolation method (5.22) lead to a shift-variant blur K with kernel $k(x, y)$, and the deblurring model becomes

$$\min_u E[u \mid u_0, K] = \alpha \int_\Omega |Du| + \frac{\lambda}{2} \int_\Omega (K[u] - u_0)^2 dx. \tag{5.25}$$

Next we discuss the solutions and solution methods to this model.

5.4.2   Existence and Uniqueness

The spirit of the following presentation could be found in many works, e.g., Chambolle and Lions [56] and Acar and Vogel [1].

Assume that the image domain Ω is a bounded Lipschitz domain in $\mathbb{R}^2$. In addition, we have the following conditions.

Condition 1. The ideal image $u \in BV(\Omega)$.

Condition 2. The blurry and noisy observation $u_0 \in L^2(\Omega)$.

Condition 3. The linear blur $K : L^1(\Omega) \to L^2(\Omega)$ is bounded, injective, and satisfies the DC-condition $K[1] \equiv 1$.

Conditions 1 and 2 are apparently necessary for the energy formulation (5.25) to make sense. The injective condition is also necessary for the uniqueness of optimal deblurring.

Theorem 5.2 (Existence and Uniqueness of BV Deblurring). *Under the preceding three conditions, the optimal deblurred estimation $u_* = \operatorname{argmin} E[u \mid u_0, K]$ in model (5.25) exists and is unique.*

Proof. Uniqueness is more straightforward. The TV Radon measure is a homogeneous norm, and thus convex (but not strictly). On the other hand, $\|v - g\|^2$ is strictly convex in v for any given g in L^2. Therefore, $E[u_0 \mid u, K] = \|K[u] - u_0\|^2$ is convex since K is linear, and is strictly convex if and only if K is injective, which is indeed part of Condition 3. In combination, the model is strictly convex and its minimizer has to be unique if it indeed exists.

For the existence part, consider any minimizing sequence $(u_n \mid n = 1, 2, \ldots)$ of $E[u \mid u_0, K]$, which must exist since, for example, $E[1 \mid u_0, K] < \infty$. Then their TV

$$\mathrm{TV}(u_n) = \int_\Omega |Du_n|, \qquad n = 1, 2, \ldots$$

are uniformly bounded. From Poincaré's inequality in two dimensions [3, 117, 137, 193],

$$\int_\Omega |u_n - \langle u_n \rangle| dx \le C(\Omega) \int_\Omega |Du_n| \quad \text{for some constant } C, \tag{5.26}$$

one concludes that $g_n = u_n - \langle u_n \rangle$ is bounded in $L^1(\Omega)$. Since the blur $K : L^1 \to L^2$ is continuous,

$$K[g_n] = K[u_n] - \langle u_n \rangle \qquad \text{(by the DC-condition)}$$

must be bounded in L^2. But $K[u_n]$ is bounded according to Condition 2 and the boundedness of $E[u_n \mid u_0, K]$, implying that $\langle u_n \rangle$ must be a bounded sequence.

By Poincaré's inequality (5.26) again, this leads to the boundedness of u_n in $L^1(\Omega)$ and hence in $BV(\Omega)$ as well. By the L^1 precompactness of a bounded BV-set, there exists a subsequence, for convenience still denoted by $(u_n \mid n = 1, 2, \ldots)$, which converges to some u_* in $L^1(\Omega)$. By the lower semicontinuity of the TV Radon measure under the L^1-topology,

$$\int_\Omega |Du_*| \le \liminf_{n \to \infty} \int_\Omega |Du_n|. \tag{5.27}$$

On the other hand, since $K : L^1(\Omega) \to L^2(\Omega)$ is continuous, one must have

$$\int_\Omega (K[u_*] - u_0)^2 dx = \lim_{n \to \infty} \int_\Omega (K[u_n] - u_0)^2 dx. \tag{5.28}$$

In combination of (5.27) and (5.28), one concludes that

$$E[u_* \mid u_0, K] \leq \liminf_{n \to \infty} E[u_n \mid u_0, K],$$

and consequently u_* has to be a minimizer, which completes the proof.   □

We conclude this section with a partial characterization of the optimal deblurring.

Corollary 5.3 (The Mean Constraint). *Following the assumptions of the preceding theorem, the unique minimizer u_* must automatically satisfy the mean constraint $\langle K[u_*] \rangle = \langle u_0 \rangle$.*

Statistically, this is a natural inference from the blur model

$$u_0 = K[u] + n$$

since the noise has zero mean.

Proof. Based on the unique minimizer u_*, define a single-variable function of $c \in \mathbb{R}$ by

$$e(c) = E[u_* - c \mid u_0, K].$$

Then $c_* = \mathrm{argmin} e(c)$ has to minimize

$$\int_\Omega (K[u_*] - u_0 - c)^2 dx \qquad \text{since } K[c] = c.$$

As a result, the unique minimizer $c_* = \langle K[u_*] - u_0 \rangle$. On the other hand, c_* has to be zero since $u_* - c_* = u_*$ due to uniqueness. Therefore,

$$\langle K[u_*] \rangle = \langle u_0 \rangle,$$

which is the assertion.   □

5.4.3   Computation

Computation of the variational deblurring model (5.25) has been studied in many works (e.g., [1, 56, 257, 258]). Most of them are more or less inspired by the formal Euler–Lagrange equation associated with $E[u \mid u_0, K]$:

$$\alpha \nabla \cdot \left[\frac{\nabla u}{|\nabla u|} \right] - \lambda K^*[K[u] - u_0] = 0 \qquad (5.29)$$

with Neumann adiabatic condition $\partial u / \partial n = 0$ along the boundary $\partial \Omega$. Equation (5.29) holds in the distributional sense; i.e., for any compactly supported smooth test function ϕ, the solution satisfies

$$\alpha \left\langle \nabla \phi \, , \, \frac{\nabla u}{|\nabla u|} \right\rangle + \lambda \langle K[\phi] \, , \, K[u] - u_0 \rangle = 0.$$

an out–of–focus image   deblurred image (with known PSF)

Figure 5.6. *Deblurring an out-of-focus image (with known PSF).*

The nonlinear degenerate elliptic equation (5.29) is often regularized to

$$\alpha \nabla \cdot \left[\frac{\nabla u}{|\nabla u|_a} \right] - \lambda K^*[K[u] - u_0] = 0, \tag{5.30}$$

where the notation $|x|_a$ denotes $\sqrt{x^2 + a^2}$ for some fixed positive parameter a. This regularized version corresponds to the minimization of the modified deblurring model

$$E_a[u \mid u_0, K] = \alpha \int_\Omega \sqrt{|Du|^2 + a^2} + \frac{\lambda}{2} \int_\Omega (K[u] - u_0)^2 dx, \tag{5.31}$$

which is closely connected to the minimum surface problem [137]. Notice that the surface area measure in the first term is defined in the distributional sense as similar to the TV Radon measure [117, 137].

The regularized nonlinear equation (5.30) is then often solved by some iterative scheme after a natural linearization procedure. For example, the most popular scheme is, based on the current best estimation $u^{(n)}$, to solve for $u^{(n+1)}$ the following linearized equation:

$$\alpha \nabla \cdot \left[\frac{\nabla u^{(n+1)}}{|\nabla u^{(n)}|_a} \right] - \lambda K^*[K[u^{(n+1)}] - u_0] = 0 \tag{5.32}$$

with Neumann boundary condition. Notice that given $u^{(n)}$, the linear operator

$$L_n = -\alpha \nabla \cdot \frac{1}{|\nabla u^{(n)}|_a} \nabla + \lambda K^* K$$

is positive definite. This is the natural extension of the lagged (diffusivity) fixed-point algorithm [1, 56, 62] discussed previously in Section 4.5.5.

Figures 5.6, 5.7, and 5.8 demonstrate the performance of the above model and algorithm on three typical examples.

image blurred by horizontal hand jittering

deblurred image (with known PSF)

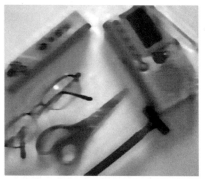

Figure 5.7. *Deblurring an image blurred by horizontal hand jittering.*

image blurred by horizontal hand jittering

deblurred image (with known PSF)

Figure 5.8. *Another example of restoring an image blurred by motion.*

5.5   Variational Blind Deblurring with Unknown PSF

In this section, we develop variational deblurring models when the blur PSF is unknown, a scenario often nicknamed "blind deblurring" in the literature [124, 188, 326]. As analogous to statistical estimation theory, we shall classify such models into ones that are *parametric* or *nonparametric*, or equivalently, *partially blind* or *completely blind*.

5.5.1   Parametric Blind Deblurring

First, consider the scenario when the unknown linear blur belongs to a known parametric family

$$\mathcal{K} = \{K_\theta \mid \theta \in I \subseteq \mathbb{R}^d\},$$

where $\theta = (\theta_1, \ldots, \theta_d)$ denotes a d-dimensional parametric vector and varies on a subset or domain I in $\mathbb{R}^d$. One is therefore not completely "blind" to the blur operator, and the uncertainty lies in choosing the right parameter θ_*. For instance, if $\mathcal{K}$ is a family of linear shift-invariant blurs, then each K_θ is uniquely associated with a parametric PSF $k(x \mid \theta)$. The Gaussian family is a familiar example:

$$g(x \mid \theta) = \frac{1}{2\pi\theta} \exp\left(-\frac{x_1^2 + x_2^2}{2\theta}\right), \qquad \theta \in I = (0, \infty), \tag{5.33}$$

where in statistics θ precisely embodies the variance σ^2.

If the blur is generated by a complex physical system, the parameter θ is often determined by the physical constants of that system, as manifest in formulae (5.6) and (5.7) for the out-of-focus blur model. In the case of atmospheric blur, for another example, the parameter could be well associated with the turbulence activities of the atmosphere, such as temperature, humidity, etc.

To deblur a blurry observation with additive Gaussian white noise

$$u_0 = K_\theta[u] + n, \tag{5.34}$$

both the ideal image u and the unknown parameter θ have to be estimated. According to the Bayesian estimation theory briefly outlined in the beginning of the preceding section, deblurring is to maximize the posterior probability

$$p(u, \theta \mid u_0), \qquad \text{or equivalently}, \qquad p(u_0 \mid u, \theta) p(u, \theta).$$

Since the ideal image and the blur mechanism of the imaging system are commonly independent, one has $p(u, \theta) = p(u)p(\theta)$. Thus in terms of the logarithmic energy formulation $E = -\log p$, deblurring becomes the minimization of

$$E[u, \theta \mid u_0] = E[u_0 \mid u, \theta] + E[u] + E[\theta]. \tag{5.35}$$

The first two terms can be safely copied from the nonblind deblurring model in the preceding section. Thus it suffices to incorporate some appropriate model for the parameter distribution $p(\theta)$ or $E[\theta]$.

Now consider the situation when $u \in \mathrm{BV}(\Omega)$, $\theta \in I \subseteq R^d$, and $E[\theta] = \phi(\theta)$ for some suitable function ϕ. Then the deblurring model is explicitly given by

$$E[u, \theta \mid u_0] = \alpha \int_\Omega |Du| + \frac{\lambda}{2} \int_\Omega (K_\theta[u] - u_0)^2 dx + \phi(\theta). \tag{5.36}$$

We shall assume that $\phi(\theta)$ is bounded below: $\phi(\theta) \geq M > -\infty$ for all $\theta \in I$. Otherwise it can diminish the role of the first two terms in (5.36) and distort the real intention of the model. As an example, consider the Gaussian family in (5.33). Suppose the variance θ is subject to the exponential distribution with density function

$$p(\theta) = a \exp(-a\theta), \qquad \theta \in I = (0, \infty) \quad \text{for some } a > 0. \tag{5.37}$$

Then

$$\phi(\theta) = E[\theta] = -\ln p(\theta) = a\theta + const.,$$

which is clearly bounded below.

Following Theorem 5.2 in the preceding section, it shall be naturally assumed that for each $\theta \in I$, K_θ is injective and satisfies the DC-condition, $K_\theta[1] = 1$. Then for any given θ, the conditional minimizer

$$\hat{u}_\theta = \text{argmin } E[u \mid u_0, K_\theta] = \text{argmin } \alpha \int_\Omega |Du| + \frac{\lambda}{2} \int_\Omega (K_\theta[u] - u_0)^2 dx \qquad (5.38)$$

always exists and is unique by Theorem 5.2.

With the conditional minimizer, the original model (5.36) is then reduced to an optimization problem on the parameter domain $I \subseteq \mathbb{R}^d$:

$$\min_{\theta \in I} e(\theta) \quad \text{with} \quad e(\theta) = E[\hat{u}_\theta, \theta \mid u_0].$$

The convexity of $e(\theta)$ is generally not guaranteed, and consequently the global minimizer $(\theta_*, \hat{u}_{\theta_*})$ can be nonunique.

The existence of solutions to the parametric deblurring model (5.36) will be studied in the upcoming section in a more general setting (see Theorem 5.6). Much of the formulation and mathematical analysis in the continuum setting is new in the literature, to the best knowledge of the authors.

Computationally, there exists a more popular approach for minimizing $E[u, \theta \mid u_0]$, which is often called *alternating minimization*, or the *zigzag* approach. It appears in the image processing literature frequently whenever the objectives involve two or more unknowns, e.g., the Mumford–Shah segmentation model involving both the image u and its unknown edge set Γ (or edge signature function z in its Γ-convergence approximation) [11, 12, 76, 77, 116, 226], and the image dejittering problem involving both the image u and the unknown horizontal jitters s [276].

To proceed, one starts with some initial guess $\theta^{(0)}$, which could be drawn from argmin $\phi(\theta)$ for instance. Then one successively obtains the alternating sequence (between u and θ) of conditional minimizers

$$\theta^{(0)} \to u^{(0)} \to \theta^{(1)} \to u^{(1)} \to \cdots \qquad (5.39)$$

by solving, for $n = 0, 1, \ldots,$

$$u^{(n)} = \text{argmin } E[u \mid u_0, \theta^{(n)}], \quad \text{followed by}$$

$$\theta^{(n+1)} = \text{argmin } E[\theta \mid u_0, u^{(n)}], \quad \text{where} \qquad (5.40)$$

$$E[\theta \mid u_0, u] = \frac{\lambda}{2} \int_\Omega (K_\theta[u] - u_0)^2 dx + \phi(\theta).$$

Notice the Markov property of the zigzag sequence (5.39), i.e., in the language of conditional probabilities,

$$\text{Prob}(\theta^{(n+1)} \mid u^{(n)}, \theta^{(n)}, u^{(n-1)}, \ldots) = \text{Prob}(\theta^{(n+1)} \mid u^{(n)}),$$

$$\text{Prob}(u^{(n)} \mid \theta^{(n)}, u^{(n-1)}, \theta^{(n-1)}, \ldots) = \text{Prob}(u^{(n)} \mid \theta^{(n)}).$$

Also notice that the step $\theta^{(n)} \to u^{(n)}$ is unique following Theorem 5.2, while the step of conditional parameter estimation $u^{(n)} \to \theta^{(n+1)}$ can be nonunique. One could enforce the uniqueness by some sort of selection schemes, e.g.,

$$\theta^{(n+1)} = \text{argmin } \{\phi(\theta) \mid \theta \in \text{argmin } E[\theta \mid u_0, u^{(n)}]\},$$

provided that $\phi(\theta)$ is strictly convex.

Theorem 5.4 (Alternating Minimization Is Monotone). *For each $n \geq 0$,*

$$E[u^{(n+1)}, \theta^{(n+1)} \mid u_0] \leq E[u^{(n)}, \theta^{(n)} \mid u_0].$$

Proof. It is left to the reader to easily verify that

$$E[u^{(n+1)}, \theta^{(n+1)} \mid u_0] \leq E[u^{(n)}, \theta^{(n+1)} \mid u_0] \leq E[u^{(n)}, \theta^{(n)} \mid u_0]. \quad \square$$

Let $B(L^1, L^2) = B(L^1(\Omega), L^2(\Omega))$ denote the Banach space of all bounded linear operators from $L^1(\Omega)$ to $L^2(\Omega)$ endowed with the operator norm.

Theorem 5.5 (Convergence of Alternating Minimization). *Assume that*

(a) *the blur parametrization*

$$K : I \subseteq \mathbb{R}^d \rightarrow B(L^1, L^2), \quad \theta \rightarrow K_\theta$$

   is a continuous mapping; and

(b) *$\phi(\theta)$ is lower semicontinuous in $\theta \in I$.*

Then, if as $n \rightarrow \infty$,

$$u^{(n)} \rightarrow u_* \;\; in \;\; L^1(\Omega) \;\; and \;\; \theta^{(n)} \rightarrow \theta_* \in I,$$

the limit pair (u_*, θ_*) must satisfy

$$\begin{aligned}
u_* &= \text{argmin } E[u \mid u_0, \theta_*], \\
\theta_* &= \text{argmin } E[\theta \mid u_0, u_*].
\end{aligned} \tag{5.41}$$

Proof. For any two admissible pairs (u, θ) and (u_*, θ_*) in $\text{BV}(\Omega) \times I$,

$$\begin{aligned}
\|K_\theta[u] - K_{\theta_*}[u_*]\|_2 &\leq \|K_\theta[u] - K_{\theta_*}[u]\|_2 + \|K_{\theta_*}[u] - K_{\theta_*}[u_*]\|_2 \\
&\leq \|K_\theta - K_{\theta_*}\| \times \|u\|_1 + \|K_{\theta_*}\| \times \|u - u_*\|_1.
\end{aligned}$$

Therefore, as $\theta \rightarrow \theta_*$ and $u \rightarrow u_*$ in L^1, $K_\theta[u] \rightarrow K_{\theta_*}[u_*]$ in L^2.

By the algorithm of alternating minimization (5.40), for each n,

$$E[u^{(n)} \mid u_0, \theta^{(n)}] \leq E[u \mid u_0, \theta^{(n)}] \quad \forall u \in \text{BV}(\Omega).$$

That is,

$$\alpha \int_\Omega |Du^{(n)}| + \frac{\lambda}{2} \|K_{\theta^{(n)}}[u^{(n)}] - u_0\|_2^2 \leq \alpha \int_\Omega |Du| + \frac{\lambda}{2} \|K_{\theta^{(n)}}[u] - u_0\|_2^2.$$

Coupled with the lower semicontinuity of the TV measure in L^1-topology and the continuity property just inferred in the preceding paragraph, this gives, as $n \rightarrow \infty$,

$$\alpha \int_\Omega |Du_*| + \frac{\lambda}{2} \|K_{\theta_*}[u_*] - u_0\|_2^2 \leq \alpha \int_\Omega |Du| + \frac{\lambda}{2} \|K_{\theta_*}[u] - u_0\|_2^2,$$

or equivalently, $E[u_* \mid u_0, \theta_*] \leq E[u \mid u_0, \theta_*]$ for any $u \in \mathrm{BV}(\Omega)$. This proves the first identity in (5.41). By the lower semicontinuity condition on ϕ, the second identity can be proven in the same manner.   □

Notice that the continuity on blur parametrization is strong but not baseless. Consider the shift-invariant Gaussian family (5.33) on $\Omega = \mathbb{R}^2$ for instance. By Young's inequality [193], one has

$$\|(K_\theta - K_{\theta'})[u]\|_2 = \|(g(x \mid \theta) - g(x \mid \theta')) * u\|_2 \leq \|g(x \mid \theta) - g(x \mid \theta')\|_2 \|u\|_1.$$

Therefore,

$$\|K_\theta - K_{\theta'}\| \leq \|g(x \mid \theta) - g(x \mid \theta')\|_2.$$

For the Gaussian family, the latter obviously converges to zero for any $\theta' > 0$, and $\theta \to \theta'$.

In terms of the first formal variations,

$$\frac{\partial}{\partial u} E[u_* \mid u_0, \theta_*] = \frac{\partial}{\partial u} E[u_*, \theta_* \mid u_0],$$

$$\frac{\partial}{\partial \theta} E[\theta_* \mid u_0, u_*] = \frac{\partial}{\partial \theta} E[u_*, \theta_* \mid u_0].$$

Thus the limit (u_*, θ_*) does satisfy the system of equilibrium equations of the original deblurring model $E[u, \theta \mid u_0]$, and consequently offers a good candidate for optimal deblurring. In particular, if $E[u, \theta \mid u_0]$ is strictly convex as a functional of $(u, \theta) \in \mathrm{BV}(\Omega) \times I$, then (u_*, θ_*) has to be the unique global minimizer.

5.5.2   Parametric–Field-Based Blind Deblurring

Now suppose the PSF $k(x, y)$ of a linear blur operator K is given in the form of

$$k(x, y) = g(y \mid x, \theta(x)) \tag{5.42}$$

for some known family of functions $g(y \mid x, \theta)$ defined for

$$x, y \in \Omega, \quad \text{and} \quad \theta : \Omega \to I \subseteq \mathbb{R}^d.$$

Thus θ is pixel-dependent, instead of being a constant vector. For each given parameter field θ, we shall still label the blur by K_θ or k_θ.

For example, let $\theta(x) = (m(x), \sigma(x)) \in \mathbb{R}^2 \times \mathbb{R}^+$, and define

$$g(y \mid x, \theta(x)) = g(y \mid m(x), \sigma(x)) = \frac{1}{2\pi\sigma^2(x)} \exp\left(-\frac{(y - m(x))^2}{2\sigma^2(x)}\right).$$

At each pixel $x \in \Omega = \mathbb{R}^2$, this is a Gaussian centered at $m(x)$ with variance $\sigma^2(x)$. Suppose as in most situations that $m(x) \equiv x$ for any $x \in \mathbb{R}^2$. Then one can simply define $\theta(x) = \sigma(x)$ and reduce the above parametric-field model to

$$g(y \mid x, \theta(x)) = \frac{1}{2\pi\theta(x)} \exp\left(-\frac{(y - x)^2}{2\theta(x)}\right).$$

Physically, such families of Gaussian PSFs can well model spatially varying blurs, which are often caused by media inhomogeneity (as for large-scale remote sensing through water or air) or velocity nonuniformity of fast moving objects in a scene.

Following the same line of reasoning as for the deblurring model (5.35), one attempts to minimize the posterior energy in the form of

$$E[u, \theta \mid u_0] = E[u_0 \mid u, \theta] + E[u] + E[\theta],$$

provided that the blur mechanism is independent of image contents. What is new here is that $\theta = \theta(x)$ is an unknown field instead of an unknown constant. As a result, field characteristics can be built into the prior model on θ. For instance, if the field is assumed to be smoothly distributed, then one could impose

$$E[\theta] = \int_\Omega [\beta |\nabla \theta|^2 + \phi(\theta)] dx. \tag{5.43}$$

If, for example, $\phi(\theta) = \kappa(1 - |\theta|^2)^2$ for some large parameter κ, then $E[\theta]$ happens to be closely connected to Landau and Ginsburg's celebrated theory of superconductivity and phase transitions [37] and has been well studied by the mathematical community (see, e.g., Modica [219], Kohn and Sternberg [179], and Kohn and Strang [180]). Generally, $\phi(\theta)$ equals $- \ln p(\theta)$ from the probabilistic point of view (see, e.g., (5.37)). Driven by real situations, one could also consider the more involved but general case when the field $\theta(x)$ itself is shift-variant, in which case

$$\phi = \phi(\theta(x) \mid x) = - \ln p(\theta(x) \mid x).$$

Assume that the ideal image u belongs to $\mathrm{BV}(\Omega)$ and the parameter field θ is smoothly distributed as specified by (5.43). The deblurring model $E[u, \theta \mid u_0]$ is then specifically given by

$$\alpha \int_\Omega |Du| + \frac{\lambda}{2} \int_\Omega (K_\theta[u] - u_0)^2 dx + \int_\Omega (\beta |\nabla \theta|^2 + \phi(\theta)) dx. \tag{5.44}$$

Here $\theta : \Omega \to I \subseteq \mathbb{R}^d$ is a d-dimensional field parametrizing the blur K_θ.

Theorem 5.6 (Existence of Deblurring by Model (5.44)). *Suppose that*

(A) *the ideal image $u \in \mathrm{BV}(\Omega)$ and the observation $u_0 \in L^2(\Omega)$;*

(B) *the parametric field $\theta \in H^1(\Omega, I)$, and I is a closed domain of $\mathbb{R}^d$;*

(C) *the potential $\phi : I \to \mathbb{R}$ is lower semicontinuous, bounded below: $\inf \phi(\theta) > -\infty$ and satisfies*

$$A|\theta| \le \phi(\theta) + M \le B(1 + |\theta|)^q \qquad \forall \theta \in I \tag{5.45}$$

for some positive constants A, B, M, and $q \in [1, \infty)$; and

(D) *the parametric blur operator satisfies the DC-condition $K_\theta[1] \equiv 1$; in addition, assume that the parametrization procedure*

$$K : H^1(\Omega, I) \to B(L^1, L^2), \quad \theta \to K_\theta,$$

is L^2-Lipschitz continuous, i.e., for any $\theta, \theta' \in H^1(\Omega, I)$,

$$\|K_\theta - K_{\theta'}\| \leq L\|\theta - \theta'\|_{L^2} \quad \text{for some fixed constant } L. \tag{5.46}$$

Then the minimizer to the deblurring model $E[u(x), \theta(x) \mid u_0]$ in (5.44) exists.

We first make two comments on the motivations of the conditions before proceeding to the proof.

(1) Condition (C) requires that ϕ be bounded below. Otherwise, there would exist a trivial minimizing sequence $(u_n \equiv 0, \theta_n)$ with $\phi(\theta_n) \to -\infty$ as $n \to \infty$.

(2) The compatibility between conditions (B) and (C) is guaranteed by Sobolev's inequality [193] in two dimensions:

$$\|\theta\|_{L^q} \leq C(q, \Omega)\|\theta\|_{H^1} \quad \forall q \in [1, \infty),$$

which guarantees that for any $\theta \in H^1(\Omega, I)$, $\int_\Omega \phi(\theta(x))dx < \infty$.

To our best knowledge, the formulation and proof of the theorem are new in the literature.

Proof of Theorem 5.6. First, notice that for any $s \in I$, $E[u \equiv 0, \theta \equiv s \mid u_0] < \infty$. Therefore, there must exist a minimizing sequence $(u_n, \theta_n) \in \text{BV}(\Omega) \times H^1(\Omega, I), n = 1, 2, \ldots$ such that

$$E[u_n, \theta_n \mid u_0] \to \inf E[u, \theta \mid u_0] > -\infty, \qquad n \to \infty.$$

By the lower bound condition of ϕ in (5.45),

$$\int_\Omega (\beta|\nabla\theta_n|^2 + A|\theta_n|)dx, \qquad n = 1, 2, \ldots$$

must be bounded. By Poincaré's inequalities [3, 117, 137, 193], this implies that (θ_n) is a bounded sequence in $H^1(\Omega, I)$. Then by the Sobolev embedding theorem [3, 193], there is a subsequence of (θ_n), for simplicity still denoted by (θ_n), such that

$$\theta_n(x) \to \theta_*(x) \quad \text{in } L^2(\Omega), \quad n \to \infty.$$

Since I is closed, $\theta_*(x) \in I$. By the lower semicontinuity property of Sobolev norms, the limit θ_* must belong to $H^1(\Omega, I)$. With possibly another round of subsequence refinement, one could further assume that $\theta_n \to \theta_*$ almost surely on Ω. Then by the lower semicontinuity properties on both ϕ and Sobolev norms, in combination with Fatou's lemma [126, 193] for $f_n = \phi(\theta_n)$ (which is uniformly bounded below on the finite domain Ω), one has

$$\beta \int_\Omega |\nabla\theta_*|^2 dx + \int_\Omega \phi(\theta_*(x))dx \leq \liminf_{n\to\infty} \beta \int_\Omega |\nabla\theta_n|^2 dx + \int_\Omega \phi(\theta_n(x))dx. \tag{5.47}$$

By the Poincaré inequality

$$\int_\Omega |u - \langle u \rangle|dx \leq C\int_\Omega |Du|, \qquad \text{with } C \text{ independent of } u, \tag{5.48}$$

$g_n = u_n - \langle u_n \rangle$ must be bounded in $L^1(\Omega)$. On the other hand, by the Lipschitz condition (5.46) on K_θ, (K_{θ_n}) has to be bounded in $B(L^1, L^2)$ since (θ_n) belong to H^1 as just established above. Thus bounded in $L^2(\Omega)$ must be the following sequence:

$$K_{\theta_n}[g_n] = K_{\theta_n}[u_n] - \langle u_n \rangle \quad \text{by the DC-condition.}$$

On the other hand, from the original model,

$$\|K_{\theta_n}[u_n]\|_2 \leq \|u_0\|_2 + \sqrt{2E_n/\lambda}, \qquad E_n = E[u_n, \theta_n \mid u_0],$$

implying that $(K_{\theta_n}[u_n])$ is bounded in L^2. Therefore, the scalar sequence $(\langle u_n \rangle)$ has to be bounded, which in return via the Poincaré inequality (5.48), implies that (u_n) is a bounded sequence in $\mathrm{BV}(\Omega)$. By the precompactness of bounded BV sets in L^1, there exists a subsequence, still denoted by (u_n) for convenience, and some $u_* \in \mathrm{BV}(\Omega)$, such that

$$u_n \to u_* \quad \text{in } L^1, \quad \text{and} \quad \int_\Omega |Du_*| \leq \liminf_{n \to \infty} \int_\Omega |Du_n|. \tag{5.49}$$

To sum up, possibly with several consecutive rounds of subsequence refinement if necessary, we have found a minimizing sequence $(u_n, \theta_n) \in \mathrm{BV}(\Omega) \times H^1(\Omega)$, such that

$$(u_n, \theta_n) \to (u_*, \theta_*) \quad \text{in } L^1 \times L^2,$$

for some $(u_*, \theta_*) \in \mathrm{BV}(\Omega) \times H^1(\Omega)$. Then the Lipschitz condition (5.46) necessarily guarantees that

$$K_{\theta_n}[u_n] \to K_{\theta_*}[u_*] \quad \text{in } L^2,$$

which, in combination with both (5.47) and (5.49), immediately implies that (u_*, θ_*) must be a minimizer. $\square$

5.5.3 Nonparametric Blind Deblurring

Suppose now that the linear blur K is completely unknown except that

1. it satisfies the DC-condition $K[1] = 1$, and

2. it satisfies certain spatial constraints to be characterized later.

Then the deblurring task is conceivably much more challenging than the previous cases. Instead of estimating a few parameters or a parametric field, now one has to reconstruct an *operator*.

In what follows, we shall consider only the shift-invariant case when the image domain Ω is $\mathbb{R}^2$, and the linear blur is defined by its PSF $k(x)$, $x \in \mathbb{R}^2$. Then the estimation of a blur operator is reduced to that of a function.

In the Bayesian framework, one is to minimize the posterior energy

$$E[u, k \mid u_0] = E[u] + E[u_0 \mid u, k] + E[k],$$

assuming that the blur mechanism does not depend on image contents.

In the case of BV images and Gaussian white noise, one has

$$E[u] = \alpha \int_{\mathbb{R}^2} |Du|, \qquad E[u_0 \mid u, k] = \frac{\lambda}{2} \int_{\mathbb{R}^2} (k * u - u_0)^2 dx.$$

Thus the key to successful deblurring lies in the proper modeling of the blur prior $E[k]$.

In situations where the blur is known to be smooth, e.g., a Gaussian, one may naturally enforce the Sobolev regularity

$$E[k] = \beta \int_{\mathbb{R}^2} |\nabla k|^2 dx.$$

This was indeed the model studied by You and Kaveh [326].

The Double-BV Blind Deblurring Model of Chan and Wong

On the other hand, in motion blurs or out-of-focus blurs arising from ideal diffraction-free lenses, as discussed in the beginning of this chapter, the PSFs are typically compactly supported with sharp cutoff boundaries. For such a class of blurs, as for images with sharp edges, the TV regularity seems more appealing,

$$E[k] = \beta \int_{\mathbb{R}^2} |Dk|.$$

This choice leads to the blind deblurring model first studied by Chan and Wong [77]:

$$E[u, k \mid u_0] = \alpha \int_{\mathbb{R}^2} |Du| + \beta \int_{\mathbb{R}^2} |Dk| + \frac{\lambda}{2} \int_{\mathbb{R}^2} (k * u - u_0)^2 dx, \qquad (5.50)$$

which, for convenience, shall be referred to as the *double-BV blind deblurring model*.

For the infinite domain $\Omega = \mathbb{R}^2$, the BV norm is conventionally defined as [137, 117]

$$\|u\|_{\mathrm{BV}} = \|u\|_{L^1(\mathbb{R}^2)} + |Du|(\mathbb{R}^2). \qquad (5.51)$$

While most results on BV functions in the literature are for bounded domains, it is worthwhile to pay extra attention to the complexity arising from unboundedness.

1. First, for example, one could easily cook a radially symmetric smooth function $g(x) = g(r)$ that equals r^{-2} as $r = |x| = \sqrt{x_1^2 + x_2^2} \to \infty$. Thus it cannot belong to $L^1(\mathbb{R}^2)$. On the other hand, $|g|^2 = r^{-4}$ and $|\nabla g| = |\partial g / \partial r| = 2r^{-3}$ as $r \to \infty$. Therefore, $g \in L^2(\mathbb{R}^2)$ and $|Dg|(\mathbb{R}^2) < \infty$. This situation cannot happen on any bounded domain.

2. Second, regular compactness theorems on bounded domains can fail on $\mathbb{R}^2$. Recall that on any bounded Lipschitz domain Ω, a bounded sequence from BV(Ω) must be precompact in $L^1(\Omega)$ [117, 137]. When $\Omega = \mathbb{R}^2$, this assertion becomes false. For example, take any compactly supported smooth function $\phi(x) \neq 0$ on $\mathbb{R}^2$, and define

$$g_n(x_1, x_2) = \phi(x_1 - n, x_2), \qquad n = 1, 2, \ldots.$$

Then it is trivial to see that

$$\|g_n\|_{BV} \equiv \|\phi\|_{BV}, \qquad n = 1, 2, \ldots.$$

As a result, (g_n) is a bounded sequence in $BV(\mathbb{R}^2)$. Suppose a subsequence (g_{n_k}) converges to some g_* in $L^1(\mathbb{R}^2)$. Then possibly with another round of subsequence refinement, one could assume that (g_{n_k}) converges to g_* almost everywhere. Now that ϕ is compactly supported, it is plain to see that $g_n(x) \to 0$ for any $x \in \mathbb{R}^2$. Thus $g_* \equiv 0$. But $g_{n_k} \to g_* = 0$ in L^1 is impossible since

$$\int_{\mathbb{R}^2} |g_{n_k}(x) - 0| dx \equiv \int_{\mathbb{R}^2} |\phi(x)| dx > 0, \quad n = 1, 2, \ldots.$$

We now first extend a Poincaré inequality from bounded domains to $\mathbb{R}^2$.

Theorem 5.7 (Poincaré's Inequality for $BV(\mathbb{R}^2)$). *Suppose u belongs to $BV(\mathbb{R}^2)$ with finite BV norm defined as in (5.51). Then $u \in L^2(\mathbb{R}^2)$, and more specifically,*

$$\|u\|_{L^2(\mathbb{R}^2)} \leq C |Du|(\mathbb{R}^2) \qquad \text{for some constant } C \text{ independent of } u.$$

Proof. By regular Poincaré inequalities [3, 137, 193], there exists a *fixed* constant C, such that for any open disk B_R centered at the origin, and any function $g \in BV(B_R)$,

$$\|g - \langle g \rangle_R\|_{L^2(B_R)} \leq C |Dg|(B_R) \quad \text{with} \quad \langle g \rangle_R = \frac{1}{|B_R|} \int_{B_R} g(x) dx.$$

It is remarkable and crucial that C does not depend on R (due to the right scaling law on both sides [117, 193]).

For any $u \in BV(\mathbb{R}^2)$ and any $R > 0$, define $g = u|_{B_R}$, and apply the above regular inequality:

$$\|u - \langle u \rangle_R\|_{L^2(B_R)} \leq C |Du|(B_R) \qquad \forall R > 0.$$

Notice that

$$\langle u \rangle_R = \frac{1}{|B_R|} \int_{B_R} u(x) dx \quad \Rightarrow \quad |\langle u \rangle_R| \leq \frac{\|u\|_{L^1(\mathbb{R}^2)}}{|B_R|}.$$

Therefore,

$$\|u\|_{L^2(B_R)} \leq C |Du|(B_R) + |\langle u \rangle_R| \times \|1\|_{L^2(B_R)} \leq C |Du|(B_R) + \frac{\|u\|_{L^1(\mathbb{R}^2)}}{|B_R|^{1/2}}.$$

Since both $|Du|$ and u^2 could be treated as nonnegative measures on $\mathbb{R}^2$, passing $R \to \infty$ proves the theorem. □

For the double-BV blind deblurring model

$$\min E[u, k \mid u_0] = \alpha \int_{\mathbb{R}^2} |Du| + \beta \int_{\mathbb{R}^2} |Dk| + \frac{\lambda}{2} \int_{\mathbb{R}^2} (k * u - u_0)^2 dx, \qquad (5.52)$$

we now impose the following natural conditions.

Condition A. The observation $u_0 \in L^2(\mathbb{R}^2) \cap L^\infty(\mathbb{R}^2)$.

Condition B. The ideal image u belongs to $\mathrm{BV}(\mathbb{R}^2)$.

Condition C. The blur PSF k belongs to $\mathrm{BV}(\mathbb{R}^2)$ and satisfies the DC-condition

$$\int_{\mathbb{R}^2} k(x)dx = 1.$$

The L^2 constraint in Condition A naturally comes from the data model in (5.52), while the L^∞ constraint is satisfied by most real imaging devices and is convenient for mathematical analysis.

On the other hand, according to the Poincaré inequality just established in Theorem 5.7, Condition B implies that $u \in L^2(\mathbb{R}^2)$. Therefore, according to Young's inequality [193],

$$\|k * u\|_{L^2(\mathbb{R}^2)} \leq \|k\|_{L^1(\mathbb{R}^2)} \|u\|_{L^2(\mathbb{R}^2)}.$$

Together with the assumption that $u_0 \in L^2(\mathbb{R}^2)$, this makes the data fitting term in (5.52) finite and well defined.

On the Uniqueness of Blind Deblurring

The investigation into the uniqueness issue helps further polish the modeling of blind deblurring.

First, we show that there are several hidden symmetries in the double-BV deblurring model (5.52), as stated in the next three theorems. Such symmetries, as in many other areas of mathematics, could lead to the nonuniqueness of solutions.

Theorem 5.8 (Image-PSF Uncertainty). *Suppose (u_*, k_*) is a minimizer to the double-BV deblurring model (5.52) with (α, β, λ) and under Conditions A, B, and C. Assume in addition that*

$$m = \int_{\mathbb{R}^2} u_*(x)dx = \beta/\alpha.$$

Then $(u_+, k_+) = (mk_*, u_*/m)$ must be a minimizer as well for the same set of parameters and under Conditions A, B, and C.

Proof. It is trivial to verify that $E[u_+, k_+ \mid u_0] = E[u_*, k_* \mid u_0]$ and k_+ satisfies the DC-condition. $\square$

On the other hand, for any given $a = (a_1, a_2) \in \mathbb{R}^2$, define the shifting operator

$$S_a : g(x) \to S_a[g] = g(x - a) \quad \text{for any measurable function } g.$$

Then just like differential operators, one has

$$S_a[k * u] = S_a[k] * u = k * S_a[u].$$

On the other hand, for any $u, k \in BV(\mathbb{R}^2)$,

$$\int_{\mathbb{R}^2} |DS_a[u]| = \int_{\mathbb{R}^2} |Du| \text{ and } \int_{\mathbb{R}^2} S_a[k]dx = \int_{\mathbb{R}^2} kdx.$$

Therefore the following theorem emerges naturally.

Theorem 5.9 (Dual-Translation Uncertainty). *Suppose* (u_*, k_*) *is a minimizer to the double-BV deblurring model* (5.52) *with* (α, β, λ) *and under Conditions* A, B, *and* C. *Then for any* $a \in \mathbb{R}^2$, $(S_a[u], S_a[k])$ *is a minimizer as well for the very same model.*

To gain further insights into the nature of nonuniqueness arising from the double-BV deblurring model, consider now an easier but intimately related model—the double-Sobolev blind deblurring model

$$E_2[u, k \mid u_0] = \frac{\alpha}{2} \int_{\mathbb{R}^2} |\nabla u|^2 dx + \frac{\beta}{2} \int_{\mathbb{R}^2} |\nabla k|^2 dx + \frac{\lambda}{2} \int_{\mathbb{R}^2} (k * u - u_0)^2 dx, \qquad (5.53)$$

where it has been assumed that both the image and PSF belong to the Sobolev space $H^1(\mathbb{R}^2)$ and that $k \in L^1(\mathbb{R}^2)$ satisfies the DC-condition $\langle k, 1 \rangle = 1$.

Recall that the unitary Fourier transform of a function $g(x)$ on $\mathbb{R}^2$ is defined by

$$G(\omega) = G(\omega_1, \omega_2) = \int_{\mathbb{R}^2} g(x) e^{-i2\pi\omega \cdot x} dx.$$

Then the fundamental properties give

$$\int_{\mathbb{R}^2} |G(\omega)|^2 d\omega = \int_{\mathbb{R}^2} |g(x)|^2 dx \text{ and } \int_{\mathbb{R}^2} |\nabla g(x)|^2 dx = 4\pi^2 \int_{\mathbb{R}^2} \omega^2 |G(\omega)|^2 d\omega$$

with $\omega^2 = |\omega|^2 = \omega_1^2 + \omega_2^2$.

Let $U(\omega)$, $K(\omega)$, and $U_0(\omega)$ denote the (unitary) Fourier transform of u, k, and u_0, respectively. Then the Fourier transform of $k * u$ becomes a direct product $K(\omega)U(\omega)$. Therefore, in the domain of spatial frequency $\omega = (\omega_1, \omega_2)$, the double-Sobolev blind deblurring energy $E_2[u, k \mid u_0]$ becomes $E_2[U, K \mid U_0] =$

$$2\pi^2\alpha \int_{\mathbb{R}^2} \omega^2 |U(\omega)|^2 d\omega + 2\pi^2\beta \int_{\mathbb{R}^2} \omega^2 |K(\omega)|^2 d\omega + \frac{\lambda}{2} \int_{\mathbb{R}^2} |K(\omega)U(\omega) - U_0(\omega)|^2 d\omega. \quad (5.54)$$

The DC-condition on the PSF now is simply $K(0) = 1$. Furthermore, on the image domain, u, k, and u_0 are all real. Therefore one requires that both U and K satisfy the conjugate condition

$$\bar{U}(\omega) = U(-\omega) \text{ and } \bar{K}(\omega) = K(-\omega), \qquad \omega \in \mathbb{R}^2. \qquad (5.55)$$

We are now ready to state a nonuniqueness theorem which is more general than Theorem 5.9.

Theorem 5.10 (Dual-Phase Uncertainty). *Let* $(u_*, k_*) \in H^1(\mathbb{R}^2) \times H^1(\mathbb{R}^2)$ *be a minimizer to the double-Sobolev blind deblurring model* (5.53) *with* (α, β, λ). *Let*

$$\phi(\omega) : \mathbb{R}^2 \to \mathbb{R}, \qquad \omega \to \phi(\omega),$$

be any real smooth phase factor that is odd: $\phi(-\omega) = -\phi(\omega)$. *Then*

$$(u_+, k_+) = \textit{Inverse Fourier Transforms of } (U_*(\omega)e^{i\phi(\omega)}, K_*(\omega)e^{-i\phi(\omega)})$$

is a minimizer as well for the very same model.

Proof. It is straightforward to verify on the Fourier domain that

$$E[u_+, k_+ \mid u_0] = E[u_*, k_* \mid u_0],$$

and that both u_+ and k_+ are indeed real. Furthermore, k_+ satisfies the DC-condition since

$$\int_{\mathbb{R}^2} k_+ dx = K_+(0) = K_*(0)e^{-i\phi(0)} = K_*(0) = 1. \quad \square$$

By taking $\phi(\omega) = a \cdot \omega = a_1\omega_1 + a_2\omega_2$ for any fixed $a = (a_1, a_2) \in \mathbb{R}^2$, one recovers the dual-translation uncertainty stated in Theorem 5.9.

To make solutions unique, it is therefore desirable to impose further conditions to break up the potential symmetries. On the other hand, the example of noncompactness designed right above Theorem 5.7 also suggests the hidden risk of nonexistence of solutions under the translation symmetry. Therefore, the discussion converges to an interesting point; i.e., symmetry breaking seems beneficial to the study of both uniqueness and existence.

The Existence Theorem

Before investigating the existence property, let us first polish Poincaré's inequality in Theorem 5.7 by dropping off the L^1 condition.

Theorem 5.11 (Poincaré's Inequality). *For any $u \in L^2(\mathbb{R}^2)$, the following Poincaré inequality holds:*

$$\|u\|_{L^2(\mathbb{R}^2)} \le C|Du|(\mathbb{R}^2) \quad \textit{for some constant } C \textit{ independent of } u.$$

Notice that the L^2 condition automatically implies that $u \in L^1_{\text{loc}}$, and consequently the TV Radon measure is well defined though it might be infinite. On the other hand, the finiteness of the L^2 norm appears necessary due to counterexamples like $u \equiv 1$.

Proof. Since both the L^2 norm and the TV Radon measure are continuous under the mollification procedure [117, 137], it suffices to prove the theorem when $u \in L^2(\mathbb{R}^2) \cap C^1(\mathbb{R}^2)$.

Define a compactly supported and radially symmetric function ϕ by

$$\phi(x) = \begin{cases} 1, & |x| < 1, \\ 0, & |x| \ge 2, \\ 2 - |x|, & 1 \le |x| \le 2. \end{cases}$$

Then $0 \le \phi(x) \le 1$ for any $x = (x_1, x_2) \in \mathbb{R}^2$. For any radius $R > 0$, define

$$\phi_R(x) = \phi(x/R), \qquad \text{which is compactly supported.}$$

Then $\nabla \phi_R(x)$ is supported on $R \le |x| \le 2R$, on which it equals $1/R$, and

$$\int_{\mathbb{R}^2} |\nabla \phi_R(x)|^2 dx = 2\pi \int_R^{2R} \frac{1}{R^2} r dr = 3\pi.$$

For any given $u \in L^2(\mathbb{R}^2)$, and $R > 0$, define $u_R(x) = \phi_R(x)u(x)$. Then at any $x \in \mathbb{R}^2$, $|u_R(x)|^2$ monotonically converges to $|u(x)|^2$ as $R \to \infty$. By the monotone convergence theorem [193],

$$\|u\|_{L^2(\mathbb{R}^2)} = \lim_{R \to \infty} \|u_R\|_{L^2(\mathbb{R}^2)}.$$

Since each u_R is compactly supported, Theorem 5.7 implies that

$$\|u\|_{L^2(\mathbb{R}^2)} \le C \liminf_{R \to \infty} |Du_R|(\mathbb{R}^2). \tag{5.56}$$

On the other hand, by the product rule,

$$\nabla(\phi_R u) = \phi_R \nabla u + u \nabla \phi_R,$$

and consequently,

$$\int_{\mathbb{R}^2} |\nabla u_R| dx \le \int_{\mathbb{R}^2} |\nabla u| dx + \int_{\mathbb{R}^2} |u| |\nabla \phi_R| dx. \tag{5.57}$$

Now that ϕ_R is supported on $R \le |x| \le 2R$ or the ring $B_{2R} \setminus B_R$, one has

$$\int_{\mathbb{R}^2} |u| |\nabla \phi_R| dx \le \|u\|_{L^2(B_{2R} \setminus B_R)} \|\nabla \phi_R\|_{L^2(\mathbb{R}^2)} = \sqrt{3\pi} \, \|u\|_{L^2(B_{2R} \setminus B_R)},$$

which converges to zero as $R \to \infty$ since $u \in L^2(\mathbb{R}^2)$. In combination with (5.56) and (5.57), this establishes the theorem. □

Motivated by Theorems 5.7 and 5.11, we now define the space BV_2 by

$$BV_2(\mathbb{R}^2) = \{u \in L^2(\mathbb{R}^2) \mid |Du|(\mathbb{R}^2) < \infty\}.$$

Then by Theorem 5.7, $BV(\mathbb{R}^2) \subseteq BV_2(\mathbb{R}^2)$. The larger space BV_2 shall play a natural role for the blind deblurring model to be discussed below.

We are now in a well-informed position to study the existence of the double-BV blind deblurring model

$$E[u, k \mid u_0] = \alpha \int_{\mathbb{R}^2} |Du| + \beta \int_{\mathbb{R}^2} |Dk| + \frac{\lambda}{2} \int_{\mathbb{R}^2} (k * u - u_0)^2 dx. \tag{5.58}$$

As clear from the preceding discussion as well as motivated by real applications, it is important to break the symmetric role of the image u and PSF k in the model. The following conditions will be assumed for the study of existence.

Condition (a). Observation $u_0 \in L^2(\mathbb{R}^2) \cap L^\infty(\mathbb{R}^2)$.

Condition (b). Image $u \in \mathrm{BV}_2(\mathbb{R}^2)$, and $\|u\|_{L^\infty} \leq \|u_0\|_{L^\infty}$.

Condition (c). PSF $k \in \mathrm{BV}(\mathbb{R}^2)$, nonnegative, and satisfies the DC-condition $\langle k, 1 \rangle = 1$.

The L^∞ assumption on the observation is often valid in most real applications since most imaging devices have a maximum saturation level. The control on the L^∞ norm of u in Condition (b) seems natural as well since u_0 is already "overshooting" due to spontaneous noise. It is like the maximum principle for linear elliptic equations [117] to ensure stability, or from the information theory point of view [93], it amounts to saying that no independently new information (with respect to the observed data) should be created in data processing. Finally, besides the necessary DC-condition, in Condition (c), k is required to be nonnegative, leading to what is called *moving average* in signal processing [237]. The nonnegativity condition is certainly satisfied by most blur models including motion blurs and out-of-focus blurs addressed in the beginning.

The constraints put differently on u and k help break their symmetric role in the model. However, it is easy to check that even under Conditions (b) and (c), the dual-translation uncertainty addressed by Theorem 5.9 is still not gotten rid of, since both sets of conditions are still translation-invariant.

To eradicate the translation duality, one needs to prevent from "floating" at least one of the two targets: the ideal image u or the PSF k. Images by definition can virtually be any functions, while most PSFs are indeed centered around the origin (corresponding to moving averages near the vicinities of each pixel). It thus become natural to have k fixed instead of u.

In Chan and Wong's work [77], the following centrosymmetry condition is imposed:

Condition (d'). The PSF is centrosymmetric: $k(-x) = k(x)$.

From the linear operator point of view, this amounts to requiring that the blur $K[u]$ is Hermitian. Numerical evidences in [77] seem to suggest that this condition can stably lead to unique deblurring solutions, or at least in a local sense (i.e., local minima). But general theoretical support has not yet been developed.

For what follows, to encourage the PSF to be highly concentrated near the origin, we impose the last condition.

Condition (d). There exist some nonnegative function $F(x) \in L^1(\mathbb{R}^2)$ and some positive radius $R > 0$, so that

$$0 \leq k(x) \leq F(x) \quad \forall x \in \mathbb{R}^2 : |x| \geq R. \tag{5.59}$$

Notice that here the knowledge of R and $F(x)$ for $|x| \geq R$ is treated as known. For example, if $F(x) \equiv 0$ for all $|x| \geq R$, Condition (d) amounts to requiring that k is compactly supported on the disk $B_R = \{x \in \mathbb{R}^2 : |x| < R\}$.

Theorem 5.12 (Existence of Double-BV Blind Deblurring). *Under Conditions* (a), (b), (c), *and* (d), *the minimizers to the double-BV blind deblurring model* (5.58) *exist.*

Proof. Let $R > 0$ be introduced as in Condition (d), and define

$$k_R(x) = \frac{1}{|B_R|} 1_{|x|<R}(x) = \frac{1}{\pi R^2} 1_{|x|<R}(x).$$

Then, $k_R \geq 0$ satisfies the DC-condition, and

$$\int_{\mathbb{R}^2} |Dk_R| = \frac{2\pi R}{\pi R^2} = \frac{2}{R} < \infty.$$

In particular, for the special image-PSF pair $(u \equiv 0, k_R)$,

$$E[u \equiv 0, k_R \mid u_0] = \beta \int_{\mathbb{R}^2} |Dk_R| + \frac{\lambda}{2} \|u_0\|_{L^2}^2 < \infty.$$

Therefore, there must exist a minimizing sequence (u_n, k_n) to the double-BV blind deblurring energy, subject to Conditions (a) through (d).

By Poincaré's inequality in Theorem 5.11, (u_n) must be a bounded sequence in $L^2(\mathbb{R}^2)$. Then on any fixed bounded (Lipschitz) domain Ω of $\mathbb{R}^2$, by Schwartz's inequality,

$$\|u_n\|_{L^1(\Omega)} \leq \|u_n\|_{L^2(\Omega)} \times \sqrt{|\Omega|}.$$

Therefore, restricted on Ω, (u_n) is bounded in BV(Ω) for any bounded Ω. Then by the L^1 precompactness of bounded sets of BV functions on bounded domains [137, 193], in combination with Cantor's diagonal selection procedure [193], one could find a subsequence of (u_n), for convenience still labelled by (u_n), and some $u_* \in L^1_{\text{loc}}(\mathbb{R}^2)$, such that on any finite disk $B_\rho = \{x \in \mathbb{R}^2 : |x| < \rho\}$,

$$u_n \to u_* \quad \text{in} \quad L^1(B_\rho).$$

In particular, with possibly another round of subsequence refinement, one could assume that

$$u_n(x) \to u_*(x), \qquad \text{almost everywhere in } \mathbb{R}^2. \tag{5.60}$$

Then by the lower semicontinuity of the TV Radon measure under L^1_{loc}-topology [137], one has

$$\int_{\mathbb{R}^2} |Du_*| \leq \liminf_{n \to \infty} \int_{\mathbb{R}^2} |Du_n|. \tag{5.61}$$

Since all these results are only based upon the boundedness of the TV Radon measure, they hold for the PSF sequence (k_n) as well, which shall be assumed from now on. In particular, there exists $k_* \in L^1_{\text{loc}}(\mathbb{R}^2)$, such that

$$k_n \to k_* \quad \text{in any} \quad L^1(B_\rho), \quad \text{and almost surely in } \mathbb{R}^2. \tag{5.62}$$

In addition,

$$\int_{\mathbb{R}^2} |Dk_*| \leq \liminf_{n \to \infty} \int_{\mathbb{R}^2} |Dk_n|. \tag{5.63}$$

Let $M = \|u_0\|_{L^\infty(\mathbb{R}^2)}$. Then Condition (b) implies that

$$|u_n(y)| \leq M, \quad n = 1, 2, \ldots, \quad \forall y \in \mathbb{R}^2. \tag{5.64}$$

For any fixed $x \in \mathbb{R}^2$, define $k^x(y) = k(x - y)$, and k_n^x and k_*^x similarly. Define $r = R + |x|$. Then

$$k * u(x) = \langle k^x(y), u(y) \rangle = \langle k^x(y), u(y) \rangle_{B_r} + \langle k^x(y), u(y) \rangle_{B_r^c}, \qquad (5.65)$$

where $B_r^c = \mathbb{R}^2 \setminus B_r$ denotes the complement.

Restricted on B_r, the property in (5.62) implies that

$$k_n^x(y) \to k_*^x(y) \quad \text{in } L^1(B_r).$$

By Lebesgue's dominated convergence theorem, in combination with (5.60) and (5.64),

$$\langle k_*^x, u_n \rangle_{B_r} \to \langle k_*^x, u_* \rangle_{B_r}, \quad n \to \infty.$$

On the other hand,

$$|\langle k_n^x, u_n \rangle_{B_r} - \langle k_*^x, u_n \rangle_{B_r}| \le M \| k_n^x - k_*^x \|_{L^1(B_r)} \to 0, \quad n \to \infty.$$

Therefore, we have established

$$\langle k_n^x, u_n \rangle_{B_r} \to \langle k_*^x, u_* \rangle_{B_r}, \quad n \to \infty. \qquad (5.66)$$

On the complement $y \in B_r^c$ (with $r = R + |x|$),

$$|y - x| \ge |y| - |x| > r - |x| = R.$$

Then by Condition (d),

$$|k_n^x(y)| = |k_n(x - y)| \le F(x - y) = F^x(y) \qquad \forall n \text{ and } y \in B_r^c.$$

Since $F \in L^1(\mathbb{R}^2)$, for each given x, one must have $F^x \in L^1(B_r^c)$. Using $M F_x(y)$ as the majorant and applying Lebesgue's dominated convergence theorem to $(k_n^x(y) u_n(y))$ on B_r^c, one has

$$\langle k_n^x(y), u_n(y) \rangle_{B_r^c} \to \langle k_*^x(y), u_*(y) \rangle_{B_r^c}, \quad n \to \infty. \qquad (5.67)$$

In combination with (5.66) and (5.67), the decomposition identity (5.65) implies that

$$k_n * u_n(x) \to k_* * u_*(x) \quad \forall x \in \mathbb{R}^2.$$

Then by applying Fatou's lemma [193] to the pointwise convergent nonnegative sequence

$$e_n(x) = (k_n * u_n - u_0(x))^2, \quad n = 1, 2, \ldots,$$

one has

$$\int_{\mathbb{R}^2} e_*(x) dx \le \liminf_{n \to \infty} \int_{\mathbb{R}^2} e_n(x) dx.$$

In combination with (5.61) and (5.63), this leads to

$$E[u_*, k_* \mid u_0] \le \liminf_{n \to \infty} E[u_n, k_n \mid u_0],$$

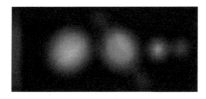

Figure 5.9. *A computational example for the double-BV blind deblurring model (by Chan and Wong [77]). Left: the blurry image; Right: the deblurred image.*

implying that (u_*, k_*) has to be a minimizer pair, if it indeed satisfies Conditions (b) through (d), which shall be validated one by one as follows.

Due to pointwise convergency, one has $\|u_*\|_{L^\infty} \le \|u_0\|_{L^\infty}$. Furthermore, by Fatou's lemma and Poincaré's inequality in Theorem 5.11,

$$\|u_*\|_{L^2} \le \liminf_{n \to \infty} \|u_n\|_{L^2} \le \liminf_{n \to \infty} |Du_n|(\mathbb{R}^2) < \infty.$$

This implies that, in combination with (5.61), $u_* \in \mathrm{BV}_2(\mathbb{R}^2)$ and satisfies Condition (b).

Similarly, k_* must belong to $\mathrm{BV}(\mathbb{R}^2)$, $k_* \ge 0$, and satisfy Condition (d). The DC-condition

$$\langle k_* , 1 \rangle = 1$$

must hold due to Condition (d) for the minimizing sequence (k_n) and their L^1-convergence to k_* on any bounded domain of $\mathbb{R}^2$.

Therefore, (u_*, k_*) is indeed a minimizer to the double-BV blind deblurring model (5.58), subject to Conditions (b) through (d). □

Computationally, the double-BV blind deblurring model (5.58) can be implemented via the alternating minimization (AM) algorithm (see (5.40)). More details can be found in [77, 229]. Figure 5.9 is a computational example from Chan and Wong [77].

Chapter 6
Image Inpainting

Interpolation has been a significant topic in a number of areas including numerical analysis; computational PDEs; approximation theory; real, complex, and harmonic analysis; and signal processing.

In image processing, image interpolation is such a fundamental problem that there have been numerous prior works in existence. In the engineering literature, for instance, one witnesses the following samples from a large pool: image interpolation [13, 181, 182], image replacement [156, 316], error concealment [161, 187], and image editing [111]. In mathematical image and vision analysis, image interpolation has also been studied systematically in the remarkable works of Nitzberg, Mumford, and Shiota for segmentation with depth and edge completion [234], Masnou and Morel for level-line completion [213, 214], and Caselles, Morel, and Sbert for axiomatic interpolation based on second order PDEs [50]. To our best knowledge, the work of Masnou and Morel [214], which won the best-student-paper award in ICIP '98, was the first work performing variational *image* interpolation as inspired by Nitzberg, Mumford, and Shiota's variational model for *edge* completion [234].

The word *inpainting* is an artistic synonym for *image interpolation* and has been circulated for quite a while among museum restoration artists [312]. It was first transplanted into digital image processing in the remarkable work by Bertalmio et al. [24], which has stimulated the recent wave of interest in numerous problems related to image interpolation, including the works by Chan and Shen and their collaborators.

The current chapter presents several inpainting models based upon the Bayesian, variational, PDE, as well as wavelet approaches. Numerous applications of inpainting techniques in digital and information technologies are also discussed.

The presentation of the current chapter attempts to organize the topics according to the logical mathematical structure espoused in Chapters 1, 2, and 3, i.e., from the general Baysian/variational principles to their associated Euler–Lagrange PDEs. We will also discuss other approaches that do not fit into this framework strictly but have been very important and successful, including the third order nonlinear inpainting PDE by Bertalmio et al. [24] and its Navier–Stokes interpretation [23], and the axiomatic approach of Caselles, Morel, and Sbert [50]. Inpainting of Markov random fields (as first heuristically employed in the well-known paper by Efros and Leung [110]) will also be briefly discussed in the end, and other more complex but powerful stochastic approaches to pattern-theoretic inpainting can be found, e.g., in the work of Guo, Zhu, and Wu [148].

6.1   A Brief Review on Classical Interpolation Schemes

A general image inpainting problem can be described as follows. Normally an ideal image $u^0 = u^0(x)$ is defined on a complete image domain $x = (x_1, x_2) \in \Omega$. Due to imperfect image acquisition, transmission, and numerous other factors, however, there exists a subset $D \subseteq \Omega$ such that the image information on D is missing (e.g., due to wireless loss) or unavailable (e.g., due to opaqueness and occlusion). Furthermore, even the observable or accessible portion $u^0\big|_{D^c}$ of the image on the complement $D^c = \Omega \setminus D$ is often degraded by noise or blur. The goal of image inpainting is to reconstruct the entire ideal image from such incomplete and often degraded observable data (see Figure 6.1). Therefore, inpainting is in essence a 2-D interpolation problem.

To be more self-contained and complete, we first briefly review the rich classical literature on signal or function interpolation. In the next section, we shall then explain why most conventional interpolation schemes become insufficient for image inpainting applications.

For more details on the classical literature of signal interpolation, we refer the reader to the monographs by Walsh [313] on polynomial and rational interpolation, de Boor [99] on spline interpolation, and Wahba [311] on thin-plate splines.

6.1.1   Polynomial Interpolation

Classical polynomial interpolation (in one dimension) is stated as follows: given $n + 1$ distinct nodes

$$\Gamma = \{a = x_0 < x_1 < \cdots < x_n = b\}$$

and the values of an unknown signal f on these nodes

$$f_0 = f(x_0), \quad f_1 = f(x_1), \quad \ldots, \quad f_n = f(x_n),$$

find the unique polynomial $p(x)$ in the $(n + 1)$-dimensional linear space

$$P_n = \{q(x) \mid q(x) = a_0 + a_1 x + \cdots + a_n x^n\},$$

such that

$$p(x_i) = f(x_i), \quad i = 0 : n.$$

Then the unknown signal $f(x)$ is approximated by $p(x)$.

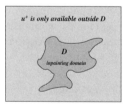

Figure 6.1. *The goal of inpainting is to reconstruct the ideal image u on the* entire domain *based on the incomplete and often degraded data u^0 available outside the missing (or inpainting) domain D.*

The solution exists uniquely and can be expressed explicitly via the Lagrange basis:

$$L_i(x) = \frac{\prod_{j \neq i}(x - x_j)}{\prod_{j \neq i}(x_i - x_j)}, \quad i = 0 : n.$$

Each Lagrange function has the canonical interpolant property

$$L_i(x_j) = \delta_{i,j} = 1 \quad \text{if } j = i; \quad 0 \quad \text{otherwise.} \tag{6.1}$$

Then the unique polynomial interpolant $p \in P_n$ for a given data f_i's is given by

$$p(x) = \sum_{i=0}^{n} f_i L_i(x).$$

Algebraically clean and elegant, this theoretical approach is, however, computationally unpleasant when the number n of nodes is not small. In applications it often occurs that one would like to add more control nodes to an existing set Γ. The above formulae do not reveal any obvious way to construct the new interpolant based on the existing ones. Clever algorithms, however, do exist for computing $p(x)$ progressively, such as *Newton's divided differences* and Neville's algorithm [287]. We also refer the reader to the recent work of Olver for further extensions of these schemes [236].

Furthermore, when n is large, the high order polynomial interpolant $p(x)$ would inevitably become oscillatory even though the original target function $f(x)$ may not. This is mainly due to the fact that polynomial interpolation does not satisfy the *maximum principle*:

$$\|p(x)\|_{L^\infty[a,b]} \leq \|f(\Gamma)\|_{l^\infty}, \quad f(\Gamma) = (f(x_0), f(x_1), \ldots, f(x_n)), \tag{6.2}$$

where $f(\Gamma)$ is considered as an ordered sequence. Overshooting is therefore common in polynomial interpolation.

Finally, we formulate a more general polynomial interpolation problem. Let Γ be a given finite set of nodes as above, and

$$\boldsymbol{m} : \Gamma \to \{0, 1, 2, \ldots\}, \quad \boldsymbol{m} = (\boldsymbol{m}_0, \ldots, \boldsymbol{m}_n),$$

a multiplicity vector which assigns $\boldsymbol{m}_i$ to each node x_i. Define

$$|\boldsymbol{m}| = \boldsymbol{m}_0 + \boldsymbol{m}_1 + \cdots + \boldsymbol{m}_n.$$

Given a nodes set Γ and $\boldsymbol{m}$, define for any smooth function $f(x)$ on $[a, b]$ the allocation map $\Gamma^{\boldsymbol{m}} : f \to \Gamma^{\boldsymbol{m}}(f)$ by

$$\Gamma^{\boldsymbol{m}}(f) = (f(x_0), f'(x_0), \ldots, f^{(m_0-1)}(x_0); \ldots \ldots; f(x_n), \ldots, f^{(m_n-1)}(x_n)). \tag{6.3}$$

Then a general polynomial interpolation problem can be stated as follows:

$$\text{given } \Gamma^{\boldsymbol{m}}(f), \text{ find } p(x) \in P_{|\boldsymbol{m}|-1}, \text{ such that } \Gamma^{\boldsymbol{m}}(p) = \Gamma^{\boldsymbol{m}}(f). \tag{6.4}$$

If $\boldsymbol{m} = (1, 1, \ldots, 1)$, it reproduces the above Lagrange interpolation problem. For a general $\boldsymbol{m}$, it is the Hermitian interpolation problem. The solution always exists uniquely, and progressive constructive algorithms are available as well (see, e.g., [287]).

6.1.2 Trigonometric Polynomial Interpolation

If one knows a priori that the target unknown signal $f(x)$ is periodic, the trigonometric polynomial interpolants then become more ideal than ordinary polynomials since the latter are not periodic.

For convenience, after a possible linear rescaling of x, assume that $f(x)$ is 2π-periodic. Define the trigonometric polynomial space

$$T_n = \text{span}\{1, \cos x, \sin x, \ldots, \cos nx, \sin nx\}.$$

Given a set of $2n + 1$ nodes

$$\Gamma : 0 \le x_0 < x_1 < \cdots < x_{2n} < 2\pi,$$

the interpolation problem can then be stated as follows:

find the unique trigonometric polynomial $t(x) \in T_n$ such that $t(\Gamma) = f(\Gamma)$,   (6.5)

where $f(\Gamma)$ or $t(\Gamma)$ is defined as in (6.2). The solution exists and is unique [287].

As inspired by digital signal processing [237], the z-transform is a useful tool to make the connection between trigonometric polynomial interpolants and ordinary polynomial interpolants in the preceding section. First, notice that in terms of complex coefficients, T_n is equivalently spanned by

$$T_n = \text{span}\{1, e^{\pm ix}, \ldots, e^{\pm inx}\}.$$

The z-transform is given by

$$z = e^{ix}, \quad z^k = e^{ikx}, \quad \text{and} \quad z_k = e^{-ix_k}, \quad k = 0 : 2n.$$

Then the interpolant space T_n and the nodes set Γ become

$$T_n^z = \text{span}\{1, z^{\pm 1}, \ldots, z^{\pm n}\} \quad \text{and} \quad \Gamma^z = \{z_0, z_1, \ldots, z_{2n}\}.$$

On the complex plane under the z-transform, T_n^z becomes a linear space of Laurent polynomials, and the nodes set is along the unit circle S^1. Then the trigonometric polynomial interpolation problem becomes a Laurent polynomial interpolation problem:

find the unique z-Laurent polynomial $q(z) \in T_n^z$ such that $q(\Gamma^z) = f(\Gamma^z)$.   (6.6)

Furthermore, if one defines

$$z^n f(\Gamma^z) = (z_k^n f(z_k) \mid k = 0 : 2n),$$

and $P_{2n}(z)$ denotes the ordinary z-polynomial space as in the preceding section, then the trigonometric interpolation problem becomes a genuine polynomial one on the complex plane:

find the unique polynomial $p(z) \in P_{2n}(z)$ such that $p(\Gamma^z) = z^n f(\Gamma^z)$,   (6.7)

from which the polynomial interpolation theory guarantees the existence and uniqueness of trigonometric interpolants.

A special case of the z-transform technique is the x-transform, as very useful in designing various finite impulse response (FIR) digital filters in both digital signal processing and wavelet theory (see, e.g., Oppenheim and Schafer [237], Shen and Strang [280, 281, 282] and Shen, Strang, and Wathen [284]). In these applications, the target function $F(\omega)$ is the frequency response of an FIR filter to be designed, and

$$\Gamma = \{\omega_0, \omega_1, \ldots, \omega_n\}$$

specifies a set of frequencies on which desired values are given:

$$F(\Gamma) = (F_0 = F(\omega_0), \ldots, F_n = F(\omega_n)).$$

If the filter is symmetric and real as in many applications, then $F(\omega) = F(-\omega)$ and is real as well. As a result, it suffices to specify only the values for some $\Gamma \subseteq [0, \pi]$ and restrict to the cosine interpolants:

$$T_n^c = \text{span}\{1, \cos\omega, \ldots, \cos n\omega\} = \text{span}\{1, \cos\omega, \ldots, \cos^n \omega\}.$$

Define the x-transform $\omega \to x = \cos\omega = (z + \bar{z})/2$, under which

$$\Gamma \to \Gamma^x = \cos(\Gamma) = \{x_0, x_1, \ldots, x_n\} \subseteq [0, 1] \quad \text{and} \quad T_n^c \to P_n = \text{span}\{1, x, \ldots, x^n\}.$$

Thus trigonometric interpolation becomes ordinary real polynomial interpolation.

Finally, for the general trigonometric interpolation problem (6.5), when the nodes are equally spaced, the coefficients of the interpolant $t(x)$ and the given data $f(\Gamma)$ are clearly connected by the discrete Fourier transform and the celebrated FFT algorithm.

6.1.3 Spline Interpolation

Splines improve polynomial interpolants based on the spirit of Taylor expansion, which says that *locally* any smooth function is a polynomial plus some high order residue. Thus a general smooth function looks like a collection of locally valid polynomials smoothly glued together. The gluing mechanism frees the interpolants from the restriction of being global polynomials, and thus is more flexible and faithful for approximating local variations.

As before, let $\Gamma : a = x_0 < x_1 < \cdots < x_n = b$ denote the nodes set, and let

$$\Gamma(f) = f(\Gamma) = (f(x_0), f(x_1), \ldots, f(x_n))$$

be the samples of an unknown smooth signal on Γ. More generally, for any positive integer r, define

$$\Gamma^r(f) = (f^{(s)}(x_k) \mid s = 0 : r - 1, \quad k = 0 : n),$$

which, in terms of the map $\Gamma^m(f)$ introduced in the preceding section, corresponds to $m = (r, r, \ldots, r)$. Furthermore, for any two positive integers α and m, define the spline space of interpolants

$$S_m^\alpha(\Gamma) = \{s(x) \in C^\alpha[a, b] \ : \ s(x)\big|_{[a,b]\backslash\Gamma} \in P_m\}, \tag{6.8}$$

where for any open set I, the notation $s(x)\big|_I \in P_m$ means that for any $x_0 \in I$, there is a neighborhood $J \subseteq I$ of x_0 on which $s(x)$ is identical to some polynomial in P_m. Then it is easy to see that $s(x)$ must be a *single* polynomial on any interval (x_k, x_{k+1}), $k = 0 : n - 1$, and these n localized polynomials are glued together at the nodes in Γ to achieve global C^α-smoothness.

A general spline interpolation problem is then formulated as follows: *given a nodes set Γ and sampled data $\Gamma^r(f)$ of some unknown smooth function f, find a spline $s \in S_m^\alpha(\Gamma)$, such that $\Gamma^r(f) = \Gamma^r(s)$.*

Apparently, there must exist some constraints among r, α, and m for the problem to be well posed, i.e, ensuring the existence and uniqueness of a spline interpolant. To proceed, focus on any particular interval $I_k = (x_k, x_{k+1})$, and let $p_k = s\big|_{I_k}$ denote the polynomial on I_k. Since $p_k \in P_m$, it has $m + 1$ degrees of freedom endowed through its $m + 1$ coefficients. Meanwhile, p_k has to satisfy two types of constraints:

(A) the *fitting* constraints at ∂I_k and (B) the *regularity* constraints for $s \in C^\alpha$.

The first imposes $2r$ constraints with r ones demanded by each endpoint. The second seems to add $\alpha + 1$ constraints at each endpoint to match each adjacent polynomial. With r conditions already specified in (A), the number of regularity constraints (B) is then reduced to $\alpha + 1 - r$ at each endpoint. However, this does not mean that the net number of regularity constraints for p_k would be $2(\alpha + 1 - r)$, simply because that unlike (A), the $\alpha + 1 - r$ regularity constraints at each endpoint are of a *free-boundary* nature! That is, they are not *fixed* constraints but ones coupled to the adjacent polynomials. Therefore, these number of constraints should be equally split between p_k and its adjacent neighbor at that endpoint. Consequently the net number of regularity constraints (type (B)) on p_k is $\alpha + 1 - r$, as if $(\alpha + 1 - r)/2$ ones from either end.

In combination, the total number of constraints on p_k is

$$2r + \alpha + 1 - r = \alpha + r + 1.$$

Thus the natural condition for existence and uniqueness is

$$m + 1 = \alpha + r + 1 \quad \text{or} \quad m = \alpha + r \qquad (r \geq 1). \tag{6.9}$$

Furthermore, for the two global endpoints $a = x_0$ and $b = x_n$, the above analysis also indicates that uniqueness would require $(\alpha + 1 - r)/2 = (m + 1)/2 - r$ number of extra (boundary) conditions to be imposed at each endpoint. Thus m must be an odd integer. Furthermore, $m \geq 2r - 1$ as a direct consequence of type (A) constraints.

Under the conditions of (6.9) and $m \geq 2r - 1$ being odd, it is known in spline theory that the spline interpolant uniquely exists for any given data $\Gamma^r(f)$. For many applications in computational sciences (e.g., computer graphics and numerical PDEs), only the function values are usually directly available, which implies the importance of $r = 1$.

When $m = 1$, (6.9) then requires $r = 1$ and $\alpha = 0$. Since $(m + 1)/2 - r = 0$, no extra boundary conditions are required at a or b. Then the spline interpolant is simply the unique *piecewise linear* function whose graph passes through and makes turns only at (x_k, f_k)'s.

When $m = 3$ and $r = 1$, one obtains the celebrated *cubic* splines. By (6.9), the regularity index is $\alpha = m - r = 2$, implying that cubic splines are C^2 functions. Moreover, since $(m + 1)/2 - r = 1$, one extra condition is needed at each boundary node $x_0 = a$ or $x_n = b$, which could be imposed as $s''(a) = s''(b) = 0$, the inflection-point condition.

When $m = 3$, the above conditions also allow $r = 2$, which is, however, uninteresting since the spline interpolation problem on Γ is then decoupled to ordinary cubic polynomial interpolation on each interval $I_k = [x_k, x_{k+1}]$, $k = 0 : n - 1$.

When $m = 5$ and $r = 1$, one obtains *quintic* splines, of which the regularity is $\alpha = 4$, and the number of extra constraints needed at each boundary endpoint is $(m + 1)/2 - r = 2$. When $m = 5$ and $r = 2$, $\alpha = 3$ and one extra condition is required at each of the two boundary points. The last permissible case when $m = 5$ and $r = 3$ is again uninteresting due to its decoupling nature.

We refer the reader to de Boor [99] for further details on numerous computational and analytical structures of splines.

6.1.4 Shannon's Sampling Theorem

A signal $f(x) \in L^2(\mathbb{R})$ is said to be bandlimited if its Fourier transform is compactly supported. By the Paley–Wiener theorem [96], a bandlimited signal must be an entire function $f(z)$ defined on the whole complex plane.

After a proper dilation, such a signal $f(x)$ can be assumed bandlimited within $(-\pi, \pi)$. Let $F(\omega)$ denote its Fourier transform. Then

$$1_{(-\pi, \pi)}(\omega) \cdot F(\omega) = F(\omega), \quad \omega \in \mathbb{R}.$$

Let $F_p(\omega)$ denote the periodic extension of $F(\omega)$, i.e.,

$$F_p(\omega) = \sum_{n=-\infty}^{\infty} F(\omega + 2n\pi), \quad \omega \in \mathbb{R}.$$

Then one still has

$$1_{(-\pi, \pi)}(\omega) \cdot F_p(\omega) = F(\omega), \quad \omega \in \mathbb{R}. \tag{6.10}$$

In order to return to the x-domain, notice that the inverse Fourier transform of $1_{-\pi, \pi}(\omega)$ is

$$\frac{1}{2\pi} \int_{-\pi}^{\pi} e^{ix\omega} d\omega = \frac{\sin(\pi x)}{\pi x} = \mathrm{sinc}(x),$$

and the inverse Fourier transform of a periodic function is a sequence $c_. = (c_n)$:

$$c_n = \frac{1}{2\pi} \int_{-\pi}^{\pi} F_p(\omega) e^{in\omega} d\omega = \frac{1}{2\pi} \int_{\mathbb{R}} F(\omega) e^{in\omega} d\omega = f(n).$$

That is, c_n is precisely the sampling of f at $x = n$, which is well defined since f is entire (and in particular continuous). Since multiplication becomes convolution under inverse Fourier transform, eventually the identity (6.10) leads to

$$\mathrm{sinc}(x) * c_. = f(x) \quad \text{or} \quad \sum_{n \in \mathbb{Z}} f(n) \, \mathrm{sinc}(x - n) = f(x).$$

This is exactly the celebrated sampling and interpolation theorem of Shannon.

Theorem 6.1 (Shannon's Canonical Sampling/Interpolation Theorem). *Suppose an* L^2
function $f(x)$ *is bandlimited to* $(-\pi, \pi)$. *Then* $f(x)$ *has an entire representative which
satisfies the perfect interpolation reconstruction:*

$$f(x) = \sum_{n \in \mathbb{Z}} f(n) \operatorname{sinc}(x - n).$$

Shannon's interpolation theorem has profound implication in modern wavelet interpolation theory, of which we now give a very brief account.

Suppose the Fourier transform $G(\omega)$ of a general L^2 signal $g(y)$ is bandlimited onto
$(-\Omega, +\Omega)$. Define

$$F(\omega) = G\left(\frac{\Omega \omega}{\pi}\right),$$

and $f(y)$ is the inverse Fourier transform of F. Then f is bandlimited to the canonical
interval $(-\pi, \pi)$, and

$$f(y) = \frac{\pi}{\Omega} g\left(\frac{\pi y}{\Omega}\right).$$

Therefore by Shannon's theorem (Theorem 6.1),

$$g\left(\frac{\pi y}{\Omega}\right) = \sum_{n \in \mathbb{Z}} g\left(\frac{n\pi}{\Omega}\right) \operatorname{sinc}(y - n).$$

Making a change of variables, $x = y\pi/\Omega$, one has the general sampling theorem of Shannon:

$$g(x) = \sum_{n \in \mathbb{Z}} g\left(\frac{n\pi}{\Omega}\right) \operatorname{sinc}\left(\frac{\Omega}{\pi} x - n\right). \tag{6.11}$$

In particular, if $\Omega = 2^j \pi$ with $j \in \mathbb{Z}$, one has

$$g(x) = \sum_{n \in \mathbb{Z}} g(2^{-j} n) \operatorname{sinc}(2^j x - n).$$

Define as in wavelet theory

$$s_{j,n}(x) = 2^{j/2} \operatorname{sinc}(2^j x - n), \qquad j, n \in \mathbb{Z}.$$

Then for each given j, $(s_{j,\cdot})$ is an orthonormal basis for the Hilbert subspace

$$V_j = \{f \in L^2(\mathbb{R}) \mid f \text{ is bandlimited within } (-2^j \pi, 2^j \pi)\}.$$

For any general L^2 function f, define for each j,

$$f_j(x) = \sum_{n \in \mathbb{Z}} \langle f, s_{j,n} \rangle s_{j,n}(x) \in V_j.$$

Then it is easy to see that in the Fourier domain,

$$F_j(\omega) = F(\omega) \cdot 1_{(-2^j \pi, 2^j \pi)}(\omega)$$

is the spectral truncation of F. Therefore, as $j \to \infty$, $F_j \to F$ in L^2, and so is $f_j \to f$.
Modern wavelet approximation and interpolation essentially polish Shannon's sampling
theorem along this line [96, 281, 290].

Extensions of Shannon's sampling theorem can be found, for example, in the works
of Frazier, Jawerth, and Weiss [127] and Smale and Zhou [285].

6.1.5   Radial Basis Functions and Thin-Plate Splines

Radial basis functions are popular interpolants for interpolating scattered spatial data, such as in image processing, computer graphics, and statistical data analysis [311].

Let $\Gamma = \{x_1, \ldots, x_n\} \subseteq \mathbb{R}^2$ be a discrete set of spatial locations on which the values of an unknown function f is given by

$$f(\Gamma) = \{f_1 = f(x_1), \ldots, f_n = f(x_n)\}.$$

Let $\phi(r) = \phi(|x|)$ be a radially symmetric function. Popular choices in the literature include

$$
\begin{aligned}
\text{Gaussian}: \quad & \phi(r) = e^{-r^2/a^2}, \\
\text{reciprocal quadratic}: \quad & \phi(r) = \frac{1}{1 + a^2 r^2}, \\
\text{multiquadratic}: \quad & \phi(r) = \sqrt{1 + a^2 r^2}, \\
\text{thin-plate spline}: \quad & \phi(r) = r^2 \ln r.
\end{aligned}
\tag{6.12}
$$

A radial basis interpolant is to have the reconstruction of f given by the following form:

$$\hat{f}(x) = \sum_{k=1}^{n} \lambda_k \phi(|x - x_k|), \tag{6.13}$$

so that $\hat{f}(x_k) = f(x_k) = f_k, k = 1 : n$. These n conditions generally uniquely determine the existence of the "potential" constants $\lambda_1, \ldots, \lambda_n$ (see, e.g., Michelli [217]). It is clear that computationally the problem is reduced to a linear symmetric system of n by n.

Furthermore, to be able to exactly reproduce some lower order polynomials, the radial basis interpolant $\hat{f}$ often takes the more general form of

$$\hat{f}(x) = p_m(x) + \sum_{k=1}^{n} \lambda_k \phi(|x - x_k|), \tag{6.14}$$

where $p_m \in P_m$ is a polynomial of degree no greater than m. To ensure uniqueness, these new degrees of freedom have to be controlled by the same number of suitably designed new constraints other than the fitting conditions $\hat{f}(x_k) = f_k$'s. This is often achieved via the *orthogonality condition*,

$$\langle x^\alpha \rangle_{\lambda, \Gamma} = \sum_{x_k \in \Gamma} \lambda_k x_k^\alpha = 0, \quad |\alpha| \leq m,$$

where $|\alpha| = \alpha_1 + \alpha_2$ in two dimensions when the multiplicity index $\alpha = (\alpha_1, \alpha_2)$. Notice that in the language of probability or measure theory, if one defines the signed measure

$$\mu_{\lambda, \Gamma} = \sum_{k-1}^{n} \lambda_k \delta(x - x_k),$$

which is atomically supported on Γ, then the orthogonality condition is equivalent to the vanishing-moment condition as in wavelet theory [96, 290]:

$$\langle x^\alpha \rangle_{\lambda,\Gamma} = \langle x^\alpha , \ \mu_{\lambda,\Gamma} \rangle = 0.$$

The vanishing-moment condition is apparently equivalent to

$$\langle q_m \rangle_{\lambda,\Gamma} = \sum_{x_k \in \Gamma} \lambda_k q_m(x_k) = 0 \qquad \forall q_m \in P_m.$$

Therefore, under any basis of P_m, the number of new degrees of freedom equals the number of new constraints, and the general version (6.14) is again reduced to a linear symmetric system.

The next question is how to choose the degree m of the polynomial component in some optimal way. This is often achieved by analyzing the growth rate of the interpolant $\hat{f}(x)$ as $|x| \to \infty$, especially when the radially symmetric function $\phi(r)$ blows up when $r \to \infty$, e.g., multiquadratic functions or thin-plate splines. For small m, the growth rate is set by $\phi(r)$, while for large m, the polynomial growth rate dominates. Therefore, in between, there could exist some optimal m_0, such that the net growth rate is the lowest among all m. This valley phenomenon is made possible by the vanishing-moment condition when one expands $\phi(|x - x_k|)$'s using Taylor expansion near $x = \infty$.

Finally, let us specifically focus on one of the most popular radial basis functions—the thin-plate splines (in two dimensions).

Consider a thin plate under minor bending from its flat planar shape, so that its shape can be represented as the graph of a 2-D function (on its flat plane Ω): $u = u(x)$, $x = (x_1, x_2) \in \Omega \subseteq \mathbb{R}^2$. The thin-plate energy is defined as

$$E[u] = \frac{1}{2} \int_\Omega (u_{x_1 x_1}^2 + 2u_{x_1 x_2}^2 + u_{x_2 x_2}^2) dx_1 dx_2 = \frac{1}{2} \int_\Omega \text{trace}(H^2) dx, \qquad (6.15)$$

where $H = D^2 u$ denotes the Hessian matrix of u. Since all the second order derivatives are involved, mathematically it demands $u \in H^2(\Omega)$, the Sobolev space of all functions whose derivatives up to the second order ones are all square-integrable.

For convenience we now denote u_{x_i, x_j} simply by u_{ij}. Then using Einstein's summation rule,

$$E[u] = \frac{1}{2} \int_\Omega u_{ij} u_{ij} dx.$$

The first order variation $u \to u + \delta u$ leads to

$$\delta E = \int_\Omega u_{ij} \delta u_{ij} dx = \int_\Omega u_{iijj} \delta u dx = \int_\Omega \Delta^2 u \ \delta u dx,$$

under the natural boundary conditions $\partial \Delta u / \partial \nu = 0$, $\partial \nabla u / \partial \nu = (0, 0)$ along $\partial \Omega$.

Therefore, in the interior a thin plate with minimal energy must satisfy the double harmonic equation

$$\Delta^2 u(x) = 0, \quad x \in \Omega. \qquad (6.16)$$

In the 1-D case the equilibrium equation is precisely $u''''(x) \equiv 0$, implying that u has to be locally a cubic polynomial. Therefore thin-plate splines, or solutions to the double harmonic equation, naturally generalize the notion of cubic splines in one dimension to two dimensions.

One now looks for a radially symmetric solution $u(x) = \phi(r)$ with $r = |x|$. Then the double harmonic equation (6.16) becomes

$$\frac{1}{r}\frac{\partial}{\partial r}r\frac{\partial}{\partial r}\Delta\phi = 0,$$

implying that $\Delta\phi = a'\ln r + b'$ for some free constants a' and b'. Applying the radial form of the Laplacian operator again, one has

$$\frac{1}{r}\frac{\partial}{\partial r}r\frac{\partial}{\partial r}\phi = a'\ln r + b',$$

and therefore, the general form of a radially symmetric solution is

$$\phi(r) = (ar^2 + b)\ln r + cr^2 + d, \qquad a, b, c, d \in \mathbb{R}.$$

In particular, modulo quadratic polynomials, the only globally C^1 solution is

$$\phi(r) = ar^2 \ln r, \quad a \neq 0,$$

which can be called the *mother* thin-plate spline, as inspired by *mother* wavelets in wavelet theory [96, 290].

Unlike 1-D cubic splines which are C^2, thin-plate splines are only C^1. Denote $x/|x| = \hat{r}$. Then

$$\nabla\phi = \hat{r}\frac{\partial}{\partial r}\phi = a(2r\ln r + r)\hat{r} = a(\ln x^2 + 1)x,$$

$$D^2\phi = a\frac{2x}{x^2} \otimes x + a(\ln x^2 + 1)I_2 = 2a(\hat{r} \otimes \hat{r} + (\ln r + 1/2)I_2),$$

where I_2 denotes the identity matrix. This clearly shows that the Hessian $D^2 u$ blows up at $r = 0$ with a logarithmic singularity. Therefore ϕ is only C^1. On the other hand, since logarithmic singularities are integrable, indeed one has $\phi \in H^2_{\text{loc}}(\mathbb{R}^2)$.

Since the double Laplacian equilibrium equation (6.16) is translation-invariant, for any given finite set Γ of scattered spatial locations,

$$\hat{f} = \sum_{x_k \in \Gamma} \lambda_k \phi(|x - x_k|), \quad \lambda_k \in \mathbb{R},$$

must satisfy the equilibrium equation as well for any $x \in \mathbb{R}^2 \setminus \Gamma$. Thus $\hat{f}$ shall be called a thin-plate spline, generated from the *mother* thin-plate spline ϕ.

Furthermore, all cubic 2-D polynomials are trivial solutions to the equilibrium equation (but could be radially asymmetric locally), and a more general thin-plate spline can be in the form of (6.14):

$$\hat{f} = p_m(x) + \sum_{x_k \in \Gamma} \lambda_k \phi(|x - x_k|), \quad \lambda_k \in \mathbb{R},$$

where the polynomial $p_m \in P_m$ with $m = 0, 1, 2, 3$. The corresponding vanishing-moment condition discussed above must be imposed. A straightforward analysis shows that $m = 1$ gives the lowest growth rate near $x = \infty$—the linear order of $O(|x|)$.

6.2   Challenges and Guidelines for 2-D Image Inpainting

6.2.1   Main Challenges for Image Inpainting

Compared with all the aforementioned classical interpolation problems, the main challenges of 2-D image inpainting or interpolation lie in three aspects:

(A) domain complexity,

(B) image complexity, and

(C) pattern complexity.

Domain Complexity

For 2-D images, the missing inpainting domains could be very arbitrary depending on the particular applications at hand.

For text removal, inpainting domains consist of various fonts of the 26 characters (for English), 10 numerics, and several punctuation signs. For disocclusion in computer vision, inpainting domains are determined by the objects on the foregrounds, which in real life can have any shapes and sizes. For fine art retouching in museums, missing domains often correspond to the cracks on ancient paintings, which could occur quite randomly due to bad weather conditions or natural aging of pigments. For digital superresolution or zooming, on the other hand, missing information is scattered (often uniformly in space) across the entire image domains, and the inpainting regions look more like porous media, i.e., scattered blank holes surrounded by available image features.

Unlike most classical interpolation problems briefly reviewed above, the available image information is therefore often given on complicated sets instead of finite discrete ones. These complex sets could contain 2-D subdomains, 1-D (in terms of Hausdorff measure) structures such as regular curve segments, and atomic or isolated points. An ideal inpainting scheme should be able to simultaneously benefit from all these different types of available information, in order to interpolate or reconstruct the original images as faithfully as possible.

Image Complexity

The complexity of images as functions causes further challenges for image inpainting.

At coarse scales, as in multiresolution wavelet analysis, images could be well approximated by Sobolev smooth functions. But in small scales, images are full of localized details spatially organized into coherent structures. For human and computer vision, it is often these singular features of images, e.g., edge jumps, corners, T-junctions, and features of fractal dimensions, that convey crucial visual information. An ideal inpainting scheme thus has to respect these geometric or inhomogeneous features. The main challenge from modeling and computational points of view is that there seems to be no single Banach or Hilbert function space that could conveniently manage all these fine properties.

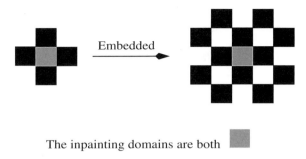

The inpainting domains are both ▨

Figure 6.2. *The effect of local and global pattern recognition on image inpainting: the black color seems to be a reasonable inpainting solution in the left panel, while for the right chessboard pattern, the white color becomes more plausible (Chan and Shen [67]).*

Pattern Complexity

On the other hand, a realistic inpainting scheme cannot be merely built upon the fine properties of images as *functions*. It must also respect visually meaningful patterns (e.g., mirror symmetry [278]).

Imagine, for example, a human face image with the entire area of the left eye and its eyebrow missing. Without any prior knowledge that it depicts a human face, a general inpainting scheme reasonably does the following: first, inspect the available skin tone information in the surrounding vicinity, and then on the missing area fill in the average tone with minor variation to smoothly match the available information. However, this would result in a horrible face image.

In this imaginary scenario, even any kindergarten kid can come up with a much better and more "logical" solution, i.e., simply copying the right eye pattern available or its mirror image with respect to the nose-mouth central axis. However, such trivial human inpainting activity already involves some crucial ingredients of intelligence, i.e., (a) the *on-site* recognition that the image (despite its incompleteness) depicts a human face and (b) the *off-site* prior knowledge that a typical human face has approximate mirror symmetry [278].

Thus the inpainting problem inherits the very same challenges of pattern recognition and artificial intelligence [67]. Figures 6.2 and 6.3 display two examples that highlight such challenges.

6.2.2 General Guidelines for Image Inpainting

Vision research has been generally classified into different levels, low, middle, and high, though there exist no clear-cut boundaries. Tasks with low complexities such as denoising and image enhancement, or most problems in image processing, belong to low-level vision. On the other hand, inference-oriented and learning adapted tasks, such as pattern recognition, classification, and organization, are typical high-level vision problems. Most contemporary works have been primarily focused on low-level or middle-level ones, because high-level ones are built upon them and in practice are still more challenging in terms of both modeling and computation.

"E 3" or "B" ?

Figure 6.3. *The effect of aspect ratios on image inpainting* [67].

The same guidelines work for image inpainting. In this book, we shall mainly focus on low-level inpainting models and algorithms. More specifically, by low-level inpainting, we mean the following [67].

(a) (Locality) Inpainting is *local*: the missing information is to be inpainted based only on the image information available in the vicinities of missing areas.

(b) (Functionality) Inpainting is *functional*: the inpainting models or algorithms depend only on the properties of images as *functions*, not on any high-level pattern recognition inputs.

On the other hand, even at the low levels, the inpainting models must share certain common features in order to be practically useful.

(c) (Automation) Inpainting must be as *automatic* as possible. The less human input is demanded, the more powerful the models are for real applications.

(d) (Genericity) Inpainting should be able to deal with as *generic* images as possible, meaning that as long as information loss is indeed local, most generic incomplete images can be successfully inpainted to certain satisfactory precision.

(e) (Stability) Inpainting must be *stable*, meaning that it must have built-in mechanisms to resist any minor degradation of the available image information such as noise and blur, which are very common in applications.

We hope that these descriptive guidelines, refined from our previous experience on the inpainting project, can be very helpful to readers who wish to make further novel contributions to the modeling and computation of image inpainting. In the rest of the chapter, we will present several inpainting models which are more or less influenced by these guidelines.

6.3 Inpainting of Sobolev Images: Green's Formulae

To develop a rigorous mathematical framework for inpainting, as well practiced in numerical analysis, we start from simple settings in which the accuracy of inpainting can be well studied. This is the case when the target images are smooth Sobolev functions.

Let u^0 be a smooth image function defined on a 2-D domain Ω (a rectangular domain, typically). Denote by D the domain to be inpainted, d its diameter, and the restriction of u^0 on D by $u^0|_D$. Then to inpaint is to construct a good approximation u_D to $u^0|_D$.

An inpainting scheme is said to be of *linear* order, or simply linear inpainting, if for any smooth test image u^0, as the diameter d of the inpainting region D shrinks to 0,

$$\|u_D - u^0|_D\|_\infty = O(d^2). \tag{6.17}$$

Similarly, an inpainting scheme is said to be of kth order if

$$\|u_D - u^0|_D\|_\infty = O(d^{k+1}). \tag{6.18}$$

Smooth Inpainting via Green's Second Formula

Recall that for the 1-D case, harmonic functions on an interval have to be linear. Therefore, 1-D linear inpainting can be carried out equivalently by harmonic interpolants, which provides the key to 2-D smooth inpainting. In [67], Chan and Shen proposed to apply Green's second formula.

Let Δ denote the Laplacian

$$\Delta u := \frac{\partial^2 u}{\partial x^2} + \frac{\partial^2 u}{\partial y^2}.$$

Then Green's second formula on D is

$$\int_D (u\Delta v - v\Delta u)dxdy = \int_\Gamma \left(u\frac{\partial v}{\partial \boldsymbol{n}} - v\frac{\partial u}{\partial \boldsymbol{n}} \right) ds, \tag{6.19}$$

where $\boldsymbol{n}$ is the outward normal of Γ, and s is the length parameter.

Take $G(z_0, z)$ to be the Green's function for the grounded Poisson equation on D. That is, for any "source" point $z_0 = (x_0, y_0) \in D$, as a function of the "field" point $z = (x, y) \in D$, $G(z_0, z)$ solves

$$-\Delta G = \delta(z - z_0), \qquad G|_\Gamma = 0.$$

Applying Green's second formula to $(u = u^0(z), v = -G(z_0, z))$, one has

$$u^0(z_0) = \int_\Gamma u^0(z(s))\frac{\partial(-G(z_0, z))}{\partial \boldsymbol{n}}ds + \int_D G(z_0, z)\left(-\Delta u^0(z)\right)dz, \tag{6.20}$$

where $dz = dxdy$.

In (6.20), denote the first term on the right by $u^h(z_0)$ and the second term by $u^a(z_0)$. Then u^h is the harmonic extension of $f = u^0|_\Gamma$, and

$$d\omega_{z_0} = \frac{\partial(-G(z_0, z))}{\partial \boldsymbol{n}}ds$$

is the harmonic measure of Γ associated with a source point z_0.

The antiharmonic component $u^a := u^0 - u^h$ satisfies the Poisson equation

$$\Delta u^a(z) = \Delta u^0(z), \qquad z \in D; \qquad \text{and} \quad u^a|_\Gamma = 0. \tag{6.21}$$

Numerically, the Poisson equation is favored over the direct integration formulation since one can profit from many numerical PDE schemes and their fast solvers.

To analyze inpainting accuracy for smooth images, we turn to the geometry of a 2-D domain encoded into its associated Green's function. The following results on Green's functions are standard in the classical potential theory. We put them down here due to the increasingly important role played by the complex potential theory in signal and image processing (see, e.g., [284]).

Theorem 6.2. *Let d denote the diameter of a domain D and $G(z_0, z)$ the associated Green's function for the Poisson equation. Then*

$$\int_D G(z_0, z)dxdy \leq \frac{d^2}{4}.$$

The proof is based upon two simple lemmas.

Lemma 6.3 (Comparison Lemma). *Suppose $D_1 \subseteq D_2$, and $G_1(z_0, z)$ and $G_2(z_0, z)$ are their associated Green's functions. Then for all $z_0, z \in D_1$,*

$$G_1(z_0, z) \leq G_2(z_0, z).$$

Proof. For any $z_0 \in D_1$, define

$$g(z) = G_2(z_0, z) - G_1(z_0, z).$$

Then along the boundary of D_1,

$$g(z) = G_2(z_0, z) \geq 0,$$

since the grounded Green's function is always nonnegative. Moreover, $g(z)$ is harmonic inside D_1 because the logarithm singularities at z_0 cancel out. Therefore, $g(z) \geq 0$ for all $z \in D_1$ due to the *extremum principle* of harmonic functions: the minimum is always achieved along the boundary (Gilbarg and Trudinger [132]). This proves the lemma. □

Lemma 6.4. *Suppose B_1 is the unit disk centered at 0, and $G_1(z_0, z)$ is its Green's function. Then*

$$\int_{B_1} G_1(z_0, z)dxdy = \frac{1 - |z_0|^2}{4}$$

for all $z_0 \in B_1$.

Proof. Consider the Poisson equation on B_1:

$$-\Delta u = 1, \qquad u\big|_{\partial B_1} = 0.$$

It is easy to see that the unique solution is

$$u(z) = \frac{1 - |z|^2}{4} = \frac{1 - x^2 - y^2}{4}.$$

On the other hand, by Green's second formula,

$$u(z_0) = \int_{B_1} G_1(z_0, z)(-\Delta u(z))dxdy = \int_{B_1} G_1(z_0, z)dxdy.$$

This verifies the lemma. (Since we do know that

$$G_1(z_0, z) = \frac{-1}{2\pi} \ln \left| \frac{z - z_0}{1 - \overline{z_0}z} \right|,$$

the lemma can also be worked out by evaluating the integral explicitly.)   □

We are now ready to prove Theorem 6.2.

Proof. Take any single point $w \in D$, and let B_d denote the disk centered at w with radius d. Then

$$D \subseteq B_d.$$

Let $G_d(z_0, z)$ denote the Green's function for B_d. Then Lemma 6.3 shows that

$$G(z_0, z) \leq G_d(z_0, z)$$

for all z_0 and z in D. For simplicity, let us assume that $w = 0$. Then we have the scaling law

$$G_d(z_0, z) = G_1\left(\frac{z_0}{d}, \frac{z}{d}\right), \tag{6.22}$$

where G_1, as in Lemma 6.4, is the Green's function for B_1. (This scaling law is true only for the 2-D case.) Therefore, by Lemma 6.4, for any $z_0 \in D$,

$$\int_D G(z_0, z)dxdy \leq \int_D G_d(z_0, z)dxdy \leq \int_{B_d} G_d(z_0, z)dxdy$$

$$= \int_{B_d} G_1\left(\frac{z_0}{d}, \frac{z}{d}\right)dxdy = d^2 \int_{B_1} G_1\left(\frac{z_0}{d}, z'\right)dx'dy'$$

$$= d^2 \frac{1 - |z_0/d|^2}{4} \leq \frac{d^2}{4},$$

as asserted by the theorem. (The last step is due to the assumption that $w = 0 \in D$ and $z_0 \in D$. If this is not the case, then simply replace z_0 and z by $z_0 - w$ and $z - w$, and the proof still holds.) This completes the proof.   □

Based on this theorem, one can easily establish the accuracy orders for the above inpainting schemes based on Green's second formula.

(a) **Linear inpainting via harmonic extension.** Suppose that $u^0\big|_D$ is inpainted via the harmonic extension, i.e., $u_D = u^h$. It must be a linear inpainting scheme, i.e.,

$$\|u^h - u^0\big|_D\|_\infty = O(d^2),$$

as the diameter $d \to 0$. This can be easily shown as follows.

According to (6.20), the error of the harmonic inpainting is exactly the antiharmonic component u^a. Since u^0 is a fixed smooth function, there exists a constant M such that

$$|\Delta u^0(z)| \le M$$

for all $z \in D$. Then for any $z_0 \in D$, by Theorem 6.2,

$$|u^a(z_0)| \le M \int_D G(z_0, z)dz \le \frac{Md^2}{4}.$$

This validates the assertion.

(b) **Cubic inpainting via Green's formula.** To improve the accuracy, we must also inpaint the "detail" component u^a missed by the harmonic inpainting. The idea carries the same flavor as the multiresolution synthesis in wavelet decomposition or coding [96, 290].

Let u_D^Δ be *any* linear inpainting of $\Delta u^0|_D$ (via the harmonic scheme, for example). Then we inpaint $u^a|_D$ by u_D^a according to the integration formula

$$u_D^a(z_0) = \int_D G(z_0, z)(-u_D^\Delta(z))dz, \tag{6.23}$$

or equivalently, by solving the grounded Poisson equation

$$-\Delta u_D^a(z) = -u_D^\Delta(z), \qquad z \in D; \quad u_D^a|_\Gamma = 0.$$

Finally, by adding this new detail to the harmonic inpainting, we derive a more accurate inpainting u_D to the original smooth test image u^0:

$$u_D(z) = u^h(z) + u_D^a(z). \tag{6.24}$$

Theorem 6.5 (Cubic Inpainting). *If u_D^Δ is a linear inpainting of Δu^0 on D (unnecessarily being harmonic), then (6.23) and (6.24) define a* cubic *inpainting of u^0, i.e.,*

$$\|u_D - u^0|_D\|_\infty = O(d^4).$$

Proof. By Green's second formula, for any $z_0 \in D$,

$$u_D(z_0) - u^0|_D(z_0) = \int_D G(z_0, z)\left(-u_D^\Delta(z) + \Delta u^0(z)\right) dxdy.$$

Since $u_D^\Delta(z)$ is a linear inpainting of $\Delta u^0(z)$, there exists a constant M, independent of the inpainting domain D, such that

$$|u_D^\Delta(z) - \Delta u^0(z)| \le Md^2$$

for all $z \in D$. Hence,

$$\left|u_D(z_0) - u^0|_D(z_0)\right| \le Md^2 \int_D G(z_0, z)dxdy.$$

The proof is then complete by Theorem 6.2.   □

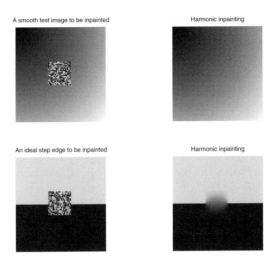

Figure 6.4. *Harmonic inpainting of a smooth image ($u = r = \sqrt{x^2 + y^2}$) and an ideal step edge.*

In the above cubic inpainting process, if the linear inpainting u_D^Δ of $\Delta u^0|_D$ is realized by the harmonic inpainting, then the cubic inpainting is in fact a biharmonic inpainting. That is, $u_D(z)$ solves the following biharmonic boundary value problem:

$$\Delta^2 u_D = 0, \qquad u_D\big|_\Gamma = u^0\big|_\Gamma, \qquad \Delta u_D\big|_\Gamma = \Delta u^0\big|_\Gamma.$$

As in the classical approximation theory, the above smooth inpainting models have allowed rigorous error analysis. They also shed some light on the nature of the inpainting problem. In most applications, however, such models are less practical because of the following:

(a) Images (even nontexture ones) are *deterministically* nonsmooth functions. They contain edges and discontinuities (see the lower panel in Figure 6.4).

(b) Images are often degraded by noise or blur.

The inpainting models to be developed in the coming sections partially resolve these issues. We start with how to improve the above Sobolev inpainting models by incorporating more geometric ingredients.

6.4   Geometric Modeling of Curves and Images

The performance of geometric inpainting models crucially depends on what types of geometric information are incorporated and how they are actually integrated into the models. This section addresses some generic ways of constructing and incorporating geometric information.

6.4.1   Geometric Curve Models

The most important geometry for image analysis resides within edges. From Marr's classical work on primal sketch [211] to Donoho's *geometric* wavelet analysis [107], edges always stay in the core of many issues: image coding and compression, image restoration, and segmentation and tracking, just to name a few. Therefore, it is of fundamental importance to understand how to mathematically model edges and curves.

From the Bayesian point of view, this is to establish a probability distribution $\text{Prob}(\Gamma)$ over "all" curves. An instant example coming to mind is the Brownian motion and its associated Wiener measure [164]. The problem is that Brownian paths are parameterized curves (by "time") and are even almost surely nowhere differentiable. For image analysis, however, edges are intrinsic (1-D) manifolds, and their regularity is an important visual cue.

According to Gibbs' energy formulation, we are also to look for a suitable energy form $e[\Gamma]$. It is always convenient to first start with a discrete version. Digitally, a 1-D curve Γ can be represented by a chain of ordered sample points

$$x_0, x_1, \ldots, x_N,$$

dense enough to ensure reasonable approximation. Working directly with such chains of finite length, one needs to define appropriate energy forms

$$e[x_0, x_1, \ldots, x_N].$$

In what follows, guided by several natural axioms, we shall construct two of the most useful planer curve models: the length energy and Euler's elastica energy.

Axiom 1. Euclidean invariance.

Let $Q \in O(2)$ (conventionally called a rotation, though including all reflections), and let $c \in \mathbb{R}^2$ be an arbitrary point. Euclidean invariance consists of two parts: the rotational invariance

$$e[Qx_0, Qx_1, \ldots, Qx_N] = e[x_0, x_1, \ldots, x_N]$$

and the translation invariance

$$e[x_0 + c, x_1 + c, \ldots, x_N + c] = e[x_0, x_1, \ldots, x_N].$$

Axiom 2. Reversal invariance.

It requires that

$$e[x_0, \ldots, x_N] = e[x_N, \ldots, x_0],$$

which means that the energy does not depend on the orientation of the curve.

Axiom 3. p-point accumulation ($p = 2, 3, \ldots$).

This is fundamentally a rule on the *local* interaction or coupling of pixels. A p-point accumulative energy satisfies the accumulation law

$$e[x_0, \ldots, x_n, x_{n+1}] = e[x_0, \ldots, x_n] + e[x_{n-p+2}, \ldots, x_{n+1}]$$

for all $n \geq p - 2$. Through cascading, one easily establishes the following proposition.

Proposition 6.6. *Suppose e is p-point accumulative. Then for any $N \geq p - 1$,*

$$e[\boldsymbol{x}_0, \ldots, \boldsymbol{x}_N] = \sum_{n=0}^{N-p+1} e[\boldsymbol{x}_n, \ldots, \boldsymbol{x}_{n+p-1}].$$

Thus, for example, a 2-point accumulative energy must be in the form of

$$e[\boldsymbol{x}_0, \ldots, \boldsymbol{x}_N] = e[\boldsymbol{x}_0, \boldsymbol{x}_1] + e[\boldsymbol{x}_1, \boldsymbol{x}_2] + \cdots + e[\boldsymbol{x}_{N-1}, \boldsymbol{x}_N];$$

and a 3-point accumulative energy satisfies

$$e[\boldsymbol{x}_0, \ldots, \boldsymbol{x}_N] = e[\boldsymbol{x}_0, \boldsymbol{x}_1, \boldsymbol{x}_2] + e[\boldsymbol{x}_1, \boldsymbol{x}_2, \boldsymbol{x}_3] + \cdots + e[\boldsymbol{x}_{N-2}, \boldsymbol{x}_{N-1}, \boldsymbol{x}_N].$$

Generally, a p-point accumulative energy e is completely determined by its fundamental form

$$e[\boldsymbol{x}_0, \ldots, \boldsymbol{x}_{p-1}].$$

In what follows, we study the cases of $p = 2$ and $p = 3$.

6.4.2   2-, 3-Point Accumulative Energies, Length, and Curvature

We first study 2-point accumulative energies.

Proposition 6.7. *A Euclidean invariant 2-point accumulative energy must be in the form of*

$$e[\boldsymbol{x}_0, \ldots, \boldsymbol{x}_N] = \sum_{n=0}^{N-1} f(|\boldsymbol{x}_{n+1} - \boldsymbol{x}_n|)$$

for some nonnegative function $f(s)$.

Proof. It suffices to show that

$$e[\boldsymbol{x}_0, \boldsymbol{x}_1] = f(|\boldsymbol{x}_1 - \boldsymbol{x}_0|).$$

Translation invariance leads to

$$e[\boldsymbol{x}_0, \boldsymbol{x}_1] = e[0, \boldsymbol{x}_1 - \boldsymbol{x}_0] = F(\boldsymbol{x}_1 - \boldsymbol{x}_0)$$

with $F(\boldsymbol{x}) = e[0, \boldsymbol{x}]$. Then rotational invariance further implies that

$$F(Q\boldsymbol{x}) \equiv F(\boldsymbol{x}), \quad Q \in O(2), \boldsymbol{x} \in \mathbb{R}^2.$$

Thus if we define $f(s) = F((s, 0))$, then $F(\boldsymbol{x}) = f(|\boldsymbol{x}|)$. $\square$

If in addition, we impose the following axiom.

Axiom 4. Linear additivity.

For any $\alpha \in (0, 1)$, and for $\boldsymbol{x}_1 = \alpha \boldsymbol{x}_0 + (1 - \alpha)\boldsymbol{x}_2$,

$$e[\boldsymbol{x}_0, \boldsymbol{x}_2] = e[\boldsymbol{x}_0, \boldsymbol{x}_1] + e[\boldsymbol{x}_1, \boldsymbol{x}_2].$$

Then it is easy to show that the energy is unique up to a multiplicative constant.

Theorem 6.8. *A continuous and Euclidean invariant 2-point accumulative energy e with linear additivity must be the* length *energy, i.e.,*

$$e[x_0, \ldots, x_N] = c \sum_{n=0}^{N-1} |x_n - x_{n+1}|$$

for some fixed positive constant c.

For a summable curve Γ, as $N \to \infty$ and the sampling size

$$\max_{0 \le n \le N-1} |x_n - x_{n+1}|$$

tends to zero, such digital energy converges to the length.

Next we study 3-point accumulative energies.

To determine the fundamental form $e[x_0, x_1, x_2]$, first recall Frobenius' classical theorem [39]. The three points x_0, x_1, x_2 live in $\mathbb{R}^6 = \mathbb{R}^2 \times \mathbb{R}^2 \times \mathbb{R}^2$, and the dimension of a Euclidean orbit is 3: 1 from the rotation group and 2 from the translation group. Therefore, Frobenius' theorem applied to the Euclidean invariance gives the following proposition.

Proposition 6.9. *One can find exactly three independent joint invariants, I_1, I_2, and I_3, such that $e[x_0, x_1, x_2]$ is a function of them.*

Define

$$a = |x_1 - x_0|, \quad b = |x_2 - x_1|, \quad c = |x_2 - x_0|.$$

Then the ordered triple (a, b, c) is apparently Euclidean invariant, and two chains $[x_0, x_1, x_2]$ and $[y_0, y_1, y_2]$ are Euclidean congruent if and only if they share the same (a, b, c). Thus there must exist a nonnegative function $F(a, b, c)$ such that

$$e[x_0, x_1, x_2] = F(a, b, c).$$

Define the two elementary symmetric functions of a and b:

$$A_1 = \frac{a + b}{2} \quad \text{and} \quad B_1 = ab. \tag{6.25}$$

The reversal invariance implies the symmetry of F with respect to a and b. Thus e has to be a function of A_1, B_1, and c:

$$e[x_0, x_1, x_2] = f(A_1, B_1, c).$$

Let s denote the half perimeter of the triangle (x_1, x_2, x_3),

$$s = A_1 + \frac{c}{2},$$

and Δ its area:

$$\Delta = \sqrt{s(s - a)(s - b)(s - c)} = \sqrt{s(s - c)(s^2 - 2A_1 s + B_1)}.$$

Then one can define the digital curvature at x_1 [39, 40, 31] by

$$\kappa_1 = 4\frac{\Delta}{B_1 c} = \frac{\sin \theta_1}{c/2},$$ (6.26)

where θ_1 is the angle facing the side $[x_0, x_2]$. It is shown by Calabi, Olver, and Tannenbaum [40] that for a generic smooth curve and a fixed point x_1 on it, as $a, b \to 0$,

$$\kappa_1 = \kappa(x_1) + O(|b - a|) + O(a^2 + b^2),$$

where $\kappa(x_1)$ is the absolute curvature at x_1.

Now it is easy to see that κ_1, A_1, B_1 is a complete set of joint invariants for both the Euclidean and reversal invariances, and

$$e[x_0, x_1, x_2] = g(\kappa_1, A_1, B_1).$$

Therefore, we have proved the following result.

Theorem 6.10. *A 3-point accumulative energy e with both Euclidean and reversal invariances must be in the form of*

$$e[x_0, \ldots, x_N] = \sum_{n=1}^{N-1} g(\kappa_n, A_n, B_n).$$

Further notice that, as the sampling size $a, b = O(h), h \to 0$ at a fixed point $x_1 \in \Gamma$,

$$\kappa_1 = O(1), \quad A_1 = O(h), \quad B_1 = O(h^2).$$

If one assumes that g is a smooth function of its arguments, Taylor expansion with respect to the infinitesimals A_1 and B_1 leads to

$$g(\kappa_1, A_1, B_1) = \phi(\kappa_1)A_1 + \psi(\kappa_1)B_1 + \cdots$$ (6.27)

for some functions $\phi, \psi, \ldots$. In the linear integration theory, by neglecting all the nonlinear high order infinitesimals, one ends up with

$$g(\kappa_1, A_1, B_1) = \phi(\kappa_1)A_1.$$

Therefore we have derived the following corollary.

Corollary 6.11. *Suppose Γ is a regular C^2 curve, and the size of its chain coding approximation $[x_0, x_1, \ldots, x_N]$,*

$$h = \max_{0 \le n \le N-1} |x_n - x_{n+1}|,$$

tends to zero. In addition, following Theorem 6.10, assume that g is at least C^1. Then as far as the continuum limit is concerned, there is only one class of 3-point accumulative energy with both Euclidean and reversal invariances, which is given by

$$e[x_0, \ldots, x_N] = \sum_{n=1}^{N-1} \phi(\kappa_n)A_n,$$ (6.28)

with ϕ defined as in (6.27), the digital arc length element A's as in (6.25), and the digital curvature κ's as in (6.26). And as $h \to 0$, it converges to

$$e[\Gamma] = \int_\Gamma \phi(\kappa)ds,$$

where ds is the arc length element along Γ.

Notice that the C^2 assumption on Γ is necessary for the curvature feature κ to be well defined and continuous. The C^1 assumption on g justifies the Taylor expansion in (6.27), as well as the definability and continuity of $\phi(\kappa)$, so that the Riemann sum in (6.28) indeed converges to $e[\Gamma]$.

As an example, if one takes $\phi(\kappa) = \alpha + \beta\kappa^2$ for two fixed weights α and β, the resulting energy is called the elastica energy, which was studied by Euler in modeling the shape of a torsion-free thin rod in 1744 [222] and was first seriously employed in computer vision by Mumford [222] and Nitzberg, Mumford, and Shiota [234]. If $\beta = 0$, the elastica energy degenerates to the length energy.

6.4.3　Image Models via Functionalizing Curve Models

Once a curve model $e[\Gamma]$ is established, it can be "lifted" to an image model by direct functionalization and the level-set approach.

Let $u(x)$ be an image defined on a domain $\Omega \subseteq \mathbb{R}^2$. For the moment assume that u is smooth so that almost surely for each gray value λ, the level set

$$\Gamma_\lambda = \{x \in \Omega : u(x) = \lambda\}$$

is a smooth 1-D manifold. (Such values are said to be *regular* in differential topology [218], and the set of all regular values are well known to be open and dense.) Let $w(\lambda)$ be an appropriate nonnegative weight function. Then based on a given *curve* model $e[\Gamma]$, one can construct an *image* model:

$$E[u] = \int_{-\infty}^{\infty} e[\Gamma_\lambda]w(\lambda)d\lambda.$$

For example, $w(\lambda)$ could be set to 1 to reflect human perceptual sensitivity. This is justified as follows. Consider a bundle of level sets whose gray values are concentrated over $[\lambda, \lambda + \Delta\lambda]$. If $\Delta\lambda$ is small, then the image appears smooth over the region made of these level sets, and is thus less sensitive to perception. The energy assigned to such bundles should be small accordingly. On the other hand, if $\Delta\lambda$ is large, for example in the situation when the bundle contains a sharply transitory edge, then the level sets carry important visual information and the associated energy should be large as well. Therefore, the Lebesgue measure $d\lambda$ is already perceptually motivated and $w(\lambda)$ could indeed be set to 1, which we shall assume in what follows. (On the other hand, if u and λ are understood as light intensity values (or photon counts in the quantum setting), then the recent works by Shen [275] and Shen and Jung [279] show that it is also desirable to take $w(\lambda) = 1/\lambda$ in the spirit of a well-known visual perception rule called *Weber's law*.)

Suppose we take the length energy in Theorem 6.8 as the curve model; then the resulting image model

$$E[u] = \int_{-\infty}^{\infty} \text{length}(\Gamma_\lambda) d\lambda$$

is exactly Rudin, Osher, and Fatemi's TV model [258, 257]:

$$E[u] = \int_\Omega |\nabla u| dx.$$

This is because for a smooth image u, along any level set Γ_λ,

$$d\lambda = |\nabla u| d\sigma, \quad \text{length}(\Gamma_\lambda) = \int_{\Gamma_\lambda} ds,$$

with ds and $d\sigma$ denoting the arc lengths of the level sets and their dual gradient flows, which are orthogonal to each other. In particular,

$$ds d\sigma = dx = dx_1 dx_2$$

is the area element, and the "lifted" energy is indeed the TV measure

$$E[u] = \int_{-\infty}^{\infty} \int_{\Gamma_\lambda} |\nabla u| d\sigma ds = \int_\Omega |\nabla u| dx.$$

The above derivation is in a formal level and can be rigorously established based on the theory of BV functions [137], where the length of a level set is replaced by the perimeter of its associated region and the Sobolev norm by the TV Radon measure. Then the lifting process gives precisely the famous co-area formula of Fleming and Rishel [125], De Giorgi [135], and Giusti [137], as introduced in Section 2.2.3.

Similarly, suppose we take the curvature curve model in Corollary 6.11; then the lifted image model becomes

$$E[u] = \int_\Omega \phi(\kappa) |\nabla u| dx = \int_\Omega \phi\left(\left| \nabla \cdot \left[\frac{\nabla u}{|\nabla u|} \right] \right| \right) |\nabla u| dx. \tag{6.29}$$

Especially, if $\phi(s) = \alpha + \beta s^2$, it yields the elastica image model introduced for image inpainting by Chan, Kang, and Shen [61], as inspired by Mumford [222] and Nitzberg, Mumford, and Shiota [234]. Prior to [61], Masnou and Morel also employed $\phi(s) = 1 + |s|^p$ (with $p \geq 1$) for image disocclusion by the means of dynamic programming [213, 214].

Rigorous theoretical study of the second order geometric energy (6.29) turns out to be much more challenging than the TV measure and the co-area formula. De Giorgi conjectured that the elastica model is some sort of singular limit of geometric measures, and Bellettini, Dal Maso, and Paolini of De Giorgi's school have indeed conducted some remarkable preliminary analysis [21].

6.4.4 Image Models with Embedded Edge Models

The second approach to construct image models from curve models is based on the object-edge free-boundary (or mixture) model, as proposed by Mumford and Shah [226] and Geman and Geman [130]. In such image models, the curve model is embedded to weigh the energy from edges, i.e., abrupt jumps in images.

For example, Mumford and Shah's original image model employs the length curve model

$$E[u, \Gamma] = \int_{\Omega \setminus \Gamma} | \nabla u|^2 dx + \alpha \text{length}(\Gamma).$$

Here Γ denotes edge collection. Unlike the TV image model, once the singular set Γ is singled out, Sobolev smoothness can be legally imposed on the rest of the image domain.

The Mumford–Shah image model has been very successful in image segmentation and denoising. For image inpainting, as Esedoglu and Shen discussed in [116], it is intrinsically insufficient for faithful interpolation. Therefore, a new image model called Mumford–Shah–Euler is proposed in [116] based on Euler's elastica curve model

$$E[u, \Gamma] = \int_{\Omega \setminus \Gamma} | \nabla u|^2 dx + \int_{\Gamma} (\alpha + \beta \kappa^2) ds,$$

where the elastica energy is embedded to enforce the second order geometric regularity of the edges.

Likewise in the functionalization approach, the Mumford–Shah model could be properly studied in the framework of *special functions with bounded variations* (SBVs), as beautifully done by De Giorgi, Carriero, and Leaci [136], and Dal Maso, Morel, and Solimini [94], and later by many others as well (also see Chapter 7). The "edge" set Γ is then replaced by the weaker jump set of an SBV image, and accordingly its length energy by the 1-D Hausdorff measure $\mathcal{H}^1$. On the other hand, rigorous study on the Mumford–Shah–Euler image model encounters the very same difficulty as in the elastica image model. The main challenge is again rooted in the lack of proper functional spaces that have the second order geometry (i.e. the curvature) intrinsically built in. The spaces of BV and SBV are only of first order.

Nevertheless in practice, with suitable numerical conditioning and approximation techniques, all these free-boundary geometric image models are quite effective in numerous real applications. We now discuss how to carry out inpainting based on these image models.

6.5 Inpainting BV Images (via the TV Radon Measure)

6.5.1 Formulation of the TV Inpainting Model

In [67], the authors first explored the Bayesian idea for the inpainting problem, as an alternative to the PDE approach invented by Bertalmio et al. [24]. The image model employed in [67] is the well-known Rudin–Osher–Fatemi BV image model, as first proposed for denoising and deblurring [258, 257] in the preceding two chapters. In addition, to our best knowledge, the notion of interpolating BV images first appeared in the award winning work of Masnou and Morel [214]. However, unlike [67], in [214] the incomplete images were assumed noiseless and belonging to an even more regular subspace of BV.

The TV inpainting model is to minimize the posterior energy

$$E_{\text{tv}}[u|u^0, D] = \int_{\Omega} | \nabla u|dx + \frac{\lambda}{2} \int_{\Omega \setminus D} (u - u^0)^2 dx. \tag{6.30}$$

Define the masked Lagrange multiplier

$$\lambda_D(x) = \lambda \cdot 1_{\Omega \setminus D}(x). \tag{6.31}$$

Then the steepest descent equation for the energy is

$$\frac{\partial u}{\partial t} = \nabla \cdot \left[\frac{\nabla u}{|\nabla u|}\right] + \lambda_D(x)(u^0 - u), \tag{6.32}$$

which is a diffusion-reaction type of nonlinear equation. To justify the drop of the boundary integral coming from the variational process, the associated boundary condition along $\partial\Omega$ has to be adiabatic: $\partial u/\partial \vec{v} = 0$, where $\vec{v}$ denotes the normal direction of the boundary.

In [61], the existence of a minimizer of E_{tv} in the BV space is established based on the direct method of calculus of variation. The uniqueness, however, is generally not guaranteed. An example is given in [61]. Nonuniqueness, from the vision point of view, reflects the uncertainty of human visual perception in certain situations, and thus should not be cursed in terms of faithful modeling. In the Bayesian framework of statistical decision making, the nonuniqueness often results from the multimodality of the decision function or the a posteriori probability.

For the digital realization of model (6.32), the degenerate diffusion coefficient $1/|\nabla u|$ is always conditioned to

$$\frac{1}{|\nabla u|_a}, \quad |\nabla u|_a = \sqrt{a^2 + |\nabla u|^2}$$

for some small positive constant a. From the energy point of view, it amounts to the minimization of the modified E_{tv}:

$$E_{tv}^a[u] = \int_\Omega |\nabla u|_a + \frac{\lambda}{2}\int_{\Omega \setminus D}(u - u^0)^2 dx. \tag{6.33}$$

This energy form connects image inpainting to the classical problem of *nonparametric minimal surfaces* [137]. In fact, in the (x, y, z) space, the first term of $E_{tv}^a[u]$, up to the multiplicative constant a, is exactly the area of the surface

$$z = z(x, y) = u(x, y)/a.$$

In the case when the available part u^0 is noise-free, we have

$$\lambda = \infty, \quad z|_{\Omega \setminus D} = z^0|_{\Omega \setminus D}.$$

Thus we end up with the exact minimal surface problem on the inpainting domain D:

$$\min \int_D \sqrt{1 + |\nabla z|^2} dx \quad \text{with} \quad z = z^0 \text{ along } \partial D.$$

Here along the boundary, $z|_{\partial D}$ is understood as the trace from the interior. Since this Dirichlet problem might not be solvable for general inpainting domains D (see [137] for example), as far as inpainting is concerned, one may formulate a weaker version even for the noise-free case:

$$\min \int_D \sqrt{1 + |\nabla z|^2} + \frac{\mu}{2} \int_{\partial D} (z - z^0)^2 d\mathcal{H}^1,$$

where μ is a large positive weight and $d\mathcal{H}^1$ the 1-D Hausdorff measure of ∂D. Then the existence of a minimum can be easily established based on the direct method. This is also a standard relaxation technique in the study of the minimal surface problems [137].

Compared with all the other variational inpainting schemes, the TV model has the lowest complexity and easiest digital implementation. It works remarkably well for all *local* inpainting problems such as digital zooming, superresolution, and text removal. But for large-scale problems, the TV inpainting model suffers from its origin in the length curve energy. One major drawback is its failure to realize the connectivity principle in visual perception as discussed in [68].

6.5.2 Justification of TV Inpainting by Visual Perception

Following [67], we now further justify the TV inpainting model through a well-known class of illusions in visual perception. The vision phenomenon we are to discuss is best illustrated through the example of *Kanizsa's Entangled Woman and Man*, which is one of the many artistic inventions of Kanizsa [163]. Its importance for the mathematical understanding and modeling of human vision was first emphasized in Nitzberg, Mumford, and Shiota's systematic work on disocclusion [234]. We have plotted a simpler version in Figure 6.5 and name it "Kanizsa's Entangled Man."

Figure 6.5 shows how our visual perception can subconsciously contradict common knowledge in life. What we perceive is a man entangled in the fence. Knowing by common sense that he is behind the fence does not erase this false perception. As Nitzberg, Mumford, and Shiota [234] wrote, "Simply put, we navigate in the world successfully by seeing what's in front of what independently of knowing what's what." We now apply the TV inpainting model to explain such a stubborn best guess by our visual perception.

Kanizsa's entangled man

Figure 6.5. *Can the TV inpainting model explain Kanizsa's Entangled Man?*

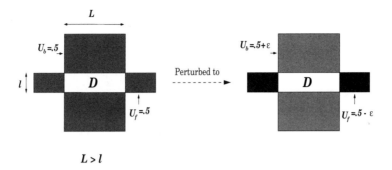

$$L > l$$

Figure 6.6. *The model for Kanizsa's Entangled Man.*

The contradiction occurs inside the circled region in Figure 6.5: the "fact" is that the upper body of the man is behind the fence, while our perception strongly prefers the opposite scenario. It is apparently caused by the same color shared by the fence and the upper body. So the puzzle is, Why does human perception prefer to assign the controversial intersection to the upper body?

Kanizsa's original explanation was based on the modal and amodal completion accomplished by the shortest edge continuation between T-junctions. Here we show that the TV inpainting model offers another similar explanation. While in practice the detection of T-junctions often relies on the sharpness of edges, our functional approach based on the variational principle thus seems to be more general.

First, we simplify the problem to the left image in Figure 6.6. The vertical and horizontal bars model separately the upper body and the fence. Notice the length scales $L > l$, and in Figure 6.5, L is roughly a triple of l. Assume that the two bars share the same gray level $u_b = u_f = 1/2$ (with "b" and "f" tracking the "body" and "fence" variables). The uncertain region is denoted by D.

Outside D, let us make a small perturbation of the two gray levels:

$$u_b = 1/2 \rightarrow u_b = 1/2 + \epsilon, \qquad u_f \rightarrow u_f = 1/2 - \epsilon$$

for some small positive gray value ϵ (see the image on the right panel in Figure 6.6). Now treat D as an inpainting domain, and denote by u_D the optimal solution on D obtained from the TV inpainting model with $\lambda = \infty$ (since there is no noise) and E the complement of D. A simple calculation shows that

$$u_D = u_b = 1/2 + \epsilon, \tag{6.34}$$

which coincides with our "stubborn" perception. In another word, the TV model is consistent with the "algorithm" performed by our visual neurons.

In fact, it is easy to see that the optimal solution u_D must be a constant, c, say. Then the maximum principle [63] requires that $u_f \leq c \leq u_b$. The TV of u_D on the closure of D concentrates along the four edges and equals (Giusti [137])

$$2 \times (|u_f - c| * l + |u_b - c| * L) = [(1 + 2\epsilon)L - (1 - 2\epsilon)l] - (L - l)c. \tag{6.35}$$

We do not care about the TV measure on E because it is a fixed quantity for this noise-free inpainting problem. To minimize the TV norm as given in (6.35), the only choice is $c = u_b = 1/2 + \epsilon$ since $L > l$. This proves the claim.

6.5.3 Computation of TV Inpainting

The great news about the TV inpainting model is that computationally one can immediately adopt the same computational schemes elaborated in Section 4.5.5 for Rudin, Osher, and Fatemi's TV denoising model, with some necessary modifications.

First, instead of a uniform Lagrange potential λ in Rudin, Osher, and Fatemi's TV denoising model, one needs only to replace it by a *variable* scalar field $\lambda_D(x)$ with $x \in \Omega$ so that

$$\lambda_D(x) = 0, \quad x \in D; \quad 1, \quad x \in \Omega \setminus D.$$

Furthermore, if the noises on the available image data are not homogeneous, one can even allow $\lambda_D(x)$ to be a more general scalar function on $\Omega \setminus D$.

Unlike for image denoising, inpainting schemes usually converge significantly slower due to the lack of constraints in missing regions, as well as the critical spatial correlations among data that take time to surface. To reduce computational burdens and speed up the schemes, it is also desirable to replace the complement $\Omega \setminus D$ by a small neighborhood U of D with $U = E \cup D$, where the extended (skirt) area $E \subseteq \Omega \setminus D$ can be determined as follows.

If the available portion of an incomplete image is clean or the noise involved is negligible, E can simply be the boundary of the inpainting domain D. Otherwise, to extract robust image information from the available noisy data, one can choose E with a reasonable size, e.g., several pixels wide.

Next we discuss some major applications of the TV inpainting model in zooming and superresolution, edge-based sparse image coding, and numerous other areas of digital and information technologies [67].

6.5.4 Digital Zooming Based on TV Inpainting

Digital zoom-in has wide applications in digital photography, image superresolution, data compression, etc. Zoom-out is a process of losing details, or in the framework of wavelets and multiresolution analysis, a process of projections from fine scales to coarser ones [96, 290]. Zoom-in, on the other hand, is the inverse problem of zoom-out, and thus belongs to the general category of image restoration problems.

A (dyadic) single-level zoom-in from a given digital image u^0 of size n-by-m is to reconstruct a new digital image u of size $2n$-by-$2m$ (2 is typical but not unique), so that u^0 can be the single-level zoom-out of u. Thus it is important to know the exact form of the zoom-out operator. Typically, the zoom-out operator consists of two steps: a lowpass filtering (or local smooth averaging) of the fine scale image u, followed by a downsampling process leading to the zoom-out u^0 on a coarser grid, a scenario much less strange in wavelet theory [290]. In what follows, we shall assume a direct downsampling zoom-out. That is, the filter is a Dirac δ, and thus the zoom-out is simply a restriction from a $2n$-by-$2m$ grid to its n-by-m double-spaced subgrid.

Unlike for inpainting on block domains, continuous modeling becomes less appropriate for the digital setting of zoom-in's. A similar problem has been addressed earlier by Chan, Osher, and Shen [63] and Osher and Shen [242] for image denoising and enhancement, where a self-contained digital theory for the TV denoising has been developed and studied. Here we follow the same framework to construct a zoom-in model, which is exactly the digital version of the continuous TV inpainting model.

Let Ω denote the fine grid on which the zoom-in u is to be defined. The grid for the given coarse-scale image u^0 is denoted by Ω_0, which is a subgrid of Ω. As in the practice of Markov random fields [33], assign a neighborhood system to Ω, so that each pixel $\alpha \in \Omega$ has its neighborhood N_α, a collection of "nearby" pixels (excluding α itself). For example, we can assign a *rectangular* neighborhood system so that if $\alpha = (i, j)$, then N_α consists of the four pixels $(i, j \pm 1)$, $(i \pm 1, j)$.

At each pixel α, define the local variation as

$$|\nabla_\alpha u| = \sqrt{\sum_{\beta \in N_\alpha} (u_\beta - u_\alpha)^2}.$$

Also define the extended Lagrange multiplier λ_e as a function on the fine grid Ω:

$$\lambda_e(\alpha) = \begin{cases} \lambda, & \alpha \in \Omega_0; \\ 0 & \text{otherwise.} \end{cases}$$

Then the digital TV zoom-in model is to minimize the digital energy E_λ over all possible fine-scale images u:

$$E_\lambda[u] = \sum_{\alpha \in \Omega} |\nabla_\alpha u| + \sum_{\alpha \in \Omega} \frac{\lambda_e(\alpha)}{2} (u_\alpha - u_\alpha^0)^2. \tag{6.36}$$

For the purpose of comparison, one may also try the digital *harmonic* zoom-in model:

$$E_\lambda^h[u] = \sum_{\alpha \in \Omega} \frac{1}{2} |\nabla_\alpha u|^2 + \sum_{\alpha \in \Omega} \frac{\lambda_e(\alpha)}{2} (u_\alpha - u_\alpha^0)^2. \tag{6.37}$$

As established in [63], the minimization of the digital TV zoom-in energy can be carried out by repeatedly applying the so-called digital TV filter $u \to v = F(u)$: at each pixel α,

$$v_\alpha = F_\alpha(u) = \sum_{\beta \in N_\alpha} h_{\alpha\beta}(u) u_\beta + h_{\alpha\alpha}(u) u_\alpha^0,$$

where the exact formulae for the filter coefficients $h_{\alpha\beta}$'s depend on the input u and λ_e, and are worked out in [63]. Starting with an arbitrary initial guess $u^{(0)}$ for the zoom-in, we polish its quality by iterating the digital TV filter: $u^{(n)} = F(u^{(n-1)})$. As n goes to ∞, $u^{(n)}$ converges to the "best" digital zoom-in of u^0.

As we have noticed, the digital TV zoom-in model (6.36) is almost identical to the continuous TV inpainting model (6.30). The reason we prefer the self-contained digital framework lies in the facts that it is independent of numerical PDE schemes one applies and always permits a solution (since we are working with finite-dimensional data). The technical difficulty with the continuous modeling is that existence is unguaranteed, as discussed by Caselles, Morel, and Sbert [50]. The most understandable case is when we choose the H^1 regularity, analogous to the digital version (6.37). Then in the noise-free case, the continuous model is equivalent to finding a harmonic function u on a continuous 2-D domain Ω, which interpolates the given data u^0 on a finite set of pixels. But for harmonic extensions, it is a well-known ill-posed problem to impose both the boundary condition and any 0-dimensional constraints, mainly due to the maximum principle [117, 132].

6.5.5 Edge-Based Image Coding via Inpainting

In this section, we discuss a very interesting new application of the inpainting technique to edge-based image coding and compression.

Ever since Marr [210], edge has always been playing a crucial role in vision and image analysis, from the classical theory of zero crossings to the more recent theory of wavelets. In image coding, for example, the performance of a scheme is very much determined by its reaction to edges. This viewpoint is better supported by the mainstream development in the current wavelet theory for image coding: the invention of curvelets and beamlets by Donoho's school [41, 107], Pennec and Mallat's bandlets [248], and Cohen et al.'s tree coding scheme [88].

It will be digressing too much if we intend to explore here the vast literature of image coding and compression. Instead, we now introduce the inpainting approach to (lossy) image coding and compression based on the edge information.

The encoding stage consists of three steps.

– (Edge detection E) Apply an edge detector (Canny's for example) to detect the edge collection E of a given image u^0. E is typically a set of digital pixels or curves, without good geometric regularities. In addition, we also demand the physical boundary of the entire image domain Ω to belong to the edge collection.

– (Edge tube T) Next, fixing a small constant ϵ, we generate the ϵ-neighborhood T of the edge collection, or as we prefer to call it, *an edge tube*. Digitally, T can be a 1- or 2-pixel thickening of E (see Figure 6.12).

– (Encoding) Finally, we encode the addresses of the tube pixels and use high bit rate to accurately code the gray values on the tube $u^0|_T$.

This encoding scheme creates a large area of "empty seas" where the image information has been wiped out, and thus achieves a high compression rate. In the absence of strong textures and small-scale features, the edge collection consists of 1-D piecewise smooth curves. Thus as ϵ tends to zero, the area of the tube T goes to zero, which theoretically leads to an infinite compression ratio. Inevitably, such a high compression ratio passes the reconstruction challenge to the decoding scheme. Here we employ the digital TV inpainting scheme to "paint" the uncoded missing information.

To decode, we apply the digital TV inpainting model to the tube T and the gray value data $u^0|_T$:

$$\min_u \left[\sum_{\alpha \in \Omega} |\nabla_\alpha u| + \sum_{\alpha \in \Omega} \frac{\lambda_T(\alpha)}{2}(u_\alpha - u^0_\alpha)^2 \right], \tag{6.38}$$

where the extended Lagrange multiplier is

$$\lambda_T(\alpha) = \lambda, \quad \alpha \in T; \qquad 0, \quad \alpha \in \Omega\backslash T.$$

Unlike JPEG or JPEG2000, here the decoding is realized by a variational reconstruction, instead of by a direct inverse transform such as the discrete cosine transform or the fast wavelet transform.

The TV norm here has its intrinsic significance. Since during the encoding stage, we do not demand any regularity condition on the edge collection, typically E is a messy set without good geometric regularities. Thus the TV norm in the decoding process can straighten the wavy edges and improve their visual quality.

In Figure 6.12 of the next section, we show a typical example of image decoding based on the TV inpainting model (6.38).

6.5.6   More Examples and Applications of TV Inpainting

For all the inpainting examples of this section, the inpainting domains are given to the algorithm, and are initially painted with random guesses, for both the iterative filtering algorithm and the time marching scheme.

Inpainting a Noisy Step Edge and Occluded Bars

See Figures 6.7 and 6.8. In the first example, a noisy step edge has been inpainted faithfully by the TV inpainting model. For the second, the occluded bars are recovered (i.e., disocclusion) as expected.

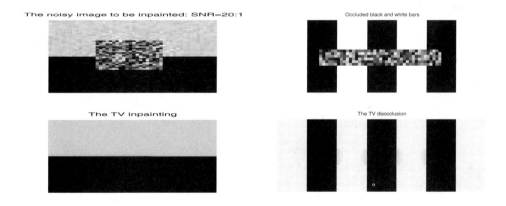

Figure 6.7. *Inpainting a noisy edge.*   **Figure 6.8.** *Inpainting occluded bars.*

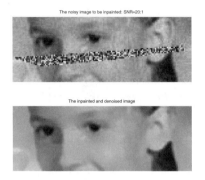

Figure 6.9. *Inpainting a noisy face.*   **Figure 6.10.** *Inpainting for text removal.*

Inpainting for Scratch Removal

See Figure 6.9. The image represents the scanned noisy data of an old scratched photo. As promised, the TV inpainting model can simultaneously denoise the available part of the photo and fill in the missing features. This is the beauty of the TV inpainting: in both the model and algorithm, denoising and inpainting are coherently integrated.

Inpainting for Text Removal

See Figure 6.10. The text string "Lake & Me" has been removed and the original features occluded by these letters are inpainted. Note that the black rim around the right arm of the T-shirt is not successfully restored by the TV inpainting. The "failure" is due to the scale factor discussed in Section 6.2. The inpainting scale (i.e., the width of a letter in this case) is larger than that of the feature (i.e., the black rim).

Digital Zoom-In

See Figure 6.11. We apply both the digital TV zoom-in (6.36) and harmonic zoom-in (6.37) to the test image "Lamp" from the image bank of Caltech's Computational Vision Group. It is clear that the TV zoom-in model produces much better visual output in terms of edge sharpness and boundary regularity.

Edge Decoding by Inpainting

In Figure 6.12, we have shown an example of the inpainting approach for image decoding based on the edge information. The edge detector we have employed belongs to Canny, which is now a standard MATLAB® built-in function. The thickening width described in the previous section is one pixel. This highly lossy coding scheme certainly loses some details of the original image. But remarkably, it does faithfully capture the most essential visual information of the image.

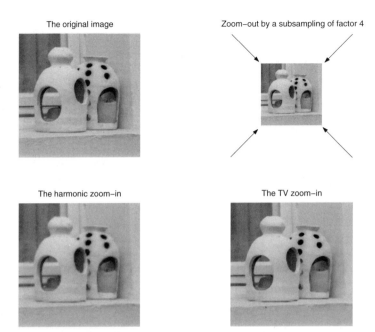

Figure 6.11. *Digital harmonic zoom-in and TV zoom-in (Chan and Shen [67]).*

6.6 Error Analysis for Image Inpainting

The TV inpainting as well as other inpainting methods have demonstrated many successful applications. Their ultimate performance often depends on the geometry of inpainting domains. In [59], Chan and Kang provide some error analysis for image inpainting problems, deepening the preliminary results on harmonic inpainting already discussed in Section 6.3.

In general, it has been known from numerous computational results that inpainting models usually work better for narrow inpainting domains than thick or fat ones. As shown in Figure 6.13, even though the inpainting regions in the two test scenarios share the same total areas, the inpainting outputs are quite different. The narrower one (with a large aspect ratio) leads to much better performance, under the same inpainting model.

As in Section 6.3, a smooth image u can be expressed by the Green's function on a given inpainting domain D,

$$u(z_0) = -\int_{\partial D} \phi(s)\frac{\partial(G(z_0, z(s)))}{\partial \boldsymbol{n}}ds + \int_D f(z)G(z_0, z)dz,$$

where $\phi(s)$ denotes the restriction of u along ∂D, and $f = -\Delta u$ is the interior source field on D. The first term is the harmonic inpainting based only on the boundary information, while the second one is the antiharmonic term and is the error for the harmonic inpainting scheme. By considering Green's functions on ellipses, Chan and Kang show that the error is bounded by the smaller width of an extremal ellipse covering the inpainting domain D.

The original image

Edge tube from Canny's detector

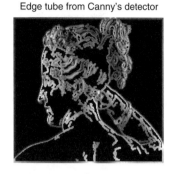

The initial guess

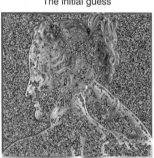

The TV inpainting

Figure 6.12. *Edge decoding by TV inpainting (Chan and Shen* [67]; *also see the recent pattern-theoretic approach by Guo, Zhu, and Wu* [148]).

Theorem 6.12 (Chan and Kang [59]). *For a given inpainting domain D, let B_e denote an ellipse that covers D with maximum aspect ratio between a and b ($a \geq b$) and with the smallest area. Then, for any $z_0 = (x_0, y_0) \in D$,*

$$\mathrm{err}(z_0) \leq \frac{Mb^2}{2},$$

where M bounds the regularity of u : $|\Delta u(z)| \leq M$.

By properly defining the notion of *local widths* w, one can show that the error is bounded by the maximum of such widths over D. A local width $w(z)$ at a pixel $z \in D$ is defined as the shortest distance between the intersections of boundary ∂D and a straight line passing through z [59].

Theorem 6.13 (Chan and Kang [59]). *Let $w_{\max}$ denote the absolute maximum (among all w's) of a given inpainting domain D. Then for all $z \in D$, the pointwise intensity u is*

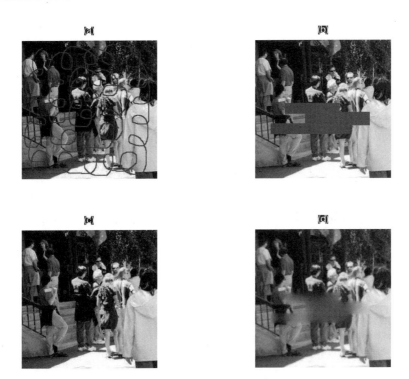

Figure 6.13. *The aspect ratios of inpainting domains influence the performance of inpainting schemes (Chan and Kang [59]).*

bounded by

$$u(z) \le M \frac{w_{\max}^2}{8},$$

where M is the same as in the previous theorem.

Therefore, when harmonic inpainting is applied to a smooth image u, the pointwise intensity error at any point $z \in D$ is bounded by the absolute maximum of the local widths of D. This is consistent with numerous numerical observations.

For piecewise constant images using the TV inpainting scheme, $u(z)$ at any pixel $z \in D$ can have a value quite different from the neighboring pixels due to the emergence of edges. Therefore, Chan and Kang [59] focus on possible *error regions* rather than pointwise intensity errors. An error region R is where an inpainting output and the original image are substantially different. The main tool is the level-curve analysis.

There are many different ways for interpolated level curves to meet with the boundaries of inpainting domains. Chan and Kang consider two cases: when incomplete level lines are uniquely matched and when multiple connections are possible. In the first case, the area of the error region R is a function of b, k_i, and θ_i, where b is the shortest distance between the level lines, k_i the curvature, and θ_i the direction of each level line. If two incomplete level curves belong to one circle, then $|R| = g_1(b, \kappa)$, where g_1 is the area of the region surrounded by the base b and the curve with curvature $\kappa = \kappa_1 = \kappa_2$. If two *straight* level lines have an intersection inside D, then $|R| = g_2(b, \theta) = \mathcal{O}(b^2\theta)$, where g_2 is the area of a triangle defined by b and the intersection between level lines. Finally, if the two (curved or straight) level curves have an intersection inside D, then $|R| = g_3(b, \theta_i, \kappa_i)$, where g_3 denotes the area surrounded by b and curvature-based extension of the two level lines.

Theorem 6.14 (Chan and Kang [59]). *The area of the error region $|R|$ is a function of the distance between level curves b, the curvature κ_i, and the direction θ_i:*

$$|R| = f(b, \kappa_i, \theta_i),$$

where f is one of three forms g_1, g_2, or g_3 mentioned above.

Even if the explicit formula of the error area is very involved, the theorem gives valuable understanding on the size of the error region R by only observing level lines outside D. The total error for a piecewise constant image u depends on the area of R,

$$\text{err} = |R|\partial I = f(b, \kappa_i, \theta_i)\partial I,$$

where $\partial I = I_{\max} - I_{\min}$ denotes the maximum intensity difference along ∂D. If there are multiple possible connections among the level curves, the best estimation for the error region R is the polygon connecting all the intersections between ∂D and the level lines.

We refer the interested reader to Chan and Kang [59] for more detailed analysis.

6.7 Inpainting Piecewise Smooth Images via Mumford and Shah

The idea of applying the Mumford–Shah image model to inpainting and image interpolation first appeared in Tsai, Yezzi, and Willsky [299], and Chan and Shen [67], and has been recently studied again by Esedoglu and Shen [116] based on the Γ-convergence theory.

The model is to minimize the posterior energy

$$E_{\text{ms}}[u, \Gamma|u^0, D] = \frac{\gamma}{2}\int_{\Omega\backslash\Gamma}|\nabla u|^2 dx + \alpha\text{length}(\Gamma) + \frac{\lambda}{2}\int_{\Omega\backslash D}(u - u^0)^2 dx, \qquad (6.39)$$

where γ, α, and λ are positive weights. Notice that if D is empty, i.e., there is no spatially missing domain, then the model is exactly the classical Mumford–Shah denoising and segmentation model [226]. Also, notice that unlike the previous two models, it outputs two objects: the completed and cleaned image u, and its associated edge collection Γ.

For a given edge layout Γ, variation of $E_{\text{ms}}[u|\Gamma, u^0, D]$ gives

$$\gamma\Delta u + \lambda_D(x)(u^0 - u) = 0 \quad \text{on } \Omega\backslash\Gamma, \qquad (6.40)$$

with the natural adiabatic condition $\partial u/\partial\vec{v} = 0$ along both Γ and $\partial\Omega$.

Denote the solution to the elliptic equation (6.40) by u_Γ. Then the steepest descent infinitesimal move of Γ for $E_{\text{ms}}[\Gamma|u_\Gamma, u^0, D]$ is given by

$$\frac{dx}{dt} = \left(\alpha\kappa + \left[\frac{\gamma}{2}|\nabla u_\Gamma|^2 + \frac{\lambda_D}{2}(u_\Gamma - u^0)^2\right]_\Gamma\right)\vec{n}. \qquad (6.41)$$

Here $x \in \Gamma$ is an edge pixel and $\vec{n}$ the normal direction at x. The symbol $[g]_\Gamma$ denotes the jump of a scalar field $g(x)$ across Γ:

$$[g]_\Gamma(x) = \lim_{\sigma \to 0^+} (g(x + \sigma\vec{n}) - g(x - \sigma\vec{n})).$$

The sign of the curvature κ and the direction of the normal $\vec{n}$ are coupled so that $\kappa\vec{n}$ points to curvature center of Γ at x.

Note that the curve evolution equation (6.41) is a combination of the *mean curvature motion* [119]

$$dx/dt = \alpha\kappa\vec{n}$$

and a field-driven motion specified by the second term. The field-driven motion attracts the curve toward the expected edge set, while the mean curvature motion makes sure that the curve does not develop ripples and stays smooth.

Like the TV inpainting model, inpainting based on the Mumford–Shah image model is of second order. But the extra complexity comes from its free boundary nature. In [67, 299], the level-set method of Osher and Sethian [241] is proposed.

In Esedoglu and Shen [116], a simpler numerical scheme is developed based on the Γ-convergence theory of Ambrosio and Tortorelli [11, 12] and Modica and Mortola [220].

In the Γ-convergence theory, the 1-D edge Γ is approximately represented by its associated signature function

$$z : \Omega \to [0, 1],$$

which is nearly 1 almost everywhere except on a narrow (specified by a small parameter ϵ) tubular neighborhood of Γ, where it is close to 0. The posterior energy $E_{\mathrm{ms}}[u, \Gamma|u^0, D]$ is approximated by

$$\begin{aligned} E_\epsilon[u, z|u^0, D] = & \frac{1}{2} \int_\Omega \lambda_D(x)(u - u^0)^2 dx + \frac{\gamma}{2} \int_\Omega z^2 |\nabla u|^2 dx \\ & + \alpha \int_\Omega \left(\epsilon|\nabla z|^2 + \frac{(1-z)^2}{4\epsilon} \right) dx. \end{aligned} \tag{6.42}$$

Taking variation on u and z separately yields the Euler–Lagrange system:

$$\lambda_D(x)(u - u^0) - \gamma \nabla \cdot (z^2 \nabla u) = 0, \tag{6.43}$$

$$(\gamma|\nabla u|^2)z + \alpha \left(-2\epsilon \Delta z + \frac{z-1}{2\epsilon} \right) = 0 \tag{6.44}$$

with the natural adiabatic boundary conditions along $\partial\Omega$ (due to the boundary integrals coming from integration by parts):

$$\frac{\partial u}{\partial\vec{v}} = 0, \qquad \frac{\partial z}{\partial\vec{v}} = 0.$$

Define two elliptic operators acting on u and z separately:

$$L_z = -\nabla \cdot z^2 \nabla + \lambda_D/\gamma, \tag{6.45}$$

$$M_u = (1 + 2(\epsilon\gamma/\alpha)|\nabla u|^2) - 4\epsilon^2 \Delta. \tag{6.46}$$

Figure 6.14. *Inpainting based on the Γ-convergence approximation* (6.42) *and its associated elliptic system* (6.47).

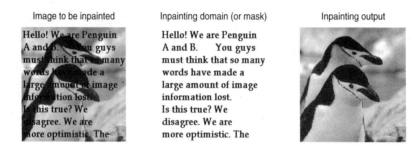

Figure 6.15. *Text erasing by inpainting based on the Mumford–Shah image model.*

Then the system of Euler–Lagrange equations (6.43) and (6.44) is simply written as

$$L_z u = (\lambda_D/\gamma)u^0 \quad \text{and} \quad M_u z = 1. \tag{6.47}$$

This coupled system can be solved easily by any efficient elliptic solver and an iterative scheme. Two digital examples are included in Figures 6.14 and 6.15.

6.8   Image Inpainting via Euler's Elasticas and Curvatures

6.8.1   Inpainting Based on the Elastica Image Model

In [61], Chan, Kang, and Shen proposed to improve the TV inpainting model by using the elastica image model

$$E[u] = \int_\Omega (\alpha + \beta \kappa^2)|\nabla u|dx, \quad \kappa = \nabla \cdot \left[\frac{\nabla u}{|\nabla u|}\right].$$

The elastica inpainting model is thus to minimize the posterior energy

$$E_e[u|u^0, D] = \int_\Omega \phi(\kappa)|\nabla u|dx + \frac{\lambda}{2}\int_{\Omega \backslash D}(u - u^0)^2 dx, \tag{6.48}$$

where $\phi(s) = \alpha + \beta s^2$. As explained by Chan, Kang, and Shen [61], the variational inpainting model proposed by Ballester et al. [17] is closely related to this elastica model but not exactly equivalent.

We must point out that prior to Chan, Kang, and Shen [61], Masnou [213] and Masnou and Morel [214] also proposed the regularity energy,

$$E_p[u] = \int_\Omega (1 + |\kappa|^p)|\nabla u|dx, \quad p \geq 1,$$

for disoccluding noiseless images. Both works [61, 214] were similarly inspired by Mumford [222] and Nitzberg, Mumford, and Shiota [234]. Computationally, Masnou [213] and Masnou and Morel [214] employed dynamic programming instead of the computational PDE approach.

By calculus of variation, it is shown in [61] that the steepest descent equation is given by

$$\frac{\partial u}{\partial t} = \nabla \cdot \vec{V} + \lambda_D(x)(u^0 - u), \tag{6.49}$$

$$\vec{V} = \phi(\kappa)\vec{n} - \frac{\vec{t}}{|\nabla u|} \frac{\partial(\phi'(\kappa)|\nabla u|)}{\partial \vec{t}}. \tag{6.50}$$

Here $\vec{n}, \vec{t}$ are the normal and tangent directions:

$$\vec{n} = \frac{\nabla u}{|\nabla u|}, \quad \vec{t} = \vec{n}^\perp, \quad \frac{\partial}{\partial \vec{t}} = \vec{t} \cdot \nabla.$$

Notice that the coupling of $\vec{t}$ and $\partial/\partial \vec{t}$ in (6.50) makes it safe to take any direction of $\vec{n}^\perp$ for $\vec{t}$. The natural boundary conditions along $\partial\Omega$ are

$$\frac{\partial u}{\partial \vec{v}} = 0 \quad \text{and} \quad \frac{\partial(\phi'(\kappa)|\nabla u|)}{\partial \vec{v}} = 0.$$

The vector field $\vec{V}$ is called the flux of the elastica energy. Its decomposition in the natural orthogonal frame $(\vec{n}, \vec{t})$ in (6.50) has significant meaning in terms of microinpainting mechanisms.

(i) The normal flow $\phi(k)\vec{n}$ carries the feature of an important inpainting scheme invented earlier by Chan and Shen called *curvature driven diffusion* (CDD) [68]. CDD was discovered in looking for micromechanisms that can realize the *connectivity principle* in visual perception [68, 163, 234].

(ii) The tangential component can be written as

$$\vec{V}_t = -\left(\frac{1}{|\nabla u|^2} \frac{\partial(\phi'(\kappa)|\nabla u|)}{\partial \vec{t}}\right) \nabla^\perp u,$$

and its divergence is

$$\nabla \cdot \vec{V}_t = \nabla^\perp u \cdot \nabla \left(\frac{-1}{|\nabla u|^2} \frac{\partial(\phi'(\kappa)|\nabla u|)}{\partial \vec{t}}\right)$$

since $\nabla^\perp u$ is divergence-free. Define the smoothness measure

$$L_\phi = \frac{-1}{|\nabla u|^2} \frac{\partial(\phi'(\kappa)|\nabla u|)}{\partial \vec{t}}.$$

Then the tangent component is in the form of the transport inpainting mechanism as originally invented by Bertalmio et al. [24]: $\nabla \cdot \vec{V}_t = \nabla^\perp u \cdot \nabla(L_\phi)$. Notice that here L_ϕ is a third order smoothness quantity. In equilibrium when $\nabla \cdot \vec{V}_t = 0$, the smoothness measure L_ϕ has to remain constant along the level sets of u. On the inpainting domain D where image information is missing, this means that the existing information L_ϕ on $\Omega \backslash D$ is transported into D along the level sets of u. Compared with Bertalmio et al.'s practical choice of Laplacian $L = \Delta u$, we believe that L_ϕ provides a more natural and geometry motivated "messenger."

Pure transport of Bertalmio et al. [24] can lead to shock development as well known in the study of conservation laws, while pure CDD of Chan and Shen [68] is only motivated by the connectivity principle in vision research and lacks theoretical support. The elastica inpainting PDE (6.49) therefore combines their strength and offers a theoretical root. (Another way to stabilize Bertalmio et al.'s transport mechanism is to add viscosity, which leads to the work of Bertalmio, Bertozzi, and Sapiro on connecting inpainting to the Navier–Stokes equation in fluid dynamics [23]. On the other hand, another way to integrate the transport mechanism into Chan and Shen's CDD diffusion scheme is via an axiomatic approach as explored in [70].)

For the numerical realization of the model, we mention the following aspects. More detail can be found in [61]. Two digital examples are illustrated in Figure 6.16.

(a) To accelerate the convergence of the steepest descent marching (6.49) toward its equilibrium solution, one can adopt the Marquina–Osher method [209] by adding a nonnegative "time correcting factor" $T = T(u, |\nabla u|)$:

$$\frac{\partial u}{\partial t} = T \cdot \left(\nabla \cdot \vec{V} + \lambda_D(x)(u^0 - u) \right).$$

For instance, take $T = |\nabla u|$. As shown in [209], such a simple technique can substantially improve the numerical marching size and speed up the convergence.

(b) As in the TV inpainting model, for the computation of κ and $\vec{V}$, $1/|\nabla u|$ is always conditioned to $1/|\nabla u|_a$ to avoid a zero denominator.

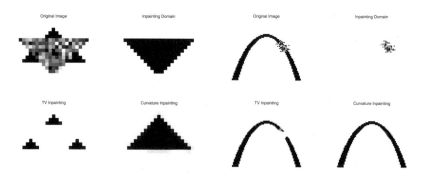

Figure 6.16. *Two examples of elastica inpainting, as compared with TV inpainting. In the case of large aspect ratios [68], the TV inpainting model fails to comply to the connectivity principle.*

(c) To more efficiently denoise and propagate sharp edges, classical numerical techniques from computational fluid dynamics (CFD) can be very useful, including those originally designed for capturing shocks. Techniques adopted in [61] are the *upwind scheme* and the *min-mod* scheme [240].

6.8.2 Inpainting via Mumford–Shah–Euler Image Model

Like the TV image model, the Mumford–Shah image model is insufficient for large-scale image inpainting problems due to the embedded length curve energy. To improve, Esedoglu and Shen [116] proposed the inpainting scheme based on the Mumford–Shah–Euler image model.

In this model, the posterior energy to be minimized is

$$E_{\mathrm{mse}}[u, \Gamma | u^0, D] = \frac{\gamma}{2} \int_{\Omega \backslash \Gamma} |\nabla u|^2 dx + \int_{\Gamma} (\alpha + \beta \kappa^2) ds + \frac{\lambda}{2} \int_{\Omega \backslash D} (u - u^0)^2 dx, \quad (6.51)$$

where the length energy in E_{ms} has been upgraded to Euler's elastica energy.

As in the previous inpainting model, for a given edge layout Γ, the Euler–Lagrange equation for $E_{\mathrm{mse}}[u | \Gamma, u^0, D]$ is

$$\gamma \Delta u + \lambda_D(x)(u^0 - u) = 0, \qquad x \in \Omega \backslash \Gamma, \quad (6.52)$$

with the adiabatic condition along Γ and $\partial \Omega$: $\partial u / \partial \vec{v} = 0$.

For the solution u_Γ to this equation, the infinitesimal steepest descent move of Γ is given by [61, 222, 189]

$$\frac{dx}{dt} = \alpha \kappa - \beta \left(2 \frac{d^2 \kappa}{ds^2} + \kappa^3 \right) + \left[\frac{\gamma}{2} |\nabla u_\Gamma|^2 + \frac{\lambda_D}{2} (u_\Gamma - u^0)^2 \right]_\Gamma. \quad (6.53)$$

The meaning of the symbols is the same as in the previous section.

The digital implementation of this fourth order nonlinear evolutionary equation is highly nontrivial. The challenge lies in finding an effective numerical representation of the 1-D object Γ and robust ways to compute its geometry, i.e., the curvature and its differentials.

In Esedoglu and Shen [116], the equation is numerically implemented based on the Γ-convergence approximation of De Giorgi's conjecture [135]. As for the previous Mumford–Shah image model, Γ-convergence approximation leads to simple elliptic systems that can be solved efficiently in computation.

De Giorgi [135] conjectured to approximate Euler's elastica curve model

$$e(\Gamma) = \int_{\Gamma} (\alpha + \beta \kappa^2) ds$$

by an elliptic integral of the signature z (the two constants α and β may vary):

$$E_\epsilon[z] = \alpha \int_\Omega \left(\epsilon |\nabla z|^2 + \frac{W(z)}{4\epsilon} \right) dx + \frac{\beta}{\epsilon} \int_\Omega \left(2\epsilon \Delta z - \frac{W'(z)}{4\epsilon} \right)^2 dx, \quad (6.54)$$

where $W(z)$ can be the symmetric double-well function

$$W(z) = (1 - z^2)^2 = (z + 1)^2 (z - 1)^2. \quad (6.55)$$

Unlike the choice of $W(z) = (1 - z)^2$ for the Mumford–Shah image model, here the edge layout Γ is embedded as the zero level set of z. Asymptotically, as $\epsilon \to 0^+$, a boundary layer grows to realize the sharp transition between the two well states $z = 1$ and $z = -1$.

Then the original posterior energy E_{mse} on u and Γ can be replaced by an elliptic energy on u and z:

$$E_\epsilon[u, z|u^0, D] = \frac{\gamma}{2} \int_\Omega z^2 |\nabla u|^2 dx + E_\epsilon[z] + \frac{1}{2} \int_\Omega \lambda_D (u - u^0)^2 dx. \tag{6.56}$$

For a given edge signature z, variation on u in $E_\epsilon[u|z, u^0, D]$ gives

$$\lambda_D(u - u^0) - \gamma \nabla \cdot (z^2 \nabla u) = 0 \tag{6.57}$$

with the adiabatic boundary condition $\partial u / \partial \vec{v} = 0$ along $\partial \Omega$. For the solution u, the steepest decent marching of z for $E_\epsilon[z|u, u^0, D]$ is given by

$$\frac{\partial z}{\partial t} = -\gamma |\nabla u|^2 z + \alpha g + \frac{\beta W''(z)}{2\epsilon^2} g - 4\beta \Delta g, \tag{6.58}$$

$$g = 2\epsilon \Delta z - \frac{W'(z)}{4\epsilon}, \tag{6.59}$$

again with the Neumann adiabatic conditions along the boundary $\partial \Omega$:

$$\frac{\partial z}{\partial \vec{v}} = 0 \qquad \text{and} \qquad \frac{\partial g}{\partial \vec{v}} = 0.$$

Equation (6.58) is of fourth order for z, with the leading head $-8\epsilon\beta\Delta^2 z$. Thus, to ensure stability, an explicit marching scheme would require $\Delta t = O((\Delta x)^4/\epsilon\beta)$. There are a couple of ways to stably increase the marching size. First, as inspired by Marquina and Osher [209], one can add a time correcting factor (as in Section 6.8.1):

$$\frac{\partial z}{\partial t} = T(\nabla z, g|u) \left(-\gamma |\nabla u|^2 z + \alpha g + \frac{\beta W''(z)}{2\epsilon^2} g - 4\beta \Delta g \right),$$

where $T(\nabla z, g, |u|)$ is a suitable positive scalar, for example, $T = |\nabla z|$ [209].

The second alternative is to turn to implicit or semi-implicit schemes. Equation (6.58) can be rearranged to

$$\frac{\partial z}{\partial t} + \gamma |\nabla u|^2 z - 2\alpha\epsilon\Delta z + 8\beta\epsilon\Delta^2 z = -\frac{\alpha}{4\epsilon} W'(z) + \frac{\beta W''(z)}{2\epsilon^2} g + \frac{\beta}{\epsilon} \Delta W'(z), \tag{6.60}$$

or simply

$$\frac{\partial z}{\partial t} + L_u z = f(z),$$

where L_u denotes the positive definite elliptic operator (u-dependent)

$$L_u = \gamma |\nabla u|^2 - 2\alpha\epsilon\Delta + 8\beta\epsilon\Delta^2,$$

and $f(z)$ is the entire right-hand side of (6.60). Then a semi-implicit scheme can be designed as follows: at each discrete time step n,

$$(1 + \Delta t L_u)z^{(n+1)} = z^{(n)} + \Delta t f(z^{(n)}),$$

where the positive definite operator $1 + \Delta t L_u$ is numerically inverted based on many fast solvers [139, 288]. A digital example is given in Figure 6.17.

Figure 6.17. *Inpainting based on the Mumford–Shah–Euler image model can satisfactorily restore a smooth edge as expected.*

6.9 Inpainting of Meyer's Texture

In *computer graphics*, "texture" is almost a synonym for "image," referring to any visually meaningful spatial pattern either regular or irregular. In image analysis and processing, though there still lacks a uniform definition, textures generally refer to those image patterns that appear to be stochastic in terms of spatial distribution (i.e., random fields [130, 328]), oscillatory in terms of functional behavior [216], or atomic and multiscale in terms of pattern composition. Here we discuss textures in the latter sense.

Textures are universal in images and essential for image objects to be felt real and authentic. Therefore, proper texture modelling has remained for a long while a challenging but fundamental task in image processing and analysis [130, 328, 329]. Simply put in terms of the Bayesian or variational frameworks, only good texture models lead to good image processors that can effectively deal with complex images.

A comprehensive discussion on texture inpainting would run out of the focus of the current book, and in what follows we discuss only some issues related to the variational inpainting models built upon Meyer's recent texture models proposed in [216] (also see Section 4.5.7).

In the context of image denoising, Meyer proposed the $u + v + w$ image model

$$u^0(x) = u(x) + v(x) + w(x), \qquad x = (x_1, x_2),$$

where u^0 denotes an observed image and the three components are

(a) the cartoonish component u, which is assumed to be BV;

(b) the texture component v, which is oscillatory and to be modelled;

(c) the white noise component w, which is oscillatory as well but visually unattractive.

Focusing on the oscillatory behavior of textures, Meyer's new contribution is to model the texture component v by some functional spaces or spaces of generalized functions (i.e., distributions) that can properly encode oscillations. One major model is the following space of generalized functions:

$$G = \{v = \mathrm{div}(\boldsymbol{g}) \mid \boldsymbol{g} = (g_1, g_2) \in L^\infty(\Omega, \mathbb{R}^2)\},$$

where the divergence operator

$$\mathrm{div}(\boldsymbol{g}) = \nabla \cdot \boldsymbol{g} = \partial_{x_1} g_1 + \partial_{x_2} g_2$$

is applied in the distributional sense. That is, for any test function ϕ on the image domain Ω,

$$\langle \nabla \cdot \boldsymbol{g} , \phi \rangle = - \int_\Omega \boldsymbol{g} \cdot \nabla \phi \, dx.$$

The texture norm in G is defined via the minimax approach:

$$\|v\|_* = \inf \left\{ \|\boldsymbol{g}\|_{L^\infty} = \sup_\Omega \sqrt{g_1^2 + g_2^2} \mid v = \nabla \cdot \boldsymbol{g}, \ \boldsymbol{g} \in L^\infty(\Omega, \mathbb{R}^2) \right\}.$$

Since $L^\infty = (L^1)^*$ is a dual space, by the weak compactness of dual spaces, the norm is in fact reachable by some compatible $\boldsymbol{g}$ for any given texture $v \in G$. In addition, $\| \bullet \|_*$ is indeed a norm since the constraint $v = \nabla \cdot \boldsymbol{g}$ is linear and $L^\infty(\Omega, \mathbb{R}^2)$ by itself a normed space. We refer the reader to Section 4.5.7 for the earlier coverage of the space G.

For convenience, we shall call the vector field $\boldsymbol{g}$ the *texture flow* compatible with v if $v = \nabla \cdot \boldsymbol{g}$.

Under the data model $u^0 = u + v + w \in L^2$ with Gaussian white noise, a general denoising scheme based on the prior models

$$u \in \mathrm{BV} \quad \text{and} \quad v \in G$$

would be to minimize the following posterior energy:

$$E_{\mathrm{meyer}}[u, v \mid u^0] = \alpha \int_\Omega |Du| + \beta \|v\|_* + \lambda \int_\Omega (u^0 - u - v)^2 dx.$$

Notice that by the Sobolev embedding in two dimensions, one has $\mathrm{BV} \subseteq L^2$. Thus this variational denoising model necessarily requires that the texture v belongs to L^2 since both u^0 and u do. An equivalent variational formulation in terms of texture flows is given by

$$E_{\mathrm{meyer}}[u, \boldsymbol{g} \mid u^0] = \alpha \int_\Omega |Du| + \beta \|\boldsymbol{g}\|_\infty + \lambda \int_\Omega (u^0 - u - \nabla \cdot \boldsymbol{g})^2 dx.$$

Vese and Osher [309] made a p-approximation to the above energy:

$$E_{(p)}[u, \boldsymbol{g} \mid u^0] = \alpha \int_\Omega |Du| + \beta \|\boldsymbol{g}\|_p^p + \lambda \int_\Omega (u^0 - u - \nabla \cdot \boldsymbol{g})^2 dx.$$

Their numerical computation showed that in the case of denoising, even $p = 2$ already leads to some interesting results for certain classes of textures. When $p = 2$, for the energy to make sense it suffices to assume that g_1 and g_2 both belong to the Sobolev class $H^1(\Omega)$.

For image and texture inpainting, the natural adaptation from the above variational model is to minimize

$$E_{(p)}[u, g \mid u^0, D] = \alpha \int_\Omega |Du| + \beta \|g\|_p^p + \lambda \int_{\Omega \backslash D} (u^0 - u - \nabla \cdot g)^2 dx, \qquad (6.61)$$

when the image information is missing on D. Notice that the inpainting is given by $u + \nabla \cdot g$ on the entire domain.

We claim that such a texture model lacks geometric correlation and can only lead to a trivial solution to the texture component on the missing domain. This again shows the subtle difference between denoising and inpainting.

Suppose (u^*, g^*) is a pair of minimizers to the inpainting model (6.61) on the entire image domain Ω. We claim that $g^* \equiv 0$ on the missing domain D, which makes the above variational texture inpainting less uninteresting.

First, g^* must be the minimizer to the conditional energy

$$E_{(p)}[g \mid u^0, D, u^*] = \beta \int_\Omega |g|^p dx + \lambda \int_{\Omega \backslash D} (u^0 - u^* - \nabla \cdot g)^2 dx,$$

which can be written as

$$E_{(p)}[g \mid u^0, D, u^*] = \int_D \beta |g|^p dx + \int_{\Omega \backslash D} \left(\beta |g|^p + \lambda (u^0 - u^* - \nabla \cdot g)^2 \right) dx.$$

Assume that the inpainting domain D is closed and its boundary ∂D is Lipschitz continuous, so that for any sufficiently small $\varepsilon > 0$, there exists a smooth function $\phi_\varepsilon \in [0, 1]$ on Ω which equals 1 on $\Omega \backslash D$ and 0 for any $x \in \Omega$ with $\text{dist}(x, \Omega \backslash D) \geq \varepsilon$. Define $g_\varepsilon^* = \phi_\varepsilon g^*$. Then on $\Omega \backslash D$, $g_\varepsilon^* \equiv g^*$ and $\nabla \cdot g_\varepsilon^* \equiv \nabla \cdot g^*$. Since g^* is a minimizer to $E_{(p)}[g \mid u^0, D, u^*]$, one must have

$$\int_D \beta |g^*|^p dx \leq \int_D \beta |g_\varepsilon^*|^p dx = \int_D \beta |g^*|^p |\phi_\varepsilon|^p dx.$$

Now that $\varepsilon > 0$ is arbitrary and the right-hand tends to zero as $\varepsilon \to 0$, it indeed must be true that $\int_D |g^*|^p dx = 0$, or equivalently, $g^* \equiv 0$ on D, almost surely. As a result, the inpainted texture on the missing domain $v^* = \nabla \cdot g^* = 0$, which is uninteresting and unfaithful in most applications.

This analysis shows that unlike the classical tasks of denoising and segmentation, variational texture inpainting requires image models to explicitly encode spatial or geometrical correlations. Lack of short-range or long-range correlation often fails to yield faithful reconstruction or synthesis of the missing textures from the given ones nearby.

To conclude, Meyer's texture model could be very useful for image decomposition but inapplicable for *direct* variational inpainting. It is, however, possible, as recently done by Bertalmio et al. [25], to inpaint images *indirectly* by combining Meyer's texture decomposition with suitable texture synthesis algorithms.

6.10   Image Inpainting with Missing Wavelet Coefficients

In the wireless communication of JPEG2000 images [157], it could happen that certain wavelet packets are randomly lost during the transmission process. Recovering the original images from their incomplete wavelet transforms naturally falls into the scope of image inpainting.

Inspired by the preceding successful variational inpainting models in the pixel domain, one may try as well to adapt for inpainting the existing variational denoising schemes on the wavelet domain. But much to one's surprise, such an attempt fails to work effectively. We claim that the Besov image models, which are crucial in the analysis of wavelet-based denoising and compression schemes [106, 109, 101, 102], become ineffective for variational inpainting with missing wavelet coefficients. For simplicity we shall analyze only the 1-D case, but the 2-D situation is essentially the same.

Given a regular multisolution analysis (see Section 2.6) in L^2 with mother wavelet $\psi(x)$ and shape (or scaling) function $\phi(x)$ [96, 290], let $d_{j,k} = d_{j,k}(u)$ denote the wavelet coefficients of a given image u:

$$u(x, y) = \sum_{j \geq -1, k} d_{j,k}(u)\psi_{j,k}(x),$$

where (in one dimension) for any resolution $j \geq 0$,

$$\psi_{j,k}(x) = 2^{j/2}\psi(2^j x - k), \qquad k \in \mathbb{Z}.$$

For notational convenience, for $j = -1$, we have set

$$\psi_{-1,k} = \phi_{0,k} = \phi(x - k), \qquad k \in \mathbb{Z}.$$

As a result, $(d_{-1,k} \mid k)$ are in fact the lowpass coefficients, which are often separately denoted by $(c_{0,k} \mid k)$ in the literature.

For the least square mechanism to take effect, in addition, we assume that the multiresolution is *orthonormal* so that continuous white noises in the pixel domain are represented by discrete white noises in the wavelet domain.

Theorem 6.15 (Insufficiency of Wavelet-Based Image Models). *Suppose*

$$E_{\mathrm{w}}[u] = E_{\mathrm{w}}[|d_{j,k}(u)| \ : \ j \geq -1, k \in \mathbb{Z}]$$

is a type of image regularity which is monotonically increasing with respect to each argument $t_{j,k} = |d_{j,k}|$. Let D denote the collection of indices (j, k) for which the associated wavelet coefficients are missing and $d^0 = (d^0_{j,k} \mid (j, k) \in D^c)$ the set of available wavelet coefficients which could be degraded by Gaussian white noise. Then any minimizer u^* to the following variational inpainting model:

$$E[u \mid d^0, D] = E_{\mathrm{w}}[u] + \frac{\lambda}{2} \sum_{(j,k) \in D^c} (d^0_{j,k} - d_{j,k}(u))^2$$

must satisfy

$$d^*_{j,k} = d_{j,k}(u^*) \equiv 0 \quad \forall (j, k) \in D.$$

The proof is straightforward and left out. The problem raised by the theorem is that no matter what the original wavelet coefficients are, the above variational inpainting model always restores them by filling in zeros. As a result, missing edge segments in the pixel domain are inevitably blurred due to such bandpass filtering.

In particular, this leads to the unpleasing conclusion that the *Besov image models* fail to produce meaningful inpainting models in the above variational setting, since a Besov norm in $B_q^\alpha(L^p)$ can indeed be equivalently characterized via the wavelet coefficients (see Section 3.3.3):

$$E_w[u] = \|u\|_{B_q^\alpha(L^p)} = \left(\sum_{j \geq -1} 2^{jq(\alpha+1/2-1/p)} \|d_j,\|_{l^p}^q \right)^{1/q},$$

which apparently satisfies the condition of the theorem. Here $d_{j,} = (d_{j,k} \mid k \in \mathbb{Z})$ denotes the sequence of wavelet coefficients at each resolution level j. (In two dimensions, the factor $1/2 - 1/p$ should be multiplied by 2.)

The failure of the Besov image models for inpainting is rooted in the lack of spatial correlation among wavelet coefficients, which, however, has been good news in the classical applications of denoising and compression. That is, wavelet representation, like the spectral decomposition of Hermitian operators, has conventionally served as the diagonalization procedure for the denoising and compression operators [55]. But diagonalization is bad news for inpainting since interpolation demands the very opposite property—dediagonalization or coupling of information. Only via coupling can the lost information be possibly restored from what is available.

To remedy such deficiency, we propose to explicitly employ geometric image models to enforce spatial interactions between the existing and missing wavelet coefficients. Taking the BV image model for example, one ends up with the following variational inpainting model in mixed domains, i.e., both the pixel domain and the wavelet domain:

$$\min E[u \mid d^0, D] = \int_\Omega |Du| + \frac{\lambda}{2} \sum_{(j,k) \in D^c} (d_{j,k}^0 - d_{j,k}(u))^2. \tag{6.62}$$

Noticing that

$$d_{j,k}(u) = \langle u, \psi_{j,k} \rangle \quad \text{and} \quad \frac{\partial d_{j,k}(u)}{\partial u} = \psi_{j,k},$$

we work out the Euler–Lagrange equation for the mixed variational model (6.62):

$$0 = -\nabla \cdot \left[\frac{\nabla u}{|\nabla u|} \right] + \lambda \sum_{(j,k) \in D^c} (d_{j,k}(u) - d_{j,k}^0)\psi_{j,k}. \tag{6.63}$$

Define $T = T_D$ to be the linear *bandpass filter* on the wavelet domain

$$T_D u = \sum_{(j,k) \in D^c} d_{j,k}(u)\psi_{j,k}.$$

That is, T_D is the *partial* resolution of the identity:

$$T_D = \sum_{(j,k) \in D^c} |\psi_{j,k}\rangle\langle\psi_{j,k}|,$$

lost w−coeff: 5% for coarse band & 50% for detail bands   TV inpainting with lost wavelet components

Figure 6.18. *An example of inpainting a noisy and incomplete BV image with missing wavelet components using the model* (6.64) *(Chan, Shen, and Zhou* [74]).

borrowing the bra-ket notations from quantum mechanics. In particular, T_D is nonnegative. Then the Euler–Lagrange equation can be rewritten as

$$0 = - \nabla \cdot \left[\frac{\nabla u}{|\nabla u|} \right] + \lambda T_D[u - u^0]. \qquad (6.64)$$

Pay attention to the beauty of the new model (6.64): formally it looks like the ordinary TV denoising model except that the Lagrange weight λ is to be upgraded to a linear operator. For more theoretical analysis (on existence and uniqueness), numerical implementation, and computational performance on this mixture model, we refer the reader to the recent work by Chan, Shen, and Zhou [74]. Figures 6.18 and 6.19 show two generic numerical examples. Readers are also referred to several other interesting works on regularized wavelet compression, denoising, or interpolation [43, 42, 78, 79, 80, 81, 197, 200].

lost w−coeff: 10% for coarse band & 50% for detail bands   TV inpainting with lost wavelet components

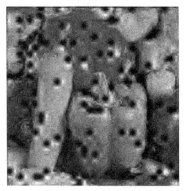

Figure 6.19. *Another example of inpainting a noisy and incomplete BV image with missing wavelet components using the model* (6.64) *(Chan, Shen, and Zhou* [74]).

6.11 PDE Inpainting: Transport, Diffusion, and Navier–Stokes

So far, we have introduced several inpainting models that are fundamentally Bayesian or variational. In this section, we explore the PDE inpainting machinery.

6.11.1 Second Order Interpolation Models

In the beautiful work [50] of Caselles, Morel, and Sbert, image interpolation was for the first time viewed in a systematic way. In particular, their axiomatic approach lays out a solid mathematical foundation for image interpolation via second order PDEs. This section gives only a brief review on the major outcomes of their axiomatic interpolation approach, and interested readers are encouraged to read the original paper.

Consider the canonical lattice pixel domain $\Omega = (h\mathbb{Z}) \times (h\mathbb{Z})$ with grid size h. Denote a general pixel (ih, jh) by $\alpha, \beta, \ldots$, and $u_\alpha = u(ih, jh)$. For the moment, we shall assume that the continuum image $u(x)$, $x \in \mathbb{R}^2$, is smooth.

Let N_α denote the canonical Cartesian neighborhood of each pixel $\alpha = (ih, jh)$, i.e.,

$$N_\alpha = \{\beta \in \Omega \mid \beta \neq \alpha, \|\beta - \alpha\|_1 = h\} = \{((i \pm 1)h, jh), (ih, (j \pm 1)h)\},$$

where $\|x\|_1 = |x_1| + |x_2|$ denotes the l^1 norm.

The Mean Interpolant and Harmonic Images

Suppose u_α is missing, while $u|_{N_\alpha}$ is available. Then the *mean* interpolant is to approximate u_α by the mean value of u_{N_α}:

$$\hat{u}_\alpha = \text{mean } u(N_\alpha) = \frac{1}{4} \sum_{\beta \in N_\alpha} u_\beta.$$

More generally, if u is missing on some pixel domain D, the mean interpolant $\hat{u}$ defined on D is the one satisfying

$$\hat{u}_\alpha = \text{mean}(u(N_\alpha \setminus D) \cup \hat{u}(N_\alpha \cap D)) \qquad \forall \alpha \in D. \qquad (6.65)$$

Thus for any *interior* missing pixel $\alpha = (ih, jh)$ with $N_\alpha \subseteq D$, $\hat{u}$ satisfies

$$0 = \frac{\hat{u}_{(i+1)h, jh} + \hat{u}_{(i-1)h, jh} - 2\hat{u}_{ih, jh}}{h^2} + \frac{\hat{u}_{ih, (j+1)h} + \hat{u}_{ih, (j-1)h} - 2\hat{u}_{ih, jh}}{h^2}.$$

Passing h to 0 leads to the Laplacian equation

$$\Delta \hat{u}(x) = 0, \quad x = \alpha = (ih, jh) \text{ fixed}. \qquad (6.66)$$

Therefore, in the continuum language, the mean interpolant is precisely the harmonic interpolant, assuming the continuum image is harmonic on any missing open domain.

As mentioned previously for TV inpainting, while in the discrete setting the mean interpolant (6.65) is well defined for *any* missing set D, the harmonic interpolant in the continuum limit is not, mainly due to the *maximum principle*. For example, it is generally ill-posed trying to construct a harmonic interpolant inside a disk with the values along its circular boundary as well as on its center specified independently. There exists no harmonic interpolant if the central value is different from the average along the circle.

The Median Interpolant and Curvature

Following the above notations, the *median* interpolant $\hat{u}$ is defined by

$$\hat{u}_\alpha = \text{median}(u(N_\alpha \setminus D) \cup \hat{u}(N_\alpha \cap D)). \tag{6.67}$$

Thus for an *interior* missing pixel α with $N_\alpha \subseteq D$,

$$\hat{u}_\alpha = \text{median}(\hat{u}(N_\alpha)).$$

Define the local l^1 energy at any interior missing pixel α by

$$e_\alpha[\hat{u}] = \frac{1}{h} \sum_{\beta \in N_\alpha} |\hat{u}_\beta - \hat{u}_\alpha|.$$

As is well known in statistics, the median interpolant then must satisfy

$$\hat{u}_\alpha = \underset{v_\alpha}{\text{argmin}} \ e_\alpha[v_\alpha \mid v(N_\alpha) = \hat{u}(N_\alpha)]. \tag{6.68}$$

In particular, define the global energy

$$E[\hat{u} \mid D] = h \sum_{\alpha \sim \beta : \alpha \in \Omega, \beta \in D} |\hat{u}_\alpha - \hat{u}_\beta|.$$

Then by (6.68), the median interpolant $\hat{u}$ must be at least a local minimum to E given D and u outside.

On the other hand, if we assume that u and D are regular enough and $h \to 0$, then up to some multiplicative constant, the discrete energy converges to (by noticing that $h = \frac{1}{h} \cdot h^2$)

$$E[\hat{u} \mid D] = \int_D (|\hat{u}_{x_1}| + |\hat{u}_{x_2}|)dx. \tag{6.69}$$

Therefore, the Euler–Lagrange equilibrium equation requires

$$\nabla \cdot (A \nabla \hat{u})(x) = 0, \qquad x \in D,$$

where the diffusivity matrix $A = \text{diag}(|\hat{u}_{x_1}|^{-1}, |\hat{u}_{x_2}|^{-1})$ is generally anisotropic. Notice that both the equilibrium equation and the energy (6.69) are *not* rotationally invariant; i.e., they depend on the specific directions that set up the lattice domain.

In order to establish a continuum description of the interpolant $\hat{u}$ that is rotationally invariant, we now define the median interpolant without referring to a specific Cartesian lattice. For any $h \ll 1$, let $B_h(\mathbf{0})$ denote the disk of radius h centered at $\mathbf{0} = (0, 0)$. Let v

be a random position *uniformly* distributed in $B_h(\mathbf{0})$. $\hat{u}$ is said to be a median interpolant on D if it satisfies the following: for any $x \in D$,

$$\hat{u}(x) = \operatorname*{argmin}_{\lambda} \; \mathrm{E}_v |\hat{u}(x+v) - \lambda| h^{-1}, \qquad (6.70)$$

where the expectation operator E_v is on the uniformly random position $v \in B_h(\mathbf{0})$. Assume that $\hat{u}$ is smooth at x. Then

$$\hat{u}(x+v) - \hat{u}(x) = v \cdot \nabla \hat{u}(x), \qquad \operatorname{mod} h^2, \qquad h \ll 1.$$

Thus at any $x \in D$, $\hat{u}$ locally minimizes

$$\mathrm{E}_v |\hat{u}(x+v) - \hat{u}(x)| h^{-1} = |\nabla \hat{u}(x)| \, \mathrm{E}_v |v \cdot n| h^{-1} = \frac{2}{3} |\nabla \hat{u}(x)|, \qquad (6.71)$$

where $n = \nabla \hat{u} / |\nabla \hat{u}|$. On the other hand, (6.70) is simply the pointwise decoupled version of

$$\hat{u}(x) = \operatorname*{argmin}_{\lambda(x)} \; \mathrm{E}_v \int_D |\hat{u}(x+v) - \lambda(x)| h^{-1} dx$$

since E_v and the integral on x commute. Therefore, the asymptotic relation (6.71) as $h \to 0$ implies that the median interpolant $\hat{u}$ minimizes (at least locally) the energy (up to a multiplicative factor 2/3):

$$E[\hat{u} \mid D] = \int_D |\nabla \hat{u}| dx, \quad \text{i.e., the TV measure.}$$

In particular, the first variation leads to the Euler–Lagrange equation

$$0 = \nabla \cdot \left[\frac{\nabla \hat{u}}{|\nabla \hat{u}|} \right](x) = \kappa(x), \quad x \in D, \qquad (6.72)$$

where $\kappa(x)$ is the curvature of the level set $\hat{u} \equiv \hat{u}(x)$ at x. Or, in terms of the Hessian operator $H = D^2 \hat{u}$, and tangent $t = n^\perp = \nabla^\perp \hat{u} / |\nabla \hat{u}|$,

$$0 = D^2 \hat{u}(t, t)(x), \quad x \in D. \qquad (6.73)$$

In short, the median interpolant is equivalent to, in the deterministic language, the minimizer of the TV energy.

The major drawback of either (6.72) or (6.73) is that, given the boundary data of an unknown image u along ∂D, the optimal inpainting $\hat{u}$ on D may not exist. Caselles, Morel, and Sbert constructed a good example in [50].

The Gradient-Equalizer Interpolant

The name *gradient-equalizer* is given by the authors of the current book for convenience.

By far the mean and median interpolants lead to, separately,

$$\Delta \hat{u}(x) = 0 \text{ and } D^2 \hat{u}(t, t)(x) = 0 \quad \forall x \in D,$$

where D is the missing inpainting domain.   Since $t(x)$ and $n(x)$ is a local orthonormal frame, from linear algebra, one has

$$\Delta\hat{u} = \text{trace}(D^2 u) = D^2\hat{u}(t, t) + D^2\hat{u}(n, n).$$

Arising naturally is the question of whether it is possible to have an interpolant $\hat{u}$ satisfying

$$D^2\hat{u}(n, n) = 0, \qquad n = \frac{\nabla\hat{u}}{|\nabla\hat{u}|}. \tag{6.74}$$

The answer is not only affirmative but also surprising since in some sense this interpolant is better than the mean or median interpolant, as thoroughly explained by Caselles, Morel, and Sbert [50].

The major advantages of the gradient-equalizer interpolant (6.74) are

(a) unlike the harmonic interpolant, the gradient-equalizer allows scattered pixelwise image data; and

(b) unlike the zero-curvature interpolant (6.72) which may not exist for certain given image data on certain domains, the gradient-equalizer interpolant always exists.

We refer the reader to [50] for detailed explanation.

Like the mean and median interpolants, the gradient-equalizer allows direct discrete construction as follows.

Let $x \in D$ be an interior pixel in the missing inpainting domain D.   Suppose that an optimal interpolant $\hat{u}$ satisfies the following property. Assume $\hat{u}$ is smooth at x, and $\nabla\hat{u}(x) \neq 0$. Then locally near x, $(e_1 = t(x), e_2 = n(x))$ consist into an orthonormal frame. Suppose that the interpolant $\hat{u}$ is optimal in the following minimax sense:

$$\hat{u}(x) = \underset{\lambda}{\text{argmin}} \ \max\{|\hat{u}(x \pm he_1) - \lambda|, |\hat{u}(x \pm he_2) - \lambda|\}. \tag{6.75}$$

Since $e_1 = t$ is the tangent direction of the level set,

$$\hat{u}(x + he_1) = \hat{u}(x - he_1) = \hat{u}(x) + O(h^2).$$

On the other hand, along the normal direction $e_2 = n$,

$$\hat{u}(x \pm he_2) = \hat{u}(x) \pm h|\nabla\hat{u}(x)| + O(h^2).$$

Thus the optimality (6.75) must imply the exact identity

$$\hat{u}(x + he_2) - \hat{u}(x) = \hat{u}(x) - \hat{u}(x - he_2) \quad \text{or} \quad \frac{\hat{u}(x + hn) + \hat{u}(x - hn) - 2\hat{u}(x)}{h^2} = 0.$$

This is the interpolating algorithm first employed by Casas and Torres [46] and also discussed in [50]. Passing $h \to 0$, one obtains precisely the gradient-equalizer interpolant

$$D^2\hat{u}(n, n)(x) = 0, \quad x \in D.$$

Finally, we explain why this interpolant is called gradient-equalizer (also see [50]).

Theorem 6.16. *Suppose $\hat{u}$ is C^2 at x. Let $x(s)$ denote the gradient line through x defined by the gradient flow n,*

$$\frac{dx}{ds} = n(x(s)) = \frac{\nabla u}{|\nabla u|}(x(s)), \quad x(0) = x.$$

Define $\phi(s) = u(x(s))$. Then $\phi(s)$ is a linear function of s: $\phi(s) = a + bs$ near $s = 0$.

First, notice that since $|n| \equiv 1$, s is automatically the arc length parameter. Then the theorem basically claims that $|\nabla u|(x(s))$ $(= \phi'(s) = b)$ remains constant (or equalized) along the gradient line. So comes the name *gradient-equalizer*.

Proof. Simply notice that $\phi'(s) = |\nabla u(x(s))|$, and

$$\phi''(s) = n \cdot \nabla_x |\nabla u(x)| = D^2 u(n, n) = 0.$$

Therefore $\phi(s)$ must be linear. $\quad\square$

The gradient-equalizer interpolant was mathematically studied by Aronsson [14] and Jensen [159] for interpolating Lipschitz-continuous functions. We refer the reader to the work of Caselles, Morel, and Sbert [50] for more properties.

6.11.2   A Third Order PDE Inpainting Model and Navier–Stokes

Despite the long traditions of image interpolation, the recent wave of interest in image interpolation, or *image inpainting*, very much started from the third order nonlinear PDE inpainting model of Bertalmio et al. [24].

This model is based on the brilliant intuition of information transport along broken level lines, or *isophotes* as called in optics. Let $L : u \to L[u]$ denote some differential operators, linear or nonlinear, and it is called the information measure in [24]. Suppose a pixel x in the image domain Ω is a regular point of u so that $\nabla u \neq 0$. Define $\mathbf{n}(x) = \nabla u / |\nabla u|(x)$ to be the unit normal and $\mathbf{t}(x) = \mathbf{n}^{\perp}(x)$ the unit tangent of the isophote passing through x. Then Bertalmio et al.'s model is to solve the evolutionary PDE

$$u_t = \mathbf{t} \cdot \nabla L,$$

or its scaled version:

$$u_t = \nabla^{\perp} u \cdot \nabla L.$$

Bertalmio et al. made the special but convenient choice of $L = \Delta u$ as the information measure, which leads to the third order nonlinear evolutionary PDE:

$$u_t = \nabla^{\perp} u \cdot \nabla(\Delta u). \tag{6.76}$$

Thus in essence this is a progressive inpainting scheme, with image quality gradually improved as the artificial time t increases.

The model was then implemented on the inpainting domain $x = (x_1, x_2) \in D$, with some proper initial inpainting guess $u(x, t = 0)$. While initially unclear on what should be the proper boundary conditions for (6.76), the authors cleverly worked with a narrow stripe along ∂D for digital implementation.

On the other hand, as well known in fluid dynamics, nonlinear *transport* or *advection* equations (e.g., the Burgers equation [2]) could easily lead to shocks. Thus in the original numerical implementation of the model, Bertalmio et al. employed another necessary mechanism that helped stabilize the computation—to hybrid the transport model (6.76) with some nonlinear diffusion scheme of Perona–Malik-type [251]:

$$u_t = \nabla \cdot (A(\nabla u) \nabla u). \tag{6.77}$$

Diffusion stabilizes and better conditions the transport mechanism (6.76).

The whole theoretical picture of the above practice did not come clear until Bertalmio, Bertozzi, and Sapiro [23] made the connection between the hybrid of (6.76) and (6.77) and the Navier–Stokes equation for 2-D incompressible fluids.

Recall that when a 2-D flow is incompressible, its velocity field $v : \Omega \to \mathbb{R}^2$ is divergence-free:

$$\nabla \cdot v = v_{1,x_1} + v_{2,x_2} = 0, \quad v_{i,x_j} = \partial v_i / \partial x_j. \tag{6.78}$$

On the other hand, the scalar vorticity ω (i.e., the projection of the 3-D vorticity vector onto the $\hat{z}$-direction perpendicular to the flow plane) is given by

$$\omega = \hat{z} \cdot \nabla \times v = v_{2,x_1} - v_{1,x_2}. \tag{6.79}$$

Therefore, if one defines $v^\perp = (v_2, -v_1)$ as the imaginary normal flow to v, then

$$\hat{z} \cdot \nabla \times v^\perp = -(v_{1,x_1} + v_{2,x_2}) = -\nabla \cdot v = 0,$$

implying that $v^\perp$ is curl-free. Then by the Gauss–Green–Stokes theorem, $v^\perp$ must be a gradient flow for some function u: $\nabla u = v^\perp$. In fluid dynamics, u is called the *stream function* since its level lines are tangent to the original flow v.

In terms of the stream function, the vorticity scalar in (6.79) is simply the Laplacian

$$\omega = \nabla \cdot (v^\perp) = \nabla \cdot (\nabla u) = \Delta u.$$

On the other hand, the vorticity equation for 2-D incompressible flows is known to be [2]

$$\omega_t + v \cdot \nabla \omega = \nu \Delta \omega, \tag{6.80}$$

where the pressure-gradient field in the Navier–Stokes equation has been annihilated by the curl operator, and ν denotes isotropic viscosity.

Therefore, the right-hand side of Bertalmio et al.'s inpainting model (6.76) is precisely the second transport term in the vorticity equation (6.80):

$$v \cdot \nabla \omega = \nabla^\perp u \cdot \nabla(\Delta u).$$

On the other hand, the Perona–Malik mollification (6.77), though only of second order in u, can at least be qualitatively explained via the role of viscosity $\nu \Delta \omega$ in the vorticity equation. In fact, Bertalmio, Bertozzi, and Sapiro [23] even suggested to have the ordinary viscosity term in the vorticity equation (6.80) replaced by the Perona–Malik viscosity

$$\nu \nabla \cdot A(|\nabla \omega|) \nabla \omega.$$

For more details on computation and analysis, we refer the reader to the original papers of Bertalmio, Bertozzi, and Sapiro [23] and Bertalmio et al. [24].

6.11.3 TV Inpainting Revisited: Anisotropic Diffusion

Following Section 6.5, recall that the Euler–Lagrange equation of the TV inpainting energy
is given by

$$\frac{\partial u}{\partial t} = \nabla \cdot \left[\frac{\nabla u}{|\nabla u|} \right] + \lambda_e(u - u^0), \qquad (6.81)$$

valid on the entire image domain Ω. The extended Lagrange multiplier $\lambda_e = \lambda(1 - \chi_D)$,
where χ_D is the characteristic function (or mask) of the inpainting domain D. Therefore,
inside the inpainting domain, the model employs a simple anisotropic diffusion process:

$$\frac{\partial u}{\partial t} = \nabla \cdot \left[\frac{\nabla u}{|\nabla u|} \right], \qquad (6.82)$$

which has been studied extensively (see [258, 257, 221]). The application of anisotropic
diffusions in image denoising and enhancement now has become a classical topic since
Perona and Malik [251] (also see [317, 221]).

From (6.81), in the absence of noise (i.e., $\lambda_e = \infty$ outside the inpainting domain),
the equilibrium inpainting of the TV model is indeed morphologically invariant since the
right-hand side of (6.82) is exactly the curvature of the isophotes and is independent of the
relative gray values. On the other hand, if one requires the entire time evolution (6.82)
to be morphologically invariant, then the factor $|\nabla u|$ should be added to balance the time
derivative

$$\frac{\partial u}{\partial t} = |\nabla u| \, \nabla \cdot \left[\frac{\nabla u}{|\nabla u|} \right],$$

which is exactly the *mean curvature motion* [221], and is also very useful for the speeding
up of numerical convergence, as studied by Marquina and Osher [209] recently.

Despite its many advantages in analysis, implementation, and complexity, the TV
inpainting model has also two major drawbacks. The first one is that the TV model is only
a linear interpolant; i.e., the broken isophotes are interpolated by straight lines. Thus it can
generate corners along the inpainting boundary. The second one is that TV often fails to
make the connection of *widely* separated parts of a whole object, due to the high cost of
long-distance communication [67, 61] (see Figure 6.20).

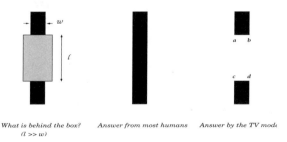

What is behind the box?　　Answer from most humans　　Answer by the TV mod
(l >> w)

Figure 6.20. *TV fails to realize the* connectivity principle *in inpainting problems
with large scales (or aspect ratios).*

6.11.4   CDD Inpainting: Curvature Driven Diffusion

The failure of the TV inpainting on the *connectivity principle* [67] due to the high cost on long-distance connection inspired the curvature driven diffusion (CDD) inpainting model of Chan and Shen [68].

The CDD inpainting model is a further refinement of the TV anisotropic diffusion (6.81). To encourage long-distance connections, the CDD employs the curvature information for the diffusion. It is based on the simple observation (such as from Figure 6.20) that when the TV gets lazy in connection, the edge isophotes typically contain corners (a, b, c, d in Figure 6.20) which have large curvatures. Thus, from the optimistic point of view, large curvatures can be incorporated into the diffusion process to "push" out the false edges (ab and cd in Figure 6.20) formed in the TV diffusion:

$$\frac{\partial u}{\partial t} = \nabla \cdot \left(\frac{g(\kappa)}{|\nabla u|} \nabla u \right), \qquad \kappa = \nabla \cdot \left[\frac{\nabla u}{|\nabla u|} \right], \qquad (6.83)$$

where $g : R \to [0, +\infty)$ is a continuous function satisfying $g(0) = 0$ and $g(\pm\infty) = +\infty$. The introduction of $g(\kappa)$ is to penalize large curvatures and encourage small ones (or flatter and smoother isophotes), since $D = g(\kappa)/|\nabla u|$ denotes the diffusion strength. A simple example would be $g(s) = |s|^p$ for some positive power p. Figure 6.21 shows one example of CDD inpainting, where even very weak edges are connected successfully (like the shadow of the nose).

CDD inpainting is a third order PDE model, and is indeed morphologically invariant since both the curvature κ and the normal vector $\vec{n}$ are. The model encourages long-distance connections. But one drawback of the TV inpainting model still stays. That is, the isophotes are still approximated by straight lines.

It is this drawback that has eventually driven Chan, Kang, and Shen [61] to the re-investigation of the earlier proposal of Masnou and Morel [214] on image interpolation based on Euler's elastica energy discussed earlier, as well as the following quasi-axiomatic approach.

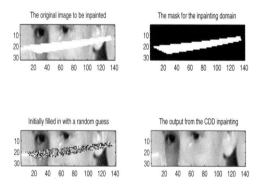

Figure 6.21. *An example of CDD inpainting for scratch removal (Chan and Shen [68]).*

6.11.5 A Quasi-axiomatic Approach to Third Order Inpainting

Based on the experience gained from all the above works, in this section, we derive a new third order inpainting PDE from a set of principles or axioms. From the mathematical point of view, the axiomatic approach is an important step in the big blueprint for putting image processing on a firm mathematical foundation. Previous works can be found in [6, 50].

Geometric Representation of Differentials: The Curvature κ and Deviation Rate σ

Given an image u, its Cartesian differentials up to the second order are given by

$$\nabla u = \begin{pmatrix} u_x \\ u_y \end{pmatrix}, \qquad D^2 u = \begin{bmatrix} u_{xx} & u_{xy} \\ u_{yx} & u_{yy} \end{bmatrix}. \tag{6.84}$$

They are easy to compute if the image u is given in the x- and y-coordinates, yet less ideal from the invariant (or geometric) point of view. For example, if the observer rotates by some angle, then both ∇u and $D^2 u$ change. Another simpler reason for the less idealness is that for a given image u, the x- and y-directions have no specific significance as far as visual information is concerned.

However, near a regular pixel of a given image u, we do have two orthogonal directions that come naturally with the image itself: the normal $\boldsymbol{n}$ and the tangent $\boldsymbol{t}$. Let $\boldsymbol{p} = \nabla u = p\,\boldsymbol{n}$ ($p \geq 0$) and $H = D^2 u$ denote the Cartesian differentials. We make the following transform from $R^2 \backslash \{(0, 0)\} \times R^{2 \times 2}$ to $R^+ \times S^1 \times R^{2 \times 2}$:

$$(\boldsymbol{p}, H) \rightarrow \left(p,\ \boldsymbol{n},\ \frac{1}{p}[\boldsymbol{t}, \boldsymbol{n}]^T H[\boldsymbol{t}, \boldsymbol{n}] \right) = (p,\ \boldsymbol{n},\ G). \tag{6.85}$$

Apparently the transform is invertible and smooth (where $p \neq 0$). The transformed differentials have nicer geometric or morphological properties:

(a) $p = |\boldsymbol{p}| = |\nabla u|$ is rotationally invariant while $\boldsymbol{n}$ is morphologically invariant.

(b) More importantly, the new second order differential matrix G carries much more explicit geometric information about the image. The first diagonal of G

$$\frac{1}{p} \boldsymbol{t}^T H \boldsymbol{t} = \frac{1}{|\nabla u|} D^2 u(\boldsymbol{t}, \boldsymbol{t}) := \kappa$$

is exactly the scalar curvature of the oriented (by the gradient) isophotes. It is a geometric quantity characterizing each individual isophote, and thus is both rotationally and morphologically invariant. The off-diagonal of G

$$\frac{1}{p} \boldsymbol{t}^T H \boldsymbol{n} = \frac{1}{|\nabla u|} D^2 u(\boldsymbol{t}, \boldsymbol{n}) := \sigma$$

is also a rotationally and morphologically invariant scalar, which has played almost no role in the classical scale-space or filtering theory due to the ellipticity constraint [6, 50]. However, as shown below, for inpainting, it can play an important role for the

transportation mechanism. In this paper, we shall call this scalar the *deviation rate* of
the image or the associated isophotes. It can easily be shown that

$$\sigma = \frac{1}{|\nabla u|} \frac{\partial |\nabla u|}{\partial t} = \frac{\partial (\ln |\nabla u|)}{\partial t},$$

from which the rotational and morphological invariances are immediate. (To the best
knowledge of the authors, the deviation rate σ was first mentioned in the classical paper
of Rudin and Osher [257] on TV-based image denoising and deblurring. The name
deviation rate is given here for the first time, however.) The last diagonal of G

$$\frac{1}{p} \, \boldsymbol{n}^T \, H \, \boldsymbol{n} = \frac{1}{|\nabla u|} D^2 u(\boldsymbol{n} \, , \boldsymbol{n}) = \frac{1}{|\nabla u|} \Delta u - \kappa$$

is only rotationally invariant and generally not morphologically invariant.

By considering images u of the general quadratic form

$$u = \frac{1}{2} \, \boldsymbol{x}^T \, H \, \boldsymbol{x} + \boldsymbol{p}^T \, \boldsymbol{x} + c,$$

we can easily establish the following theorem with the help of the one-to-one transform (or
change of variables) (6.85).

Theorem 6.17. *Let $f = f(\nabla u, D^2 u)$ be a function of up to the second order differentials.
Then f is morphologically invariant if and only if it can be written in the form of*

$$f = f(\boldsymbol{n}, \, \kappa, \, \sigma).$$

If, furthermore, f is also rotationally invariant, then

$$f = f(\kappa, \sigma).$$

*In other words, f is both rotationally and morphologically invariant if and only if it is a
function of the curvature κ and the deviation rate σ.*

Axiomatic Approach to Third Order PDE Inpainting

As inspired by all the previous four inpainting models, we look for a third order inpainting
PDE of the divergence form

$$\frac{\partial u}{\partial t} = \nabla \cdot \vec{V}.$$

Therefore, the flux field $\vec{V}$ shall be of second order only:

$$\vec{V} = \vec{V}(\nabla u, D^2 u).$$

It can be naturally decomposed in the normal and tangent directions:

$$\vec{V} = f \, \boldsymbol{n} + g \, \boldsymbol{t} \, ,$$

and

$$f = f(\nabla u, D^2 u), \qquad g = g(\nabla u, D^2 u).$$

Axiom 1. Morphological invariance.

This first axiom requires that the equilibrium equation $0 = \nabla \cdot \vec{V}$ is morphologically invariant. Since both n and t are already morphologically invariant, it amounts to saying that

both f and g are morphologically invariant.

Then by Theorem 6.17, we must have

$$f = f(n, \kappa, \sigma) \qquad \text{and} \qquad g = g(n, \kappa, \sigma). \tag{6.86}$$

Axiom 2. Rotational invariance.

The second axiom requires that the equilibrium equation $0 = \nabla \cdot \vec{V}$ is rotationally invariant. Since all the following scalars and operators are rotationally invariant,

$$\nabla \cdot n, \quad \nabla \cdot t, \quad n \cdot \nabla, \quad \text{and} \quad t \cdot \nabla,$$

it requires that both f and g are rotationally invariant. Therefore, by Theorem 6.17, we must have

$$f = f(\kappa, \sigma) \qquad \text{and} \qquad g = g(\kappa, \sigma). \tag{6.87}$$

The following two axioms or principles are imposed on the normal flux fn and tangential flux gt individually. (It is more inspired by all the practical approaches discussed above, rather than by the *superimposition principle*, which we do not have due to nonlinearity.)

Axiom 3. Stability principle for the pure diffusion.

As is well known in the PDE theory, backward diffusion is unstable. Thus this principle asks for the stability of the pure diffusion term

$$\frac{\partial u}{\partial t} = \nabla \cdot (f n) = \nabla \cdot \left(\frac{f}{|\nabla u|} \nabla u \right).$$

Stability requires that $f \geq 0$, or the strong stability $f \geq a > 0$.

Axiom 4. Linearity principle for the pure transport.

For the pure transportation term

$$\frac{\partial u}{\partial t} = \nabla \cdot (g \, t),$$

as learned from the drawback of Bertalmio et al.'s model, we now impose the *linear interpolation* constraint, or simply, the linearity principle. First, notice that

$$\nabla \cdot (g \, \boldsymbol{t} \,) = \nabla \cdot ((g|\nabla u|^{-1})\nabla^{\perp} u) = \nabla^{\perp} u \cdot \nabla(g|\nabla u|^{-1})$$

$$= |\nabla u| \, \boldsymbol{t} \, \cdot \nabla(g|\nabla u|^{-1}) = |\nabla u| \, \frac{\partial}{\partial \boldsymbol{t}}(g|\nabla u|^{-1}).$$

The linearity principle means that there must exist some smoothness measure L so that

$$g|\nabla u|^{-1} = \frac{\partial L}{\partial \boldsymbol{t}}, \tag{6.88}$$

and thus the equilibrium solution u satisfies

$$\frac{\partial^2 L}{\partial \boldsymbol{t}^{\,2}} = 0.$$

Therefore, along any inpainted isophote, L must be linear: $L = a + bs$, where s denotes the arc length parameter of the isophote, and a and b are two constants that are determined by the L values at the two boundary pixels. Recall that Bertalmio et al.'s pure transport model demands a constant value for the smoothness measure along any inpainted isophote. But for a generic image function u, level lines of u (i.e., isophotes) are generally different from those of L.

Since g is a second order feature, by (6.88) L must only involve the first order differential ∇u, or $L = L(\nabla u)$. Furthermore, since g, $|\nabla u|$, and $\partial/\partial \boldsymbol{t}$ are all rotationally invariant, so must L by (6.88), which means $L = L(|\nabla u|)$. Therefore,

$$g = |\nabla u| \frac{\partial L(|\nabla u|)}{\partial \boldsymbol{t}} = |\nabla u|^2 L'(|\nabla u|) \frac{1}{|\nabla u|} \frac{\partial |\nabla u|}{\partial \boldsymbol{t}} = |\nabla u|^2 L'(|\nabla u|) \, \sigma.$$

Together with (6.87), it implies that

$$|\nabla u|^2 L'(|\nabla u|) = a, \qquad \text{a constant.}$$

(Notice that g/σ is a function of κ and σ only, and from the transform (6.85), generically, $p = |\nabla u|$ is independent of κ and σ.) Therefore,

$$L(|\nabla u|) = -a|\nabla u|^{-1} + b \qquad \text{and} \quad g = a \, \sigma = a \, \frac{\partial (\ln |\nabla u|)}{\partial \boldsymbol{t}}.$$

In summary, we have established the following theorem.

Theorem 6.18. *Under the previous four principles, a third order inpainting model in the divergence form must be given by*

$$\frac{\partial u}{\partial t} = \nabla \cdot (f(\kappa, \sigma) \, \boldsymbol{n} + a\sigma \, \boldsymbol{t} \,), \tag{6.89}$$

where a is a nonzero constant, $f(\kappa, \sigma)$ a positive function, and

$$\kappa = \nabla \cdot \left(\frac{\nabla u}{|\nabla u|} \right) \quad and \quad \sigma = \frac{\partial (\ln |\nabla u|)}{\partial \boldsymbol{t}}$$

the scalar curvature and the deviation rate.

For instance, as inspired by Euler's elastica inpainting model discussed earlier, one can choose $f = a + b\kappa^2$ for two positive constants a and b, or even $f = \exp(c\kappa^2)$ for some positive constant c. As discussed in Section 6.11.4 for the CDD model, such choices penalize large curvatures and thus realize the connectivity principle [61, 68].

6.12 Inpainting of Gibbs/Markov Random Fields

Let $(\Omega, \mathcal{N})$ be a neighborhood system, on which an image random field u is defined (see Section 3.4.4). Let $\alpha, \beta, \ldots \in \Omega$ denote typical pixels or nodes, and $\mathcal{N}_\alpha, \mathcal{N}_\beta, \ldots$ their neighbors.

Let $D \subseteq \Omega$ be a subset of pixels on which image information u is missing. u is assumed to be available outside D. A natural inpainting scheme is then the *maximum likelihood estimator* (MLE):

$$\hat{u}_D = \underset{u_D}{\operatorname{argmax}} \ p(u_D \mid u(\Omega \setminus D)), \tag{6.90}$$

which is optimal ranging over all marginal fields u_D's on the missing set D.

Assume that u is a Gibbs/Markov image random field with respect to the neighborhood system $\mathcal{N}$. Define the boundary of D by

$$\partial D = \{\beta \in \Omega \setminus D \mid \text{ there exists some } \alpha \in D, \text{ such that } \beta \in \mathcal{N}_\alpha\}.$$

Then the Markovian property reduces the MLE (6.90) to

$$\hat{u}_D = \underset{u_D}{\operatorname{argmax}} \ p(u_D \mid u(\partial D)), \tag{6.91}$$

which is a *boundary value problem*.

In terms of computation, one can solve (6.91) iteratively: $\hat{u}_D^{(n)} \to \hat{u}_D^{(n+1)}$. As inspired by numerical linear algebra [138], for example, one could try the *Jacobi*-type iteration

$$\hat{u}_\alpha^{(n+1)} = \underset{u_\alpha}{\operatorname{argmax}} \ p(u_\alpha \mid (u \vee \hat{u}^{(n)})(\mathcal{N}_\alpha)), \quad \alpha \in D,$$

where the $\vee$ notation stands for

$$(u \vee \hat{u}^{(n)})(\mathcal{N}_\alpha) = \{u_\gamma \mid \gamma \in \mathcal{N}_\alpha \cap \partial D\} \cup \{\hat{u}_\beta^{(n)} \mid \beta \in \mathcal{N}_\alpha \cap D\}.$$

Alternatively, one could first assign a convenient order to all the missing pixels of D,

$$D = \{\alpha_1, \alpha_2, \ldots, \alpha_m\} \text{ with } D_{>k} = \{\alpha_i \mid i > k\} \text{ and } D_{<k} = \{\alpha_j \mid j < k\},$$

and then employ the *Gauss–Seidel*-type iteration [138]:

$$\hat{u}_{\alpha_k}^{(n+1)} = \underset{u_{\alpha_k}}{\operatorname{argmax}} \ p(u_{\alpha_k} \mid (u \vee \hat{u}^{(n)} \vee \hat{u}^{(n+1)})(\mathcal{N}_{\alpha_k})), \quad k = 1 : m,$$

where, as in the Jacobi case, $(u \vee \hat{u}^{(n)} \vee \hat{u}^{(n+1)})(\mathcal{N}_{\alpha_k})$ stands for

$$\{u_\beta \mid \beta \in \mathcal{N}_{\alpha_k} \cap \partial D\} \cup \{\hat{u}_\beta^{(n)} \mid \beta \in \mathcal{N}_{\alpha_k} \cap D_{>k}\} \cup \{\hat{u}_\beta^{(n+1)} \mid \beta \in \mathcal{N}_{\alpha_k} \cap D_{<k}\}.$$

When the Markov random field is expressed in terms of Gibbs' cliquish potentials V_C's (see Section 3.4.4), one has

$$p(u_\alpha \mid u(\mathcal{N}_\alpha)) = \frac{1}{Z_\alpha} e^{-\sum_{C:\alpha \in C} V_C(u_\alpha, u(\mathcal{N}_\alpha))} \quad \text{with}$$

$$Z_\alpha = Z_\alpha(u(\mathcal{N}_\alpha)) = \sum_{u_\alpha \in \Lambda} e^{-\sum_{\alpha \in C} V_C(u_\alpha, u(\mathcal{N}_\alpha))},$$

where Λ is the shade or color space, assumed to be finite (e.g., 16 bit). Therefore, a single-pixel inpainting problem with only u_α missing can be solved via energy minimization:

$$\hat{u}_\alpha = \operatorname*{argmin}_{u_\alpha} \sum_{C:\alpha \in C} V_C(u_\alpha, u(N_\alpha)).$$

When the missing set D is a domain containing more than one missing pixel, this can be implemented in the same spirit of Jacobi or Gauss–Seidel iteration just explained above. For example, for the Jacobi scheme [138],

$$\hat{u}_\alpha^{(n+1)} = \operatorname*{argmin}_{u_\alpha} \sum_{C:\alpha \in C} V_C(u_\alpha, (u \vee \hat{u}^{(n)})(\mathcal{N}_\alpha)), \quad \alpha \in D.$$

Notice that the local partition function Z_α does not participate in the computation.

In [72], Chan and Shen also discuss some information-theoretic aspects of the inpainting of Markov random fields. For more discussion on the role of Gibbs/Markov random fields in image analysis and processing and the stochastic approach to inpainting, we refer the reader to Geman and Geman [130], Mumford [224], and the work by Guo, Zhu, and Wu [148].

The notion of interpolating Markov random fields has been the key ingredient in the work of Efros and Leung [110] for texture synthesis. The main challenge for practical implementations lies in the effective learning of the Markov local structures from the available image samples. Efros and Leung cleverly approximated such local structures by heuristically comparing the local windows near missing pixels with those available. We refer the reader to the original work [110] for further details.

Chapter 7

Image Segmentation

Image segmentation is the bridge between low-level vision/image processing and high-level vision. Its goal is to partition a given image into a collection of "objects," built upon which other high-level tasks such as object detection, recognition, and tracking can be further performed. In this chapter, we discuss several important and interconnected models pertinent to the segmentation task, including Active Contours, Geman and Geman's mixture model, and Mumford and Shah's free boundary model. From imaging and graphics points of view, segmentation is also an *inverse* problem, i.e., from images to the perception of objects, instead of from objects to the acquisition of images. The current chapter thus starts with a mathematical model or theory for the *forward* problem, as done in the previous chapters for denoising and deblurring.

7.1 Synthetic Images: Monoids of Occlusive Preimages

In this first section, we develop a simplified mathematical theory or model for synthesizing images from individual objects. Without the complication of 3-D real imaging environments, the theory focuses on the topological and algebraic structures of image generation. Though only restricted to binary images, it provides a reasonable *forward* problem for the segmentation task. We have especially emphasized the important role of occlusion in vision.

7.1.1 Introduction and Motivation

In human and computer vision, the occlusion phenomenon plays a key role in successful retrieval of 3-D structural information from 2-D images projected onto the retinas. Its importance has been repeatedly emphasized by many giants in vision sciences, including David Marr in computer vision and artificial intelligence [210], Gaetano Kanizsa in Gestalt and cognitive vision [163], and David Mumford in mathematical and statistical modeling of visual perception [191, 226, 234].

The left panel of Figure 7.1 shows a popular image in vision research, for which the lack of occlusion cues causes a perceptual illusion; i.e., two or more distinct 3-D scenes can be interpreted from the image. The right panel on the other hand shows the importance of occlusion cues in the visual perception of 3-D knots as in knot theory [253].

309

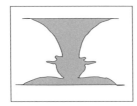

Figure 7.1. *Role of occlusion in visual perception. Left panel: a gray vase against a bright background or two opposite human faces against a gray background? This is a typical illusion problem caused by the lack of occlusion cues;   Right panel (a trefoil): the role of occlusion in knot theory* [253].

The occlusion phenomenon has motivated numerous research works in mathematical image and vision analysis, especially by David Mumford, together with his students and colleagues. In the monograph [234], Nitzberg, Mumford, and Shiota invented variational models for the disocclusion task as well as boundary interpolation, which has also inspired the recent wave of interest in image inpainting and geometric interpolation [61, 67, 116, 273]. In [191], Lee, Mumford, and Huang employed the occlusion mechanism to simulate image formation of natural scenes, and discovered the remarkable agreement, in terms of both qualitative and quantitative properties (e.g., scale invariance), between such simulated images and complex natural ones. Occlusion is also a key factor leading to the logical faith in the literature that natural images are nonstationary random fields or non-Sobolev functions globally. As a result, mixture image models have been proposed to handle such images in the celebrated works of Geman and Geman [130] and Mumford and Shah [226], especially for the tasks of image restoration and segmentation.

In [277], Shen takes a different approach towards occlusion-based image synthesis. Instead of the aforementioned analytical, functional, or stochastic methods, a simpler occlusion model is developed based on the point-set topology, and both its *topological* and *algebraic* properties are further explored. The major discovery is the following: with a proper topological definition of preliminary images (or *preimages*, sketched images before the applications of colors or shades), as well as a binary operation called "occlu" on them (denoted by $A \dashv B$), the set of all preimages constitute into a noncommutative monoid, i.e., a noncommutative semigroup with an identity.

The current section is mainly mathematically oriented, and readers in more applied sciences can safely skip it in the first place.

7.1.2 Monoids of Occlusive Preimages

Definition 7.1 (Preimages). *A preliminary image (in $\mathbb{R}^2$), abbreviated to "a preimage," is a pair (a, γ) that satisfies*

(1) *a and γ are both* closed *subsets of $\mathbb{R}^2$ (but unnecessarily being compact);*

(2) *$\partial a \subseteq \gamma \subseteq a$; and*

(3) γ *is σ-finite under 1-D Hausdorff measure $\mathcal{H}^1$.*

Here by σ-finite we mean that for any compact subset K of $\mathbb{R}^2$,

$$\mathcal{H}^1(\gamma \cap K) < \infty.$$

It requires γ not to be too complex locally, as inspired by the celebrated variational segmentation model of Mumford and Shah [226].

For convenience, sometimes we shall use the notation a_γ, b_δ for preimages (a, γ), (b, δ), or capital letters A, B if the topological details are less concerned than their algebraic relations.

Definition 7.2 (Support and Pattern). *For a preimage (a, γ), a is called its* support *and γ its* pattern.

We now define a binary operation called "occlu," which is denoted by $\dashv$ and pronounced as in the English words "occlusion" or "occlude."

Definition 7.3 ((a, γ) occlu (b, δ)). *Let $a_\gamma = (a, \gamma)$ and $b_\delta = (b, \delta)$ be any two preimages. Then a_γ occlu b_δ is defined as*

$$a_\gamma \dashv b_\delta = (a \cup b, \gamma \cup (\delta \setminus a^\circ)) := (c, \eta) = c_\eta, \tag{7.1}$$

where a° denotes the topological interior of the set a. We shall call $a_\gamma \dashv b_\delta$ the occlusion *of a_γ to b_δ (see Figure 7.2 for an example).*

Theorem 7.4. *The occlusion of two preimages is still a preimage.*

Proof. Recall in topology [169] that the union and joint of any two closed sets are still closed. Thus c and η in (7.1) are both closed, since

$$\delta \setminus a^\circ = \delta \cap (a^\circ)^c,$$

where the superscript c stands for the complement operation. Thus condition (1) is satisfied in the definition of preimages.

One also has in general topology, for any two sets a and b,

$$\partial(a \cup b) \subseteq \partial a \cup \partial b.$$

Furthermore, since $a^\circ \subseteq (a \cup b)^\circ$ and $\partial a \cap a^\circ = \phi$,

$$\partial(a \cup b) \subseteq (\partial a \cup \partial b) \setminus a^\circ = \partial a \cup (\partial b \setminus a^\circ).$$

Therefore,

$$\partial c \subseteq \gamma \cup (\delta \setminus a^\circ)(= \eta) \subseteq a \cup b = c.$$

This verifies condition (2) in the definition of preimages.

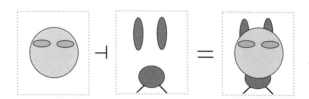

Figure 7.2. *An example of two preimages a_γ and b_δ and their occlusion $a_\gamma \dashv b_\delta$. Complex image patterns in the real world often originate from simple objects via occlusion.*

Finally, by the subadditivity of general measures, for any compact set K,

$$\mathcal{H}^1(\eta \cap K) \le \mathcal{H}^1((\gamma \cup \delta) \cap K) \le \mathcal{H}^1(\gamma \cap K) + \mathcal{H}^1(\delta \cap K) < \infty,$$

which verifies condition (3).   □

Theorem 7.5. *The occlusion operation is associative; i.e., for any three preimages $a_\gamma = (a, \gamma), b_\delta = (b, \delta)$, and $c_\eta = (c, \eta)$,*

$$a_\gamma \dashv (b_\delta \dashv c_\eta) = (a_\gamma \dashv b_\delta) \dashv c_\eta.$$

Proof. By definition,

$$a_\gamma \dashv (b_\delta \dashv c_\eta) = (a \cup b \cup c, \ \gamma \cup (\delta \cup \eta \setminus b^\circ) \setminus a^\circ), \tag{7.2}$$

$$(a_\gamma \dashv b_\delta) \dashv c_\eta = (a \cup b \cup c, \ \gamma \cup (\delta \setminus a^\circ) \cup \eta \setminus (a \cup b)^\circ). \tag{7.3}$$

(To avoid too many parentheses, the set subtraction operation "$\setminus$" is assumed to have first priority in computation compared with other set operations such as union $\cup$ and joint $\cap$.) It then suffices to show that the two patterns are identical. For the first pattern, one has

$$\gamma \cup (\delta \cup \eta \setminus b^\circ) \setminus a^\circ = \gamma \cup (\delta \setminus a^\circ) \cup (\eta \setminus b^\circ) \setminus a^\circ, \tag{7.4}$$

where the last group in the unions

$$(\eta \setminus b^\circ) \setminus a^\circ = \eta \setminus (b^\circ \cup a^\circ) \supseteq \eta \setminus (a \cup b)^\circ, \tag{7.5}$$

since $a^\circ \cup b^\circ \subseteq (a \cup b)^\circ$. This completes half of the proof; i.e., the pattern of the right-hand side contains that of the left in the theorem.

For the other half, let us investigate how much on earth could be possibly left out in the inclusion relation (7.5). Applying the set identity

$$(X \setminus A) \setminus (X \setminus B) = (X \cap B) \setminus A,$$

one has

$$(\eta \setminus (b^\circ \cup a^\circ)) \setminus (\eta \setminus (a \cup b)^\circ) = (\eta \cap (a \cup b)^\circ) \setminus (a^\circ \cup b^\circ) \subseteq (a \cup b)^\circ \setminus (a^\circ \cup b^\circ).$$

For this last set,

$$(a \cup b)^\circ \setminus (a^\circ \cup b^\circ) \subseteq \overline{a \cup b} \setminus (a^\circ \cup b^\circ) = (\bar{a} \cup \bar{b}) \setminus (a^\circ \cup b^\circ)$$
$$\subseteq (\partial a \cup \partial b) \setminus (a^\circ \cup b^\circ) \subseteq (\partial a \cup \partial b) \setminus a^\circ$$
$$= \partial a \cup (\partial b) \setminus a^\circ \subseteq \gamma \cup (\delta \setminus a^\circ).$$

Thus what could be potentially missing in the inclusion relation (7.5) is already contained in the first two commonly shared terms in (7.3) and (7.4), which completes the proof. □

Lemma 7.6. *Two preimages a_γ and b_δ satisfy*

$$a_\gamma \dashv b_\delta = a_\gamma$$

if and only if $b \subseteq a$.

Proof. If the occlusion identity holds, then in terms of the supports, $a \cup b = a$, which immediately implies $b \subseteq a$.

Now suppose $b \subseteq a$. Then in terms of the patterns,

$$\gamma \subseteq \gamma \cup (\delta \setminus a^\circ) \subseteq \gamma \cup (b \setminus a^\circ) \subseteq \gamma \cup (a \setminus a^\circ) = \gamma \cup \partial a = \gamma.$$

This establishes the occlusion identity. □

Lemma 7.7. *A universal right identity element c_η, i.e., for any preimage a_η in $\mathbb{R}^2$,*

$$a_\gamma \dashv c_\eta = a_\gamma,$$

has to be the empty preimage (ϕ, ϕ), or simply denoted by ϕ.

Proof. By the preceding lemma, a right identity element $c_\eta = (c, \eta)$ has to satisfy

$$c \subseteq a \quad \forall \text{ closed set } a \text{ in } \mathbb{R}^2.$$

In particular, $a = \phi$ implies $c = \phi$. Then $\eta = \phi$ since $\eta \subseteq c = \phi$. □

It is also easy to verify that the empty preimage $\phi = (\phi, \phi)$ is a left identity as well. Therefore, it is a genuine (double-sided) identity element.

To conclude, we have established the following theorem.

Theorem 7.8 (Monoids of Occlusive Preimages). *Any set $\mathcal{I}$ of preimages is a semigroup if it is closed under the occlusion operation; i.e., for any $a_\gamma, b_\delta \in \mathcal{I}$, $a_\gamma \dashv b_\delta \in \mathcal{I}$. In addition, if $\mathcal{I}$ contains the empty preimage $\phi = (\phi, \phi)$, it is a monoid.*

In particular, the set of all preimages on $\mathbb{R}^2$ forms a monoid, which is apparently the largest preimage monoid, and will be called the *universal monoid* of preimages.

It is easy to see that generally a preimage monoid is noncommutative, which is mainly due to the pattern part since the support part is commutative (i.e., $a \cup b = b \cup a$). For instance, for any two preimages a_γ and b_δ with $b \subseteq a$,

$$a_\gamma \dashv b_\delta = (a, \gamma) \quad \text{and} \quad b_\delta \dashv a_\gamma = (a, \delta \cup \gamma \setminus b^\circ).$$

Thus as long as $\delta \subsetneqq \gamma$, a_γ and b_δ are not commutative.

It is also trivial to show that for the universal monoid of preimages, the center C consists only of the identity element ϕ.

We now discuss an identity that most explicitly reveals the algebraic structure of preimage monoids.

Theorem 7.9 (Fundamental Identity of Occlusion). *For any two preimages A and B, one has*

$$A \dashv B \dashv A = A \dashv B. \tag{7.6}$$

Proof. Suppose $A = (a, \gamma)$ and $B = (b, \delta)$. Then by definition,

$$A \dashv B = (a \cup b, \gamma \cup \delta \setminus a^\circ).$$

Since $a \subseteq a \cup b$, by Lemma 7.6,

$$(A \dashv B) \dashv A = A \dashv B. \quad \square$$

Unlike the identity in Lemma 7.6 which involves the topological constraint $b \subseteq a$, the fundamental identity can be understood as a purely algebraic identity. Thus it could play a role similar to, for example,

$$Q^T Q = I_n \quad \text{for the } n \times n \text{ rotaion group; or,}$$

$$[a, [b, c]] + [b, [c, a]] + [c, [a, b]] = 0 \quad \text{for a Lie algebra.}$$

In particular we have the following.

Corollary 7.10. *The following identities hold for any preimages $A, B, \ldots$:*

(i) (Projection) $A \dashv A = A$.

(ii) (Nonrepetition)

$$A \dashv \cdots \dashv B \dashv \cdots \dashv C \dashv B = A \dashv \cdots \dashv B \dashv \cdots \dashv C.$$

Recall in linear algebra that any square matrix P satisfying $P^2 = P$ is called a projection, which has inspired the name of the first identity. On the other hand, from the vision point of view, occlusion is indeed a genuine projection; i.e., objects on the foreground are projected onto those on the background.

Proof. The projection identity follows directly from the fundamental identity (7.6) by taking $B = \phi = (\phi, \phi)$, the identity preimage.

The nonrepetition identity also follows directly from the fundamental identity. $\quad \square$

7.1.3 Mimimal and Prime (or Atomic) Generators

Definition 7.11 (Generators). *Let $\mathcal{I}$ be a preimage monoid. A subset $S \subseteq \mathcal{I}$ is said to be a generator of the monoid if for any $a_\gamma \in \mathcal{I}$, there exists a finite sequence of preimages*

$$b_\delta, \ldots, c_\eta \in S,$$

such that

$$a_\gamma = b_\delta \dashv \cdots \dashv c_\eta.$$

If so, $\mathcal{I}$ is said to be generated from S.

Theorem 7.12. *Given any set S of preimages, there exists a* unique *preimage monoid $\mathcal{I}_* = \mathcal{I}_*(S)$ that is generated from S and is* minimal *in the sense that*

$$\mathcal{I}_*(S) \subseteq \mathcal{I} \quad \text{for any preimage monoid } \mathcal{I} \text{ that contains } S.$$

Proof. Uniqueness is trivial since the minimality condition requires that any two minimum monoids contain each other.

Existence is guaranteed by the following construction, which is standard in abstract algebra. Define

$$\mathcal{I}_* = \{(b_1, \gamma_1) \dashv \cdots \dashv (b_n, \gamma_n) \mid n = 0, 1, \ldots, \ (b_k, \gamma_k) \in S, k = 1 : n\},$$

with the agreement that $n = 0$ corresponds to the identity element $\phi = (\phi, \phi)$. It is then easy to verify that $\mathcal{I}_*$ is closed under the occlusion operation and hence is indeed a preimage monoid. Its minimality is also crystal clear since any of its elements belongs to any monoid that contains S. $\square$

Theorem 7.13 (Size Bound of Preimages). *Suppose S is a finite set of preimages with $\#S = n$ elements. Then the preimage monoid $\mathcal{I}_*(S)$ generated by S is a finite set as well, and*

$$\#\mathcal{I}_*(S) \le \sum_{k=0}^{n} (n)_k,$$

where $(n)_k = n(n-1) \cdots (n-k+1)$ with $(n)_0 = 1$.

Proof. According to the properties of projection and nonrepetition in Corollary 7.10, and the construction in the preceding theorem, any element $Z \in \mathcal{I}_*$ can be written in the form of

$$Z = A \dashv B \dashv \cdots \dashv C \tag{7.7}$$

with preimages $A, B, \ldots, C$ belonging to S and being *distinct*.

For each integer k, there are $\binom{n}{k}$ different ways of selecting k preimages from S, followed by $k! = k(k-1) \cdots 1$ permutations for each selection to assemble a general preimage in $\mathcal{I}_*(S)$ by (7.7). Therefore

$$\#\mathcal{I}_* \le \sum_{k=0}^{n} \binom{n}{k} k! = \sum_{k=0}^{n} (n)_k. \quad \square$$

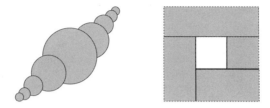

Figure 7.3. *Left: a diskette preimage; Right: a planar preimage.*

We now define some interesting classes of preimage monoids based on their generators.

(a) (Diskette preimage monoid) Define the generator set

$$S_d = \{(B_r(x), \partial B_r(x)) \mid r \geq 0, x = (x_1, x_2) \in \mathbb{R}^2\},$$

consisting of all closed disks on the plane (see Figure 7.3). Then $\mathcal{I}_{\text{disk}} = \mathcal{I}_*(S_d)$ shall be called the *diskette preimage monoid*.

(b) (Planar preimage monoid) Define the generator set

$$S_p = \{(P, \partial P) \mid P = \{y \in \mathbb{R}^2 \mid n \cdot (y - x) \geq 0\}, n \in S^1, x \in \mathbb{R}^2\},$$

consisting of all half-planes (see Figure 7.3). Then $\mathcal{I}_{\text{plane}} = \mathcal{I}_*(S_p)$ shall be called the *planar preimage monoid*. (Here S^1 denotes the unit circle.)

(c) (Convex preimage monoid) Define the generator set

$$S_c = \{(E, \partial E) \mid E \subseteq \mathbb{R}^2 \text{ is convex}\}.$$

Then $\mathcal{I}_{\text{conv}} = \mathcal{I}_*(S_c)$ shall be called the *convex preimage monoid*. It is clear that both the diskette and planar monoids are submonoids of the convex monoid.

(d) (Smooth preimage monoid) Define the generator set

$$S_s = \{(M, \partial M) \mid M \text{ is a connected } C^{(2)} \text{ submanifold with borders}\}. \tag{7.8}$$

That is, as in differential topology [218], for each boundary point $x = (x_1, x_2) \in \partial M$, there are an open neighborhood U_x and a C^2 invertible map ϕ that map U_x onto $\mathbb{R}^2$, so that

$$\phi(U_x \cap M) = \{(x_1, x_2) \mid x_2 \geq 0\}, \quad \text{i.e., the upper half-plane.}$$

Then we shall call $\mathcal{I}_{\text{smooth}} = \mathcal{I}_*(S_s)$ the *smooth preimage monoid*. The C^2 regularity condition has been imposed so that curvature along the boundaries is well defined.

Notice that although the above generator sets are all quite regular, they can already generate very complex preimages and patterns. The underlying motivation and philosophy are therefore clearly rooted in the fundamental fact of physics: the complex physical world arises from its simple generators of basic particles such as quarks and protons.

Definition 7.14 (Minimal Generating Sets). *Suppose S generates a preimage monoid $\mathcal{I}$.* *Then S is said to be* minimal *if*

$$A \notin \mathcal{I}_*(S \setminus \{A\}) \qquad \forall A \in S.$$

That is, no proper subset of S alone can regenerate the entire monoid $\mathcal{I}$.

Definition 7.15 (Prime or Atomic Preimages). *An element a_γ in a preimage monoid $\mathcal{I}$ is said to be* prime *or* atomic *if*

$$a_\gamma \notin \mathcal{I}_*(\mathcal{I} \setminus \{a_\gamma\}).$$

Let $\mathcal{A}(\mathcal{I})$ denote the collection of all prime or atomic preimages, and it will be called the atomic set *of $\mathcal{I}$.*

Notice that if $\mathcal{I}$ is compared to the (commutative) monoid of natural numbers under multiplication, then a prime or atomic preimage is analogous to a prime number. The following proposition is evident from the definitions.

Proposition 7.16. *For a given preimage monoid, it is always true that $\mathcal{A}(\mathcal{I}) \subseteq S(\mathcal{I})$ for any minimal generating set $S(\mathcal{I})$.*

Definition 7.17 (Regular Preimages). *A preimage (a, γ) is said to be* regular *if its 2-D Hausdorff measure (identical to the 2-D Lebesgue measure in $\mathbb{R}^2$) $\mathcal{H}^2(a)$ is nonzero, and $\partial a = \partial(a^\circ)$. Otherwise it is said to be* degenerate.

Theorem 7.18. *A preimage (a, γ) is regular if and only if $a \neq \phi$ and $a = \overline{a^\circ}$.*

Proof. First, suppose (a, γ) is regular. Then $a \neq \phi$ since $\mathcal{H}^2(a) > 0$, and

$$a = \partial a \cup a^\circ = \partial a^\circ \cup a^\circ = \overline{a^\circ}.$$

Conversely, suppose $a \neq \phi$ and $a = \overline{a^\circ}$. Then $a^\circ \neq \phi$, implying that

$$\mathcal{H}^2(a) \geq \mathcal{H}^2(a^\circ) > 0.$$

Furthermore, since

$$a = \partial a \cup a^\circ \quad \text{and} \quad \overline{a^\circ} = a^\circ \cup \partial a^\circ,$$

and $\partial a \cap a^\circ = \phi$, $a = \overline{a^\circ}$ must imply that

$$\partial a \subseteq \partial a^\circ \subseteq \partial a,$$

which concludes the proof. $\square$

For more topological, geometric, and algebraic properties of the preimage monoids, we refer the reader to Shen [277]. To some extent, segmentation can be considered as the inverse problem of such image synthesis processes.

7.2   Edges and Active Contours

Objects in images differ from each other via their boundaries or edges, which has made *edge detection* or *extraction* one of the oldest yet still the most fundamental tasks in vision and image analysis.

Though primarily arising in image analysis and processing, we must point out that edge detection and adaptivity have also been pivotal in many other areas such as numerical analysis of spectral data (see, e.g., Tadmor and Tanner [295, 296]).

7.2.1   Pixelwise Characterization of Edges: David Marr's Edges

Like any general pattern recognition problem, edge detection crucially depends on

   (i) a sound definition of the edge feature or pattern; and

   (ii) a good algorithm for extracting such edges.

The two are intimately correlated, however.

Edges are traditionally recognized as the collection of pixels where the gradients are noticeably large. Thus, for example, a simple edge detector can be defined by

$$\Gamma = \Gamma_u(p) = \{x \in \Omega \: : \: |\nabla u(x)| \geq p\}, \tag{7.9}$$

where $\Omega \subseteq \mathbb{R}^2$ denotes an image domain, u a given image on Ω, and p some suitable threshold.

This naive edge detector can be criticized from two aspects. First, it is oversensitive to noise. Suppose $u = v + n$ is the superposition of a clean image v with some additive noise n. Then the detector (7.9) fails to distinguish genuine edge pixels from noisy pixels. That is, almost surely (from the probability point of view), the detected edge set $\Gamma_u(p)$ would be the entire domain Ω, regardless of what the embedded clean image v is.

The second more deadly blow to the edge detector (7.9) is that it is *not intrinsic*, since it depends on an external threshold p. In particular, it is not invariant under a linear "flashing": $u \to \lambda u$ with $\lambda \in (0, \infty)$, because $\Gamma_{\lambda u} \neq \Gamma_u$ for a generic image u and λ. To human vision, u and λu, however, seem to share the same set of edges.

These drawbacks are nevertheless remediable. To watch out for possible noise interference, one may first apply some mollifier to the image, e.g., the Gaussian kernel and mollification:

$$u \to u_\sigma = g_\sigma * u \;\; \text{with} \;\; g_\sigma(x) = g_\sigma(x_1, x_2) = \frac{1}{2\pi\sigma^2} \exp\left(-\frac{x^2}{2\sigma^2}\right). \tag{7.10}$$

To make the detector intrinsic, on the other hand, one may look for *homogeneous* constraints instead of the hard thresholding formula (7.9), e.g., a formulation like

$$\Gamma = \Gamma_u = \{x \in \Omega \mid \mathcal{L}(u_\sigma)(x) = 0\},$$

where the operator $\mathcal{L}$ is homogeneous:

$$L(\lambda u_\sigma) = \lambda^\alpha \mathcal{L}(u_\sigma) \quad \text{for some fixed} \;\; \alpha.$$

In one dimension, $u_x(x)$ could only reach its extrema at inflection locations where $u_{xx} = 0$. A natural generalization to two dimensions is to replace the second derivative by the Laplacian operator

$$\mathcal{L} = \Delta = \frac{\partial^2}{\partial x_1{}^2} + \frac{\partial^2}{\partial x_2{}^2}.$$

Then the associated edge detector is given by

$$\Gamma_u = \{x \in \Omega \mid \Delta u_\sigma(x) = (\Delta g_\sigma) * u(x) = 0\}, \tag{7.11}$$

which is precisely David Marr's zero-crossing theory of edges [210, 211], and resists to minor noises.

More generally in two dimensions, the second order information is expressed by the Hessian matrix

$$H_u = \begin{bmatrix} u_{xx} & u_{xy} \\ u_{yx} & u_{yy} \end{bmatrix}, \qquad H_{\lambda u} = \lambda H_u. \tag{7.12}$$

The Laplacian Δu is exactly trace(H_u). Denote $\mathbf{n} = \nabla u / |\nabla u|$ the unit normal, and consider

$$\frac{\partial^2 u}{\partial \mathbf{n}^2} \text{ as the genuine 2-D generalization of } u_{xx} \text{ in one dimension.}$$

Then

$$\begin{aligned} \frac{\partial u}{\partial \mathbf{n}} &= \mathbf{n} \cdot \nabla u = |\nabla u|, \\ \frac{\partial^2 u}{\partial \mathbf{n}^2} &= \mathbf{n} \cdot \nabla(|\nabla u|) = H_u(\mathbf{n}, \mathbf{n}), \end{aligned} \tag{7.13}$$

where the Hessian has been treated as a bilinear operator (or $H_u(\mathbf{n}, \mathbf{n}) = \mathbf{n}^T H_u \mathbf{n}$ by the matrix-vector notion). Thus, an alternative to Marr's edge detector is

$$\Gamma_u = \{x \in \Omega \mid H_{u_\sigma}(\nabla u_\sigma, \nabla u_\sigma) = 0 \text{ and } \nabla u_\sigma \neq 0\}. \tag{7.14}$$

Notice that it is indeed homogeneous $\Gamma_{\lambda u} = \Gamma_u$ since

$$H_{\lambda v}(\nabla(\lambda v), \nabla(\lambda v)) = \lambda^3 H_v(\nabla v, \nabla v).$$

We refer the reader to the remarkable axiomatic interpretation of this edge detector by Caselles, Morel, and Sbert [50] in the context of image interpolation.

It is also interesting to point out that one of the most successful edge detectors, *Canny's edge detector* [44, 100], is specified by

$$\Gamma_{u,\tau} = \{x \in \Omega \ : \ |\nabla u_\sigma|(x) \text{ is a local maximum along } \mathbf{n}, \text{ and } |\nabla u_\sigma| \geq \tau\},$$

where $\tau > 0$ is a threshold level. Notice that

$$H_{u_\sigma}(\nabla u_\sigma, \nabla u_\sigma)(x) = 0$$

is a necessary condition for $|\nabla u_\sigma|(x)$ being a local maximum along the normal, as clear from (7.13).

7.2.2 Edge-Regulated Data Models for Image Gray Values

The main shortcoming of pixelwise edge detection is the lack of explicit correlation among different edge pixels. Without being polished by extra postprocessing steps, edges detected in such ways often contain many unwanted ripples or spurious segments, and they lack global spatial consistency to human vision.

A beautiful yet simple way to integrate spatial regularity into pixelwise edge detection is realized by models of *Active Contours*, or often nicknamed "Snakes," as invented by Kass, Witkin, and Terzopoulos [165]. Active Contours are based on the principle of variational optimization, or stochastically, Bayesian inference.

As mentioned many times in previous chapters, a Bayesian estimation scheme relies on two pieces of information—the prior knowledge model and the generative data model. The current section will primarily focus on the latter, while the prior model (for edges) will be studied in the next section.

In the Bayesian framework, the goal of a generative data model is to describe how data or observations should look when the target feature is present. In terms of images and their edge features, it means to model an image u when the precise information about its edge set Γ is given, i.e., the conditional distribution $p(u \mid \Gamma)$.

To proceed, we think of edges as hidden features of images, and we model it by a binary random field γ on the given image domain Ω, which could be the ideal 2-D lattice $\mathbb{Z}^2$ after a uniform scaling. Thus for any pixel $x \in \Omega$,

$$\gamma(x) = 1 \quad \text{if } x \text{ is an edge pixel;} \quad 0 \quad \text{otherwise.}$$

Consequently for any given γ, the physical edge set is $\Gamma = \gamma^{-1}(1)$.

We must point out that classical Active Contour models specify only the behavior of edge pixels, i.e.,

$$p(u \mid \gamma(x) = 1) \quad \text{for any fixed pixel } x \in \Omega. \tag{7.15}$$

In the models of Geman and Geman [130] and Mumford and Shah [226] (to be discussed later in this chapter) the data models of nonedge pixels are also investigated, i.e.,

$$p(u \mid \gamma(x) = 0) \quad \text{for any fixed pixel } x \in \Omega.$$

To model (7.15), i.e., how an image u should look if a given x is known to be its edge pixel, one tries the Gibbs formula:

$$p(u \mid \gamma(x) = 1) = \frac{1}{Z} e^{-\mu g(x, u, \nabla u, \dots)}, \tag{7.16}$$

where

(a) μ is the parameter adjusting the virtual inverse "temperature" (Section 2.3),

(b) g is the "energy" function which may depend on pixel locations as well as derivatives of u, and

(c) Z is the partition function for probability normalization (whose rigorous definition on infinite lattices could involve renormalization procedures [225, 321]).

Thus the mission is to properly model the energy function g.

To narrow down possible candidates for g, we impose the following three axioms as inspired by human vision.

(i) (Spatial shift invariance) $g(x + a, u(x + a), \ldots) = g(x, u(x), \ldots)$ under any constant spatial shift $x \rightarrow x + a$.

(ii) (Gray-level shift invariance) $g(x, \lambda + u, \ldots) = g(x, u, \ldots)$ under any constant gray-level shift $u \rightarrow \lambda + u$.

(iii) (Rotational invariance) $g(Qx, u(Q(x)), \ldots) = g(x, u(x), \ldots)$ for any planar rotation $Q \in O(2)$.

Spatial shift invariance implies that g cannot explicitly depend on x, i.e., $g = g(u, \nabla u, \ldots)$. Gray-level shift invariance then requires that g be independent of u: $g = g(\nabla u, \ldots)$. Finally, the rotational invariance implies that

$$g(Q^T \nabla u, \ldots) = g(\nabla u, \ldots) \quad \forall Q \in O(2).$$

Therefore, the energy function must be given by

$$g = g(|\nabla u|, \kappa_1, \kappa_2, \ldots),$$

where κ_1 and κ_2 are the two eigenvalues of the Hessian matrix H_u, which are the complete set of rational invariants since H_u is symmetric. In particular since $\Delta u = \kappa_1 + \kappa_2$,

$$g = g(|\nabla u|, \Delta u)$$

could be an energy form satisfying all the previous axioms.

The style of such axiomatic approaches in image analysis and processing has been greatly promoted and developed by Jean-Michel Morel and his colleagues (see, e.g., [6, 50]). It provides an efficient mathematical way of thinking, as well as of computation.

Following the existent literature of Active Contours, from now on we shall specifically focus on the first order energy $g = g(|\nabla u|)$ and the generative data model:

$$p(u \mid \gamma(x) = 1) = p(|\nabla u| \mid \gamma(x) = 1) = \frac{1}{Z} \exp(-\mu g(|\nabla u|(x))), \quad x \in \Omega. \quad (7.17)$$

In particular, the formula implies that given the information that x is an edge pixel, only the behavior of u on a vicinity of x is influenced (i.e., $|\nabla u|$).

On the other hand, to be consistent with the preceding subsection, the gradient $|\nabla u|(x)$ should be as large as possible at any edge pixel x. This is equivalent to saying in the opposite direction that a pixel x has a larger chance of becoming an edge pixel if $|\nabla u|$ is larger, which motivates the following condition:

$$\frac{\partial p(u \mid \gamma(x) = 1)}{\partial |\nabla u|} > 0, \quad \text{or equivalently,} \quad \frac{\partial g(|\nabla u|)}{\partial |\nabla u|} < 0. \quad (7.18)$$

Thus g has to be a decreasing function of $|\nabla u|$. Typical examples in the literature include the Cauchy decay

$$g(p) = \frac{1}{1 + ap^2}, \quad p = |\nabla u|, \quad a > 0,$$

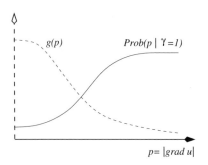

Figure 7.4. *On an edge pixel x (with $\gamma(x) = 1$), $p = |\nabla u|(x)$ is more likely to be large according to (7.17).*

the Gaussian decay

$$g(p) = e^{-bp^2}, \quad p = |\nabla u|, \quad b > 0,$$

and their close variants (see Figure 7.4). To be resistant to noise, ∇u shall be replaced by ∇u_σ as in the preceding subsection. The celebrated Snake model of Kass, Witkin, and Terzopoulous [165], on the other hand, allows g to be negative, and simply takes $g(p) = -p^2$, which of course also satisfies the condition in (7.18).

7.2.3   Geometry-Regulated Prior Models for Edges

Given an image u, the extraction of its edge set Γ could be generally treated as a Bayesian posterior estimation problem:

$$\max_{\Gamma} p(\Gamma \mid u) = p(u \mid \Gamma)p(\Gamma)/p(u),$$

where $p(u)$ is simply a probability normalization constant once u is given. Thus in terms of the logarithmic likelihood or Gibbs' formal energy $E = -\ln p$, one is to minimize the posterior energy:

$$E[\Gamma \mid u] = E[u \mid \Gamma] + E[\Gamma]. \tag{7.19}$$

The data model can be built upon the pixelwise edge model developed in the preceding subsection by independent combinations, i.e.,

$$p(u \mid \Gamma) = \prod_{x \in \Gamma} p(|\nabla u|(x) \mid \gamma(x) = 1),$$

or equivalently in terms of the energy,

$$E[u \mid \Gamma] = \mu \sum_{x \in \Gamma} g(|\nabla u|(x)) \Longrightarrow \mu \int_{\Gamma} g(|\nabla u|)d\mathcal{H}^1 \tag{7.20}$$

in the continuum limit after proper scaling, where $\mathcal{H}^1$ denotes the 1-D Hausdorff measure of Γ.

The prior model $E[\Gamma]$ has to properly encode geometric regularity of Γ to ensure visually meaningful appearance of extracted edges. There are a number of ways to proceed.

Brownian Paths

One could attempt to model edges by the most general Brownian paths. Consider an edge Γ as a discrete 2-D Brownian path (sampled with equal time intervals):

$$\Gamma = [x_0, x_1, \ldots, x_N], \quad x_k \in \Omega \subseteq \mathbb{R}^2,$$

or equivalently, a homogeneous Markov random walk with transition probability specified by

$$p(x_{k+1} \mid x_k) = \frac{1}{2\pi\sigma^2\Delta t} e^{-\frac{(x_{k+1}-x_k)^2}{2\sigma^2\Delta t}},$$

where σ^2 denotes the 1-D variance and Δt the sample time interval. It shall be assumed that the total walking time $T = N \times \Delta t$ is fixed.

From the Markov property, one has

$$p(\Gamma) = p([x_0, \ldots, x_N]) = p(x_0)p(x_1 \mid x_0) \cdots p(x_N \mid x_{N-1}).$$

Thus, with initial position x_0 fixed, it leads to the characterization of the associated discrete energy

$$E_2[\Gamma] = \frac{1}{2\sigma^2} \sum_{k=0}^{N-1} \frac{(x_{k+1} - x_k)^2}{\Delta t}, \tag{7.21}$$

up to an additive constant which depends only on T, Δt, and σ.

Let $\Delta t \to 0$, and $N = T/\Delta t \to \infty$. Then on average (by taking expectation),

$$\mathrm{E}(E_2[\Gamma]) = \frac{1}{2\sigma^2\Delta t} \sum_{k=0}^{N-1} \mathrm{E}(x_{k+1} - x_k)^2 = N \to \infty.$$

That is, an average Brownian path has very large energy E_2 when $\Delta t = T/N \to 0$, implying that average Brownian paths are too rough and irregular to become probable edges under E_2, which should be the case since Brownian paths are almost surely nowhere differentiable [164].

Sobolev Edges

Edges with low E_2 energies are therefore much more regular than average Brownian paths. More specifically, assume that

$$x'(k\Delta t) = \lim_{\Delta t \to 0} \frac{x_{k+1} - x_k}{\Delta t} \quad \text{exists for any fixed } t = k\Delta t \in (0, T).$$

Then as $\Delta t \to 0$, the energy E_2 converges to the continuum Sobolev energy, still denoted by E_2 for simplicity,

$$E_2[\Gamma] = \frac{\lambda}{2} \int_0^T x'(t)^2 dt \quad \text{with } \lambda = \frac{1}{\sigma^2}. \tag{7.22}$$

Thus E_2 is well defined for all Sobolev parametric paths, i.e., $x(t) = (x_1(t), x_2(t))$ with

$$x_1(t), x_2(t) \in H^1(0, T).$$

First Order Euclidean Edges: Length Energy

One major problem with the Sobolev energy E_2 is that it is not geometric. That is, for a given segment of edge Γ, $E_2[\Gamma]$ depends on the parametrization procedure. More specifically, suppose Γ is originally parameterized by $x(t)$ with $t \in (0, T)$. Let $r = g(t) : (0, T) \rightarrow (0, R)$ be a smooth and increasing function with

$$g'(t) > 0, \quad g(0) = 0 \text{ and } g(T) = R,$$

so that $x(r) = x(g^{-1}(r))$ reparameterizes the edge Γ. Then generally,

$$\int_0^T x'(t)^2 dt = \int_0^R x'(r)^2 g'(t) dr \neq \int_0^R x'(r)^2 dr.$$

This motivates the following theorem.

Theorem 7.19 (The Length Energy). *Let $\phi : \mathbb{R}^2 \rightarrow [0, \infty)$ be a continuous and nonnegative function. Suppose the edge energy defined by*

$$E_\phi[\Gamma] = E_\phi[x(t) \mid t \in (0, T)] = \int_0^T \phi(x'(t)) dt$$

does not depend on parametrization for any given smooth edge segment Γ. In addition, suppose it is Euclidean-invariant in the sense that for any rotation $\Gamma \rightarrow Q\Gamma$:

$$x(t) \rightarrow y(t) = Qx(t), \quad Q \in O(2),$$

$E_\phi[Q\Gamma] = E_\phi[\Gamma]$. *Then $\phi(v) = \alpha|v|$ for any $v \in \mathbb{R}^2$ and some nonnegative constant α.*

Proof. By taking any parametrization $x(t) = vt$ with $v \in \mathbb{R}^2$ fixed and $t \in (0, 1)$, the Euclidean invariance implies that $\phi(v) = \phi(Qv)$ for any rotation $Q \in O(2)$. Thus one must have $\phi(v) = \phi(|v|)$.

On the other hand, for any given parametrization $x(t) = vt$ with $t \in (0, T)$ and $v \in \mathbb{R}^2$ fixed, consider the reparameterization $y(t) = x(Tt) = Tvt$ with $t \in (0, 1)$. Then the condition on parametrization independence implies that

$$\int_0^1 \phi(|y'(t)|) dt = \int_0^T \phi(|x'(t)|) dt,$$

or simply, $\phi(T|v|) = T\phi(|v|)$. In particular, $\phi(T) = T\phi(1) = \alpha T$ with $\alpha = \phi(1) \geq 0$. Therefore $\phi(v) = \phi(|v|) = \alpha|v|$ by taking $T = |v|$. $\square$

Thus this simple theorem implies that the length energy

$$E_1[\Gamma] = \alpha \text{ length}(\Gamma) = \alpha \int_\Gamma |dx| = \alpha \int_0^T |x'(t)| dt$$

is the unique type of first order (i.e., only involving x') energy that satisfies the two geometric conditions: parametrization independence and rotational invariance. More generally, E_1 can be the 1-D Hausdorff measure $\mathcal{H}^1$ up to a multiplicative constant c.

Second Order Euclidean Edges: Euler's Elastica

Second order Euclidean geometric regularitiy can be imposed via curvature κ, which leads to Euler's elastica edge model

$$E_2[\Gamma] = \int_\Gamma (\alpha + \beta\kappa^2)d\mathcal{H}^1 \tag{7.23}$$

for two positive parameters α and β. This is the model first proposed by Euler in 1744 to model the shape of a torsion-free thin rod [196]. In approximation theory, Birkhoff and De Boor [27] referred to its equilibrium shapes as "nonlinear splines" for the purpose of data fitting or interpolation. It was David Mumford who first introduced the model into computer vision for interpolating missing smooth edge segments due to occlusion [222, 234]. We have also briefly discussed it in the preceding chapter on image inpainting.

Suppose Γ is at least C^2. Then any of its connected components can be parameterized by the arc length s, and $d\mathcal{H}^1 = ds$. Under the arc length parametrization $s \to x(s) = (x_1(s), x_2(x))$, the elastica energy becomes

$$E_2[\Gamma] = \int_\Gamma (\alpha + \beta|\ddot{x}|^2)|\dot{x}|ds.$$

Notice the similarity between Euler's elastica energy and the elastic energy first employed in the Snake model of Kass, Witkin, and Terzopoulos [165]:

$$E_{\text{KWT}}[x(t) \mid 0 \le t \le 1] = \int_0^1 (\alpha|x'(t)|^2 + \beta|x''(t)|^2)dt. \tag{7.24}$$

In the case of arc length parametrization they are identical. However, unlike Euler's elastica energy, E_{KWT} is not geometric since it depends on the parametrization $x(t)$.

One major feature of Euler's elastica model is that it prevents a closed edge from collapsing into a single point since small radius implies large curvature. More specifically, one could easily verify the following result.

Theorem 7.20. *Let C_r denote the circle centered at the origin with radius $r > 0$, and define $h(r) = E_2[C_r]$ to be the elastica energy with positive weights α and β for all $r > 0$. Then*

$$r_{\min} = \operatorname{argmin} h(r) = \sqrt{\beta/\alpha} > 0.$$

An alternative to prevent closed edges from collapsing into points is to add some kind of artificial pressure in the interior of a closed edge (see, e.g. [90, 158, 294]). Most pressure fields are image dependent and are therefore not prior models.

7.2.4 Active Contours: Combining Both Prior and Data Models

With the preparation in the preceding two subsections, we are now ready to introduce the Snakes or Active Contour models [28, 47, 75, 165, 245, 247, 261] using the Bayesian combination of the prior and data models.

In the Bayesian framework, edge extraction from a given image u is to minimize the posterior energy

$$E[\Gamma \mid u] = E[\Gamma] + E[u \mid \Gamma].$$

We have established the general form of a first order data model

$$E[u \mid \Gamma] = \mu \int_{\Gamma} g(|\nabla u|(x)) d\mathcal{H}^1$$

with $g(p) = (1+ap^2)^{-1}, g(p) = \exp(-bp^2)$, or as in Kass, Witkin, and Terzopoulos's [165] original Snakes model, $g(p) = -p^2$. Properly combined with the prior models for edges just established, one can easily assemble some interesting Active Contour models.

For example, the length prior model $E_1[\Gamma]$ leads to

$$E_1[\Gamma \mid u] = \alpha \int_{\Gamma} ds + \mu \int_{\Gamma} g(|\nabla u|(x)) ds, \tag{7.25}$$

and Euler's elastica prior leads to

$$E_2[\Gamma \mid u] = \int_{\Gamma} (\alpha + \beta \kappa^2) ds + \mu \int_{\Gamma} g(|\nabla u|(x)) ds. \tag{7.26}$$

On the other hand, using the nongeometric prior E_{KWT} in (7.24), one obtains the original Snakes model of Kass, Witkin, and Terzopoulos [165]:

$$E_{KWT}[x(r) \mid u, 0 \le r \le 1] = \int_0^1 (\alpha|x'(r)|^2 + \beta|x''(r)|^2) dr + \mu \int_0^1 g(|\nabla u|(x(r))) \, dr. \tag{7.27}$$

In applications ∇u is always replaced by its mollified version ∇u_σ, using the standard Gaussian kernel of variance σ^2.

Furthermore, if one defines

$$G(x \mid u) = \alpha + \mu g(|\nabla u|) \ge \alpha > 0, \tag{7.28}$$

then the Active Contour model E_1 leads to Caselles, Kimmel, and Sapiro's *Geodesic Active Contour* model [49]:

$$E_G[\Gamma \mid u] = \int_{\Gamma} G(x(s) \mid u) ds, \tag{7.29}$$

where s is the Euclidean arc length. The name of the model is motivated by the following geometric consideration. On the planar domain Ω, instead of the Euclidean length element ds, one modifies the planar geometry in a *conformal* manner so that the new arc length $d_G s$, or equivalently the *first fundamental form* (see Section 2.1) of the new (Riemannian) geometry is given by

$$d_G s^2 = G^2 ds^2 = G(x \mid u)^2 (dx_1^2 + dx_2^2).$$

Then $E_G[\Gamma \mid u]$ is precisely the new total length of Γ according to the new geometry:

$$E_G[\Gamma \mid u] = \int_{\Gamma} d_G s.$$

In geometry, a path with shortest length among all perturbations is called a *geodesic*.

Next we discuss how to compute these Active Contour models.

7.2.5 Curve Evolutions via Gradient Descent

The above variational Active Contour models are typically solved via gradient descent based curve evolutions. For convenience, for a given image u and data model $g(p)$, we shall write $\Phi(x) = g(|\nabla u_\sigma|(x))$, a scalar field over the image domain $x \in \Omega$.

For the E_1 model (7.25), first variation under infinitesimal variation along the curve $x \to x + \delta x$ leads to

$$\delta E_1[\Gamma \mid u] = \alpha \int_\Gamma \delta(ds) + \mu \int_\Gamma \Phi \, \delta(ds) + \mu \int_\Gamma (\nabla\Phi \cdot \delta x) ds, \qquad (7.30)$$

where s specifically denotes the Euclidean arc length parameter. Let T and N denote the unit tangent and normal along the curve, and κ the scalar curvature which is coupled to the normal so that $\dot{T} = \kappa N$ points to the *center of curvature*.

From $ds^2 = dx \cdot dx$, one has $ds\,\delta(ds) = dx \cdot \delta(dx)$. Since variation and differentiation commute and $dx = T\,ds$, one has

$$\delta(ds) = T \cdot d(\delta x).$$

Thus by integration by parts along the fixed reference edge Γ (closed without endpoints),

$$\int_\Gamma \delta(ds) = \int_\Gamma T \cdot d(\delta x) = -\int_\Gamma dT \cdot \delta x = -\int_\Gamma \kappa N \cdot \delta x \, ds.$$

Similarly,

$$\int_\Gamma \Phi\delta(ds) = -\int_\Gamma d(\Phi T) \cdot \delta x = -\int_\Gamma (\dot{\Phi}T + \Phi\dot{T}) \cdot \delta x \, ds.$$

Under directional derivatives, the gradient has orthonormal decomposition

$$\nabla\Phi = \frac{\partial\Phi}{\partial T}T + \frac{\partial\Phi}{\partial N}N \ \text{ and } \ \frac{\partial\Phi}{\partial T} = \dot{\Phi}.$$

In combination, the explicit formula for the first variation of E_1 in (7.30) is

$$\delta E_1[\Gamma \mid u] = -\int_\Gamma (\alpha + \mu\Phi)\kappa N \cdot \delta x ds + \mu \int_\Gamma \Phi_N N \cdot \delta x ds,$$

where $\Phi_N = N \cdot \nabla\Phi = \partial\Phi/\partial N$ denote the normal (of Γ) derivative of the field Φ.

Introducing t as the artificial curve evolution time, then the gradient descent equation for the E_1 Active Contour model is given by

$$\frac{\partial x}{\partial t} = (\alpha + \mu\Phi)\kappa N - \mu\Phi_N N, \quad t > 0, \qquad (7.31)$$

which is a PDE since $x = x(s; t)$ depending on both t and the arc length parameter s. For convenience, at each time t the active contour can be denoted by Γ_t, parameterized by its arc length s.

Notice the clean structure of the evolution equation (7.31). The first term signifies the field-modulated *mean curvature motion* [40, 119]

$$\frac{\partial x}{\partial t} = (\alpha + \mu\Phi)\kappa N$$

to shorten the curve and mollify undesirable local ripples. The second term represents curve-modulated *autonomous particle motion*

$$\frac{dx}{dt} = -\mu \Phi_N(x) N(x),$$

and the modulation is by the edge curve Γ via its normal N. Compared with the classical autonomous system (an ODE system) $x'(t) = -\nabla \Phi(x)$, the modulation introduces bias towards the normal direction of the current active contour Γ_t.

Together, the active contour evolves to the "valleys" of the external field Φ, while maintaining its smoothness. By the design of g or Φ, these valleys have been laid out along the potential edges of a given image u. In more details, when the active contour matures and stops further significant evolution, then by (7.31) one must have

$$(\alpha + \mu\Phi)\kappa - \mu\Phi_N \approx 0, \qquad \text{everywhere along } \Gamma.$$

If near $x \in \Gamma$ the edge is indeed smooth and flat so that $\kappa \approx 0$, one must have $\Phi_N(x) = N \cdot \nabla\Phi(x) = 0$, implying that x indeed belongs to the stationary troughs of Φ.

We close the discussion on the E_1 model by pointing out that in the language of Geodesic Active Contours, with $G = \alpha + \mu\Phi$, the evolution equation simply becomes

$$\frac{\partial x}{\partial t} = \kappa G N - G_N N. \tag{7.32}$$

An example of such curve evolution is displayed in Figure 7.5.

Similarly, by the works of Mumford [222], Langer and Singer [189], or Chan, Kang, and Shen [61], one could establish the gradient descent equation for the elastica Active Contour model E_2 in (7.26):

$$\frac{\partial x}{\partial t} = (\alpha + \mu\Phi)\kappa N - \beta(2\ddot{\kappa} + \kappa^3)N - \mu\Phi_N N, \quad t > 0. \tag{7.33}$$

The first two composite terms arise from the elastica edge energy, which makes the equation essentially of fourth order in the space variable s since κ is already of second order. Numerical computation of such a high order nonlinear equation is conceivably challenging.

As in finite element methods, one then observes the advantage of Kass, Witkin, and Terzopoulos's Snake model E_{KWT} in (7.27) based on Sobolev norms in H^2. Suppose the snakes are spatially parameterized by $r \in [0, 1]$ so that $x = x(r; t)$ at each time t. It is then easy to work out its gradient descent equation:

$$\frac{\partial x}{\partial t} = \alpha x''(r; t) - \beta x''''(r; t) - \frac{\mu}{2}\nabla\Phi(x), \quad t > 0, \ 0 \le r \le 1,$$

where the superscript apostrophe's denote derivatives with respect to r, and a factor of 2 has been divided on the right-hand side.

One major drawback with the above active contour models is that there often exist many local minima, and the converged contours depend sensitively on the initial ones started with. Region-based Active Contour models can diminish such negative effects, which will be introduced after the next subsection.

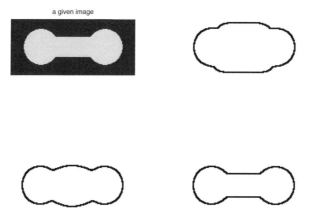

a given image

Figure 7.5. *An example of geodesic active contouring: the given image and three different stages of the contour evolution by (7.32).*

7.2.6 Γ-Convergence Approximation of Active Contours

In mathematical image processing, the technique of Γ-convergence approximation has been introduced and developed mainly for the Mumford–Shah segmentation model which will be discussed later, and the main credit shall go to the remarkable works of Ambrosio and Tortorelli [11, 12].

The work presented below is novel, to the best knowledge of the authors, in the literature of Active Contours, though inheriting the very same spirit of Ambrosio and Tortorelli's work.

We now specifically focus on the Geodesic Active Contour model (7.28) and (7.29)

$$E_G[\Gamma] = \int_\Gamma G(x \mid u)ds, \quad G(x \mid u) = \alpha + \mu g(|\nabla u|(x)), \qquad (7.34)$$

where as before $g(p)$ satisfies

$$g(0) = 1, \quad g(+\infty) = 0, \quad \text{and} \quad g'(p) < 0.$$

As a result, $G \geq \alpha > 0$.

The idea of Γ-convergence approximation is to approximate a 1-D edge set Γ by a smooth edge "canyon" function $z : \Omega \to [0, 1]$, which ideally should behave like

$$z(x) \approx 1 \quad \text{for } x \text{ away from } \Gamma; \text{ and } \approx 0, \quad x \text{ is in a close vicinity of } \Gamma. \qquad (7.35)$$

For such a smooth but transitional function, it could be expected after some calculation [11, 12] that the 1-D Hausdorff measure $d\mathcal{H}^1 = ds$ along Γ can be well approximated (in the measure-theoretic sense) by a 2-D measure (modulating a multiplicative factor of $1/2$)

$$d\nu_\varepsilon = \left(\varepsilon |\nabla z|^2 + \frac{(z-1)^2}{4\varepsilon} \right) dx, \quad \varepsilon \ll 1. \qquad (7.36)$$

The small parameter ε is naturally connected to the transition bandwidth of z in the vicinity of Γ. In physics, dv_ε is a particular type of the celebrated phase-field models of Ginsburg and Landau [133].

If one indeed went ahead to approximate the model $E_G[\Gamma]$ (7.34) by

$$\tilde{E}_G[z] = \int_\Omega G(x \mid u) \left(\varepsilon |\nabla z|^2 + \frac{(z-1)^2}{4\varepsilon} \right) dx,$$

it would be too naive to believe that it alone can actually work for active contouring. The reason is plain: the Ginsburg–Landau measure dv_ε could well encode information of an edge set Γ if and only if the ideal behavior described in (7.35) is indeed realized by z. But the latter is not explicitly enforced by $\tilde{E}_G[z]$. In fact, the global minimum is trivial to see: $E_G[z \equiv 1] = 0$!

What has been missing in the approximate model $\tilde{E}_G$ regarding the enforcement of the ideal behavior in (7.35)? With small ε, it is clear from the second term in $\tilde{E}_G$ that $z \approx 1$ measured by the Lebesgue measure (or in the L^2 sense). However, z is yet not explicitly forced to drop to zero in the vicinity of Γ.

This consideration leads to the following polished version of approximation:

$$E_G[z] = \int_\Omega G(x \mid u) \left(\varepsilon |\nabla z|^2 + \frac{(z-1)^2}{4\varepsilon} \right) dx + \beta \int_\Omega \frac{z^2}{G(x \mid u) - \alpha} dx \qquad (7.37)$$

for some $\beta > 0$. Notice that $G - \alpha = \mu g$ could be replaced by any of its powers $|G - \alpha|^p$. For a given image u, near its sharp edges, $p = |\nabla u| \to \infty$ implies that $G(x \mid u) - \alpha \to 0^+$. Thus the newly added second term explicitly forces z to drop to zero along the edges of the given image u.

Notice a few key features of the Γ-convergence approximation model $E_G[z]$:

(i) It is self-contained, i.e., depending only on the image-based scalar field $G(x|u)$.

(ii) Compared with the original Geodesic Active Contour model (7.34), the new approximate model is about the optimization of a 2-D function z. More importantly, the new energy $E_G[z]$ is quadratic (or *elliptic*) in z and can be more easily solved.

Under the infinitesimal variation $z(x) \to z + \delta z$, it could be worked out that the first functional derivative of $E_G[z]$ is

$$\frac{1}{2} \frac{dE_G[z]}{dz} = -\varepsilon \nabla \cdot (G \nabla z) + \frac{(z-1)G}{4\varepsilon} + \frac{\beta z}{G - \alpha},$$

under the Neumann adiabatic condition $\partial z / \partial \boldsymbol{n} = 0$. Thus the optimal edge canyon function for the unknown edge Γ could be computed by either solving directly the Euler–Lagrange equation

$$-\varepsilon \nabla \cdot (G \nabla z) + \frac{(z-1)G}{4\varepsilon} + \frac{\beta z}{G - \alpha} = 0, \quad x \in \Omega,$$

or solving the gradient descent evolutionary equation for $z = z(x; t)$

$$\frac{\partial z}{\partial t} = \varepsilon \nabla \cdot (G \nabla z) - \frac{(z-1)G}{4\varepsilon} - \frac{\beta z}{G - \alpha}, \quad t > 0, \ x \in \Omega,$$

with some initial guess $z(x; 0)$ and the Neumann boundary condition. Notice that both equations are linear and could be easily solved numerically using any efficient elliptic solvers.

7.2.7   Region-Based Active Contours Driven by Gradients

Region-based Active Contour models can be developed in the same framework of Bayesian inference [75, 246]. Compared with curve-based or localized Active Contour models, region-based ones typically behave more stable and have nontrivial local minima that are often visually meaningful.

All previous Active Contour models have been developed based on the data model for individual edge pixels:

$$p(u \mid \gamma(x) = 1) = \frac{1}{Z}e^{-\mu g(x, u(x), \nabla u(x))}, \tag{7.38}$$

where as in (7.16), edge has been treated as a hidden binary pattern.

On the other hand, to specify an edge Γ is equivalent to specifying its segmented regions on the image domain Ω:

$$\Omega \setminus \Gamma = \cup_{i=1}^{N} \Omega_i,$$

where Ω_i's are disjoint *connected components*, which is unique once Γ is given. That is, in terms of the edge pattern indicator γ, to specify the image behavior for $\gamma(x) = 1$ amounts to specifying that for $\gamma(y) = 0$. But the latter is fundamentally region-based, and so comes the name *region-based Active Contours*.

Along the same line as the data model in (7.38), we now assume that at any nonedge pixel $x \in \Omega$, the data model is also in the form of Gibbs' formula

$$p(u \mid \gamma(x) = 0) = \frac{1}{Z}e^{-\mu \phi(x, u(x), \nabla u(x), \dots)},$$

where ϕ is a new potential function to be specified.

As before, under the conditions of translation invariance, rotational invariance, and gray-scale shift invariance, one could assume that

$$\phi = \phi(|\nabla u|, \kappa_1, \kappa_2, \dots),$$

where κ_1 and κ_2 are the two eigenvalues of the Hessian matrix H_u, etc. From now on, we shall only focus on the first order model $\phi = \phi(p)$ with $p = |\nabla u|$.

The behavior of the potential functions $g(p)$ and $\phi(p)$ should be conceivably different, because the former specifies the gradient behavior (of an image) *along* edges while the latter away from edges. Following the classical notion of edges, $\phi(p)$ should penalize large image gradients to reflect less dramatic transitions at nonedge pixels. In particular, $\phi(p)$ should be an increasing function p. After ground-level normalization, we could assume, for example,

$$\phi(0) = 0, \quad \phi(+\infty) = +\infty, \quad \text{and} \ \phi \text{ is monotonically increasing on } \mathbb{R}^+.$$

For example, $\phi(p) = p^2$.

Assuming independency of the gradient behavior at different nonedge pixels, one then obtains a global data model from a given edge Γ:

$$p(u \mid \Gamma) = p(u \mid \gamma) = \prod_{x \in \Omega \setminus \Gamma} p(\nabla u(x) \mid \gamma(x) = 0) = \frac{1}{Q}e^{-E[u|\Gamma]}$$

for some normalization partition number Q, and

$$E[u \mid \Gamma] = \mu \sum_{x \in \Omega \setminus \Gamma} \phi(|\nabla u|(x)) \rightarrow \mu \int_{\Omega \setminus \Gamma} \phi(|\nabla u|) dx$$

in the continuum limit after some proper scaling (on μ and dx).

A general region-based Active Contour model is given by the Bayesian posterior energy

$$E[\Gamma \mid u] = E[\Gamma] + E[u \mid \Gamma].$$

Thus in the common case when the prior model is defined by the length and $\phi(p) = p^2/2$, one has

$$E[\Gamma \mid u] = \alpha \text{ length}(\Gamma) + \frac{\mu}{2} \int_{\Omega \setminus \Gamma} |\nabla u|^2 dx. \tag{7.39}$$

As in the previous Active Contour models, ∇u should be generally replaced by its mollified version ∇u_σ.

It is remarkable that the region-based Active Contour model (7.39) is already very similar to the celebrated segmentation model of Mumford and Shah [226], which will be studied in later sections. From the Active Contour point of view, the Mumford–Shah model further polishes (7.39) by explicitly dealing with noise, instead of leaving noise to the Gaussian mollifier $u \rightarrow u_\sigma$.

7.2.8 Region-Based Active Contours Driven by Stochastic Features

So far all the above Active Contour models, whether curve-based or region-based, have been developed within the thinking frame that edges could be completely characterized by gradients. These models have been quite successful in numerous applications.

On the other hand, in some applications such as medical imaging and astronomical imaging, objects in an image could have no sharp-gradient induced edges at all. But human vision could often still isolate these objects and roughly sketch their boundaries. This motivates Active Contour models that are *not* built upon gradients, or Active Contour models without edges (as named by Chan and Vese [75]). In this book, we shall call such models *Active Contour models without gradients*.

However, visual identification of vague edges or boundaries has to rely on certain recognizable features. Therefore, we will generally refer to such models as *Active Contour models driven by features*. Of course image gradient is a special example of image features. Below we will make the term "feature" more specific, and stochastic analysis will become the main powerful tool.

We first briefly highlight the stochastic view on edge detection. Near a natural ocean beach, the boundaries between water and sandy beach, or between the sandy beach and its inland grassland, are often not clear-cut. Nevertheless most of us can still pretty robustly outline their approximate boundaries on a satellite image or an image taken above from a helicopter. The underlying inference procedure in the human mind is believed to be mainly based on stochastic reasoning, since the images of water, sandy beaches, and grasslands are generally not smooth functions but much closer to stochastic random fields (Section 3.4). The human vision system is superior in robustly spotting distinguishable visual features (e.g., color, density, and texture orientation) and in using them as objector classifiers. For such images, the deterministic notion of gradient or Laplacian seems less appealing. This is the perceptual foundation for region-based Active Contour models driven by stochastic features.

Image Random Fields, Visual Filters, and Features

First, consider a homogeneous image random field u, assumed to be well defined in the entire plane $\Omega = \mathbb{R}^2$ to avoid unnecessary boundary complication. Such an image contains no stochastic boundary since everywhere the image looks exactly the same (from the statistical point of view). More specifically, a random field u on $\mathbb{R}^2$ is said to be *homogeneous* or equivalently *translation-invariant* if

$$\text{Prob}(u(x_1) \in A_1, \ldots, u(x_N) \in A_N) = \text{Prob}(u(x_1 - a) \in A_1, \ldots, u(x_N - a) \in A_N) \tag{7.40}$$

for any finite number of pixels $x_1, \ldots, x_N \in \mathbb{R}^2$, any fixed translation $a \in \mathbb{R}^2$, and any collection of shades or color sets $A_1, \ldots, A_N$.

Without causing much confusion, we shall use the symbols u and v to represent both random fields and their particular samples.

A *local feature* F of a sample field u is first of all a vector-valued map from the image domain $\Omega = \mathbb{R}^2$ to some d-dimensional vector space $\mathbb{R}^d$ (or the feature space):

$$F(x \mid u) \in \mathbb{R}^d \qquad \forall x \in \Omega, \quad \text{or simply } F(\cdot \mid u) : \Omega \to \mathbb{R}^d.$$

The locality property is characterized by the following: for any two sample fields u and v,

$$u = v \text{ on any } open \text{ set } U \subseteq \Omega \text{ implies} \quad F(x \mid u) \equiv F(x \mid v) \ \forall x \in U. \tag{7.41}$$

For example, if both u and v are smooth, then the gradient field $F(x \mid u) = \nabla u(x)$ is a 2-D local feature. For random fields on discrete pixel lattices, locality can be similarly defined via local connectivity structures, or equivalently, the neighborhood system in the case of Gibbs or Markov random fields (see Section 3.4.4).

In addition, the feature is also assumed to be *translation-invariant*:

$$F(x - a \mid u(\cdot)) = F(x \mid u(\cdot - a)) \quad \forall a \in \mathbb{R}^d, \ x \in a + \Omega.$$

As in classical signal analysis [237], it is easy to show that if F is *linear* in u; then translation invariance necessarily demands F to be a linear filtering process with some generalized kernel, which could be as ordinary as a Gaussian filter, or as generalized as the differential operator $\nabla = (\partial/\partial x_1, \partial/\partial x_2)$. As discussed in Section 3.4.6, for image and vision analysis, the family of Gabor filters have also been particularly powerful.

Following these assumptions, if the image u is a random field, so naturally becomes the feature field $F(x \mid u)$ since each sample image leads a feature distribution. If furthermore u is homogeneous, so must be F due to the translation invariance, and one could define its mean and covariance matrix,

$$\text{E}F(x \mid u) = m \in \mathbb{R}^d \ \text{ and } \ \text{E}((F - m) \otimes (F - m)) = A \ \forall x \in \Omega, \tag{7.42}$$

which are independent of individual pixels.

In image and vision analysis, the reason one often prefers working with some well-designed features instead of the given images is that the gray values themselves could be highly oscillatory and carry large variances. For a well-designed feature F, the covariance matrix could be significantly small so that the human vision system can easily detect and differentiate the mean levels m. The orientation feature is such an example for straw images or fingerprints.

Definition 7.21 (White Gaussian Feature). *Let u be a homogeneous image random field and $F = F(x \mid u)$ a d-dimensional homogeneous feature field defined above. F is said to be a* white Gaussian feature *if*

(i) *any single-pixel marginal distribution $F(x \mid u)$ is a Gaussian $N(m, A)$;*

(ii) *for any two disjoint finite pixel sets U and V, the two random vectors $F(U \mid u)$ and $F(V \mid u)$ are independent, where*

$$F(V \mid u) = \{ F(z \mid u) \mid z \in V \}.$$

At first sight, the white nature of F seems quite unnerving since it is built upon a nonwhite image field u. The orientation feature of discrete Brownian motions (or Markov random walks), however, provides such an example.

The following characterization directly results from the definition.

Proposition 7.22. *For a white Gaussian feature $F(x \mid u)$ with mean m and covariance matrix A, for any finite set V of pixels,*

$$\mathrm{Prob}(F(V \mid u)) = \prod_{x \in V} \frac{1}{\sqrt{(2\pi)^d |A|}} e^{-\frac{1}{2}(F(x)-m)^T A^{-1}(F(x)-m)} = \frac{1}{Z} e^{-E[F(V)|u]},$$

$$E[F(V) \mid u] = \frac{1}{2} \sum_{x \in V} (F(x) - m)^T A^{-1}(F(x) - m) \tag{7.43}$$

$$\to \frac{1}{2} \int_V (F(x) - m)^T A^{-1}(F(x) - m) dx$$

in the continuum limit with proper scaling on A and dx if V becomes a domain. Here $|A|$ denotes the determinant of A, and F and m have been written as column vectors.

Piecewise Homogeneous Image Random Fields and Features

We are now ready to discuss region-based Active Contour models for stochastic edges.

Definition 7.23 (Piecewise Homogeneous Image Random Fields). *An image random field u on an image domain Ω is said to be* piecewise homogeneous *if there exists a closed set $\Gamma \subseteq \Omega$ with finite 1-D Hausdorff measure such that $\Omega \setminus \Gamma$ consists of finitely many (nonempty) connected components $\Omega_1, \ldots, \Omega_N$, and there exist N homogeneous image random fields $u_1, \ldots, u_N$ on the plane $\mathbb{R}^2$, so that*

$$u\big|_{\Omega_i} = u_i\big|_{\Omega_i}, \qquad i = 1 : N.$$

In addition, these random fields are independent.

For convenience, we shall identify $u|_{\Omega_i}$ with each u_i and call u_i a *homogeneous patch* of u. Furthermore, it shall be assumed that there exists a homogeneous feature $\boldsymbol{F}$ so that for each homogeneous patch u_i, $\boldsymbol{F}_i(x) = \boldsymbol{F}(x \mid u_i)$ is white and Gaussian.

By the assumption on independence, the global data model for feature distribution given an edge set Γ is in the form of

$$E[\boldsymbol{F} \mid \Gamma] = E[\boldsymbol{F} \mid \Omega_i, i = 1 : N] = \sum_{i=1}^{N} E[\boldsymbol{F}_i(\Omega_i)].$$

By (7.43), under the assumption of white Gaussian features,

$$E[\boldsymbol{F} \mid \Gamma] = \frac{1}{2} \sum_{i=1}^{N} \int_{\Omega_i} (\boldsymbol{F}_i(x) - \boldsymbol{m}_i)^T A_i^{-1} (\boldsymbol{F}_i(x) - \boldsymbol{m}_i) dx, \qquad (7.44)$$

where $\boldsymbol{m}_i$'s and A_i's are the means and covariance matrices of $\boldsymbol{F}_i$'s. In particular, this establishes the following result.

Theorem 7.24. *Let* $1_i(x)$ *denote the characteristic function for* Ω_i *of each patch* u_i. *Define a matrix and vector-valued spatial functions* $A(x)$ *and* $\boldsymbol{m}(x)$ *by*

$$A(x) = \sum_{i=1}^{N} A_i 1_i(x) \quad \text{and} \quad \boldsymbol{m}(x) = \sum_{i=1}^{N} \boldsymbol{m}_i 1_i(x), \qquad (7.45)$$

and $\boldsymbol{F}(x) = \boldsymbol{F}(x \mid u)$ *for any* $x \in \Omega \setminus \Gamma$ *(which is well defined due to the locality condition in (7.41)). Then the data model is*

$$E[\boldsymbol{F} \mid \Gamma] = \frac{1}{2} \int_{\Omega \setminus \Gamma} (\boldsymbol{F}(x) - \boldsymbol{m}(x))^T A(x)^{-1} (\boldsymbol{F}(x) - \boldsymbol{m}(x)) dx. \qquad (7.46)$$

In particular, if the feature patches are all scalar Gaussians in the feature space $\mathbb{R}^d$ *with* $A_i = \lambda_i^{-1} I_d$, *where* I_d *denotes the identity matrix of* d *by* d, *one has*

$$E[\boldsymbol{F} \mid \Gamma] = \frac{1}{2} \int_{\Omega \setminus \Gamma} \lambda(x) (\boldsymbol{F}(x) - \boldsymbol{m}(x))^2 dx, \qquad (7.47)$$

where $\lambda(x) = \lambda_i(x)$ *for any* $x \in \Omega_i$. *If furthermore the feature patches share the same single-component variance* $\sigma^2 = \lambda^{-1}$, *one arrives at the uniform formula*

$$E[\boldsymbol{F} \mid \Gamma] = \frac{\lambda}{2} \int_{\Omega \setminus \Gamma} (\boldsymbol{F}(x) - \boldsymbol{m}(x))^2 dx. \qquad (7.48)$$

Active Contours for Piecewise Homogeneous White Gaussian Features

For stochastic edges arising from piecewise homogeneous image random fields, region-based Active Contour models are developed based on their features, instead of directly on the given gray-level images.

Following the variational/Bayesian framework for edge detection,

$$\min_{\Gamma} E[\Gamma | F] = E[\Gamma] + E[F | \Gamma],$$

an Active Contour model, in the case of the length prior and scalar white Gaussian feature patches (7.47), is explicitly given by

$$E[\Gamma | F] = \alpha \text{ length}(\Gamma) + \frac{1}{2} \int_{\Omega \backslash \Gamma} \lambda(x)(F(x) - m(x)^2 dx, \qquad (7.49)$$

where the inverse variance $\lambda(x)$ and the mean $m(x)$ are both piecewise constant with possible jumps only along Γ.

Treating both $\lambda(x)$ and $m(x)$ as unknowns besides edge set Γ, one ends up with the more complicated problem of minimizing $E[\Gamma, \lambda(x), m(x) | F]$, as still given by the right-hand side of (7.49).

There is an easy justification for rejecting $\lambda(x)$ as a working variable, because otherwise

$$(\Gamma = \phi, \lambda \equiv 0, m(x)) = \text{argmin } E[\Gamma, \lambda(x), m(x) | F]$$

is always a trivial global minimizer with an empty edge set. Since λ is inversely proportional to the variance, it amounts to saying that the given image and feature have zero signal-to-noise ratio (SNR) so that there is no reliable information at all. That is, the whole image is simply disregarded as garbage, which is of course too naive to be practically useful.

It is, however, not the Bayesian framework that discourages $\lambda(x)$ from becoming a working variable but that in deriving energy formulae like (7.49), we have invariably thrown away the information on the partition function (e.g., Z in (7.43)), which contains the crucial *prior* information on λ. Thus if one insists on treating $\lambda(x)$ as an unknown to be optimized, a prior model $E[\lambda(x)]$ must be included as well.

Thus in the literature, $\lambda(x)$ is often treated as a tunable parameter λ (instead of an unknown), just like α for the length prior in (7.49). Then the Active Contour model (7.49) becomes

$$E[\Gamma, m(x) | F] = \alpha \text{ length}(\Gamma) + \frac{\lambda}{2} \int_{\Omega \backslash \Gamma} (F(x) - m(x)^2 dx, \qquad (7.50)$$

where the piecewise constant mean feature field $m(x)$ is indeed treated as an unknown.

Adding $m(x)$ as an unknown does not significantly increase the complexity of both the model and its computation, as clarified by the following theorem.

Theorem 7.25. *For each current edge estimation Γ that partitions Ω into N disjoint connected components $\Omega_1, \ldots, \Omega_N$, the optimal $m(x)$ is explicitly given by*

$$m_i = \frac{1}{|\Omega_i|} \int_{\Omega_i} F(x) dx, \quad i = 1 : N.$$

That is, m_i's are the empirical means of F on the patches.

The proof is trivial based on least square optimizations. The result itself is consistent with the original meaning of m from the Bayesian rationale of models (7.50) or (7.49). Thus one could write

$$m = m(x | \Gamma)$$

to indicate that there is an explicit formula for m once Γ is given. As a result, the model (7.50) is reduced to

$$E[\Gamma \mid F] = \alpha \text{ length}(\Gamma) + \frac{\lambda}{2} \int_{\Omega \backslash \Gamma} (F(x) - m(x \mid \Gamma))^2 dx, \qquad (7.51)$$

which is purely about the unknown edge set Γ again, and thus an Active Contour model.

As an example, we now introduce Active Contour models without gradients as developed by Chan and Vese [75], Chan, Sandberg, and Vese [64, 65], and Sandberg, Chan, and Vese [260].

First, by taking $F(x) = u(x)$, i.e., no essential filtering, the general model (7.51) leads to Chan and Vese's model [75]

$$E[\Gamma \mid u] = \alpha \text{ length}(\Gamma) + \frac{\lambda}{2} \int_{\Omega \backslash \Gamma} (u(x) - m(x \mid \Gamma))^2 \, dx. \qquad (7.52)$$

For RGB color images or more generally a multichannel image $u(x) = (u_1(x), \ldots, u_d(x))$, by taking $F = u$ directly without filtering, one has Chan, Sandberg, and Vese's vectorial model [64]

$$E[\Gamma \mid u] = \alpha \text{ length}(\Gamma) + \frac{\lambda}{2} \int_{\Omega \backslash \Gamma} (u(x) - m(x \mid \Gamma))^2 dx.$$

Finally, let

$$\{f_\lambda(x) = f_{\sigma, \theta, k}(x) \mid \lambda = (\sigma, \theta, k) \in \Lambda\} \qquad (7.53)$$

be a finite set of linear Gabor filters characterizing quantized scale σ, orientation θ, and spatial wave number k. For any given image u, define a vectorial feature field

$$F(x) = F(x \mid u) = \{f_\lambda * u(x) \mid \lambda \in \Lambda\}.$$

Then model (7.51) is what Sandberg, Chan, and Vese have employed for Active Contours on texture images [65, 260].

For more detailed discussion as well as computational strategies and examples, we refer the reader to the work of Chan and Vese [75, 76]. Figures 7.6 and 7.7 have shown two generic examples to illustrate the remarkable performance of the above models.

An attempt to unify classical active contours and region growing algorithms has been made in the remarkable papers by Zhu and Yuille and their collaborators [303, 330], where

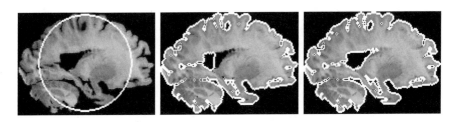

Figure 7.6. *An example of Chan and Vese's Active Contour model (7.52) without gradients (i.e., region based and driven by mean fields): three different evolution stages for a sectional brain image (from Chan and Vese [75]).*

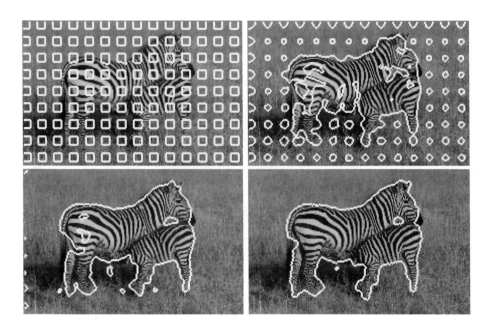

Figure 7.7. *An example of texture segmentation by combining Chan and Vese's Active Contour model (7.52) and Gabor filters (7.53) (shown at increasing times; see [65, 260]).*

the authors propose a *region competition* algorithm based on the Bayesian principle as well as the *minimum description length* (MDL) criterion. Segmentation based upon pattern-theoretic analysis of contours and textures can also be found in the work by Malik et al. [201].

7.3   Geman and Geman's Intensity-Edge Mixture Model

Explored in this section is the celebrated Gibbs fields approach to image restoration and segmentation proposed by Geman and Geman [130]. It is a hidden Markov model that defines images as random intensity fields regulated by their hidden edge patterns. In what follows we have slightly reformulated the theory to fit the flow of the current chapter and book. We refer the reader to the seminal paper by Geman and Geman [130] for more details on both the theory and its stochastic computation.

7.3.1   Topological Pixel Domains, Graphs, and Cliques

As before, let Ω denote the set of pixels on which an intensity image u is defined. We shall use u_a to denote the intensity value at a pixel $a \in \Omega$. Let E denote the set of hidden undirected edges in the graph-theoretic sense (as contrast to the *edges* of objects in images). That is,

$$E \subseteq \Omega \times \Omega \text{ and } (a, b) \in E \Leftrightarrow (b, a) \in E.$$

For convenience, we shall also use the notation (a, b) to denote the set $\{a, b\}$. Then (Ω, E) constitute a graph structure in combinatorial theory.

Equivalently, for each pixel $a \in \Omega$, define its neighborhood by

$$\mathcal{N}_a = \{b \in \Omega \mid b \neq a, (a, b) \in E\}.$$

Let $\mathcal{N} = \{\mathcal{N}_a \mid a \in \Omega\}$ denote the neighborhood system. Then the graph structure (Ω, E) is equivalent to the neighborhood structure $(\Omega, \mathcal{N})$. The notion of neighborhood explicitly conveys the topological concept of "closeness," which is beneficial for modelling spatial correlations of image information. For convenience, we shall also denote it by $a \sim b$ if $(a, b) \in E$, or equivalently $b \in \mathcal{N}_a$.

Recall from Section 3.4.4 that a clique C of (Ω, E) is a subset of Ω of which any two distinct pixels a and b directly communicate:

$$\forall a, b \in C, \quad a \neq b \Rightarrow \alpha = (a, b) \in E.$$

Let $\mathcal{C} = \mathcal{C}(\Omega, E)$ denote the collection of all cliques of (Ω, E).

Furthermore, to develop regularity conditions for image edges, one could even introduce a neighborhood system $\mathcal{N}^E$ for the graph edge set E, so that for each graph edge $\alpha \in E$, its neighborhood $\mathcal{N}_\alpha^E$ is properly defined. Let $\mathcal{C}^E = \mathcal{C}(E, \mathcal{N}^E)$ denote the collection of all cliques as done for $(\Omega, \mathcal{N})$.

In graph theory, there is a natural and unique neighborhood system $\mathcal{N}^*$ for the edge set E of a graph (Ω, E) or $(\Omega, \mathcal{N})$. That is, for any two graph edges $\alpha, \beta \in E$,

$$\alpha \sim \beta \quad \text{if and only if there exists some pixel } a \in \Omega : \ a \in \alpha, a \in \beta. \tag{7.54}$$

Then the resulted graph $(E, \mathcal{N}^*)$ is said to be the *dual graph* of $(\Omega, \mathcal{N})$ or (Ω, E). The duality is manifest in the analogy between (7.54) and

$$a \sim b \quad \text{if and only if there exists some edge } \alpha \in E : \ a \in \alpha, b \in \alpha.$$

Algebraically and combinatorially elegant, the neighborhood system of a dual graph is unnecessarily the ideal structure for image and vision analysis. The freedom must be kept open regarding the graph structure of $(E, \mathcal{N}^E)$ given (Ω, E) or $(\Omega, \mathcal{N})$.

7.3.2   Edges as Hidden Markov Random Fields

An image edge distribution Γ is a hidden Markov random field on the graph edge set E, with a properly defined neighborhood system $\mathcal{N}^E$ as just discussed above.

Γ is considered as a stochastic map: $E \to Q$ with the range space

$$Q_m = \{0\} \cup \{e^{i\pi \frac{k}{m}} \mid k = 0 : m - 1\}, \tag{7.55}$$

where for any graph edge $\alpha = (a, b) \in E$, $\Gamma_\alpha = 0$ means that pixels a and b of the *graph* edge α are not actually cut apart by an *image* edge. On the other hand, $\Gamma_\alpha = e^{i\pi k/m}$ means that a and b are separated by an image edge in the orientation of $\theta = \pi k/m$.

For convenience, when $|\Gamma_\alpha| = 1$, we shall call the pair of data (α, Γ_α) *an edgel*, abbreviated for an (image) **edge el**ement. Thus an edgel is always supported on some graph edge $\alpha \in E$, but not all graph edges support an actual (image) edgel.

Q_2, which was the main example in [130], could be treated as *binary* on a *Cartesian* image lattice $\Omega = \mathbb{Z}^2$ due to the following practical "exclusion principle": an edgel between two *horizontal* adjacent pixels is generically more likely to be *vertical* instead of being *horizontal*. And the dual statement for two *vertical* adjacent pixels is similarly true. Therefore, for Q_2, an edge distribution Γ would essentially be an on-off binary pattern.

By Section 3.4.4, the edge random field Γ, supported on a graph $(E, \mathcal{N}^E)$, can be Markovian with respect to the neighborhood system $\mathcal{N}^E$ if and only if when it is a Gibbs field with energy composition in the form of

$$E[\Gamma] = \sum_{C \in \mathcal{C}^E} V_C^E(\Gamma), \qquad (7.56)$$

where for each edge clique C, $V_C^E(\Gamma)$ is a local potential dependent only on $\Gamma(\alpha), \alpha \in C$.

Following Geman and Geman [130], let us study a concrete example to put the above theory in real context.

Consider the standard pixel lattice $\Omega = \mathbb{Z}^2$ with the "cross" neighborhood system (Figure 7.8):

$$\mathcal{N}_a = \{b \in \mathbb{Z}^2 \mid 0 < \|b - a\|_1 \le 1\},$$

where if $a = (i, j)$, $\|a\|_1$ is defined as $|i| + |j|$. Explicitly,

$$\mathcal{N}_a = \{(i, j \pm 1), (i \pm 1, j)\} \quad \forall a = (i, j) \in \mathbb{Z}^2.$$

On the plane $\mathbb{R}^2$, physically identify each edge $\alpha = (a, b)$ by its midpoint $(a + b)/2$. Then the (graph) edge set E itself becomes a rotated 2-D Cartesian lattice with

$$E = \{(i, j + 1/2) \mid (i, j) \in \mathbb{Z}^2\} \cup \{(i + 1/2, j) \mid (i, j) \in \mathbb{Z}^2\}.$$

Define its neighborhood system by, for any $\alpha \in E$,

$$\mathcal{N}_\alpha^E = \{\beta \in E \mid 0 < \|\beta - \alpha\|_1 \le 1\}.$$

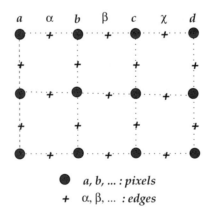

$\bullet \quad a, b, \ldots : pixels$

$+ \quad \alpha, \beta, \ldots : edges$

Figure 7.8. *A pixel lattice* $\Omega = \{a, b, \ldots\}$ *and an edge lattice* $E = \{\alpha, \beta, \ldots\}$.

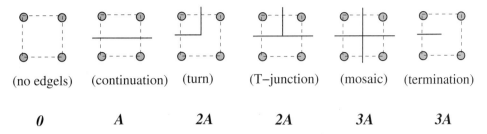

(no edgels)   (continuation)   (turn)   (T–junction)   (mosaic)   (termination)

0   *A*   *2A*   *2A*   *3A*   *3A*

Figure 7.9. *Six binary edgel configurations on a maximal edge clique and their empirical potentials $V_C^E(\Gamma)$'s assigned by Geman and Geman* [130] *(where A is a constant).*

Under this neighborhood system $\mathcal{N}^E$, maximal cliques are rotated squares which can be conveniently labelled by $(i, j) \in \mathbb{Z}^2$ (referring to Figure 7.8):

$$C_{(i,j)}^\delta = (i, j) + \delta(1/2, 1/2) + \{(0, \pm 1/2), (\pm 1/2, 0)\} \subseteq E, \quad \delta = 0, 1. \quad (7.57)$$

Here the notation $a + B$ stands for $\{a + b \mid b \in B\}$.

As one example in [130], Geman and Geman employed the binary orientation resolution Q_2 in (7.55) and defined the cliquish potentials V_C^E in (7.56) to be specifically concentrated upon the classes of maximal cliques of $C_{(i,j)}^1$ defined in (7.57).

The cliquish potential $V_C^E(\Gamma)$ is assumed to be rotationally invariant (restricted to 90-degree rotations which keep the pixel lattice $\mathbb{Z}^2$ invariant), as inspired by human vision. Then there are essentially *six* different edgel configurations on a maximal clique $C_{(i,j)}^1$, as plotted in Figure 7.9 (copied from Geman and Geman [130] and rearranged) and named by

(no edgels), (continuation), (turn), (T-junction), (mosaic), and (termination),

respectively. Geman and Geman assigned their potentials $V_C^E(\Gamma)$ empirically with the following nondecreasing values (given in the same order):

$$0, \quad A, \quad 2A, \quad 2A, \quad 3A, \quad 3A, \quad (7.58)$$

for some positive constant A. As intuitively consistent with the behavior of natural images, such potential values encourage no edgels or simpler ones.

Ideally, one should learn these potentials from image databanks. On the other hand, deterministic modeling, which is less faithful but often yields reasonably good approximation, can also shed some light on the general regularity of image edges. As an interesting observation, for example, consider closed touring around all the six edge configurations as illustrated in Figure 7.10. For each route γ_i, $i = 0 : 5$, compute its total curvature *inside* the squares by ignoring the turns made at the four sides of the squares:

$$K_i = K(\gamma_i) = \int_{\gamma_i \text{ in the interior of the square}} |\kappa|\, ds,$$

where ds is the arc length element and κ the curvature. Then one has (Figure 7.10)

$$0, \quad 0, \quad \pi, \quad \pi, \quad 2\pi, \quad \pi.$$

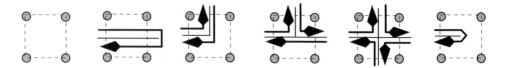

Figure 7.10. *The total curvatures (in the interior of the pixel squares) of closed tours around the six edge configurations qualitatively match Geman and Geman's empirical choice of potentials in Figure 7.9.*

Except for the last configuration, it well matches the qualitative behavior of Geman and Geman's empirical choice in (7.58) (and the first two zeros can be further distinguished by taking into account the number of edgels in the clique).

7.3.3   Intensities as Edge-Regulated Markov Random Fields

With the edgel field Γ well modelled above, the image intensity field u on the pixel graph (Ω, E) or $(\Omega, \mathcal{N})$ is then modelled as a conditional Markov random field $p(u \mid \Gamma)$ regulated by Γ. In terms of Gibbs' energy and potential formulation,

$$E[u \mid \Gamma] = \sum_{C \in \mathcal{C}} V_C(u \mid \Gamma),$$

where $\mathcal{C} = \mathcal{C}(\Omega, \mathcal{N})$ denotes the collection of all cliques of Ω under topology $\mathcal{N}$.

In the examples that Geman and Geman worked on, the potentials are in fact often restricted to the simple pairwise cliques (or *doubletons* [130]):

$$E[u \mid \Gamma] = \sum_{a \sim b} V_{(a,b)}(u \mid \Gamma) = \sum_{\alpha \in E} V_\alpha(u \mid \Gamma).$$

The pairwise potentials are then further reduced to the following canonical form:

$$V_\alpha(u \mid \Gamma) = (1 - |\Gamma_\alpha|)\phi(|u_b - u_a|), \quad \alpha = (a, b) \in E.$$

Therefore, if the two pixels of a *graph* edge α are indeed separated by an edgel (i.e., $|\Gamma_\alpha| = 1$), the contribution by u_a and u_b to the overall intensity energy $E[u \mid \Gamma]$ is then nullified. On the other hand, when no edgel is present, a single-variable potential function ϕ measures the energy contribution solely based on the difference of intensities along the graph edge α.

One could symbolically write, as in *spectral graph theory* [63, 87],

$$|u_b - u_a| = \left|\frac{\partial u}{\partial \alpha}\right|, \quad \text{as the gradient along } \alpha = (a, b).$$

Then

$$V_\alpha(u \mid \Gamma) = (1 - |\Gamma_\alpha|)\phi\left(\left|\frac{\partial u}{\partial \alpha}\right|\right), \tag{7.59}$$

and the total conditional intensity energy

$$E[u \mid \Gamma] = \sum_{\alpha \in E \setminus \Gamma} \phi \left(\left| \frac{\partial u}{\partial \alpha} \right| \right), \tag{7.60}$$

where $E \setminus \Gamma = \{\alpha \in E \mid \Gamma_\alpha = 0\}$ is the set of graph edges that are nonedges.

7.3.4 Gibbs' Fields for Joint Bayesian Estimation of u and Γ

In combination of the models in the preceding two subsections, the mixture prior model is given by

$$E[u, \Gamma] = E[u \mid \Gamma] + E[\Gamma]$$
$$= \sum_{C \in \mathcal{C}} V_C(u \mid \Gamma) + \sum_{C \in \mathcal{C}^E} V_C^E(\Gamma). \tag{7.61}$$

And in the special simple choice of pairwise intensity cliques (7.60),

$$E[u, \Gamma] = \sum_{\alpha \in E \setminus \Gamma} \phi \left(\left| \frac{\partial u}{\partial \alpha} \right| \right) + \sum_{c \in \mathcal{C}^E} V_C^E(\Gamma). \tag{7.62}$$

Assume that u^0 is an image observation, generated from an ideal target image u after degradations by some linear or nonlinear deterministic distortion operator $K : u \to K[u]$ (such as a blur), and some independent Gaussian white noise with zero mean and variance σ^2:

$$u_a^0 = K[u]_a + n_a \qquad \forall a \in \Omega.$$

Then up to a constant ground level adjusting, the data model is given by

$$E[u^0 \mid u] = \frac{1}{2\sigma^2} \sum_{a \in \Omega} (K[u]_a - u_a^0)^2.$$

In combination with the mixture prior model (7.62), this leads to the posterior Gibbs energy under Bayesian inference:

$$E[u, \Gamma \mid u^0] = E[u_0 \mid u, \Gamma] + E[u \mid \Gamma] + E[\Gamma]$$
$$= \frac{1}{2\sigma^2} \|K[u] - u^0\|_{l^2(\Omega)}^2 + \sum_{\alpha \in E \setminus \Gamma} \phi \left(\left| \frac{\partial u}{\partial \alpha} \right| \right) + \sum_{C \in \mathcal{C}^E} V_C^E(\Gamma). \tag{7.63}$$

When the deterministic distortion operator K is local (e.g., compactly supported blurs), then this posterior energy is still in the form of a Gibbs energy, with the neighborhood system properly enlarged on the pixel domain Ω [130]. As a result, the Bayesian model (7.63) could be computed by stochastic algorithms such as Gibbs' sampler and simulated annealing. For further details on both analysis and stochastic computation of the model, we refer the reader to the seminal paper by Geman and Geman [130]. Interested readers are also referred to the book of Blake and Zisserman [29] and the approximate models therein that combine the last two terms (i.e., prior models) in (7.63) into a single nonconvex energy functional. General mixture image modeling can also be found in the work of Jepson and Black [160].

7.4 The Mumford–Shah Free-Boundary Segmentation Model

In this section, we explore the theory, computation, and some recent extensions of the celebrated segmentation model of Mumford and Shah [226]. In particular, we have paid special attention to the asymptotic limits of the Mumford–Shah model, which were carefully developed in the original paper [226] but have somehow been overshadowed by the existence theories and computational methods in the literature.

7.4.1 The Mumford–Shah Segmentation Model

The Mumford–Shah segmentation model (M.–S. model) could be considered as the deterministic refinement of Geman and Geman's image restoration model (7.63).

Assume that the image domain Ω is a bounded Lipschitz domain in $\mathbb{R}^2$, instead of a discrete graph. Let $u_0 \in L^\infty(\Omega)$ (or $L^2(\Omega)$) be the observed image sample. In the deterministic setting, an edge set Γ is a *relatively closed* subset of Ω, with finite 1-D Hausdorff measure. The Gibbs energy in Geman and Geman's model (7.63),

$$E[\Gamma] = \sum_{C \in \mathcal{C}^E} V_C(\Gamma),$$

is naturally replaced by the "length" energy:

$$E[\Gamma] = \alpha \mathcal{H}^1(\Gamma) \quad \left(= \alpha \int_\Gamma ds, \quad \text{when } \Gamma \text{ is regular} \right).$$

On the other hand, the Γ-regulated intensity model in (7.63) is also revised to

$$E[u \mid \Gamma] = \int_{\Omega \backslash \Gamma} \phi(|\nabla u|) dx, \quad dx = dx_1 dx_2.$$

Notice that in the continuum limit, a lattice Ω and its graph edge set E are treated identical.

Therefore, keeping the same data model as in Geman and Geman's model, one formally derives the following image recovery model:

$$E[u, \Gamma \mid u_0] = \alpha \mathcal{H}^1(\Gamma) + \int_{\Omega \backslash \Gamma} \phi(|\nabla u|) dx + \frac{\lambda}{2} \int_\Omega (K[u] - u_0)^2 dx,$$

where K is a linear or nonlinear image distortion operator (e.g., optical blur). As in Mumford and Shah's original paper [226], in this section we shall only work with the most common choice of

$$\phi(p) = \frac{\beta}{2} p^2, \quad \text{and} \quad K = \text{Id}, \quad \text{the identity operator},$$

which leads to the celebrated segmentation model often simply referred to as *the Mumford–Shah model*:

$$E_{\text{ms}}[u, \Gamma \mid u_0] = \alpha \mathcal{H}^1(\Gamma) + \frac{\beta}{2} \int_{\Omega \backslash \Gamma} |\nabla u|^2 dx + \frac{\lambda}{2} \int_\Omega (u - u_0)^2 dx. \tag{7.64}$$

We first make two logistic comments on the model.

(a) As far as energy minimization is concerned, only the relative ratios $\alpha : \beta : \lambda$ make a contribution. But just as in *projective geometry* [128], it is often convenient to directly work with the three "homogeneous" parameters (as compared to *homogeneous coordinates* in projective geometry), especially for asymptotic analysis when ∞'s are of particular interest (see later subsections).

(b) There are $3! = 3 \times 2 \times 1 = 6$ different orders to write the Mumford–Shah model (7.64). In this section, we shall always stick to the same exact order as in (7.64), as inspired by its probability origin,

$$p(u, \Gamma \mid u_0) = p(\Gamma)p(u \mid \Gamma)p(u_0 \mid u, \Gamma)/p(u_0),$$

or more generally, the *telescoping formula* in probability,

$$p(A_1, A_2, \ldots, A_N) = p(A_1)p(A_2 \mid A_1) \cdots p(A_N \mid A_{N-1}, \ldots, A_1),$$

for any events $A_1, \ldots, A_N$.

Next we discuss the admissible definition domain for the M.–S. model. Since Γ is assumed to be relatively closed in Ω, $\Omega \setminus \Gamma$ must be an open set. Thus the second term in the model naturally demands the Sobolev regularity condition,

$$\nabla u \in L^2(\Omega \setminus \Gamma) \ \text{ or } \ u \in H^1(\Omega \setminus \Gamma).$$

Since the observation $u_0 \in L^\infty(\Omega) \subseteq L^2(\Omega)$, the third term indeed demands $u \in L^2(\Omega)$, which is guaranteed by the Sobolev condition $u \in H^1(\Omega \setminus \Gamma)$, and that Γ is a dx-null set. In combination, the admissible definition domain for the M.–S. model (7.64) is

$$\mathcal{D}_{\mathrm{ms}} = \{(u, \Gamma) \mid u \in H^1(\Omega \setminus \Gamma), \mathcal{H}^1(\Gamma) < \infty, \ \Gamma \text{ is relatively closed in } \Omega\}. \quad (7.65)$$

For both theoretical as well as practical purposes, it is also interesting to study the 1-D M.–S. model on a finite interval $x \in I = (a, b)$:

$$E_{\mathrm{ms}}[u, \Gamma \mid u_0] = \alpha \# \Gamma + \frac{\beta}{2} \int_{I \setminus \Gamma} (u_x)^2 dx + \frac{\lambda}{2} \int_I (u - u_0)^2 dx, \quad (7.66)$$

where $\# \Gamma = \mathcal{H}^0(\Gamma)$ is the zero-dimensional Hausdorff counting measure. Like for image segmentation, this model could be equally useful for studying the compositional structures of 1-D piecewise stationary signals (such as bar code scanning [323]).

7.4.2 Asymptotic M.–S. Model I: Sobolev Smoothing

As well practiced in fluid dynamics [2] or the study of complex systems, it is often helpful to consider the asymptotic limits of a complex model when some of its parameters tend to extreme values. For the M.–S. model (7.64), the asymptotic approach was first developed in the original seminal paper [226], though paid less attention to later in the literature.

In the following three subsections, we shall consider separately three asymptotic limits of the M.–S. model, all of which are important for image processing and often rediscovered later independently by other researchers in different contexts. In this section, we shall first consider the asymptotic limit of the M.–S. model when the Hausdorff parameter

$$\alpha \to \infty, \quad \text{while keeping } \beta, \lambda \text{ fixed.}$$

This is the relatively easier case compared with the other two.

Define

$$E_{\text{ms}}^{011}[u \mid u_0] = \frac{\beta}{2} \int_\Omega |\nabla u|^2 dx + \frac{\lambda}{2} \int_\Omega (u - u_0)^2 dx, \tag{7.67}$$

which is formally obtained from the M.–S. model (7.64) by having both Γ and the first term dropped off.

Notice that E_{ms}^{011} is precisely the classical Sobolev smoothing model, very useful for observations generated from smooth signals. Due to the quadratic terms and their convexity, the following theorem is plain to see.

Theorem 7.26. *Suppose $u_0 \in L^\infty(\Omega)$. Then E_{ms}^{011} has a* unique *minimizer $u^{011} \in H^1(\Omega)$, which satisfies the linear elliptic equation*

$$-\beta \Delta u + \lambda(u - u_0) = 0, \quad x \in \Omega; \quad \frac{\partial u}{\partial v} = 0 \text{ along } \partial\Omega$$

in the distributional sense.

Furthermore, classical regularity estimation for elliptic equations [117, 132] implies that as long as $\partial\Omega$ is regular enough, $u^{011} \in C^{1,s}(\Omega)$ is Hölder continuous.

Having both β and λ fixed, let $(u_\alpha, \Gamma_\alpha)$ denote a minimizer to E_{ms} for any given α (assuming it exists, which will be discussed in later subsections). Define

$$E(\alpha) = E_{\text{ms}}[u_\alpha, \Gamma_\alpha \mid u_0, \alpha] = \min E_{\text{ms}}[u, \Gamma \mid u_0, \alpha], \quad h(\alpha) = \mathcal{H}^1(\Gamma_\alpha),$$

and $E^{011} = E_{\text{ms}}^{011}[u^{011} \mid u_0] = \min E_{\text{ms}}^{011}[u \mid u_0]$.

Theorem 7.27. *Following the above definitions, one has*

(1) $E(\alpha) \le E^{011}$ *and $h(\alpha) \le \alpha^{-1} E^{011}$ for any $\alpha > 0$;*

(2) $E(\alpha)$ *is Lipschitz continuous on any $[a, \infty)$ with $a > 0$; and*

(3) $E(\alpha)$ *is nondecreasing while $h(\alpha)$ is nonincreasing in α.*

Proof.

(1) follows directly from $h(\alpha) \le \alpha^{-1} E(\alpha)$, and

$$E(\alpha) \le E_{\text{ms}}[u^{011}, \phi \mid u_0, \alpha] = E_{\text{ms}}^{011}[u^{011} \mid u_0] = E^{011},$$

where $\Gamma = \phi$ denotes the empty edge set.

To prove (2) and (3), we first establish the following fact:

$$h(\alpha') \leq \frac{E(\alpha') - E(\alpha)}{\alpha' - \alpha} \leq h(\alpha) \quad \forall \alpha' > \alpha > 0. \tag{7.68}$$

It is easy to see that (2) and (3) are direct consequences of (7.68), and the Lipschitz bound in (2) can be taken to be $h(a) = \mathcal{H}^1(a)$ on any $[a, \infty)$.

To prove (7.68), first we have, for any $\alpha' > \alpha$,

$$\begin{aligned}
E(\alpha) &\leq E_{\text{ms}}[u_{\alpha'}, \Gamma_{\alpha'} \mid u_0, \alpha] \\
&= -(\alpha' - \alpha)\mathcal{H}^1(\Gamma_{\alpha'}) + E_{\text{ms}}[u_{\alpha'}, \Gamma_{\alpha'} \mid u_0, \alpha'] \\
&= -(\alpha' - \alpha)h(\alpha') + E(\alpha'),
\end{aligned} \tag{7.69}$$

which establishes the lower bound control in (7.68). On the other hand,

$$\begin{aligned}
E(\alpha') &\leq E_{\text{ms}}[u_\alpha, \Gamma_\alpha \mid u_0, \alpha'] \\
&= (\alpha' - \alpha)\mathcal{H}^1(\Gamma_\alpha) + E_{\text{ms}}[u_\alpha, \Gamma_\alpha \mid u_0, \alpha] \\
&= (\alpha' - \alpha)h(\alpha) + E(\alpha),
\end{aligned} \tag{7.70}$$

which establishes the upper bound in (7.68) and completes the proof. $\quad\square$

As a result of (1) and (3), the optimal edge set Γ_α becomes shorter and shorter as $\alpha \to \infty$, and eventually vanishes. Since

$$\begin{aligned}
u_\alpha &= \text{argmin } E_{\text{ms}}[u \mid u_0, \Gamma_\alpha], \\
u^{011} &= \text{argmin } E_{\text{ms}}^{011}[u \mid u_0] = E_{\text{ms}}[u \mid u_0, \phi],
\end{aligned} \tag{7.71}$$

it therefore becomes intuitively evident that the optimal M.–S. segmentation u_α will get closer and closer to the Sobolev solution u^{011}. (A precise characterization of such closeness relies on the dependence of the solution to the free-boundary elliptic problem

$$-\beta \Delta u_\alpha + \lambda(u_\alpha - u_0) = 0, \quad x \in \Omega \setminus \Gamma_\alpha; \quad \frac{\partial u_\alpha}{\partial \nu} = 0 \text{ along } \partial\Omega \cup \Gamma_\alpha$$

on Γ_α when Γ_α is close to an $\mathcal{H}^1$-null set.)

7.4.3 Asymptotic M.–S. Model II: Piecewise Constant

Following [226], we now investigate the asymptotic behavior of the M.–S. model

$$E_{\text{ms}}[u, \Gamma \mid u_0] = \alpha\mathcal{H}^1(\Gamma) + \frac{\beta}{2}\int_{\Omega \setminus \Gamma} |\nabla u|^2 dx + \frac{\lambda}{2}\int_\Omega (u - u_0)^2 dx \tag{7.72}$$

when the Sobolev parameter $\beta \to \infty$ while keeping the other two, α and λ, fixed.

Likewise in the preceding subsection, define

$$E_{\text{ms}}^{101}[u, \Gamma \mid u_0] = \alpha\mathcal{H}^1(\Gamma) + \frac{\lambda}{2}\int_{\Omega \setminus \Gamma} (u - u_0)^2 dx, \tag{7.73}$$

and restrict it in the admissible space

$$\mathcal{D}_{\mathrm{ms}}^{101} = \{(u, \Gamma) \; : \; Du|_{\Omega \setminus \Gamma} = 0, \; \Gamma \text{ is closed in } \Omega \text{ and } \mathcal{H}^1(\Gamma) < \infty, \} \subseteq \mathcal{D}_{\mathrm{ms}},$$

where Du denotes the TV vectorial Radon measure. Since $\nabla u = 0$ on $\Omega \setminus \Gamma$, E_{ms}^{101} is the restriction of the M.–S. model E_{ms} in $\mathcal{D}_{\mathrm{ms}}^{101}$.

Furthermore, if

$$\Omega \setminus \Gamma = \cup_{i=1}^N \Omega_i$$

is the unique decomposition (ignoring permutation orders) of connected components, then

$$u|_{\Omega_i} \equiv u_i \text{ must be a constant, } \; i = 1 : N.$$

Thus $\mathcal{D}_{\mathrm{ms}}^{101}$ consists of piecewise constant images that are compatible to Γ. On the other hand, it is well known in least square approximations that

$$\operatorname*{argmin}_{u_i \in \mathbb{R}} \int_{\Omega_i} (u_0 - u_i)^2 dx = \frac{1}{|\Omega_i|} \int_{\Omega_i} u_0 dx = \langle u_0 \rangle_{\Omega_i}, \text{ the empirical mean.}$$

For any given edge set Γ, define the Γ-adapted averaging of u_0 by

$$\langle u_0 \rangle_\Gamma = \sum_{i=1}^N \langle u_0 \rangle_{\Omega_i} 1_{\Omega_i}(x), x \in \Omega,$$

which is piecewise constant and belongs to $\mathcal{D}_{\mathrm{ms}}^{101}$. In essence E_{ms}^{101} then becomes an energy purely about the edge set Γ:

$$E_{\mathrm{ms}}^{101}[\Gamma \mid u_0] = \alpha \mathcal{H}^1(\Gamma) + \frac{\lambda}{2} \int_{\Omega \setminus \Gamma} (u_0 - \langle u_0 \rangle_\Gamma)^2 dx. \qquad (7.74)$$

Thus it is reduced to an Active Contour model, i.e., a model relying only on the unknown edge set, and has indeed been rediscovered by Chan and Vese [75], who name it *Active Contours without (Gradient) Edges*, as discussed earlier in Section 7.2.

The main result could be stated as follows (also see Mumford and Shah [226]).

Theorem 7.28. E_{ms}^{101} *is the asymptotic limit of* E_{ms} *as* $\beta \to \infty$ *(with* α *and* γ *fixed).*

We shall gradually clarify the exact meaning of the asymptotics. First, we state a number of fine properties of the reduced model E_{ms}^{101}.

Definition 7.29 (Isolated Segment). *Suppose* $\Gamma \subseteq \Omega$ *is relatively closed and* $\mathcal{H}^1(\Gamma) < \infty$. *A subset* $\gamma \subseteq \Gamma$ *is said to be an isolated segment if*

(a) $\mathcal{H}^1(\gamma) > 0$,

(b) $\mathrm{dist}(\gamma, (\Gamma \cup \partial\Omega) \setminus \gamma) > 0$, *and*

(c) *there exists a neighborhood* $Q \subseteq \Omega \setminus (\Gamma \setminus \gamma)$ *of* γ *such that* $Q \setminus \gamma$ *is connected.*

Thus it is evident that an isolated segment must be topologically closed and cannot contain any *closed* loop (such as a circle) as a subset.

Theorem 7.30. *Suppose* Γ^* *is a minimizer to* E_{ms}^{101} *for a given* $u_0 \in L^2(\Omega)$. *Then* Γ^* *cannot contain any isolated segment.*

As Mumford and Shah demonstrated in [226], if (u^*, Γ^*) is a minimizer pair for the general M.–S. model E_{ms}, it could happen that Γ^* contains crack-tips and therefore isolated segments. Such an occurrence is partially endorsed by the compensation from the gradient term $\int_{\Omega \backslash \Gamma} |\nabla u|^2 dx$, which, however, plays no role in E_{ms}^{101}.

Proof. Otherwise suppose $\gamma \subseteq \Gamma^*$ is an isolated segment. Define $\Gamma^\dagger = \Gamma^* \backslash \gamma$. Then $\alpha \mathcal{H}^1(\Gamma^\dagger) < \alpha \mathcal{H}^1(\Gamma^*)$. On the other hand, we claim that almost surely (with respect to $dx = dx_1 dx_2$)

$$\langle u_0 \rangle_{\Gamma^\dagger}(x) = \langle u_0 \rangle_{\Gamma^*}(x), \, x \in \Omega. \tag{7.75}$$

As a result, we must have $E_{ms}^{101}[\Gamma^\dagger \mid u_0] < E_{ms}^{101}[\Gamma^* \mid u_0]$, contradicting to the minimizer role of Γ^*.

Thus it suffices to establish (7.75). Take any neighborhood Q of γ satisfying the last condition in the definition. Then there must exist a unique connected component, say Ω_i^*, of $\Omega \backslash \Gamma^*$, such that $Q \backslash \gamma \subseteq \Omega_i^*$. Define

$$\Omega_i^\dagger = \Omega_i^* \cup \gamma = \Omega_i^* \cup Q,$$

which is clearly open and connected since it is the relative closure of Ω_i^* in $\Omega_i^\dagger$.

Therefore, $\Omega \backslash \Gamma^*$ and $\Omega \backslash \Gamma^\dagger$ share the same set of connected components except for Ω_i^* and $\Omega_i^\dagger$. But the difference between this pair is a Lebesgue null set γ, and thus one must have

$$\langle u_0 \rangle_{\Omega_i^*} = \langle u_0 \rangle_{\Omega_i^\dagger},$$

and $\langle u_0 \rangle_{\Gamma^*}(x) = \langle u_0 \rangle_{\Gamma^\dagger}(x)$ almost surely on Ω, which is precisely (7.75). $\square$

Following the same line as the preceding section, define

$$E^{101} = \min_{\Gamma} E_{ms}^{101}[\Gamma \mid u_0],$$

which must be finite since the no-edge model $E_{ms}^{101}[\phi \mid u_0] < \infty$ (assuming $u_0 \in L^\infty(\Omega)$ or $L^2(\Omega)$). Having α and λ fixed, define for each Sobolev parameter $\beta > 0$,

$$E(\beta) = \min_{(u,\Gamma) \in \mathcal{D}_{ms}} E_{ms}[u, \Gamma \mid u_0, \beta],$$

and assume that (u_β, Γ_β) is an optimal segmentation pair for E_{ms} and

$$s(\beta) = \int_{\Omega \backslash \Gamma_\beta} |\nabla u_\beta|^2 dx.$$

Then the following theorem can be established in exactly the same fashion as Theorem 7.27.

Theorem 7.31. *Following the above definitions,*

(a) $E(\beta) \leq E^{101}$ and $s(\beta) \leq \beta^{-1} E^{101}$,

(b) $E(\beta)$ *is Lipschitz continuous on any* $[b, \infty)$ *with* $b > 0$, *and*

(c) $E(\beta)$ *is nondecreasing and* $s(\beta)$ *nonincreasing on* $\beta \in (0, \infty)$.

Let
$$\Omega \setminus \Gamma_\beta = \cup_i \Omega_i$$

denote the decomposition of connected components. Assume that Γ_β is regular enough so that the Poincaré inequality [3, 117, 193] holds on each component:

$$\int_{\Omega_i} (w - \langle w \rangle_{\Omega_i})^2 dx \leq C_i \int_{\Omega_i} |\nabla w|^2 dx \quad \forall w \in H^1(\Omega_i),$$

where $C_i = C_i(\Omega_i)$ is independent of w. Define $R_\beta = R_{\Gamma_\beta} = \sup_i C_i$. Then

$$\int_\Omega (u_\beta - \langle u_\beta \rangle_{\Gamma_\beta})^2 dx \leq R_\beta \int_{\Omega \setminus \Gamma_\beta} |\nabla u_\beta|^2 dx \leq \beta^{-1} R_\beta E^{101}. \tag{7.76}$$

Therefore, as long as Γ_β's are regular enough so that R_β's are bounded, or more generally $R_\beta = o(\beta)$ as $\beta \to \infty$, one has

$$\int_\Omega (u_\beta - \langle u_\beta \rangle_{\Gamma_\beta})^2 dx \to 0, \quad \beta \to \infty.$$

(Notice that in reality both C_i's and R_β's depend on detailed characterizations of the optimal edge sets Γ_β's, which like the regularity theory of minimal surfaces [137] is highly involved, and could be found in [226]. Generally these are geometric constants closely connected to the isoperimetric constants of the domains.)

Furthermore, a tighter control on the Sobolev norm $s(\beta)$ can be established.

Theorem 7.32. *Let* R_β *be defined as in* (7.76). *Then*

$$s(\beta) = \int_{\Omega \setminus \Gamma_\beta} |\nabla u_\beta|^2 dx \leq C R_\beta \beta^{-2},$$

where $C = C(\lambda, \|u_0\|_{L^\infty(\Omega)}, |\Omega|)$ *is independent of* β. *As a result,* $s(\beta) = O(\beta^{-2})$ *if* R_β *is bounded, and* $o(\beta^{-1})$ *if* $R_\beta = o(\beta)$.

Proof. Since (u_β, Γ_β) is a minimizing pair, one has

$$E_{\mathrm{ms}}^{101}[\langle u_\beta \rangle_{\Gamma_\beta}, \Gamma_\beta \mid u_0] = E_{\mathrm{ms}}[\langle u_\beta \rangle_{\Gamma_\beta}, \Gamma_\beta \mid u_0] \geq E_{\mathrm{ms}}[u_\beta, \Gamma_\beta \mid u_0].$$

That is,

$$\alpha \mathcal{H}^1(\Gamma_\beta) + \frac{\lambda}{2} \|\langle u_\beta \rangle_{\Gamma_\beta} - u_0\|_2^2 \geq \alpha \mathcal{H}^1(\Gamma_\beta) + \frac{\beta}{2} s(\beta) + \frac{\lambda}{2} \|u_\beta - u_0\|_2^2.$$

Let $M = \|u_0\|_\infty < \infty$. Then one must have $\|u_\beta\|_\infty \leq M$. Thus,

$$
\begin{aligned}
\frac{\beta}{2} s(\beta) &\leq \frac{\lambda}{2} \left(\| \langle u_\beta \rangle_{\Gamma_\beta} - u_0 \|_2^2 - \| u_\beta - u_0 \|_2^2 \right) \\
&\leq \frac{\lambda}{2} \left(\| \langle u_\beta \rangle_{\Gamma_\beta} - u_0 \|_2 + \| u_\beta - u_0 \|_2 \right) \| u_\beta - \langle u_\beta \rangle_{\Gamma_\beta} \|_2 \\
&\leq 2\lambda M \sqrt{|\Omega|} \, \| u_\beta - \langle u_\beta \rangle_{\Gamma_\beta} \|_2 \\
&\leq 2\lambda M \sqrt{|\Omega|} \sqrt{R_\beta} \sqrt{s(\beta)},
\end{aligned}
\tag{7.77}
$$

where the last step follows from the Poincaré inequality (7.76). Therefore,

$$
\sqrt{s(\beta)} \leq \sqrt{C} \beta^{-1} \sqrt{R_\beta}, \quad \text{with} \quad C = 16\lambda^2 \|u_0\|_\infty^2 |\Omega|,
\tag{7.78}
$$

which completes the proof. $\quad\square$

Corollary 7.33. *Suppose $R_\beta = o(\beta)$ (i.e., growing slower than β as $\beta \to \infty$). Then $(\langle u_\beta \rangle_{\Gamma_\beta}, \Gamma_\beta) \in \mathcal{D}_{ms}^{101}$ asymptotically minimizes E_{ms}^{101} in the sense that*

$$
E_{ms}^{101}[\langle u_\beta \rangle_{\Gamma_\beta}, \Gamma_\beta \mid u_0] = \min_{(u,\Gamma) \in \mathcal{D}_{ms}^{101}} E_{ms}^{101}[u, \Gamma \mid u_0] + O(\beta^{-1} R_\beta).
$$

In particular if R_β is bounded, the asymptotic residual is $O(\beta^{-1})$.

Proof. From (7.77) in the above proof,

$$
\frac{\lambda}{2} \left| \, \| \langle u_\beta \rangle_{\Gamma_\beta} - u_0 \|_2^2 - \| u_\beta - u_0 \|_2^2 \, \right| \leq 2\lambda M \sqrt{|\Omega|} \sqrt{R_\beta} \sqrt{s(\beta)} \leq \frac{C}{2} \beta^{-1} R_\beta,
$$

where the last step follows from (7.78). Therefore,

$$
\begin{aligned}
E_{ms}^{101}[\langle u_\beta \rangle_{\Gamma_\beta}, \Gamma_\beta \mid u_0] &= E_{ms}[\langle u_\beta \rangle_{\Gamma_\beta}, \Gamma_\beta \mid u_0, \beta] \\
&= E_{ms}[u_\beta, \Gamma_\beta \mid u_0, \beta] + O(\beta^{-1} R_\beta) \\
&\leq \min_{(u,\Gamma) \in \mathcal{D}_{ms}^{101}} E_{ms}[u, \Gamma \mid u_0, \beta] + O(\beta^{-1} R_\beta) \\
&= \min_{(u,\Gamma) \in \mathcal{D}_{ms}^{101}} E_{ms}^{101}[u, \Gamma \mid u_0] + O(\beta^{-1} R_\beta).
\end{aligned}
$$

This clearly implies the corollary. $\quad\square$

7.4.4 Asymptotic M.–S. Model III: Geodesic Active Contours

Following Mumford and Shah's original paper [226], we investigate the asymptotic behavior as $\lambda \to \infty$ of the M.–S. segmentation model:

$$
E_{ms}[u, \Gamma \mid u_0] = \alpha \mathcal{H}^1(\Gamma) + \frac{\beta}{2} \int_{\Omega \setminus \Gamma} |\nabla u|^2 dx + \frac{\lambda}{2} \int_\Omega (u - u_0)^2 dx.
\tag{7.79}
$$

Unlike the preceding two asymptotic limits, one shall see that it is natural to also rescale α according to $\alpha = \alpha_0 \sqrt{\varepsilon}$ with $\varepsilon = \lambda^{-1} \to 0$ and α_0 fixed, which is of course not so obvious at this point.

Assume that $u_0 \in C^{1,1}(\Omega)$ and $\Gamma \in C^{1,1}$ are both first order Lipschitz continuous. Define

$$E_{ms}^{110}[\Gamma \mid u_0, \alpha_0] = \alpha_0 \mathcal{H}^1(\Gamma) - \beta \int_\Gamma \left(\frac{\partial u_0}{\partial n} \right)^2 ds = \int_\Gamma \left[a_0 - \beta \left(\frac{\partial u_0}{\partial n} \right)^2 \right] ds, \quad (7.80)$$

which is a *Geodesic Active Contour* model since it is a line integral along Γ for a given u_0.

Mumford and Shah [226] established the following remarkable asymptotic behavior as $\varepsilon = \lambda^{-1} \to 0$.

Theorem 7.34 (Mumford and Shah's Asymptotic Theorem [226]). *Let $\alpha_0 = \alpha / \sqrt{\varepsilon}$, $\lambda = 1/\varepsilon$, and β be fixed. For each given Γ, let u_Γ denote the optimal image for $E_{ms}[u \mid u_0, \Gamma]$. Then*

$$E_{ms}[u_\Gamma, \Gamma \mid u_0] = \sqrt{\varepsilon} E_{ms}^{110}[\Gamma \mid u_0, \alpha_0] + \frac{\beta}{2} \int_\Omega |\nabla u_0|^2 dx$$
$$- \sqrt{\varepsilon} \frac{\beta}{2} \int_{\partial \Omega} \left(\frac{\partial u_0}{\partial n} \right)^2 ds + O(\varepsilon \log \varepsilon^{-1}). \quad (7.81)$$

Since for a given u_0, the second and third terms in (7.81) are independent of Γ, the above theorem therefore establishes E_{ms}^{110} as the asymptotic limit of the M.–S. segmentation model as $\lambda \to \infty$ (i.e., $\varepsilon \to 0$) with $\alpha_0 = \alpha \sqrt{\lambda}$ and Γ fixed.

The proof of Theorem 7.34 involves many technical details and we refer to Mumford and Shah's seminal work [226] for readers who are interested in this topic. In what follows, we take an easier but less rigorous approach to gain a feeling why the theorem is so through the 1-D M.–S. model:

$$E_{ms}[u, \Gamma \mid u_0] = \alpha \# \Gamma + \frac{\beta}{2} \int_{I \setminus \Gamma} (u_x)^2 dx + \frac{\lambda}{2} \int_I (u - g)^2 dx, \quad (7.82)$$

where $x \in I$ is an interval domain, and $u_0(x) = g(x)$.

Our major tool will be asymptotic analysis, based on the theory of both regular and singular perturbations (see, e.g., Bender and Orszag [22]), in particular, the *boundary layer method* which is known to be very powerful in classical fluid mechanics.

For any fixed Γ, $u_\Gamma = \operatorname{argmin} E_{ms}[u \mid u_0, \Gamma]$ must solve the elliptic system

$$-\beta u_{xx} + \lambda(u - g) = 0, \quad x \in I \setminus \Gamma, \quad \text{and} \quad u_x(s) = 0 \quad \forall s \in \Gamma \cup \partial I.$$

For convenience, assume that $J = (0, 1)$ is a typical connected component of $I \setminus \Gamma$ and $\{0, 1\} \subseteq \Gamma$. Without loss of generality, also assume that $\beta = 1$. We then intend to analyze the behavior of $u = u_\Gamma$ on $J = (0, 1)$ as $\lambda = \varepsilon^{-1} \to +\infty$, which solves the boundary value problem:

$$-\varepsilon u_{xx} + u = g, \quad x \in (0, 1), \quad \text{and} \quad u_x(0) = u_x(1) = 0. \quad (7.83)$$

Notice that it is a *singular perturbation problem*; namely, the nature of the system with nonzero perturbation parameter ε is different from the reference system with $\varepsilon = 0$.

Let $D = d/dx$ denote the differential operator. Away from the two boundary ends,

$$u = (1 - \varepsilon D^2)^{-1} g = (1 + \varepsilon D^2 + O(\varepsilon^2))g = g + \varepsilon g_{xx} + O(\varepsilon^2), \qquad (7.84)$$

provided that g is smooth enough.

Near a boundary end, say $s = 0$, one then "zooms in" and rescales the system according to boundary layer analysis. Assume the layer is restricted in $(0, \delta)$ for some δ with $0 < \delta \ll 1$ to be determined later.

Then the boundary layer approximation to system (7.83) is given by

$$-\varepsilon u_{xx} + u = g, \quad x \in (0, \delta), \quad \text{with } u_x(0) = 0, \ u(\delta) = g(\delta). \qquad (7.85)$$

Notice that at the interior end of the boundary layer, the boundary condition comes from the interior solution (7.84), up to a residue of order $O(\varepsilon)$.

Expand $g(x)$ within the thin boundary layer using Taylor's expansion:

$$g(x) = g(0) + g'(0)x + O(x^2) = ax + O(x^2), \quad a = g'(0),$$

where it has been assumed for convenience that $g(0) = 0$ (otherwise simply having u replaced by $u - g(0)$). We shall also *only* consider the generic case when $a \neq 0$. Thus the boundary layer system (7.85) is reduced to

$$-\varepsilon u_{xx} + u = ax + O(\delta^2), \quad x \in (0, \delta), \quad \text{with } u_x(0) = 0, \ u(\delta) = a\delta + O(\delta^2). \quad (7.86)$$

Let $r(x) = u(x) - ax$, and rescale

$$x = \sqrt{\varepsilon}t \quad \text{and} \quad \delta = \sqrt{\varepsilon}A, \quad \text{with } t \in (0, A); \quad \text{and} \quad \phi(t) = \frac{r(\sqrt{\varepsilon}t)}{a\sqrt{\varepsilon}},$$

where the scaled boundary layer range $A \gg 1$ is yet to be determined. Then the boundary layer system is further reduced to

$$-\phi_{tt} + \phi = O(\eta), \quad t \in (0, A), \quad \text{with } \phi_t(0) = -1 \text{ and } \phi(A) = O(\eta), \qquad (7.87)$$

with $\eta = \delta^2/(a\sqrt{\varepsilon})$. In order for this renormalized boundary layer system to have a leading order solution which is independent of η, we therefore must require

$$\eta = \frac{\delta^2}{a\sqrt{\varepsilon}} \ll 1, \quad \text{or equivalently,} \quad A \ll \varepsilon^{-1/4}.$$

Now that the renormalized system (7.87) is a regular perturbation system, its solution could be easily found to be

$$\phi(t) = e^{-t} + O(\eta), \quad t \in (0, A).$$

Therefore, the boundary layer solution is eventually given by

$$u(x) = ax + a\sqrt{\varepsilon}\, e^{-\frac{x}{\sqrt{\varepsilon}}} + o(\sqrt{\varepsilon}), \quad 0 < x < A\sqrt{\varepsilon} \text{ and } 1 \ll A \ll \varepsilon^{-1/4}. \qquad (7.88)$$

The boundary layer solution (7.88) and the interior solution (7.84) enable us to estimate the terms in the M.–S. model (7.82). Still assume that $J = (0, 1)$ is a typical connected component of $I \setminus \Gamma$. We shall estimate the contributions from both the edge points. Taking $s = 0$ for example, one intends to estimate (again assuming $\beta = 1$)

$$\frac{1}{2} \int_0^{1/2} u_x^2 dx + \frac{\lambda}{2} \int_0^{1/2} (u - g)^2 dx$$

or its constant renormalization

$$\left[\frac{1}{2} \int_0^{1/2} u_x^2 dx - \frac{1}{2} \int_0^{1/2} g_x^2 dx \right] + \frac{\lambda}{2} \int_0^{1/2} (u - g)^2 dx.$$

First, based on the interior solution (7.84), it is easy to establish that the interior contribution is in the order of $O(\varepsilon)$:

$$\frac{1}{2} \int_{A\sqrt{\varepsilon}}^{1/2} (u_x^2 - g_x^2) dx + \frac{\lambda}{2} \int_{A\sqrt{\varepsilon}}^{1/2} (u - g)^2 dx = O(\varepsilon).$$

Second, by using the boundary solution (7.88), one could similarly work out the boundary layer contributions to be

$$\frac{1}{2} \int_0^{A\sqrt{\varepsilon}} \left(u_x^2 - g_x^2 \right) dx = -\frac{3}{4} a^2 \sqrt{\varepsilon} + o(\sqrt{\varepsilon}),$$

$$\frac{\lambda}{2} \int_0^{A\sqrt{\varepsilon}} (u - g)^2 dx = \frac{a^2 \sqrt{\varepsilon}}{4} + o(\sqrt{\varepsilon}),$$

where $a = g_x(0)$. Hence the net boundary layer contribution is

$$\frac{1}{2} \int_0^{A\sqrt{\varepsilon}} \left(u_x^2 - g_x^2 \right) dx + \frac{\lambda}{2} \int_0^{A\sqrt{\varepsilon}} (u - g)^2 dx = -\frac{1}{2} a^2 \sqrt{\varepsilon} + o(\sqrt{\varepsilon}).$$

Compared with the interior contribution, the boundary layer thus dominates.

On the other hand, a typical edge point like $s = 0 \in \Gamma$ makes contributions to either connected component of its two sides, bringing its total leading contribution to $-a^2 \sqrt{\varepsilon} = -g_x(s)^2 \sqrt{\varepsilon}$. But the contribution remains to be $-\frac{1}{2} a^2 \sqrt{\varepsilon}$ at the two global endpoints ∂I of the entire interval domain I.

Thus in combination, we have established the 1-D version of Mumford and Shah's remarkable asymptotic result in Theorem 7.34:

$$E_{ms}[u_\Gamma, \Gamma \mid g] = \sqrt{\varepsilon} \int_\Gamma (\alpha_0 - \beta g_x^2) d\mathcal{H}^0 - \frac{\beta \sqrt{\varepsilon}}{2} \int_{\partial I} g_x^2 d\mathcal{H}^0 + \frac{\beta}{2} \int_I g_x^2 dx + o(\sqrt{\varepsilon}),$$

where $\mathcal{H}^0$ is the Hausdorff counting measure. In particular, for a fixed Γ, the M.–S. functional indeed asymptotically converges to the *Active Point Process* model (as compared to the Active Contour model on 2-D image domains):

$$E_{ms}^{110}[\Gamma \mid g] = \int_\Gamma (\alpha_0 - \beta g_x^2) d\mathcal{H}^0.$$

We refer the interested reader to Mumford and Shah [226] for more details on the asymptotics. Next we discuss the uniqueness of M.–S. optimal segmentations.

7.4.5 Nonuniqueness of M.–S. Segmentation: A 1-D Example

Nonuniqueness of the M.–S. segmentation is caused by the nonconvexity of the model, especially due to its free-boundary and geometric nature. In this section, we explicitly construct a simple 1-D example to demonstrate the nonuniqueness to the 1-D M.–S. model:

$$E_{ms}[u, \Gamma \mid u_0] = \alpha \# \Gamma + \frac{\beta}{2} \int_{I \setminus \Gamma} u_x^2 dx + \frac{\lambda}{2} \int_I (u - u_0)^2 dx. \tag{7.89}$$

To indicate parameter dependence, we shall also write

$$E_{ms}[u, \Gamma \mid u_0] = E_{ms}[u, \Gamma \mid u_0, \alpha, \beta, \lambda].$$

Let $I = (0, 1)$ be the unit interval and $u_0 = g(x) = -1_{(0,1/2]}(x) + 1_{(1/2,1]}(x)$ the Haar mother wavelet [96, 290]. Let us investigate the behavior of M.–S. model for g: $E_{ms}[g, \Gamma \mid g, \alpha, \beta, \lambda]$.

(a) Suppose $\# \Gamma > 0$. Then

$$E_{ms}[u, \Gamma \mid g, \alpha, \beta, \lambda] \geq \alpha \# \Gamma \geq \alpha,$$

and the lower bound α could indeed be achieved when

$$\Gamma = \{1/2\} \quad \text{and} \quad u \equiv g \quad \text{on } I \setminus \Gamma.$$

(b) Suppose $\# \Gamma = 0$ or, equivalently, $\Gamma = \phi$ is empty. Then

$$E_{ms}[u, \phi \mid g, \alpha, \beta, \lambda] = E_{ms}^{011}[u \mid g, \beta, \lambda] = \frac{\beta}{2} \int_I u_x^2 dx + \frac{\lambda}{2} \int_I (u - g)^2 dx.$$

Now that the latter is a strictly convex functional, the minimizer $u_{\beta,\lambda}$ exists and is unique, and

$$m = m(\beta, \lambda) = E_{ms}^{011}[u_{\beta,\lambda} \mid g, \beta, \lambda] > 0.$$

In combination, one could then conclude that when

$$\alpha = m = m(\beta, \lambda),$$

there are at least two different sets of optimal M.–S. segmentations:

$$(u = g \big|_{I \setminus \Gamma}, \Gamma = \{1/2\}) \quad \text{and} \quad (u = u_{\beta,\lambda}, \Gamma = \phi).$$

7.4.6 Existence of M.–S. Segmentation

For the M.–S. segmentation model

$$E_{ms}[u, \Gamma \mid u_0] = \alpha \mathcal{H}^1(\Gamma) + \frac{\beta}{2} \int_{\Omega \setminus \Gamma} |\nabla u|^2 dx + \frac{\lambda}{2} \int_\Omega (u - u_0)^2 dx, \tag{7.90}$$

the existence issue has drawn much attention in its theoretical study. The existence of classical (or strong) solutions in any dimension was first established by De Giorgi, Carriero, and Leaci [136], and Dal Maso, Morel, and Solimini in [94] used different approaches to prove the existence of solutions for 2-D image domains. We refer the reader to these remarkable original works for more details, as well as the more recent ones by Ambrosio, Fusco, and Pallara [8, 9], Ambrioso and Pallara [10], and David [98].

In what follows, we shall only outline some major ideas in the existence analysis. There are mainly two key ingredients, as similar to the classical minimal surface problem [137].

(a) Establish the compactness and lower semicontinuity properties of the M.–S. model in some weak formulation, which guarantees the existence of weak solutions.

(b) Characterize the regularity of weak solutions and show that weak solutions are in fact regular enough to become classical (strong) solutions.

The first step was established by Ambrosio [7], and the key tool is the space of SBV, *special functions with bounded variations*, as briefly introduced in Section 3.6.6. Recall that a general 2-D BV image u allows the measure-theoretic orthogonal decomposition

$$Du = \nabla_L u + J_u + D_c u,$$

corresponding to the Lebesgue continuous gradient, weighted 1-D Hausdoff measure supported along the jump set S_u, and singular Cantor measure, respectively. An SBV image is a special BV image whose Cantor part vanishes. As first suggested by De Giorgi, restricted in SBV the M.–S. model (7.90) allows the natural weak formulation:

$$E_{ms}^w[u \mid u_0] = \alpha \mathcal{H}^1(S_u) + \frac{\beta}{2}\int_\Omega (\nabla_L u)^2 dx + \frac{\lambda}{2}\int_\Omega (u - u_0)^2 dx.$$

Then the properties in (a) established by Ambrosio [7] guarantee the existence of weak solutions.

Let $u^* \in$ SBV be a weak solution in SBV. A natural way to obtain a strong solution is to take the edge set Γ^* to be the relative closure of S^* in Ω, the jump set of u^*. It is not guaranteed, however, that the closure of a general set A with finite 1-D Hausdorff measure is also regular enough to have finite 1-D Hausdorff measure. Here is one example to show that it is possible $\mathcal{H}^1(\bar{S}) = \infty$ even though $\mathcal{H}^1(S) < \infty$.

Example (See Figure 7.11). Let $\Omega = (0, 1)^2$ be the unit square image domain. For each scale level $k = 0, 1, 2, \ldots$, define a binary grid supported on the nodes:

$$x_{ij}^{(k)} = \left(\frac{i}{2^{k+1}}, \frac{j}{2^{k+1}}\right), \quad i, j \in \{1, 3, 5, \ldots, 2^{k+1} - 1\} = G_k.$$

Notice that at each scale level k, there are totally $\#G_k \times \#G_k = 4^k$ grid nodes. Choose any positive sequence (r_k) so that

$$\sum_{k=0}^\infty 4^k r_k = M < \infty.$$

At each node $x_{ij}^{(k)}$, let $C_{ij}^{(k)}$ denote the circle that is centered at $x_{ij}^{(k)}$ and with radius r_k. Finally, define

$$S_N = \cup_{k=0:N, (i,j) \in G_k} C_{ij}^{(k)} \quad \text{and} \quad S = \lim_{N \to \infty} S_N.$$

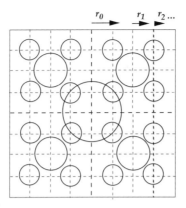

Figure 7.11. *Visualization of the example: the set S consisting of the circles at all scale levels has the weird property* $\mathcal{H}^1(S) < \infty$ *but* $\mathcal{H}^1(\bar{S}) = \infty$, *since* $\bar{S} = \Omega$.

Then by the monotone convergence of a general measure,

$$\mathcal{H}^1(S) = \lim_{N \to \infty} \mathcal{H}^1(S_N) = \lim_{N \to \infty} \sum_{k=0}^{N} 4^k 2\pi r_k = 2\pi M < \infty,$$

where we have used the fact that any two *distinct* circles can only intersect at an $\mathcal{H}^1$-null set (in fact, at most two points). But on the other hand, it is clear that S is dense in Ω, and its relative closure $\bar{S} = \Omega$. As a result $\mathcal{H}^1(\bar{S}) = \infty$.

This example clearly demonstrates the potential obstacle passing from the weak solution u^* and its jump set S^* to a strong solution by taking $\Gamma = \overline{S^*}$. Further detailed regularity characterization of the weak solution and its jump set therefore must be properly investigated. This task is accomplished by the following regularity characterization of a weak solution [136].

Theorem 7.35 (2-D Version of Jump Set Regularity). *There exist three constants* $C_1, C_2,$ *and R, such that*

$$C_1 r \le \mathcal{H}^1(S^* \cap B_r(x)) \le C_2 r \quad \forall x \in S^*, \ B_r(x) \subseteq \Omega, \ and \ r \le R.$$

By the language of *geometric measure theory* [195], the $\mathcal{H}^1$ upper and lower densities of S^* at x, $\rho_{\pm}^1(S^*, x)$, are both of order 1:

$$\rho_+^1(S^*, x) = \limsup_{r \to 0} \frac{\mathcal{H}^1(S^* \cap B_r(x))}{2r} \quad \text{and} \quad \rho_-^1(S^*, x) = \liminf_{r \to 0} \frac{\mathcal{H}^1(S^* \cap B_r(x))}{2r}.$$

What this theorem reveals is that the jump set S^* of a weak solution cannot be as dilute as the weird example just constructed above. The lower bound requires the mass (according to $\mathcal{H}^1$) of S^* be well concentrated everywhere along S^*, thus prohibiting its wandering on the 2-D domain. In particular, after some measure-theoretic argument it leads to $\mathcal{H}^1(\overline{S^*} \setminus S^*) = 0$, suggesting that $(u^*, \Gamma = \overline{S^*})$ is indeed a strong solution to the M.–S. segmentation (that $u^* \in H^1(\Omega \setminus \Gamma)$ is obvious from the weak formulation and $u^* \in \mathrm{SBV}$).

We refer the reader to the aforementioned references for a further detailed account on the general issues of existence. Below we prove the existence theorem for 1-D Mumford–Shah segmentations, which are much simpler than high-dimensional cases.

Assume for simplicity that the image domain is the unit interval $I = (0, 1)$, and denote by Γ_u the jump set of an image u on I.

Theorem 7.36 (Existence of Optimal M.–S. Segmentation in One Dimension). *Suppose an observed gray-scale image $u_0 \in L^\infty(I)$, and define the admissible space*

$$\mathcal{D}_{\mathrm{ms}} = \{u(x) \ : \ \|u\|_\infty \leq \|u_0\|_\infty, \ \#\Gamma_u < \infty, \ u \in H^1(I \setminus \Gamma_u)\}.$$

Then the minimizer in $\mathcal{D}_{\mathrm{ms}}$ exists to the M.–S. segmentation model:

$$E_{\mathrm{ms}}[u, \Gamma \mid u_0] = \alpha \#\Gamma + \frac{\beta}{2} \int_{I \setminus \Gamma} |u_x|^2 dx + \frac{\lambda}{2} \int_I (u - u_0)^2 dx.$$

Proof.

(a) First, notice that $E_{\mathrm{ms}}[u \equiv 0, \Gamma = \phi \mid u_0] < \infty$. Thus one can assume that there is a minimizing sequence $\{u_n\}_{n=1}^\infty \subseteq \mathcal{D}_{\mathrm{ms}}$ whose E_{ms} energies are bounded by some finite value, say, M.

(b) Let Γ_n denote the associated jump set of u_n. Then $\{\#\Gamma_n\}$ is uniformly bounded. With a possible subsequence refinement, one could assume that $\#\Gamma_n \equiv N$ for $n = 1, 2, \ldots$, and that

$$\Gamma_n = \{x_1^{(n)} < x_2^{(n)} < \cdots < x_N^{(n)}\} \subseteq I.$$

By the precompactness of bounded sequences in $\mathbb{R}$, with possibly another round of subsequence refinement, one could assume that there exists a limiting set (possibly a multiset)

$$\Gamma^* = \{x_1^* \leq x_2^* \leq \cdots \leq x_N^*\} \subseteq \bar{I} = [0, 1],$$

and for each $j = 1 : N, x_j^{(n)} \to x_j^*$ as $n \to \infty$.

(c) For any $\varepsilon > 0$, define the (relatively) closed ε-neighborhood of Γ^* in $I = (0, 1)$ by

$$\Gamma_\varepsilon^* = \{y \in I \ : \ \mathrm{dist}(y, \Gamma^*) \leq \varepsilon\},$$

and its open complement $I_\varepsilon = I \setminus \Gamma_\varepsilon^*$. Then as $\varepsilon \to 0$, I_ε monotonically expands to I. For any fixed ε, there exists an n_ε, so that for any $n > n_\varepsilon$, u_n's are bounded in $H^1(I_\varepsilon)$ since

$$\|u_n\|_{H^1(I_\varepsilon)}^2 = \int_{I_\varepsilon} u_n^2(x)dx + \int_{I_\varepsilon} (u_n'(x))^2 dx \leq \|u_0\|_\infty^2 + \frac{2M}{\beta},$$

as long as Γ_n starts to be included within Γ_ε^*.

(d) Choose any sequence (ε_k) with $\varepsilon_k \to 0$ as $k \to \infty$. For ε_1, by the compactness of $H^1(I_{\varepsilon_1})$ in $L^2(I_{\varepsilon_1})$ [212], one could refine a subsequence of $(n)_{n=1}^{\infty}$, denoted by $(n \mid 1)_{n=1}^{\infty}$, so that $(u_{(n|1)})_{n=1}^{\infty}$ is a Cauchy sequence in $L^2(I_{\varepsilon_1})$.

Repeating this process, for each step $k \geq 2$, one could find a subsequence $(n|k)$ of $(n|k-1)$ so that $(u_{(n|k)})_{n=1}^{\infty}$ is a Cauchy sequence in $L^2(I_{\varepsilon_k})$. Finally, define $u_k^* = u_{(k|k)}$, $k = 1 : \infty$.

(e) Then it is clear that there exists a unique $u^* \in L_{\text{loc}}^2(I \setminus \Gamma^*)$, so that $u_k^* \to u^*$ in any $L^2(I_{\varepsilon})$. In particular,

$$\|u^*\|_{\infty} \leq \|u_0\|_{\infty}.$$

Furthermore, by the L^2-lower semicontinuity of Sobolev norms, on any I_{ε},

$$\int_{I \setminus \Gamma^*} |(u^*)'|^2 dx = \sup_{\varepsilon} \int_{I_{\varepsilon}} |(u^*)'|^2 dx \leq \sup_{\varepsilon} \liminf_{k \to \infty} \int_{I_{\varepsilon}} |(u_k^*)'|^2 dx$$

$$\leq \liminf_{k \to \infty} \int_{I \setminus \Gamma_{(k|k)}} |(u_k^*)'|^2 dx.$$

Since (u_k^*) is a minimizing sequence, we conclude that $u^* \in H^1(I \setminus \Gamma^*)$, $\Gamma_{u^*} \subseteq \Gamma^*$, and $u^* \in \mathcal{D}_{\text{ms}}$.

(f) With a possible subsequence refinement, one could assume

$$u_k^*(x) \to u^*(x), \quad \text{a.e.} \quad x \in I.$$

Then, by $\|u_k^*\|_{\infty} \leq \|u_0\|_{\infty}$ and *Lebesgue's dominated convergence theorem*,

$$\int_I (u^* - u_0)^2 dx = \lim_{k \to \infty} \int_I (u^* - u_0)^2 dx.$$

(g) In combination of the last two itemized results, we arrive at

$$E_{\text{ms}}[u^*, \Gamma_{u^*} \mid u_0] \leq \liminf_{k \to \infty} E_{\text{ms}}[u_k^*, \Gamma_{u_k^*} \mid u_0].$$

Since (u_k^*) is a minimizing sequence, $u^* \in \mathcal{D}_{\text{ms}}$ has to be a minimizer being sought. □

7.4.7 How to Segment Sierpinski Islands

As a concrete example, let us now investigate how the M.–S. segmentation model behaves for a particular image of interest, which we shall nickname *Sierpinski Islands*, obtained from the classical Sierpinski gasket (see, e.g., Mandelbrot [206]) by a contraction rescaling.

Let the image domain Ω be an open triangle. Construct on it the classical Sierpinski gasket by the iterated digging process: digging out the central and closed (relatively in Ω) quarter-sized triangle in each remaining or new connected component (see the left panel of Figure 7.12).

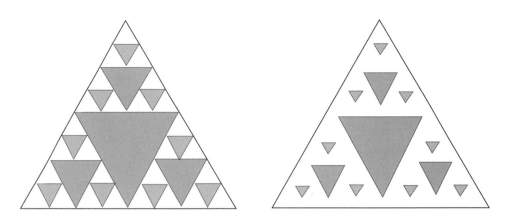

Figure 7.12. *Left panel: the complement G of the classical Sierpinski gasket (Mandelbrot [206]) consists of all the shaded open triangles (excluding their sides).* *Right panel: Sierpinski Islands $G(\rho)$ is the open set obtained from G by contracting each triangle of G with some suitable rate controlled by some $\rho \in (0, 3/2)$ (see the text). And the target image u_ρ discussed in this section is the indicator function of $G(\rho)$.*

Let G denote the open set consisting of all the open triangles (excluding their sides) which have been dug out during the construction process. Therefore,

$$\text{the classical Sierpinski gasket refers to} \quad \overline{\Omega} \setminus G.$$

Since the Sierpinski gasket is a Lebesgue null set (with respect to $dx = dx_1 dx_2$), $|G| = |\Omega|$.

Furthermore, G as an ensemble of triangles is naturally *stratified* according to the scales

$$G = G_1 \cup G_2 \cup \cdots \cup G_k \cup \cdots ,$$
$$G_k = \{T \in G \ : \ |T| = |\Omega|/4^k\}, \quad k = 1, 2, \ldots ,$$

where T denotes any triangle of G. Then $\#G_k = 3^{k-1}$ for any $k \geq 1$. Furthermore,

$$\mathcal{H}^1(\partial T_k) = \mathcal{H}^1(\partial \Omega)/2^k \quad \forall T_k \in G_k, \ k = 1, 2, \ldots .$$

For any triangle T, let $c(T) \in T$ denote its mass center. Fix any $\rho \in (0, 3/2)$. Define the contracted versions of G_k's by

$$G_k(\rho) = \{c(T_k) + (T_k - c(T_k)) \cdot (2/3)^k \rho^k \mid T_k \in G_k\}, \quad k = 1, 2, \ldots ,$$

and $G(\rho) = G_1(\rho) \cup G_2(\rho) \cup \cdots$. We shall call $G(\rho)$ Sierpinski Islands (see Figure 7.12).

Let $u_\rho(x) = 1_{G(\rho)}(x), x \in \Omega$, denote the indicator function of $G(\rho)$ on Ω, which shall also be called Sierpinski Islands. We are interested in the M.–S. segmentation of u_ρ:

$$(u_*, \Gamma_*) = \operatorname{argmin} E_{\text{ms}}[u, \Gamma \mid u_\rho] = \operatorname{argmin} E_{\text{ms}}[u, \Gamma \mid u_\rho, \alpha, \beta, \lambda, \Omega].$$

First, assume that the perfect segmentation is reached:

$$u_*(x) = u_\rho(x), \quad x \in \Omega \setminus \Gamma_*; \quad \text{and} \quad \Gamma_* = \partial G(\rho).$$

Then

$$E_{\text{ms}}[u_*, \Gamma_* \mid u_\rho] = \alpha \mathcal{H}^1(\Gamma_*).$$

On the other hand,

$$
\begin{aligned}
\mathcal{H}^1(\partial G(\rho)) &= \sum_{k=1}^{\infty} \mathcal{H}^1(\partial G_k(\rho)) \\
&= \sum_{k=1}^{\infty} (2/3)^k \rho^k \mathcal{H}^1(\partial G_k) \\
&= \sum_{k=1}^{\infty} (2/3)^k \rho^k \sum_{T_k \in G_k} \mathcal{H}^1(\partial T_k) \qquad (7.91) \\
&= \sum_{k=1}^{\infty} (2/3)^k \rho^k \times 3^{k-1} \times 2^{-k} \mathcal{H}^1(\partial \Omega) \\
&= \frac{1}{3} \mathcal{H}^1(\partial \Omega) \sum_{k=1}^{\infty} \rho^k = \frac{\rho}{3(1-\rho)} \mathcal{H}^1(\partial \Omega),
\end{aligned}
$$

if $\rho \in (0, 1)$, otherwise equals ∞ for all $\rho \in [1, 3/2)$. Therefore, we have the following claim.

Proposition 7.37. *Perfect segmentation under the M.–S. model is impossible for any Sierpinski Islands image u_ρ with $\rho \in [1, 3/2)$.*

This, however, does not necessarily imply that perfect segmentation can be realized for any $\rho \in (0, 1)$. The following analysis shall help us further understand what could happen to a multiscale image such as the Sierpinski Islands.

Theorem 7.38. *Perfect segmentation is impossible for any Sierpinski Islands image u_ρ even with $\rho \in (0, 1)$.*

Proof. For each integer $N = 1, 2, \ldots$, define

$$G^{(N)} = G^{(N)}(\rho) = G_1(\rho) \cup G_2(\rho) \cup \cdots \cup G_N(\rho).$$

Let $u_{\rho,N}$ denote the indicator function $G^{(N)}$ and

$$u_{\rho,N}^c = u_\rho - u_{\rho,N},$$

which is the indicator function of the remaining islands in $G_{N+1}(\rho), G_{N+2}(\rho), \ldots$. In some sense, $u_{\rho,N}$ cannot see these remaining small-scale islands. Then

$$
\begin{aligned}
E_{\text{ms}}[u_{\rho,N}, \partial G^{(N)} \mid u_\rho, \alpha, \beta, \lambda] &= \alpha \mathcal{H}^1(\partial G^{(N)}) + \frac{\lambda}{2} \int_\Omega (u_{\rho,N}^c)^2 dx \\
&= \alpha \mathcal{H}^1(\partial G^{(N)}) + \frac{\lambda}{2} \sum_{k>N} |G_k(\rho)| \\
&= \alpha \mathcal{H}^1(\partial G^{(N)}) + \left(\frac{\rho^2}{3}\right)^{N+1} \frac{\lambda/2}{3 - \rho^2}.
\end{aligned}
$$

On the other hand, for the perfect segmentation $(u_\rho, \partial G(\rho))$, as in (7.91)

$$
\begin{aligned}
E_{\mathrm{ms}}[u_\rho, \partial G(\rho) \mid u_\rho, \alpha, \beta, \lambda] &= \alpha \mathcal{H}^1(\partial G(\rho)) \\
&= \alpha \mathcal{H}^1(\partial G^{(N)}(\rho)) + \alpha \sum_{k > N} \mathcal{H}^1(\partial G_k(\rho)) \\
&= \alpha \mathcal{H}^1(\partial G^{(N)}) + \rho^{N+1} \frac{\alpha/3}{1 - \rho}.
\end{aligned}
$$

Therefore, for any fixed set of positive M.–S. parameters (α, β, λ), for sufficiently large N,

$$
E_{\mathrm{ms}}[u_{\rho, N}, \partial G^{(N)} \mid u_\rho, \alpha, \beta, \lambda] < E_{\mathrm{ms}}[u_\rho, \partial G(\rho) \mid u_\rho, \alpha, \beta, \lambda],
$$

implying that perfect segmentation, which respects every detail in every scale, cannot be realized under the M.–S. segmentation.   ☐

In fact, the competition between regional energy and boundary energy in the Sierpinski Islands is a common phenomenon in general M.–S. segmentation computations. It shows that isolated and scattered small-scale features are better treated as noise than genuine features.

On the other side of the token, it is worth mentioning that exact segmentation is indeed possible for an ideal binary image $u_0 = 1_G(x)$ when (i) the bounded domain G has smooth boundary, and (ii) the fitting weight λ in the M.–S. model is large enough. This is the remarkable result of Alberti, Bouchitté, and Dal Maso [4].

7.4.8   Hidden Symmetries of M.–S. Segmentation

In this section, we discuss certain symmetries hidden in the M.–S. model

$$
E_{\mathrm{ms}}[u, \Gamma \mid u_0] = \alpha \mathcal{H}^1(\Gamma) + \frac{\beta}{2} \int_{\Omega \backslash \Gamma} |\nabla u|^2 dx + \frac{\lambda}{2} \int_\Omega (u - u_0)^2 dx. \tag{7.92}
$$

To indicate domain dependence, we shall also occasionally write it as $E_{\mathrm{ms}}[u, \Gamma \mid u_0, \Omega]$, or to indicate parameter dependence, $E_{\mathrm{ms}}[u, \Gamma \mid u_0, \alpha, \beta, \gamma]$. Let

$$
(u_*, \Gamma_*) = \operatorname{argmin} E_{\mathrm{ms}}[u, \Gamma \mid u_0]
$$

denote any minimizer (with a fixed set of α, β, and λ and on a given domain Ω).

Euclidean Invariance

For any $a \in \mathbb{R}^2$ and rotation $Q \in O(2)$, define the Euclidean transform:

$$
x \to y = Q(x + a): \quad x \in \Omega \to y \in \Omega' = Q(\Omega + a).
$$

Then one must have the Euclidean invariance of the M.–S. segmentation

$$
(u_*(Q^T y - a), Q(\Gamma_* + a)) = \operatorname{argmin} E_{\mathrm{ms}}[v(y), \Gamma \mid v_0(y), \Omega'],
$$

where $v_0(y) = u_0(Q^T y - a)$. This is plain to see since all three components

$$
\mathcal{H}^1(\Gamma), \quad \int_{\Omega \backslash \Gamma} |\nabla u|^2 dx, \quad \text{and} \quad \int_\Omega (u - u_0)^2 dx
$$

are invariant under Euclidean transforms.

Gray-Level Shift Invariance

Let $m \in \mathbb{R}$ be any fixed gray level. Then it is plain to see that

$$E_{ms}[u + m, \Gamma \mid u_0 + m] = E_{ms}[u, \Gamma \mid u_0].$$

In particular in terms of optimal segmentation,

$$u_0 \to u_0 + m \Rightarrow (u_*, \Gamma_*) \to (u_* + m, \Gamma_*),$$

which is called the gray-level shift invariance. Therefore, one could for convenience always assume that a given observation has zero mean:

$$m = \langle u_0 \rangle = \frac{1}{|\Omega|} \int_\Omega u_0(x)dx = 0.$$

However, the celebrated Weber's law in vision psychology and psycophysics [121, 315] indicates that to human vision, visual inference is adapted to different mean fields. As a result, for instance, an edge segment in u_0 is much more difficult to be recognized in $u_0 + 100$. For more discussion on this interesting topic and development along this line, we refer the reader to Shen [275] and Shen and Jung [279].

Constant Flashing Invariance

Model a constant flashing (as for digital cameras) by

$$u_0 \to \theta u_0 \qquad \text{for some fixed constant } \theta \in [1, \infty).$$

Then one has the constant flashing invariance:

$$E_{ms}[\theta u, \Gamma \mid \theta u_0, \alpha, \beta, \lambda] = E_{ms}[u, \Gamma \mid u_0, \alpha, \theta^2 \beta, \theta^2 \lambda].$$

In particular, by taking $\theta = -1$ and into consideration the preceding gray-level shift invariance as well, one has, for any $m \in \mathbb{R}$,

$$u_0 \to m - u_0 \quad \Rightarrow \quad (u_*, \Gamma_*) \to (m - u_*, \Gamma_*).$$

Assume that all gray levels are bounded between 0 and 1. Then the transformation $1 - u$ is what for old analog films is known as the negative of u. Therefore, the M.–S. model is negative-invariant as well.

Domain Additivity

Let $\Gamma_0 \subseteq \Omega$ be a relatively closed set, with locally finite 1-D Hausdorff measure. Then Γ_0 is a Lebesgue null set (with respect to $dx = dx_1 dx_2$). Assume that

$$\Omega \setminus \Gamma_0 = \Omega_1 \cup \Omega_2$$

is a decomposition of two nonempty disjoint open components, each of which could further contain many connected components. For any admissible M.–S. edge $\Gamma \subseteq \Omega$, define

$$\gamma_1 = \Gamma \cap \Omega_1, \quad \gamma_0 = \Gamma \cap \Gamma_0, \quad \text{and} \quad \gamma_2 = \Gamma \cap \Omega_2.$$

Then one has the property of domain additivity

$$E_{\text{ms}}[u, \Gamma \mid u_0, \Omega] = \alpha \mathcal{H}^1(\gamma_0) + E_{\text{ms}}[u_1, \gamma_1 \mid u_{0,1}, \Omega_1] + E_{\text{ms}}[u_2, \gamma_2 \mid u_{0,2}, \Omega_2], \quad (7.93)$$

where u_i and $u_{0,i}$ denote the restrictions of u and u_0 on Ω_i, $i = 1, 2$. Seemingly trivial, this property has, however, played an important role in Ambrosio and Tortorelli's Γ-convergence theory for the Mumford–Shah model [11, 12].

7.4.9 Computational Method I: Γ-Convergence Approximation

The main computational challenge arises from the free-boundary nature of the M.–S. model. In this section, we discuss the approach by Γ-convergence approximation, as proposed by Ambrosio and Tortorelli [11, 12]. The level-set approach will be introduced in the next section. Other computational approaches based on finite differences or finite elements can be found in Chambolle [52, 53], or based on multiscale transitions in Koepfler, Lopez, and Morel [178].

The main idea of Γ-convergence approximation is to encode the 1-D edge feature Γ by a 2-D edge signature function

$$z = z_\varepsilon(x), \quad x = (x_1, x_2) \in \Omega \to [0, 1],$$

where ε is a small positive parameter controlling the degree of approximation. To signify the edge set, z is close to 1 almost everywhere on Ω, except in the vicinity of Γ where it sharply (controlled by ε) drops close to 0.

Therefore, if z is plotted as an image, Γ shall be easily recognizable from the narrow dark stripes on the image domain Ω, whose bandwidth is controlled by ε. On the other hand, the graph of z (in three dimensions) looks like a plateau ($z \simeq 1$) with canyons ($z \simeq 0$ along Γ). Thus z shall also be called the *canyon function*.

The remarkable observation, as already mentioned in the section on Active Contours, is that the 1-D Hausdorff measure $E[\Gamma] = \alpha \mathcal{H}^1(\Gamma)$ can be well approximated by the Ginzburg–Landau energy [133]:

$$E_\varepsilon[z] = \alpha \int_\Omega \left(\frac{\varepsilon |\nabla z|^2}{2} + \frac{(z-1)^2}{2\varepsilon} \right) dx, \quad (7.94)$$

provided that $z = z_\varepsilon$ indeed carries the aforementioned structures.

First, it is relatively easier to see that $E_\varepsilon[z]$ provides an asymptotic upper bound for $E[\Gamma]$. This follows from the geometric inequality

$$E_\varepsilon[z] \geq \alpha \int_\Omega |\nabla z||z - 1| dx = \frac{\alpha}{2} \int_\Omega |\nabla w| dx, \quad (7.95)$$

where $w = (1 - z)^2$ is the edge *wall* function since its graph looks like walls (along Γ) standing on the ground level. Notice that the last integral is precisely the *TV* of the wall function, for which one has the co-area formula of Fleming and Rishel [125], and De Giorgi [134] (see also Section 2.2),

$$\int_\Omega |Dw| = \int_\Omega |\nabla w| dx = \int_0^1 \text{length}(w \equiv s) ds.$$

Thus as long as the wall is narrow and rises from $w \simeq 0$ to $w \simeq 1$ monotonically on either side of Γ, for each $s \in (0, 1)$, the level set $(w \equiv s)$ consists of two curves which are as if copied from Γ. As a result,

$$\int_{\Omega} |\nabla w| dx \simeq 2 \, \text{length}(\Gamma),$$

which is the assertion of asymptotic upper bound.

The above analysis also points to the way of truly achieving the upper bound. The geometric inequality in (7.95) can be achieved when

$$\sqrt{\varepsilon} |\nabla z| = \frac{1-z}{\sqrt{\varepsilon}} \quad \text{or} \quad |\nabla z| = \frac{1-z}{\varepsilon}. \tag{7.96}$$

Assume that $\Gamma \in C^{1,1}$ so that its vicinity allows the natural curvilinear coordinates

$$(s, t) \rightarrow x(s, t) = x(s) + t N(s), \quad t \in (-\delta, \delta),$$

where $x(s)$ is the arc length parametrization of Γ, $N(s)$ its normal, and δ a small range (controlled by ε and to be specified below). Let $z(s, t) = z(x(s, t))$. If Γ is to be designed as the level line of z with the lowest value, one must have $z_s(s, 0) = 0$. As a result, to the accuracy of $O(\varepsilon)$ by Taylor expansion,

$$|\nabla z(s, t)| = |z_t(s, t)| \quad \forall t \in (-\delta, \delta).$$

Design z symmetrically with respect to t; then (7.96) is reduced to the following system (parameterized by s) of linear ODEs:

$$\frac{dz}{dt} = \frac{1-z}{\varepsilon}, \quad t \in (0, \delta), \quad \text{and} \quad z(s, 0) = 0,$$

whose solutions are plain to see:

$$z(s, t) = 1 - e^{-\frac{t}{\varepsilon}}, \quad t \in [0, \delta).$$

In particular, as long as δ satisfies $\varepsilon \ll \delta \ll 1$, the rising of z close to 1 near δ is indeed realized.

In combination, the asymptotic approximation of $E_{\varepsilon}[z]$ to $E[\Gamma]$ has been established, under the above specific design of the edge canyon function $z = z_{\varepsilon}$.

Furthermore, the Sobolev term in the M.–S. model also allows a natural approximation:

$$\frac{\beta}{2} \int_{\Omega \setminus \Gamma} |\nabla u|^2 dx \simeq \frac{\beta}{2} \int_{\Omega} z^2 |\nabla u|^2 dx,$$

since $z = z_{\varepsilon}$ almost vanishes along Γ. (Often z^2 is replaced by $z^2 + o_{\varepsilon}$ with a positive constant o_{ε} tending to zero faster than ε. o_{ε} can enforce uniform ellipticity [11, 12].)

Thus one naturally arrives at the Γ-convergence approximation of the M.–S. model as proposed by Ambrosio and Tortorelli [11, 12]:

$$E_{\text{ms}}[u, z \mid u_0, \varepsilon] = \frac{\alpha}{2} \int_{\Omega} (\varepsilon |\nabla z|^2 + \varepsilon^{-1}(1-z)^2) dx + \frac{\beta}{2} \int_{\Omega} z^2 |\nabla u|^2 dx + \frac{\lambda}{2} \int_{\Omega} (u - u_0)^2 dx. \tag{7.97}$$

a given noisy image   optimal image estimation u   associated edge canyon z

Figure 7.13. *An example of Γ-convergence-based approximation to the M.–S. segmentation model (7.97): the optimal image estimation $u = u_\varepsilon(x)$ and its associated edge "canyon" function $z = z_\varepsilon(x)$. Computation has been based on the alternating minimization scheme (7.98).*

That $E_{\mathrm{ms}}[u, z \mid u_0, \varepsilon] \to E_{\mathrm{ms}}[u, \Gamma \mid u_0]$ in the Γ-convergence sense is proven by Ambrosio and Tortorelli [11, 12]. Interested readers are referred to their works for further detailed mathematical analysis.

The good news is that under Γ-convergence approximation (7.97), both conditionals are quadratic functionals on u and z separately:

$$E_{\mathrm{ms}}[u \mid z, u_0, \varepsilon] = \frac{\beta}{2} \int_\Omega z^2 |\nabla u|^2 dx + \frac{\lambda}{2} \int_\Omega (u - u_0)^2 dx,$$

$$E_{\mathrm{ms}}[z \mid u, u_0, \varepsilon] = \frac{\alpha}{2} \int_\Omega (\varepsilon |\nabla z|^2 + \varepsilon^{-1}(1 - z)^2) dx + \frac{\beta}{2} \int_\Omega z^2 |\nabla u|^2 dx.$$

Their first variations lead to the Euler–Lagrange system of elliptic equations

$$-\beta \nabla \cdot (z^2 \nabla u) + \lambda(u - u_0) = 0,$$

$$\alpha(-\varepsilon \Delta z + \varepsilon^{-1}(z - 1)) + \beta |\nabla u|^2 z = 0,$$

with Neumann boundary conditions along $\partial\Omega$, both of which are conditionally linear. These two equations can be easily integrated numerically based on proper elliptic solvers and iteration schemes, for example, by the alternating minimization (AM) scheme which amounts to $z^{(n)} \to u^{(n)} \to z^{(n+1)}$:

$$u^{(n)} = \mathrm{argmin}\ E_{\mathrm{ms}}[u \mid z^{(n)}, u_0, \varepsilon],$$
$$z^{(n+1)} = \mathrm{argmin}\ E_{\mathrm{ms}}[z \mid u^{(n)}, u_0, \varepsilon].$$

$$(7.98)$$

See [116, 207, 208, 279], for example, for detailed numerical implementation of the AM scheme. Figure 7.13 shows a typical numerical example.

7.4.10   Computational Method II: Level-Set Method

The level-set method was invented by Osher and Sethian in their remarkable paper [241] in 1987, and it has become ever since a powerful tool for computing front propagations and interface motions. The method especially excels in its unique capabilities of handling topological changes. Its application to the numerical computation of M.–S. segmentation was first introduced by Chan and Vese [75, 76] and Tsai, Yezzi, and Willsky [299]. This section gives a brief introduction to these works. For more details on the general level-set methods, readers are referred to the excellent sources [202, 243, 239, 269, 268, 300, 327].

By the level-set method, a curve Γ is represented as the zero level set of a $C^{0,1}$ or Lipschitz continuous function ϕ:

$$\Gamma = \{x \in \Omega \mid \phi(x) = 0\} = \phi^{-1}(0).$$

As in differential topology [218], 0 should be the *regular value* of ϕ, meaning that for any $x \in \phi^{-1}(0)$, $\nabla \phi(x) \neq 0$. Then Γ becomes a 1-D submanifold embedded in $\Omega \subseteq \mathbb{R}^2$, which of course can consist of many disjoint connected components or loops. The function ϕ is often conveniently called the *level-set function*.

On the other hand, by the *implicit function theorem*, Γ is locally homeomorphic to the real line in $\mathbb{R}^2$. In particular, Γ cannot contain any crack-tips, as called by Mumford and Shah [226]. Crack-tips are, however, possible optimal solutions to the M.–S. segmentation [226], though quite rare in most practical applications.

Similarly, if Γ is represented by a level-set function ϕ, it cannot contain vertices, i.e., points where more than two smooth segments of Γ intersect. In particular, it cannot contain any T-junctions or Y-junctions. As proven by Mumford and Shah [226], Y-junctions with 120 degrees apart between any two branches are plausible solutions in optimal M.–S. segmentations. Vertices are, however, representable using multiphase level-set formulations [76, 73].

Suppose Γ is represented by ϕ. Define

$$\Omega^\pm = \{x \in \Omega \mid \pm \phi(x) > 0\}.$$

Then $\Omega = \Omega^+ \cup \Gamma \cup \Omega^-$, and generally Ω^+ and Ω^- can both further contain many connected components.

Let $H(z) = 1_{z>0}(z)$ denote the Heaviside 0-1 function for $z \in \mathbb{R}$. Then the two indicators

$$1_{\Omega^\pm}(x) = H(\pm \phi(x)).$$

In particular, by the perimeter formula [137],

$$\mathcal{H}^1(\Gamma) = \text{Per}(\Omega^+) = \int_\Omega |D 1_{\Omega^+}| = \int_\Omega |DH(\phi)|,$$

which is the level-set representation for the length energy.

Furthermore, since $H(z) + H(-z) = 1$ for any $z \neq 0$, one has

$$H(-\phi(x)) = 1 - H(\phi(x)) \quad \forall x \in \Omega \setminus \Gamma.$$

Also notice that in terms of distributional derivatives,

$$DH(\phi) = \delta(\phi) \nabla \phi,$$

where $\delta(z) = H'(z)$ is Dirac's delta measure.

In practical numerical computation, $H(z)$ is often substituted by any of its mollified version such as $H_\sigma(z) = g_\sigma * H(z)$, as mollified by a Gaussian with variance $\sigma^2 \ll 1$. Then Dirac's delta function is also mollified to a smooth peak such as

$$\delta_\sigma(z) = H'_\sigma(z) = g_\sigma * H'(z) = g_\sigma * \delta(z) = g_\sigma(z),$$

i.e., a Gaussian peak. Chan and Vese's computational results in [75, 76] demonstrated that such mollification is very effective in actual level-set computations. The more recent paper by Engquist, Tornberg, and Tsai [113] exclusively discussed how to numerically compute the Dirac's delta function.

In combination, under the level-set formulation, the M.–S. segmentation model,

$$E_{\mathrm{ms}}[u, \Gamma \mid u_0] = \alpha \mathcal{H}^1(\Gamma) + \frac{\beta}{2} \int_{\Omega \setminus \Gamma} |\nabla u|^2 dx + \frac{\lambda}{2} \int_\Omega (u - u_0)^2 dx, \qquad (7.99)$$

becomes a model on the two image patches $u^\pm$ on $\Omega^\pm$ and the level-set function ϕ, which represents Γ:

$$\begin{aligned}
E_{\mathrm{ms}}[u^+, u^-, \phi \mid u_0] = & \alpha \int_\Omega |DH(\phi)| + \int_\Omega \left(\frac{\beta}{2} |\nabla u^+|^2 + \frac{\lambda}{2}(u^+ - u_0)^2 \right) H(\phi) dx \\
& + \int_\Omega \left(\frac{\beta}{2} |\nabla u^-|^2 + \frac{\lambda}{2}(u^- - u_0)^2 \right) H(-\phi) dx.
\end{aligned}$$
$$(7.100)$$

For given Γ, or equivalently ϕ, the optimal image patches $u^\pm$ can be integrated from the elliptic system:

$$-\beta \Delta u^\pm + \lambda(u^\pm - u_0) = 0, \ x \in \Omega^\pm \quad \text{with Neumann bounday conditions.}$$

Here $+$ or $-$ must be taken uniformly along the formula (and the same rule applies in all subsequent formulae).

On the other hand, for any current best estimators $u^\pm$, define

$$e^\pm(x) = \frac{\beta}{2} |\nabla u^\pm|^2 + \frac{\lambda}{2}(u^\pm - u_0)^2, \quad x \in \Omega^\pm.$$

Then the first variation of (7.100) on $\phi(x) \to \phi(x) + \varepsilon(x)$ with $|\varepsilon| \ll 1$ gives

$$\text{first variation of } E_{\mathrm{ms}} = -\alpha \int_\Omega \delta(\phi) \nabla \cdot \left(\frac{\nabla \phi}{|\nabla \phi|} \right) \varepsilon dx + \int_\Omega e^+ \delta(\phi) \varepsilon dx - \int_\Omega e^- \delta(-\phi) \varepsilon dx.$$

Since for Dirac's delta function, $\delta(-z) = \delta(z)$, one obtains the formal differential

$$\frac{\partial E_{\mathrm{ms}}}{\partial \phi} = -\alpha \delta(\phi) \nabla \cdot \left(\frac{\nabla \phi}{|\nabla \phi|} \right) + [e]\delta(\phi) \quad \text{with Neumann boundary condition,}$$

where $[e] = e^+ - e^-$. Since $[e]$ is a multiplier to $\delta(\phi)$, only the values of $[e]$ at $\phi = 0$ or Γ make contributions. Both $e^+|_\Gamma$ and $e^-|_\Gamma$ are therefore understood as their traces along Γ. Thus the steepest descent marching scheme for $\phi(x, t)$ is given by

$$\frac{\partial \phi}{\partial t} = \alpha \delta(\phi) \nabla \cdot \left(\frac{\nabla \phi}{|\nabla \phi|} \right) - [e]\delta(\phi)$$

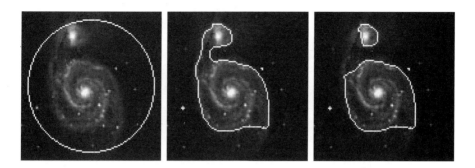

Figure 7.14. *An example of M.–S. segmentation using the level-set algorithm by Chan and Vese* [75, 76].

with Neumann boundary condition along $\partial\Omega$. Notice that the equation is essentially local along $\Gamma = \phi^{-1}(0)$. Computationally as stated earlier, δ is replaced by its mollified version, say δ_σ, with essential bandwidth proportional to σ (as in the Gaussian case). Then the computation is carried out in a narrow stripe along Γ with the indicated bandwidth. We refer the reader to Chan and Vese [75, 76] for more details on numerical implementation. Figure 7.14 shows a typical computational example.

7.5 Multichannel Logical Segmentation

In this section, we outline the recent efforts of Sandberg and Chan in developing logical segmentation schemes for multichannel images [259]. Other numerous extensions and novel applications of the Mumford–Shah model could be found, e.g., in [325].

In a multichannel image $u(x) = (u_1(x), u_2(x), \ldots, u_n(x))$, a single physical object can leave different traces in different channels. For example, Figure 7.15 shows a two-channel image containing a triangle which is, however, incomplete in each individual channel. For this example, most conventional segmentation models for multichannel images [64, 65, 145, 263, 330] would output the complete triangle, i.e., the union of both channels. The union is just one of the several possible logical operations for multichannel

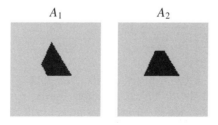

Figure 7.15. *A synthetic example of an object in two different channels. Notice that the lower left corner of A_1 and the upper corner of A_2 are missing.*

$$A_1 \cup A_2 \qquad\qquad A_1 \cap A_2 \qquad\qquad A_1 \cap \neg A_2$$

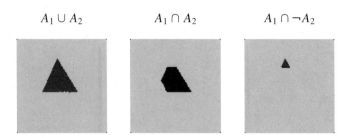

Figure 7.16. *Different logical combinations for the sample image: the union, the intersection, and the differentiation.*

images. For example, the intersection and the differentiation are also very common in applications, as illustrated in Figure 7.16.

First, we define two logical variables to encode the information inside and outside the contour Γ separately for each channel i:

$$z_i^{in}(u_0^i, x, \Gamma) = \begin{cases} 1 & \text{if } x \text{ is inside } \Gamma \text{ and not on the object,} \\ 0 & \text{otherwise;} \end{cases}$$

$$z_i^{out}(u_0^i, x, \Gamma) = \begin{cases} 1 & \text{if } x \text{ is outside } \Gamma \text{ and on the object,} \\ 0 & \text{otherwise.} \end{cases}$$

Such different treatments are motivated by the energy minimization formulation. Intuitively speaking, in order for the active contour Γ to evolve and eventually capture the *exact* boundary of the targeted logical object, the energy should be designed so that both partial capture and overcapture lead to high energies (corresponding to $z_i^{out} = 1$ and $z_i^{in} = 1$ separately). Imagine that the target object is the tumor tissue, then in terms of decision theory, over and partial captures correspond to *false alarms* and *misses* separately. Both are to be penalized.

In practice, we do not have the precise information of "the object," which is exactly to be segmented. One possible way to approximate z_i^{in} and z_i^{out} is based on the interior (Ω^+) and exterior (Ω^-) averages $c_i^{\pm}$ in channel i:

$$z_i^{in}(u_0^i, x, \Gamma) = \frac{|u_0^i(x) - c_i^+|^2}{\max_{y \in \Omega^+} |u_0^i(y) - c_i^+|^2} \quad \text{for } x \in \Omega^+;$$

$$z_i^{out}(u_0^i, x, \Gamma) = \frac{|u_0^i(x) - c_i^-|^2}{\max_{y \in \Omega^-} |u_0^i(y) - c_i^-|^2} \quad \text{for } x \in \Omega^-.$$

The desired truth table can then be described using the z_i^{in}'s and z_i^{out}'s. In Table 7.1, we have shown three examples of logical operations for the two-channel case. Notice that "true" is represented by 0 inside Γ. It is so designed to encourage energy minimization when the contour tries to capture the targeted object inside.

We then design continuous objective functions to smoothly interpolate the binary truth table. This is because in practice, as mentioned above, the z's are approximated and take

Table 7.1. *The truth table for the two-channel case. Notice that inside* Γ *"true" is represented by* 0. *It is so designed to encourage the contour to enclose the targeted logical object at a lower energy cost.*

			Truth table for the two-channel case				
	z_1^{in}	z_2^{in}	z_1^{out}	z_2^{out}	$A_1 \cup A_2$	$A_1 \cap A_2$	$A_1 \cap \neg A_2$
x inside Γ	1	1	0	0	1	1	1
(or $x \in \Omega^+$)	1	0	0	0	0	1	1
	0	1	0	0	0	1	0
	0	0	0	0	0	0	1
x outside Γ	0	0	1	1	1	1	0
(or $x \in \Omega^-$)	0	0	1	0	1	0	1
	0	0	0	1	1	0	0
	0	0	0	0	0	0	0

continuous values. For example, the possible interpolants for the union and intersection can be

$$f_{A_1 \cup A_2}(x) = \sqrt{z_1^{in}(x) z_2^{in}(x)} + (1 - \sqrt{(1 - z_1^{out}(x))(1 - z_2^{out}(x)))},$$

$$f_{A_1 \cap A_2}(x) = 1 - \sqrt{(1 - z_1^{in}(x))(1 - z_2^{in}(x))} + \sqrt{z_1^{out}(x) z_2^{out}(x)}.$$

The square roots are taken to keep them of the same order as the original scalar models. It is straightforward to extend the two-channel case to more general n-channel ones.

The energy functional E for the logical objective function f can be expressed by the level-set function ϕ. Generally, as just shown above, the objective function can be separated into two parts,

$$f = f(z_1^{in}, z_1^{out}, \ldots, z_n^{in}, z_n^{out}) = f_{in}(z_1^{in}, \ldots, z_n^{in}) + f_{out}(z_1^{out}, \ldots, z_n^{out}).$$

The energy functional is then defined by

$$E[\phi | c^+, c^-] = \mu \text{length}(\phi = 0) + \lambda \int_\Omega \left[f_{in}(z_1^{in}, \ldots, z_n^{in}) H(\phi) \right.$$
$$\left. + f_{out}(z_1^{out}, \ldots, z_n^{out})(1 - H(\phi)) \right] dx.$$

Here each $c^\pm = (c_1^\pm, \ldots, c_n^\pm)$ is in fact a multichannel vector. The associated Euler–Lagrange equation is similar to the scalar model

$$\frac{\partial \phi}{\partial t} = \delta(\phi) \left[\mu \text{div}\left(\frac{\nabla \phi}{|\nabla \phi|} \right) - \lambda \left(f_{in}(z_1^{in}, \ldots, z_n^{in}) - f_{out}(z_1^{out}, \ldots, z_n^{out}) \right) \right],$$

with suitable boundary conditions as before. Even though the form often looks complicated for a typical application, its implementation is very similar to that of the scalar model.

Channel A_1 Initial Contour   Final Contour

Channel A_2 Initial Contour   Final Contour

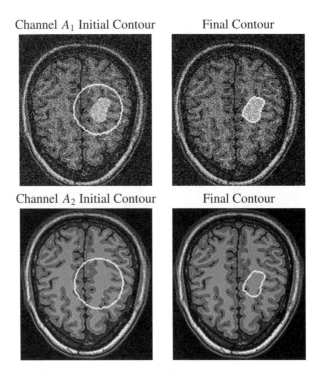

Figure 7.17. *Region-based logical model on a medical image. In the first channel A_1, the noisy image has a "brain tumor," while channel A_2 does not. The goal is to spot the tumor that is in channel A_1, but not in A_2, i.e., the differentiation $A_1 \cap \neg A_2$. In the right column, we observe that the tumor has been successfully captured.*

Numerical results support our above efforts. Figure 7.15 shows two different occlusions of a triangle. We are able to successfully recover the union, the intersection, and the differentiation of the objects in Figure 7.16 using our model. In Figure 7.17, we have a two-channel image of the brain. One noisy channel contains a tumor, while the other is benign. The images are not registered. We want to find $A_1 \cap \neg A_2$ so that the tumor can be observed. This happens to be a very complicated example as there are a lot of features and textures. However, the model performs quite impressively.

Bibliography

[1] R. Acar and C. R. Vogel. Analysis of total variation penalty methods for ill-posed problems. *Inverse Problems*, 10:1217–1229, 1994.

[2] D. J. Acheson. *Elementary Fluid Dynamics*. Clarendon Press, Oxford, 1990.

[3] R. A. Adams and J. J. F. Fournier. *Sobolev Spaces*. Academic Press, Amsterdam, second edition, 2003.

[4] G. Alberti, G. Bouchitté, and G. Dal Maso. The calibration method for the Mumford-Shah functional and free-discontinuity problems. *Calc. Var. Partial Differential Equations*, 16:299–333, 2003.

[5] G. Alberti and C. Mantegazza. A note on the theory of SBV functions. *Boll. Un. Mat. Ital.* B(7), 11:375–382, 1997.

[6] L. Alvarez, F. Guichard, P.-L. Lions, and J.-M. Morel. Axioms and fundamental equations of image processing. *Arch. Rational Mech. Anal.*, 123:199–257, 1993.

[7] L. Ambrosio. A compactness theorem for a new class of functions of bounded variation. *Boll. Un. Mat. Ital.* B(7), 3:857–881, 1989.

[8] L. Ambrosio, N. Fusco, and D. Pallara. Partial regularity of free discontinuity sets II. *Ann. Scuola Norm. Sup. Pisa Cl. Sci.* (4), 24:39–62, 1997.

[9] L. Ambrosio, N. Fusco, and D. Pallara. *Functions of Bounded Variations and Free Discontinuity Problems*. Oxford University Press, New York, 2000.

[10] L. Ambrosio and D. Pallara. Partial regularity of free discontinuity sets I. *Ann. Scuola Norm. Sup. Pisa Cl. Sci.* (4), 24:1–38, 1997.

[11] L. Ambrosio and V. M. Tortorelli. Approximation of functionals depending on jumps by elliptic functionals via Γ-convergence. *Comm. Pure Appl. Math.*, 43:999–1036, 1990.

[12] L. Ambrosio and V. M. Tortorelli. On the approximation of free discontinuity problems. *Boll. Un. Mat. Ital.* B(7), 6:105–123, 1992.

[13] S. Armstrong, A. Kokaram, and P. J. W. Rayner. Nonlinear interpolation of missing data using min-max functions. *IEEE Int. Conf. Nonlinear Signal and Image Processings*, 1997.

373

[14] G. Aronsson. Extension of functions satisfying Lipschitz conditions. *Ark. Mat.*, 6:551–561, 1967.

[15] G. Aubert and P. Kornprobst. *Mathematical Problems in Image Processing.* Springer-Verlag, New York, 2001.

[16] G. Aubert and L. Vese. A variational method in image recovery. *SIAM J. Numer. Anal.*, 34:1948–1979, 1997.

[17] C. Ballester, M. Bertalmio, V. Caselles, G. Sapiro, and J. Verdera. Filling-in by joint interpolation of vector fields and grey levels. *IEEE Trans. Image Process.*, 10:1200–1211, 2001.

[18] G. Battle. Phase space localization theorem for ondelettes. *J. Math. Phys.*, 30:2195–2196, 1989.

[19] P. Belik and M. Luskin. Approximation by piecewise constant functions in a BV metric. *Math. Models Methods Appl. Sci.*, 13:373–393, 2003.

[20] G. Bellettini, V. Caselles, and M. Novaga. The total variation flow in R^n. *J. Differential Equations*, 184:475–525, 2002.

[21] G. Bellettini, G. Dal Maso, and M. Paolini. Semicontinuity and relaxation properties of a curvature depending functional in 2D. *Ann. Scuola Norm. Sup. Pisa Cl. Sci. (4)*, 20:247–297, 1993.

[22] C. M. Bender and S. A. Orszag. *Advanced Mathematical Methods for Scientists and Engineers.* McGraw-Hill, New York, 1978.

[23] M. Bertalmio, A. L. Bertozzi, and G. Sapiro. Navier-Stokes, fluid dynamics, and image and video inpainting. *IMA Preprint 1772*, 2001, www.ima.umn.edu/preprints/jun01.

[24] M. Bertalmio, G. Sapiro, V. Caselles, and C. Ballester. Image inpainting. In *Computer Graphics (SIGGRAPH 2000)* 2000.

[25] M. Bertalmio, L. Vese, G. Sapiro, and S. Osher. Simultaneous structure and texture image inpainting. *UCLA CAM Tech. Report*, 02-47, 2002.

[26] A. L. Bertozzi and J. B. Greer. Low-curvature image simplifiers: Global regularity of smooth solutions and Laplacian limiting schemes. *Comm. Pure Appl. Math.*, 57:1–27, 2004.

[27] G. Birkhoff and C. R. De Boor. Piecewise polynomial interpolation and approximation. In *Approximation of Functions*, H. Garabedian, ed., Elsevier, Amsterdam, pages 164–190, 1965.

[28] A. Blake and M. Isard. *Active Contours.* Springer-Verlag, New York, 1998.

[29] A. Blake and A. Zisserman. *Visual Reconstruction.* MIT Press, Cambridge, MA, 1987.

[30] P. Blomgren and T. F. Chan. Color TV: Total variation methods for restoration of vector-valued images. *IEEE Trans. Image Process.*, 7:304–309, 1998.

[31] M. Boutin. Numerically invariant signature curves. *Int. J. Comput. Vision*, 40:235–248, 2000.

[32] S. Boyd and L. Vandenberghe. *Convex Optimization*. Cambridge University Press, Cambridge, UK, 2004.

[33] P. Brémaud. *Markov Chains: Gibbs Fields, Monte Carlo Simulation, and Queues*. Springer-Verlag, New York, 1998.

[34] W. L. Briggs, V. E. Henson, and S. F. McCormick. *A Multigrid Tutorial*. SIAM, Philadelphia, second edition, 2000.

[35] P. J. Burt and E. H. Adelson. The Laplacian pyramid as a compact image code. *IEEE Trans. Commun.*, 31:532–540, 1983.

[36] R. B. Buxton. *Introduction to Functional Magnetic Resonance Imaging—Principles and Techniques*. Cambridge University Press, Cambridge, UK, 2002.

[37] G. Caginalp. An analysis of a phase-field model of a free boundary. *Arch. Rational Mech. Anal.*, 92:205–245, 1986.

[38] T. Cai and J. Shen. Boundedness is redundant in a theorem of Daubechies. *Appl. Comput. Harmon. Anal.*, 6:400–404, 2003.

[39] E. Calabi, P. J. Olver, C. Shakiban, A. Tannenbaum, and S. Haker. Differential and numerically invariant signature curves applied to object recognition. *Int. J. Comput. Vision*, 26:107–135, 1998.

[40] E. Calabi, P. J. Olver, and A. Tannenbaum. Affine geometry, curve flows, and invariant numerical approximations. *Adv. Math.*, 124:154–196, 1996.

[41] E. J. Candès and D. L. Donoho. Curvelets and reconstruction of images from noisy radon data. In *Wavelet Applications in Signal and Image Processing* VIII, A. Aldroubi, A. F. Laine, M. A. Unser, eds., Proc. SPIE 4119, 2000.

[42] E. J. Candès and T. Tao. Near optimal signal recovery from random projections: Universal encoding strategies? *Preprint*, 2004.

[43] E. J. Candès and F. Guo. New multiscale transforms, minimum total variation synthesis: Applications to edge-preserving image reconstruction. *Signal Processing*, 82:1519–1543, 2002.

[44] J. F. Canny. Computational approach to edge detection. *IEEE Trans. Pat. Anal. Mach. Intell.*, 8:34–43, 1986.

[45] J. L. Carter. *Dual methods for TV-based image restoration (Ph.D. Thesis 2001)*. Also *UCLA CAM Tech. Report*, 02-13, 2002.

[46] J. R. Casas and L. Torres. Strong edge features for image coding. In *Mathematical Morphology and Its Applications to Image and Signal Processing,* R. W. Schafer, P. Maragos, and M. A. Butt, eds., Kluwer, Boston, pages 443–450, 1996.

[47] V. Caselles, F. Catte, T. Coll, and F. Dibos. A geometric model for active contours. *Numer. Math.,* 66:1–31, 1993.

[48] V. Caselles, B. Coll, and J.-M. Morel. Topographic maps. *Preprint CEREMADE,* 1997.

[49] V. Caselles, R. Kimmel, and G. Sapiro. Geodesic active contours. In *Fifth International Conf. on Computer Vision (ICCV'95),* pages 694–699, 1995.

[50] V. Caselles, J.-M. Morel, and C. Sbert. An axiomatic approach to image interpolation. *IEEE Trans. Image Process.,* 7:376–386, 1998.

[51] F. Catté, P.-L. Lions, J.-M. Morel, and T. Coll. Image selective smoothing and edge detection by nonlinear diffusion. *SIAM J. Numer. Anal.,* 29:182–193, 1992.

[52] A. Chambolle. Image segmentation by variational methods: Mumford and Shah functional and the discrete approximations. *SIAM J. Appl. Math.,* 55:827–863, 1995.

[53] A. Chambolle. Finite-differences discretizations of the Mumford-Shah functional. *M2AN Math. Model. Numer. Anal.,* 33:261–288, 1999.

[54] A. Chambolle. An algorithm for total variation minimization and applications. *J. Math. Imaging Vision,* 20:89–97, 2004.

[55] A. Chambolle, R. A. DeVore, N.-Y. Lee, and B. J. Lucier. Nonlinear wavelet image processing: Variational problems, compression and noise removal through wavelet shrinkage. *IEEE Trans. Image Process.,* 7:319–335, 1998.

[56] A. Chambolle and P. L. Lions. Image recovery via total variational minimization and related problems. *Numer. Math.,* 76:167–188, 1997.

[57] R. H. Chan, C.-W. Ho, and M. Nikolova. Salt-and-pepper noise removal by median-type noise detectors and edge-preserving regularization. *IEEE Trans. Image Process.,* to appear.

[58] T. F. Chan, G. H. Golub, and P. Mulet. A nonlinear primal-dual method for total variation-based image restoration. *SIAM J. Sci. Comput.,* 20:1964–1977, 1999.

[59] T. F. Chan and S.-H. Kang. An error analysis on image inpainting problems. *J. Math. Imag. Vision,* to appear.

[60] T. F. Chan, S.-H. Kang, and J. Shen. Total variation denoising and enhancement of color images based on the CB and HSV color models. *J. Visual Comm. Image Rep.,* 12:422–435, 2001.

[61] T. F. Chan, S.-H. Kang, and J. Shen. Euler's elastica and curvature-based inpainting. *SIAM J. Appl. Math.,* 63:564–592, 2002.

[62] T. F. Chan and P. Mulet. On the convergence of the lagged diffusivity fixed point method in total variation image restoration. *SIAM J. Numer. Anal.*, 36:354–367, 1999.

[63] T. F. Chan, S. Osher, and J. Shen. The digital TV filter and nonlinear denoising. *IEEE Trans. Image Process.*, 10:231–241, 2001.

[64] T. F. Chan, B. Sandberg, and L. Vese. Active contours without edges for vector-valued images. *J. Visual Comm. Image Rep.*, 11:130–141, 1999.

[65] T. F. Chan, B. Sandberg, and L. Vese. Active contours without edges for textured images. *UCLA Department of Mathematics CAM Report*, 02-28, 2002.

[66] T. Chan and J. Shen. Variational restoration of nonflat image features: Models and algorithms. *SIAM J. Appl. Math.*, 61:1338–1361, 2000.

[67] T. F. Chan and J. Shen. Mathematical models for local nontexture inpaintings. *SIAM J. Appl. Math.*, 62:1019–1043, 2002.

[68] T. F. Chan and J. Shen. Nontexture inpainting by curvature driven diffusions (CDD). *J. Visual Comm. Image Rep.*, 12:436–449, 2001.

[69] T. F. Chan and J. Shen. Bayesian inpainting based on geometric image models. In *Recent Progress in Comput. Applied PDEs,* Kluwer, New York, pages 73–99, 2002.

[70] T. F. Chan and J. Shen. Inpainting based on nonlinear transport and diffusion. In *Inverse Problems, Image Analysis, and Medical Imaging.* Volume 313 of *Contemp. Math.*, Z. Nashed and O. Scherzer, eds., AMS, Providence, RI, pages 53–65, 2002.

[71] T. F. Chan and J. Shen. On the role of the BV image model in image restoration. In *Recent Advances in Scientific Computing and Partial Differential Equations*, Volume 330 of *Contemp. Math.*, S. Y. Cheng, C.-W. Shu, and T. Tang, eds., AMS, Providence, RI, pages 25–41, 2003.

[72] T. F. Chan and J. Shen. Variational image inpainting. *Comm. Pure Appl. Math.*, 58:579–619, 2005.

[73] T. F. Chan, J. Shen, and L. Vese. Variational PDE models in image processing. *Notices Amer. Math. Soc.*, 50:14–26, 2003.

[74] T. F. Chan, J. Shen, and H.-M. Zhou. Total variation wavelet inpainting. *J. Math. Imag. Vision*, to appear.

[75] T. F. Chan and L. A. Vese. Active contours without edges. *IEEE Trans. Image Process.*, 10:266–277, 2001.

[76] T. F. Chan and L. A. Vese. A level set algorithm for minimizing the Mumford-Shah functional in image processing. In *Proceedings of the 1st IEEE Workshop on "Variational and Level Set Methods in Computer Vision"*, pages 161–168, 2001.

[77] T. F. Chan and C. K. Wong. Total variation blind deconvolution. *IEEE Trans. Image Process.*, 7:370–375, 1998.

[78] T. F. Chan and H.-M. Zhou. Optimal construction of wavelet coefficients using total variation regularization in image compression. *UCLA CAM Tech. Report*, 00-27, 2000.

[79] T. F. Chan and H.-M. Zhou. Total variation improved wavelet thresholding in image compression. *Proc. Int. Conf. Image Proc.*, Volume 2, pages 391–394, Vancouver, Canada, 2000.

[80] T. F. Chan and H.-M. Zhou. ENO-wavelet transforms for piecewise smooth functions. *SIAM J. Numer. Anal.*, 40:1369–1404, 2002.

[81] T. F. Chan and H.-M. Zhou. Total variation minimizing wavelet coefficients for image compression and denoising. *SIAM J. Sci. Comput.*, submitted.

[82] D. Chandler. *Introduction to Modern Statistical Mechanics*. Oxford University Press, New York, Oxford, 1987.

[83] S. Chaudhuri and A. N. Rajagopalan. *Depth from Defocus: A Real Aperture Imaging Approach*. Springer-Verlag, New York, 1999.

[84] Y.-G. Chen, Y. Giga, and S. Goto. Uniqueness and existence of viscosity solutions of generalized mean curvature flow equations. *J. Differential Geom.*, 33:749–786, 1991.

[85] S. S. Chern, W. H. Chen, and K. S. Lam. *Lectures on Differential Geometry*. World Scientific, River Edge, NJ, 1998.

[86] C. K. Chui. *Introduction to Wavelets*. Academic Press, Boston, MA, 1992.

[87] F. R. K. Chung. *Spectral Graph Theory*. AMS, Providence, RI, 1994.

[88] A. Cohen, W. Dahmen, I. Daubechies, and R. DeVore. Harmonic analysis of the space BV. *Rev. Mat. Iberoamericana*, 19:235–263, 2003.

[89] A. Cohen, I. Daubechies, B. Jawerth, and P. Vial. Multiresolution analysis, wavelets, and fast algorithms on an interval. *Compt. Rend. Acad. Sci. Paris*, A, 316:417–421, 1992.

[90] L. D. Cohen. Note: On active contour models and balloons. *CVGIP: Image Understanding*, 53:211–218, 1991.

[91] R. R. Coifman and Y. Meyer. Remarques sur l'analyse de Fourier à fenêtre. *C. R. Acad. Sci. Paris Sér. I Math.*, 312:259–261, 1991.

[92] P. Concus, R. Finn, and D. A. Hoffman. *Geometric Analysis and Computer Graphics*. Springer-Verlag, New York, 1990.

[93] T. M. Cover and J. A. Thomas. *Elements of Information Theory*. John Wiley & Sons, New York, 1991.

[94] G. Dal Maso, J.-M. Morel, and S. Solimini. A variational method in image segmentation: Existence and approximation results. *Acta Math.*, 168:89–151, 1992.

[95] I. Daubechies. Orthogonal bases of compactly supported wavelets. *Comm. Pure. Appl. Math.*, 41:909–996, 1988.

[96] I. Daubechies. *Ten Lectures on Wavelets*. Volume 61 of CBMS-NSF Regional Conference Series in Applied Mathematics. SIAM, Philadelphia, 1992.

[97] I. Daubechies, S. Jaffard, and J.-L. Journé. A simple Wilson orthonormal basis with exponential decay. *SIAM J. Math. Anal.*, 22:554–572, 1991.

[98] G. David. *Singular Sets of Minimizers for the Mumford-Shah Functional*. Birkhäuser, Berlin, 2005.

[99] C. de Boor. *A Practical Guide to Splines*. Springer-Verlag, New York, 1978.

[100] R. Deriche. Using Canny's criteria to derive a recursively implemented optimal edge detector. *Int. J. Comput. Vision*, 1:167–187, 1987.

[101] R. A. DeVore, B. Jawerth, and B. J. Lucier. Image compression through wavelet transform coding. *IEEE Trans. Inform. Theory*, 38:719–746, 1992.

[102] R. A. DeVore, B. Jawerth, and V. Popov. Compression of wavelet coefficients. *Amer. J. Math.*, 114:737–785, 1992.

[103] M. do Carmo. *Differential Geometry of Curves and Surfaces*. Prentice–Hall, Englewood Cliffs, NJ, 1976.

[104] D. C. Dobson and F. Santosa. Recovery of blocky images from noisy and blurred data. *SIAM J. Appl. Math.*, 56:1181–1198, 1996.

[105] D. C. Dobson and C. R. Vogel. Convergence of an iterative method for total variation denoising. *SIAM J. Numer. Anal.*, 34:1779–1791, 1997.

[106] D. L. Donoho. De-noising by soft-thresholding. *IEEE Trans. Inform. Theory*, 41:613–627, 1995.

[107] D. L. Donoho and X. Huo. Beamlets and multiscale image analysis. In *Multiscale and Multiresolution Methods*, volume 20 of *Lect. Notes Comput. Sci. Eng.*, Springer-Verlag, Berlin, pages 149–196, 2002.

[108] D. L. Donoho and X. Huo. BeamLab and reproducible research. *Int. J. Wavelets Multiresolut. Inf. Process.*, 2:391–414, 2004.

[109] D. L. Donoho and I. M. Johnstone. Ideal spacial adaption by wavelet shrinkage. *Biometrika*, 81:425–455, 1994.

[110] A. A. Efros and T. K. Leung. Texture synthesis by non-parametric sampling. In *IEEE International Conference on Computer Vision*, Corfu, Greece, pages 1033–1038, 1999.

[111] J. H. Elder and R. M. Goldberg. Image editing in the contour domain. *IEEE Conf. CVPR*, pages 374–381, 1998.

[112] G. Emile-Male. *The Restorer's Handbook of Easel Painting*. Van Nostrand Reinhold, New York, 1976.

[113] B. Engquist, A.-K. Tornberg, and R. Tsai. Discretization of Dirac delta functions in level set methods. *UCLA CAM Tech. Report*, 04-16, 2004.

[114] J. L. Ericksen. Equilibrium theory of liquid crystals. In *Advances in Liquid Crystals*, Academic Press, New York, pages 233–299, 1976.

[115] S. Esedoglu and R. March. Segmentation with depth but without detecting junctions. *J. Math. Imaging Vision*, 18:7–15, 2003.

[116] S. Esedoglu and J. Shen. Digital inpainting based on the Mumford-Shah-Euler image model. *European J. Appl. Math.*, 13:353–370, 2002.

[117] L. C. Evans. *Partial Differential Equations*. AMS, Providence, RI, 1998.

[118] L. C. Evans and R. F. Gariepy. *Measure Theory and Fine Properties of Functions*. CRC Press, Boca Raton, FL, 1992.

[119] L. C. Evans and J. Spruck. Motion of level sets by mean curvature. *J. Differential Geom.*, 33:635–681, 1991.

[120] O. Faugeras and R. Keriven. Scale-spaces and affine curvature. In *Proc. Europe-China Workshop on Geometrical Modelling and Invariants for Computer Vision*, R. Mohr and C. Wu, eds., pages 17–24, 1995.

[121] G. T. Fechner. Über ein wichtiges psychophysiches Grundgesetz und dessen Beziehung zur Schäzung der Sterngrössen. Abk. k. Ges. Wissensch. *Math.-Phys.*, K1, 4, 1858.

[122] D. J. Field. Relations between the statistics of natural images and the response properties of cortical cells. *J. Opt. Soc. Amer.*, 4:2379–2394, 1987.

[123] D. J. Field. Scale-invariance and self-similar wavelet transforms: An analysis natural scenes and mammalian visual systems. In *Wavelets, Fractals and Fourier Transforms*, M. Farge, et al., eds., Oxford University Press, Oxford, UK, 1993.

[124] D. Fish, A. Brinicombe, and E. Pike. Blind deconvolution by means of the Richardson-Lucy algorithm. *J. Opt. Soc. Amer. A*, 12:58–65, 1996.

[125] W. H. Fleming and R. Rishel. An integral formula for total gradient variation. *Arch. Math.*, 11:218–222, 1960.

[126] G. B. Folland. *Real Analysis—Modern Techniques and Their Applications*. John Wiley & Sons, New York, second edition, 1999.

[127] M. Frazier, B. Jawerth, and G. Weiss. *Littlewood-Paley Theory and the Study of Function Spaces*. Number 79 in *CBMS-NSF Regional Conference Series in Mathematics*. AMS, Providence, RI, 1991.

[128] L. E. Garner. *An Outline of Projective Geometry.* North–Holland, New York, 1981.

[129] D. Geman and C. Yang. Nonlinear image recovery with half-quadratic regularization. *IEEE Trans. Image Process.*, 4:932–946, 1995.

[130] S. Geman and D. Geman. Stochastic relaxation, Gibbs distributions, and the Bayesian restoration of images. *IEEE Trans. Patt. Anal. Mach. Intell.*, 6:721–741, 1984.

[131] W. Gibbs. *Elementary Principles of Statistical Mechanics.* Yale University Press, 1902.

[132] D. Gilbarg and N. S. Trudinger. *Elliptic Partial Differential Equations.* Springer-Verlag, New York, 1983.

[133] V. L. Ginzburg and L. D. Landau. On the theory of superconductivity. *Soviet Phys. JETP*, 20:1064–1082, 1950.

[134] E. De Giorgi. Complementi alla teoria della misura $(n-1)$-dimensionale in uno spazio n-dimensionale. *Sem. Mat. Scuola Norm. Sup. Pisa*, 1960-61.

[135] E. De Giorgi. Frontiere orientate di misura minima. *Sem. Mat. Scuola Norm. Sup. Pisa*, 1960-61.

[136] E. De Giorgi, M. Carriero, and A. Leaci. Existence theorem for a minimization problem with free discontinuity set. *Arch. Rational Mech. Anal.*, 108:195–218, 1989.

[137] E. Giusti. *Minimal Surfaces and Functions of Bounded Variation.* Birkhäuser, Boston, 1984.

[138] G. H. Golub and C. F. Van Loan. *Matrix Computations.* The Johns Hopkins University Press, Baltimore, MD, 1983.

[139] G. H. Golub and J. M. Ortega. *Scientific Computing and Differential Equations.* Academic Press, Boston, MA, 1992.

[140] R. C. Gonzalez and R. E. Woods. *Digital Image Processing.* Addison–Wesley, New York, 1992.

[141] J. W. Goodman. *Introduction to Fourier Optics.* McGraw–Hill, New York, 1968.

[142] Y. Gousseau and J.-M. Morel. Are natural images of bounded variation?, *SIAM J. Math. Anal.*, 33:634–648, 2001.

[143] U. Grenander. *Lectures in Pattern Theory.* I. II. *and* III. Springer-Verlag, 1976-1981.

[144] G. R. Grimmett. A theorem on random fields. *Bull. London Math. Soc.*, 5:81–84, 1973.

[145] F. Guichard. A morphological affine and Galilean invariant scale space for movies. *IEEE Trans. Image Process.*, 7:444–456, 1998.

[146] F. Guichard, L. Moisan, and J.-M. Morel. A review of P.D.E. models in image processing and image analysis. *J. Phys.* IV *France*, 12:Pr1–137, 2002.

[147] F. Guichard and J.-M. Morel. Partial differential equations and image iterative filtering. In *Tutorial at the International Conference of Image Processing*, Washington D.C., 1995.

[148] C.-E. Guo, S.-C. Zhu, and Y. Wu. A mathematical theory of primal sketch and sketchability. In *Proc. Int. Conf. Comput. Vision*, Nice, France, 2003.

[149] J. W. Hardy. *Adaptive Optics for Astronomical Telescopes*. Oxford University Press, New York, 1998.

[150] D. J. Heeger, E. P. Simoncelli, and J. A. Movshon. Computational models of cortical visual processing. *Proc. Natl. Acad. Sci. USA*, 93:623–627, 1996.

[151] A. D. Hillery and R. T. Chin. Iterative Wiener filters for image restoration. *IEEE Trans. Signal Process.*, 39:1892–1899, 1991.

[152] D. H. Hubel and T. N. Wiesel. Receptive fields, binocular intersection and functional architecture in the cat's visual cortex. *Journal of Physiology*, 160:106–154, 1962.

[153] P. J. Huber. *Robust Statistics*. Wiley-Interscience, New York, 2003.

[154] R. A. Hummel. Representations based on zero-crossings in scale-space. In *Proc. IEEE CVPR*, pages 204–209, 1986.

[155] X. Huo and J. Chen. JBEAM: multiscale curve coding via beamlets. *IEEE Trans. Image Process.*, to appear.

[156] H. Igehy and L. Pereira. Image replacement through texture synthesis. In *Proceedings of IEEE Int. Conf. Image Processing*, 1997.

[157] ISO/IEC JTC 1/SC 29/WG 1, ISO/IEC FDIS 15444-1. Information technology-JPEG 2000 image coding system: Core coding system [WG 1 N 1890], 2000.

[158] J. Ivins and J. Porrill. Statistical snakes: Active region models. *Fifth British Machine Vision Conference (BMVC'94)* University of York, England, pages 377–386, 1994.

[159] R. Jensen. Uniqueness of Lipschitz extensions: Minimizing the sup-norm of the gradient. *Arch. Rational Mech. Anal.*, 123:51–74, 1993.

[160] A. D. Jepson and M. J. Black. Mixture models for image representation. *PRECARN ARK Project Tech. Report ARK96-PUB-54*, 1996.

[161] K.-H. Jung, J.-H. Chang, and C. W. Lee. Error concealment technique using data for block-based image coding. *SPIE*, 2308:1466–1477, 1994.

[162] R. E. Kalman. A new approach to linear filtering and prediction problems. *Trans. ASME J. Basic Eng.*, 82:34–45, 1960.

[163] G. Kanizsa. *Organization in Vision*. Praeger, New York, 1979.

[164] I. Karatzas and S. E. Shreve. *Brownian motion and stochastic calculus*. Springer-Verlag, New York, 1997.

[165] M. Kass, A. Witkin, and D. Terzopoulos. Snakes: Active contour models. *Intl. J. Comput. Vision*, 1:321–331, 1987.

[166] A. K. Katsaggelos and N. P. Galatsanos, editors. *Signal Recovery Techniques for Image and Video Compression and Transmission*. Kluwer, Norwell, MA, 2004.

[167] A. K. Katsaggelos and M. G. Kang. Iterative evaluation of the regularization parameter in regularized image restoration. *J. Visual Comm. Image Rep.*, 3:446–455, 1992.

[168] J. Keener and J. Sneyd. *Mathematical Physiology*. Volume 8 of *Interdisciplinary Applied Mathematics*. Springer-Verlag, New York, 1998.

[169] J. L. Kelley. *General Topology*. Springer-Verlag, New York, 1997.

[170] D. Kersten. High-level vision and statistical inference. In *The New Cognitive Neurosciences*, M. S. Gazzaniga, ed., MIT Press, Cambridge, MA, pages 353–363, 1999.

[171] S. Kichenassamy. The Perona–Malik paradox. *SIAM J. Appl. Math.*, 57:1328–1342, 1997.

[172] B. Kimia, A. Tannenbaum, and S. Zucker. On the evolution of curves via a function of curvature, I: The classical case. *J. Math. Anal. Appl.*, 163:438–458, 1992.

[173] R. Kimmel. *Numerical Geometry of Images*. Springer-Verlag, New York, 2003.

[174] R. Kimmel, R. Malladi, and N. Sochen. Images as embedded maps and minimal surfaces: Movies, color, texture, and volumetric medical images. *Int. J. Comput. Vision*, 39:111–129, 2000.

[175] R. Kimmel, N. Sochen, and J. Weickert, editors. *Scale-Space Theories in Computer Vision*. Lecture Notes in Computer Science. Springer-Verlag, Berlin, 2005.

[176] D. C. Knill and W. Richards. *Perception as Bayesian Inference*. Cambridge University Press, Cambridge, UK, 1996.

[177] R. Koenker and I. Mizera. Penalized triograms: Total variation regularization for bivariate smoothing. *J. Roy. Statist. Soc. Ser. B*, 66:145–163, 2004.

[178] G. Koepfler, C. Lopez, and J.-M. Morel. A multiscale algorithm for image segmentation by variational method. *SIAM J. Numer. Anal.*, 31:282–299, 1994.

[179] R. V. Kohn and P. Sternberg. Local minimizers and singular perturbations. *Proc. Roy. Soc. Edinburgh Sect. A*, 111:69–84, 1989.

[180] R. V. Kohn and G. Strang. Optimal design and relaxation of variational problems. I, II, III. *Comm. Pure Appl. Math.*, 39:113–137, 139–182, 353–377, 1986.

[181] A. C. Kokaram, R. D. Morris, W. J. Fitzgerald, and P. J. W. Rayner. Detection of missing data in image sequences. *IEEE Trans. Image Process.*, 11:1496–1508, 1995.

[182] A. C. Kokaram, R. D. Morris, W. J. Fitzgerald, and P. J. W. Rayner. Interpolation of missing data in image sequences. *IEEE Trans. Image Process.*, 11:1509–1519, 1995.

[183] S. M. Konishi, A. L. Yuille, J. M. Coughlan, and S.-C. Zhu. Fundamental bounds on edge detection: An information theoretic evaluation of different edge cues. In *Proceedings CVPR*, Fort Collins, CO, 1999.

[184] P. Kornprobst, R. Deriche, and G. Aubert. Image coupling, restoration and enhancement via PDE's. *ICIP*, Volume 2, Washington, DC, pages 458–461, 1997.

[185] R. Kronland-Martinet, J. Morlet, and A. Grossmann. Analysis of sound patterns through wavelet transforms. *Int. J. Patt. Rec. Art. Intell.*, 1:273–301, 1988.

[186] N. V. Krylov. An analytic approach to SPDEs. In *Stochastic Partial Differential Equations: Six Perspectives*, AMS, Providence, RI, pages 185–242, 1999.

[187] W. Kwok and H. Sun. Multidirectional interpolation for spatial error concealment. *IEEE Trans. Consumer Electron.*, 39:455–460, 1993.

[188] R. L. Lagendijk, A. M. Tekalp, and J. Biemond. Maximum likelihood image and blur identification: A unifying approach. *Optical Eng.*, 29:422–435, 1990.

[189] J. Langer and D. A. Singer. The total squared curvature of closed curves. *J. Differential Geom.*, 20:1–22, 1984.

[190] M. R. Leadbetter, G. Lindgren, and H. Rootzen. *Extremes and Related Properties of Random Sequences and Processes*. Springer-Verlag, New York, 1983.

[191] A. B. Lee, D. Mumford, and J. Huang. Occlusion models for natural images: A statistical study of a scale-invariant Dead Leaves Model. *Int. J. Comput. Vision*, 41:35–59, 2001.

[192] J. S. Lee. Digital image enhancement and noise filtering by use of local statistics. *IEEE Trans. Patt. Anal. Mach. Intell.*, 2:165–168, 1980.

[193] E. H. Lieb and M. Loss. *Analysis*. AMS, Providence, RI, second edition, 2001.

[194] J. S. Lim. *Two-Dimensional Signal and Image Processing*. Prentice–Hall, Upper Saddle River, NJ, 1989.

[195] F. H. Lin and X. P. Yang. *Geometric Measure Theory: An Introduction*. International Press, Boston, MA, 2002.

[196] A. E. H. Love. *A Treatise on the Mathematical Theory of Elasticity*. Dover, New York, fourth edition, 1927.

[197] F. Malgouyres. *Increase in the Resolution of Digital Images: Variational Theory and Applications*. Ph.D. thesis, Ecole Normale Supérieure de Cachan, Cachan, France, 2000.

[198] F. Malgouyres. A noise selection approach of image restoration. In *SPIE International Conference on Wavelets* IX, Volume 4478, M. Unser, A. Laine, and A. Aldroubi, eds., San Diego, pages 34–41, 2001.

[199] F. Malgouyres. Mathematical analysis of a model which combines total variation and wavelet for image restoration. *Journal of Information Processes*, 2:1–10, 2002.

[200] F. Malgouyres and F. Guichard. Edge direction preserving image zooming: A mathematical and numerical analysis. *SIAM, J. Numer. Anal.*, 39:1–37, 2001.

[201] J. Malik, S. Belongie, T. Leung, and J. Shi. Contour and texture analysis for image segmentation. *Int. J. Comput. Vision*, 43:7–27, 2001.

[202] R. Malladi, J. A. Sethian, and B. Vemuri. Shape modeling with front propagation: A level set approach. *IEEE Trans. Pat. Anal. Mach. Intell.*, 17:158–175, 1995.

[203] S. Mallat. Applied mathematics meets signal processing. *Doc. Math.*, Extra Vol. I:319–338, 1998.

[204] S. Mallat. *A Wavelet Tour of Signal Processing*. Academic Press, New York, 1998.

[205] H. S. Malvar. *Signal Processing with Lapped Transforms*. Artech House, Boston, MA, 1992.

[206] B. B. Mandelbrot. *The Fractal Geometry of Nature*. W. H. Freeman, New York, 1982.

[207] R. March. Visual reconstruction with discontinuities using variational methods. *Image Vision Comput.*, 10:30–38, 1992.

[208] R. March and M. Dozio. A variational method for the recovery of smooth boundaries. *Image Vision Comput.*, 15:705–712, 1997.

[209] A. Marquina and S. Osher. Explicit algorithms for a new time dependent model based on level set motion for nonlinear deblurring and noise removal. *SIAM. J. Sci. Comput.*, 22:387–405, 2000.

[210] D. Marr. *Vision*. Freeman, San Francisco, 1980.

[211] D. Marr and E. Hildreth. Theory of edge detection. *Proc. Roy. Soc. London* B, 207:187–217, 1980.

[212] J. T. Marti. *Introduction to Sobolev Spaces and Finite Element Solution of Elliptic Boundary Value Problems*. Academic Press, London, 1986.

[213] S. Masnou. Filtrage et desocclusion d'images par méthodes d'ensembles de niveau. Thèse, Université Paris-Dauphine, 1998.

[214] S. Masnou and J.-M. Morel. Level-lines based disocclusion. In *Proceedings of 5th IEEE Int. Conf. on Image Process.*, Chicago, pages 259–263, 1998.

[215] Y. Meyer. *Wavelets and Operators*. Cambridge University Press, Cambridge, UK, 1992.

[216] Y. Meyer. *Oscillating Patterns in Image Processing and Nonlinear Evolution Equations*, volume 22 of *University Lecture Series*. AMS, Providence, RI, 2001.

[217] C. A. Michelli. Interpolation of scattered data: Distance matrices and conditionally positive definite functions. *Constr. Approx.*, 2:11–22, 1986.

[218] J. W. Milnor. *Topology from the Differentiable Viewpoint*. Princeton University Press, Princeton, NJ, revised edition, 1997.

[219] L. Modica. The gradient theory of phase-transitions and the minimal interface criterion. *Arch. Rational Mech. Anal.*, 98:123–142, 1987.

[220] L. Modica and S. Mortola. Un esempio di Gamma-convergenza. *Boll. Un. Mat. Ital. B* (5), 14:285–299, 1977.

[221] J.-M. Morel and S. Solimini. *Variational Methods in Image Segmentation*, volume 14 of *Progress in Nonlinear Differential Equations and Their Applications*. Birkhäuser, Boston, 1995.

[222] D. Mumford. Elastica and computer vision. In *Algebraic Geometry and Its Applications*, C. L. Bajaj, ed., Springer-Verlag, New York, pages 491–506, 1994.

[223] D. Mumford. The Bayesian rationale for energy functionals. Chapter 5 in *Geometry Driven Diffusion in Computer Vision*, Kluwer, Norwell, MA, pages 141–153, 1994.

[224] D. Mumford. Pattern theory: The mathematics of perception. In *Int. Congress Mathematicians (ICM)*, Volume I, Beijing, 2002.

[225] D. Mumford and B. Gidas. Stochastic models for generic images. *Quart. Appl. Math.*, 59:85–111, 2001.

[226] D. Mumford and J. Shah. Optimal approximations by piecewise smooth functions and associated variational problems. *Comm. Pure Appl. Math.*, 42:577–685, 1989.

[227] J. D. Murray. *Mathematical Biology*. Springer-Verlag, New York, 1993.

[228] E. Nelson. *Dynamical Theories of Brownian Motion*. Princeton University Press, Princeton, NJ, 1967.

[229] M. K. Ng, R. J. Plemmons, and F. Pimentel. A new approach to constrained total least squares image restoration. *Linear Algebra Appl.*, 316:237–258, 2000.

[230] M. Nielsen, P. Johansen, O.F. Olsen, and J. Weickert, eds. *Scale-Space Theories in Computer Vision*, volume 1682 of *Lecture Notes in Computer Science*. Springer-Verlag, Berlin, 1999.

[231] M. Nikolova. Minimizers of cost-functions involving nonsmooth data-fidelity terms. Application to the processing of outliers. *SIAM J. Numer. Anal.*, 40:965–994, 2002.

[232] M. Nikolova. A variational approach to remove outliers and impulse noise. *J. Math. Imaging Vision*, 20:99–120, 2004.

[233] J. C. C. Nitsche. *Lectures on Minimal Surfaces*, Volume 1. Cambridge University Press, Cambridge, UK, 1989.

[234] M. Nitzberg, D. Mumford, and T. Shiota. *Filtering, Segmentation, and Depth*. Volume 662 of *Lecture Notes in Comp. Sci.*, Springer-Verlag, Berlin, 1993.

[235] B. K. Oksendal. *Stochastic Differential Equations*. Springer-Verlag Telos, Berlin, sixth edition, 2003.

[236] P. J. Olver. On multivariate interpolation. *IMA Tech. Report 1975*, University of Minnesota, 2004.

[237] A. V. Oppenheim and R. W. Schafer. *Discrete-Time Signal Processing*. Prentice–Hall, Englewood Cliffs, NJ, 1989.

[238] A. V. Oppenheim and A. S. Willsky. *Signals and Systems*. Prentice–Hall, Englewood Cliffs, NJ, 1996.

[239] S. Osher and N. Paragios. *Geometric Level Set Methods in Imaging, Vision and Graphics*. Springer-Verlag, New York, 2002.

[240] S. Osher and L. I. Rudin. Feature-oriented image enhancement using shock filters. *SIAM J. Numer. Anal.*, 27:919–940, 1990.

[241] S. Osher and J. A. Sethian. Fronts propagating with curvature-dependent speed: Algorithms based on Hamilton-Jacobi formulations. *J. Comput. Phys.*, 79:12–49, 1988.

[242] S. Osher and J. Shen. Digitized PDE method for data restoration. In *Analytical-Computational Methods in Applied Mathematics*. G. A. Anastassiou, ed., Chapman & Hall/CRC, Boca Raton, FL, 2000.

[243] S. J. Osher and R. P. Fedkiw. *Level Set Methods and Dynamic Implicit Surfaces*. Springer-Verlag, New York, 2002.

[244] G. C. Papanicolaou. Mathematical problems in geophysical wave propagation. In *Proceedings of the International Congress of Mathematicians*, volume ICM 98 I of *Documanta Mathematica*, Berlin, pages 241–265, 1998.

[245] N. Paragios and R. Deriche. Geodesic active contours and level sets for detection and tracking of moving objects. *IEEE Trans. Patt. Anal. Mach. Intell.*, 22:266–280, 2000.

[246] N. Paragios and R. Deriche. Geodesic active regions: A new paradigm to deal with frame partition problems in computer vision. *Int. J. Visual Comm. Image Rep.*, 13:249–268, 2002.

[247] N. Paragios and R. Deriche. Geodesic active regions and level set methods for supervised texture segmentation. *Int. J. Comput. Vision*, 46:223–247, 2002.

[248] E. L. Pennec and S. Mallat. Image compression with geometrical wavelets. In *Proc. of IEEE ICIP*, Volume 1, pages 661–664, 2000.

[249] A. P. Pentland. A new sense for depth of field. *IEEE Tran. Pat. Anal. Mach. Intell.*, 9:523–531, 1987.

[250] P. Perona. Orientation diffusions. *IEEE Trans. Image Process.*, 7:457–467, 1998.

[251] P. Perona and J. Malik. Scale-space and edge detection using anisotropic diffusion. *IEEE Trans. Patt. Anal. Mach. Intell.*, 12:629–639, 1990.

[252] T. Poggio and S. Smale. The mathematics of learning: Dealing with data. *Notices Amer. Math. Soc.*, 50:537–544, 2003.

[253] V. Prasolov and A. Sossinsky. *Knots, Links, Braids, and 3-Manifolds*. AMS, Providence, RI, 1997.

[254] C. Price, P. Wambacq, and A. Oosterlinck. Applications of reaction-diffusion equations to image processing. In *3rd Int. Conf. Image Processing and Its Applications*, pages 49–53, 1989.

[255] M. C. Roggemann and B. Welsh. *Imaging Through Turbulence*. CRC Press, Boca Raton, FL, 1996.

[256] B. M. Romeny. *Geometry-Driven Diffusion in Computer Vision*. Kluwer, Norwell, MA, 1994.

[257] L. Rudin and S. Osher. Total variation based image restoration with free local constraints. In *Proc. 1st IEEE ICIP*, Volume 1, pages 31–35, 1994.

[258] L. Rudin, S. Osher, and E. Fatemi. Nonlinear total variation based noise removal algorithms. *Phys. D*, 60:259–268, 1992.

[259] B. Sandberg and T. F. Chan. Logic operations for active contours on multi-channel images. *UCLA Department of Mathematics CAM Report*, 02-12, 2002.

[260] B. Sandberg, T. F. Chan, and L. Vese. A level-set and Gabor-based active contour algorithm for segmenting textured images. *UCLA Department of Mathematics CAM Report*, 02-39, 2002.

[261] G. Sapiro. Color snakes. *Computer Vision and Image Understanding*, 68:247–253, 1997.

[262] G. Sapiro. *Geometric Partial Differential Equations and Image Analysis*. Cambridge University Press, Cambridge, UK, 2001.

[263] G. Sapiro and D. L. Ringach. Anisotropic diffusion of multi-valued images with applications to color filtering. *IEEE Trans. Image Process.*, 5:1582–1586, 1996.

[264] G. Sapiro and A. Tannenbaum. Affine invariant scale-space. *Int. J. Comput. Vision*, 11:25–44, 1993.

[265] W. F. Schreiber. *Fundamentals of Electronic Imaging Systems.* Springer-Verlag, New York, 1986.

[266] G. M. Schuster, X. Li, and A. K. Katsaggelos. Shape error concealment using Hermite splines. *IEEE Trans. Image Process.*, 13:808–820, 2004.

[267] J. Serra. *Image Analysis and Mathematical Morphology.* Academic Press, London, 1982.

[268] J. A. Sethian. A marching level set method for monotonically advancing fronts. *Proc. Natl. Acad. Sci. USA*, 93:1591–1595, 1996.

[269] J. A. Sethian. *Level Set Methods and Fast Marching Methods.* Cambridge University Press, Cambridge, UK, 2nd edition, 1999.

[270] J. Shah. A common framework for curve evolution, segmentation and anisotropic diffusion. In *CVPR,* Los Alamitos, CA, pages 136–142, 1996.

[271] J. Shah. Elastica with hinges. *J. Visual Comm. Image Rep.*, 13:36–43, 2002.

[272] C. E. Shannon. A mathematical theory of communication. *The Bell System Technical Journal*, 27:379–423, 623–656, 1948.

[273] J. Shen. Inpainting and the fundamental problem of image processing. *SIAM News*, 36, 2003.

[274] J. Shen. A note on wavelets and diffusions. *J. Comput. Anal. Appl.*, 5:147–159, 2003.

[275] J. Shen. On the foundations of vision modeling I. Weber's law and Weberized TV restoration. *Phys. D*, 175:241–251, 2003.

[276] J. Shen. Bayesian video dejittering by BV image model. *SIAM J. Appl. Math.*, 64:1691–1708, 2004.

[277] J. Shen. On the foundations of vision modeling III. Noncommutative monoids of occlusive images. *J. Math. Imag. Vision*, to appear.

[278] J. Shen. On the foundations of vision modeling II. Mining of mirror symmetry of 2-D shapes. *J. Visual Comm. Image Rep.,* 16:250–270, 2005.

[279] J. Shen and Y.-M. Jung. Weberized Mumford-Shah model with Bose-Einstein photon noise. *Appl. Math. Optim.*, to appear.

[280] J. Shen and G. Strang. Asymptotic analysis of Daubechies polynomials. *Proc. Amer. Math. Soc.*, 124:3819–3833, 1996.

[281] J. Shen and G. Strang. Asymptotics of Daubechies filters, scaling functions and wavelets. *Appl. Comput. Harmon. Anal.*, 5:312–331, 1998.

[282] J. Shen and G. Strang. The asymptotics of optimal (equiripple) filters. *IEEE Trans. Signal Process.*, 47:1087–1098, 1999.

[283] J. Shen and G. Strang. On wavelet fundamental solutions to the heat equation—heatlets. *J. Differential Equations*, 161:403–421, 2000.

[284] J. Shen, G. Strang, and A. Wathen. The potential theory of several intervals and its applications. *Appl. Math. Optim.*, 44:67–85, 2001.

[285] S. Smale and D.-X. Zhou. Shannon sampling and function reconstruction from point values. *Bull. Amer. Math. Soc. (N.S.)*, 41:279–305, 2004.

[286] G. Steidl, J. Weickert, T. Brox, P. Mrázek, and M. Welk. On the equivalence of soft wavelet shrinkage, total variation diffusion, total variation regularization, and SIDEs. *SIAM J. Numer. Anal.*, 42:686–713, 2004.

[287] J. Stoer and R. Bulirsch. *Introduction to Numerical Analysis*. Springer-Verlag, New York, 1992.

[288] G. Strang. *Introduction to Applied Mathematics*. Wellesley–Cambridge Press, Wellesley, MA, 1993.

[289] G. Strang. *Introduction to Linear Algebra*. Wellesley–Cambridge Press, Wellesley, MA, third edition, 1998.

[290] G. Strang and T. Nguyen. *Wavelets and Filter Banks*. Wellesley–Cambridge Press, Wellesley, MA, 1996.

[291] W. A. Strauss. *Partial Differential Equations: An Introduction*. John Wiley and Sons, New York, 1992.

[292] R. Strichartz. *A Guide to Distribution Theory and Fourier Transforms*. CRC Press, Ann Arbor, MI, 1994.

[293] D. M. Strong and T. F. Chan. Edge-preserving and scale-dependent properties of total variation regularization. *Inverse Problems*, 19:165–187, 2003.

[294] G. D. Sullivan, A. D. Worrall, R. W. Hockney, and K. D. Baker. Active contours in medical image processing using a networked SIMD array processor. In *First British Machine Vision Conference*, pages 395–400, 1990.

[295] E. Tadmor and J. Tanner. Adaptive mollifiers—High resolution recovery of piecewise smooth data from its spectral information. *Found. Comput. Math.*, 2:155–189, 2002.

[296] E. Tadmor and J. Tanner. Adaptive filters for piecewise smooth spectral data. *Preprint*, 2004.

[297] B. Tang, G. Sapiro, and V. Caselles. Color image enhancement via chromaticity diffusion. *Elect. Comp. Eng. Dept. Tech. Report*, University of Minnesota, 1999.

[298] A. N. Tikhonov. Regularization of incorrectly posed problems. *Soviet Math. Dokl.*, 4:1624–1627, 1963.

[299] A. Tsai, Jr. A. Yezzi, and A. S. Willsky. Curve evolution implementation of the Mumford-Shah functional for image segmentation, denoising, interpolation and magnification. *IEEE Trans. Image Process.*, 10:1169–1186, 2001.

[300] R. Tsai and S. Osher. Level set methods and their applications in image science. *Commun. Math. Sci.*, 1:623–656, 2003.

[301] D. Tschumperlé and R. Deriche. Diffusion tensor regularization with constraints preservation. In *IEEE Computer Society Conference on Computer Vision and Pattern Recognition*, Kauai Marriott, Hawaii, 2001.

[302] D. Tschumperlé and R. Deriche. Regularization of orthonormal vector sets using coupled PDE's. In *Proceedings of IEEE Workshop on Variational and Level Set Methods in Computer Vision*, pages 3–10, 2001.

[303] Z. Tu and S. C. Zhu. Image segmentation by data-driven Markov chain Monte Carlo. *IEEE Trans. Pat. Anal. Mach. Intell.*, 24:657–673, 2002.

[304] A. M. Turing. The chemical basis of morphogenesis. *Philos. Trans. R. Acad. Sci. London* Ser. B, 237:37–72, 1952.

[305] G. Turk. Generating textures on arbitrary surfaces using reaction-diffusion. In *Computer Graphics (SIGGRAPH '91)* Volume 25, pages 289–298, 1991.

[306] H. Urkowitz. *Signal Theory and Random Processes*. Artech House, Boston, MA, 1983.

[307] V. Vapnik. *The Nature of Statistical Learning Theory*. Springer-Verlag, New York, 1995.

[308] L. A. Vese. A study in the BV space of a denoising-deblurring variational problem. *Appl. Math. Optim.*, 44:131–161, 2001.

[309] L. A. Vese and S. J. Osher. Modeling textures with total variation minimization and oscillating patterns in image processing. *UCLA CAM Tech. Report*, 02-19, 2002.

[310] C. Vogel. *Computational Methods for Inverse Problems*. Volume 23 of Frontiers in Applied Mathematics. SIAM, Philadelphia, 2002.

[311] G. Wahba. *Spline Models for Observational Data*. Volume 59 of CBMS-NSF Regional Conference Series in Applied Mathematics. SIAM, Philadelphia, 1990.

[312] S. Walden. *The Ravished Image*. St. Martin's Press, New York, 1985.

[313] J. L. Walsh. *Interpolation and Approximation*. AMS, New York, 1935.

[314] Z. Wang, B. C. Vemuri, Y. Chen, and T. H. Mareci. A constrained variational principle for direct estimation and smoothing of the diffusion tensor field from complex DWI. *IEEE Trans. Medical Imaging*, 23:930-939, 2004.

[315] E. H. Weber. De pulsu, resorptione, audita et tactu. *Annotationes anatomicae et physiologicae*, Koehler, Leipzig, 1834.

[316] L.-Y. Wei and M. Levoy. Fast texture synthesis using tree-structured vector quantization. Preprint, Computer Science, Stanford University, 2000; Also in *Proceedings of SIGGRAPH*, 2000.

[317] J. Weickert. *Anisotropic Diffusion in Image Processing*. Teubner-Verlag, Stuttgart, Germany, 1998.

[318] J. Weickert, B.M. ter Haar Romeny, and M.A. Viergever. Efficient and reliable schemes for nonlinear diffusion filtering. *IEEE Trans. Image Process.*, 7:398–410, 1998.

[319] C.-F. Westin, S. E. Maier, H. Mamata, A. Nabavi, F. A. Jolesz, and R. Kikinis. Processing and visualization of diffusion tensor MRI. *Medical Image Analysis*, 6:93–108, 2002.

[320] N. Wiener. *Extrapolation, Interpolation, and Smoothing of Stationary Time Series*. MIT Press, Cambridge, MA, 1964.

[321] K. G. Wilson. The renormalization group and critical phenomena I: Renormalization group and the Kadanoff scaling picture. *Phys. Rev.*, 4:3174, 1971.

[322] A. Witkin. Scale space filtering—a new approach to multi-scale description. In *Image Understanding*, R. Ullmann, ed., Ablex, NJ, pages 79–95, 1984.

[323] T. Wittman. Lost in the supermarket: Decoding blurry barcodes. *SIAM News*, 37, 2004.

[324] P. Wojtaszczyk. *A Mathematical Introduction to Wavelets*. Volume 37 of London Mathematical Society Student Texts. Cambridge University Press, Cambridge, UK, 1997.

[325] A. J. Yezzi and S. Soatto. Deformotion: Deforming motion, shape average and the joint registration and approximation of structures in images. *Int. J. Comput. Vision*, 53:153–167, 2003.

[326] Y. You and M. Kaveh. A regularization approach to joint blur identification and image restoration. *IEEE Trans. Image Process.*, 5:416–428, 1996.

[327] H. K. Zhao, T. F. Chan, B. Merriman, and S. Osher. A variational level set approach to multiphase motion. *J. Comput. Phys.*, 127:179–195, 1996.

[328] S. C. Zhu and D. Mumford. Prior learning and Gibbs reaction-diffusion. *IEEE Trans. Patt. Anal. Mach. Intell.*, 19:1236–1250, 1997.

[329] S. C. Zhu, Y. N. Wu, and D. Mumford. Minimax entropy principle and its applications to texture modeling. *Neural Computation*, 9:1627–1660, 1997.

[330] S. C. Zhu and A. Yuille. Region competition: Unifying snakes, region growing, and Bayes/MDL for multi-band image segmentation. *IEEE Trans. Patt. Anal. Mach. Intell.*, 18:884–900, 1996.

Index